South and West Coasts of Ireland

Sailing Directions

What joy to sail the crested sea and watch the waves beat white upon the Irish shore!

Saint Columba, 563 AD

Irish Cruising Club

Sailing Directions

for the

South and West Coasts of Ireland

Information gathered by members of the Irish Cruising Club, supplemented by the contributions of many others who sail, live and work around the coasts of Ireland

14th Edition
2016

Norman Kean
Editor

with a Foreword by **Roger Millard**

formerly Regional Geographic Manager, British Isles and English Channel United Kingdom Hydrographic Office

ICC Publications Ltd

First published (South and South-West Coasts) 1930
New editions 1946, 1962 (South and West Coasts), 1966, 1974, 1983, 1990, 1993, 1996,
2001, 2006, 2008, 2013

This 14th Edition published 2016

© Irish Cruising Club Publications Ltd.

ISBN 978 0 9558 199 6 4

All rights reserved. No part of this publication may be reproduced, transmitted or used in any form by any means – graphic, electronic or mechanical, including photocopying, recording, taping or information storage and retrieval systems or otherwise – without the prior permission of Irish Cruising Club Publications Ltd.

Aerial photographs © Kevin Dwyer and other photographs © Geraldine Hennigan except where separately acknowledged.

Designed and typeset by Irish Cruising Club Publications Ltd

Printed by W & G Baird Ltd, Greystone Press, Antrim, Northern Ireland BT41 2RS

Irish Cruising Club Publications Ltd
Burren, Kilbrittain, County Cork P72 PN50
email: sales@iccsailingbooks.com
www.iccsailingbooks.com

Cover: *Blind Harbour, Co.Waterford; Clare Island, Co.Mayo*

Frontispiece: *Ardnakinna Point and Pipers Sound, Bantry Bay*

Title pages: **Peel Castle** *heads out towards the Fastnet Rock*

Opposite: *East Grove Quay, Cork Harbour*

Contents

Foreword 9
Preface 10
Acknowledgements 11
Disclaimer 12
Introduction 13

Chapter 1	Rosslare to Cork Harbour	28
Chapter 2	Cork Harbour to Crookhaven	70
Chapter 3	Mizen Head to Bantry Bay	118
Chapter 4	Dursey Sound to Cahersiveen	144
Chapter 5	Valentia to the Shannon	178
Chapter 6	Loop Head to Slyne Head	208
Chapter 7	Slyne Head to Erris Head	252
Chapter 8	Broad Haven to Rathlin O'Birne	298
Chapter 9	Rathlin O'Birne to Bloody Foreland	322
Chapter 10	Crossing to and from England and Wales	348

Appendix 1	Paper Charts and Admiralty Publications	352
Appendix 2	Maritime Safety Information	353
Appendix 3	Symbols and Abbreviations	355
Appendix 4	Tidal Streams	356
Appendix 5	Distances Table	361
Appendix 6	Irish Language Glossary	362
Appendix 7	Customs and Immigration Requirements	364

Index 365

Foreword

Having recently retired from a long career at the UK Hydrographic Office, involved in the production of navigational charts and publications, I was delighted to be asked to contribute a Foreword to this excellent publication.

In my final professional post as Geographic Manager, British Isles and the English Channel, the main objective of my role was to ensure that accurate and relevant information was included in Admiralty publications about these waters. The sources for new information vary greatly, from major Irish and British Government surveying programmes such as INFOMAR, through to crofters looking out of cottage windows at the sea and reporting observed changes. Modern technology such as depths gathered by multi-beam survey vessels, aircraft and satellites can provide volumes of data as never before possible. Many of the major programmes are, however, primarily aimed at the areas frequented by larger vessels.

A question I was often asked was "Is there still a place for small-craft users to supply reports of navigational changes to the Admiralty?" The answer to this is emphatically Yes (a good format to provide the information is to use a Hydrographic Note, available on the UKHO website). Observations that have an element of "ground-truth" are more meaningful than data collected by remote methods. Personally I would much prefer a report of a rock in a remote bay or narrow passage to be made by someone in a small boat with a leadline, or even in welly boots, with a stick, rather than remotely, from a satellite. In this regard, many observations made while gathering information to compile the ICC Sailing Directions have also resulted in the publication of Notices to Mariners to bring Admiralty charts and publications up to date.

The excellently laid out information contained in the ICC Sailing Directions supplements Admiralty Publications. Although aimed at small-craft users it has many admirers from major marine institutions.

In the first place it is an excellent guide to help the small-craft sailor plan where and when he or she would like to visit, considering the type of craft being handled. Secondly it provides a lot of local up to date information that might not be so important to larger vessels within port areas. It is also able to provide details of seasonal or temporary facilities and activities. On top of these advantages I find it a fascinating read, and I am sure you will also enjoy it.

Roger Millard CMarTech FIMarEST

formerly Regional Geographic Manager, British Isles and English Channel
United Kingdom Hydrographic Office

Taunton
January 2016

Opposite: The Old Head of Kinsale

Preface

Harry Donegan

Bob Berridge

Wallace Clark

Sailing Directions for the South and South-west Coasts of Ireland were first compiled by Harry Donegan, a founder member of the Irish Cruising Club, and were published (for the use of Club members) in 1930. They were revised in 1946 by his son, Harry Junior, and for the first time offered for sale to the public. Paul Campbell, Bob Berridge, Roger Bourke and Wallace Clark then expanded the Directions to include the west coast, and the third edition, this time covering the South and West Coasts, was published in 1962. Over the following 51 years the book went through a further ten editions, with new information provided by recreational sailors (ICC members and non-members alike), professional seafarers, Government agencies and many others. The ICC was a pioneer in the use of aerial photographs as an aid to navigation.

For the present edition, the south coast has been comprehensively researched again, by land and sea. Information on facilities, navigational aids and shoreside amenities everywhere has once again been brought up to date. Contributions have been received from amateur and professional mariners, the Irish Lights, harbourmasters and harbour engineers. The latest relevant hydrographic survey information from the ongoing INFOMAR programme is included, with details of many previously uncharted dangers. 92 of the photographs are new.

Since the last edition was published, many navigational aids have been upgraded, including such features as AIS transmitters. A new marina is under construction at Cobh, and pontoons have been provided at Dunmore East, Aghada, Passage West, Castletownbere, Bantry, Whiddy Island, Portmagee and Rosmoney. Significant changes have taken place in the channel to Dungarvan, where pontoon facilities have also been greatly improved. Dredging and improvements have taken place at Kilrush, Dunmore East and North Harbour, Cape Clear. Spike Island in Cork Harbour, for long a forbidden Government preserve, has been opened up to visitors and is a fascinating place to visit.

Additional advice on the use of electronic charts is provided, and a short chapter has been added on crossings to and from England and Wales. The sister volume for the East and North Coasts has for many years included advice on sailing *to* Great Britain, but (considering that most of our readers live there) it is appropriate to provide guidance also on crossing *from* our neighbouring island. Clearly - by definition - almost all those readers will be making the crossing.

Aerial photographs are by Kevin Dwyer, and sea-level photographs by Geraldine Hennigan, unless individually acknowledged.

Acknowledgements

Thanks are due to the staff of the UK Hydrographic Office in Taunton, especially Christine Walton, hydrographer responsible for the charting of Ireland, and to her predecessor Roger Millard, now retired, for his generous Foreword. Thanks to the staff of the Commissioners of Irish Lights in Dun Laoghaire, especially Robert McCabe, Harry McClenahan, Deirdre Lane and Mark Devlin; to Sean Cullen and the crew of RV *Keary*; to Harbourmasters Phil Murphy of Kilmore Quay, Harry McLoughlin of Dunmore East, Cormac McGinley of Castletownbere and Brian Sheridan of Galway; to Kim Roberts of Kilrush Marina; to coastal engineers Gearoid O'Shea, Kevin Boyle and Cathal Sweeney; to Maeve Bell, Alex Blackwell, Seamus Butler, Ken Cashman, John Clementson, Brian Cudmore, Eleanor Cudmore, Dick Lincoln, Paddy McGlade, Paul McSorley, W.M.Nixon, Donal Walsh and Padraic Whooley. It seems unjust for the publication of a new edition to consign to obscurity some of those whose contribution has been invaluable in the past, but their names are too numerous to list again. Suffice it to say that this book represents the work of scores if not hundreds of people, over many years.

Niall Quinn has been generous in extending the use of his two successive yachts, both named *Aircín*, and both pictured several times on the following pages. The first a Sirius 38, the second an Ovni 395, both were used to survey the west coast. Thanks to Club Commodore Peter Killen and the flag officers and committee of the ICC, whose support has been unfailing.

As a respected aid to navigation, Kevin Dwyer's beautiful aerial photographs once again add distinction and clarity to the Directions. For her photographs like the one below, her enthusiasm for the task and her infinite forbearance, I am again indebted to my wife Geraldine.

Norman Kean   **February 2016**

Inishnabro and Tearaght, Blasket Islands

Disclaimer

Please read this and the Introduction which follows before using this book as an aid to navigation. The statement below is essential to a proper understanding of the book and to the safety of your vessel and crew.

The Flag Officers and Members of the Irish Cruising Club, and the Editor, together with Irish Cruising Club Publications Ltd and its Directors and Members draw the special attention of purchasers and readers of this volume of Sailing Directions to the following. Coastal cruising, passage-making or any other activity upon the sea carries inherent risks. Such risks are increased by the passage of time as channels vary, conspicuous objects are repainted or become obscured, and many other changes occur. In many places around this coast the accuracy of charts is not equal to the precision of global positioning satellite systems. It is impracticable to check all of the information contained in this volume on a continuous basis. The publishers assume no obligation to amend or update this publication. This volume is intended as an aid to recreational sailing and cruising, to be used by skilled, competent and prudent sailors in conjunction with up-to-date cartographic, textual, mechanical and electronic aids and equipment. Whilst all reasonable care has been exercised in its compilation and editing, it is not warranted to be completely accurate nor error-free in every respect, nor is it practicable for it to be so. The above-mentioned persons do not accept any liability or responsibility for any loss, damage or injury to property or persons arising or allegedly arising out of any error, inaccuracy, mis-statement in or omission from these Sailing Directions.

Additions and Corrections

Additions and corrections are always welcome and may be sent to the publishers at Burren, Kilbrittain, Co.Cork P72 PN50, phone +353 23 884 6891, e-mail sales@iccsailingbooks.com. Amendments and updates are published on the Irish Cruising Club Publications website, www.iccsailingbooks.com. The reader is strongly advised to refer to these before embarking on a cruise, and readers are encouraged to sign up on the website for periodic newsletters and notifications.

Beeves Rock lighthouse, in the Shannon estuary (Chapter 5)

Introduction

Roundstone, Co.Galway (chapter 6)

The south and west coasts of Ireland are among the finest cruising grounds in the world, blessed with wonderful and varied scenery and warmed by the North Atlantic Drift. The south coast is 130 miles by sea from Land's End, 250 miles from the north coast of France, or the Clyde, and a long day's sail of 60 miles from Dublin or Milford Haven. It can claim to be the cradle of yachting as a sport, and is the setting for several of its most prestigious events. The west coast is wild, remote and spectacular, and yet only 48 hours' sailing from England, France, Scotland or the Irish Sea.

This book is primarily aimed at the recreational sailor, with a vessel in the range 6 to 18 metres in length, having a draft of 2·4 metres or less, a reliable engine, an echosounder and GPS, probably a chartplotter but not necessarily radar.

PORTS and HARBOURS

From the bustle of the historic cities to the stark and lonely grandeur of the remoter islands, the south and west coasts of Ireland have the full range of ports, harbours and anchorages. There are several fine marinas, but this cruising ground most richly rewards those who are confident in using good anchors and can deal with the rise and fall of the tide alongside an old stone pier. Many places are accessible by day and night in all

Towns and Villages; Weather

Baltimore (Chapter 2)

weathers, but many can be reached only in daylight and a few only in specific weather conditions. Access to most places is free of tidal restrictions. There are numerous small piers and jetties, old and new, some with deep water and some drying. In recent years many of the older piers have been renovated and extended, but not all of these improvements have been reflected on the Admiralty charts.

The coast is for the most part cliffbound, with splendid sandy bays and long, sheltered inlets, and is breathtakingly beautiful in every inch of its length.

TOWNS and VILLAGES

The major population centres are the cities of Waterford, Cork, Limerick and Galway but the towns of New Ross, Dungarvan, Youghal, Cobh, Kinsale, Skibbereen, Bantry, Castletownbere, Kenmare, Cahersiveen, Dingle, Kilrush, Clifden, Westport, Belmullet, Sligo, Donegal and Killybegs are all locally pre-eminent, and many smaller villages are significant as well. Of the true islands, 21 have permanent populations, including Sherkin (114), Heir (29), Cape Clear (124), Long Island (10), Bere Island (216), Whiddy (20), Dursey (3), the Aran Islands of Inishmore (845), Inishmaan (157) and Inisheer (249), Inishbofin (160), Inishturk (53), Clare Island (168), Inishlyre (4), Inishbiggle (25) and Arranmore (514). Several of these, and many others, have seasonal or occasional residents, including Great Blasket, with its one faithful inhabitant who returns every summer. Although frequently described as Ireland's largest island, Achill (2,569) is linked to the mainland by a bridge, as are Valentia (665), Great Island in Cork Harbour and many of the islands on the south coast of Connemara.

WEATHER

The famously capricious Irish weather is, in general, free of extremes. The climate is maritime, and is characterised by the passage of Atlantic depressions, with rapidly changing weather conditions. A typical depression produces lowering clouds and a rising south-east wind, followed by more-or-less continuous rain and a gradual veer to the south or south-west. The passage of the cold front is often quite sudden, with a clearance to showers and an abrupt veer in the wind to west or north-west. This may all happen within twelve hours and be followed by a day or two of moderating winds and

Weather

Bray Head, Valentia Island (Chapter 4)

sunshine as a ridge of high pressure passes, before the cycle begins again. But equally, an anticyclone can dominate for days or weeks at a time and the weather can be glorious, with cloudless skies, warm sunshine and limitless visibility. Summer winds blow from the west and south-west about 40% of the time. The mean daytime temperature is about 18°C in June, July and August, and the coast of Kerry gets about 100 mm of rain per month. Fog is relatively uncommon, averaging one or two days in the month. The one predictable feature is unpredictability, at least more than a few days ahead; but that said, it must be declared that weather forecasts, from both Irish and British Met services, are accurate and reliable. The Irish sea-area forecasts are regularly broadcast by the Coastguard on VHF and by local and national radio stations, and Irish and British forecasts are both transmitted on Navtex. More specific details of weather forecast sources are listed in Appendix 2.

A typical two weeks' summer cruise can be expected to include a day weatherbound somewhere, but it is also common to find yachts held up for days at the east end of the south coast waiting for a persistent west or south-west wind to change in their favour. If crossing from England or France it is often wise to make landfall further west, so as to have options if the weather does not co-operate. The best way to be weatherproof, so to speak, is to start at Baltimore, from where a cruise can be shaped almost regardless of wind direction.

Severe storms are unusual in summer, but do happen, the infamous Fastnet Race storm of August 1979 being remembered for its deadly consequences. The sea state in winds of force 9 and 10 can be awesome and dangerous, especially close to the salient points and in wind-over-tide conditions.

Despite its apparent exposure to the south-west, the south coast does not in general experience a heavy swell. On that coast, the less common east and south-east winds can produce an unpleasantly short and lumpy sea. On the west coast – from Cape Clear northwards – the prevailing ocean swell from the west is seldom absent, but its long rhythmic roll is not difficult to deal with. There are many so-called "breakers" on the west coast – rocks with anything from a metre to 10 metres of water, or even more, which cause the seas to break. As a rule of thumb, the height of the breaker will at least equal

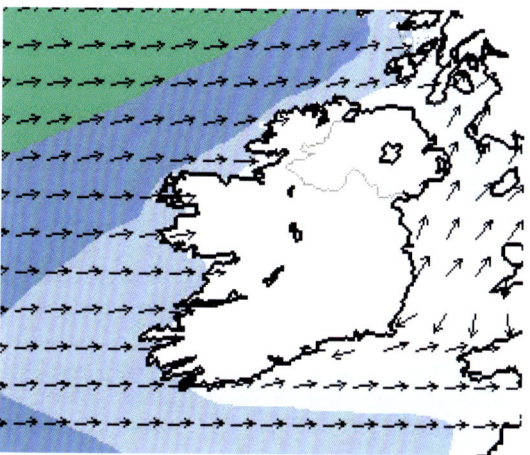

Typical summer swell pattern around Ireland, with the prevailing swell from almost due west. Note how the regime changes at Malin and Mizen Heads. Colours denote wave height; white less than 0·5m, green 3 to 4m. (courtesy of www.passageweather.com)

15

Weather; Tides

Summer Cove, Kinsale (Chapter 2)

A tremendous spectacle: breaker on Cod Rock, Dunworley Bay, Co.Cork (L and centre), in gale conditions and 5m swell (unusually) from the SE. The rock has 8m of water over it and the breaker is 8 to 10m high

the depth of water over the rock. No hard and fast guidance can be given about when these hazards may be approached and when they must be avoided, but if in doubt stay well clear. Such a rock will often form "blind breakers", the sea rising into a steep pinnacle before subsiding without actually breaking. These are usually clear from leeward but hard to see from the windward side. A big breaker offshore in a heavy swell is a tremendous spectacle.

In many places the swell conditions are as important as the wind in determining the feasibility of passages. Swell forecasts from a site such as www.passageweather.com repay study.

The seawater surface temperature offshore rises from 12°C in May to 16°C in September, and in the recesses of the longer inlets may reach 20°C or more in a warm summer. Daylight hours are long in summer; at the solstice the sun rises over Cork at 0510 and sets at 2155.

TIDES

The tidal rise and fall averages 3·5m at springs and 2·5m at neaps, and is remarkably uniform all around the south and west coasts, the range being slightly greater in the upper reaches of the estuaries and at Galway. There is an amphidromic point close to the east coast 25 miles north of Carnsore Point, which has the effect of reducing the range at Rosslare to 1·6m at springs and 0·6m at neaps. All round these coasts, spring high tides occur morning and evening, and neap high tides around midday and midnight. There are no anomalous tides; the tidal curves are everywhere more or less sinusoidal, so the rule of twelfths can be applied.

For simplicity, no distinction is drawn here between tidal constants at neaps and springs, or low and high water, and a single average is usually quoted. In most places the resulting approximation is only a few minutes. Likewise, while the use of Tarbert as a Tidal Standard Port for the Shannon estuary gives marginally greater accuracy, Galway is used here in the interests of simplicity.

The main flood stream divides west of the Kenmare River, and flows north on the west coast and east on the south coast. Tidal streams are noticeable but for the most part not very strong, and the only tidal gate is the Bull's Mouth, at the north end of Achill Sound. The strongest tides are naturally

Navigational Aids; Charts

around the headlands and in narrow channels, with spring rates of about 2 knots at most headlands, 3 to 4 knots in some of the narrow channels and 5 knots or more at the Bull's Mouth. Strong and persistent winds may increase the rate of the streams by up to half a knot and the duration of flow or ebb by as much as an hour.

Details of tidal streams are given in Appendix 4 and throughout the text.

NAVIGATIONAL AIDS

The coastal marks throughout Ireland are maintained by the Commissioners of Irish Lights, and harbour marks by harbour authorities, marina owners or the County Councils. In some places privately- or locally-maintained marks exist, and these are described wherever they are considered reliable. IALA System A (red to port) is used in Ireland, and the standard of provision and maintenance is very high. The principal lights are on the Tuskar Rock, Hook Head, Ballycotton Island, Roche's Point, the Old Head of Kinsale, Galley Head, the Fastnet Rock, Mizen Head, Sheep's Head, the Bull, the Great Skellig, Tearaght, Loop Head, Inisheer, Eeragh, Slyne Head, Achillbeg, Black Rock, Eagle Island, Rathlin O'Birne, Arranmore and Tory Island. The conventional direction of lateral buoyage offshore changes at the Bull Rock, north-west of Dursey. The power and the range of some of the major lights are being reduced, but not so as to concern the recreational sailor. The standard and number of inshore marks have dramatically improved in recent years. Audible fog signals have been discontinued, and the major lights are no longer shown by day in fog.

The most significant recent technical advance has been the introduction of AIS (Automatic Identification Systems), for which transmitters are fitted to many lighthouses and buoys, a continuing programme. These are identified in the text. The first permanent "virtual" AIS beacon, transmitting an AIS signal as if it comes from a location where there is no physical object, has already been established in the North Channel; an economical way of providing a navigational aid in a difficult spot.

Characteristics of lights and buoys are described using the same standard abbreviations as in the Admiralty List of Lights. Arcs of visibility are expressed from seaward.

Tarbert lighthouse, Co.Kerry (chapter 5)

CHARTS

Seven Admiralty or four Imray charts, on scales between 1:150,000 and 1:200,000, cover the coast and are useful for planning purposes and passagemaking. On some parts of the south coast there are, in fact, no larger-scale charts. For cruising the coast, the largest-scale charts are almost always essential, both for safety and for the fullest enjoyment of the experience. The few exceptions are some of the large-scale harbour plans. The coast from Rosslare to Bantry Bay is comprehensively covered by three Small Craft Folios. The Imray charts offer an economical and convenient alternative on part of the south coast, but west of Galley Head and north of Cape Clear, the Admiralty charts or Folios are indispensible. The text gives more specific advice, and Appendix 1 (page 352) gives a complete listing of Admiralty and Imray products for the area.

Much of the coast of Ireland has not been surveyed since the mid-19th century, and many of the charts are still based, at least in part, on the old data. This includes Imray as well as Admiralty charts, and the chartplotter

*Irish Lights Vessel **Granuaile** (Commissioners of Irish Lights)*

17

Charts; Electronic charts

North Harbour, Cape Clear Island (Chapter 2)

Fort Mitchel, Spike Island (Chapter 2)

products directed at the leisure market. Satellite-derived positions are more accurate than the charted data in many places, and the UK Hydrographic Office has issued a standard caution to the effect that reliance should not be placed upon satellite-derived positions in relation to several of the charts of the Irish coast. There are certain places where the charts are as much as 90m out of position, and blind trust in a chartplotter can have unfortunate consequences. The Marine Institute, together with the Geological Survey of Ireland, is undertaking a major survey project of the inshore waters. New and accurate information is continually being published, and new editions of 26 of the Admiralty charts of the south and west coasts have been issued since 2009. But the standard advice to the prudent navigator still applies with full force in the waters around Ireland. Keep a good look-out, maintain good traditional pilotage, and do not place undue reliance upon GPS when in close proximity to the coast or charted dangers.

To landward, the Ordnance Survey maps are excellent and up-to-date, and provide detail not only for exploration ashore but landmark-spotting from seaward. On the smaller scale the 1:250,000 scale Holiday Map is recommended. For intimate details of the land, including the minor road network and locations of hundreds of antiquities, the 1:50,000 scale Discovery Series is excellent.

ELECTRONIC CHARTS

The standard chartplotter packages include all the largest-scale information, but bear in mind when using chartplotters that the data displayed is never any better than that on the paper charts, and that only a hairsbreadth fuse stands between the navigator and the loss of this vital information. Electronic chart packages aimed at yachts are officially "not to be used for navigation", a fact often overlooked. Always carry the paper charts or Folios as a backup.

Such vector electronic charts are normally based on rasterized versions of the paper ones. They normally contain no original survey information, and they reproduce any errors and limitations of the paper charts, and add a few of their own. Source and age of survey data are not readily accessible. Horizontal and vertical datums are assumed to be "standard", but this can be difficult to confirm. Position errors from paper charts are perpetuated but cautions are omitted or hard to find. Soundings, "nature of seabed" information and spurious artefacts on paper charts may be misrepresented on

Ballycotton Sound, showing the pitfalls of over-magnification on a chartplotter, in this case by a factor of eight. At the scale here (approximately 1:18,000) the high water mark (taken from the OS at 1:2,500) is accurate, but everything else is derived from AC2049 at 1:150,000. Over-magnification to this extent on a plotter screen results in a misleading picture. The straight line SSW-NNE through the sound is a track of a safe transit in deep water. Compare the plan and photographs on page 57.

Pilotage; Anchoring, mooring and berthing

Kinsale (Chapter 2)

electronic ones as specific hazards. Precise terrestrial data may be used to draw the high water mark, which can add a misleading impression of overall accuracy and precision. Where the best paper chart is on a small scale, it is not valid to magnify the electronic chart to a larger scale. On zooming out, or on selecting a particular level of detail for the display, hazards and navigational aids may disappear, change or lose detail. All of the above issues arise on the coasts described in this book. Notwithstanding the above, electronic charts are an extremely valuable navigational aid here if used properly.

PILOTAGE

A clear and unambiguous visual transit is the best position line. On this coast, the traditional ones are described on the Admiralty charts, but many of them are no longer clear or were never clear to begin with. Many of the better transits have been photographed, but for many dangers, safe clearing latitudes, longitudes or waypoints have been provided. Waypoints are given for ports, anchorages and those channels where GPS is more than usually helpful. Where the waypoint symbol ⊕ appears beside the position data in the text, the position will be found on the appropriate plan, marked with the same symbol. They are identified by two-letter abbreviations, which should be self-explanatory. These points or position lines should always be cross-checked on a chart. Where the camera symbol 📷 appears in the lists of Dangers, Lights and Marks, a photograph of the object in question will be found either at the appropriate point in the text or on the page number specified.

The plans are intended to illustrate the text, and should not be used for navigation; that is to say that they do not necessarily show all the dangers, and that bearings, courses, clearing lines and positions should not be taken from them unless these are specified in figures.

Depths and heights on the plans are in metres, and the plans are oriented north-south (true). Depths are reduced to Lowest Astronomical Tide. Bearings quoted in the text and on the plans refer to true North. Magnetic variation in the region is 3° to 5°W (2015), decreasing 11' annually. These Directions run from south-east to north-west. To avoid needless repetition of descriptive material, they sometimes require the reader to skip to the next section or paragraph to find the approach to a harbour from the other direction, and the reader sailing from north-west to south-east will inevitably be flipping back and forward occasionally.

ANCHORAGE, MOORING and BERTHING

In most places on this coast, anchorage, where it is available, is free. Good ground tackle is essential, and that includes an ample scope of chain as opposed to all-rope or a nominal length of chain next to the anchor. In most places the holding ground is good, and it should be borne in mind that many reports pre-date the present generation of high-performance anchors. Weed and kelp may

19

Anchorage, mooring and berthing

Lawrence Cove, Bere Island (Chapter 3)

The Little Skellig (Chapter 4) is one of the world's largest gannetries (photo Tom McDonnell)

occasionally be a problem, and care must be taken to ensure that the anchor is well bedded in and not merely hooked in the weed. This involves going astern on the anchor, gently at first but then more and more forcefully until full astern, while keeping an eye on a transit on the beam. Lift and re-lay if not satisfied.

There are marinas at Kilmore Quay, Waterford, New Ross, Crosshaven, East Ferry, Cobh, Monkstown, Kinsale, Lawrence Cove, Cahersiveen, Dingle, Fenit, Kilrush, Galway and Rossaveal, and more modest pontoon facilities at Dunmore East, Dungarvan, Spike Island, Passage West, Aghada, Cork City, Courtmacsherry, Baltimore, Sherkin, Castletownbere, Bantry, Whiddy Island, Portmagee, Knightstown, Foynes, Rosmoney and Sligo. Many of the harbours described have proposals for infrastructure developments. Where projects seem likely to be realised within the next few years, they are mentioned so that the intending visitor may check the latest information on the ICC website, www.irishcruisingclub.com. Visitors' moorings are maintained in certain places by the County Councils and private businesses. The Council moorings are usually designed for 15 tonnes displacement and are equipped with large rigid yellow buoys which may or may not have pickup ropes and/or bridles attached – care should be taken to distinguish between these! A line simply run through the shackle on the top of a buoy and cleated on either bow can chafe through in a few hours: use a fisherman's hitch, a chain bridle with the shackle secured by wire or a cable tie, or a rope bridle with a short length of chain spliced in.

There may be a charge for the use of visitors' moorings; if so the details are often on a tag attached to the buoy. These Directions cannot give any assurances about the condition of these moorings, and visitors use them entirely at their own risk. Bear in mind also that many yacht insurance policies place the onus for checking visitors' moorings on the user. Piers and harbours may charge dues for visitors; when they do, a typical level is €10 or €15 per night. Marina charges are generally higher.

In the following pages, when an anchorage is described as being sheltered (or not) from certain wind directions, the sense is always clockwise, so for example "W to NE" means "W through N to NE". A "mile" is the nautical mile of ten cables or 1,854 metres. Distances on land are specified in kilometres.

PASSAGEMAKING

On most parts of this coast harbours and anchorages are closely spaced, but there are no good harbours on the west coast of County Clare, and the popular option for those not wishing to explore the Shannon estuary is the 75-mile direct passage from the Blaskets or Smerwick to the Aran Islands or further to the mainland coast of Connemara. The crossing is straightforward and most yachts can make it in a long day's sail.

The beaten track also leads 55 to 75 miles direct across the mouth of Donegal Bay, from Portnafrankagh or Broad Haven to Teelin, Church Pool or Aran Sound; this is a pity, since Donegal Bay offers many attractive ports of call.

A table of distances around the coast is given in Appendix 5.

SAILING ROUND IRELAND

Many each year prove to themselves that Ireland is indeed an island. A typical circumnavigation takes four weeks but with a few long passages included it can be done in three or fewer. Other things being equal, a case – as follows – can be made for an anticlockwise course. As a typical depression passes to the north-west of Ireland, the southerly winds are accompanied by rain and low clouds. After the cold front, the wind veers, often to west or north-west. Sailing south on the west coast, it may be as well to sit out the southerly in a welcoming harbour, and then continue southwards in fair wind and sunshine. On the long south coast, the prevailing winds will be favourable; while the east coast will provide a lee from strong winds from south-west to north-west. Bear in mind that on the west and north coasts between Valentia and Malin Head, there is a more-or-less continuous swell, usually from the west, which is heightened by strong winds far out at sea, whereas on the south coast, and particularly on the east coast, light winds bring calm seas.

Much depends on the starting point; whether or not the cruise is to be interrupted and the yacht left somewhere for a while; and on the intended choice of places to visit.

A Coast Guard helicopter lands on the sand at low tide, Courtmacsherry. (Chapter 2). These aircraft have now been replaced by Sikorsky S92s.

RADIO COMMUNICATIONS and SEARCH & RESCUE

Garda Costa na hÉireann, the Irish Coast Guard, has its National Maritime Operations Centre and Marine Rescue Coordination Centre in Dublin, and Marine Rescue Sub-Centres at Malin Head (Co. Donegal) and Valentia Island (Co. Kerry). These three stations maintain a continuous listening watch on VHF, including VHF DSC. MRSCs Malin Head and Valentia also listen on MF and are Navtex broadcast stations. There are sixteen remotely controlled transmission sites which are individually named. The Coast Guard stations provide regular weather forecasts, navigational warnings and traffic lists, and coordinate search and rescue. The RNLI has all-weather lifeboat stations at Rosslare, Kilmore Quay, Dunmore East, Ballycotton, Courtmacsherry, Baltimore, Castletownbere, Valentia, Fenit, Kilronan, Clifden, Achill Island, Ballyglass and Arranmore. Clifden has a 17-knot Mersey lifeboat, and the others 25-knot Tamars, Severns or Trents. Inshore lifeboats are stationed at Fethard, Tramore, Helvick, Youghal, Crosshaven, Kinsale, Union Hall, Kilrush, Galway, Clifden, Westport, Sligo and Bundoran. There are affiliated local inshore rescue services at Tramore, Bunmahon, Schull, Bantry, Derrynane, Ballybunion and Kilkee. Airborne rescue is provided by Irish Coast Guard helicopters based at Sligo, Shannon, Waterford and Dublin and by UK Coastguard helicopters from Newquay in Cornwall.

More details of Coast Guard Radio Stations and S & R facilities are given in Appendix 2.

Commercial Shipping; Fishing

Derrynane, one of the most beautiful anchorages on the coast (Chapter 4; photo Kevin Dwyer)

(bottom R) Rope culture of mussels, Roaringwater Bay, Co.Cork

(below) Fish cages in Bantry Bay

COMMERCIAL SHIPPING

There are Traffic Separation Schemes off the Tuskar and Fastnet Rocks, in which the usual International Rules apply. Rosslare is a busy RoRo port, Waterford has a large container terminal, and Cork is a major international port with constant traffic in oil and chemical tankers, container ships, passenger ferries and general cargo ships. Cork is also the headquarters of the Irish Naval Service, with eight patrol vessels based at Haulbowline Island. Foynes, in the Shannon estuary, is a major cargo port, and very large colliers supply Money Point power station. Crude oil tankers, including some very large ones, use Whiddy Island terminal in Bantry Bay. Cargo vessels also visit New Ross, Youghal, Kinsale, Fenit, Limerick, Galway, Sligo and Killybegs, and cruise ships, including very large ones, visit Cork, Waterford, Galway, Killybegs and the large inlets of the south-west. Coastwise shipping traffic is constant if not heavy on the south coast, but light on the west.

There are small car ferries in Waterford Harbour (between Ballyhack and Passage East and across King's Channel), in Cork Harbour (between Passage West and Rushbrooke), in Berehaven (between Castletownbere and Bere Island and from Pontoon Pier to Lawrence Cove), from Reenard Point to Valentia, across the Shannon between Killimer and Tarbert, and from Burtonport to Arranmore. Passenger ferries sail from Baltimore to Sherkin and Cape Clear, from Galway, Rossaveal and Doolin to the Aran Islands and from Bunbeg to Tory Island. Ferries also run from Schull to Cape Clear, Cunnamore Pier to Heir Island, Bantry to Whiddy Island, Cleggan to Inishbofin and Inishturk and Roonagh Quay to Inishturk and Clare Island. Tourist boats take day-trippers from the mainland to Spike Island, the Skelligs, the Blaskets and Garinish Island. Dursey Island is unique in being served not by boat but by a cable car.

FISHING

The fishing industry in Ireland and the UK is facing challenges, but fishing is still vitally important. In fishing harbours yachts are rightly expected to accord priority to fishing vessels and their requirements. Killybegs, Castletownbere, Dunmore East, Rossaveal and Dingle are designated Fishery Harbour Centres, Kilmore Quay and Union Hall have significant fleets, and Ballycotton, Helvick, Crosshaven, Kinsale and Baltimore are also important.

The principal fishery close inshore is for shellfish – lobsters, crabs and prawns – and pot markers are met almost everywhere. These are usually orange plastic buoys, but dan buoys with black flags are also used. They generally mark the ends of a long string of pots on the bottom. It is normally safe to pass within a boat's length of a buoy, but beware of excess floating ropes, which can be very long. Buoys may also be tied in tandem to deal with a fast tidal stream - avoid sailing between two buoys close together. Sea angling

Diving; Traditional Boats; Wildlife

The **bád mór** (Galway hooker) **MacDuach** at Kinvara, Co.Galway (Chapter 6). Most hookers are gaff cutter rigged on a single mast (photo W.M.Nixon)

is a thriving tourist business in many places; the boats often work to a regular timetable and the skippers appreciate having their normal berths left available. In return, they are often the handiest source of wonderfully fresh fish.

Fish farming is carried out in many places on this coast. Locations of many fish farms are noted in the text, but these can change at short notice, so a good look-out is required. Fish farms are usually, but not always, marked by yellow buoys with flashing yellow lights. Parallel rows of buoys – usually grey or blue plastic barrels – indicate rope culture of mussels. There are shellfish beds in some places, with oysters and scallops cultivated, where anchoring and running aground are frowned upon.

It is often convenient to raft up with fishing boats in harbour, but if doing this, a little courtesy and common sense are the key, as are good fenders and a willingness to keep antisocial hours. If in doubt, consult the harbourmasters for guidance. In many places, facilities for yachts and fishing boats are well segregated anyway.

DIVING

The coast is liberally strewn with wrecks, some ancient, many casualties of the great 20th-century wars, and the largest of all, the giant ore carrier *Kowloon Bridge*, which foundered on the Stags off Toe Head in 1986, with her cargo of 169,000 tonnes of iron ore. These wrecks are a magnet for divers, and diving boats, usually large rigid inflatables, are commonly seen. They display the blue and white International Code flag A, and should be given a wide berth. Baltimore is a major centre for this activity. Unauthorised salvage of artefacts from wrecks more than 100 years old is illegal in Ireland.

TRADITIONAL BOATS

The west coast has a rich heritage of traditional boat design, and few places in the world have so many of these vessels still in routine use. In many places, the sea provided the means of communication and transport, while the harsh natural and economic environment forced a frugality of design and materials, and great ingenuity. At one end of the scale is the classic, heavy Galway hooker, the *bád mór* or "big boat", 40 feet long, with its cod's-head-and-mackerel-tail lines, its characteristic tumblehome and its gaff rig, tan or black sails, long bowsprit and long sweeping boom. At the other end of the scale is the *curach*, ancient in design and feather-light, its principal member the gunwale rather than the keel; traditionally canvas-covered, most of them are now skinned in GRP. The *curach adhmaid* or "wooden currach" is currach-like in shape but carvel-built in wood, and heavy. With added outboard motors, both types of currach are ubiquitous in Connemara as shellfish boats.

WILDLIFE

Whales and dolphins are common around Ireland, and bottlenose and common Atlantic dolphins, harbour porpoises, and fin and minke whales are often seen. Humpback

Otters are often seen along the shore (photo John Campbell)

Wildlife; Place Names

Humpback whale off Hook Head, Co.Wexford (Chapter 1) (photo Padraig Whooley)

Basking sharks as they are usually observed in calm weather (photo Emmett Johnston)

Grey seal pup on Great Saltee Island

whales are becoming more common and basking sharks are making a significant comeback. Sunfish are not uncommon and leatherback turtles are sometimes reported. Jellyfish sometimes occur in huge numbers (and may even block engine cooling intakes) and at other times are nowhere to be seen – nobody knows why. The harmless moon jelly is the commonest, but blue and compass jellyfish are also seen, and occasionally the stinging lion's mane and mauve stinger. Sea anglers catch mackerel, pollack, whiting, ling, cod, haddock, dogfish, congers and small sharks. Grey and common seals are plentiful, and otters are often seen along the shore.

Vast numbers of seabirds nest around the south and west coasts. These include the various species of gulls and terns, kittiwakes, guillemots, razorbills, cormorants and shags; and the now-ubiquitous fulmar, which sixty years ago was very rare. The Little Skellig is one of the world's largest gannetries. About 180,000 pairs of storm petrels – a third of the world population – nest on the offshore islands, which also have huge colonies of Manx shearwaters. The birds come ashore only after dark, so many visitors (and predators!) are unaware of their presence, but rafts of them may be met at sea. There are several large puffin colonies. Puffins are easiest to observe on Skellig Michael, where they are very tame, but they disperse to sea in July. Cape Clear Island has a noted bird observatory.

In the estuaries herons, egrets, oystercatchers and curlews abound, and waders arrive for the winter. Ireland is, in general, blessed in its freedom from aggressive and venomous creatures of all sizes, only partly thanks to Saint Patrick and his fine work on the snake population, now (as is well known) zero. There are few if any mosquitoes, even in a warm summer, and the south coast is mercifully free of that scourge of Scotland, the midge.

PLACE NAMES

Almost all the place names on this coast are derived from Irish Gaelic, and their English transliterations may be variable in spelling or usage. Many charted names are plainly misspelt, such as "Skull" for Schull, Co. Cork, and some have two equally valid spellings, such as Cahersiveen/Caherciveen (Co. Kerry). This can lead to confusion. It appears to be a uniquely Irish phenomenon, and it probably dates back to the original Ordnance Survey of Ireland in the 1830's. It must be assumed that the authorities whom the surveyors of the time consulted – probably the landowners or clergymen – had individualistic opinions on the matter. Be that as it may, the Admiralty charts usually (but not always) follow the OS spelling. Where this is locally regarded as incorrect, the text uses the local name but refers to the charted name, for example "Rossaveal (Rossaveel on the chart)".

Many places have two distinct names, for example Garinish and Ilnacullen, which refer to the same island, while many names occur more than once. There are three Inishturks, at least three Gar(i)nishes and seven Horse Islands. Sometimes the chart gives a place one name and the OS map another.

Appendix 6 lists many of the placename elements, with their Gaelic derivations and English translations.

Supplies; Pubs and Restaurants

Quirky placename conventions; the English version is given as "Castletown Bearhaven" on the charts

SUPPLIES

Availability of supplies of all kinds is detailed in the text. There are at least small shops of some kind in most villages, and for a major restock, Dungarvan, Castletownbere and Dingle offer perhaps the best combination of convenience by sea and proximity to the supermarket, while Youghal, Kinsale, Union Hall, Baltimore, Schull, Bantry, Kilrush, Galway, Sligo and Killybegs come a close second. Connemara and the coast of Mayo are notably short of accessible sources of supply. There are some very capable boatyards, but large chandleries only in Cork, Skibbereen and Killybegs. There are sailmakers in Crosshaven, Kinsale, Schull, Galway and Sligo. Fuel is not hard to come by, but in the remoter places may require a little forethought. Although (at the time of writing in 2015) the European Commission has filed a case against Ireland in the European Court for its continued arrangements whereby yachts can use fuel "intended for fishing vessels", it remains legal in Ireland for leisure craft to use marked (untaxed/agri/tractor) diesel, which is dyed green. Tankers, and all marina and harbourside pumps, dispense green diesel. In general, in the text, this is what is meant by "diesel". However leisure craft must pay the additional tax, in respect of all marked diesel used for propulsion. The self-declaration must be made and the extra tax remitted direct to the Revenue Commissioners by March 1 of the year following purchase. See www.revenue.ie, using the search key "private pleasure navigation", for details and applicable tax rates. Yachtsmen are strongly advised to retain on board all receipts and tax documents for fuel, which may be subject to Customs audit. Petrol (gasoline) is available only at roadside filling stations, all of which sell taxed (road or "white") diesel as well. Some of them also have a green diesel pump, and most of them sell bottled gas (propane or butane). Gas may pose problems of compatibility of fittings. If all else fails, the Irish standard fittings (which differ from the British ones) are easily bought. Camping Gaz, while expensive, can be obtained in many places.

PUBS and RESTAURANTS

Ireland is legendary for the warmth of its welcome, and nowhere is this more marked than in its pubs, of which there are thousands. The pub is the local meeting-place where the best *craic* is often to be found. This Irish term, which derives from English but has developed to the point where it has no longer a direct English translation, describes the mix of conversation, banter, jokes, ribbing, argument and laughter that has made the Irish pub and its customers a worldwide success story. It is in the pub that the curiosity of the island is seen in its highest form – "are you on holiday?" is not a straight question

Croagh Patrick overlooks Rosmoney and Mayo SC

Waste Disposal; Communications; Customs and Immigration; Travel

but an invitation to share your life story and your opinions, and in return to have the questioner reciprocate.

Equally, the quality of restaurants is outstanding. It would be a full-time job to stay current with the phone numbers, let alone the merits of individual establishments, so this book does not attempt it – the cruising sailor should carry an up-to-date tourist guide book as well and make full use of the tourist information facilities listed.

WASTE DISPOSAL

Dumping of any waste overboard in Irish waters is forbidden by law. The paucity of waste disposal facilities in ports and harbours has been the focus of much well-deserved criticism, and any opportunity to use a recycling facility should be seized, although it goes without saying that disposing of waste on the islands, even in an authorised facility, is inconsiderate. In some places tagged rubbish bags are available from shops for a standard charge; these may be filled and left for collection. The law does not, however, require holding tanks for sewage on yachts, and in consequence there are very few pumpout stations. Most marinas and harbours prohibit the use of on-board heads while in port, and it is only common courtesy to use the facilities on shore.

COMMUNICATIONS

Mobile phone signal is available in most places up to five miles offshore, and 4G coverage is improving, but there are still some blank spots both afloat and ashore, depending on the provider network. It may be assumed that every house, shop and pub has a telephone anyway. Broadband is always available in marinas, and in restaurants and pubs as well as public facilities such as libraries.

CUSTOMS and IMMIGRATION

For most yachts arriving from other EU countries there is normally no requirement to report to Customs, and there are no passport formalities between the UK and Ireland. However the authorities are vigilant and well-equipped, their major preoccupations being drugs, firearms, illegal immigrants and the protection of Ireland's vital farming industry from illicit or diseased plants and animals. For an official statement of the requirements, see Appendix 7, page 364.

TRAVEL

These parts of Ireland can be reached by road or rail from Dublin or points north or south. There are ferries from England, Wales and France to Dublin, Rosslare and Cork. Dublin, Waterford, Cork, Derry, Farranfore (Kerry), Knock (Mayo), Carrickfin (Donegal) and Shannon (Clare) have flights from airports in Great Britain and beyond. Inishmore, Inishmaan and Inisheer (Aran Islands) have connections by air with the mainland.

Rosslare, Waterford, Cork, Tralee, Limerick, Galway, Westport, Ballina, Sligo and Belfast have train connections with Dublin, and bus services are widespread and comprehensive. Car rental offices tend to be concentrated in the cities, at the airports and at Rosslare Harbour. There is a dense network of minor roads, and almost every mainland anchorage is reachable by road. For detailed routes, timetables and fares to and around Ireland, as anywhere else, consult the Internet.

The authorities are vigilant and well-equipped; LÉ **Samuel Beckett** *of the Irish Naval Service, off the Old Head of Kinsale. Probably not Waiting for Godot...*

Cruising Ireland

Tearaght, Blasket Islands, Co.Kerry (Chapter 5)

"CRUISING IRELAND"

Cruising Ireland – A Companion to the Irish Cruising Club Sailing Directions by Mike Balmforth and Norman Kean, published in 2012, provides a wealth of additional fascinating background information on the whole coast of Ireland, with 650 stunning photographs by 58 different photographers. Complementing this, the more technical pilot book, it is an invaluable guide to planning a cruise. References to chapter and page numbers in *Cruising Ireland* are contained throughout this volume.

ISBN 978 0 9558 199 3 3, 256 pages in hardback, *Cruising Ireland* is available from booksellers and chandlers or from our website www.iccsailingbooks.com, price £29.95 / €37.50.

"...enough to have any reader rooting for the lifejacket....the stories behind the extensive art on Wicklow's harbour wall, behind Kinsale's connection with Robinson Crusoe, behind the 'jaunty tilt' to the leaning tower of Waterford's Ardmore.

"Chris Stillman writes about Valentia's tetrapods and Padraig Whooley extols the best whale watching waters in Europe, while Libby Purves and Tim Severin are among guest contributors. The photographs, by Kevin Dwyer, Geraldine Hennigan and many ICC members and friends resemble nothing less than postcards from paradise."

Lorna Siggins, The Irish Times

"...rich not just in sailing lore but also in historical information...The photographs are a feast for the eyes....If you are going to cruise in Ireland it would be silly to set off without this book."

Iain A.MacLeod, CCC Tidelines

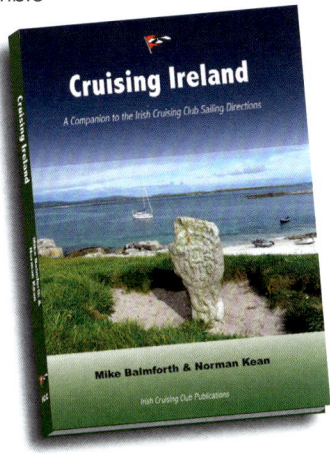

1 Rosslare to Cork Harbour

Crosshaven, the principal sailing centre in Cork Harbour and home of the Royal Cork Yacht Club, has three marinas (photo Ken Atkinson)

> **'Cruising Ireland'**
>
> The coast from Carnsore Point to Cork Harbour is described on pages 24 to 38 of **Cruising Ireland**, and Rosslare on pages 158 to 160

The south-east corner of Ireland can be a surprisingly challenging place for a yacht. The coast near Carnsore Point is unimposing, but the strong tides, offshore rocks and lack of good landmarks make for tricky pilotage, and convenient and accessible harbours are few. The ferry port of Rosslare offers reasonable anchorage in its bay and the possibility of an alongside berth. The charming village of Kilmore Quay with its busy marina, a few miles west of Carnsore Point, is often the most convenient first port of call for a yacht arriving from south-west England or from France. West of the Saltee Islands, the picture changes as the coast rises in bold cliffs, with a succession of broad bays, fine natural harbours, and few dangers offshore. Waterford Harbour was well known to the Vikings of the 10th century, and was the scene of the first Norman invasion of Ireland in 1169. Between there and Dungarvan is the "copper coast", where the metal ore was once mined below the sandstone cliffs. To the west lie Ardmore, Youghal and Ballycotton Bays and the great natural harbour of Cork.

APPROACHES to ROSSLARE

The Tuskar Rock, 6M ENE of Carnsore Point, is the principal landfall for a vessel approaching the SE corner of Ireland. The lighthouse on the Tuskar, completed in 1815, marks the entrance to St George's Channel and the Irish Sea. The area is one of strong tides, irregular seabed contours and dangerous offshore rocks, while further offshore are busy shipping lanes.

Rosslare Harbour dates from 1906 when the short-sea crossing to Fishguard was established. Today Rosslare Europort handles ferries and RoRo cargo ships of up to 30,000 tons. However the harbour is happy to accommodate yachts, provided that they are willing to deal with the constraints of a commercial port, and it is a handy place for crew changes.

28

Rosslare

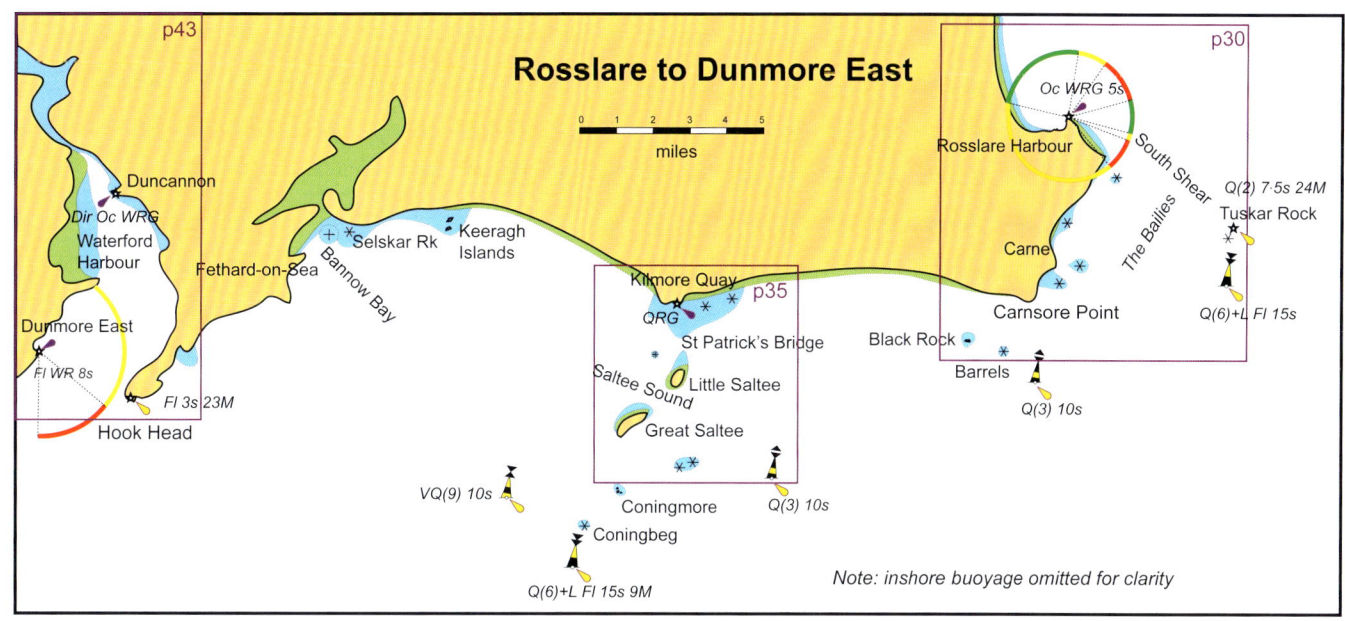

Tides – Rosslare and approaches

The stream sets NW–SE through the South Shear, SE of Rosslare, to join the main stream S of the offshore banks and NE of the Tuskar. Around the Tuskar the set is NNE–SSW. The spring rate here is 2 to 3 knots, turning N at –0100 Cobh and S at +0500 Cobh. The range at Rosslare is only 1·6m at springs and 0·6m at neaps. Constant at Rosslare (HW) +0035 Cobh, (LW) +0005 Cobh, MHWS 1·9m, MHWN 1·4m, MLWN 0·8m, MLWS 0·3m.

Paper Charts

The small-craft folios SC5621 and 5622 cover the whole of this section in full detail. In terms of individual charts, AC2049 Old Head of Kinsale to Tuskar Rock, or Imray's C57 analogously titled, cover almost all of it. AC1787 Carnsore Point to Wicklow Head or the larger-scale AC1772 Rosslare Europort and Wexford is needed for Rosslare. For exploring the Saltee Islands, AC2740 is essential. AC2046 is necessary for the Rivers Suir and Barrow above Duncannon Bar. The large-scale charts AC2071 and 2017 are optional. The 1:50,000-scale AC1765 Old Head of Kinsale to Power Head is useful, but AC1777 Port of Cork, Lower Harbour is better for Crosshaven. AC1773, Port of Cork, Upper Harbour is needed only for East Ferry and Cork city.

Traffic Separation Scheme

There is a TSS E and S of the Tuskar Rock. The S- and W-bound lane is 3 to 6M from the lighthouse, and the E- and N-bound lane 8 to 11M from the lighthouse. The lanes should be crossed at right angles, or as nearly as possible. Yachts rounding the Tuskar should use the inshore traffic zone, between the TSS and the rock. The South Shear is the main channel for ships approaching the port of Rosslare.

Tuskar Rock

The Tuskar should be given a berth of 5 cables on its E, N and W sides, more in heavy weather. On the S side, South Rock buoy should be left on the proper hand.

ROSSLARE

⊕ RL 52°15'·5N 6°20'·8W
AC1787, 1772, SC5621·15, Imray C61 and Plan
Rosslare Harbour lies opposite the southern end of the sandbanks which parallel the coast from Dublin southwards. There is anchorage in the bay to the W. The harbour is sheltered from NE through S to SW but exposed from WNW to N. Large ferries sail to Fishguard, Pembroke Dock, Roscoff and Cherbourg, and the harbour is also a busy RoRo cargo port. The Port area is required to comply with the International Ship and Port Facility Code, which may mean restricted access to the harbour from the landward side at certain hours. Subject to these provisos, yachts are welcome to use the Fishermen's Quay, on the

Tuskar Rock (photo John Clementson)

Rosslare

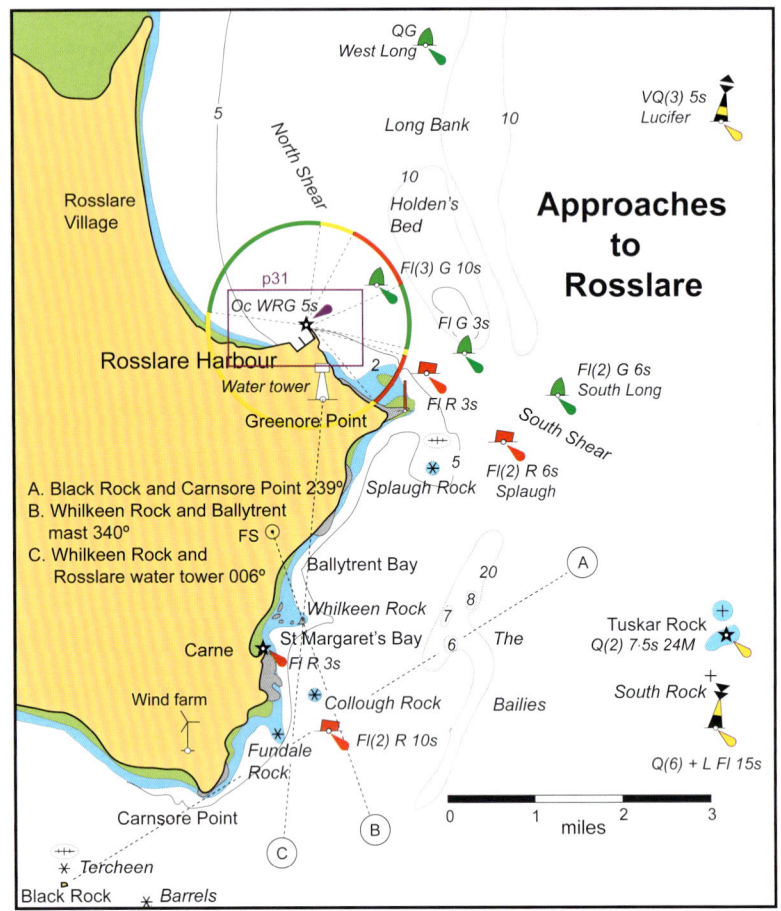

A. Black Rock and Carnsore Point 239°
B. Whilkeen Rock and Ballytrent mast 340°
C. Whilkeen Rock and Rosslare water tower 006°

Dangers – Approaches to Rosslare

Tuskar Rock (5m high), 6M ENE of Carnsore Point
Gypsy Rock, 2m, 2 cables NNW of the Tuskar
Unnamed rock, awash, 2·5 cables SSW of the Tuskar
South Rock, 2·4m, 6·5 cables SSW of the Tuskar
Splaugh Rock, extensive reef drying 0·3m, 6 cables SE of Greenore Point
Wreck, 3 cables N of Splaugh Rock
Lucifer Bank, 3·5m, **Long Bank**, 2·8m and **Holden's Bed**, 3·8m, NE of Greenore Point.
Carrick Rock, drying reef extending 3·5 cables ENE from Greenore Point

Lights and Marks

Tuskar Rock, white tower Q(2) 7·5s 33m 24M, Racon (T) 18M, AIS
South Rock buoy, S Card Q(6)+L Fl 15s, AIS, 1·5M S of the Tuskar
Lucifer buoy, E Card VQ(3) 5s, AIS, 4M ENE of Rosslare Harbour
South Long buoy, SHM Fl(2) G 6s
Splaugh buoy, PHM Fl(2) R 6s
(these two synchronised)
Carrick Rock perch, PHM, unlit
South Holdens buoy, SHM Fl G 3s
Calmines buoy, PHM Fl R 3s
(these two synchronised)
West Holdens buoy, SHM Fl(3) G 10s
Rosslare Breakwater, red tower, Oc WRG 5s 15m W13M R10M G10M; G 098°–188°, W 188°–208°, R 208°–246°, G 246°–284°, W 284°–286°, R 286°–320°, W 320°–098°. Shows a narrow white sector ESE over the main E approach through the South Shear channel, and white to the NNE over the North Shear channel and over the harbour and the shore to the SW. Red sectors show over the Long and Lucifer Banks to NE and between Splaugh and Greenore Point to the SE. Green sectors show inshore to N and NW and over Holden's Bed to the E.
Ballygeary, pole bn Oc WR 1·7s 7m 4M, R shore –152°, W 152°–200°, W (unintens) 200°–205°. Shows red to W, white to N, unintensified white close to the breakwater end.
Rosslare buoy, SHM QG

Rosslare Harbour: the Fishermen's Quay, extreme R

Rosslare to Kilmore Quay and the Saltees

SW side of the harbour, having first contacted the Port Operations tower.

Directions

From the E (South Shear Channel) leave the Tuskar light 2M to port, South Long, South Holdens and West Holdens buoys to starboard and Splaugh and Calmines buoys to port. Identify the breakwater light, and give the breakwater end a wide berth to allow space for ferries leaving. **From the S,** leave the Tuskar light 1M to starboard, then Splaugh to port and South Long to starboard as above. **From the N** (North Shear Channel), leave West Long and West Holdens buoys to port, then identify the breakwater light.

Anchorage

Anchorage is available to the W of the harbour entrance, in 3m, sand, well out of the way of the ship channel and clear of moorings (stay W and S of the starboard-hand buoy). Anchorage is prohibited within 5 cables to the N and E, and 3 cables to the W, of the breakwater head. Somewhat subject to swell.

Harbour

For an alongside berth, call Rosslare Harbour VHF Channel 14 or phone 05391 57929 or 087 232 0251. The Fishermen's Quay, on the SW side of the harbour, has 3 to 5m. The RoRo berths on the central pier and the breakwater must not be obstructed. The harbour is managed by Iarnród Éireann (Irish Railways).

Facilities

For mechanical and electrical repairs, check with the Port Operations tower. Filling stations, shops, pubs, restaurants, hotels. Train, bus and ferry connections, car rental. RNLI all-weather lifeboat station.

The small-craft harbour 4 cables W of the port almost dries at LW and is encumbered with moorings.

Rosslare Harbour from the SE: Carrick Rock perch, centre, and the breakwater light, R

ROSSLARE to KILMORE QUAY and the SALTEES

SC5621, AC1787, 2049, 2740, Imray C57

In settled weather, the waters around Carnsore Point can be like a millpond, but in adverse conditions the combination of wind over tide and the irregular bottom can throw up tumultuous seas. The Saltee Islands, S of Kilmore Quay, are surrounded by dangerous rocks, and this, combined with the low-lying and relatively featureless nature of the mainland coast here, makes for an area to be avoided in heavy weather or poor visibility. The main ship channel passes outside the Coningbeg buoy, 9M offshore, but with

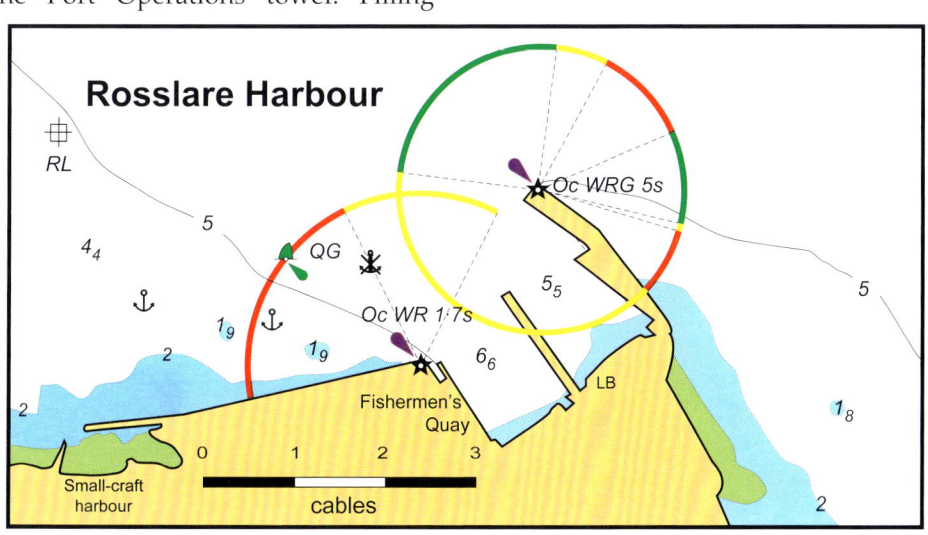

Rosslare to Kilmore Quay

careful pilotage a yacht can pass between or north of the Saltees in any reasonable weather. The classic route is across St Patrick's Bridge, a gravel bar between Little Saltee and the shore, with 2·4m at LAT and buoyed in summer. Saltee Sound, between Great and Little Saltees, has 7m but is unmarked. There is deep water south of Great Saltee, but the approach passes close to the dangerous Brandies Rocks.

Dangers – Rosslare to Kilmore Quay and the Saltees

S of Rosslare and W of the Tuskar:
Splaugh Rock (extensive reef drying 0·3m), 6 cables SE of Greenore Point
Whilkeen Rock (dries 2·5m), 4 cables offshore 2M SSW of Greenore Point
Rocks with 2·9 and 3·4m, 2·5 cables E of Whilkeen Rock
Collough Rock (awash at LWS), 5 cables offshore, 1·7M NE of Carnsore Point
The Bailies, 6 to 12m, 1M NE of Collough Rock
Fundale Rock (dries 1·2m), the outer end of a reef extending 5 cables SE from the shore, 1M NE of Carnsore Point
Between Carnsore Point and the Saltees:
The Barrels (dry 1·5m), 1·5M SW by S of Carnsore Point
Nether Rock (5m), 2 cables NW of the Barrels
Black Rock (2m high), 2·5 M SW by W of Carnsore Point
Tercheen (dries at LW), 2 cables N of Black Rock
A **dangerous wreck** 2 cables N of Tercheen
Long Bohur (4m), and **Short Bohur** (7·3m), 1·5M E of Little Saltee
The Bore (5·5m), 1M S of Long Bohur
The Brandies (dry 0·9 and 2·5m), 1·5M SE of Great Saltee
Around and between the Saltees:
Coningbeg Rock (dries 2·8m), 2·5M SSW of Great Saltee.
Coningmore Rocks (4m high), 1·5M NE of Coningbeg Rock and 1·5M S of Great Saltee
Red Bank (7·9m), 1·4M W of Coningmore Rocks, breaks in heavy weather
Whitty Rock (awash at LAT) and **Power's Rock** (0·3m) 3 cables NW of Great Saltee, and **Shoal Rock** (0·9m) 2 cables S of it.
Sebber Bridge (0·6m to 4m) boulder spit extending 7 cables N from Great Saltee
Galgee Rock (dries), 1 cable S of Little Saltee
Murroch's Rock (awash at LAT), 5 cables NW of Little Saltee
Unnamed rock (awash at LAT), 3 cables W of Little Saltee
Jackeen Rock (1·5m) 8 cables W of Little Saltee
Goose Rock (dries 2·6m), 1 cable W of Little Saltee
Forlorn Rock, 1·5m, 7 cables SW of Kilmore Quay
St Patrick's Bridge, 52°09'·2N 6°34'·9W, gravel bar with 2·4m in mid-channel, between Little Saltee and the shore SE of Kilmore Quay. The existence of several charted rocks around the Saltees is doubtful. The drying rock 4 cables SW of Great Saltee is officially labelled *ED* but the drying rock one cable SE of Little Saltee, and the three outermost rocks (two shown drying and one with less than 2m) within 3 cables N and NE of Whitty's Rock, may also be artifacts from satellite imagery. Caution is nevertheless advised when navigating in this area.

Landfall from the S and SE

Approaching the SE corner of Ireland from Land's End or the Bristol Channel, most yachts are likely to make their first call at Kilmore Quay or Dunmore East, and the natural course is to leave Coningbeg and the Saltee Islands to starboard, thus avoiding the complications of negotiating the Saltees at the end of a long and possibly tiring passage. All the approach options are described below.

Lights and Marks

Splaugh buoy, PHM Fl(2) R 6s, AIS
Calmines buoy, PHM Fl R 3s
Carne Pier, metal col Fl R 3s 6m 4M
Fundale buoy, PHM Fl(2) R 10s, 5 cables ENE of Fundale Rock
Carnsore Point, wind farm of 14 conspicuous turbines close inland of the point
Barrels buoy, E Card Q(3) 10s, AIS, 1M SE of the rocks
Coningbeg buoy, S Card Q(6) + LFl 15s 9M, Racon (G), AIS, 9 cables S of Coningbeg Rock
Bore Rocks buoy, E Card Q(3) 10s, AIS, 8 cables SE of The Bore
Red Bank buoy, W Card VQ(9) 10s, AIS, 2·6M W of Coningmore Rock
St Patrick's Bridge buoys SHM, Fl G 6s, and PHM, Fl R 6s, both these marks about 3 cables to the E of the bar. Conventional buoyage direction N and E.
Kilmore Quay fairway buoy, RWVS Iso 10s (this buoy is also on the line for St Patrick's Bridge)
Kilmore Quay breakwater end, Q RG 7m 5M, R 269°–354°, G 354°–003°, R 003°–077° shows green over approach channel from close S, red elsewhere
Kilmore Quay leading lights 008°, Oc 4s 6M, white with red stripe on grey concrete columns, front 3m, rear 6m,

Experimental buoys

A position 7 cables S of Black Rock and 2M W of the Barrels E Card buoy is used by the Irish Lights as a test location for experimental buoys. Check www.commissionersofirishlights.ie for the latest information.

Offshore weather buoy

Buoy M5, yellow, Fl(5) Y 20s, is moored 33M S of the Coningbeg Rock at 51°41'·4N 5°25'·5W

Rosslare to Kilmore Quay

Tides

Streams run at up to 3 kn at springs between Carnsore Point and Greenore Point, and through Saltee Sound, and can reach 4·5 kn over St Patrick's Bridge; elsewhere at 1·5 to 2·5 kn, Tides turn N and E at −0110 Cobh and S and W at +0510 Cobh. Over St Patrick's Bridge the E-going stream starts at −0250 Cobh.

South of the Saltees the streams are rotatory clockwise. The N and E stream begins N at −0100 Cobh, reaches its greatest rate of 1·7 kn (springs) to the ENE at +0200 Cobh, and ends SE. The S and W stream begins S at +0530 Cobh, reaches 1·9 kn (springs) W by S at −0355 Cobh, and ends NW. Slack water lasts about an hour. There are ripples near and over all the shoals. In heavy weather there are overfalls S and E of the Saltees, and steep and dangerous breakers on The Bailies, between the Tuskar Rock and Carnsore Point. Constant (Great Saltee) +0014 Cobh, MHWS 3·8m, MHWN 2·9m.

Caution

Much of the coast between Rosslare and Cork Harbour is charted only on a scale of 1:150,000. The exceptions are close S of Rosslare, around Kilmore Quay and the Saltees, in Waterford, Dungarvan and Youghal Harbours, and west of Power Head. Everywhere else, it should be borne in mind that electronic charts (which are derived from the paper ones) have no better resolution. Care must be taken not to over-zoom on the electronic charts, and to exercise particular caution in their use when in close proximity to the shore.

Black Rock (L) open S of Carnsore Point clears Collough and Fundale Rocks to the SE (transit A, plan on p30)

Rosslare water tower and Whilkeen Rock in line leads between Collough Rock and the shore (transit C, plan on p30)

Ballytrent mast and Whilkeen Rock in line clears Collough Rock to the NE (transit B, plan on p30)

Directions – Rosslare to Kilmore Quay, inshore passage

The Bailies, with their irregular rocky bottom, raise steep overfalls, and in winds of force 6 and higher against the tide, these can be dangerous. The passage between the Bailies and Collough Rock is 1M wide, and the passage between the Bailies and the Tuskar is 2M wide. In settled weather the inshore passage may be taken close E of the Calmines, Splaugh and Fundale buoys. The perch on Carrick Rock may be left half a cable to starboard, but beware then of the Calmines shoal and a shallow patch N of it. There are several short cuts: Black Rock open S of Carnsore Point 239° leads SE of Fundale and Collough Rocks. Whilkeen Rock in line with Rosslare water tower 006° astern leads between Collough Rock and the shore. The tall white mast among the trees S of Ballytrent House, in line with Whilkeen Rock 340° astern, clears Collough Rock to the NE. Note that there are rocks, with 2·9 and 3·4m, 2·5 cables E of Whilkeen Rock.

Carnsore Point is clean, and in calm weather it can be given a berth of one cable. It is identifiable in moderate to good visibility by its conspicuous wind farm. Once round the point, identify Black Rock to the SW and steer due W to leave it 7 cables to port. Identify the buoys on St Patrick's Bridge and steer to pass midway between them. The buoys are positioned 3 cables E of the Bar; if entering Kilmore Quay, hold the W'ly course to the fairway buoy, when the leading marks line up 008°.

Rosslare to Kilmore Quay

Carne Pier

Anchorage

Anchorage in winds between SW and NNW may be found in St Margaret's Bay, between Carnsore Point and Greenore Point. This is a useful and comfortable anchorage in strong NW winds, when Rosslare is exposed. There is a small drying pier at Carne (Carna on the charts), on the S side of the bay. **From the N**, leave Whilkeen Rock a cable to starboard. **From the S**, use the transits on the plan on p30 to avoid Fundale and Collough Rocks. When Carne pier bears 290°, turn in to the bay. Anchor 2 to 3 cables NE of the pier in 3 to 4m, sand. The pier is unsuitable as an alongside berth, and rocks extend 20m beyond the pier head. Shop, pub and restaurant at Carne.

Anchorage is also available in Ballytrent Bay, to the N.

Directions – Rosslare to Kilmore Quay, offshore

In heavy weather from the S, steer SE from the Splaugh buoy for a mile, then turn S, leaving the overfalls on the Bailies well to starboard. Give Carnsore Point a berth of 2M, and leave the Barrels buoy to starboard. The safest option is always to head out to sea round the Coningbeg buoy, but in moderate conditions St Patrick's Bridge and Saltee Sound are navigable, and with careful navigation a course close S of Great Saltee can be taken except in the combination of heavy weather and wind over tide.

For Saltee Sound, steer from the Barrels buoy for the N end of Little Saltee, keeping it on a bearing of not more than 270° to pass 4 cables N of Long Bohur - in other words, make good due west, and do not let the tide carry you south. When Makeston Rock (off Great Saltee) comes in line with the SE point of Great Saltee 233° (waypoint ⊕LB, 52°08'·5N 6°33'·0W, plan on p35), turn on to this course to leave the S point of Little Saltee 3 cables to starboard. Keeping this distance from Little Saltee to avoid Galgee Rock, Goose Rock and the unnamed rock W of the island, skirt the island until heading 330°, then hold this course for 4 cables through the Sound to clear Sebber Bridge. When the S end of Little Saltee bears 110° (from waypoint ⊕LS, 52°08'·15N 6°36'·0W), identify the Kilmore Quay fairway buoy, W of St Patrick's Bridge and steer towards it, passing E of Jackeen and Murroch's Rocks.

For the passage outside Great Saltee, pass 4 cables N of Long Bohur as above, then steer 225° to leave the Brandies 1M to port and the E sides of both the islands 4 cables to starboard. Do not alter course to starboard until 5 cables S of Great Saltee (waypoint ⊕GS, 52°06'·0N 6°37'·7W). Once round, and W of 6°38'W, and if heading for Kilmore Quay, steer 000° until the breakwater bears 037°. Note that a direct course from the Bore Rocks buoy to close S of Great Saltee passes dangerously close to the Brandies, and also that significant overfalls occur in the vicinity of Shoal Rock.

In strong to gale force winds between NW and NE, an inshore course to the W of Carnsore Point and across St Patrick's Bridge is normally safe, but in bad weather and darkness or fog the safest option is to stay south of the Coningbeg buoy (clearing waypoint 52°03'·0N 6°38'·6W).

Directions – passage from W to E between or outside the Saltees

Refer to the above directions for the passage from E to W. In settled conditions, the directions for St Patrick's Bridge and Carnsore Point may, as it were, be reversed.

The buoys on St Patrick's Bridge, from the N. Little Saltee, centre, Great Saltee, R

Makeston Rock and the SE point of Great Saltee in line

34

Kilmore Quay

For the passage of Saltee Sound from the W, approach with the summit of Little Saltee bearing 095°. When the E tip of Great Saltee bears 185° (at waypoint ⊕LS, 52°08'·15N 6°36'·0W), turn to starboard and steer 150° through the sound. Rounding the S point of Little Saltee, steer NE, giving the island a berth of 4 cables until its N point is well abeam, then turn due E for the Barrels buoy, 7·5M to the E.

For the passage outside Great Saltee, give the S end of the island a berth of 5 cables, then keep this distance off while rounding the island and steer to leave Little Saltee 4 cables to port. Note the comment in the preceding section about the overfalls S of Great Saltee. When the N end of Little Saltee is well abeam, turn E for the Barrels buoy.

Approaches to Kilmore Quay and Dunmore East from offshore to the south

From a position close W of the Coningbeg buoy, a course of 350° leads 3 cables W of the Coningbeg Rock. If the rock can be clearly identified when abeam (it usually shows, or breaks) it is then safe to turn on to a course of 010°, which leads 5 cables E of Red Bank and 4 cables W of Great Saltee. The safest approach to Kilmore Quay is then to stay on this course until clear well N of Little Saltee, leaving Jackeen Rock and Murroch's Rock to starboard. Then steer towards the fairway buoy W of St Patrick's Bridge until the leading beacons for Kilmore Quay are identified. For Dunmore East, a course of 292° leads from the Coningbeg buoy to Hook Head.

KILMORE QUAY

⊕KQ 52°10'N 6°35'·1W, AC2049, 2740, SC5621.16, Imray C57 and Plan

Kilmore Quay is a busy fishing harbour but has an excellent marina and welcomes yachts. The approach to the harbour, through a channel dredged to 1·9m, has little room for error. Recent winter storms have built a sandbar with 1m at LAT, immediately off the south pierhead. Deeper drafted vessels should avoid entering or leaving near LW. In winds of F6 and above between SE and SW, or in a heavy swell (particularly near LW) Dunmore East, 15M to the W, offers a safer option to the stranger.

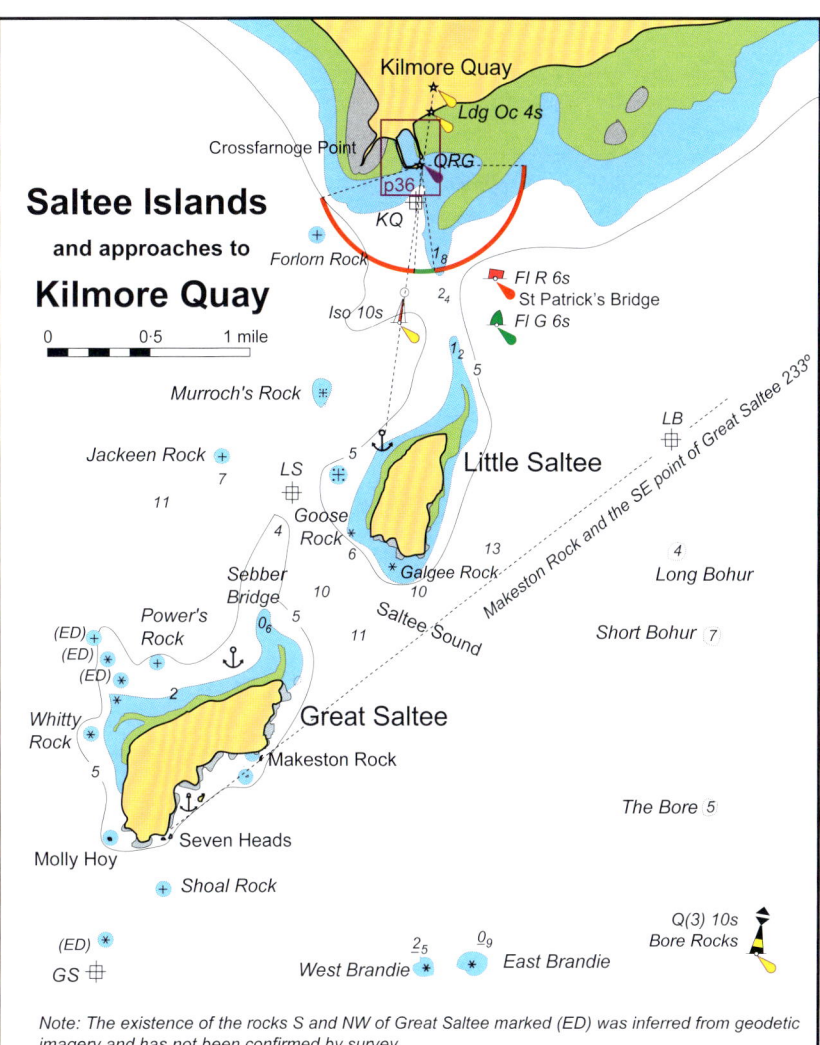

Note: The existence of the rocks S and NW of Great Saltee marked (ED) was inferred from geodetic imagery and has not been confirmed by survey.

Directions

From the E, after passing the buoys on St Patrick's Bridge, hold the W'ly course to the fairway buoy, which is on the leading line for Kilmore Quay. Steer in on the line of the leading beacons 008° until the harbour entrance is abeam, then turn in. Be alert for traffic coming out as the entrance is only 20m wide. The dredged channel to Kilmore Quay is narrow and subject to strong cross tides; care must be taken to stay on the leading line. **From Saltee Sound,** refer to the above directions for **Rosslare to Kilmore Quay – offshore. From the W,** the church building at Kilmore Quay provides the most prominent landmark, while the leading beacons are initially obscured by the pier. Give the shore at Crossfarnoge Point a berth of 5 cables to clear Forlorn Rock, then identify the fairway buoy.

Marina

The harbour, managed by Wexford County

Kilmore Quay and the Saltees

Approaching Kilmore Quay: the leading beacons, R

Kilmore Quay harbour entrance

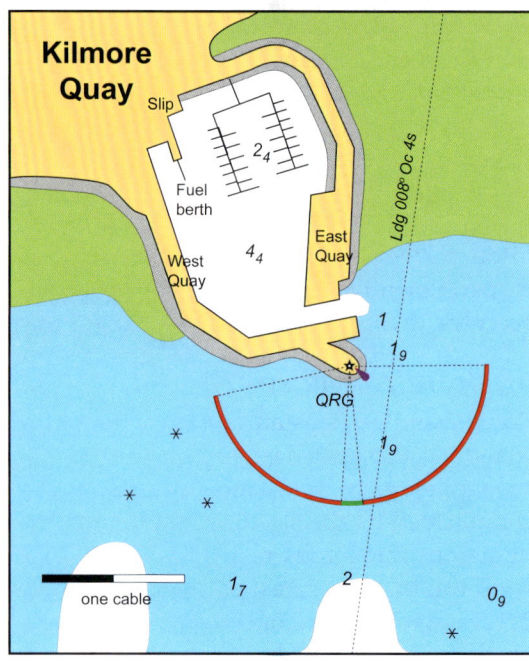

Kilmore Quay from the S

Kilmore Quay marina. The fuel pontoon, R, on the end of the pier

Council, has 4·4m alongside the E pier and 2·4m alongside the W pier, and contains a 60-berth marina with least depth 2·4m. The marina is very busy in summer and it is advisable to make contact in advance; VHF Ch 16 and 9, phone 05391 29955, e-mail harbourmaster@wexfordcoco.ie. Constant +0007 Cobh, MHWS 3·8m, MHWN 2·9m, MLWN 1·5m, MLWS 0·6m.

Facilities

Water, pumpout and shore power on the pontoons; CCTV security. Diesel (24h) by credit- or debit-card operated pump; shops, pubs, restaurants, chandlery. Buses to Wexford. Bicycle hire. Taxis 087 912 2259. Repairs, Haven Maritime 05391 29794. Mechanical, electrical and propeller repairs, Brian Kehoe 087 213 5732. Doctor. RNLI all-weather lifeboat station.

SALTEE ISLANDS

⊕LS 52°08'·15N 6°36'W, AC2740, SC5621·16

The islands are privately owned, and

36

Kilmore Quay to Dunmore East

The anchorage on the SE side of Great Saltee

Little Saltee is farmed, although neither is permanently inhabited. The somewhat eccentric owners of Great Saltee request that when they are in residence (as indicated by the standard of the Prince of the Saltees, flown from the flagstaff), visitors vacate the island by 1630 each day.

The pilotage of the islands is tricky, and is complicated by the strong tidal streams, the numerous dangerous rocks, and the lack of good transits. The latest editions (from June 2012) of AC2740 are on WGS84 datum, but on the older charts the offset in horizontal datum varied over the area of the chart. If navigating with the older chart or an electronic equivalent, do not place implicit faith in GPS in close quarters pilotage. The older charts also showed some of the above-water rocks as drying. The islands are a fascinating place to explore in good weather, home to several hundred species of birds, and offer reasonable temporary anchorages.

Anchorage

In settled conditions or moderate winds between NE and S, anchorage is available off the NW shore of Little Saltee in 4m, sand and boulders; and also off the N shore of Great Saltee, N of the buildings, in 2 to 4m, sand. In settled conditions with no swell, the bay (with 3·4m on the chart) on the SE side of Great Saltee 3 cables N of the Seven Heads Rocks provides an attractive temporary anchorage. The 2m-high rocks on the E side of the bay provide a landmark for entry.

KILMORE QUAY to DUNMORE EAST

AC2049, 2740, 2046, Imray C57

Heading W from Kilmore Quay, do not turn for Hook Head until 5 cables S of the harbour, in order to avoid Forlorn Rock. Apart from that there are no dangers on the direct passage across Ballyteige Bay and the mouth of Waterford Harbour, and Hook Head is clean and steep-to. There is a cluster of islets and a few rocks in the bay, close inshore E of Baginbun Head. Fethard-on-Sea, in Bannow Bay to the NW, has limited facilities, but Dunmore East is a significant fishing port

Hook Head from the SE

37

Dunmore East

> ### Tides
> #### Kilmore Quay to Dunmore East
> *East of Hook Head the tides set E and W, turning E at –0050 Cobh and W at +0553 Cobh. The spring rate is 1 to 1·5 kn, increasing to 2 kn or more near the Saltees and Hook Head. S of Hook Head is the Tower race, with overfalls extending several miles to the W on the W-going stream in fresh winds between SE and W. Close W of Hook Head, the ebb stream from Waterford Harbour runs S at up to 3 kn at springs. Off the entrance to Waterford Harbour the E-going stream begins at –0120 Cobh and the W-going at +0450 Cobh. Constant (Dunmore East) +0003 Cobh, MHWS 4·2m, MHWN 3·2m, MLWN 1·4m, MLWS 0·6m*

> ### Dangers
> **Forlorn Rock,** 1·5m, 4 cables SW of Crossfarnoge Point
> **Keeragh Islands,** two islets 6m high, 6 cables offshore in Ballyteige Bay
> **George Rock,** 1·2m, between the Keeragh Islands and the shore
> **Selskar Rock** (dries 2m) 3 cables SW of Clammers Point at the E end of Bannow Bay
> **Selskar Shoal,** 0·3m, 3 cables WSW of Selskar Rock
> **Brecaun Bridge,** 1·7m, reef extending 3 cables offshore, 1·5M NE of Hook Head

> ### Lights and Marks
> **Hook Head,** white tower with black bands, Fl 3s 46m 18M, Racon (K) 10M, AIS
> **Waterford** buoy, PHM Fl(3) R 10s, 1·5M E of Dunmore East
> **Dunmore East Starboard No 1** buoy, SHM QG, 1·5 cables NNE of the W pierhead
> **Dunmore East Starboard No 3** buoy, SHM Fl G 2s, 0·5 cables N of the W pierhead
> **Dunmore East, E pier head,** grey tower Fl WR 8s 13m W17M R13M, W 225°–310°, R 310°–004°, shows red to S and SE over Hook Head, white to E over the estuary
> **Dunmore East, E breakwater,** red pole beacon Fl R 2s 6m 4M
> **Dunmore East, W wharf,** green pole beacon Fl G 2s 6m 4M.

and sailing centre, accessible in all weathers by day or night, and a popular call for yachts cruising the coast.

Fethard-on-Sea

52°11'·5N 6°48'·5W

Anchorage is available in settled conditions or offshore winds in Bannow Bay, N of Baginbun Head, which is identifiable by its conspicuous tower. The village of Fethard-on-Sea lies 1M N of Baginbun Head, and has a tiny drying harbour close NW of Ingard Point. **From the E,** stay close to Ingard Point to avoid Selskar Shoal. **From the W,** give Baginbun Head a berth of 2 cables to clear the drying reefs on its E side. Anchor in 2 to 3m, sand, NW of Ingard Point. Fethard harbour may offer a convenient dinghy landing. Shops, PO and pubs at Fethard village, 3 km.

Hook Head

In settled weather, particularly with a fair tide, it is safe to pass within a cable of the shore at Hook Head, but in adverse conditions, especially with wind over tide, it is advisable to give the Hook a berth of a mile or more, particularly at night. Hook Head has the oldest lighthouse in Ireland and possibly even in the world. The 12m-diameter tower was built by the earliest Norman overlords in Ireland, probably c.1245; legend has it that St Dubhán maintained a light on Hook Head in the 5th century. The short light structure now surmounting the Norman tower dates from 1864.

DUNMORE EAST

⊕ DE 52°09'·1N 6°59'·3W
AC2049, 2046, SC5621, SC5622, Imray C57

Dunmore East is one of Ireland's principal fishing ports. The harbour is deep and sheltered, but very busy with fishing boats. However, the bays within 5 cables to the N of the harbour are fringed by high cliffs and provide anchorage well sheltered from winds between S and NE. From the E and Hook Head, identify the breakwater at Dunmore East, bearing about 315°, and steer for it. At night, stay in the red sector of the harbour light until well clear to the W of Hook Head, then come N and approach in the white sector of the light. **From the W,** give the coast a berth of 4 cables to clear Falskirt Rock (2M W) and Robin Redbreast Rock (5 cables SW).

Harbour

If intending to enter the harbour, call the HM first on VHF Ch 16 or 14 for permission. At night, note that the breakwater extends 0·5 cable to the NW of the powerful sectored light. When rounding the breakwater end, be alert for traffic leaving. The harbour was dredged

Dunmore East

Dunmore East from the SE: the breakwater, L, Waterford Harbour SC moorings, centre, and the anchorage, R

in 2015 and now has 3·6m at LAT everywhere. There are pontoons in the W corner of the harbour and alongside part of the E pier. Follow instructions from the HM if available, or raft up (with permission) to a fishing boat. The S and NW sides of the harbour have constant fishing boat traffic. The harbour is managed by the Department of Agriculture, Food and the Marine; HM phone 051 383166.

Anchorage

The best anchorage is under the cliffs in the SE-facing bay 3 cables N of the harbour, in 3 to 5m, sand. A mooring may be available in the bay close NW of the harbour mouth. Both these bays are subject to swell in strong winds from S or SE, particularly on the ebb tide in the estuary.

Constant +0002 Cobh, MHWS 4·2m, MHWN 3·2m, MLWN 1·4m, MLWS 0·6m.

Facilities

Water on the E pier; diesel by tanker (Coast to Coast Oil, phone 051 382797). Filling station 1·5 km on the Waterford road. Shops, pubs, restaurants, PO. Small chandlery. RNLI all-weather lifeboat station. Waterford Harbour Sailing Club (051 383230) has its clubhouse at the harbour; showers available. Waterford airport, 8 km.

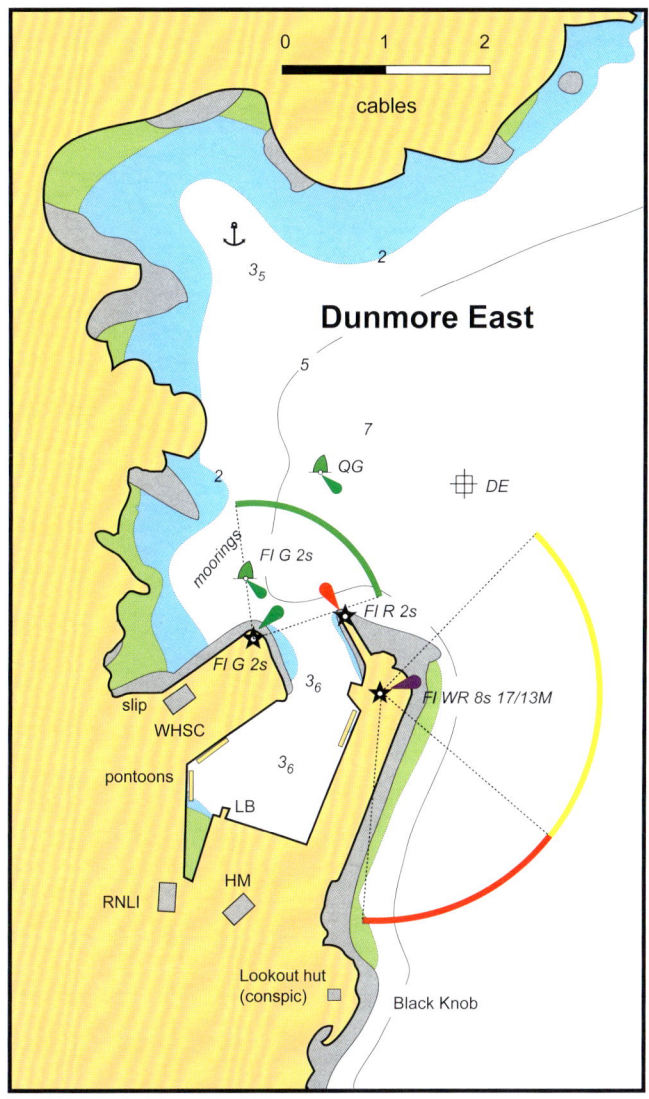

Dunmore East Harbour from the N

39

Waterford Harbour; Duncannon

Dunmore East Harbour. Pontoons (see Plan on p39) were installed after this photograph, and the one below, were taken

WATERFORD HARBOUR and NEW ROSS

AC2046, SC5621, SC5622, Imray C57

Waterford (46,700) on the River Suir is the oldest city in Ireland, starting as a Viking settlement in 914 and becoming the country's first Norman stronghold in the 12th century. Best-known in recent years for its beautiful glassware, Waterford is also a considerable general cargo and container port, and there is a convenient marina in the river. The city has many fine buildings reflecting its long and eventful history. Its name in English is derived from the Old Norse *Vatre-fjord*, "sea inlet"; the Irish name *Port Lairge* is older and unrelated. The River Suir is a well-marked deepwater ship channel leading 10M from seaward to the port of Waterford.

The River Barrow, tributary to the Suir, is spanned at its mouth by an opening railway bridge and is navigable with a least depth of 2m and good marks and lights for 10M upstream to the town of New Ross (8,150). The replica Famine emigrant ship *Dunbrody* is moored here as a museum, and there is a marina.

Duncannon

Close N of Duncannon Point there is available anchorage, sheltered from winds between NE and S. Duncannon is a small holiday village with a pier occasionally used by fishing vessels. From the S, leave Duncannon Point (with its conspicuous fort and directional light tower) and the end of the pier 0·5 cable to starboard. The pier has 0·6m at LAT at its outer end and dries at the root. The bottom alongside is rocky in places and local advice

Dunmore East from the N. Waterford Harbour SC clubhouse at the head of the slipway, R centre

Waterford Harbour

Tides - Waterford Harbour

Inside the entrance the flood begins at −0425 Cobh and the ebb at +0045 Cobh, with a spring rate off Creadan Head of 2·5 to 3 kn, less in mid-channel. Close inshore between Creadan Head and Portally Head the flood commences an hour earlier. There is a ripple on the ebb off Portally Head where the tides meet. Tidal streams are strong in the rivers, reaching 2 to 3 knots at the narrow points, the ebb often being stronger than the flood.
Constant (Waterford) +0053 Cobh, MHWS 4·5m, MHWN 3·6m, MLWN 1·2m, MLWS 0·3m.

Dangers - Waterford Harbour

The area on the W side of Waterford Harbour, from Creadan Head N to Passage East is an extensive sandbank, part of which dries, and Duncannon Spit, which also dries, extends 7 cables SSE from Duncannon Point. Apart from these and the shallows in some of the bays further upstream, there are few unexpected dangers in the rivers, and the main hazard is commercial traffic. N of Cheek Point and E of Little Island, there are groynes at right angles to the shore, and the submerged remains of fish traps. There are several obstructions with less than 1m on the E bank of the Barrow close S of New Ross. A cable area 4 cables wide crosses the estuary from Duncannon. Anchoring is prohibited here, and also between Cheek Point and Kilmokea Point.

Lights and Marks

The river channels are marked by port and starboard hand buoys Fl R and Fl G, and by the following principal marks:
Duncannon, Dir Oc WRG 4s, white tower on fort, 13m, W11M R8M G8M, G358°–001·7°, W001·7°–002·2°, R002·2°–006°, provides a leading light for traffic entering from the S. Same tower shows Oc WR 4s R119°–149°, W149°–172°, white over the channel to the N and red over the banks to the W.
Duncannon Rear, beacon Oc 6s 10M vis 000·7°– 003·2°. Provides leading line in transit with Duncannon light
Passage Spit, red piled beacon Fl WR 5s 7m W6M R5M, W shore–127°, R127°–180°, W180°–302°, R302°–shore, shows white over the channel to the NW, red over Seedes Bank and close NW and N of the beacon, white over the channel to the SE and red over the banks to the S
Parkswood Point, Fl R 4s 3m 3M
Seedes Perch, pile Fl(2) R 4s 3m 3M
Barron Quay, white post, Fl R 2s 3m
Cheek Point, white pole beacon QWR 6m 5M, W 007°–289°, R 289°–007°, shows white over the channel to the SW and N, red over Carter's Patch bank to the SE
Sheagh, beacon Fl R 3s 3m 3M
Kilmokea, beacon Fl 5s
River Barrow Railway Bridge, 2FR hor, traffic signals
Snowhill Point, ldg lts 255°, front Fl WR 2·5s 5m 3M, W 222°–020°, R 020°–057°, W 057°–107°, rear, Flour Mill Q 12m 5M. Sectored light shows white over channel to the E, red over channel to the SW and white inshore to the W
Queen's Channel ldg lts 098°, front Oc R 6s 8m 5M, black tower, white band, rear Q 15m 5M, white mast
Cove Fl WR 5s 6m W6M R4M, white tower, R 111°–161°, W 161°–234°, R234°–087°, W087°–111°. Shows red over channel to NW, white over channel to NE, red inshore over the S bank to the E
Waterford City Marina, 6x2FR vert.

Caution

Large ships can be met in the River Suir, and a sharp lookout is required at all times. Skippers of small vessels are reminded that IRPCS Rule 9 specifies that a vessel under 20m in length or a sailing vessel shall not impede larger vessels confined by a narrow channel. The Rivers Suir and Barrow above Duncannon Bar may be considered a "narrow channel" in terms of this Rule. Waterford Harbour Radio, VHF Ch 14, monitors shipping movements. A car ferry crosses the estuary between Passage East and Ballyhack.

should be taken before drying out alongside. There is a small drying harbour NE of the pier. Anchor N of the pier in 2 to 3m, sand and mud, holding reported poor. There are tidal eddies in the bay. Duncannon village has a shop, PO and pubs.

Duncannon from the S

Arthurstown to Waterford

Duncannon from the NW. The fort and lighthouse are on the point, bottom R

Duncannon pier

Arthurstown pier

Passage East. The pontoon (L) is for the use of the pilot boat

Arthurstown

Anchorage is also available off Arthurstown Pier, 1·5M NW of Duncannon Point, in 1·5 to 2m. The pier dries. Pubs at Arthurstown village.

Passage East

Passage East has a small drying harbour, a pontoon used by the pilot boat, and a car ferry slip, but there is no convenient anchorage or alongside berth. The village has pubs, shop and PO.

Ballyhack

There is a boatyard at Ballyhack (Carroll's, Ballyhack Boatyard 051 389164) offering hull (wood, metal, GRP), mechanical, electrical and electronic repairs. Slipway but no travelhoist. Anchorage is available W of the village in 2 to 3m, clear of the car ferry slip; the tides run very strongly here. The small harbour dries. Shop and pub.

River Suir – Ballyhack to Waterford

The main channel NW of Ballyhack runs close to the W shore, with Seedes Bank and Carter's Patch in mid-channel. The channel then turns W round Cheek Point and runs N of Little Island, with a training wall extending E from the island. A mid-channel course here clears all dangers, and the training wall should be left to port.

Rivers Suir and Barrow

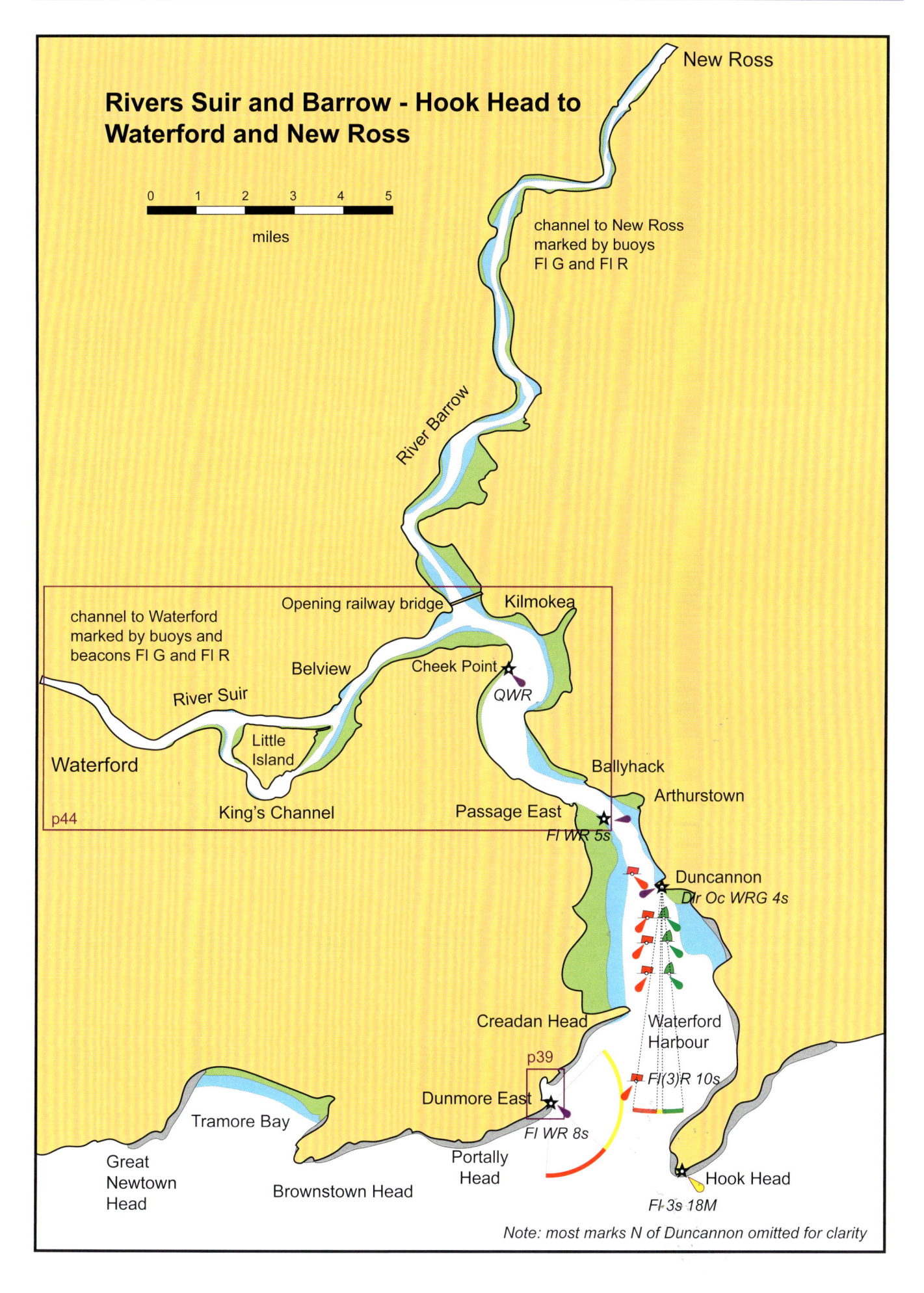

Rivers Suir and Barrow - Hook Head to Waterford and New Ross

New Ross

channel to New Ross marked by buoys Fl G and Fl R

River Barrow

Opening railway bridge — Kilmokea

channel to Waterford marked by buoys and beacons Fl G and Fl R

Belview — Cheek Point
QWR

River Suir

Waterford — Little Island

King's Channel — Passage East — Ballyhack — Arthurstown
Fl WR 5s

Duncannon
Dir Oc WRG 4s

Creadan Head

Waterford Harbour
Fl(3)R 10s

Dunmore East
Fl WR 8s

Tramore Bay

Great Newtown Head — Brownstown Head — Portally Head

Hook Head
Fl 3s 18M

Note: most marks N of Duncannon omitted for clarity

43

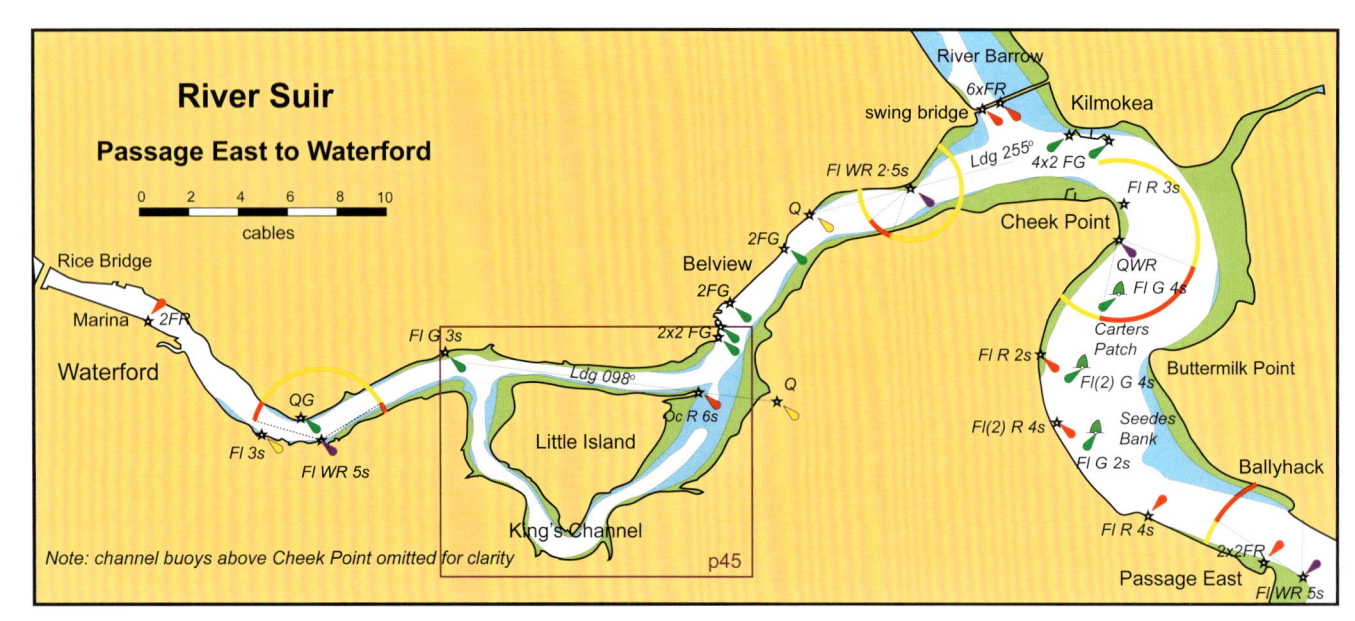

Cheek Point and King's Channel

River Suir — Passage East to Waterford

Cheek Point

There is a small drying harbour 2 cables W of the Sheagh beacon. The bar between the main channel of the Suir and the branch channel to the harbour has 1·1m at LAT. The branch channel itself and the end of the pier have 2m at LAT. The branch channel is marked by two pairs of lateral buoys QG, QR, Fl(2) G 5s and Fl(2) R 5s. Pubs ashore.

King's Channel

⊕ KC 52°15'·45N 7°04'·0W
AC2046 and Plan

The channel S of Little Island, 2M E of Waterford city centre, is navigable via its W entrance, has 20m in places, and provides a straightforward passage and a tranquil anchorage out of the strongest tides. Careful

(top) Ballyhack

(above) Cheek Point harbour

River Barrow railway bridge from the S; Kilmokea power station top R and Cheek Point harbour L centre

44

Waterford

use of the echosounder is called for when entering from the main channel of the Suir, since the sand bars doubtless shift, but the channel itself is relatively free of dangers. The W entrance is marked by a port hand buoy, and Golden Rock, 50m off the W point of the island, is marked by a starboard-hand buoy, both of these unlit (the conventional buoyage direction is westwards through the channel). From the main channel of the Suir, approach the **W entrance** steering 135° for the centre of the entrance, and as soon as the points are abeam turn S and head for the Golden Rock buoy. The deep channel 1 cable inside this entrance is only 0·5 cable wide, but widens out and deepens further in. The **E entrance** is shallower; approach on a course of 180° from a position 2 cables NE of the training wall beacon, hold this course until 0·5 cable off the SE shore, then steer for the mid-channel to the SW keeping a close watch on the depth. A chain ferry crosses the channel; avoid passing ahead or close astern of it when it is under way. Maulus Rock (0·3m) lies 50m off the W shore, 3 cables SE of the ferry slip. Anchor either NW of the ferry slip and the moorings on the W side, or E of the S tip of the island, in 3 to 4m.

Waterford City Marina

On the S side of the river close to the city centre, there is a series of long pontoons. Waterford City Marina comprises the second, third and fourth of these, labelled A, B and C. Visiting yachts should berth on pontoon C. Marina office, phone 051 309900. The tide runs past the pontoons at 3 kn at springs. Constant +0053 Cobh, MHWS 4·5m, MHWN 3·6m, MLWN 1·2m, MLWS 0·3m.

Facilities

Water and shore power on the pontoons; showers and laundry. Waterford has all the facilities of a large seaport town. Supermarkets, shops, restaurants, pubs, PO, doctors, hospital with full A&E. Car rental office opposite the marina.

River Suir above Waterford

The Rice Bridge has a closed clearance of 2·3m but is opened occasionally for commercial vessels. There are no provisions in place to have it opened for yachts, but for vessels of limited air draft, the River Suir is navigable as far as Carrick-on-Suir, 10M upriver from

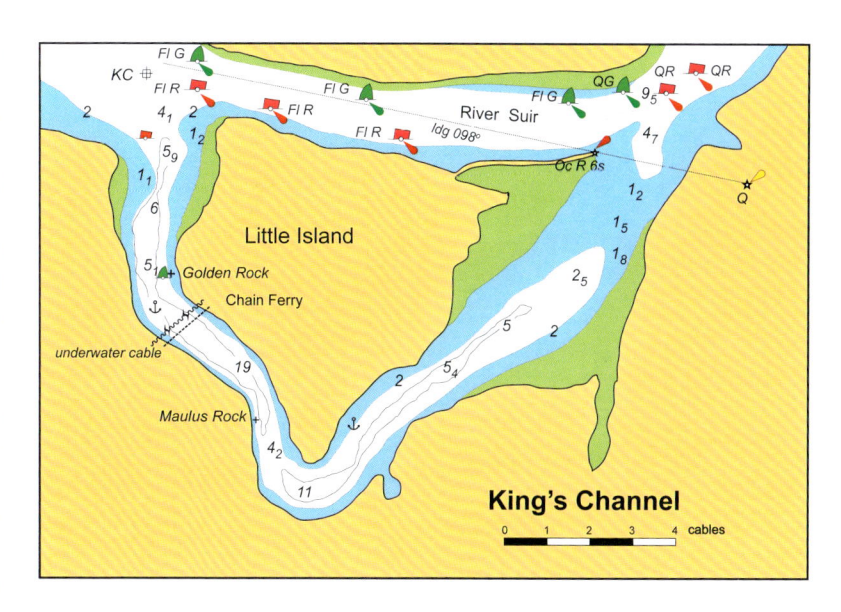

The River Suir and Waterford from the W; Rice Bridge foreground, Little Island and King's Channel upper L. The marina has acquired another two stretches of pontoon since the photograph was taken

45

New Ross

Waterford City Marina

Waterford. The new (fixed) bridge which spans the river a short distance above the Rice Bridge has 14m headroom.

River Barrow to New Ross

The River Barrow is navigable by masted yachts as far as New Ross, 10M upstream, where it is crossed by a low fixed bridge. The river is tranquil and scenic, and the town has many amenities including a 66-berth marina. It is also a commercial port and accommodates several cargo vessels each week.

At its confluence with the Suir, the Barrow is crossed by an opening railway bridge. Closed clearance is 6m. The bridge opens on request: phone 086 816 7826. At least an hour's notice is appreciated. When transiting the bridge, leave the central pivot point to port. The channel to New Ross is marked by lighted port and starboard-hand buoys and has a least depth of 2m.

New Ross – Three Sisters Marina

The marina is just downstream of the town on the E bank of the river, and has 66 berths, and a breakwater pontoon on its downstream side. Marina manager 086 388 9652. Pumpout station, water and shore power on the pontoons. Showers. Small chandlery at New Ross Boat Yard, 051 447655. Mechanical repairs, New Ross Outboards 051 421902. The town has shops, pubs, restaurants, PO, filling stations. Constant +0045 Cobh, MHWS 4·5m, MHWN 3·8m, MLWN 1·4m, MLWS 0·7m.

The bridge at New Ross has a clearance of approximately 3m at HW. Above the bridge the Barrow is navigable to St Mullins (11M), and its tributary the Nore to Inistioge (9M) with a least depth of 0·5m at LAT in the channels and two more bridges, also with approximately 3m clearance. There are pools where a deep-drafted yacht might lie afloat at both places up-river.

River Barrow railway bridge in the open position (photo Donal Walsh)

Three Sisters Marina, New Ross

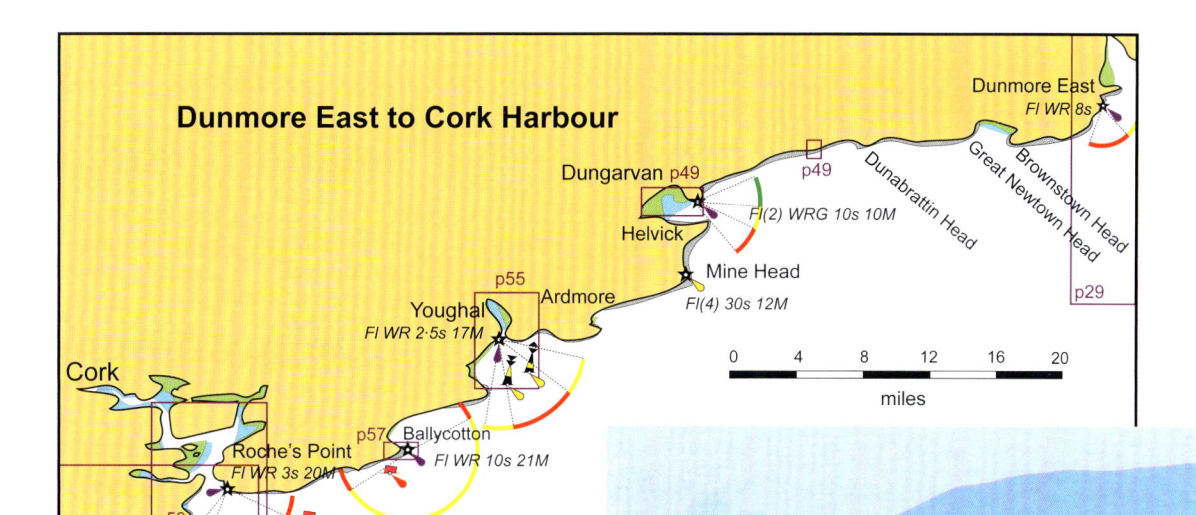

Dunmore East to Mine Head

Brownstown Head (R) and Great Newton Head (L centre) from the ESE

DUNMORE EAST to MINE HEAD

The coast between Dunmore East and Mine Head, 24M to the west, is cliffbound and penetrated by two large bays. The popular resort of Tramore stands on the first of these, but Tramore Bay faces southwest and offers no shelter from the prevailing winds. Dungarvan Harbour, facing east, although mostly occupied by drying sandbanks, has a channel leading to the historic town of Dungarvan (7,990). To the south of Dungarvan Harbour is a Gaeltacht area, centred on An Rinn (Ring) and the small fishing port of Helvick. Mine Head lighthouse, built in 1851, has the highest light elevation of any in Ireland.

Coast – Dunmore East to Dungarvan

Between Dunmore East and Brownstown Head, give the coast a berth of 4 cables to clear Robin Redbreast Rock, Falskirt Rock and Swede Rock. If heading for Cork, a course of 245° from Falskirt Rock passes S of Mine Head (and Ram Head further W). From Brownstown Head, a berth of 3 cables clears all dangers to Ballyvoyle Head, 3M NE of Dungarvan Harbour.

Boatstrand Harbour

52°08′N 7°18′W

Close NE of Dunabrattin Head is this harbour, about half a cable each way, just drying in the entrance, which faces E. Further in it is

Tides
Dunmore East to Mine Head

This section has the weakest streams on the coast, with rates nowhere exceeding 1 knot. The ENE-going stream begins at –0230 Cobh and the WSW-going at +0350 Cobh. There are at least two-hour periods of slack water.
Constant (Dungarvan) +0008 Cobh, MHWS 4·1m, MHWN 3·4m, MLWN 1·1m, MLWS 0·4m.

Dangers

Robin Redbreast Rock (dries), 0·5 cable offshore 4 cables SW of Dunmore East harbour
Falskirt Rock (dries 3m), 1 to 2 cables offshore 2M WSW of Dunmore East harbour
Swede Rock, 2·7m, 1 cable offshore 7 cables E of Brownstown Head
Carricknamone (1m high), 0·5m E of Ballynacourty Point, with drying reefs including **Carricknagaddy** extending to the shore and 7 cables NNW
Carrickapane (2m high), 8 cables N of Helvick Head
Helvick Rock, 1·4m, 4 cables NNE of Helvick harbour
The Gainers, area of shoals and rocks 2 cables across, drying up to 0·8m, centred 5 cables NNW of Helvick harbour
Whitehouse Bank and **Deadman Sand**, drying sands to the S of the channel to Dungarvan. The sands dry also to the N of the channel and there are rocks drying up to 2·6m
Unnamed stacks 15 and 7m high, 1 to 2 cables E of Helvick Head
Unnamed rock with 0·1m, 2 cables offshore 2M SW of Helvick Head
The Rogue (2·7m high), 1·5 cables E of Mine Head

47

Dungarvan

Passage planning note - shelter from the east

The coast from Dunmore East to Cork is largely open to the east. The bays at Helvick, Ardmore and Ballycotton offer shelter from the prevailing westerly weather, but an easterly wind tends to set up a short sea or a swell which makes these bays uncomfortable if not unsafe as anchorages. Youghal harbour offers access and safe anchorage but, for a yacht on passage, can mean a detour. Refer to the directions for Dungarvan and Youghal for details of feasible passage anchorages in moderate easterly weather.

Boatstrand Harbour

shallower. Pleasant temporary anchorage in settled weather is available off the harbour mouth in 3 to 5m, but beware of the reefs on either hand. The harbour was formerly used for the import of coal.

Blind Harbour

52°07′·5N 7°24′W

Blind Harbour is the more westerly of a pair of tiny enclosed coves in the cliffs 3M W of Dunabrattin Head. Barely 100m across and too small to be marked on AC2049, the cove is safe only in conditions of calm or light offshore winds and no swell. It offers a charming temporary anchorage. Approach from the SE and stay very close to the islet on the E side of the entrance. Anchor in the centre of the pool in 1·5 to 2·5m, sand. The rock in the entrance dries 2·8m.

DUNGARVAN

⊕DG 52°04′·3N 7°33′W / 52°04′·3N 7°33′·6W
AC2049, 2017, SC5622·5, Imray C57 and Plan

The channel to Dungarvan has a least depth of 0·7m to the anchorage and 0·1m to the town harbour, so for most yachts the town is accessible only above half tide, and there is a bar with 1·5m, 2 cables W of Ballynacourty

Blind Harbour from the SE; St John's Island, L. Stay close to the islet (R) on entering. Note the distinctive purple cliff behind the pool

Lights and Marks

Brownstown Head, 2 conspicuous grey towers on the headland at the SE extremity of Tramore Bay, unlit.

Great Newtown Head, 3 conspicuous white towers on the headland at the W extremity of Tramore Bay, unlit. The middle tower is surmounted by the Metal Man, a statue of a sailor in 19th-century uniform, with an outstretched arm pointing out to sea (his twin brother stands in the entrance to the port of Sligo, on the west coast)

Ballynacourty Point, white tower, Fl(2) WRG 10s 16m, W10M R8M G8M, G 245°–274°, W 274°–302°, R 302°–325°, W 325°–117°. Shows green over Carricknamone and Carricknagaddy, white over the channel from the E between Carricknamone and Carrickapane, red over Carrickapane, and white to S and W over Dungarvan Harbour

The channel to **Dungarvan** is marked by port- and starboard-hand buoys and two pairs of beacons. Changes proposed in 2015 are shown on the plan opposite.

Helvick buoy, E Card Q(3) 10s, 4 cables N of Helvick Head and 2 cables W of Helvick Rock

Mine Head, white tower with black band, Fl(4) 30s 87m 12M

Caution

The coast between Dunmore East and Dungarvan is charted only on a scale of 1:150,000. Over-zooming on electronic charts here can lead to a false impression of accuracy and precision. In particular, chartplotters cannot be used for pilotage at Boatstrand Harbour and Blind Harbour, and should be used with caution when in close proximity to the shore anywhere on this coast. At the time of writing (2015) Dungarvan Harbour is being resurveyed, but the existing published charts of the channel to Dungarvan are based on a survey of 1912. Major changes have taken place in the channel, and until the present (1998) edition of AC2017 is revised with the new data, chartplotters should be used with great caution in the entrance to Dungarvan. The plan on page 49 is not to be used for navigation, but is up to date as of 2015.

Dungarvan

Blind Harbour

Blind Harbour, in ideal weather

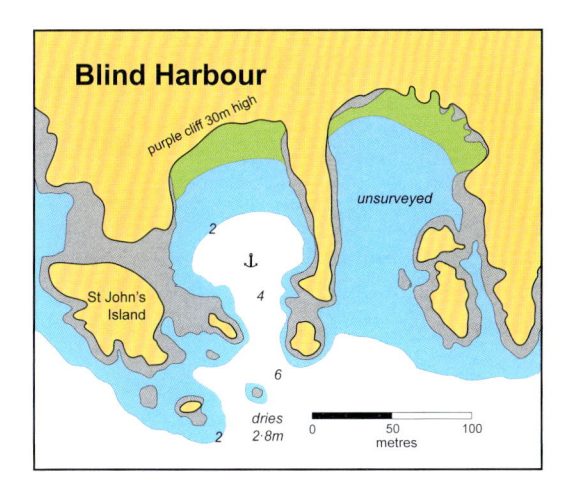

Point, which breaks in strong S and SE winds. The channel has been well marked by lit port and starboard hand buoys and beacons, but since about 2010, its course has shifted significantly, and there is an inner bar with 0·7m, 2 cables S of Ballynacourty Pier. At the time of writing (December 2015) the new buoyage has not been finalised. Dungarvan offers a warm welcome to visiting yachts and has excellent facilities within easy reach of its quayside, but depths in the town harbour are restricted. Dungarvan Sailing Club has a new 110m-long pontoon on the SW side of the town harbour.

Directions

The plan shows the new channel with the six proposed buoys for the outer channel in their provisional positions. From a position 4 cables SW of Ballynacourty Point, identify the first of the channel marks, and follow the buoys. Particular care is required at the inner bar, 2 cables S of Ballynacourty Pier. From this position identify the Davy Murray starboard-hand buoy to the W, and leave it close to starboard. The least depths in the channel are 0·7m on the inner bar and at the Whitehouse buoy. Close N of Cunnigar Point is a pool with 10m, and the tide runs strongly NE–SW across the point. The channel to the town harbour has 0·1m.

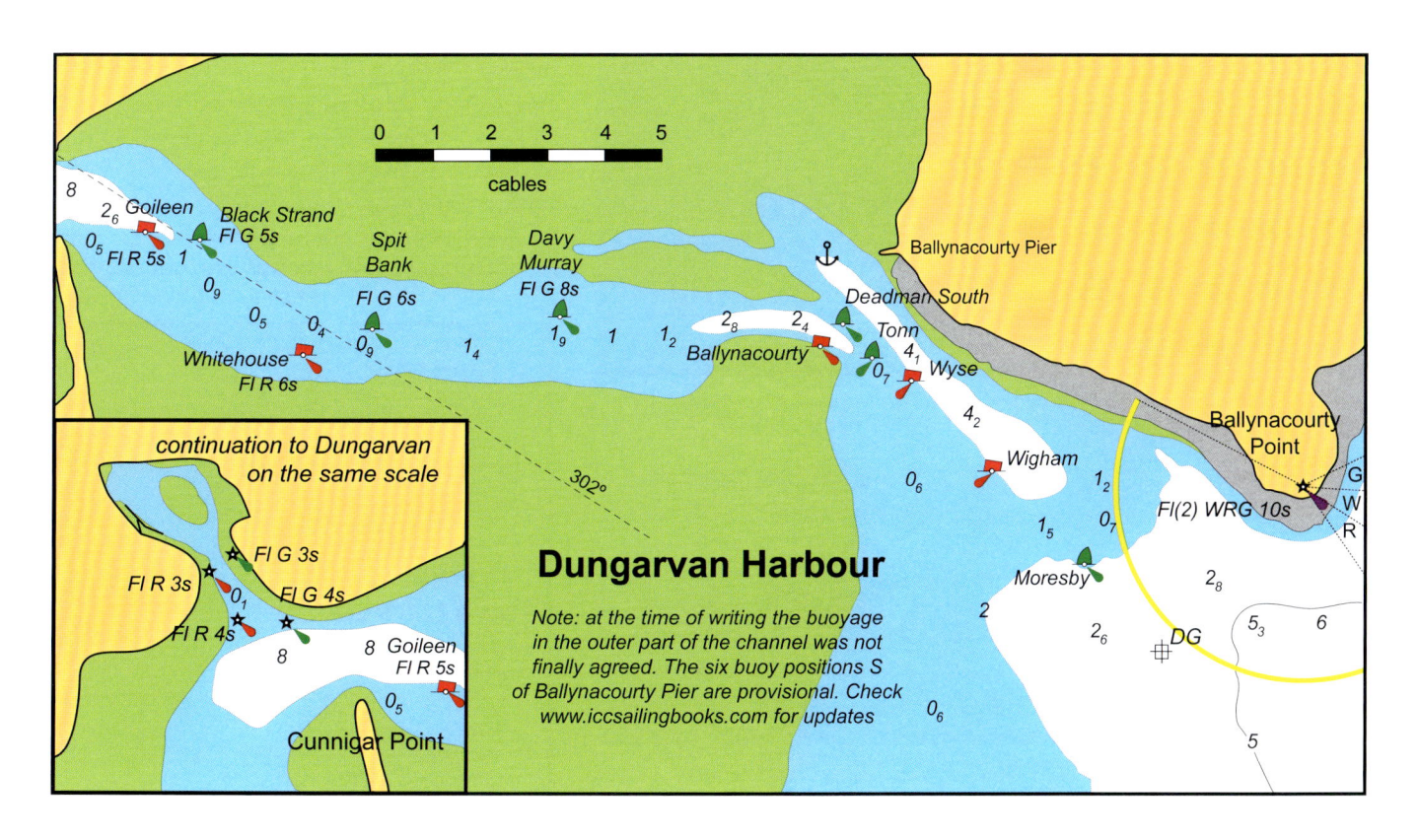

Dungarvan Harbour

Note: at the time of writing the buoyage in the outer part of the channel was not finally agreed. The six buoy positions S of Ballynacourty Pier are provisional. Check www.iccsailingbooks.com for updates

49

Dungarvan, Helvick

Tides - Dungarvan
The streams run at up to 2·5 knots at springs in the channel, and are strongest in the narrows N of Cunnigar Point, where the tide sets NE–SW across the entrance to the harbour. On the S side of the bay the streams are weaker. Constant +0008 Cobh, MHWS 4·1m, MHWN 3·4m, MLWN 1·1m, MLWS 0·4m.

Ballynacourty Point lighthouse from the S (photo Donal Walsh)

Dungarvan from the SE: Cunnigar Point, bottom centre, Abbey Point, centre L, with the town harbour beyond

Approaching Dungarvan: Black Strand and Goileen buoys, and Abbey Point, centre

Anchorage

Anchorage is available 1 cable S of Ballynacourty Pier. The tide-swept pool N of Cunnigar Point is not recommended since the bottom is rocky and fouled with old moorings. The deep water W of Cunnigar Point is fully taken up with moorings but one of these might be made available to a visiting yacht.

Dungarvan Town Harbour (see Plan)

The channel to the town harbour is marked by two pairs of pole beacons. The harbour largely dries; the one deep spot, with 5m, is occupied by a mooring. The pontoon just dries, the NW end having slightly deeper water. It is possible to dry out against the wall but the location should be checked in advance at LW.

There is a slip on the W side of the entrance suitable for trailer sailers.

Facilities

Water on pontoon. Filling station 400m. Supermarkets, shops, PO, laundry, pubs, restaurants, doctors, hospital. The supermarket is the most convenient to the harbour of any port on the south coast. Dungarvan Sailing Club, phone 058 45663, www.dungarvansailingclub.com.

HELVICK

The S side of Dungarvan Harbour, E of Helvick Head, is a sheltered anchorage in winds between SE and SW. There are visitors' moorings and a small harbour used by local fishing boats. **From the E**, leave Helvick buoy to starboard and identify the

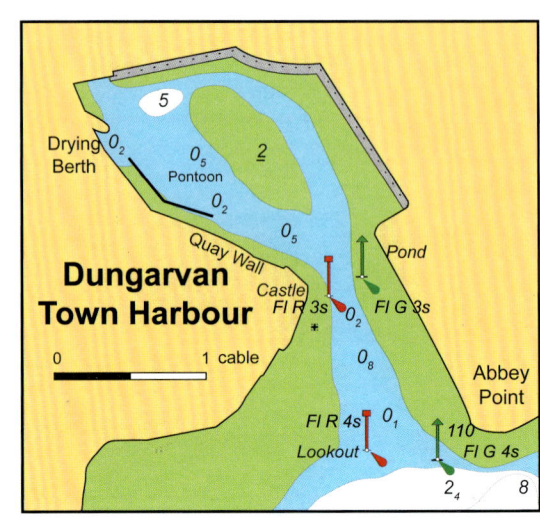

50

Dungarvan, Helvick

Entering Dungarvan : the 110 beacon, R

(below) Dungarvan town harbour. The pontoon has been replaced with a much longer one since the photograph was taken (photo Donal Walsh)

harbour breakwater to the SE. **From the SW**, the above-water rocks E of Helvick Head are clean and steep-to on their E and N sides. **From Dungarvan**, beware of the Gainers, drying rocks 3 to 5 cables NNW of Helvick harbour. The safest approach from Dungarvan is E of the Helvick buoy.

Anchorage

Anchor in 3m, sand, N of the harbour.

Harbour

The harbour, 150m by 50m, has 3m alongside its N wall and 1·5m in the entrance. A temporary berth might be available in emergency, but fishing boat traffic usually makes it impractical as an overnight stop. The entrance is 20m wide and faces W.

Facilities

Water tap on the harbour N wall. Pub 800m, shop at Helvick village, 1·5km. RNLI inshore lifeboat station in the harbour. Slip suitable for trailer sailers beside the lifeboat station.

Coast – Helvick Head to Mine Head

The coast between Helvick Head and Mine Head is bordered by 75m cliffs and should be given a berth of 3 cables to avoid offshore rocks. There are several conspicuous stacks close E of Helvick Head, and a dangerous rock with 0·1m, 2 cables offshore 2M to the SW. The Rogue, close E of Mine Head, always shows. The lighthouse tower on Mine Head is conspicuous.

Dungarvan SC new pontoon

Helvick harbour

Mine Head to Cork Harbour

Helvick harbour from the W

Mine Head from the SW; the Rogue, extreme R

Ballycotton, in the next bay to the west, is a quiet holiday and fishing village. The harbour, at the south end of the bay, is small but well-sheltered and is home to small fishing vessels and the lifeboat. Ballycotton's finest hour was the rescue of the crew of the Daunt Rock lightship in February 1936, still ranking as one of the RNLI's proudest achievements in 180 years of lifesaving.

Coast – Mine Head to Cork Harbour

The passage of 29M from Mine Head to the entrance to Cork Harbour passes S of Ram Head, Capel Island, Knockadoon Head, Ballycotton Island and Power Head, all bold and steep-to. The coast is cliffbound except in Ballycotton and Youghal Bays, and on the direct course the only significant danger is The Smiths, a dangerous drying reef S of Ballycotton, marked by a port-hand buoy. Youghal Bay has a number of hazards but they are easily avoided, and Ballycotton Bay is clean. There is a conspicuous lattice mast close N of Power Head. Approaching Cork Harbour entrance from the E, give Roche's Point a berth of 2 cables to clear the Calf Rock.

The conspicuous wreck of a crane barge lies under the cliffs close N of Ram Head.

MINE HEAD to CORK HARBOUR

AC2049, SC5622·Imray C57

The coast has wide bays between bold headlands, and few dangers offshore. West of Ram Head, the town of Youghal (pronounced "Yawl") (6,390) stands on the River Blackwater at the head of Youghal Bay. Youghal is a minor commercial port, handling cargoes of steel and timber.

Dangers
Mine Head to Cork Harbour

Longship Rock (dries 4m), 1 cable offshore 1M SW of Mine Head
Blackball Ledge, 3·4m, in Youghal Bay 8 cables S of Blackball Head
Bar Rocks, 0·6m, in Youghal Bay 1·2M SSE of Moll Goggins' Corner
Bog Rock, Clonard Rock, Barrel Rocks and **Black Rocks** (drying 0·6 to 1·8m), on the W side of Youghal Bay, 1·2 to 2·1M N of Knockadoon Head
Sound Rock, awash, between Ballycotton Island and Small Island
The Smiths (dries 0·1m), 4 cables offshore 1·5M WSW of Ballycotton Island
Wheat Rock (dries 1m), 4 cables WNW of The Smiths
Quarry Rock (dries 0·3m), and **Hawk Rock,** 2·7m, 2 cables S of Power Head
Cow Rock (2m high) and the **Calf** (dries 1·4m), extending 1 cable SW of Roche's Point

Ardmore, Youghal

Tides

Mine Head to Cork Harbour

The coastwise tidal streams are weak, seldom exceeding 1 knot, turning ENE at HW Cobh −0400 and WSW at HW Cobh +0250. HW at Youghal is essentially simultaneous with Cobh. Details of the streams in Youghal Bay and Harbour are given below.

Lights and Marks

Blackball Ledge buoy, E Card Q(3) 10s
Bar Rocks buoy, S Card Q(6)+L Fl 15s
Youghal Harbour, W side of entrance, white tower, Fl WR 2·5s 24m W17M R13M, W 183°–273°, R 273°–295°, W 295°–307°, R 307°–351°, W 351°–003°. Shows white over the harbour, red inshore S of Blackball Head, white over the channel N of Blackball Ledge, red over Blackball Ledge and the Bar Rocks, and white over the West Bar
On **Capel Island** ( ) and **Knockadoon Head** are conspicuous unlit towers
Ballycotton, black tower, Fl WR 10s 59m W18M, R14M, W 238°–048°, R 048°–238°, AIS. Shows white to seaward of Capel Island to the E and The Smiths to the W, red inshore
The Smiths buoy, PHM Fl(3) R 10s
Power buoy, S Card Q(6)+L Fl 15s, AIS
Roche's Point, white tower, Fl WR 3s 30m, W20M, R16M, R shore −292°, W 292°–016°, R 016°–033°, W(unintens) 033°–159°, R 159°–shore. Shows red to the SE over Pollock Rock, white to seaward between Pollock Rock to the E and Daunt Rock to the W, white over The Sound (entrance channel to Cork Harbour) and red inshore

Offshore Installations – Kinsale gas field

Two gas rigs are positioned 28M S of Ballycotton Island in 51°22′N 7°56′W and 8°01′W. The rigs are 2·8M apart and are surrounded by a Prohibited Area extending for 3 cables from each rig and including the area between them. The rigs exhibit R and W lights, Mo(U) 15M.

Ardmore

51°57′·3N 7°42′·5W

AC2049, SC5622·2, Imray C57

Entering Ardmore Bay from the E, beware of Black Rocks, a drying reef which extends 2 cables E from the middle of the NW shore of the bay. The two wrecks shown on AC2049 NE and SSW of Ram Head are very old and no longer a danger to navigation. The small Ardmore harbour, in the bay N of Ram Head, has 1·1m alongside its E pier wall; drying rocks extend E of the W breakwater end to within 30m of the E pier, and also near the shore on the S side of the harbour.

Anchorage

The bay is shallow close to the W shore but sheltered from winds between SW and N. Anchor in 2 to 3m, N of the harbour, sand. Shop, PO, pub, filling station.

YOUGHAL

⊕ YG 51°55′·9N 7°48′·7W

AC2049, 2071, SC5622·6, Imray C57

The port of Youghal is entered across the East Bar, with a least depth of 2·9m. **From the E**, leave the Blackball Ledge buoy to port and identify the conspicuous light tower on Moll Goggin's Corner. Steer for it, leaving East Point 1 cable to starboard, and when 2 cables short of the light tower turn to starboard and head for the W extremity of Ferry Point, steering 356°. Leave the town quays 0·5 cable to port. **From the W**, either pass E of the

Ardmore Bay and harbour from the W

53

Youghal

Youghal from the SE: Ferry Point, R

Blackball Ledge buoy as above, or else use the alternative channel across the West Bar, with a least depth of 2·4m in 2007; from a position close E of Capel Island, steer 015° for the Bar Rocks buoy, 2M NNE, and leaving the buoy close to starboard steer to leave Moll Goggin's Corner 2 cables to port.

Anchorage

- Off the quays close N of the Town Hall and outside the line of moorings in 6 to 7m. This is close to the town but subject to swell.
- The best anchorage, out of the tide and swell, is on the E side of the channel, N of the moorings close NW of Ferry Point, in 5m, sand, opposite the Commercial Quay and with the lighthouse open of Ferry Point.
- N of the moorings in the channel E of Red Bank, NE of Ferry Point, in 2m. Space is restricted.
- There are two visitors' moorings on the town side.

A temporary berth may be available on the Commercial Quay if no ships are expected; call the HM on VHF Ch 16 and 14, Mon–Fri 0900–1700, or phone 087 251 1143. The Commercial Quay has 3m, and all the other quays dry. The area E and NE of the Commercial Quay should be left clear for ships to manoeuvre.

Facilities

Filling station, supermarket, shops, pubs, restaurants, PO, doctors. Youghal Sailing Club. RNLI inshore lifeboat station.

Youghal entrance from the S: Moll Goggins' Corner and the lighthouse, centre

Youghal

Tides - Youghal

About 0·5M S of the West Bar the stream is rotatory clockwise, commencing SSW at −0605 Cobh and turning through W and N to NNE at +0020 Cobh. The stream commences SSE at +0035 Cobh, the maximum rate being 0·5 kn until +0320 Cobh. From +0320 Cobh to +0500 Cobh the rate increases to 1·5 kn. On the East Bar the rates are about the same and the times about 10 minutes later. In the entrance the flood runs from −0505 Cobh to +0130 Cobh. The maximum spring rate is 2·5 kn flood and 3 kn ebb. The ebb runs hard off Ferry Point, forming an eddy in the bight to the S of the point.
Constant +0006 Cobh, MHWS 4·1m, MHWN 3·3m, MLWN 1·3m, MLWS 0·4m.

Caution

At the time of writing (2015) Youghal Harbour is being resurveyed, but the existing published charts of the Harbour are based on a survey of 1904. Major changes have taken place in Red Bank and the channels, and until the present (1991) edition of AC2071 is revised with the new data, chartplotters should be used with great caution in the Blackwater estuary. The plan on this page is not to be used for navigation, but is based on an ICC survey carried out in 2005.

Blackwater Estuary above Youghal

Red Bank, drying up to 0·9m, occupies much of the area N and E of Ferry Point. The channel E of the bank is narrow, and dries at its N end. There is an attractive anchorage S of the road bridge at the head of the estuary, which may be reached by keeping Ferry Point open E of the lighthouse and the conspicuous square Italianate tower of the convent open E of the equally conspicuous Town Hall, until

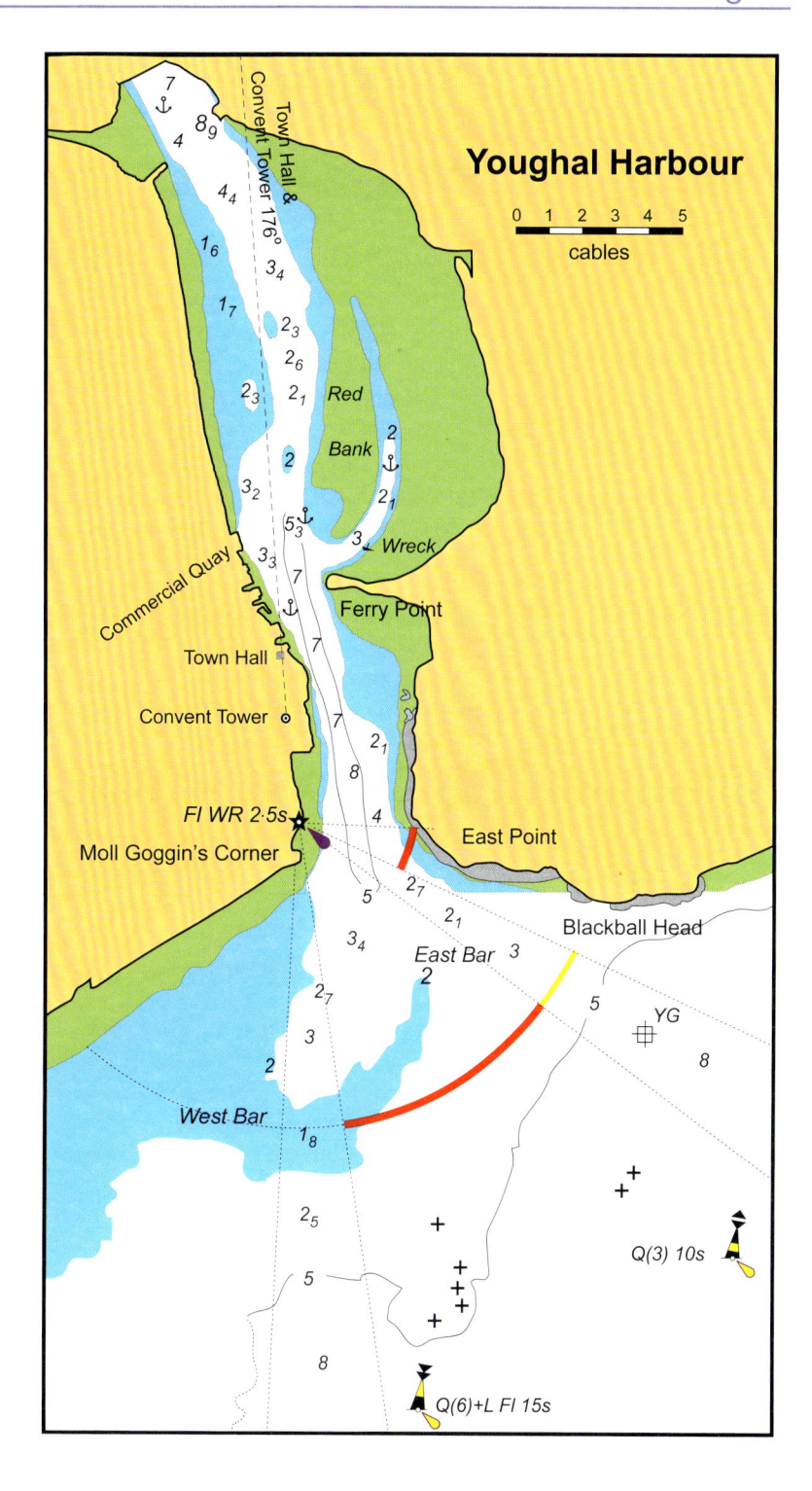

Youghal quays at HW: a timber ship at the Commercial Quay, R

Ballycotton

Capel Island from the N

within 5 cables of the NE shore. There are no rocks in the estuary, the sandbanks generally shelve gradually, and the echosounder may be used with confidence. Anchor in 4 to 7m, SE of the bridge.

River Blackwater above Youghal Bridge

The bridge has a clearance of 6·4m, and the river is navigable amid fine scenery as far as Villierstown Quay, 10M upstream. The quay is 1M N of the confluence with the River Bride. The river is not buoyed but by keeping towards the outside of bends depths of no less than 3m can be expected.

Passage Anchorages in easterly weather

Youghal harbour is always secure, but for a yacht on passage, Whiting Bay, 2·5M E of Youghal, offers a possible anchorage sheltered from moderate winds and swell from the E. Anchor in the NE corner of the bay in 2 to 4m, sand. Exposed from SE to SW. See also Capel Island, in the following paragraph.

Coast – Youghal to Roche's Point

At the SW end of Youghal Bay, Capel Island, 29m high and surmounted by an 8m tower, is 3 cables E of Knockadoon Head and clean to within 0·5 cable on its seaward side. The channel between Capel Island and Knockadoon Head has 3·7m with drying reefs on either hand; it is 1 cable wide with the deepest water slightly on the mainland side of mid-channel. The bay on the W side of Capel Island, between the reefs extending from the NW and SW points of the island, offers a possible anchorage in moderate winds and swell from the E. It is not safe in winds between SE and N.

Ballycotton Island is clean on its seaward side. Stay S of The Smiths port-hand buoy. Power buoy can be passed on either hand, and a berth of 4 cables clears all dangers from here to Roche's Point at the entrance to Cork Harbour.

BALLYCOTTON

⊕ BC 51°49'·9N 8°00'·1W
AC2049, SC5622·2, Imray C57

The village of Ballycotton faces NE from the tip of the headland W of Ballycotton Island. Its small manmade harbour is crowded with moorings, including that of the lifeboat, and a pontoon against the E wall is for the use of ferryboats taking passengers to the island. The harbour has 3·5m in the entrance but shallows rapidly inside. Its use by a visiting yacht may be regarded as emergency-only.

Anchorage

Anchor in the bay NE of the harbour entrance in 5 to 7m. There are visitors' moorings. Constant –0005 Cobh, MHWS 4·1m, MHWN 3·3m, MLWN 1·3m, MLWS 0·5m.

Facilities

Small shops, pubs, restaurants, PO. RNLI all-weather lifeboat station. Tourist boats take

Ballycotton from the NW: Ballycotton Island and lighthouse, L, the harbour entrance, centre, and the visitors' moorings, foreground

Caution

The coast between Knockadoon Head and Power Head is charted only on a scale of 1:150,000. Over-zooming on electronic charts here can lead to a false impression of accuracy and precision. In particular, chartplotters cannot be used for pilotage of Ballycotton Sound, and should be used with caution when in close proximity to the shore anywhere on this coast.

Ballycotton; Cork Harbour

Ballycotton

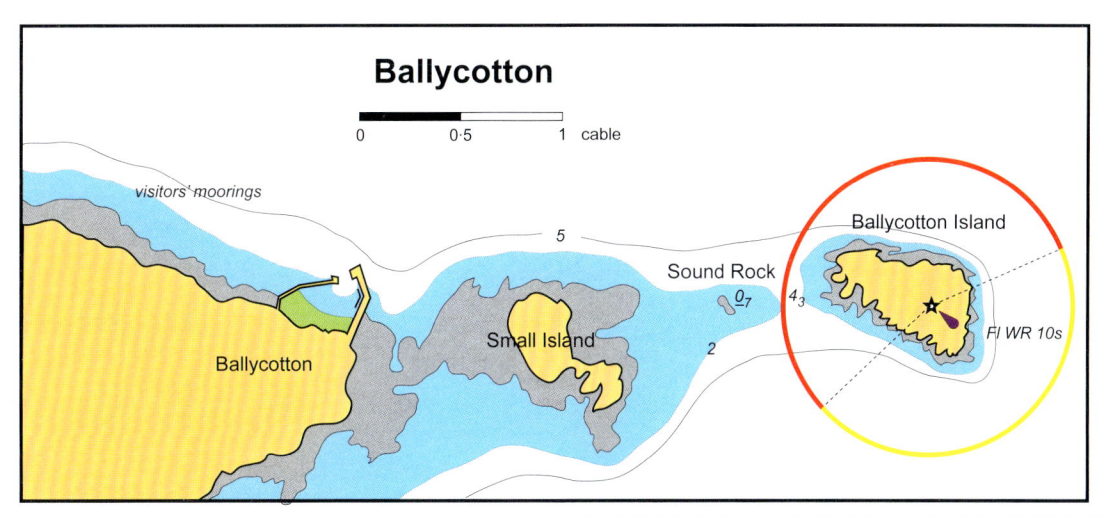

passengers to Ballycotton Island, where a lighthouse tour is available.

Ballycotton Sound

There is a least depth of 4m in the sound between Ballycotton Island and Small Island, but Sound Rock, which dries 0·7m, lies in mid-channel. The channel is navigable in settled weather, keeping to the Ballycotton Island side, although particular care must be taken to avoid lobster pots. Note also that a submarine power cable crosses the sound. The channel between Small Island and the mainland is not navigable.

CORK HARBOUR

⊕ CO 51°46'·5N 8°16'W
AC1765, 1777, SC5622, Imray C57.

Cork shares with Paris and New York the distinction of being founded on an island in the middle of its river. The city's name in the original Irish, *Corcaigh*, means a marsh, and it was amid the marshy islands of the River Lee that the first settlements here were built 1,400 years ago. The city survived centuries of power struggles, and played a leading and heroic role in the establishment of the modern Irish state. Cork today is a vibrant

Ballycotton from the NW

Ballycotton Sound from the S: Ballycotton Island, R, Small Island, L, and Sound Rock, breaking, centre

Crosshaven

Cork Harbour from the NW: Cobh, foreground with a cruise ship at the Deepwater Quay. Haulbowline Island with the naval dock R, Spike Island top centre, Whitegate oil jetty top L, Crosshaven top R and Roche's Point in the distance.

Roche's Point: The Cow, R

and prosperous place and was European Capital of Culture in 2005. The city has a population of 119,230.

Cork owes its growth and development to its fine natural harbour, on the shores of which the Royal Cork Yacht Club, the world's oldest, was founded in 1720. The harbour witnessed the departure of millions of emigrants, and it was the last port of call of the *Titanic*. Today it is a major international port and a premier centre of yachting, with its biennial Cork Week among the world's most prestigious racing events.

Cork Harbour is entered through The Sound, 8 cables wide between Roche's Point on the E and Weaver's Point on the W. The principal sailing centre in the harbour is at Crosshaven.

CROSSHAVEN

⊕ CR 51°48'·8N 8°16'·8W

AC1765, 1777, SC5622·10, Imray C57. Additional photo on p28

Entrance from seaward is straightforward. Giving either side N of Roche's Point a berth of 2 cables, identify the channel buoys. Leave Fort Meagher 1 cable to port and give the shore W of it a berth of 2 cables; leave the C2A, C2 and C4 buoys close to port and head SW into the Owenboy River between Curraghbinny and Scotchman's Point. The bottom shoals rapidly outside the buoyed channel. The C3 starboard-hand buoy appears to be very close to the S side, but stay S of it, as the N side is shoal N of the buoy. There is a 6 knot speed limit in the Owenboy upstream of the C2 buoy.

Cork Harbour

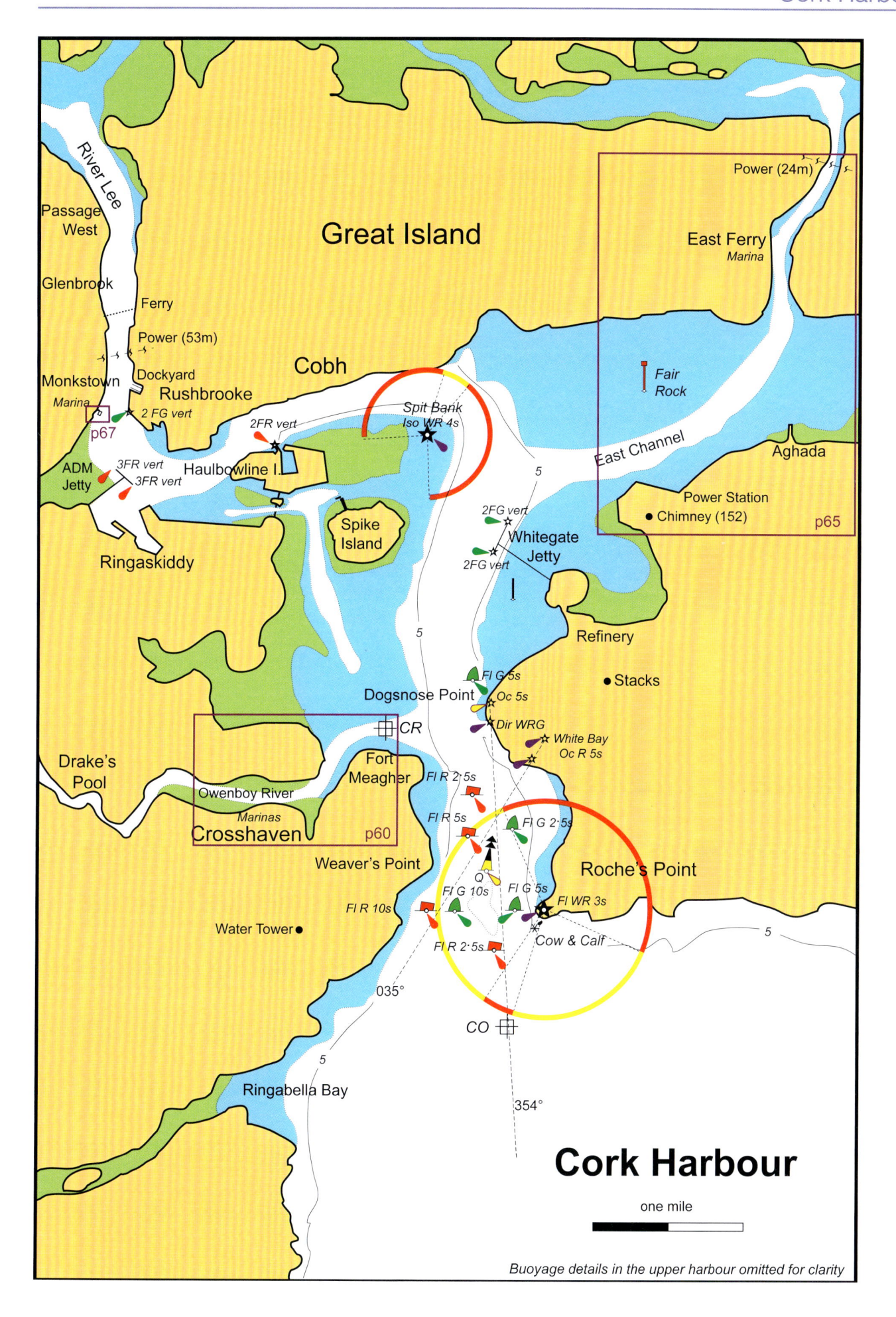

Cork Harbour

one mile

Buoyage details in the upper harbour omitted for clarity

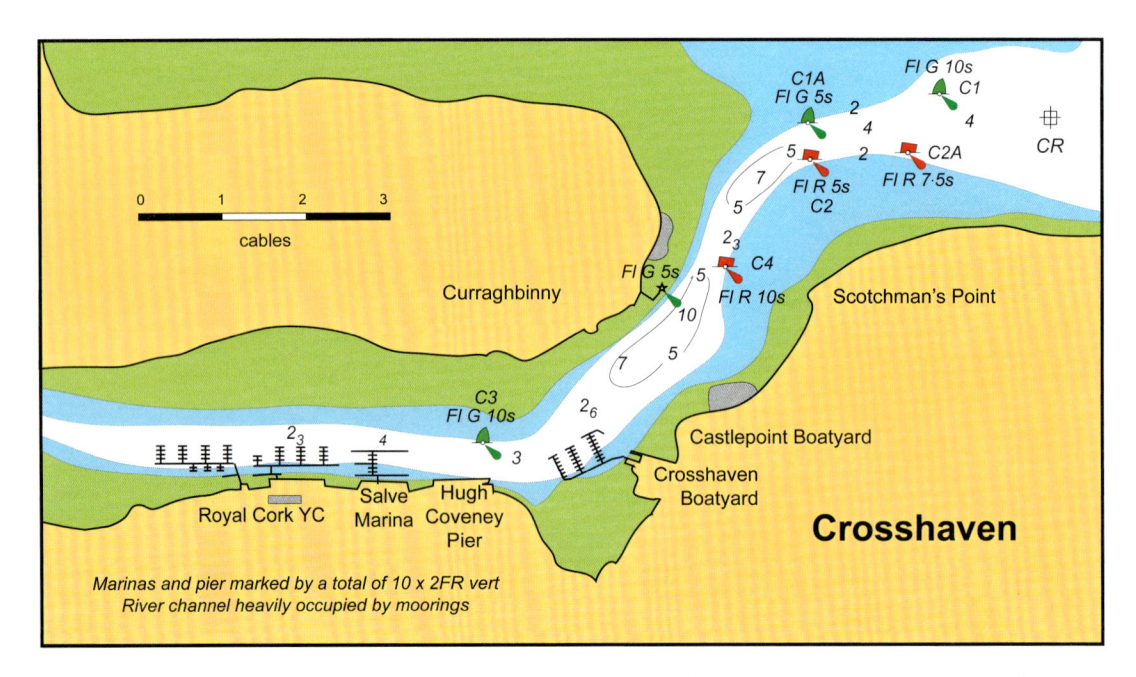

Crosshaven

Crosshaven Marinas

Crosshaven Boatyard marina has 100 berths and 20 visitors' berths; call VHF Ch 37 or phone 021 483 1161.

Salve Marina has 45 berths and 12 visitors' berths; call VHF Ch M or phone 021 483 1145. The Royal Cork Yacht Club marina has 170 berths and 30 visitors' berths; call VHF Ch M or phone 021 483 1023 or 087 244 9471.

Visitors have temporary membership of the club, with the use of showers, bar and restaurant. www.royalcork.com.

Coveney Pier

Coveney Pier (formerly known as the Town Pier) has 3·5m, and has a pontoon for alongside berthing. This is a handy stop for picking up stores, but a yacht should not be

(above) Crosshaven from the NE: buoys C2 (L) and C4 (centre)

(below) Salve and Royal Cork YC Marinas, looking upstream: the C3 buoy, centre, is close to the S side of the river

Crosshaven

Tides – Roche's Point to Crosshaven

The stream sets N–S through The Sound, reaching 1·5 kn at springs, 2 kn off Fort Meagher, and turning at HW and LW Cobh. The ebb tide in the Owenboy River at Crosshaven may continue for a short time after LW, especially after heavy rain. Persistent S winds can significantly raise the tidal levels in the harbour, and vice versa. Cobh is the Tidal Standard Port for the south coast; MHWS 4·1m, MHWN 3·3m, MLWN 1·3m, MLWS 0·4m.

Caution

Commercial and naval traffic in Cork Harbour is constant and heavy, and a sharp lookout is required at all times. Skippers of small vessels are reminded that IRPCS Rule 9 specifies that a vessel under 20m in length or a sailing vessel shall not impede larger vessels confined by a narrow channel. The whole of Cork Harbour and approaches may be considered a "narrow channel" in terms of this Rule. Small craft should when practicable stay outside the buoyed channel. There are speed limits in the Owenboy River, East Passage and the upper reach of the Lee. Cork Harbour Radio, VHF Ch 12, monitors shipping movements. For detailed advice see the Port Company's Guidance Notes for Leisure Craft on www.portofcork.ie.

"Commercial and naval traffic in Cork Harbour is constant and heavy". An inbound cruise ship passes Weaver's Point, dwarfing LÉ Roisín as she heads seaward

Dangers

The Calf (dries 1·5m) is 1 cable SW of Roche's Point, with the **Cow** (2m high) between it and the point. Apart from these, almost the only hazards in Cork Harbour are sandbanks and the ever-present traffic. The buoyage in the entrance reflects the presence of **Harbour Rock**, 5·2m, a broad shoal E of mid-channel off Roche's Point.

Lights and Marks

Cork, safe water buoy, RWVS, L Fl 10s, AIS, Racon (T), 5M S of Roche's Point
Daunt buoy, PHM Fl(2) R 6s, AIS, 7 cables offshore 4M SSW of Roche's Point
Roche's Point, white tower, Fl WR 3s 30m, W20M, R16M, R shore–292°, W 292°–016°, R 016°–033°, W (unintens) 033°–159°, R 159°–shore. Shows red over Pollock Rock, white to seaward between Pollock Rock to the E and Daunt Rock to the W, white over The Sound (entrance channel to Cork Harbour) and red inshore
Fort Davis, ldg lts 354°, Oc 5s 10M, front 29m, rear 37m, on Dogsnose Point, 1·2M N of Roche's Point. Front also shows Dir WRG 17M, FW 353°–355°
Outer Harbour Rock buoy, PHM Fl R 2·5s, 2·5 cables WSW of Roche's Point
Chicago Knoll buoy, SHM Fl G 5s, 1·5 cables NW of Roche's Point
W1 buoy, SHM Fl G 10s, 5 cables WNW of Roche's Point
W2 buoy, PHM Fl R 10s, 2 cables W of W1 and 2 cables S of Weaver's Point
The Sound buoy, N Card Q, 4 cables NW of Roche's Point
W4 buoy, PHM Fl R 5s, 3 cables ENE of Weaver's Point
W3 buoy, SHM Fl G 2·5s, 2 cables NE of W4 and 6 cables NNW of Roche's Point
White Bay, ldg lts 035°, Oc R 5s 5M, white huts with black panels, front 11m, rear 21m
W6 buoy, PHM Fl R 2·5s, 3 cables N of W4
Dogsnose Bank buoy, SHM Fl G 5s, 2 cables NW of Dogsnose Point
C1 buoy, SHM Fl G 10s, 3 cables N of Fort Meagher
C2A buoy, PHM Fl R 7·5s, 1 cable SW of C1
C2 buoy, PHM Fl R 5s, 2 cables WSW of C1
C1A buoy, SHM Fl G 5s. 0.5 cable N of C2
C4 buoy, PHM Fl R 10s, 1 cable SW of C2
C3 buoy, SHM Fl G 10s, 3 cables SW of C4
Crosshaven Boatyard Marina, 2×2FR vert
Salve Marina, 2×2FR vert
RCYC Marina, 2×2FR vert

Crosshaven, Drake's Pool

Crosshaven from the NE, with (L to R): Crosshaven Boatyard Marina, Coveney Pier, Salve Marina and the RCYC Marina

RCYC marina

left unattended without the permission of the pier manager, 086 310 0095. The pier is used by fishing vessels.

Anchorage

There is no room to anchor in the river. Visitors' moorings are available upstream of the RCYC Marina; contact the RCYC for availability.

Facilities

Water and shore power on all marina pontoons, diesel from the Boatyard Marina and Salve Marina. Shops, small supermarket, pubs, boatyards. Crosshaven Boatyard, hull (wood and GRP) and mechanical repairs. 40 tonne travelhoist, winter storage, www.crosshavenboatyard.com. Castlepoint Boatyard, phone 021 483 2154, travelhoist, winter storage. Salve Marine, phone 021 483 1145, mechanical repairs, www.sailingireland.com/salve1. Riggers, Masts & Rigging (Ireland) 021 483 3878 or 086 389 2614; Harry Lewis 087 266 7127. Sailmakers, McWilliam, phone 021 483 1505. Covers and canvaswork, Richard Marshall 021 481 2078, 086 668 6281. RNLI inshore lifeboat station. Taxis, phone 021 483 1122.

Owenboy River to Drake's Pool

The river is easily navigable for 2M upstream of Crosshaven although very crowded with moorings. The channel is close to the S side at Crosshaven and trends towards the N bank at the first bend up-river. From there on, hold mid-channel.

Two miles above Crosshaven in a wooded bend of the river is one of the most beautiful and sheltered anchorages in Ireland. This is Drake's Pool, and even though there is little if any room now to drop an anchor in it, it is worth the trip just to savour the beauty and

Drake's Pool

Drake's Pool

tranquillity of the place. The pool is almost fully taken up with moorings; the apparently available space is either shallow or has a hard shale bottom.

The river between Drake's Pool and Carrigaline, 2·5M upstream, is navigable by shallow draft vessels with local knowledge, or by dinghy, near HW.

Anchorage

Anchorage is available in 2m, in mid channel, mud, immediately W of the moorings in Drake's Pool. A tripping line is recommended.

Facilities

See under Crosshaven. Boatyard, filling stations, supermarkets, PO, pubs, restaurants, doctors at Carrigaline, 4 km.

CORK HARBOUR – CROSSHAVEN to EAST FERRY and MONKSTOWN

AC1765, 1777, 1773, SC5622·11, Imray C57

The main channel of the harbour, 4 to 5 cables wide, continues N from Fort Meagher and Dogsnose Point for 2·3M to Cobh (pronounced "Cove"), on the S side of Great Island. On the W side N of the Owenboy River, the channel is bordered by shallows and drying banks. Spike Island, with its massive star fort, lies close W of the main channel. On the E side, N of Dogsnose Point, is the conspicuous Whitegate Refinery with the jetty of its Marine Terminal projecting NW into the channel. The junction of East Channel is N of the oil jetty. This channel, with a least depth of 4·7m, leads E of Great

Dangers
Cork Harbour

N of Dogsnose Point, E of Whitegate Jetty and S of East Channel is a bank with less than 2m, and Whitegate Bay to the SE dries. On the N side of East Channel is a bank with less than 2m in places. **Fair Rock** (drying 0·2m) is 4 cables N of this channel. **Curlane Bank**, S of Spike Island, and **Oyster Bank**, SW of Haulbowline, have less than 1m, and **Spit Bank** dries. Apart from the bridge and overhead cables already mentioned, there are underwater cables and pipelines between Cobh and Haulbowline, between Haulbowline and Spike Island, and across East Channel.

Approaching within 0·5 cable of Whitegate Oil Jetty is prohibited.

Lights and Marks

The main channel is marked by port and starboard hand buoys showing Fl R and Fl G lights. Apart from these the principal marks are as follows.

Whitegate Jetty, 2×2FG vert
EF2 buoy, PHM Fl R 10s, 3 cables SSW of Fair Rock
EF1 buoy, SHM Fl G 10s, 6 cables ESE of Fair Rock.
Fair Rock, red perch, unlit
East Ferry Marina, 2×2FR vert
A2 buoy, SHM Fl(2) G 10s
A1 buoy, SHM Fl G 5s
(these two N by W of Aghada pier)
Spit Bank, piled structure on the E end of the bank, Iso WR 4s 10m, W10M R7M, shows red over the channels to S and W and a narrow white sector over the turn 📷
Haulbowline Naval Basin, 2×2FR vert
Ringaskiddy, 2×2FR vert
ADM Jetty (Ringaskiddy), 2×3FR vert
Cork Dockyard, 2FG vert
Cork Harbour Marina, 2×2FR vert

Crosshaven to East Ferry and Monkstown; Spike Island

Spit Bank light from the E: Haulbowline Island, L

Island in lovely rural surroundings. East Channel curves to the N and after 2M passes between the wooded slopes of Marloag Point and Gold Point, where it deepens to 18m. East Ferry Marina is located on the W side 0·5M N of Marloag Point. East Passage, as it has become, continues N for a further 1M with 8 to 12m, steep-to between wooded banks, to emerge into a shallow lagoon, 1M long and 2 cables wide, to the N of Great Island. Five cables N of East Ferry it is spanned by a power cable with 24m clearance at HW.

North of Spike Island is Spit Bank, drying sand 7 cables by 4, with the main channel making a 90° turn to the W around it. W of the bank on the S side of the channel is Haulbowline Island, the principal base of the Irish Naval Service and once also the site of a steelworks. The minor channel S of Haulbowline is spanned by a low bridge and overhead cables. The main ship channel passes close to the N shore at Cobh, where a marina is under construction. Continuing between Haulbowline and Great Island, the channel then turns N and narrows to 2 cables between Passage West and Rushbrooke. To the S of the channel here is the cargo, chemical, container and international ferry terminal at Ringaskiddy. Cork Dockyard, on Great Island 1M N of Ringaskiddy, is a large shiprepair facility. Opposite the Dockyard is Monkstown, with the 80-berth Cork Harbour Marina. Monkstown Creek, to the SW, dries.

SPIKE ISLAND

For over 200 years Spike Island was a military and Government preserve, with landing forbidden, and it has only recently been opened to visitors. The island is crowned by the 19th-century Fort Mitchel, used at various times as a military and naval fortress and as a prison. Tourist ferryboats now bring passengers from Cobh to the pontoon at the pier on the N side, often using the channel W and S of Haulbowline and passing under the low bridge. The channel to the N of Spike has no overhead obstructions and a least depth of 0·8m. It deepens W of the pier. There is deep water on a mid-channel course in the West Channel W of Spike, and it is easy to circumnavigate the island with suitable rise of tide. Spike is well worth a visit.

Berthing and anchorage

Although the pier and pontoon are signposted for use by licensed passenger vessels only, there is no objection to their use by yachts provided the front (N) face of the pontoon is always left free for the ferry. **Anchor** E of the pier or well south of the narrows at Paddy's Point in the West Channel. The area NW and W of the pier, between Spike, Haulbowline and Paddy's Point is fouled by submarine cables and pipes. There is a slipway for landing (also used by the cargo ferry) E of the pier, and a (drying) pier and slipway on the W side of the island.

Facilities

The island is owned by Cork County Council, whose staff welcome its visitors and run a tearoom and museum. Conducted tours are available. There is no admission charge to Fort Mitchel but it closes every day at 1730. Independent visitors must take care not to be locked in for the night, and should make themselves known to the staff. Many of the island's buildings are derelict and some may be in hazardous condition. Spike Island is a unique and special place, and visitors are requested to treat the environment and buildings with respect; do not leave litter. Dogs are not permitted on the island.

Spike Island pier and pontoon

East Channel

East Passage from the SW: Marloag Point L, Gold Point R

EAST CHANNEL

East Channel leads to East Passage, E of Great Island, and the marina at East Ferry. The entrance lies E of the No.9 channel buoy, 5 cables NNE of Whitegate Jetty. The conspicuous Aghada power station is on the SE side of the entrance. East Channel has a navigable width of at least 4 cables and a bar with 4·6m, and is marked by two lit buoys. Submarine power cables run NW from the power station to Great Island.

Directions – East Channel and East Passage

From a position 3 cables N of Whitegate jetty, steer 060° for 1·5M until East Passage, between wooded slopes, can be identified to the NE. Then steer for the mid-channel. East Passage is steep-to on both sides with 5 to 12m in mid-channel, and with its strong tides can be surprisingly subject to swell in winds between S and W. There is a 6-knot speed limit between Marloag Point and East Grove Quay.

Marina

East Ferry Marina, with 75 berths, is on the W bank 5 cables N of Marloag Point. Phone 021 481 3390.

Facilities

Water and shore power on the pontoons.

Anchorage

Anchor 5 cables further N, in 7 to 9m, clear of the moorings off East Grove Quay on the E bank. The quay has a piled extension with 1·7m at LAT, and is available as a temporary berth. Pub and restaurant at the quay. More sheltered anchorage in S to SW winds (but remote from any facilities) is available

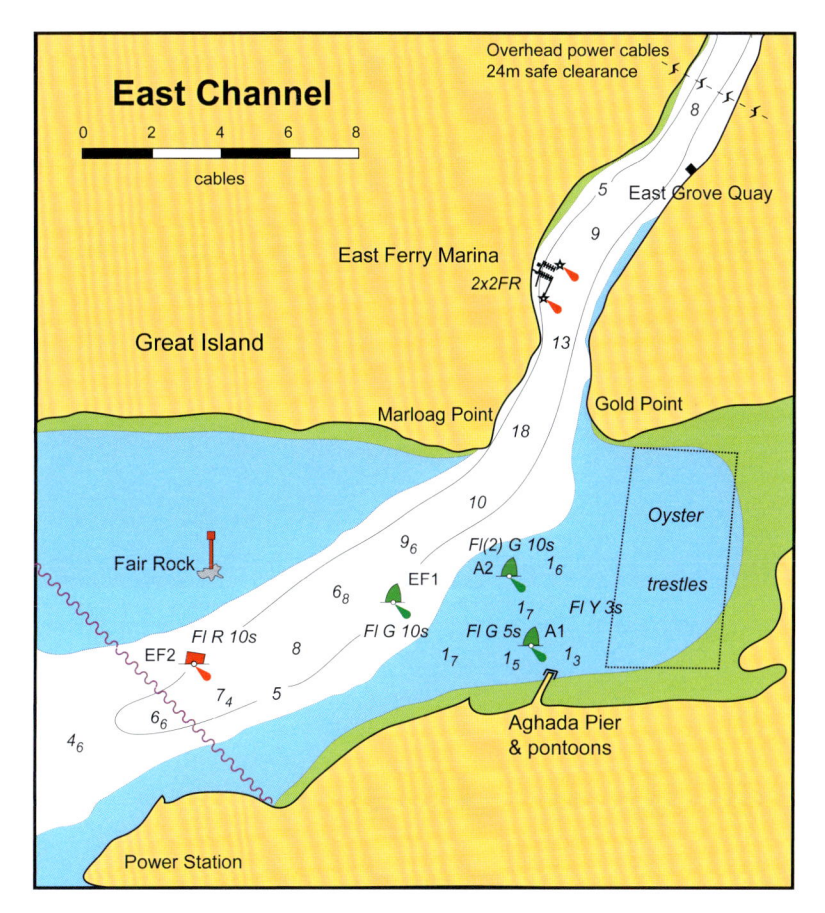

Aghada pier and pontoons

Aghada, Cobh, Monkstown

East Ferry from the N

Cobh marina - the first pontoon, June 2015

where the lagoon opens up at the N end of East Passage. The bottom here shelves gradually to the W but suddenly on the E side. The channel in the lagoon remains largely as charted, wide and deep at the E end and becoming shallow, narrow and winding towards the W.

Aghada

Aghada, on the S shore opposite East Passage, has an anchorage with 1·6m in the approach from the EF1 buoy in East Channel, and 0·6m at the pontoons at the pier head. There is almost 2m close E of the A1 and A2 buoys on the direct line from East Ferry to Aghada, but do not err E of the line as there are oyster trestles on the bank, supported by steel stakes which cover at HW. Shop and pubs near Aghada pier. Small chandlery at the Pier Service Station, 087 265 1979.

Cobh Marina

Cove Sailing Club's marina, under construction in 2015, is 400m W of the Deepwater Quay. Check the Amendments on www.iccsailingbooks.com for updates. A restaurant and bar at Cobh also has a pontoon for the use of patrons. There is no anchorage in the channel. Cobh has supermarkets, shops, restaurants, pubs, PO, banks, doctors. Cobh is the Tidal Standard Port for the south coast; MHWS 4·1m, MHWN 3·3m, MLWN 1·3m, MLWS 0·4m.

Monkstown - Cork Harbour Marina

Cork Harbour Marina, with 80 berths, is on the W side of the channel, one cable S of the old Sand Quay at Monkstown. Phone 087 250 6414, www.corkharbourmarina.ie. The marina has floating breakwaters; the tidal stream through it demands careful observation since there is an eddy close to shore.

Facilities

Water and shore power on the marina pontoons. Diesel, petrol and gas, repairs (including sails) all available by arrangement with the marina. Restaurant and bar, coffee shop at Monkstown. Cork Dockyard offers cranage and winter storage for yachts, phone 021 481 1831.

There is anchorage in 2 to 5m, on the W side of the channel opposite the dockyard and N or S of the marina.

RIVER LEE, MONKSTOWN to CORK CITY

AC1773, SC5622·12

The limit of navigation in the centre of Cork City is 6M upriver from Monkstown. Before proceeding upriver, permission must be obtained from the HM; call Cork Harbour Radio, VHF Ch 12 or phone 021 427 3125.

Monkstown and Cobh

St Colman's Cathedral dominates the skyline of Cobh. The pontoon (centre) is available for customers of the adjacent restaurant

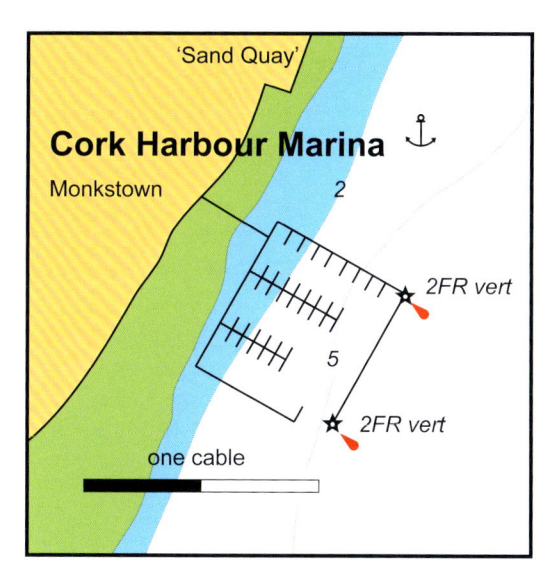

Cork Harbour Marina, Monkstown

West Passage from the S. Monkstown, L, and the dockyard at Rushbrooke, R

67

Cobh to Cork City

Haulbowline Island from the NW

Passage West pontoon

West Passage is the name given to the narrow 1M stretch running N from Monkstown between Great Island and the mainland. At Marino Point, the W tip of Great Island, it turns NW and opens out into the wide but shallow section known as Lough Mahon. The deep channel is here maintained by dredging and is less than 1 cable wide, marked by port- and starboard-hand buoys. The river narrows at Blackrock, 2M further NW, and turns W past the Tivoli container terminal. There are quays on both sides and a maintained depth of 5·2m in the uppermost reach. At the head of navigation the river divides into N and S channels, before it is spanned by the first of the city's many bridges. There is a speed limit of 6 knots in the river upstream of Blackrock Castle. This stretch is used by competitive rowing craft, and a good lookout should be kept for them.

Passage West

There is a 21-metre pontoon at Passage West, for short-stay and landing purposes only. The pontoon has a security gate, and 5·8m alongside at LAT. Passage West has shops, restaurants, pubs and PO.

Cork City Marina

This is a 100m pontoon with 4·5m alongside, at South Custom House Quay immediately downstream of the Eamon de Valera Bridge in the city centre. 24 hour security, water, shore power. The facility is operated by the Port of Cork Company. For an overnight berth contact the Port Berthing Master 021 427 3125 or outside office hours phone 021 453 0466. See www.portofcork.ie for more information and an online berth application form.

Facilities

All the amenities of a major seaport city, including a large regional hospital with full A&E facilities. Chandlery on Penrose Quay near the City Marina (Union Chandlery, phone 021 455 4334, www.unionchandlery.com), in the city centre (Matthews, phone 021 427 7633, www.matthewsofcork.com) and at Frankfield Industrial Estate, Kinsale Road

Cork City

(CH Marine, phone 021 431 5700, www.chmarine.com); electronic supplies and repairs (Dunmast Ltd, phone 021 431 8400). Ferries from Ringaskiddy to Roscoff; Cork International Airport, 5M from city centre. Train connections to Dublin, Waterford, Limerick and Tralee, bus connections to all parts of Ireland.

Cork City Marina

2 Cork Harbour to Crookhaven

Kinsale

'Cruising Ireland'
The coast from Cork Harbour to Crookhaven is described on pages 38 to 57 of **Cruising Ireland**

This beautiful coast has anchorages and harbours in abundance, and many islands large and small. There are no large towns, and no marinas west of Kinsale, but West Cork is well-populated and there is plenty to occupy the visitor ashore. The coast is mostly cliffbound, with beautiful bays and long sheltered inlets. Kinsale, magnificently situated on the estuary of the River Bandon, has a fine natural harbour and is a major tourist and sailing centre, renowned for its many restaurants and the picturesque buildings lining its ancient narrow streets. Apart from its marinas full of yachts, Kinsale has a significant fishing fleet, and handles small cargo vessels at its quay. The town is rich in history, and was the scene in 1601 of the final and decisive battle of the Anglo-Irish war of Elizabethan times, which was to establish English rule in Ireland for the next 300 years. The impressive ruins of Charles Fort, dating from the latter part of the 17th century, dominate the harbour entrance.

The Old Head of Kinsale has been marked by a lighthouse since 1665. The present tower – the third – was built in 1853. The headland has seen many shipwrecks, among them the loss of the *City of Chicago* in 1892, when the ship's master kept his engines running to hold the doomed ship against the cliffs and enable his passengers and crew to scramble ashore safely. Ten miles to the south of the Old Head, in May 1915, the *Lusitania* was torpedoed and sunk with the loss of 1,198 lives. She lies in 88 metres of water and is marked on the charts in 51°25′N 8°32′W.

Cork Harbour to Kinsale

Cork Harbour to Galley Head

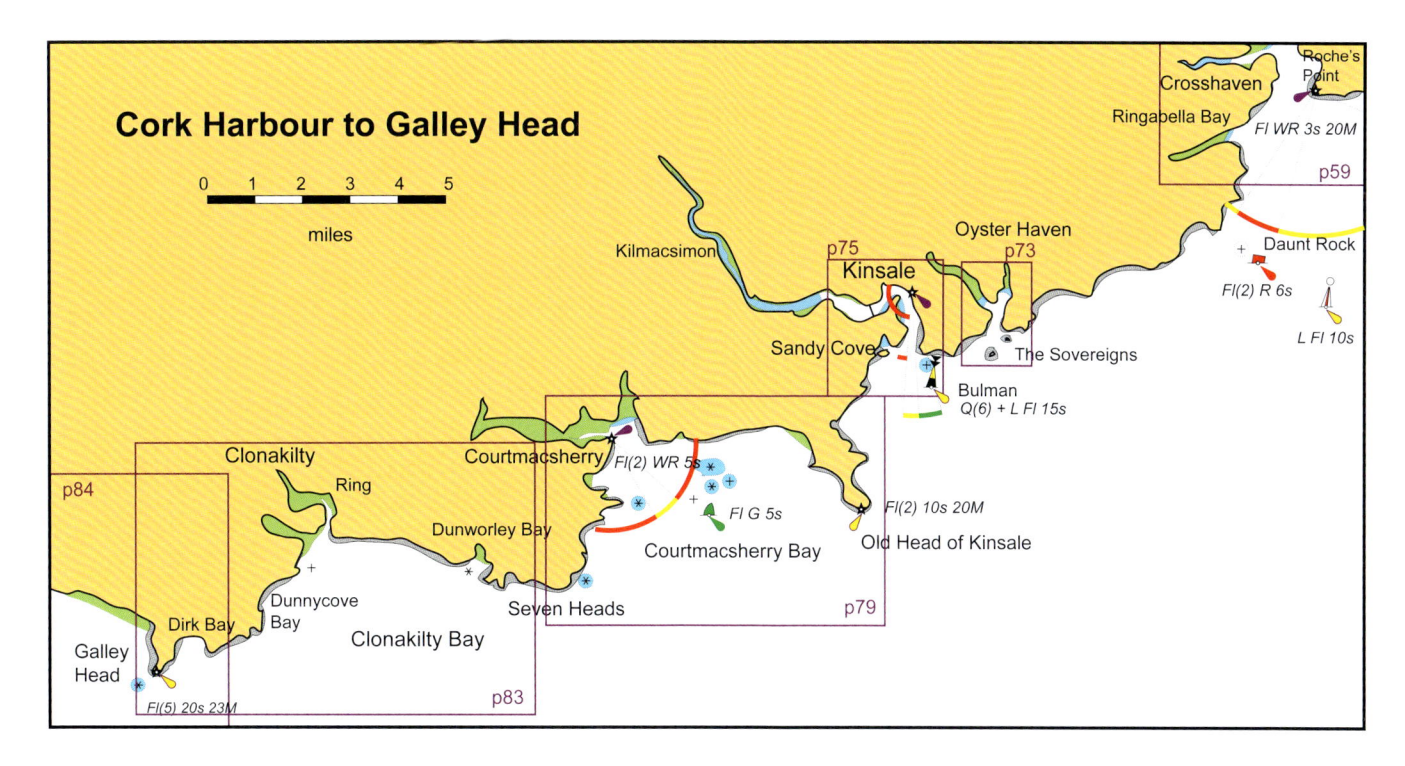

[Map showing coastline from Galley Head in the west to Roche's Point/Crosshaven in the east, including Dirk Bay, Dunnycove Bay, Clonakilty Bay, Ring, Clonakilty, Dunworley Bay, Seven Heads, Courtmacsherry, Courtmacsherry Bay, Kilmacsimon, Sandy Cove, Kinsale, Old Head of Kinsale, The Sovereigns, Bulman, Oyster Haven, Ringabella Bay, Daunt Rock. Light characteristics noted: Fl(5) 20s 23M, Fl(2) WR 5s, Fl G 5s, Fl(2) 10s 20M, Q(6)+L Fl 15s, Fl(2) R 6s, L Fl 10s, Fl WR 3s 20M. Page references p59, p73, p75, p79, p83, p84.]

Seven miles west of the Old Head, Courtmacsherry is a pretty and unspoiled village, a thriving sea angling centre and home to one of the longest-established lifeboat stations in Ireland. Further west, the village of Glandore and the fishing port of Union Hall face each other across a steep-sided and beautiful inlet. Glandore and its little stone harbour were laid out in the 1830's by the philanthropic landlord James Barry, and here was the setting for an early experiment in communal living by the notably eccentric William Thompson. This rated a mention in Marx's *Das Kapital*, but may be a little hard to imagine when in Glandore today.

Baltimore was the scene in 1631 of a raid by North African pirates, who carried off the population (at that point mostly English settlers) into slavery. The village has links, formal and informal, with its somewhat larger namesake across the Atlantic. Cecil Calvert, Lord Baltimore, founded the colony of Maryland in the early 17th century.

Between Baltimore and Mizen Head is a fabulous cruising ground of bays and islands, with the fine natural harbours of Schull and Crookhaven and many smaller harbours and anchorages. The labyrinth of channels among the islands offers good sailing (in spectacular surroundings) almost irrespective of wind direction.

Note – Tidal Streams

Between Cork and Cape Clear, the tide generally runs parallel to the coast and turns (according to all published sources, including this one) approximately two hours after high and low water at Cobh. More specific details are given below. However the timing appears to vary somewhat, and the tide is frequently observed to turn an hour or more earlier than predicted. The stream close inshore at the headlands (in any case) tends to turn earlier than offshore.

CORK HARBOUR to KINSALE

AC1765, Imray C57, SC5622·14

The coast between Cork and Kinsale is fringed by 30 to 50m cliffs, and the coastwise passage is straightforward, with the headlands clean and steep-to. Inshore of the Sovereigns, the mile-long inlet of Oyster Haven is peaceful and pretty, but is open to the south and suffers from somewhat poor holding ground. It is a centre for quiet and unobtrusive water sports.

Paper Charts

SC5622 and SC5623 cover the area described in this chapter. In terms of individual charts, the general chart AC2424 Kenmare River to Cork Harbour, or Imray's C57 Tuskar Rock to Old Head of Kinsale and C56 Old Head of Kinsale to Dingle Bay, give coverage. The Imray charts have several useful harbour plans, but AC1765, 2092, 2129 and 2184 are all essential nevertheless. AC2053 Kinsale and Oyster Haven, 2081 Courtmacsherry Bay and 3725 Baltimore Harbour are optional.

Cork Harbour to Kinsale

Ringabella Bay from the E

Tides - Cork Harbour to Kinsale

Tidal streams run parallel to the coast, turning ENE at –0420 Cobh and WSW at +0150 Cobh (but see Note on p71). The rate is 1 to 1·5 kn at springs around the headlands and 0·7 kn at the Daunt Rock. Constant (Kinsale) –0012 Cobh, MHWS 4·1m, MHWN 3·3m, MLWN 1·3m, MLWS 0·5m.

Dangers

Carrigabrochel (dries 1·8m), extending 1·8 cables offshore 1M S of Weaver's Point
Wreck 1·5 cables E of Fish Point, the S side of Ringabella Bay
Daunt Rock, 3·5m, 7 cables offshore 4M SSW of Roche's Point
Carrigadda (Long Rock), dries, extending 3·5 cables SE from the centre of Carrigadda Bay
Sovereign Patch, 2·1m, between the Little Sovereign and the shore
Harbour Rock, 0·9m, in Oyster Haven 3 cables N of Kinure Point
Bulman Rock, 0·9m, 3 cables S of Preghane Point.

Lights and Marks

Daunt buoy, PHM Fl(2) R 6s, AIS, close E of the rock
Cork, safe water buoy RWVS L Fl 10s, AIS, 1·7M ESE of the Daunt Rock
Bulman buoy, S Card Q(6)+L Fl 15s, 1 cable SW of the rock.
Old Head of Kinsale, black tower with white bands, Fl(2) 10s 72m 20M, AIS

Coastwise passage

The Daunt Rock, 4M S by W of the entrance to Cork Harbour, is a pinnacle which breaks in bad weather and is marked by a port-hand buoy. The Sovereigns, the islets marking the entrance to Oyster Haven, are bold and steep-to. From Weaver's Point, a berth of 2 cables off the headlands clears all dangers to the Little Sovereign and passes well inside the Daunt Rock. Stay outside the line between Robert's Head and Reanies Point, to avoid the drying reef Carrigadda in the bay. Passage is possible in moderate weather between the Little Sovereign and the shore, staying either N or S of mid-channel to avoid the Sovereign Patch. The W side of the entrance to Oyster Haven is clean if given a berth of 0·5 cable. Heading for Kinsale, the recommended course is S of the Bulman buoy, but passage N of the Bulman Rock is possible in settled weather by leaving Preghane Point not more than a cable to starboard. The N end of the Big Sovereign in line with Frower Point 082° leads clear N of the Bulman.

Ringabella Bay

51°46'·4N 8°18'W
Ringabella Bay, 1·6m SW of Weaver's Point, offers temporary anchorage in winds between SW and N, in 2 to 3m, sand. The inlet extends 1·2M SW, but beyond Ringabella Point it dries.

OYSTER HAVEN

⊕OH 51°41'N 8°26'·9W
AC1765, 2053, SC5622.16
Oyster Haven offers sheltered anchorage in all but S winds, when it is subject to swell.

The Sovereigns from the E: the Old Head of Kinsale in the distance, L

Oyster Haven

Oyster Haven from the S: the Big Sovereign, foreground, and the Little Sovereign, R

From the E, give Kinure Point, the E side of the entrance, a berth of a cable and head for Ferry Point on the W side to avoid Harbour Rock. The W arm of the inlet, the Belgooly River, is the more sheltered but is shoal on either side and is somewhat encumbered with moorings. The N arm is wider but more exposed and has poorer holding.

Anchorage

Anchor in 2 to 3m, either NNW of Ferry Point in mid-channel, keeping Kinure Point open of Ferry Point, or on the W side of the N arm. The holding ground is poor in weed and gravel, so care must be taken to ensure the anchor is well bedded in. Be prepared to lift it and re-lay. There are no facilities ashore.

Belgooly River above Oyster Haven

It is possible with care towards HW to take a dinghy upriver as far as Belgooly, 3M. Filling station, shop, pubs at Belgooly.

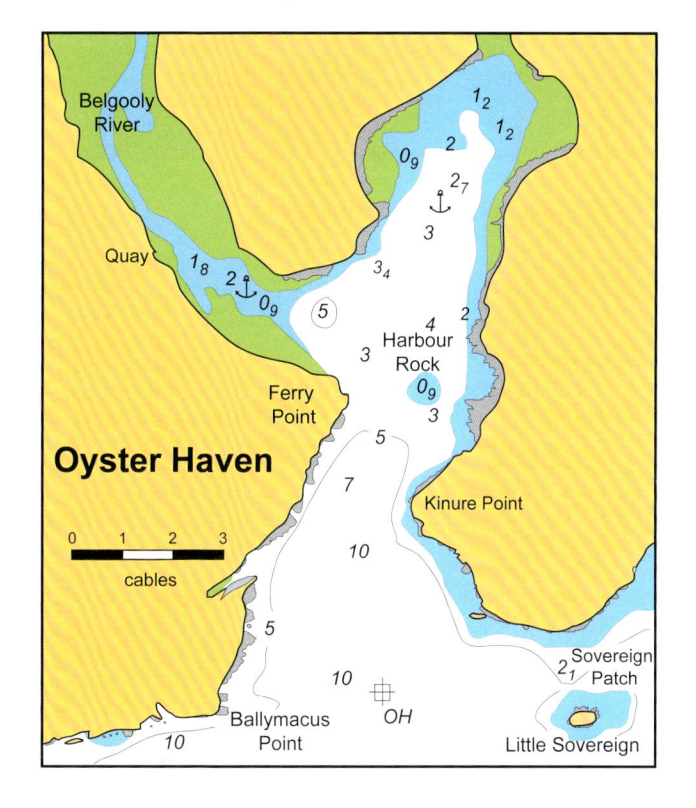

Oyster Haven from the SW: the Big Sovereign, R

Kinsale

Kinsale Harbour from the NE; Blockhouse Point, bottom L, with the ruins of James Fort on the summit; Castlepark Marina, L centre, Trident Marina, the Town Pier and the Yacht Club Marina, R. Kinsale bridge, top.

KINSALE

⊕ *KS* 51°40′·5N 8°30′·2W

AC1765, 2053, SC5622·15, Imray C56, C57. See photos also on pp 16 and 19

Kinsale Harbour, the estuary of the River Bandon, may be entered by day or night in all weathers. The approach is straightforward and well marked and lit. The Bar, with 3 to 4m, is a broad sandbank in mid-channel 8 cables within the entrance.

Directions

After clearing the Bulman, a berth of 0·5 cable clears all dangers in the entrance. Identify Charles Fort on the E side and pass between it and the Spur buoy, then leave the Spit and Crohogue buoys to port. The area S of Crohogue has many moorings. The reach SW of Crohogue, stretching 5 cables to Lobster Quay to the W and Castlepark Marina to the E, is clean and free of dangers. The area to the N and NW of the Kinsale YC Marina shoals rapidly and dries at LW. Kinsale Bridge, with 5m clearance, spans the channel 8 cables SW of Crohogue buoy. There is 7m at LAT in the SE half of the channel right up to the bridge.

Marinas

Kinsale Yacht Club Marina, with 170 berths and 50 visitors' berths, N of the Town Pier. Call VHF Ch M, 021 477 2196 or 087 678 7377, or come alongside the long outer pontoon, rafting up as permitted. The outer pontoon has 8m at LAT and with suitable notice the very largest yachts can be accommodated. Visitors have temporary membership of Kinsale YC, with showers, bar and meals. www.kyc.ie.

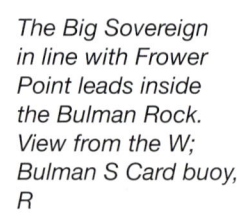

The Big Sovereign in line with Frower Point leads inside the Bulman Rock. View from the W; Bulman S Card buoy, R

Kinsale

Kinsale entrance, from the SW

Tides - Kinsale

The stream runs fairly into and out of the harbour, reaching 1·5 knots at springs and turning at HW by the shore. Constant –0012 Cobh, MHWS 4·1m, MHWN 3·3m, MLWN 1·3m, MLWS 0·5m.

Dangers

Farmer Rock (dries 0·6m), 0·5 cable offshore 3 cables S of Money Point
Spur Bank, 0·9 to 2m, SE of Blockhouse Point.

Lights and Marks

Charles Fort, white bn on the fort providing a leading light, Fl WRG 5s 18m W8M, R5M, G6M, G 348°–358°, W 358°–004°, R 004°–168°. Shows white over mid-channel
Spur buoy, PHM Fl(2) R 6s, 2 cables WNW of Charles Fort
Spit buoy, PHM QR, 4 cables N by W of Spur
Crohogue buoy, PHM Fl(3) R 10s, 2 cables WNW of Spit
Kinsale YC Marina, 2FG vert
Town Pier, 2FG vert
Fishermen's pontoon and ferry slip, 2×2FG vert
Castlepark Marina, 2×2FR vert.

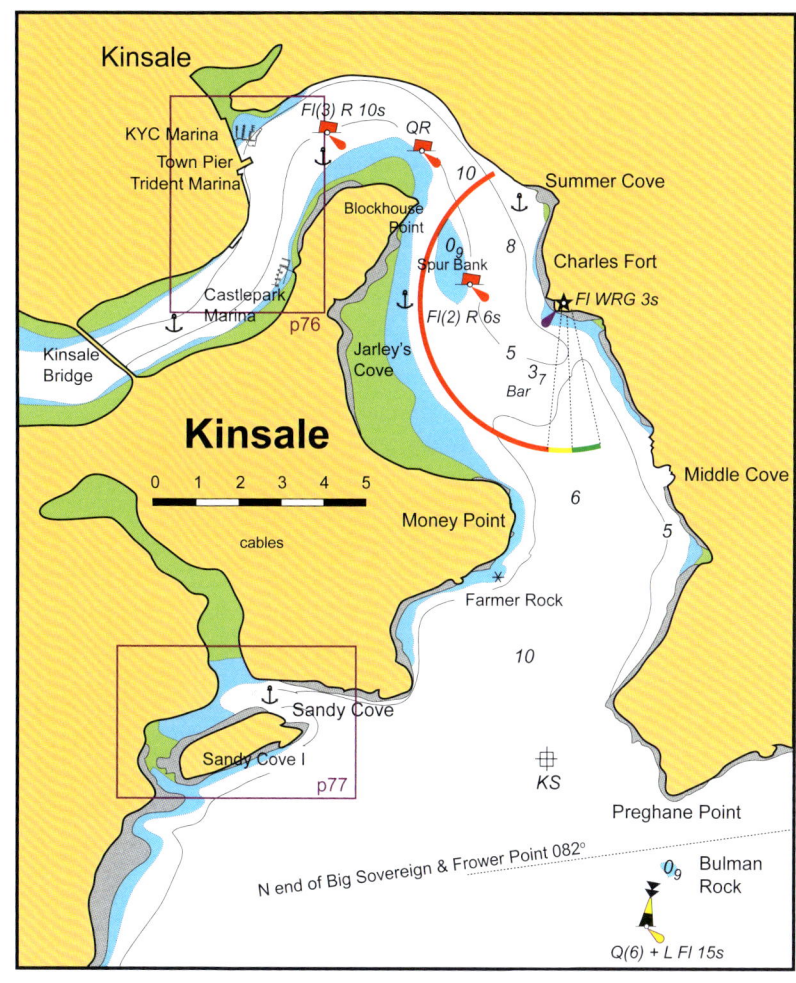

Middle Cove

Charles Fort; the light beacon is on the corner of the building, centre

75

Kinsale

Entering Kinsale; Blockhouse Point, L

Trident Marina, 6 berths, S of the Town Pier. Phone 021 477 2927.

Castlepark Marina, 70 berths and 20 visitors' berths, on the E side 3 cables SSE of the Town Pier. Call VHF Ch 6, 16 and M or phone 021 477 4959.

Harbour

The Harbour is managed by Cork County Council. The Town Pier is normally reserved for commercial, fishing and naval vessels; for a temporary berth contact the HM on VHF or by phone, 021 477 2503. The harbour cruise boat operates from the Town Pier and a jetty S of the Kinsale YC marina. There is a slipway suitable for launching trailered boats. The fishermen's pontoon, 2 cables S of the Town Quay, is strictly reserved for fishing vessels. The harbour office monitors VHF Ch 16, working channel 14. There is a speed limit of 6 knots in the harbour.

Anchorage

Anchorage immediately SE and E of the Town Pier is prohibited, to allow room for large vessels to manoeuvre. Anchor in mid-channel SW of Castlepark Marina in 5 to 7m, mud, or S of Crohogue buoy in 2 to 3m, mud and sand. The Harbour charges a fee for anchoring; this fee is also incorporated in all marina charges.

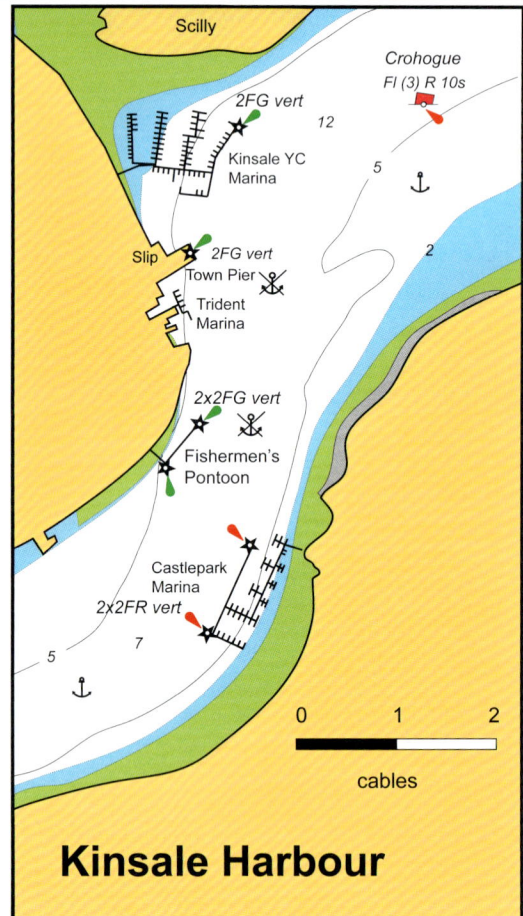

Kinsale Harbour

Summer Cove

Summer Cove, on the E shore opposite Blockhouse Point, is a delightful spot for a short visit. Anchor in 2 to 3m off the pier. There may be visitors' moorings, provided by the pub for the use of customers. The pier dries.

Kinsale Harbour; the Yacht Club marina, R, the Town Pier and Trident marina, centre, and Castlepark marina, L

76

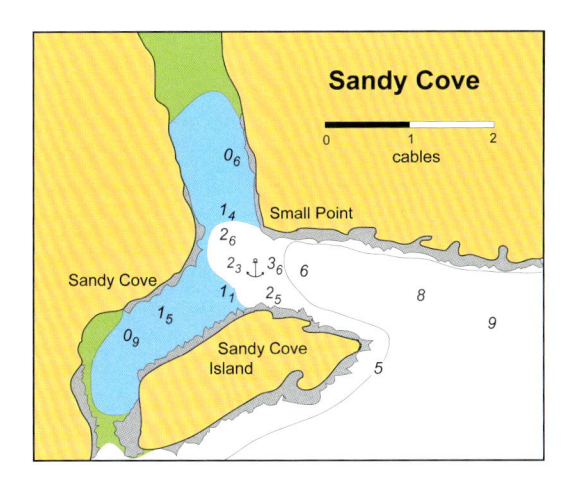

Kinsale

Middle Cove

Middle Cove, on the E side opposite Money Point, is a rocky bay in which there is a boatyard with a travelhoist dock.

Jarley's Cove

Temporary anchorage is available in 2m, off the beach on the W side S of Blockhouse Point.

Facilities

Water and shore power at all marinas. Diesel at Castlepark and Trident marinas, or by tanker on the Town Pier (Ross Oil, phone 086 258 3544). Showers at Kinsale YC. Filling station, supermarket, shops, pubs, many restaurants, PO, doctors. Car rental. Bus services to Cork, also serving Cork International Airport, 10M NE. Taxis, phone 021 477 2642 or 021 477 4900. RNLI inshore lifeboat station. Middle Cove boatyard, phone 021 477 4774, hull, mechanical, rigging, electrical and electronic repairs, 40 tonne travelhoist, winter storage. Olimpic Sails Ireland, phone 086 326 0018. Divers available. There are many tourist attractions in Kinsale and its environs; Charles Fort is particularly worth a visit.

River Bandon above Kinsale Bridge

For vessels which can clear under the bridge (7m at its S end), the river is navigable as far as Kilmacsimon, 6M from Kinsale Bridge. Hold the mid channel on the reaches and stay wide on the bends. The lower stretch is marked by several port-hand buoys. There is a boatyard at Kilmacsimon (phone 021 477 5134).

Sandy Cove

Immediately W of the entrance to Kinsale Harbour is the inlet of Sandy Cove, a cable wide and 2 cables in length and sheltered by Sandy Cove Island, 28m high. Sandy Cove offers a delightful anchorage in moderate winds between S and NE. Anchor in 4m, N of the N point of the island. The drying branch to the N, 5 cables in length, and the channel W of Sandy Cove Island may be explored by dinghy near HW. The W channel is encumbered by rocks at its S end. No facilities ashore.

Sandy Cove from the E

Sandy Cove: the yellow buoy is one of a series marking a swimming area

Kinsale to Courtmacsherry

The Old Head of Kinsale from the E

KINSALE to COURTMACSHERRY

AC1765, 2092, 2081, SC5623, Imray C56; see Plan of Courtmacsherry Bay

Bullen's Bay, 2·5M N of the Old Head, is foul for 3 cables offshore. Bream Rock, above water, is close inshore 4 cables NNE of the headland, which is steep-to. The bays to the NE and NW of the Old Head are named Holeopen Bay, East and West, and are so called because the peninsula at that point is penetrated by caves, several of which are navigable by dinghy near HW in very calm conditions. The greatest care must be taken, but the passage of the caves is an unforgettable experience. The cliffs all round the Old Head are clean to within 50m, and anchorage may be found in either bay in 9 to 11m while exploring the shore, but the yacht should not be left unattended.

Courtmacsherry Bay has a number of drying and sunken rocks, but they are well enough marked to be easily avoided. Courtmacsherry Harbour, in the NW corner of the bay, offers excellent shelter and is accessible by day or night with modest rise of tide. The bar has least depth 1·2m.

Dangers

Numerous **drying and below-water rocks** extending up to 3 cables offshore at Bullen's Bay, 2M N of the Old Head of Kinsale on the E side

In Courtmacsherry Bay:

Barrel Rock (dries 2·6m), near the middle of the bay, 1·25M from the N shore and 3·3M WNW of the Old Head of Kinsale

Black Tom, 2·3m, 6 cables W by S of Barrel Rock

Blueboy Rock, 0·2m, 4 cables E of Barrel Rock

A **sunken rock** 2 cables NE of Barrel Rock

The **Inner Barrels**, 5 cables N of Barrel Rock, an extensive patch which dries 0·5m at one point

Horse Rock (dries 3·6m), 4 cables off Barry's Point on the W shore of the bay

Drying and sunken rocks extending 3 cables offshore from Garrettstown Strand in the NE corner of the bay.

There are no dangers on the direct course from the Old Head to Seven Heads.

Lights and Marks

Old Head of Kinsale, black tower with white bands, Fl(2) 10s 72m 20M, AIS

Black Tom buoy, SHM Fl G 5s, AIS, 5 cables SSE of the rock

Barrel Rock perch, derelict but clearly visible pole beacon

Wood Point, white pole beacon, Fl (2) WR 5s 15m 5M, W 315°–332°, R to shore to E and S. The white sector leads from the SE between Black Tom and the Horse Rock

Courtmacsherry bar buoy, SHM Fl G 3s, 1 cable NNE of Wood Point.

No.1 buoy, SHM Fl G 10s
No.3 buoy, SHM Fl G 5s
No.2 buoy, PHM Fl(2) R 10s
No.5 buoy, SHM Fl(2) G 10s
No.7 buoy, SHM QG
No.9 buoy, SHM Fl G 15s
Courtmacsherry Pier, 2FR vert

Tides
Old Head of Kinsale

Off the Old Head of Kinsale and across the mouth of Courtmacsherry Bay the W-going stream makes at +0205 Cobh and the E-going stream at –0420 Cobh (but see Note on page 71). The spring rate off the Old Head is 2·5 kn. These streams form a race which extends over 1M from the Old Head, to the SW during the W-going stream and to the SE during the E-going stream. In settled weather and offshore winds, a passage close to the Head avoids the tidal slop; in heavy weather, when the race can be dangerous to smaller craft, give the Head a berth of over 2M. The stream close inshore to the N of the Head, on both sides, always runs S. Further W, the spring rate offshore is 1·5 kn, reaching 2 kn off the Seven Heads. There is little stream in Courtmacsherry Bay.

Constant (Courtmacsherry) –0018 Cobh; MHWS 3·7m, MHWN 3·0m, MLWN 1·3m, MLWS 0·5m.

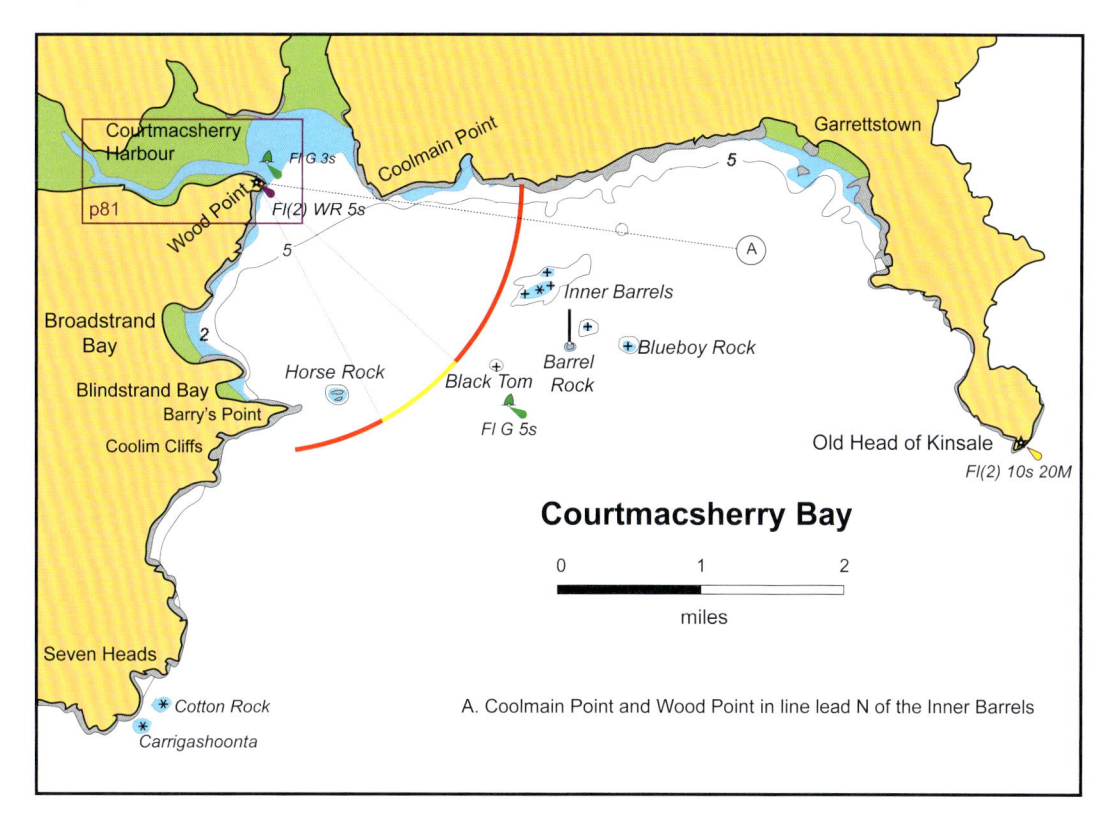

Courtmacsherry

A. Coolmain Point and Wood Point in line lead N of the Inner Barrels

COURTMACSHERRY

⊕CM 51°38′N 8°40′·5W

See Plan on p81

The harbour is entered between Wood Point and Coolmain Point. The bar at the entrance breaks in strong to gale force S or SE winds, and the entrance should not be attempted in these conditions. If unable to enter Courtmacsherry due to low tide, safe overnight anchorage, in moderate weather with winds from S through W to NW, is available in Broadstrand Bay, S of Wood Point – see below.

Directions

From the E, from a position 1 cable S of the Old Head, a course of 271° leads S of Black Tom buoy and S of all the dangers in the bay. The high ground between Barry's Point and Seven Heads (the Coolim Cliffs) will be seen ahead on this course. Leave Black Tom buoy to starboard and steer 317° for Courtmacsherry bar. If the Barrel perch can be clearly identified to the N, it is safe to take the short cut N of Black Tom in most weather conditions, leaving the Barrel perch a cable to starboard.

(below) Barrel Rock and the entrance to Courtmacsherry, from the SE. Wood Point is L of the Barrel Rock perch

(bottom) Wood Point from the SE: Courtmacsherry buoy. R

79

Courtmacsherry

Courtmacsherry from the E; the bar buoy, bottom, Wood Point, lower L, and the pier, upper R centre

Tides

Tides run at up to 3 kn at springs in the harbour, the flood starting at −0600 Cobh and the ebb at −0010 Cobh. Constant −0018 Cobh; MHWS 3·7m, MHWN 3·0m, MLWN 1·3m, MLWS 0·5m.

Courtmacsherry pontoon on an unusually busy day

There is also a passage N of the Inner Barrels, which is straightforward but not recommended to a stranger in bad weather. From a position one cable SW of the Old Head, steer 300° for 3M until 5 cables from the N shore of the bay with the tip of Wood Point in line with Coolmain Point bearing 280°. Alter course on to this transit, which leads N of the Inner Barrels, and clear of all dangers off the N shore of the bay. Approaching Coolmain Point, give it a berth of 2 cables, and continue towards Wood Point and the Courtmacsherry buoy.

From the W, give the shore NE of Seven Heads a berth of 3 cables to avoid Carrigashoonta and Cotton Rock; identify Barry's Point and Horse Rock (which almost always shows) and steer to pass in mid-channel between them.

The channel inside the bar has 2 to 4m and is marked by six lighted buoys. Follow the buoys, keeping them close aboard, and do not stray outside their line since the channel is narrow. Steer 270° from the Courtmacsherry buoy for the mid-channel between the No.2 (port-hand) and No.5 (starboard-hand) buoys, and then 210° for the No.7 buoy. The deep part of the channel extends one cable beyond the pier. There is a 6 knot speed limit in the harbour W of the No.2 port-hand buoy.

Anchorage and berthing

Anchor either NW of Ferry Point, or N of the moorings and E of the lifeboat station, leaving room for the lifeboat to pass. Good holding in 2 to 3m, stiff mud. Anchored boats will normally lie to the tide. The area in front of the pier should be kept free to allow manoeuvring room.

Beyond the pier is a 36m-long pontoon and a slipway suitable for trailer sailers. It is usually advisable to approach the pier or pontoon stemming the tide. The pontoon has 2·5m at LAT and the pier extension 4·5m. The E end of the pontoon is reserved for short-stay only. The deep channel at the pier is only 50 to 75m wide. The stone pier E of the extension has 0·9m and can be used as an alongside berth at neaps. The dock inside the pier dries. There is some fishing boat traffic at the pier, and sea angling boats leave daily in summer at 1000 and return at 1800.

Courtmacsherry provides excellent shelter in winds from S through SW to W, and moorings are in use all winter. Strong NW winds (force 7 or 8) raise a short steep chop at the pier while gale to storm force SE winds may produce a confused swell at high tide. In

Courtmacsherry

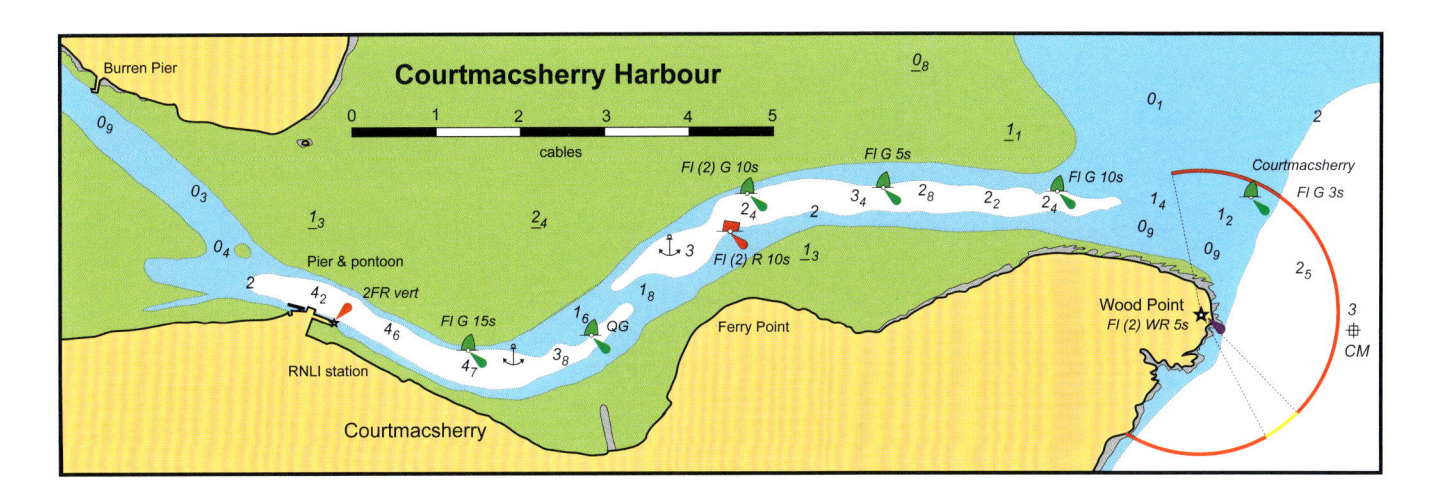

these conditions it is better to lie to an anchor.

Facilities

Pubs, hotel/restaurant in the village; diesel, water and shore power at the pontoon (for diesel contact Courtmacsherry Sea Angling 023 884 6427). Mechanical repairs, Marine Parts (Irl), 023 884 0170. RNLI all-weather lifeboat station. Buses to Cork, taxis (087 795 6055, 087 210 4964).

Argideen River to Timoleague

Burren Pier, on the N side opposite Courtmacsherry, has 0·5m at its head but is short of securing points. Near HW the river is navigable by shallow draft vessels to Timoleague, where the ruins of the 14th-century Franciscan abbey are the finest medieval monastic remains in County Cork. There is a pontoon for landing at Timoleague, and the river is marked by unlit buoys.

Courtmacsherry pier from the NE

Courtmacsherry to Glandore Harbour

Blindstrand (L) and Broadstrand Bays, from the SE. Quarry Point, centre

COURTMACSHERRY to GLANDORE HARBOUR

AC2092, SC5623, Imray C56

The passage round Seven Heads and Galley Head is straightforward, and there are no offshore dangers in Clonakilty Bay.

Broadstrand and Blindstrand Bays

51°37′N 8°40′·5W

Anchorage is available in settled weather, with winds between S and NW, in Broadstrand and Blindstrand Bays to the S of Wood Point. These bays, particularly Broadstrand, offer an alternative to Courtmacsherry in suitable weather if caught by a falling tide. Approaching from the E towards Broadstrand Bay, steer 295° from Black Tom buoy and alter course to the W when off the mouth of the bay, passing clear N of Horse Rock. Anchor in 3m, sand, on the N side of the bay. Blindstrand Bay, to the S of Quarry Point, is narrower; anchor in 3m, sand, keeping Quarry Point W of N.

Seven Heads

There is deep water in mid-channel between Horse Rock and Barry's Point. Give the shore NE of Seven Heads a berth of 3 cables to avoid Cotton Rock and Carrigashoonta. These rocks dry only 2m, not 3·1 and 3·6m as charted, and Carrigashoonta is slightly further offshore than shown on AC2081. Carrigashoonta is not marked on the smaller-scale charts.

Leganagh Point, the most E'ly of the Seven Heads, is 40m high, and has the ruin of a signal tower on its summit. A berth of 2 cables clears all dangers S of the Seven Heads.

Tides
Seven Heads to Glandore Bay

At Seven Heads and from there to Toe Head the E-going stream starts at –0420 Cobh and the W-going stream at +0205 Cobh (but see Note on page 71). Spring rate offshore is 1·5 kn, but reaches 2 kn off Seven Heads and 2·5 kn off Galley Head. There are S-going eddies on both sides of Galley Head, from which the stream sets continuously onto the Doolic Rock. There is a race extending 1·5M SSW which can be dangerous in strong SW winds even with a fair tide. There is little stream in Clonakilty or Glandore Bays. The stream runs strongly in Clonakilty Harbour and across the bar.

Constant (Castle Haven) –0028 Cobh; MHWS 3·7m, MHWN 2·9m, MLWN 1·3m, MLWS 0·6m.

Dangers

Horse Rock, dries 3·6m, 4 cables off Barry's Point
Carrigashoonta (dries 2m) and **Cotton Rock** (dries 2m), close NE of Seven Heads.
Cow Rock (dries 2·6m), in Dunworley Bay
Horse Rock (dries 0·4m), 1·25 cables N of Cow Rock
Doolic Rock (dries 3·7m), 3 cables SW of Galley Head
Sunk Rock, 0·4m, 1·5 cables SSE of Doolic Rock
Cloghna Rock, 0·9m, 6 cables offshore 1·7M NW of Galley Head

Lights and Marks

Wine Rock, green stayed perch SHM, unlit, at the entrance to Clonakilty Harbour
Galley Head, white tower Fl(5) 20s 53m 23M, visible from seaward from 256° to 065°. The light is obscured inside the line of Seven Heads on the E side and inside the line of the Stag Rocks off Toe Head to the W

For details of dangers and marks in the entrance to Glandore Harbour, see below.

Wine Rock perch. The rock is labelled "Wind Rock" on the Admiralty chart.

Clonakilty Bay

Clonakilty Bay
AC2092, SC5623 and Plan

Clonakilty Bay lies between Seven Heads and Galley Head. The bay has no harbours or anchorages which are both safe and easily accessible. Between Dunworley Bay and Ring Head are a number of drying and below-water rocks within 3 cables of the shore, and Anchor Rock, with 2·3m, lies 3 cables NE of Duneen Head.

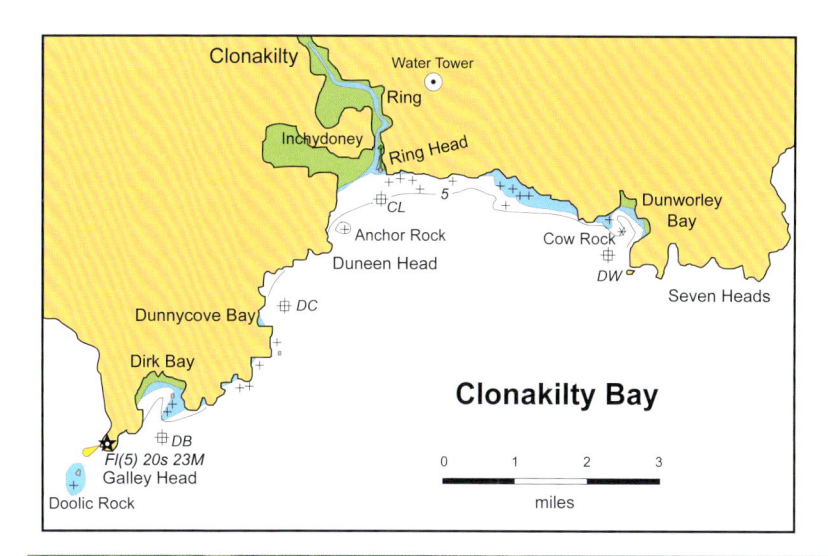

Dunworley Bay
⊕*DW* 51°34'·5N 8°46'W

This bay immediately W of Seven Heads is exposed to the SW, but offers an attractive temporary anchorage in settled or easterly weather, and has a splendid beach. Cow Rock, in the middle of the bay, normally breaks, but Horse Rock, drying 0·4m, is 1·25 cables N of Cow Rock and may not show. Give Dunworley Head a berth of 2 cables and anchor off the beach in 3 to 4m, sand.

Clonakilty Harbour
⊕*CL* 51°35'·2N 8°51'W

Clonakilty Harbour is used by small fishing craft based at Ring, NE of Inchydoney Island and 1M N of Ring Head. The bar, close W of Wine Rock (dries 0·5m), has less than 0·5m and is exposed to the S, and the channel is not deep enough for a yacht to lie afloat at LW. Entry should be attempted only in settled conditions on a high and rising tide, with great care and continuous use of the echosounder. Keep the starboard-hand perch on Wine Rock close aboard and stay 0·5 cable off the E side past South Ring. The "slip" marked close SW of Arundel Mills on AC2092 is Ring Pier, which just dries at LWS. The tide runs strongly in the channel, and there are many small-boat moorings. Restaurant and pubs at Ring; supermarkets, shops, restaurants, pubs, PO, laundry, doctors at Clonakilty, 1·8 km.

Ring (Clonakilty Harbour) from the SW

Dunnycove Bay from the E

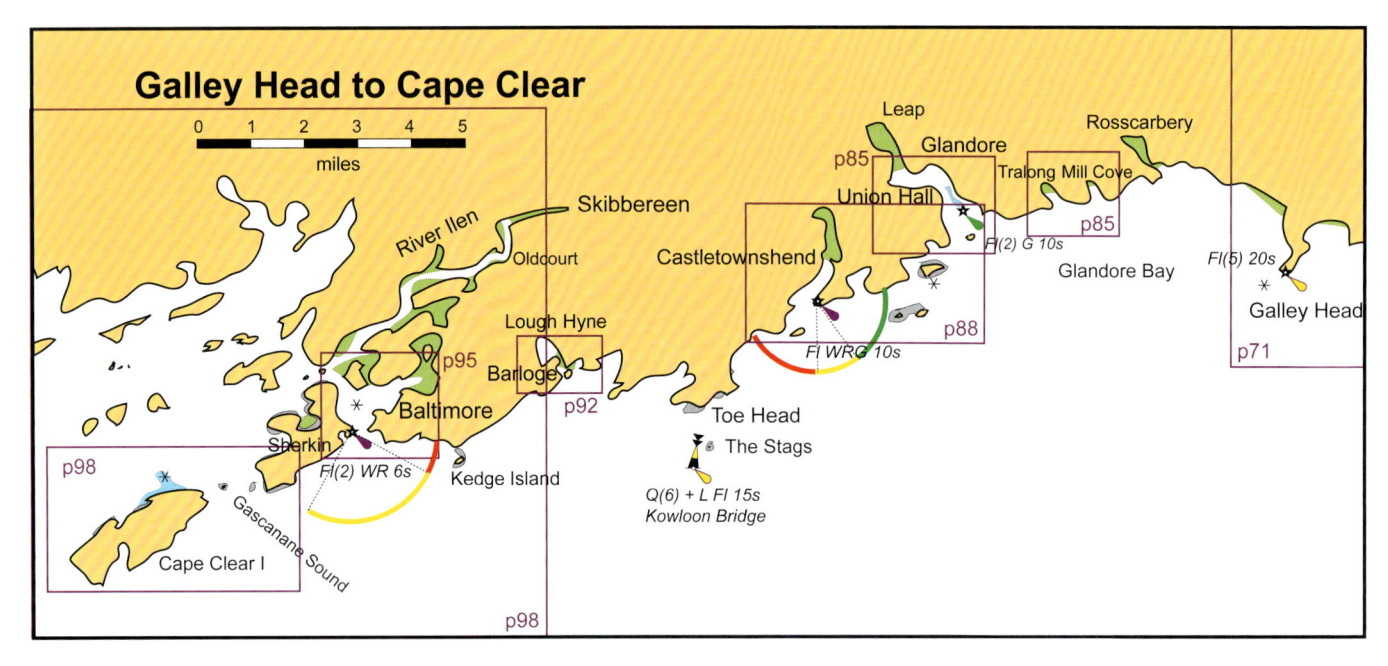

Glandore Bay

Galley Head to Cape Clear

Galley Head from the W: Doolic Rock, R

Dunnycove Bay

⊕ *DC* 51°33'·7N 8°53'·3W

This bay N of Dunnycove Point offers temporary anchorage in moderate weather and winds between SW and N. Anchor in 7m, close NW of the point.

Dirk Bay

⊕ *DB* 51°32'N 8°56'W

There is anchorage in this bay to the E of Galley Head in settled weather with winds between W and NE, and it has a splendid sandy beach in its NE corner. Enter close to the W shore to avoid Carrickduff (dries 1·5m) on the E side, with sunken rocks extending 1 cable SW from it. Anchor a cable off the beach in 3 to 5m, sand.

GLANDORE BAY

AC2092, SC5623·15, Imray C56

This bay lies between Galley Head and Toe Head, and has two excellent harbours – Glandore and Castle Haven – and some delightful smaller anchorages.

Galley Head to Glandore Harbour

Rounding Galley Head, give it a berth of at least 7 cables to clear Doolic and Sunk Rocks, or else pass inside the Doolic, keeping closer to the Head than the rock. The Head itself is steep-to. In fresh winds or poor visibility keep well outside the Doolic. A course of 283° from Galley Head leads to the entrance to Glandore Harbour.

Mill Cove and Tralong Bay

These two bays E of Glandore offer temporary anchorage in offshore weather. Mill Cove is very narrow and almost entirely taken up with small-boat moorings. Mill Cove Rock and Black Rocks, forming one cluster, are conspicuous and extend nearly 2 cables offshore to the W of Mill Cove. They are shown on the charts as drying but in fact stand 9 to 13m above HW. Tralong Bay lies 6 cables W of Mill Cove and 1M E of Goat's Head at the entrance to Glandore Harbour. The pyramidal Tralong Rock (11m high) at the W side of the entrance has rocks 0·5 cable SE of it, and between it and the shore to the

Glandore Harbour

NW. Enter in mid-channel and anchor in 3m in the middle of the bay. The head of the bay dries out. The shore between Tralong and Goat's Head is foul for a distance of 1 cable nearly all the way.

GLANDORE HARBOUR

⊕ GD 51°32'·5N 9°05'·4W
AC2092, SC5623·6, Imray C56 and Plan

The entrance lies between Goat's Head and Sheela Point. Goat's Head, on the E side, is a bluff headland, 79m high.

Dangers

Sheela's Rock (dries 1·5m), 1 cable SE of Sheela Point.
Reefs extending 1 cable W and 2 cables N and E from Adam's Island
Unnamed rock with 3m, almost in the middle of the sound between Adam's Island and Sheela Point.
A **sunken rock** between the W side of Eve Island and the shore
Unnamed rocks which partly uncover, extending 1 cable from the NE shore, 1 cable N of Grohoge Point
The Dangers, 3 drying reefs in a line NNW–SSE dividing the entrance to Glandore Harbour, 2 to 5 cables N of Eve Island
Sunk Rock, 1·5m, 1 cable N of the Dangers

Lights and Marks

Glandore SW, 5m green column, SHM, Fl(2)G 10s, on the Outer Danger rock
Outer Danger, grey perch, unlit
Middle Danger, green perch SHM, unlit
Inner Danger, green perch SHM, unlit
Sunk Rock buoy, SHM, Fl G 5s

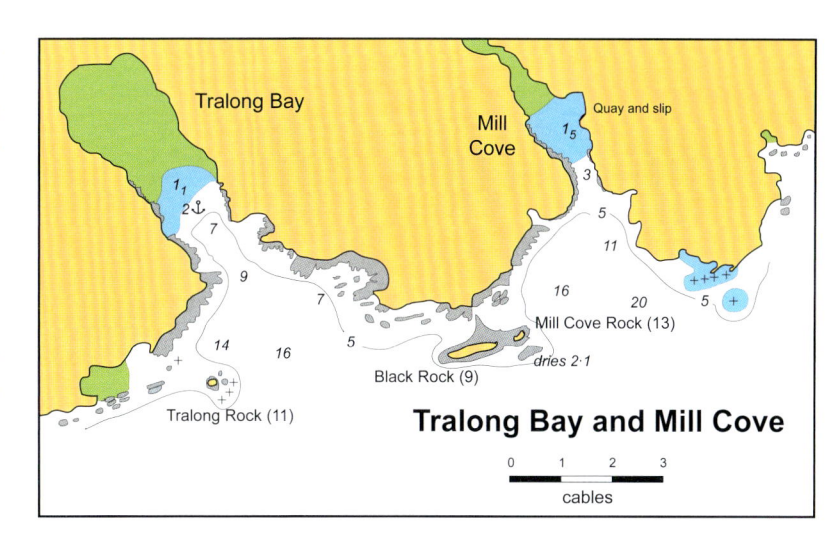

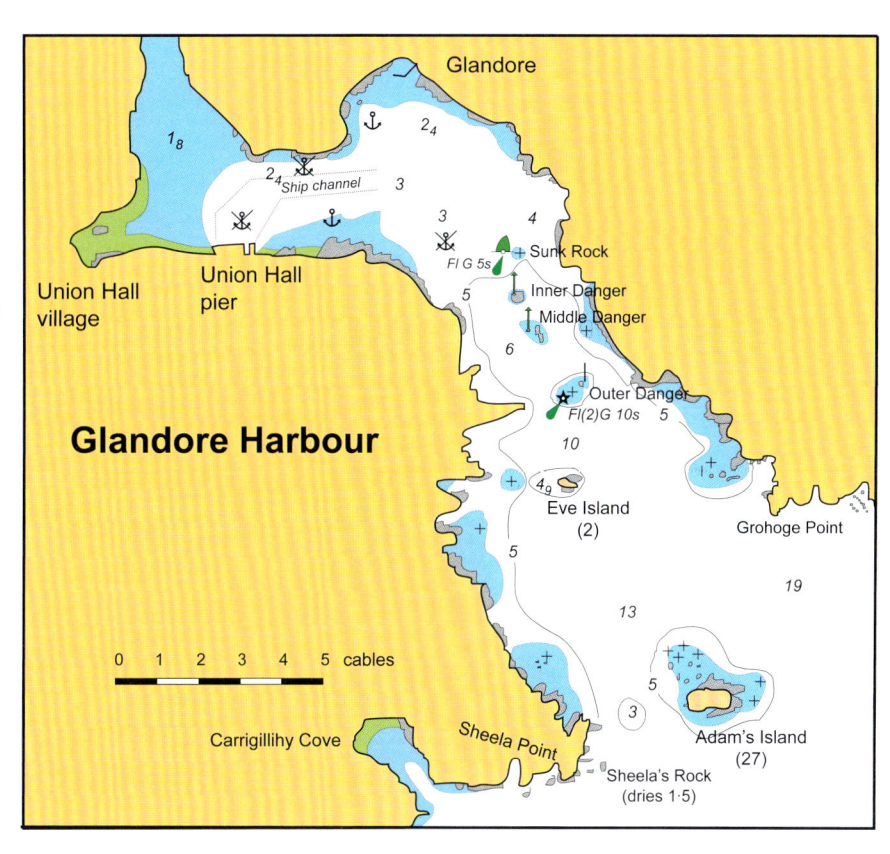

Tralong Bay and Mill Cove

Glandore Harbour

Glandore entrance marks, from the S. (L to R) Glandore SW beacon on the Outer Danger, Sunk Rock buoy, Inner Danger beacon, Middle Danger beacon and the grey perch marking the E side of the Outer Danger.

85

Glandore and Union Hall

Approaches to Glandore and Union Hall from the S: Adam's Island, lower L, Eve Island centre

Glandore Harbour from the W; Union Hall bottom R, Glandore top L

Entrance directions

From the E, steer to pass midway between Goat's Head and Adam's Island, giving the island a berth of 2 cables, then keep Eve Island close aboard to port – or as the local saying goes, avoid Adam and hug Eve. Leave Glandore SW beacon, all the marks on the Dangers, and the Sunk Rock buoy, to starboard. The derelict grey perch on the E end of the Outer Danger marks a minor channel to the NE of the Dangers, which is not recommended without local knowledge. A stranger should not attempt to pass between the separate reefs making up the Dangers. If making for Union Hall, give Coosaneigh Point, E of the pier, a berth of 1·5 cables to avoid a shoal patch extending N from the shore. From the W, give Sheela Point a berth of 1·5 cables, hold mid-channel between Sheela Point and Adam's Island and keep Eve Island close aboard to port.

86

Glandore and Union Hall

Glandore

Anchorages

- To the S and SW of the pier at Glandore, nearer to the W side of the bay in 2 to 3m, as permitted by the extensive moorings. The shelter is not good here in S to SE winds. There are visitors' moorings.
- E of Union Hall pier and a cable offshore, as shown on the plan, in 2 to 4m. The ship channel occupies the N half of the inlet at this point and should not be obstructed. Large fishing vessels enter and leave around the clock. For advice contact the HM. The tidal stream in the anchorages is slight.

Note that northward movement of the ship channel has ruled out the use of the traditional anchorage close north of it.

Union Hall

is open every day in summer, welcomes visitors, offers showers, and can advise on all local facilities. HM at Union Hall pier 028 34737, mobile 086 608 1944, VHF Ch 6.

Facilities

Water on piers at Glandore and Union Hall. Fuel by tanker at Union Hall. Shops, PO, pubs/restaurants, taxis at Union Hall. Hotel and pubs at Glandore. Buses to Cork and Skibbereen from Leap, 3 km. Filling station at Leap. Glandore Harbour Yacht Club (www.glandoreyc.com), 100m from Glandore pier,

GLANDORE HARBOUR to BALTIMORE

AC2092, 2129, SC5623 and Plan

The coast continues cliffbound and scenic, penetrated by several excellent natural harbours, with uninhabited small islands close offshore and the spectacular Stag Rocks 8 cables south of Toe Head.

Approach to Glandore Harbour from the SW; Rabbit Island, L, Stack of Beans, L centre, Adam's Island, centre

87

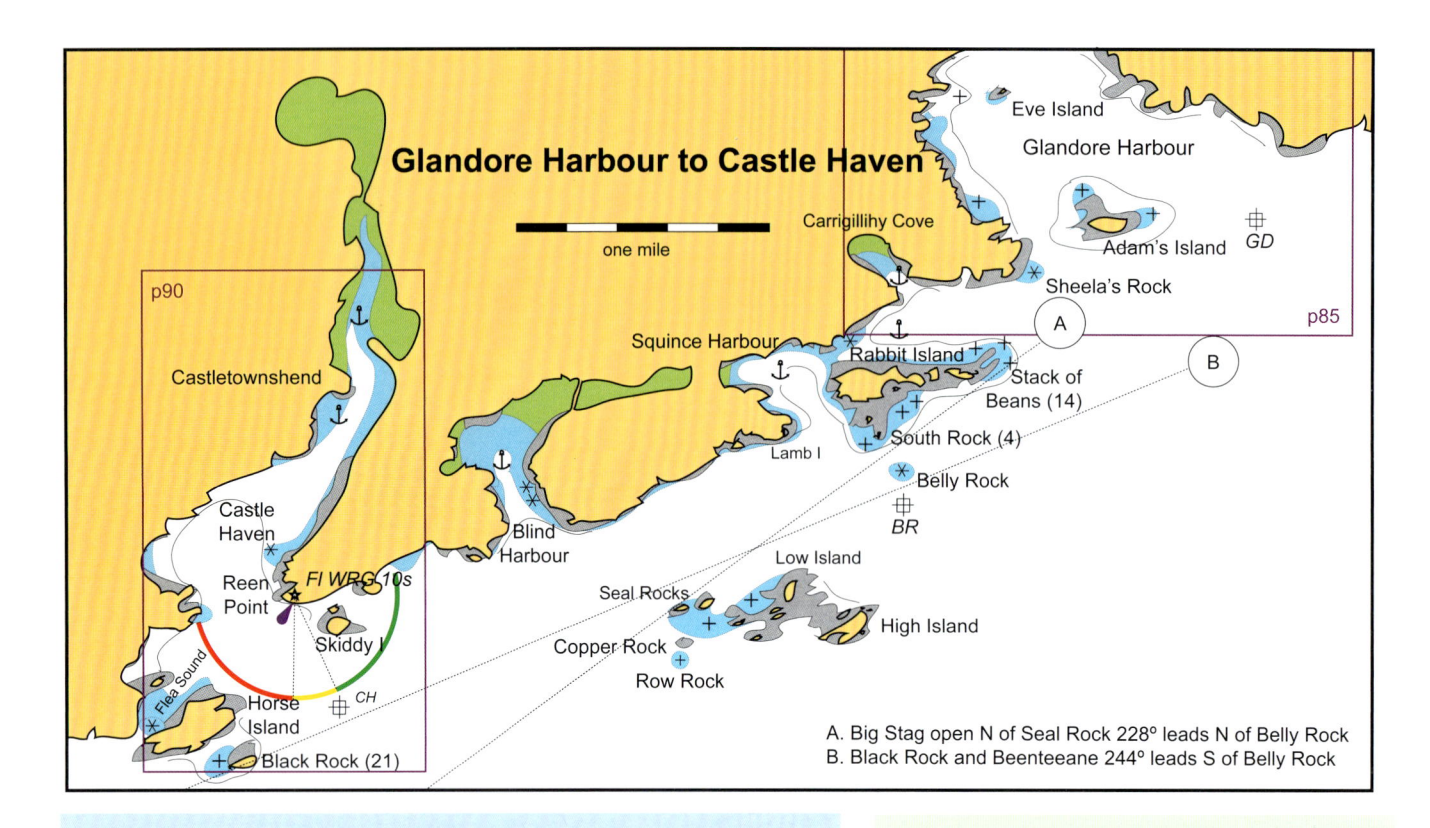

Glandore Harbour to Castle Haven

A. Big Stag open N of Seal Rock 228° leads N of Belly Rock
B. Black Rock and Beenteeane 244° leads S of Belly Rock

Tides
Glandore Bay to Baltimore

In Stag Sound, between Toe Head and the Stags, the E-going stream makes at –0435 Cobh and the W-going stream at +0150 Cobh (but see Note on page 71). The stream runs at 2 kn at springs, and there is often a confused sea in Stag Sound, especially in W winds against the ebb tide. The tides also run strongly off Kedge Island.

Constant (Baltimore) –0015 Cobh; MHWS 3·6m, MHWN 3·0m, MLWN 1·3m, MLWS 0·6m.

Dangers

Belly Rock (dries 0·4m), 1·5 cables S of South Rock, S of Rabbit Island
Copper Rock (dries 2·7m), 1·5 cables S of Seal Rocks, W of High and Low Islands
Row Rock, 2m, a cable SSW of Copper Rock.
The **wreck of the *Kowloon Bridge***, extending 2 cables SW from the Stags

Lights and Marks

Reen Point, white pillar Fl WRG 10s 9m, W5M R3M G3M, G shore –338°, W 338°–001°, R 001°– shore, shows green over Skiddy Island, white over the approach from the SSE, and red over Horse Island and Black Rock

Kowloon Bridge buoy, S Card Q(6) + L Fl 15s, AIS

Barrack Point, white tower Fl(2) WR 6s 40m W6M R3M. R 168°–294°, W 294°–038°, obscured elsewhere. Shows red over Kedge Island and Whale Rock, white over the approach to Baltimore Harbour between SE and SW

Lot's Wife, 8m pointed unlit white beacon on Beacon Point (50m), the E side of the entrance to Baltimore Harbour

Loo buoy, SHM Fl G 3s, close NW of Beacon Point.

Transit (A) on the Plan above, to pass N of Belly Rock and between it and South Rock: the Big Stag just open N of Seal Rocks 228°

Glandore Harbour to Castle Haven

Transit (B) on the Plan opposite, to pass S of Belly Rock: Black Rock in line with Beenteeane 244°

Passage NW of Rabbit Island, from the E: the mid-channel drying rock, R, with Squince Harbour beyond

Carrigillihy Cove

Glandore Harbour to Castle Haven – inshore passage

Rabbit Island, 17m high with two conspicuous notches in its profile, lies half a mile SW of Sheela Point and is foul on its E and S sides. At its E end the Stack of Beans (14m high), conical in shape, must be given a berth of 1·5 cable on its E side. The reefs S of Rabbit Island end in South Rock, 4m high and steep-to on its S side, but Belly Rock, (dries 0·4m), lies directly on the inshore course to Castle Haven, and is particularly dangerous. High Island (46m high), with Low Island (10m high), and Seal Rocks further to the W, may be regarded as one cluster which should not be approached too closely as there are rocks off and between them.

To pass S of Belly Rock, keep Black Rock (21m high, S of Castle Haven) in line with Beenteeane, the more N'ly of the twin summits on the Toe Head peninsula, bearing 244°. (Waypoint ⊕ BR 51°31'·3N 9°07'·2W is 2 cables S of Belly Rock.) To pass N of Belly Rock sail close up to South Rock with the Big Stag, S of Toe Head, just open N of Seal Rocks 228°. In poor visibility, keep Sheela Point open E of the Stack of Beans 008°, altering course to the NW only when High Island is close aboard, to pass N of Low Island and Seal Rocks. When clear S of Belly Rock and N of Seal Rocks steer for Skiddy Island at the entrance to Castle Haven. The beacon on Reen Point is not conspicuous from more than 2M away.

The passage N of Rabbit Island is navigable with great care towards HW. There is a least depth of 1·2m at the narrows, with a reef extending right across from the mainland shore, and a rocky head drying 1·6m in mid-channel. Stay 50 to 75m from the island shore at this point, on a course of 060°–240°.

Anchorages

The **channel N of Rabbit Island** offers secure anchorage in winds between S and NE, in depths of 2 to 8m, sand. **Carrigillihy Cove,** on the mainland side N of Rabbit Island, is narrow, and its inner part dries out. Drying rocks extend 50m from the shore on the W side of the entrance. Temporary anchorage is available in settled weather in 2 to 3m, no further in than the small coves on the E side of the inlet.

Squince Harbour, W of Rabbit Island, offers sheltered anchorage in offshore winds. Keep mid-channel in the entrance and anchor in 3·5 to 4m, 1·5 cables from the W shore. Squince Harbour is not secure in strong onshore winds. **Blind Harbour** lies 1M W of Squince Harbour and is also insecure in onshore winds. Keep slightly to the

Blind Harbour

Castle Haven

Castle Haven from the S; Black Rock bottom L with Horse Island and The Battery beyond, Skiddy Island centre R, Reen Point centre and Castletownshend beyond

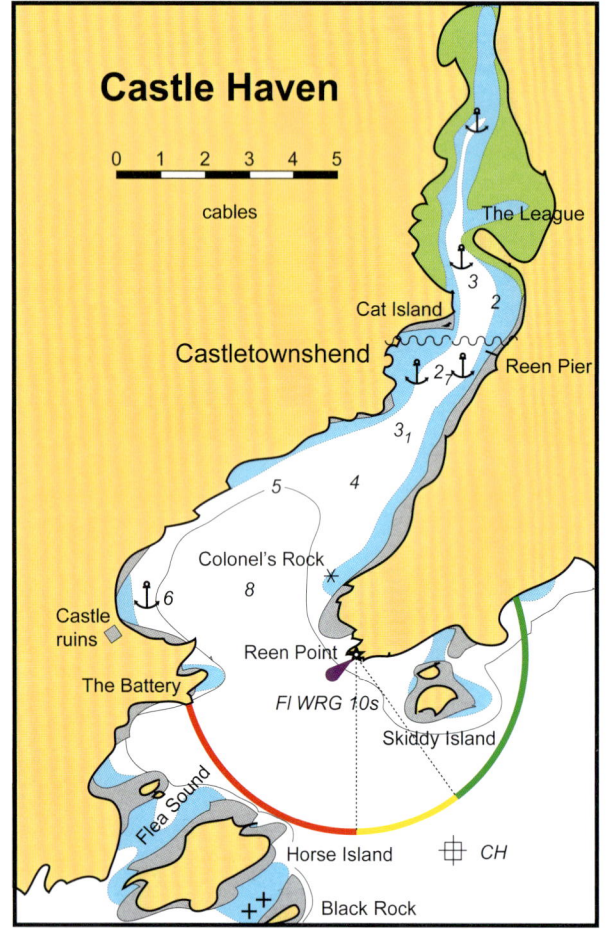

Reen Point beacon and the entrance to Castle Haven, from the SE

W shore when making the narrow entrance and anchor in the middle of the harbour in 1·5m.

Glandore Harbour to Toe Head

On the direct course pass either inside or outside High Island. If going inside, follow the directions (above) for clearing Belly Rock and then steer to pass N of Seal Rock. To pass outside High Island give it a berth of a cable.

Galley Head to Castle Haven and Toe Head

There are no dangers on the direct course between Doolic Rock and Toe Head. If bound for Castle Haven, there is no saving in distance in passing inside High Island, but if doing so, refer to the directions under *Glandore Harbour to Castle Haven – inshore passage* (above) to avoid Belly Rock.

Passing outside High Island, leave it 2 cables to starboard and hold a course S of W until Seal Rock is well abaft the beam, to clear Row Rock, before steering for Skiddy Island.

CASTLE HAVEN

⊕CH 51°30'·5N 9°10'·2W
AC2129, SC5623·14, Imray C56 and Plan

Castle Haven is an excellent natural harbour, and the inner reaches of the inlet provide nearly perfect shelter. Castletownshend, on the W shore, is a most attractive and historic village. It was named after Richard Townsend, a soldier in Cromwell's service who was granted the estate in the 1640's, but the eponymous castle was a stronghold of the O'Driscolls long before that. The "Irish RM" stories were written here by the cousins Edith Somerville and Violet Martin.

Directions

Skiddy Island, 9m high and flat-topped, with ledges extending 1 cable all round, lies 2 cables S of Reen Point. There is no passage between Skiddy Island and the shore. Horse Island, 35m high with a tower on its E side, is close to the W shore and is generally foul all round. Black Rock (21m high and conspicuous from most directions) is 2 cables SE of Horse Island and is steep-to on its S side. Enter Castle Haven between Reen Point and The Battery. Keep the Stags (S of Toe Head) and Flea Island, N of Horse Island, in line 208° astern to lead clear up the harbour. Beyond Cat Island, Castle Haven stretches

Castletownshend

Castletownshend from the anchorage S of Cat Island

a further 1·3M N between steep wooded slopes, restricted and sheltered by The League, a gravel spit extending 1·5 cables from the E shore, and sandbanks to the N of it. From here the channel, 0·5 cable wide, is close to the W shore; the lagoon at the head of the inlet dries.

Anchorage

Anchor off Castletownshend village nearer either shore, where the holding is best; there is sea-grass with limited holding in mid-channel. In strong S winds there is better shelter above Cat Island, where there is 3 to 4m in mid-channel, but the available space here is mostly occupied by moorings. Further upstream again (where an anchor is marked on the Plan) there is adequate room if a yacht is moored with a kedge; the wooded shores here are very attractive and a dinghy trip to the head of the navigation is well worthwhile. Both quays at the village dry, but are convenient for landing. The pier at Reen on the E side of the harbour is a piled concrete structure with 0·4 m at LAT at its outer end. The bay on the W side, N of The Battery, is also a feasible anchorage.

Facilities

Shop, pubs, restaurants. Water from tap on the village slip, also on Reen Pier. Petrol but no diesel.

Tides

The stream is slight off the quay but stronger above Cat Island, though a yacht will be tide-rode at times anywhere in the anchorage. Constant –0028 Cobh; MHWS 3·7m, MHWN 2·9m, MLWN 1·3m, MLWS 0·6m.

Caution

A submarine telephone cable runs across the harbour from the village slip to the slip just N of Reen Pier; avoid anchoring near this line. Above Cat Island a tripping line is strongly recommended.

Castle Haven from the SW: Castletownshend L, Reen Pier R with The League beyond

Castle Haven to Baltimore; Barloge

Flea Sound from the N: the passage is a quarter of the channel's width from the mainland side (R)

The Stags

(below) The Stags just closed behind Gokane Point leads to Barloge

(below) Approach to Barloge, from the SE: the entrance is L of Bullock Island (R)

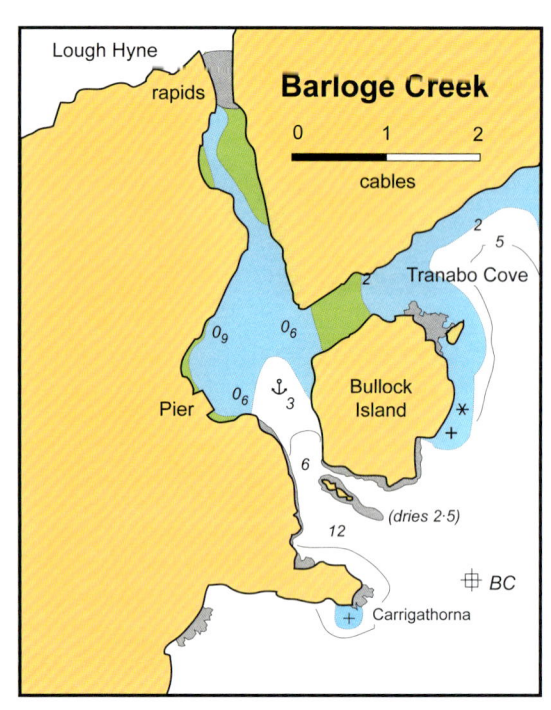

CASTLE HAVEN to BALTIMORE

AC2129, SC5623·14

Giving Horse Island and Black Rock a berth of a cable, there are no dangers on the direct course to Toe Head. There is a conspicuous ruined tower on the high ground 7 cables NE of Toe Head. Foul ground extends 3 cables from the shore close W of Toe Head, ending in the Belly Rocks, which dry.

The Stags are a group of jagged rocks 20m high, lying 7·5 cables S of Toe Head. Stag Sound, 6 cables wide, is free of danger. The colossal wreck of the ore carrier *Kowloon Bridge* lies 1 to 3 cables SW of the Stags and is marked at its SW extremity by a S Card buoy.

Flea Sound, between Horse Island and the shore, has a least depth of 0·6m and is navigable with sufficient rise of tide, keeping a quarter of the channel's width from the mainland side at the narrows.

Toehead Bay and Tragumna Bay

51°28'·7N 9°16'·7W
AC2129, SC5623·14

These bays are exposed to the prevailing winds and their shores are foul in places, but either can be a pleasant temporary anchorage in offshore winds and no swell. The best spot is the bay on the W shore of Tragumna Bay.

Barloge Creek

⊕BC 51°29'·4N 9°17'·3W
AC2129, SC5623·14, see Plan

This delightful anchorage lies inside Bullock Island and is sheltered by Carrigathorna to the S. The Stags just closed behind Gokane Point 122° leads to the entrance. Bullock Island has two prominent stands of conifers on its summit. (Tranabo Cove, which lies E of Bullock Island, is exposed to the S and is not recommended.) Enter Barloge midway between Carrigathorna and Bullock Island, and pass W of the above-water rock (2·5m high) to the SW of the island. The SE extension of this rock dries 2·5m. The entrance is deep and steep-to on both sides. Follow a mid-channel course W of the rock; the entrance is very steep-to but the creek shoals quickly once the NW face of the island opens up.

Anchorage

W of Bullock Island in 3 to 4m in good shelter, except in strong S or SE winds. Anchor clear of weed for good holding; the water is normally clear enough to spot the clean patches. The bottom is mud. An old anchor

Barloge to Baltimore

chain is reported (2013) on the bottom; a tripping line is advisable.

Lough Hyne

This lovely lake is connected to Barloge by a narrow channel which becomes a scour at half-tide. The ingoing stream makes at –0320 Cobh and the outgoing at +0115 Cobh, but these times are very susceptible to weather conditions. A visit to the Lough by dinghy is strongly recommended, as the scenery is beautiful, but beware of being unable to make way against a flood tide on the way back out – it runs at 5 to 6 knots at springs. Because of what is effectively a sill at the entrance, the flow reverses very suddenly at the turn, and within five minutes can change from one knot ebb to one knot flood. Lough Hyne was designated as Ireland's first marine nature reserve in 1981. As a half-tide lake of extraordinary depth, it has a unique ecosystem, and attracts intensive study.

Barloge to Baltimore

AC2129, SC5623·14

There are two rocks just S of Carrigathorna, so leave it at least a cable astern before turning for Kedge Island, distant 2·75M. A berth of two cables clears all dangers on the coast to the SW.

Kedge Island should be given a berth of a cable to the S. There is, however, a narrow passage 7·3m deep between the innermost rock, called Carrigatrough, and Spain Point on the mainland. This passage, no more than 50m wide, should be made only under power, and in settled conditions. The coast W of Kedge Island is generally steep-to, but

(top and above) Barloge

Passage between Spain Point and Carrigatrough (centre): Kedge Island, L

Baltimore

Baltimore from the NE; the pier and harbour bottom L, with the yacht pontoon and the Cape Clear ferry at the S pier; the S entrance and Lot's Wife, upper L; Sherkin Island, upper R; Gascanane Sound and Cape Clear Island, top R

beware of Whale Rock, which dries 1·8m and is 0·5 cable offshore and 5 cables E of the entrance to Baltimore. The conspicuous Lot's Wife beacon in line with the SW face of Black Point, 318°, leads just outside Whale Rock. The ruined Telegraph Tower on the hill (142m) NW of Spain Point is conspicuous.

BALTIMORE

⊕BL   51°28'·1N 9°23'·3W
AC2129, 3725, SC5623·13, Imray C56 and Plan

Baltimore is a fishing port, a major centre for sailing and diving, and the ferry port for the islands to the south-west. The harbour is 1M across each way, mostly between 2 and 6m deep, somewhat subject to swell in E and SE winds but offering safe anchorage. Its S entrance is straightforward and navigable in any weather, day or night. As the southwesternmost harbour in Ireland, Baltimore is often the first port of call for yachts arriving from the Azores, the Caribbean or the United States.

Tides – Baltimore Harbour

The streams run fairly through both the N and S entrances, meeting near Lousy Rocks. The flood stream runs E and SE on the N side of Sherkin Island and N on its E side commencing at +0545 Cobh. The ebb stream runs W and S, commencing at −0025 Cobh. Constant −0015 Cobh; MHWS 3·6m, MHWN 3·0m, MLWN 1·3m, MLWS 0·6m.

Dangers

Unnamed rock (drying 0·6m), 0·4 cable off Beacon Point
Loo Rock, 0·2m, 1 cable NW of Beacon Point
Rocks with 1·7m and 0·5m, close E of Barrack Point
Quarry Rock, 2·1m, 2 cables NNE of Loo Buoy
Lousy Rocks (dry 0·6 to 2·4m), in the middle of the harbour, extending 0·6 cable N and WSW from the S Card perch.
Wallis Rock, 1·6m, 3 cables W of Baltimore Pier
Ransome Rock, 2·3m, 1 cable WNW of Lousy Rocks perch
Skipjack Rock (awash), **Great Globe Rock** (2m high with ledges drying 2m extending E), **Globe Rocks** (1m high, with a rock drying 2·1m to the E), and **Cosmopoliet Rock** (dries 0·4m), all within 1 cable of the shore of Sherkin Island W of Lousy Rocks
Narrows Ledge, 0·1m, 0·5 cable off the shore of Sherkin Island at the S entrance to The Sound.

Lights and Marks

Barrack Point, white tower Fl(2) WR 6s 40m W6M R3M. R 168°–294°, W 294°–038°, obscured elsewhere. Shows red over Kedge Island and Whale Rock, white over the approach between SE and SW
Lot's Wife, 8m pointed unlit white beacon on Beacon Point (50m), the E side of the entrance
Loo buoy, SHM Fl G 3s, NW of Beacon Point
Two SHM buoys, the outer QG, the inner Fl G 4s, mark the ferry channel NW of Coney Island.
Outfall buoy, Y, unlit, S of Bull Point
Outfall buoy, Y, Fl Y 5s, NW of Bull Point
Lousy Rocks beacon, S Card perch, 12m, Q(6) + L Fl 15s
Wallis Rock buoy, PHM QR
Narrows Ledge buoy, E Card Q(3) 15s

94

Baltimore

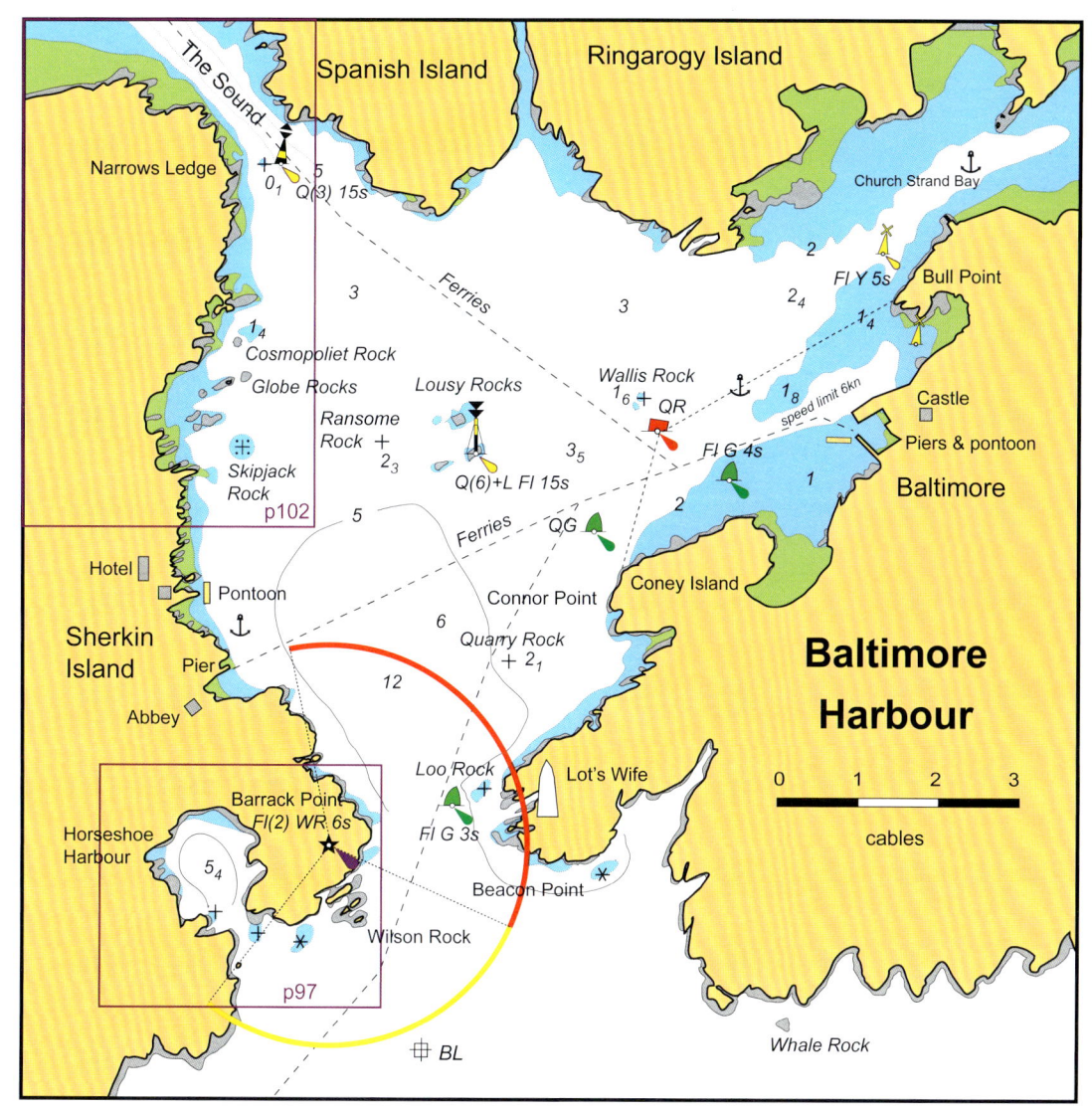

Directions

Lot's Wife is conspicuous and unmistakable. Approach the entrance with Loo buoy bearing N and leave it close to starboard. To avoid Quarry Rock steer N (towards Lousy Rocks perch) till the N pier at Baltimore comes in sight, then pass N of the two starboard-hand buoys, leaving the Lousy Rocks beacon and the Wallis Rock buoy to port. There is a speed limit of 6 knots in the area between Connor Point, Wallis Rock and Bull Point. Lousy Rocks perch should be given a berth of a cable to N and SW, and 1·5 cable to the W. Wallis Rock is 0·8 cable N by W of its buoy.

North Passage, the N exit from the harbour, between Sherkin Island and Spanish Island, is described after the directions for Cape Clear, below.

Anchorage and berthing

- NW or W of the N pier, in 2 to 3m, leaving room for fishing boats and ferries to manoeuvre. As a guide, stay NW of

Baltimore entrance, from the S; Barrack Point lighthouse, L, and Beacon Point with Lot's Wife, R. Loo buoy, centre. Mount Gabriel in the distance, extreme L

Baltimore and Sherkin

Baltimore pontoon

a line from the Wallis Rock Buoy to Bull Point. An anchor light is recommended.
- Between May and October a pontoon is moored to the end of the S pier. Contact HM 028 20123 / 087 235 1485, VHF Ch. 16 or 9.
- Visitors' moorings are available; contact HM as above, or Vincent O'Driscoll, 028 20218 / 087 244 7828. In W winds there is a good anchorage N of the pier at Abbey Strand on Sherkin Island. A pontoon is also moored here between mid-May and mid-September. Berthing charges are payable at the Islander's Rest Hotel, 028 20116.

Anchoring is not permitted in the fairway between Baltimore and Sherkin piers, N of the green buoys. The navigable water in Church Strand Bay, to the E, is entirely taken up by moorings.

There is a landing pontoon in the harbour for dinghies.

Facilities

Water on the pontoon and N pier. Shore power on the pontoon. Shop, hotel (with showers); restaurants and pubs. Diesel (contact Cotter's supermarket) and gas. Limited chandlery. HM 028 20123, mobile 087 235 1485, VHF Ch 16 & 6. Glénans Sailing School. Baltimore SC on the quay is active in July and August and also has showers. Ferries to Sherkin and Cape Clear Island. RNLI all-weather lifeboat station. Taxis. Buses to Skibbereen. The large supermarket in Skibbereen supplies the islands, delivers to Baltimore pier every morning, and will take orders from visiting yachts; phone 028 21400. Sherkin Island has water and shore power on the pontoon; hotel and pub.

Horseshoe Harbour

AC3725, SC5623·12 and Plan

This almost landlocked pool 1·5 cables across, on the S side of Sherkin Island, provides secure anchorage except in S or SE winds, but underwater rocks extend 0·5 cable southwards, W of Wilson Rock, and also from the E point of the entrance. The entrance is only 40m wide between these rocks and the cliffs to the W. From the E, give the shore a berth of 1 cable and enter on a course of 340°, keeping the W point of the entrance close aboard, and turn N when the pool opens up, to avoid a rock on the W side just inside the entrance. Approaching from the W, the shore is steep-to. Anchor in 5m, mud, in the middle of the pool. Pubs and restaurant, 1 km. Do not be caught here in strong winds between SE and SW.

BALTIMORE to CAPE CLEAR ISLAND and the FASTNET

AC 2129, 3725, SC5623·12 and Plan

Cape Clear Island's population of 124 comprises fishermen, artists, writers and many involved in the hospitality business. Cape Clear is a Gaeltacht area and the southernmost inhabited point of Ireland. It attracts Gaelic scholars, artists and the many birdwatchers who come to observe the passage of tens of thousands of seabirds on their daily flight between the coast of Kerry and their feeding grounds in the Celtic Sea. Ireland's very first saint, Ciarán, was born on

(left) Sherkin pontoon

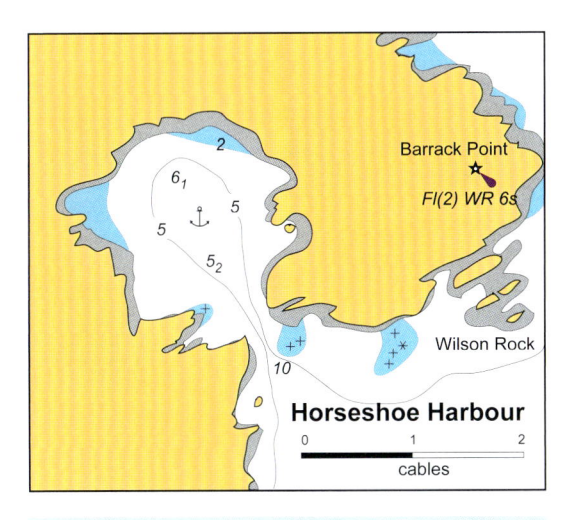

Baltimore to Cape Clear

Horseshoe Harbour

Tides
Gascanane Sound and Cape Clear

In Gascanane Sound the streams run at 3 kn springs and cause dangerous eddies, especially near the rocks in the centre. The SE-going stream makes at +0520 Cobh and the NW-going stream at –0055 Cobh.

SW of Cape Clear the streams are are not well documented, but it is probable that they run E and W between Cape Clear and the Fastnet Rock, the E-going stream starting at –0420 Cobh and the W-going stream at +0150 Cobh, spring rate 2 to 2·5 kn. Off Blananarragaun the streams are complex. It is thought that the E-going stream divides at the Bill of Cape Clear, setting NE along the N shore of the island and S to Blananarragaun (the S tip of the island), forming a large eddy E of Blananarragaun. The W-going stream forms an eddy W of Blananarragaun. The result of this is often a heavy and confused sea between the Bill of Cape Clear and Blananarragaun, off which a race is formed on both streams.

Within 1M N and S of the Fastnet Rock the streams run SSE and NNW, the E-going stream making at –0405 Cobh and the W-going stream at +0200 Cobh, spring rate 2·2 kn. With W winds the E-going stream runs for 7h and increases by 0·5 kn, and the converse with E winds. There can be a tide race with the E-going stream, extending for 1M SE of the rock.

Constant (Baltimore) –0015 Cobh; MHWS 3·6m, MHWN 3·0m, MLWN 1·3m, MLWS 0·6m.

Cape Clear about 350AD. The island is locally known as Cape Clear or simply Cape, and not (as it is labelled on the charts) Clear Island.

North Harbour, from where the ferries sail to Baltimore and Schull, is a narrow inlet on the island's northwest coast. The deep part of the harbour is very constricted, but it is a lovely spot and a popular port of call for yachts.

Gascanane Sound provides the simplest (if not always the most sheltered) route from Baltimore to North Harbour and the islands of Long Island Bay. *(For details of the North Passage from Baltimore Harbour, see page 102).*

The S shore of Sherkin Island is steep-to.

Gascanane Sound

⊕ *GS* 51°26'·9N 9°26'·9W

Gascanane Sound separates Cape Clear Island and Sherkin Island. Carrigmore and the drying Gascanane Rock lie in the middle of the sound. Gascanane Rock is a particular

Sherkin: the Abbey and ferry pier, seen from Baltimore

Horseshoe Harbour, Sherkin (photo Hazel Lewis)

97

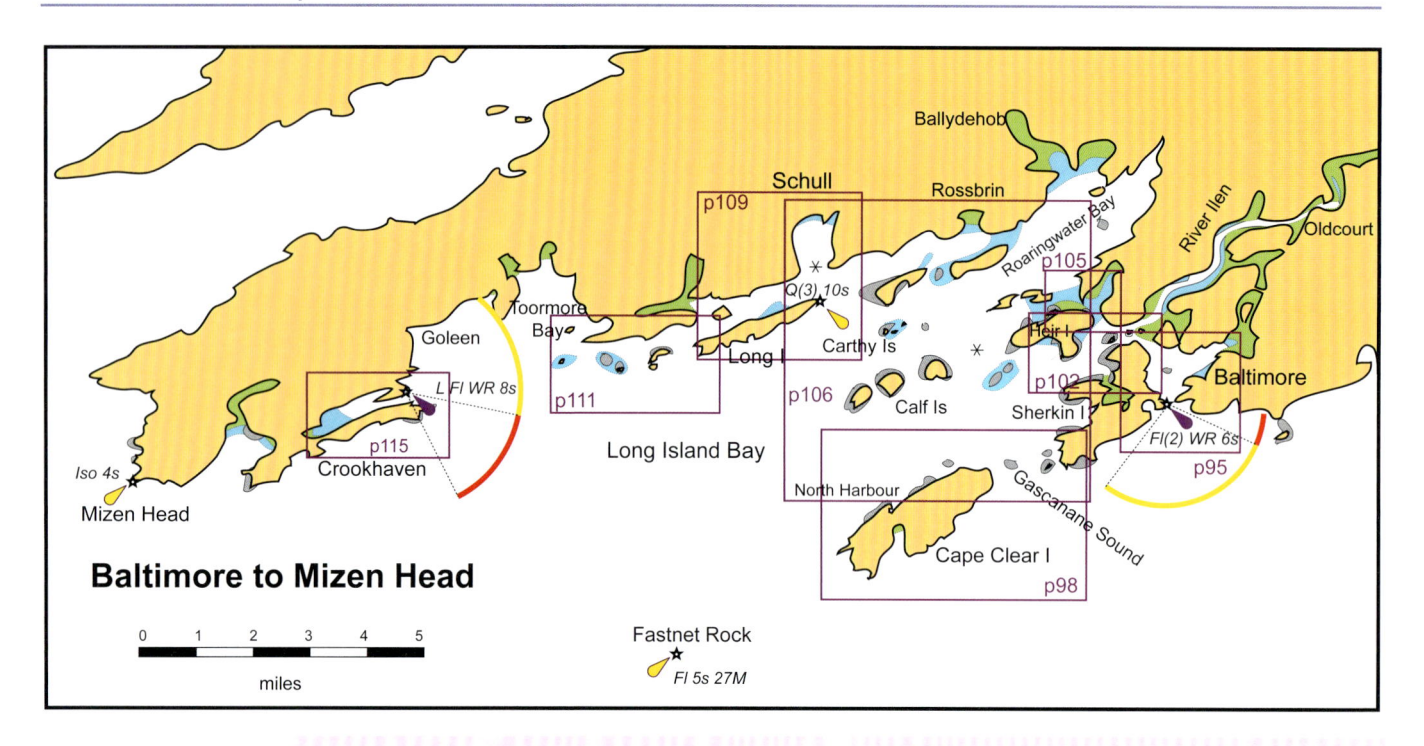

Baltimore to Cape Clear

Dangers
Gascanane Sound and Cape Clear

Carrigmore (6m high), in the middle of Gascanane Sound, with drying and underwater reefs extending 1·5 cables to the NW

Gascanane Rock (dries 1·8m), 2·5 cables W of Carrigmore

Crab Rock, reef extending 2 cables N from Illaunbrock

Avaud Rocks, drying and above-water rocks extending 0·75 cable off the NE corner of Cape Clear Island. Unnamed on charts

Drying and underwater rocks extending 1 cable SE and 0·25 cable NW from **Illauneana**

Lacklahard and **Carrigieragh,** drying and underwater reefs between 2 and 5 cables SW of Illauneana

Bullig Reef, two rocks awash at LW, 2 cables NW of Illauneana.

Tonelunga Rock (dries), 1 cable offshore near the ruins of Dún an Oir Castle, 7·5 cables from the Bill of Cape Clear.

Rock with 2·2m, 2 cables NE of Fastnet Rock

Lights and Marks

Fastnet Rock, grey tower, Fl 5s 49m 27M, Racon (G) 18M, AIS

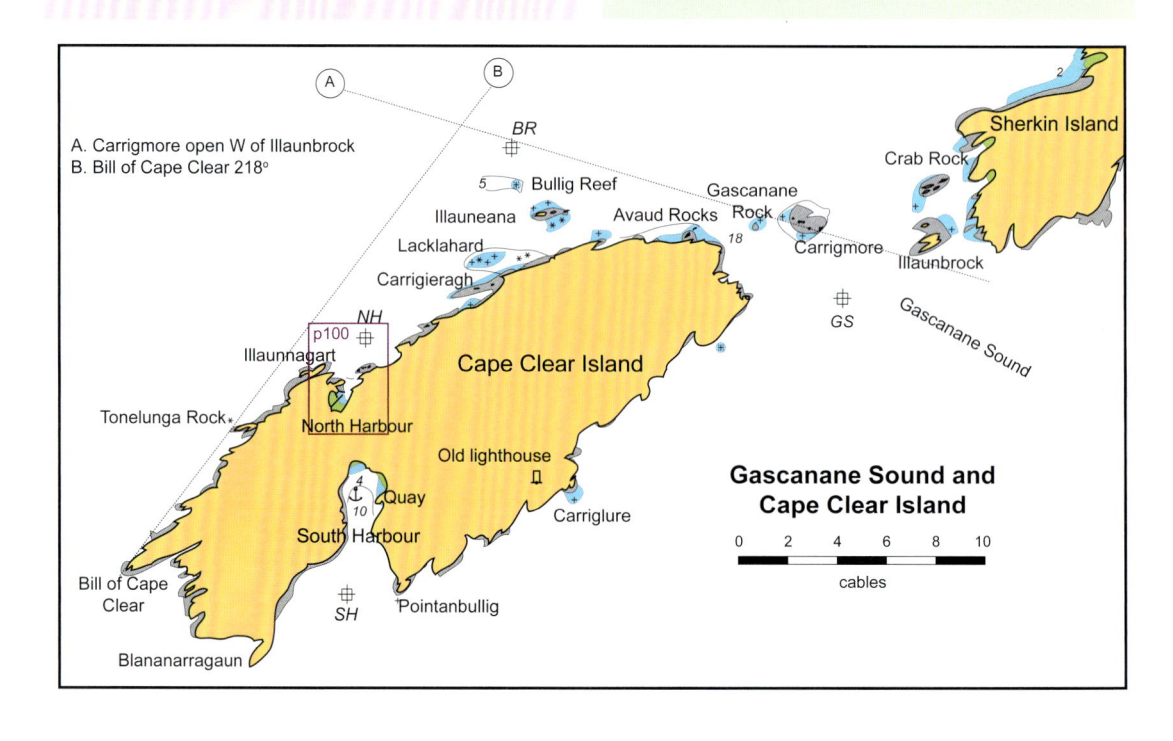

98

Gascanane Sound

danger as both tidal streams set on to it; the channel E of Carrigmore is wider and safer. Illaunbrock, off Sherkin, is steep-to on its S and W sides, but a ledge called Crab Rocks extends 2 cables N. The W channel is narrower, and the position of Avaud Rocks must be noted. A strong S or SE wind creates a turbulent sea in Gascanane Sound – especially on the S-going tide – which can be dangerous, and the Sound should not be attempted in strong to gale force winds. Local legend maintains that the sailor making a first passage of Gascanane Sound must compose a poem in its honour.

North Coast of Cape Clear Island

Illauneana (13m high), 2 cables off the N shore and 7 cables W of Gascanane Sound, has foul ground all round; to the SW, and within 2 cables of the island shore, are the dangerous Lacklahard and Carrigieragh reefs. There are narrow deep channels between Illauneana and the shore, which are used by ferryboats in settled weather, but do not be tempted to follow. Bullig Reef, with two rocks awash at LW, extends 3 cables NW of Illauneana and is a particular danger as it lies across the course from Gascanane Sound to North Harbour and Crookhaven, and from North Harbour to the N entrance to Baltimore. A waypoint of 51°27'·6N 9°29'·2W (⊕ BR on *Gascanane Sound Plan*) provides a berth of a cable to the N of Bullig Reef. The transit marked on AC2129 is no longer of use since the church on Sherkin Island cannot be identified at a distance. Carrigmore (in Gascanane Sound) open SW of Illaunbrock 107° *(see photograph)* leads clear N of Bullig Reef.

From Gascanane Sound, steer 295° for the W end of West Calf Island, leaving Illauneana 3 cables to port, and hold this course until the coast W of North Harbour opens up with the Bill of Cape Clear bearing 218° *(see photograph)*. Identify North Harbour, with the cluster of buildings behind it, and do not steer for it until it is well open. From this point a course of 265° leads to Brow Head, and 276° to Crookhaven.

In moderate conditions, it is possible to pass between Illauneana and Bullig Reef, giving Illauneana a berth of 50m on a course of 233°/053° and using waypoint 51°27'·392N 9°28'·945W. The greatest care is required.

(above) View to the W from close W of Gascanane Rock; Cape Clear Island, L, Avaud Rocks, L centre, Illauneana, R centre

(above) View from the WNW; bring Carrigmore SW of Illaunbrock 107°, centre (transit A, plan on p92). The W channel of Gascanane Sound, R, Sherkin Island, L

(above) Bill of Cape Clear bearing 218° (centre R), clears Bullig Reef (transit B, plan on p92). The Fastnet Rock may just be discerned at R

(above) View N from Cape Clear Island; Illauneana, R, and Lacklahard breaking, L centre. East Calf, top L

From the W, approaching North Harbour, beware of Tonelunga Rock, off the NW shore of the island.

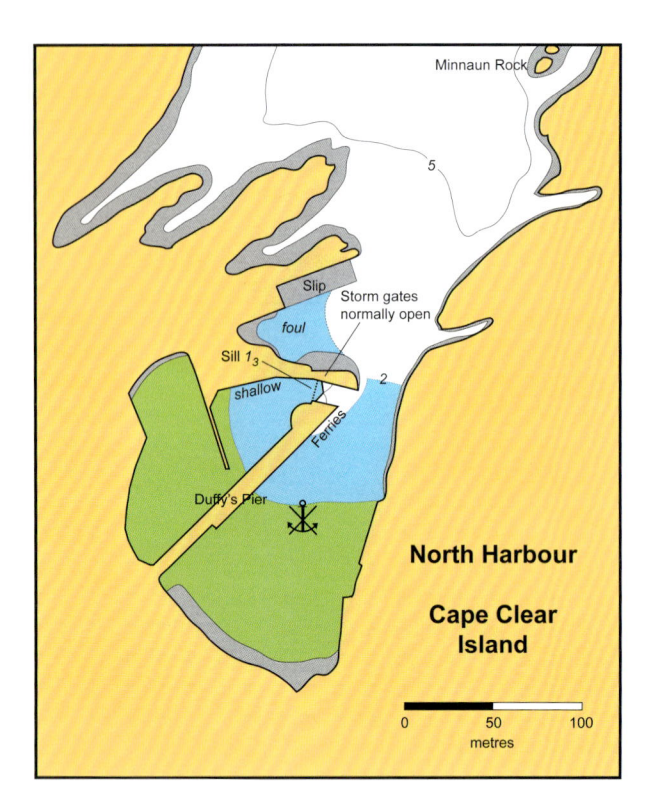

Cape Clear

Entering North Harbour

NORTH HARBOUR, CAPE CLEAR

⊕NH 51°26′·7N 9°30′·2W

No large-scale chart published; see Plan

Immediately E of the entrance to North Harbour are several above-water rocks of which Minnaun Rock is the W'most. Leave Minnaun Rock 50m to port and steer for the end of the outer (N) pier. Do not err to the NW as the bight N of the pier, beside the cargo ferry's slipway, is foul. The entrance is 25m wide and the cliffs on the SE side are clean. Most of the area of the harbour to the SW has less than 1m at LAT, and the inner harbour

Traffic Separation Scheme

There is a TSS, 6M in length, S and SE of the Fastnet. The W-bound lane is 2 to 4M from the rock and the E-bound 6 to 8M from it. The lanes should be crossed as near to right angles as possible. The inshore traffic zone extends 2M S of the rock.

Approaching North Harbour

North Harbour, Cape Clear, in June 2015 with reconstruction work almost complete. Two ferries are at the outer ferry berth on Duffy's pier. The inner basins, and the outer harbour SW of the ferry berth, mostly dry. The new slipway can be seen R, and the new storm gates just beyond the yacht, which is at the deep water berth.

100

Cape Clear and the Fastnet

South Harbour, Cape Clear

dries. Extensive repairs and reconstruction were carried out in 2014-15. Hydraulic storm gates can be used to close off the harbour basins in a heavy swell, such as can be experienced in winter gales. (The gates do not retain the water level). The best berth for a yacht is on the inside of the outer pier, where there is 2·3m at LAT. The storm gates open flush with the wall and do not obstruct berthing, but the gap is only 12m wide. The ferry berths have the only deep water on either side of Duffy's Pier. The ferries require most of the available space S of their berths for manoeuvring, which means that there is no anchorage here for shallow draft yachts. The shallow and drying part of the harbour NW of Duffy's pier has a firm level bottom for drying out, but beware of a sudden reduction in depth on the N side just beyond the gates. The first berth on the NW side of Duffy's pier, opposite the ferry, is used by a local fishing vessel and should be left free. Water on outer pier; pubs, restaurant, small shop.

South Harbour, Cape Clear

⊕ *SH* 51°25'·5N 9°30'·2W
AC2129, 2184, SC5623·12

South Harbour lies just to the E of Blananarragaun, and offers good anchorage in settled weather or in N winds. It is exposed to wind and swell between SE and SW. The anchorage is in the centre of the harbour in 4 to 6m, with good holding. Pointanbullig, on the E side of the entrance, has rocks 0·5 cable off it. In settled weather it is possible to lie alongside the quay in the SE corner, but this is not advisable for an overnight stay.

Fastnet Rock

Four miles WSW of Cape Clear is the Fastnet Rock, a lonely pinnacle 28m high. The best-known seamark in Ireland, and the logo of the Irish Cruising Club, the Fastnet lighthouse was built in 1903, replacing an earlier cast-iron tower of 1847 whose stump is still in use as a storehouse. The Fastnet tower is the tallest and widest rock lighthouse in the British Isles. The loom of the Fastnet is often the first sight of Ireland for the transatlantic sailor, and the rock is perhaps the most famous racing mark in the world.

There is a rock, with 2·2m over it, 2 cables to the NE of the Fastnet. The tidal streams set strongly around the Rock, so resist the temptation to get too close.

The Fastnet Rock

101

North Passage from Baltimore

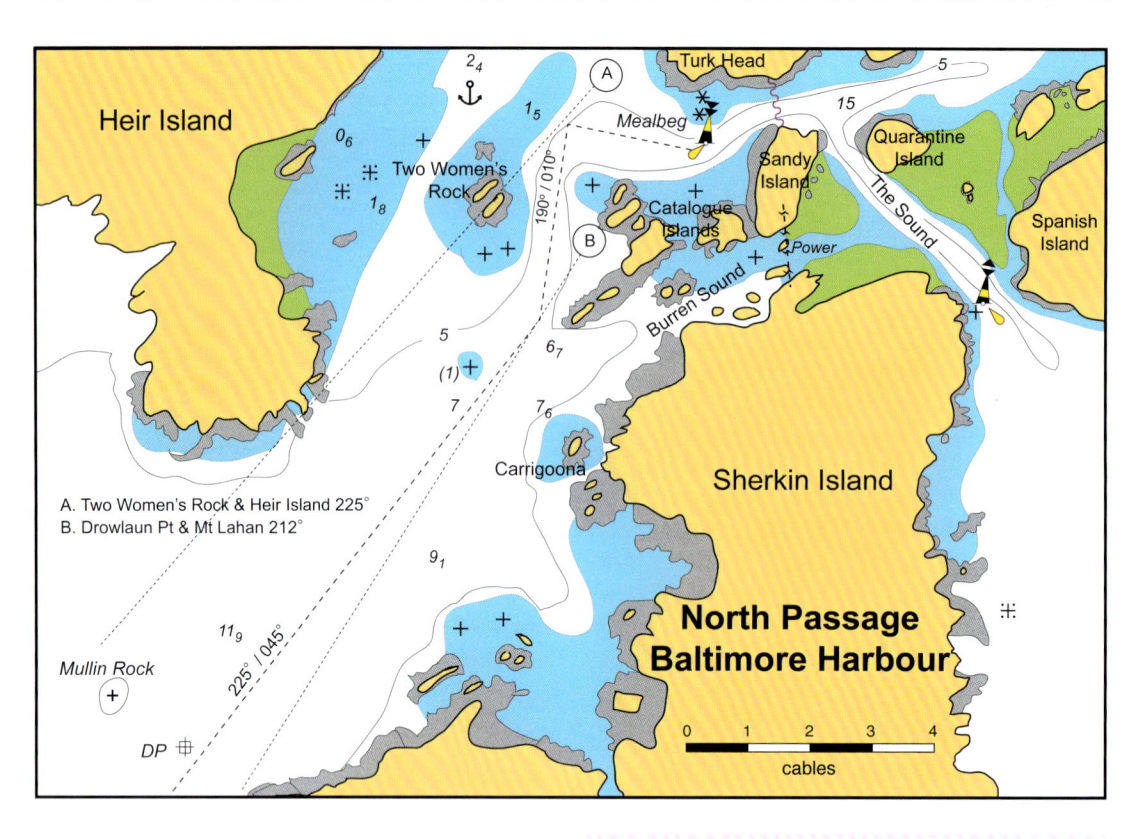

NORTH PASSAGE from BALTIMORE HARBOUR

51°29'·2N 9°23'·6W

AC2129, 3725, SC5623·12 and Plan

The North Passage provides a convenient access direct to Roaringwater Bay, avoiding Gascanane Sound. The pilotage is intricate but not unduly challenging; however the charts, including the electronic ones, are barely detailed enough. Hare Island, as it is called on the charts, is properly spelt Heir.

Directions

From Baltimore, pass either side of Lousy Rocks, giving the beacon a wide berth of 1·5 cables on its W side. Entering the Sound, between Spanish Island and Sherkin Island, leave the Narrows Ledge E Card buoy to port, identify the small Quarantine Island ahead and head for the mid-channel between it and Sandy Island to the W. Burren Sound, between Sherkin and Sandy Island appears wide at HW but is rock-strewn and spanned by a low overhead power cable. This cable continues NW across the main channel, but underwater. Burren Sound is locally known as the Postman's Passage; there is a navigable channel near HW, for vessels of limited air draft, but it requires intimate local knowledge. Note that on the charts, the power cable is incorrectly depicted as

Dangers
Baltimore North Passage and Heir Island

Mealbeg, two rocks drying 2m and 0·5m, close S of Turk Head
Two Women's Rock (above HW), 3 cables E of Heir Island, with shoals and rocks extending 2 cables N and 1 cable S
Unnamed rock, with 1m, 3 cables S of Two Women's Rock
Mullin Rock, 2·1m, 3 cables NW of Drowlaun Point, Sherkin Island
Bream Rocks (dry 1·8m), and **Greymare Rocks**, with less than 2m, forming a reef extending for 3·5 cables NE–SW, 2 cables S of Heir Island
Toorane Rocks, reef 5 cables by 2, extending NE–SW, 2 cables W of Bream Rocks. The SW part dries 2·8m and the NE part has two heads above HW.
Corrignamoe Rocks, drying rocks E and NE of Heir Island

Lights and Marks

Narrows Ledge buoy, E Card VQ(3) 5s
Mealbeg buoy, S Card Q(6)+L Fl 15s
Taylor buoy, N Card Q
Inishleigh buoy, S Card Q(6)+L Fl 15s, in the River Ilen

River Ilen

underwater all the way from Sherkin.

Giving the N shore of Sandy Island a berth of at least 30m, steer to pass close S of Mealbeg S Card buoy. Note that Mealbeg has two distinct heads; the inner head dries about 2m, but the outer head, to the SSW, is barely awash at LWS. Turn to starboard and steer 300° towards the low hill (22m) near the E end of Heir Island. When the centre of Two Women's Rock comes in line with the SE tip of Heir Island 225°, turn to port and steer 190°. Hold this course past the SW rocks of the Catalogues and until Drowlaun Point (on Sherkin) bears 212° and comes slightly to the right of Mount Lahan (77m) at the E end of Cape Clear. From this point a course of 225° will clear both the unnamed 1m rock and Mullin Rock, and pass 1·5 cables NW of Drowlaun Point (waypoint *DP*, 51°28'·7N 9°26'·2W).

Anchorage

There is reasonable anchorage in 1·5 to 2·5m in good shelter N of Two Women's Rock and between Heir Island (S of the pier) and the mainland. Fine sandy beaches. There is a substantial pier and slip at the NE point of Heir Island. Ferries run from Heir to Cunnamore Pier and (in summer) to Baltimore.

Passage from seaward

For the N entrance to Baltimore from the W, see *Schull and Cape Clear to Baltimore North Passage*, p111.

River Ilen to Oldcourt

AC2129, SC5623·12

The Ilen is navigable as far as the boatyards at Oldcourt, 4M upriver from Quarantine Island at the N end of The Sound, and 5M from Baltimore. The river is scenic and tranquil, and the trip is well worth making even if not going to one or other of the yards. AC2129 or SC5623 is essential, and though the survey of the river dates from 1846 the channel is not much changed. Passage should however be attempted only on a high and rising tide, and only in daylight. There is a minimum depth of 1m at LAT, the shallowest point being close off the N point of Inishbeg. A S Card buoy marks Bostoon Rock (dries 0·1m), E of Inishleigh.

Leave Quarantine Island close to starboard and head for Inane Point, 5 cables ENE. Leaving Inishleigh S Card buoy to port, stay 0·5 cable off Inane Point while rounding it to open up the next stretch of 1·3M to Inishbeg. As with most winding river channels, the general rule is to stay wide on the bends. Hold mid-channel on the stretch to Inishbeg, then turn wide, staying on the Inishbeg (E) side of the turn to the N. Stay mid-channel at the narrows W of Inishbeg and do not turn to starboard until the slip at Reenadhuna is almost abeam. Keeping Reenadhuna House directly astern, head for the point on the N shore opposite the slip at the N end of Inishbeg. When 1 cable from this point, turn to starboard and head for the slip on Inishbeg. Leave it 50m to starboard and head

(above) North Passage from Baltimore; view NW through The Sound, between Sandy Island (L) and Quarantine Island (R)

(above) Turk Head and Mealbeg buoy from the ESE. The outer head of Mealbeg is just covered; its position is indicated by ripples. Tidal height about 0·7m. The inner head of Mealbeg, R, and Heir Island in the background, L.

(above) Two Women's Rock (centre) in line with the SE tip of Heir Island (transit A, plan on p102); Cape Clear Island beyond, and Sherkin Island L

Drowlaun Point slightly to the R of Mount Lahan on Cape Clear Island (transit B, plan on p102)

Reenadhuna House from the S

103

Oldcourt and Skibbereen

The ferry emerges from the North Passage at Baltimore, on her way to Cape Clear. View downriver from NE of Quarantine Island, L, with Mealbeg S Cardinal buoy, extreme R. The house and poles on Sandy Island are conspicuous

Heir Island from the E; the pier, bottom R, and Two Women's Rock, lower L. The Calf Islands, top

for the jetty 2 cables E on the S bank beyond Inishbeg, leaving it 50m to starboard. From there to Oldcourt, stay in mid-channel.

Coming down-river, Quarantine Island is hard to discern until quite close; the power cable poles on Sandy Island are however prominent on the skyline.

Competitive rowing craft use the river frequently, and a good lookout should be kept for them.

Oldcourt

51°32′N 9°19′·3W

There are two boatyards at Oldcourt. O'Donovan's (Oldcourt Boats, 028 21249) has a pontoon for temporary berthing, a slipway for vessels up to 30m and 400t, and a 70-tonne travelhoist, one of the largest in Ireland. Hull (wood, metal and GRP) and mechanical repairs, mobile crane, winter storage. Hegarty's (028 22122) has a slipway for vessels up to 20m and 150t. Mobile crane, hull and mechanical repairs, winter storage. Hegarty's specialises in classic wooden boat building and restoration.

Anchorage

Anchorage is possible wherever convenient out of the main channel in the river, and temporary anchorage is possible in mid-channel at Oldcourt. An alongside berth at Oldcourt may be available by permission; phone the yards. There is a pub at Oldcourt.

Skibbereen

Above Oldcourt the river is shallower but it is possible with care to reach Skibbereen, 2·5M upstream, by dinghy near HW. In the middle of town and upstream of the iron girder footbridge, there is a landing pontoon

Goose Island Channel

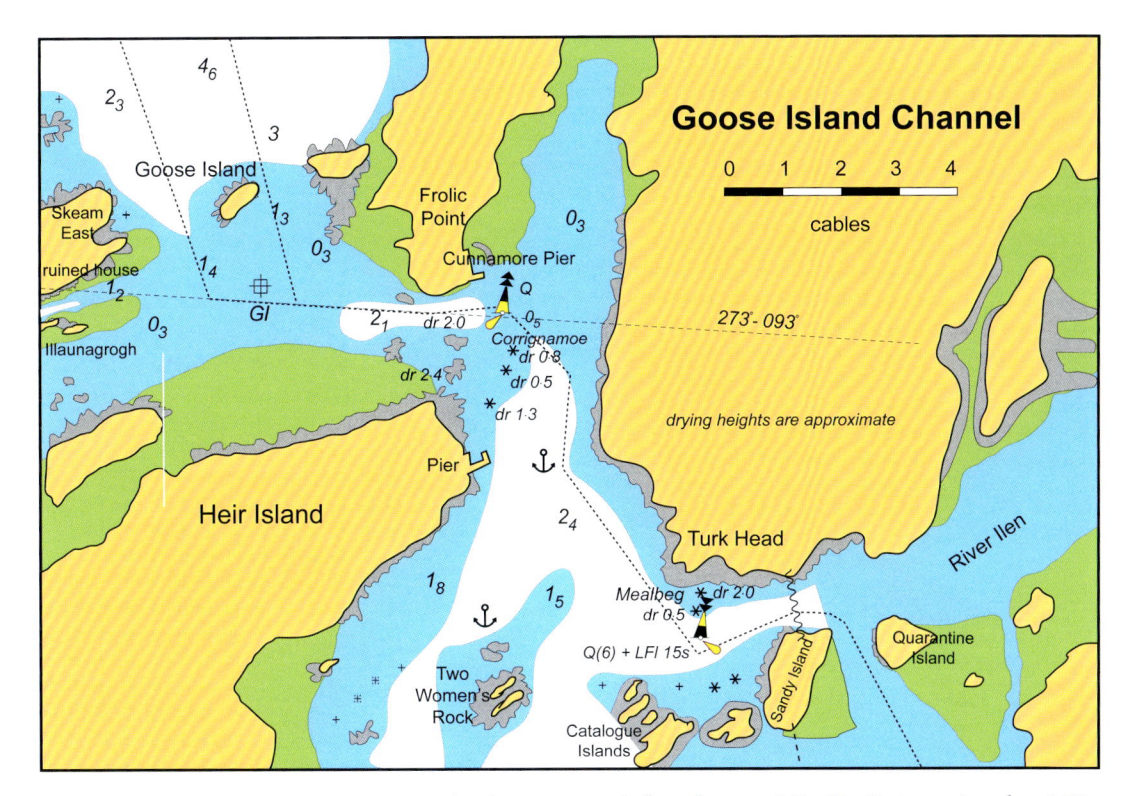

at the West Cork Hotel and steps at the head of a short tributary channel on the starboard hand. Skibbereen (2,100) has filling stations, supermarkets, shops, PO, doctors and comprehensive chandlery (CH Marine, phone 028 23190). Taxis, phone 028 22296 and 028 21258.

Passage N of Heir Island – Goose Island Channel

⊕ *GI* 51°30'·2N 9°26'W
AC2129, SC5623·12 and Plan

This passage gives direct access above half tide from Baltimore to the Skeam Islands, Roaringwater Bay and Horse Island. The wider channel, to the W of Goose Island, has 1·4m least depth while the channel to the E has 1·3m. There is little trace now of the sandspit marked on the charts to the SE of Goose I. The principal dangers in the passage from Baltimore are Mealbeg and Corrignamoe Rocks. From Baltimore N Passage and the Ilen River, pass close S of Mealbeg buoy; the outer head of the rock is almost always covered *(see photograph on p103)*. Then stay within a cable of the mainland shore to the E; at half tide the E'most of the Corrignamoe group, NE of Heir Island, will be covered. These rocks are E of a line joining Cunnamore and Heir Island piers. When the head of Cunnamore Pier bears NW, turn and steer to leave Taylor N Card buoy to port. Give Cunnamore Pier and the shore of Frolic Point a berth of 50m to avoid an offlying rock and then steer 273°, with the ruined house on Skeam East fine on the starboard bow. Pass either one-third of the channel's width to the W of Goose, or 50m from the E side of the island. There is another drying outlier one cable W of Frolic Point. The centre of Goose Island touching

(below) S Approaches to Goose Island channel; Cunnamore Pier, R, with Taylor N Card buoy.

(above) Taylor buoy and Frolic Point (R) with its offlying rock; the ruined house on Skeam East, centre L

Goose Island E channel, from the NW; Goose Island, R, with Heir Island pier beyond the leading yacht. Sandy Island and Baltimore in the distance.

105

Long Island Bay

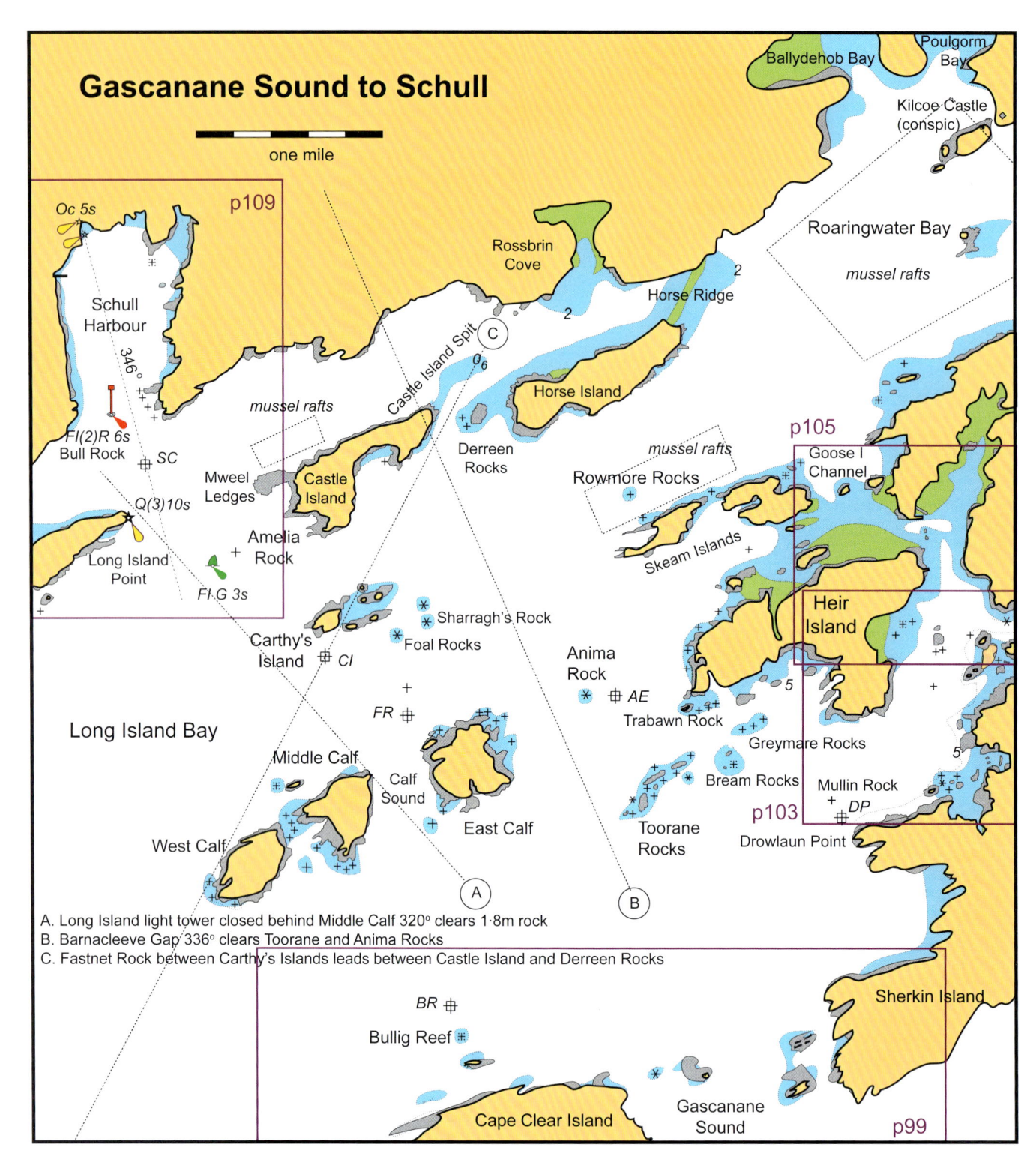

Gascanane Sound to Schull

one mile

A. Long Island light tower closed behind Middle Calf 320° clears 1·8m rock
B. Barnacleeve Gap 336° clears Toorane and Anima Rocks
C. Fastnet Rock between Carthy's Islands leads between Castle Island and Derreen Rocks

the NE point of Heir Island clears the rocks off the NE point of Skeam East. There is good anchorage off the beach on Skeam East. The narrow passage S of Skeam East, between it and Illaunagrogh, is clean, and navigable with care in mid-channel with a least depth of 1·2m at LAT at its E end. There are many half-tide rocks S of Illaunagrogh.

LONG ISLAND BAY

AC2129, 2184, SC5623·12

Long Island Bay lies between Cape Clear and Castle Point, and extends NE into Roaringwater Bay. The area offers many anchorages, lovely cruising and fascinating pilotage.

Long Island Bay

Dangers

There are many drying and underwater rocks within a cable of the shores in this area. The principal hazards further offshore are:

Bullig Reef, two rocks awash at LW, 4 cables N of Cape Clear Island.
Bream Rocks (dry 1·8m) and **Greymare Rocks**, with less than 2m, forming a reef extending for 3·5 cables NE–SW, 2 cables S of Heir Island
Toorane Rocks, reef 5 cables by 2, extending NE–SW, 2 cables W of Bream Rocks. The SW part dries 2·8m and the NE part has two heads above HW.
Anima Rock (dries 0·1m), in mid-channel between East Calf and Heir Island
Rock with 2·1m, in mid-channel between East Calf and the Carthy's Islands group
Rock with 1·8m, 2·5 cables SW of East Calf
Rock with 1·8m, 2·5 cables SW of Middle Calf
Foal Rocks (dries 2m), **Sharragh's Rock** (dries 2·8m), and a **rock** 1 cable N of Sharragh's Rock uncovering at LW, all 3 to 5 cables E of Carthy's Island.
Amelia Rock, 2·1m, 4 cables WSW of Castle Island
Rowmore Rocks, with less than 2m, 2 cables NW of West Skeam Island.
Derreen Rocks (dry 3·4m), between Horse and Castle Islands
Mweel Ledges (drying 3·6m), extending 2 cables W of Castle Island
Bull Rock (dries 1·8m), in the middle of the entrance to Schull Harbour
Baker Rock (dries 0·1m), 0·5 cable off the W shore of Schull Harbour, 1·5 cables N of Schull Point.

Tides
Long Island Bay

In the entrance to Long Island Bay, between Crookhaven and the Fastnet, the streams set E and W, the E-going stream making at –0455 Cobh and the W-going at +0115 Cobh. Spring rate is 2·5 kn around the salient points and in the narrow channels between the islands, decreasing in strength towards the head of the bay. The generally E-going stream sets SE and S through the channels between the outer islands, the W-going stream NW and N.
Constant (Schull) –0027 Cobh; MHWS 3·2m, MHWN 2·7m, MLWN 1·0m, MLWS 0·4m.

Lights and Marks

Amelia buoy, SHM Fl G 3s, AIS
Long Island Point (Copper Point), white tower Q(3) 10s 16m 8M
Schull leading lights 346°, Oc 5s 11M, front 5m rear 8m, orange triangles on white lattice masts NE of Schull pier.
Bull Rock, stayed perch PHM, Fl(2) R 6s 4m 4M
Storm Water Outfall buoy, Y, unlit, NE of Schull pier

Gascanane Sound and Cape Clear to Schull

Making N from Gascanane Sound or Cape Clear Island, course can be set W of West Calf Island or through Calf Sound, between East and Middle Calf Islands. The only danger on the course W of West Calf is the Bullig Reef (described in **North Coast of Cape Clear Island**, p99). For Calf Sound, steer first for the highest point of Middle Calf (11m). Long Island Point light tower closed behind the NE point of Middle Calf Island 320° clears the rock (with 1·8m) SW of East Calf. Hold mid-channel through the sound and when clear head for Amelia buoy 313°, distant 1·25M. The buoy and Long Island Point will be almost in line on this course, which passes to the SW of the Carthy's Island group. Carthy's Island should be given a berth of at least a cable. Give Long Island Point a berth of a cable, and leave Bull Rock perch well to port on entering Schull Harbour. Mweel Ledges extend almost 3 cables W of Castle Island, with mussel rafts N of them.

Carthy's Island group

⊕ CI 51°29'·4N 9°30'·5W (3 cables SW)
There are several dangerous rocks to the SE and E of the Carthy's Island group. If Foal and Sharragh's Rocks are not showing, a mid-channel course between the Carthy group and East Calf clears them. Near LW the 2·1m rock S of Foal Rocks may be hazardous; waypoint ⊕ FR 51°29'·3N 9°29'·7W clears it to the S.

Anchorages

There is an attractive daytime anchorage inside the Carthy's Island group. Approach through the narrow channel SE of Carthy's Island, which has least depth 3m, or else by the channel between North and South Carthy's Islands, which has 1·2m. If using this entrance, keep the N face of South Carthy's Island open so as to pass well N of Sharragh's Rock and its N outlier. This anchorage is subject to some swell if there is a sea running in the bay. It is also exposed to NW winds when the rocks NE of Carthy's Island cover as the tide rises, and the holding has been reported poor due to kelp.

Roaringwater Bay, Castle and Horse Islands

The Fastnet Rock in the gap between the Carthy's Islands leads between Castle and Horse Islands (transit C, plan on p100)

There is also an attractive anchorage off the beach (labelled "White Strand" on the chart) on the E side of East Calf. Approach steering SW and anchor in 2 to 4m, sand.

Roaringwater Bay

51°31'·5N 9°26'W

The channel E of East Calf Island is wide and deep but the dangerous Toorane and Anima Rocks lie in mid-channel. To clear W of these rocks (and E of Sharragh's Rock), steer 336° for the conspicuous Barnacleeve Gap. The Gap is just E of Mount Gabriel, which is 404m high with two conspicuous white radar domes on its summit *(see photograph)*. If bad visibility prevents this line being seen, steer for East Calf Island and approach to 1 cable off its SE point before turning on to a course of 010° to leave the foul ground E of East Calf to port and Anima Rock to starboard. Alternatively, stay close W of longitude 9°28'·4W once well clear N of Gascanane Sound. Toorane Rocks are usually marked by breakers but the westernmost heads show only at extreme LW.

Anima Rock dries only 0·1m and frequently does not break. It may be passed on its S side with the S shores of Middle and West Calf Islands just open S of East Calf Island, 250° until the W point of Horse Island bears 335°. To pass E of Anima Rock, take safe bearings on Trabawn Rock (off the SW end of Heir Island) which always shows, or use waypoint ⊕*AE* 51°29'·3N 9°27'·9W, 2·5 cables E of Anima Rock. There is a deep channel N and NE of Toorane and Greymare Rocks but this is not recommended without local knowledge.

Rowmore Rocks, N of West Skeam Island, have less than 2m but are entirely surrounded by mussel rafts which extend the length of West Skeam and halfway across the channel to the N. They are marked at their NW and NE corners by yellow buoys. Do not attempt the passage between the mussel rafts and the shore of West Skeam.

The inner part of Roaringwater Bay, NE of a line from Audley Cove to Illaunranhee, is almost entirely taken up by mussel rafts. However there is a clear passage along the NW shore, and Ballydehob and Poulgorm Bays offer attractive anchorages. Truchare Rock at the entrance to Poulgorm Bay always shows, and Kilcoe Castle is conspicuous *(see photo on p22)*. Ballydehob Bay has a drying quay immediately below the weir at the bridge, accessible by dinghy and a short walk from the village. PO, shops, pubs, restaurants, laundry.

Castle Island and Horse Island

51°30'·5N 9°29'·3W

Derreen Rocks, which dry 3·4m, lie in mid-channel between Castle and Horse Islands. Castle Island Spit, with 0·6m, extends 4 cables NE from the E end of Castle Island. There is a navigable channel with least depth 2·7m between these dangers. Approaching from Gascanane Sound with Barnacleeve Gap bearing 336° (see above, Roaringwater Bay), when the Fastnet Rock comes in transit between Carthy's Islands alter course to pass 0·5 cable SE of Castle Island. When the E end of Castle Island is abeam, steer 041° until within 2 cables of the N shore of the Sound to clear S of Castle Island Spit.

The N side of Horse Island is shoal, so it is preferable to hold closer to the mainland side of Horse Island Channel once clear of Castle Island Spit. Horse Ridge, drying 0·6m in mid-channel and 0·2m within 50m of the

Mount Gabriel (L) and Barnacleeve Gap (R) from the SE

Rossbrin

mainland shore, extends between the NE end of Horse Island and the shore to the NE. It may be crossed near HW, keeping close to the mainland side.

Rossbrin

51°31'·3N 9°28'·2W
AC2129, 2184, SC5623·12

This attractive cove with its ruined castle, 2·5M E of Schull, is substantially protected from swell, but is shallow. There is a small drying pier at the head of the bay, and a slipway in the NW corner. Rossbrin Boatyard, VHF Ch 16 or phone 028 37352, hull (wood and GRP), rigging, mechanical and electrical repairs, winter storage; travelhoist capacity 16 tonnes. Advice on visitors' moorings.

Passage SW of Castle Island

Leamcon Tower (on the 107m summit, 1·5M N of Goat Island) in line with Long Island Point beacon 281° leads between the rocks W of Castle Island and Amelia Rock, but also leads very close to the rocks SW of the SW point of Castle Island. (Historic buildings enthusiasts may wish to note that the hilltop tower is not the 15th-century Leamcon Castle; that is the ruin on Castle Point, 1·5M to the SW of the Tower.)

Leamcon tower in line with Long Island Point beacon leads between Amelia Rock and the rocks to the SW of Castle Island (transit A, plan 0n p110)

Rossbrin

Schull from the NW

109

Schull

Schull Harbour and Long Island Sound

A. Long Island Point light tower and Leamcon Tower 281° leads between Amelia Rock and the rocks W of Castle Island

SCHULL

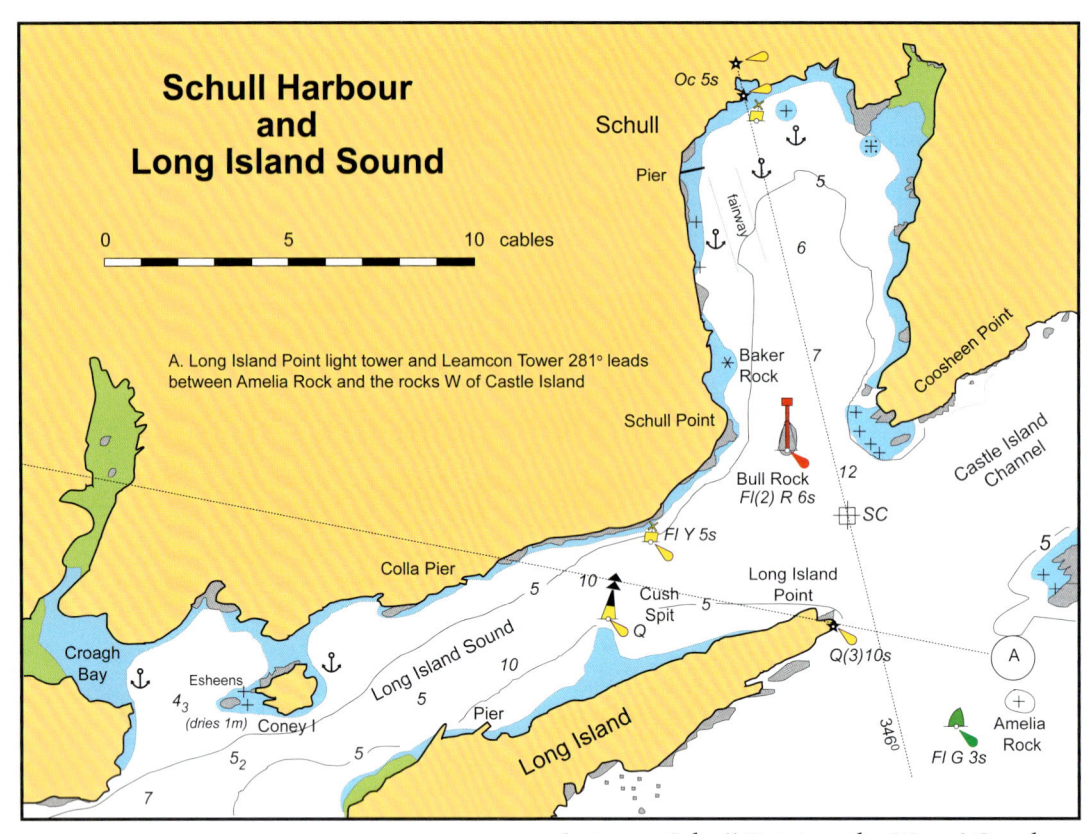

⊕ SC, 51°30'·5N 9°32'W
AC2129, 2184, SC5623·12, Imray C56 and Plan

Schull Harbour affords good shelter except in strong S or SE winds. The entrance lies between Schull Point on the W and Coosheen Point on the E. Foul ground extends 0·75 cable N of the Bull Rock perch; the rock is otherwise steep-to. The rest of the W shore is clear, but the E shore should not be approached closer than a cable. A hazardous

Schull is a popular place; the harbour and pier can be crowded at times

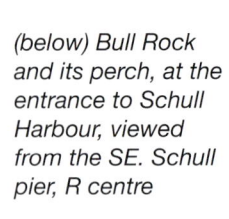

(below) Bull Rock and its perch, at the entrance to Schull Harbour, viewed from the SE. Schull pier, R centre

110

Schull to Baltimore

rock lies approximately 1·5 cables SE of the S leading beacon, near the 3·7m sounding on AC 2129 and 2184 at the head of the harbour; its position is marked by a noticeable gap in the moorings. It is a tempting but inadvisable place to anchor.

Anchorage

One cable E of the pier in 2 to 4m, good holding. An anchor light and tripping line are essential. Stay clear of the fairway to the pier, which is marked by lines of dan buoys. There are visitors' moorings on the NE side of the harbour; contact Schull Watersports for details. Constant –0027 Cobh; MHWS 3·2m, MHWN 2·7m, MLWN 1·0m, MLWS 0·4m.

There is 3m alongside the pier from the former ice plant to the head, but the pier is often occupied by fishing vessels. The main steps on the N side are used by the ferry to Cape Clear. A pontoon is available for dinghy landing, but may also be crowded in summer. At the time of writing (2015) there is planning permission for a 200-berth marina.

Facilities

Water on the pier. Diesel by tanker, phone 028 28116 or 21024. Schull Watersports keeps a range of chandlery, phone 028 28554. Sailmaker, Fastnet Sails, phone Christophe Houdaille 028 28628, mobile 086 176 2377. Shops, pubs, restaurants, bank, PO. Showers at the sailing centre. HM phone 028 28136, mobile 086 103 9105. Schull Harbour Sailing Club. Ferry to Cape Clear Island in summer.

SCHULL and CAPE CLEAR to BALTIMORE NORTH PASSAGE

AC2129, SC5623·12: see Plan on p106

Entering Calf Sound from the N, keep Long Island Point light tower closed behind the NE point of Middle Calf Island 320° to clear the 1·8m rock SW of East Calf Island. When the NW shore of Heir Island opens S of East Calf 052°, steer 090° for Drowlaun Point to clear Toorane Rocks.

From Cape Clear North Harbour, steer 012° for the middle of East Calf until Carrigmore, in the middle of Gascanane Sound, is open W of Illaunbrock 110° (waypoint ⊕BR, 51°27'·6N 9°29'·2W, *plan on p98*). Then steer 065° to pass 1·5 cables NW of Drowlaun Point (waypoint ⊕DP, 51°28'·7N 9°26'·2W, *plan on p102*). Once past Drowlaun Point, bear to starboard to bring the Point just to the right of Mount Lahan 77m) on Cape Clear Island astern, and stay on this transit until abreast the SW-most of the Catalogues. For the remainder of the passage, with plan and photographs, see the Directions for the outward passage on pp102-103.

An alternative route from Schull (with sufficient rise of tide) runs N of Heir Island and through Goose Island Channel. Refer to the Directions on p105.

Tides
Schull to Crookhaven

In Lough Buidhe, Long Island Sound and Castle Island Channel the streams make E and W at a maximum rate of 1·5 kn at springs, but E and W of Goat Island they set N and S. The stream starts S through Man of War and Goat Island Sounds and E through Long Island Sound at –0530 Cobh; it starts W through Long Island Sound and N through Goat Island and Man of War Sounds at +0030 Cobh. The E-going stream S of Long Island runs towards Sherkin Island and the North Passage to Baltimore.

Constant (Schull) –0027 Cobh; MHWS 3·2m, MHWN 2·7m, MLWN 1·0m, MLWS 0·4m.

Dangers

Esheens, reef drying up to 1m in places, extending a cable W from Coney Island
Sound Rock, dries 1·8m, a cable W of Garillaun off the W end of Long Island
Bulligmore, 0·9m, 6 cables WSW of Illaunricmonia
N and S **Barrel Rocks** (drying 1·4 and 1·8m), 2 cables E of Duharrig
Amsterdam Reef (dries 0·3m), 2 cables SSW of **Amsterdam Rock** (0·3m high, not 1·2m as charted), at the W entrance to Toormore Bay
Black Horse Rocks, (drying), extending 0·75 cable N of Alderman Rocks (9m high), on the S side of the entrance to Crookhaven

Lights and Marks

Outfall buoy, Y, Fl Y 5s, SW of Schull Point
Cush Spit buoy, N Card Q
Goat Island Little, white stone beacon, unlit
Rock Island, white tower, Fl WR 8s 20m W13M R11M, W over Long Island Bay to 281°, R 281°–340°; inside the harbour, R 281°–348°; W to shore. Shows red over safe water offshore to the SE but over Black Horse and Alderman Rocks at the entrance to Crookhaven; white to E and NE, and to the W over the harbour. AIS.
Black Horse Rocks, stayed perch N Card Q 5m 5M
Mizen Head, white tower, Iso 4s 55m 15M, AIS

111

Schull to Crookhaven

Long Island Sound and Lough Buidhe, looking W from Long Island; Goat Island Little (L, with its beacon), Goat Island (L centre), Dromadda and Duharrig centre. Rock Island lighthouse at the entrance to Crookhaven in the distance

Coney Island (R centre) seen from Long Island; Croagh Bay to the W, with Esheens reef showing

Colla Pier, on Long Island Sound west of Schull; Long Island opposite, with Long Island Point light beacon, upper L

Long Island pier

SCHULL to CROOKHAVEN

AC2184, SC5623·11, Imray C56

W of the Cush Spit buoy, Long Island Sound ("Long Island Channel" on the chart) is clean on both sides, and the S side of the island is also clean to within a cable of the shore. There are three passages to the W from Long Island Sound: Goat Island Sound, Man-of-War Sound and Barrel Sound.

The S sides of Goat Island Little and Illaunricmonia to the W are also clean, but Bulligmore, WSW of Illaunricmonia, is dangerous, especially in settled conditions when it may not be breaking. Carrigduff (close S of Long Island) open of Goat Island Little 070° leads S of Bulligmore, or stay S of 51°28'·7N.

Anchorage

Anchorage is available in 3·5m E of Coney Island, on the N side of the sound, and in Croagh Bay, W of Coney Island, giving the W side of the island a berth of 2 cables.

Anchorage is also available off the small pier on Long Island, W of Cush Spit, in 3m, sand.

Goat Island Sound

Goat Island Sound, between Long Island and Goat Island, is over 2 cables wide at its N end. Sound Rock lies a cable W of Garillaun off the W end of Long Island.

Man of War Sound

Man of War Sound, between Goat Island and Illaunricmonia is free of danger. Illaunricmonia (7m high) is clean on its S and E sides but foul to N and W. Goat and Little Goat Islands, the latter with its white beacon, are clean on their W sides.

Barrel Sound

Lough Buidhe and Long Island Sound from the W; Dromadda, bottom, with (bottom to top from lower R) Illaunricmonia, Man of War Sound, the Goat Islands, Goat Island Sound, Long Island, Castle Island and Horse Island. Coney Island centre L, Schull harbour upper L and Roaringwater Bay in the distance

Barrel Sound

Barrel Sound lies between Castle Point (on which is the conspicuous Leamcon Castle) and the islets to the NW of Illaunricmonia of which Dromadda (12m high) is the furthest N, and Duharrig (5m high) the furthest W. There is foul ground for 2·5 cables E of Duharrig where the Barrel Rocks dry 1·4 and 1·8m. Green Island, S of Castle Point has foul ground E of it and for 0·25 cable S of it. After passing down Long Island Sound continue a

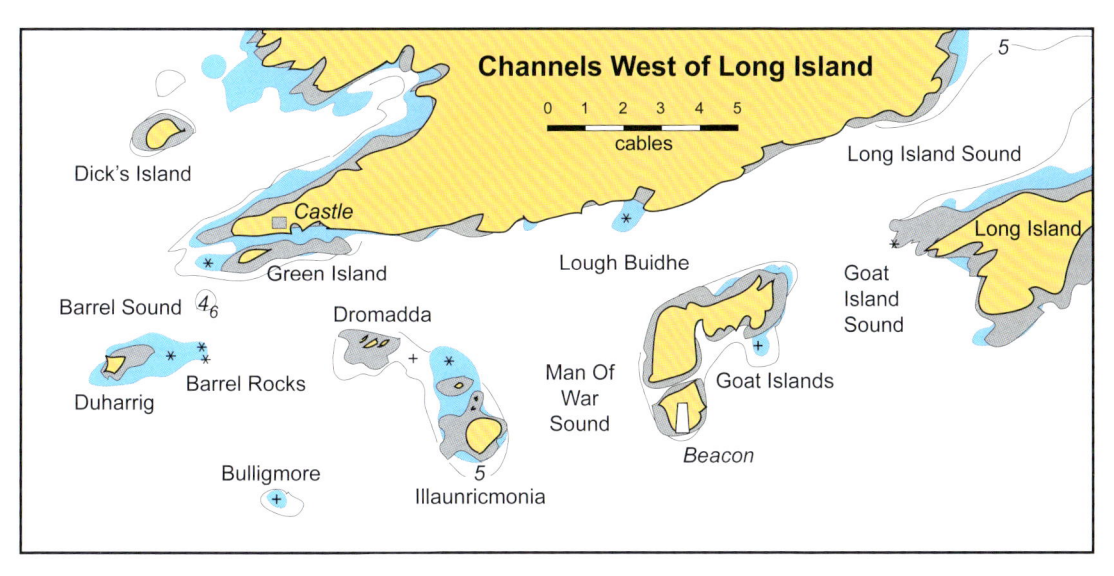

Channels West of Long Island

113

Toormore and Goleen

Barrel Sound from the WNW; Leamcon Castle (L), Dromadda in line with the Goat Islands (centre L), Illaunricmonia (centre R) and Duharrig (R). Cape Clear Island in the distance

Toormore Bay from the E

Goleen from the ESE; the church spire (L) and the entrance (centre)

Goleen, looking seaward

mid-channel course through Lough Buidhe, which lies between Goat Island and the mainland. Then steer to leave Green Island a cable to starboard and pass N of Dromadda, the Barrels and Duharrig. There are no dangers on the course from Duharrig to Crookhaven.

Toormore Bay

51°30′N 9°39′W
AC2184, SC5623·11

Amsterdam Rock marks the W side of the approach to Toormore Bay; beware the drying Amsterdam Reef, 2 cables SSW of the rock. Brow Head Tower (111m) well open S of Rock Island lighthouse, 238°, leads clear S of Amsterdam Reef. The E shore of the bay is foul and should be given a berth of 2 cables.

Anchorage

There is a delightful fine-weather anchorage in the bay N of Reenard Point, sheltered from SW to N but untenable in fresh S to SE winds. Anchor off the beach in 3m.

Goleen

51°29′·6N 9°41′·5W
AC2184, SC5623·11

One mile N of Crookhaven lighthouse there is a narrow cleft in the rocks, named "Kirealcoegea" on AC2184, which has a quay offering a temporary berth to a yacht. At the head of the inlet is Goleen village, whose church spire can be seen from some distance off, though the cleft does not become apparent till very close. The high sides provide excellent shelter from offshore breezes but the inlet is open to the SE. There are no dangers in the approach but in the entrance itself there are rocks awash at HW on the N side, so keep over to port. The quay marked on the chart is the old one; the new quay, 30m long, on the S side, is closer to the mouth of the creek,

Crookhaven

Goleen from the ESE; the church (top L) is conspicuous from seaward.

and has about 1m at LAT. A yacht should not be left unattended in case the berth is required by a fishing vessel. Turning room is very restricted, with only 40m between the quay face and the cliff opposite. There is no room to anchor and the inner part of the inlet dries. Shop, PO, pubs, restaurant at Goleen.

CROOKHAVEN

⊕ CK 51°28'·5N 9°42'W
AC2184, SC5623·11, Imray C56 and Plan

The lighthouse on Rock Island at the N side of the entrance is conspicuous. Alderman Rocks (9m high) lie from 2 to 3·5 cables offshore, E of Streek Head at the S side of the entrance. Black Horse Rocks extend 0·75 cable N of them, marked by a N Card beacon. Crookhaven offers all-round shelter although somewhat windswept in heavy weather, and is very easy to enter by day or night. The inlet is 2M long and at its entrance is 2 cables wide, but it narrows to 1·5 cables about 5 cables from the entrance and then opens up again to about 3 cables in width W of Rock Island. Both shores are steep-to, but beware of the rock (with 0·1m) 0·75 cable SW of the W point of Rock Island. This rock is not marked on AC2129. There are several old watch towers on the shores.

Streek Head is 44m high and bold, with several stacks close inshore. The largest of these, Gokane, is charted at 6m high but appears lower. Alderman Sound, W of Alderman Rocks, is navigable in the absence of swell; approaching from the S, steer due N for the mid-channel and hold this course

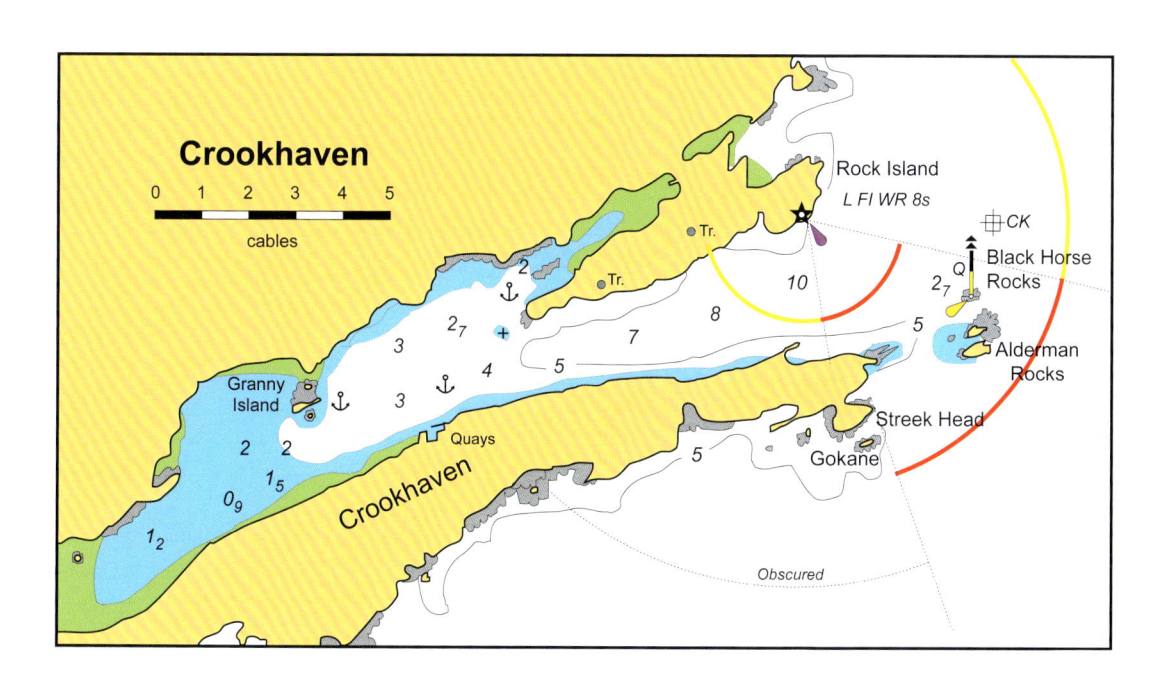

Crookhaven

Crookhaven from the E; Alderman Rocks, Streek Head and Gokane, bottom L, Crookhaven village, L centre. Brow Head top L, with Barley Cove and Mizen Head at top

until Gokane closes with Streek Head before turning to port. There is a least depth of 6·4m on this course.

Anchorage

- There are visitors' moorings in mid-channel off the village. Mooring fees payable at O'Sullivan's Bar.
- Anchor off the village and well out in the middle of the bay in 3m, good holding, but weedy in places. The available space is limited due to the number of moorings.
- In E winds, anchor N of the W point of Rock Island.
- In fresh W winds some shelter may be had in the lee of Granny Island on the N shore, NW of the village; beware of Row Rock (dries 0·3m), close S of Granny Island. Holding reported (2013) poor, in very soft mud.

Facilities

Shops, pubs, restaurants. Dinghy landing pontoon. Water on the quay. Crookhaven Sailing Club near the quay.

Alderman Sound: Gokane just open of Streek Head. View from the NE

Crookhaven

Rock Island lighthouse from the ESE; Black Horse Rocks and perch, centre

Tides
Crookhaven

There is only a slight tidal stream in the harbour. The tide sets strongly through Alderman Sound and care should be taken not to be drawn into it in calm weather. Constant –0045 Cobh; MHWS 3·3m, MHWN 2·7m, MLWN 0·9m, MLWS 0·3m.

Crookhaven (photo W.M.Nixon)

117

3 Mizen Head to Bantry Bay

Approaches to Berehaven from the S; Pipers Sound, centre, Bere Island and Berehaven R, Dunboy Bay L, Castletownbere harbour upper L centre

The south west coast of Ireland is penetrated by four long and deep inlets, geologically rias, or drowned river valleys, rather than fjords. These four – Dunmanus Bay, Bantry Bay, Kenmare River and Dingle Bay – are surrounded by spectacular mountain scenery, and the five peninsulas and their villages are renowned tourist destinations.

Mizen Head, Ireland's most southwesterly point, has a light which – somewhat surprisingly – was built as recently as 1959. The elegant bridge spanning the chasm between the shore and the lighthouse stack, however, dates from 1907, because it was built to provide access to the fog signal on the Mizen, which was on the same stack but pre-dated the lighthouse by 52 years. The one-time keepers' houses are now a lighthouse museum, with quite possibly the finest view of any museum in the world.

Dunmanus Bay is one of Ireland's less-well-travelled inlets, but is a beautiful and peaceful place with several fine anchorages.

The wide and deep inlet of Bantry Bay has been a vital commercial and strategic harbour for centuries. An abortive French invasion was aimed here in 1796, and relics of the invasion may be seen at Bantry House.

Castletownbere (Castletown Bearhaven on the charts) has traditionally been the centre of the whitefish fishery in Ireland. It is a no-nonsense place with few pretensions, but nonetheless a lovely town with a fascinating

Mizen Head to Bantry Bay

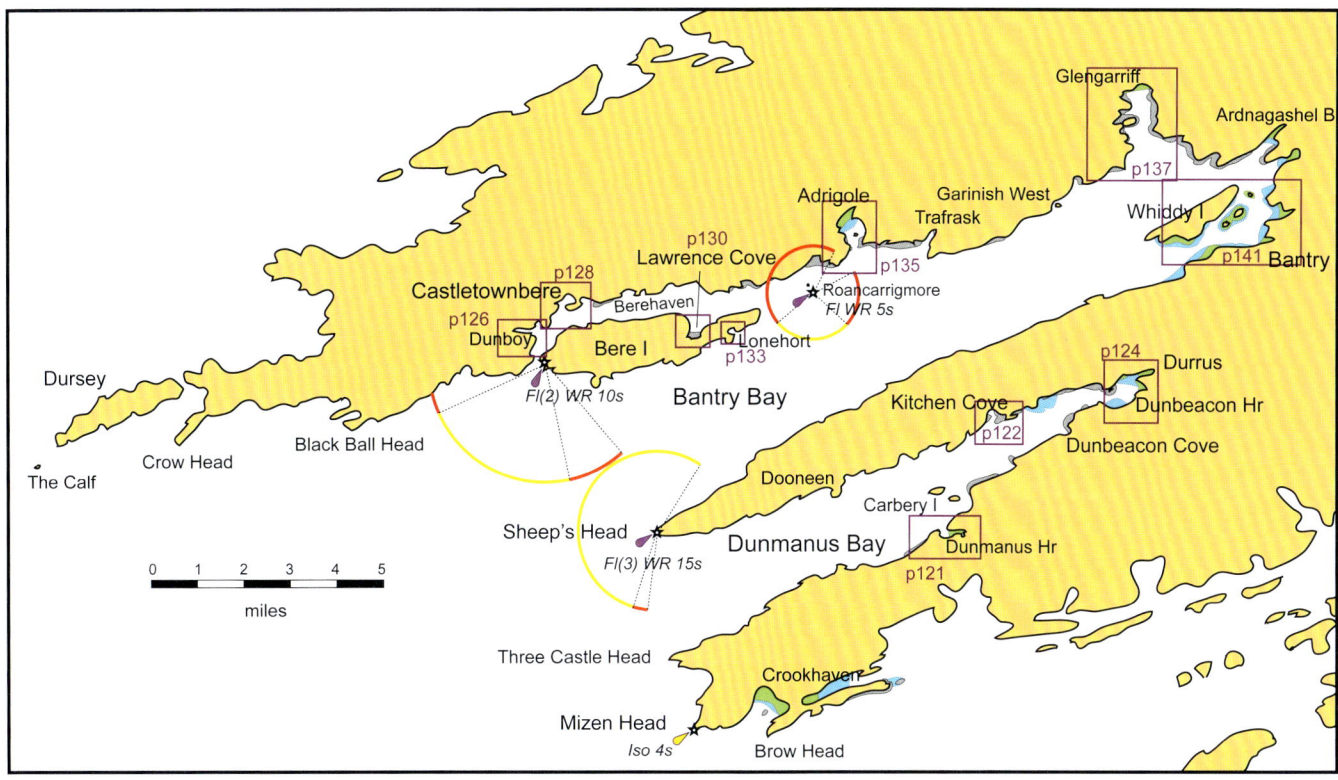

history.

The busy market town of Bantry (3,310) stands at the head of the bay, its broad harbour sheltered by Whiddy Island. At the west end of Whiddy is an oil jetty, with a tank farm ashore housing the national oil reserves. Bantry town itself is rich in history; the impressive Bantry House is open to the public and hosts regular concerts.

Facing Whiddy Island in the north-east corner of Bantry Bay is the picture-postcard natural harbour of Glengarriff, a deservedly popular destination by land and sea. The bay is sheltered by tree-clad islands, the largest of which, Ilnacullen or Garinish Island, has an extraordinary Italianate garden designed a hundred years ago by the English architect Harold Peto for the island's owner Annan Bryce. With the eccentric energy characteristic of his era, Bryce capitalised on the location's famously mild climate to turn a windswept and rocky islet into a paradise of subtropical plants, and his vision was realised by the eminent Scottish gardener Murdo MacKenzie, who managed the gardens for 43 years. Well worth a visit, the gardens are open to the public and there is a ferry to the island from the jetty at Glengarriff.

Tides
Crookhaven to Dunmanus Bay

Between Crookhaven and Mizen Head the streams set E and W. Off Mizen Head and Three Castle Head the streams run S, and NW by N, forming eddies off Three Castle Head. The S-going stream makes at −0505 Cobh and the NW-going at +0120 Cobh. The spring rate off Mizen Head is 4 kn and off Three Castle Head 3 kn, decreasing to 1·5 kn 5M offshore. This results in a race off Mizen Head, which may extend the whole way N across Dunlough Bay to Three Castle Head, and can be dangerous to smaller craft, especially with wind against tide. Tidal streams in Dunmanus Bay are almost imperceptible. Constant (Dunmanus Harbour) −0050 Cobh; MHWS 3·4m, MHWN 2·7m, MLWN 1·1m, MLWS 0·3m.

Paper Charts

The small craft folio SC5623 Bantry Bay to Kinsale covers the whole area of this chapter in detail. In terms of individual charts, on the smaller scale, AC2424 Kenmare River to Cork Harbour or Imray's C56, provide coverage. The Imray chart has several useful harbour plans, but AC2552 is essential for Dunmanus Bay and AC1838 and 1840 for Bantry Bay.

'Cruising Ireland'

Dunmanus Bay and Bantry Bay are described on pages 58 to 67 of **Cruising Ireland**

Crookhaven to Dunmanus Bay

Mizen Head from the SE: Carrignagower, breaking

CROOKHAVEN to DUNMANUS BAY

Brow Head, 1·75M E of Mizen Head, is 111m high and slopes steeply seaward. There is a ruined signal tower near its summit. Over a hundred years ago, Guglielmo Marconi built a radio station here to receive the news from America and to transmit the European news to passing liners. Between Brow Head and Mizen Head lies Barley Cove, which has the finest beach in West Cork.

Crookhaven to Mizen Head

The usual course is outside Black Horse and Alderman Rocks, but in the absence of swell Alderman Sound offers a short cut. Steer 082° for Black Horse Rocks perch until Gokane (charted 6m high) is just open of Streek Head *(see photograph on p116)*, then turn on to a course of due S in mid channel of Alderman Sound. There is a least depth of 6·4m on this course. In settled conditions Mizen Head may be approached to within a cable (but beware of Carrignagower, 5 cables ESE); however in heavy weather, especially with wind over tide, it should be given a berth of a mile.

Dunmanus Bay

AC2552, SC5623

Dunmanus Bay is 3·5M wide at its entrance between Sheep's Head and Three Castle Head, and extends 13M ENE. The bay has three good anchorages: Dunmanus Harbour, Kitchen Cove and Dunbeacon Harbour; there is also an anchorage at Dunbeacon Cove on the S shore, near the head of the bay.

Generally the outer part of the bay is steep-to and free of dangers, but **South Bullig**, 4·6m, 4 cables SW of Three Castle Head, breaks in heavy weather. Bird Island, 51m high and 3M from Three Castle Head, is close to the shore,

Dangers
Crookhaven to Dunmanus Bay

Black Horse Rocks, (drying), extending 0·75 cable N of Alderman Rocks (9m high), on the S side of Crookhaven entrance

Devil's Rock, awash at HW, in the middle of Barley Cove bay

Carrignagower, awash at HW, 1 cable offshore 5 cables ESE of Mizen Head

South Bullig, 4·6m, 4 cables SW of Three Castle Head

In Dunmanus Bay:

Carbery Breaker, 2·3m, extending 3 cables from the W end of Carbery Island

Murphy Rocks, dry 1·5m, 1·5 cables off the mainland shore E of Carbery Island

Carriglea Rock, dries 3·2m, at the W entrance to Dunbeacon Cove.

Unnamed rock with 1·7m, 3 cables offshore, 5 cables ENE of Reen Point, E of Kitchen Cove

Carrigtuil, dries 0·2m, in the bay W of Rossmore Point at the entrance to Dunbeacon Harbour

Murphy Rock, awash at LW, on the S side of Dunbeacon Harbour

Carrigbroanty, dries 0·5m, 3 cables ENE of Mannion's Island in Dunbeacon Harbour.

Lights and Marks

Mizen Head, white tower, Iso 4s 55m 15M, AIS

Sheep's Head, 7m white tower Fl(3) WR 15s 83m W15M R9M, R 011°–017° W 017°–212°, W (faint) 212°–222°, obscured elsewhere; AIS. The narrow red sector leads W of the South Bullig rock, and the light is obscured E of this

Offshore weather buoy

Weather buoy M3, yellow, Fl(5) Y 20s, 28M WSW of Mizen Head in 51°13'N 10°33'W.

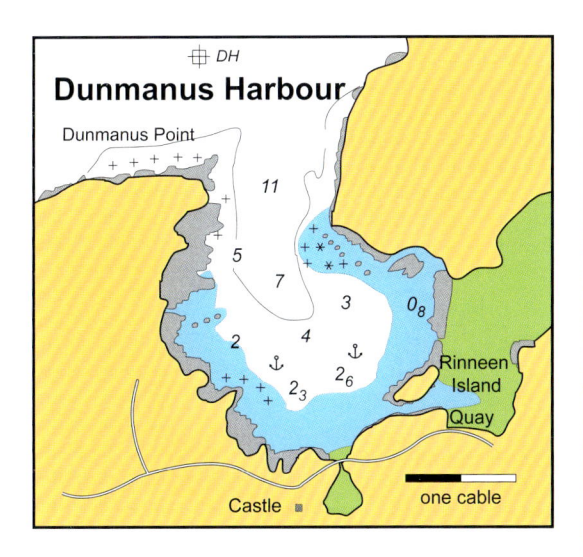

Dunmanus Harbour

and the passage inside it is foul. There are sunken rocks extending 1 cable offshore, 1M SW of Dunmanus Point.

Dunmanus Harbour

⊕ DH 51°32'·9N 9°40'W
Inset on AC2552, SC5623·6 and Plan

Dunmanus Harbour is a horseshoe bay on the south side, seven miles ENE of Three Castle Head. There are sunken rocks off the E side just inside the entrance which may extend further than on the Plan or on AC2552, and the W side is also foul, restricting the entrance to half a cable. Enter on a mid-channel course heading for a point 50m W of the ruins of Dunmanus Castle on the S shore. Anchor in the centre of the harbour in 4 to 6m, sand and soft mud. The E side of the harbour dries out. No facilities ashore. There is sometimes a roll in the harbour if the swell is running up the bay outside. Constant –0050 Cobh; MHWS 3·4m, MHWN 2·7m, MLWN 1·1m, MLWS 0·3m.

Carbery Island

Carbery Island, 15m high and 4 cables long, lies in the middle of the bay, with the smaller Furze and Cold Islands to its E. There is a single house on Carbery, occasionally occupied. Carbery Breaker extends 3 cables from the W end of the island, and the NW and SW shores are foul for 1·5 cables. The gap in Knockaughna Mt. (268m) open N of Carbery Island 080° clears Carbery Breaker to the N. There is a clear passage between Furze and Carbery Islands in mid-channel, staying within 1 cable SE of Cold Island to avoid Murphy Rocks. The other channels between the islands and E of Furze Island are foul.

Between Carbery Island and Drishane Point the S shore of the bay should not be approached closer than 2 cables. East of Drishane Point the shore is clean until Carriglea Rock is reached, at the W entrance to Dunbeacon Cove.

(above) Dunmanus Harbour from the E: Sheep's Head, top R

(below) Dunmanus Harbour and Castle

Gap in Knockaughna Mountain (L) open N of Carbery Island clears Carbery Breaker

Kitchen Cove

Dooneen Pier from the SE: note the bollard on top of the rock, L

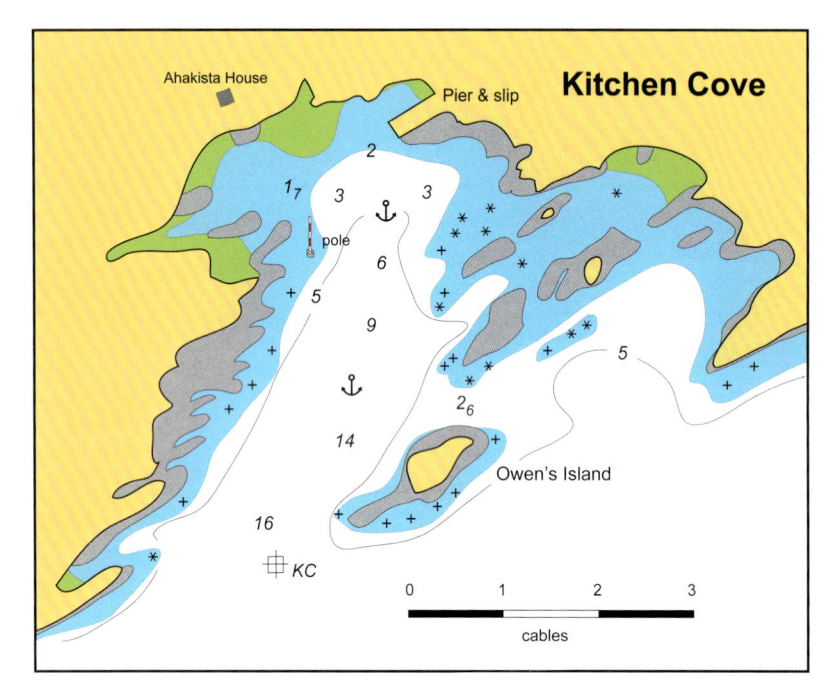

Ahakista Pier, in Kitchen Cove

Kitchen Cove: the pole beacon, L, and the pier, extreme R

North Shore of Dunmanus Bay – Sheep's Head to Kitchen Cove

If approaching from Sheep's Head the N shore is steep-to as far as Kilcrohane, opposite Carbery Island. Give Pointabulloge a berth of over 1 cable to the S and 2 cables to the W to avoid the reefs off it, and give the coast from there to Kitchen Cove a berth of a cable. Lord Bandon's Tower, a 49m folly, ("Lord Brandon's" on the chart) in the bay W of Pointabulloge, is conspicuous. Dooneen Pier, 2 cables N of Dooneen Point, might offer an intriguing temporary berth in settled weather; the pier has projecting bolts on its face, but opposite it is an above-water rock with a substantial bollard on top, and there is 5·6m of water between the pier and the rock.

Kilcrohane Pier, 1 cable N of Kilcrohane Point, is small and not recommended for alongside berthing.

Kitchen Cove

⊕ KC 51°35'·45N 9°38'·1W
Inset on AC2552, SC5623·6 and Plan

Kitchen Cove is 1·5M beyond Pointabulloge. The entrance, 2 cables wide, is between Owen's Island and the W shore. Owen's Island is a low grassy islet in front of the cove with rocks awash at HW extending 0·75 cable off its W side and 0·5 cable off its E side. All the E side of the harbour is strewn with rocks, and there is also a dangerous rock, drying 0·2m, 0·5 cable off the inner point on the W side. This rock is marked by a slim red-and-white banded pole. The N shore is wooded.

Anchorage

The best anchorage is NW of Owen's Island, midway between it and the W shore in 9m, mud. The NW corner of the bay, in front of Ahakista House, is taken up by moorings, but anchorage is available in 3 to 4m in the

122

Kitchen Cove and Dunbeacon Cove

Kitchen Cove from the SE: Owen's Island, L

centre of the bay, S of the pier. The holding is variable, good in the centre but poor on rock in the corner SE of the pier. The pier, with 1·5m at its outer end, extends 0·5 cable WSW from the rocky point where "Quay" is marked on AC2552. Water tap on the pier; pubs at Ahakista.

Kitchen Cove to Dunbeacon Harbour

There is a narrow passage N of Owen's Island, but the safe course is S of the island. Beyond Reen Point are several dangers in the middle of the bay; a rock with 1·7m lies 3 cables offshore, 5 cables ENE of Reen Point. **Doona Rock**, 7·5 cables E of Reen Point and off the S shore, with 4·9m, and another rock with 4·1m, 2 cables W of Doona Rock, may break in a heavy swell. Three Castle Head, Bird Island and the N side of Carbery Island in transit 232° lead between Doona Rock and the 1·7m rock. Good visibility is necessary for this clearing line *(see photograph)*.

Kitchen Cove

Three Castle Head, Bird Island and Carbery Island in line lead between the dangers in the upper Bay

123

Dunbeacon Harbour

Dunbeacon Harbour and Dunmanus Bay from the E; Mannion's Island, centre, Four Mile Water and Durrus pier and village, bottom. Note the mussel rafts, L

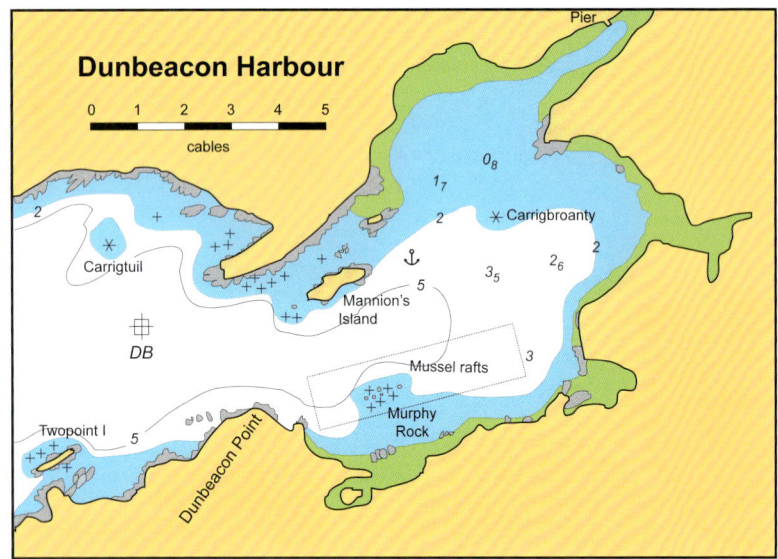

When past these dangers, the course for the entrance to Dunbeacon Harbour is clear. Give Twopoint Island, 5 cables W of Dunbeacon Point, a berth of a cable, and avoid **Carrigtuil** (dries 0·2m) in the bay W of Rossmore Point.

Dunbeacon Cove

51°35'·5N 9°35'·3W

Dunbeacon Cove may be identified by the wall of a ruined castle to the NE. The cove is small and its inner portion dries, so it offers limited shelter. Anchor midway between the E shore and Carriglea Rock in 4m, mud. Land at the quay up the cove, which dries at LW. Restaurant 1·5 km on the Durrus road.

Four Mile Water and Durrus pier, at the head of Dunmanus Bay

Dunbeacon Harbour

⊕ *DB 51°36'·4N 9°34'W*
Inset on AC2552, SC5623·6 and Plan

Dunbeacon Harbour is shallow on its N and NE sides, and is obstructed by **Murphy Rock**, awash at LW, on its S side. Halfway between Mannion's Island and the E shore is the drying rock **Carrigbroanty**. The S half of the Harbour is occupied by mussel rafts, and Murphy Rock may be avoided simply by staying N of the rafts.

Anchorage

Anchor close to the E side of Mannion's Island in 2 to 4m, with Twopoint Island in line with the S side of Mannion's Island. The pier marked at Sea Lodge on AC2552 is ruined. Durrus pier, with 0·5m at its head, lies on the N shore at the narrows of Four Mile Water, the channel leading to Durrus village from the NE corner of the bay. Durrus, 1·5 km from this pier, has shops, PO, restaurants and pubs. Constant –0040 Cobh; MHWS 3·3m, MHWN 2·6m, MLWN 1·2m, MLWS 0·5m.

Sheep's Head

Sheep's Head is 168m high with fine cliffs. The Head is steep-to but **North Bullig Rock** with 6·2m over it lies 1·5 cables to the SW and breaks in severe weather. There is less tidal stream round this head than round any of its neighbours.

Sheep's Head

Tides
Bantry Bay

The tidal streams are barely perceptible except in the entrance to Berehaven and Bantry Harbours. With strong S or SW winds a current sets into the bay around Sheep's Head. In the entrances to Berehaven the tidal streams run in from +0550 Cobh and out from –0025 Cobh; spring rate 2 kn (W entrance), 0·5 kn (E entrance).
Constant (Castletownbere) –0030 Cobh; MHWS 3·3m, MHWN 2·7m, MLWN 1·3m, MLWS 0·5m.

Dangers
Castletownbere and Approaches

Rock with 1·5m, 0·25 cable E of The Pipers, S of Pipers Point
Harbour Rock, 3·7m, in mid-channel 3·5 cables NNE of Pipers Point
Foilnaboe Rocks, a group of three drying 1·8m, 0·5 cable N of Fort Point
Rocks with 2·4m, 1·25 cables NE of Foilnaboe Rocks
Colt Rock, dries 2·1m, on the W side of the channel and NE of Dunboy Point
Little Colt Rock, dries 0·9m, between Colt Rock and the shore to the N
Walter Scott Rock, 2·7m, 2 cables S of Dinish Island
Long Point, rocky ledge, awash at HW, extending 1 cable W of Sheep Island.

Lights and Marks

Ardnakinna Point, white tower Fl(2)WR 10s 62m W14M, R9M, R 319°–348°, W 348°–066°, R 066°– shore, AIS. Shows red over the dangers off Sheep's Head and Three Castle Head and white over the safe approach from seaward
Castletownbere Port Entry Light 023°, white hut, black stripe, Dir Oc WRG 5s 7m W15M R12M G12M, G 020·5°–023°, W 023°–023·5°, R 023·5°–027·5°. Shown 24h; daylight ranges W4M R2M G2M. AIS
Castletownbere No 1 buoy, SHM QG, close NW of Foilnaboe Rocks
Colt Rock, PHM perch, Fl(2) R 10s 7·5m 5M.
Castletownbere No 2 buoy, PHM QR
Walter Scott buoy, S Card Q(6) + L Fl 15s, AIS
Sheep Islands, N Card beacon, Q 3m 3M
Castletownbere No.4 beacon PHM Fl R 5s, off Frenchman's Point
Castletownbere No.3 beacon SHM Fl G 5s, close W of Dinish Island
Cametringane Spit, red col PHM, QR
Leading beacons 008°, white pillars, red stripe, Oc blue 3s 1M, front 4m, rear 7m
RNLI pontoon, 2FR vert

Dunboy Bay

Approaches to Pipers Sound, from the SW: the Pipers, L, Ardnakinna Point lighthouse, R

BANTRY BAY

AC1838, 1840, Imray C56 and Plan

Bantry Bay is accessible from seaward by day or night in any weather. Its south shore has no harbours until Bantry is reached, but the north side has some of the finest natural harbours in Ireland.

Western Entrance to Berehaven

51°37′N 9°55′·4W

AC1840, SC5623·7. See aerial photograph on page 118

Pipers Sound lies between Fair Head (45m) on the W and Ardnakinna Point on Bere Island. Inside Ardnakinna Point, the entrance narrows to 1·75 cables between Pipers Point on the W and Naglas Point on the E. **The Pipers**, which lie close to the S extremity of Pipers Point, are high, but give Pipers Point a berth of 1 cable to avoid a rock close E of them. The Port Entry Light at Castletownbere may then be identified. The narrow white sector 023° leads up the sound E of Harbour Rock and between the No 1 and No 2 buoys. The shore N and S of Fort Point, on the island side 7 cables NNE of Naglas Point, is foul for 0·5 cable off. Sheep Islands, 5 cables NE of Fort Point, are flat and grassy, and have foul ground extending for 1·5 cables W.

Dunboy Bay

⊕DY 51°38′N 9°55′·2W

AC1840, SC5623·7 and Plan

Dunboy Bay, on the W side of Pipers Sound, provides sheltered anchorage except in E winds. The bay is dominated by Dunboy House, which was built from 1886, burned down in 1921 and has been partly restored as an hotel but is closed at the time of writing; new apartments have been built behind it, also unoccupied. The ruins of the historic Dunboy Castle are not now discernible from seaward. A rock drying 1·5m lies one cable N of Dunboy Point. Approach the anchorage midway between Colt Rock perch and

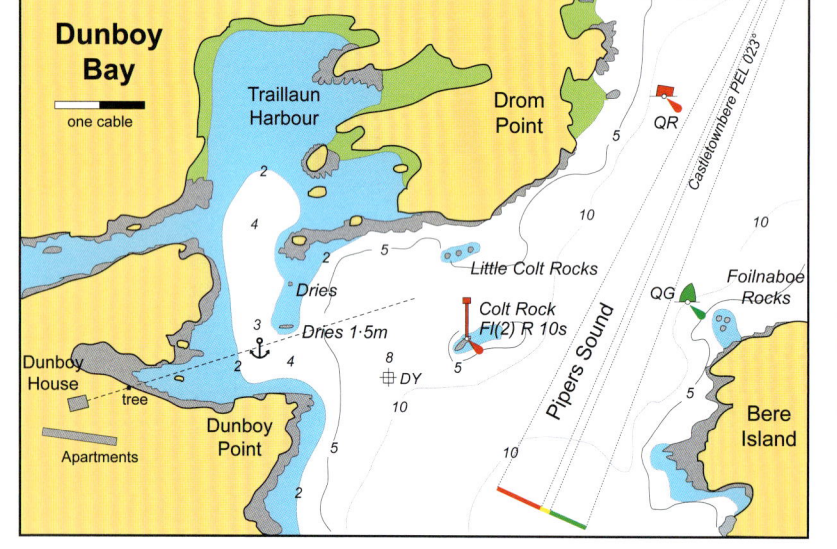

Dunboy anchorage from the NE; the restored Dunboy House, centre, with new apartment buildings behind. The front doorway of the house left of the solitary tree on the shoreline leads clear S of the drying rock, which was marked by the orange buoy, R, when this picture was taken in 2008

126

Castletownbere

Dunboy Point to avoid the drying rock and the foul ground extending 0·3 cable N from the point. The front doorway of Dunboy House left of a conspicuous solitary tree on the edge of the grass above the sea wall leads S of the rock (*see photograph*). Colt Rock should also be given a good berth all round. Anchor in 2m, NW of Dunboy Point.

There are oyster beds in Traillaun Harbour to the N of Dunboy Bay and in the SW corner of Dunboy Bay. Note that the horse topmark removed from the Colt Rock perch when it was lit in 2009 is now mounted on a red column above the E shore of Drom Point to the N. This is not a navigation mark.

Placename spellings

The charts and Ordnance Survey maps use the forms Bear Island, Bearhaven and Castletown Bearhaven. However the accepted and almost universal forms are Bere Island, Berehaven and Castletownbere.

CASTLETOWNBERE

⊕ *CT* 51°38'·7N 9°54'·5W
AC1840, SC5623·6, Imray C56 and Plan

As an important fishing port, Castletownbere offers some of the best marine technical services, and also the best and handiest supermarket, on the south-west coast. The harbour extends a welcome to yachts but has limited facilities dedicated to them. The leading marks for the harbour, unusually, show blue lights; this is to distinguish them from the background lights of the town and its traffic. The marks in line 008° lead through the entrance. The channel has a maintained depth of 6m and is 40m wide at the narrows at Came Point. The dredged area of the harbour has 8m for a width of 70m alongside the Dinish quays, and 4m on the town side. A car ferry runs from Castletownbere to a slip on Bere Island, inside the Sheep Islands and S of their beacon.

Anchorage and berthing

Priority must be given to fishing vessels, ferries and the lifeboat, but there is room to anchor and good holding in the harbour, and

Castletownbere from the SW: new entrance beacons No.3 and 4 have been built and the quays on Dinish Island have been extended since this picture was taken

Castletownbere from Pipers Sound; the PEL structure (white with black stripe), R, the No.2 port-hand buoy and No.3 and 4 beacons, L. Cametringane beacon and the inner leading marks, extreme L

127

Castletownbere

Castletownbere entrance; No.3 beacon, R, Cametringane Spit beacon, L, and the leading marks (white with red stripe), centre

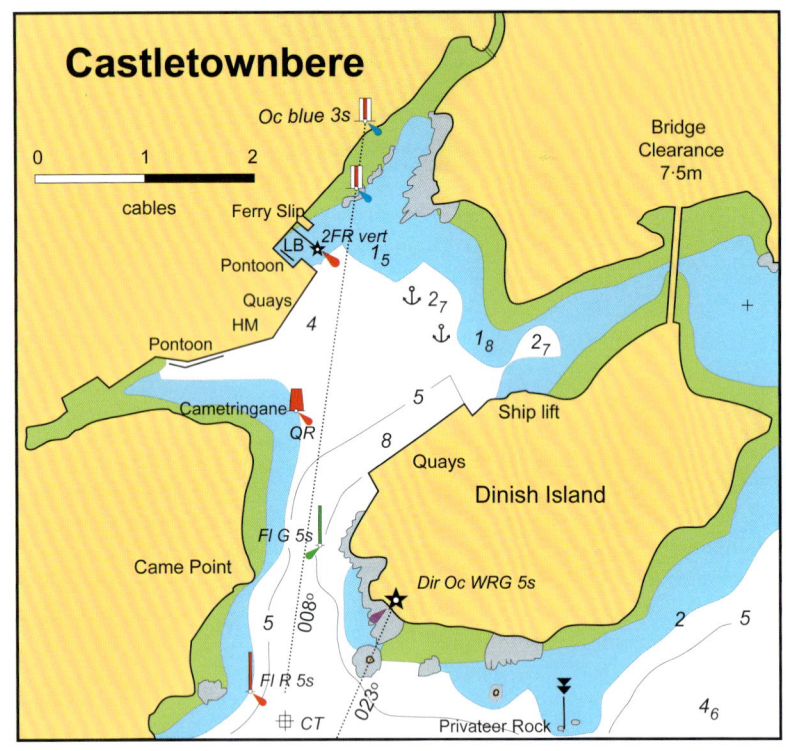

at least a temporary alongside berth can be made available for fuel, water and stores. Yachts should anchor clear of moorings, NE of a line between the ferry slip and the ship lift on Dinish Island, in 2·4m. There is an 80m pontoon at the W end of the Town Quay where yachts may berth, often rafted up to a fishing boat; contact the HM 027 70220, VHF Ch 16 and 14. The harbour limits extend beyond Castletownbere to include all of Berehaven from W and E entrances. The harbour is managed by the Department of Agriculture, Food and the Marine.

There are visitors' moorings in the bay to the E of Dinish Island (see below). The island is connected to the shore by a bridge with 7·5m clearance.

Facilities

Water on the pier, diesel by tanker. Diesel, petrol and gas at the filling station in the square, 100m from the quayside. Supermarket, shops, pubs, restaurants, hotels, PO. Bus to Bantry. Chandlery, Limar Marine, 027 70830; marine electronics,

Dinish in 2012 (photo Dept of Agriculture, Food and the Marine)

Castletownbere pontoon (photo DAFM)

Berehaven

Approaches to Castletownbere from the E: Privateer Rock perch (R), the PEL house and the No.3 beacon, centre, and the No.4 beacon, L

phone 027 70016. Marine engineers, Joe Tim O'Sullivan 027 70388, Berehaven Marine 027 70129.

BEREHAVEN

It is safe to pass in mid-channel between the Privateer Rock perch and the Walter Scott buoy; otherwise stay S of the buoy. The perch is a thin pole and carries a S topmark but is not painted as a cardinal mark. There are no dangers on the S side of Berehaven if the shore is given a berth of 1 cable. Pass N of the *Bardini Reefer* buoy or well to the S nearer the island shore; the wreck, a 4000-ton cargo ship which sank in 1982 after a fire on board, sits listing to starboard with her bows to the N and the remains of her upperworks, funnel and foremast conspicuous above HW. The isolated George Rock has over 7m of water and does not present a hazard to yachts.

There are fish cages off the Bere Island shore S of the Hornet Rock buoy and NE of the George buoy, N of Carrigavaddra and NW of Roancarrigbeg; and mussel rafts off the mainland shore outside Mill Cove and NW of the George buoy.

Castletownbere visitors' moorings

There are three visitors' moorings close W of Minane Island. These are best approached on 036° with Fort Point and Pipers Point in line astern, to avoid rocks off Dinish and to the SW of the buoys.

Mill Cove

51°39′N 9°51′·9W
AC1840, SC5623·7

Mill Cove, on the N side of Berehaven and to the N of Hornet Rock buoy, affords some shelter in N winds. Illaunboudane is a 1·5m high islet close to the E side of the entrance and there are rocks which dry 1·2 and 2·4m, 0·25 cable W and S of this. There is also a rock which dries 0·9m, 1 cable SW of Carrigagannive Point at the W side of the entrance. All the N part of the harbour dries out; anchor immediately inside the line of the E and W points of the entrance. There are oyster beds in the cove. There is a small stone pier at Sea Point E of Mill Cove.

Beal Lough is a small cove E of Sea Point which has a narrow entrance and a depth of 1·2m, soft mud bottom. A car ferry crosses from Pontoon Pier in Beal Lough to Lawrence Cove, and there is no room for a yacht to anchor. There is a sunken rock 0·5 cable SSW of the entrance.

Dangers
Berehaven

Privateer Rock, dries 1·5m, 1 cable S of Dinish Island
Volage Rock, 2·4m, 2 cables SE of Minane Island (5m high), 4 cables E of Dinish Island
Hornet Rock, 1·2m, 6 cables E of Minane Island
The **wreck** of the *Bardini Reefer*, 6 cables E of Hornet Rock
Palmer Rock, 1·8m, 1·5 cables offshore 3 cables NE of Turk Island at the entrance to Lawrence Cove.

Lights and Marks

Walter Scott buoy, S Card Q(6) + L Fl 15s
Privateer Rock perch, S Card, unlit
Hornet Rock buoy, S Card VQ(6) + L Fl 10s
Beal Lough beacon, G pillar SHM, Fl G 3s
Bardini Reefer buoy, N Card Q
George Rock, Isolated Danger Buoy Fl(2) 10s.

The Bardini Reefer wreck and its N Card buoy

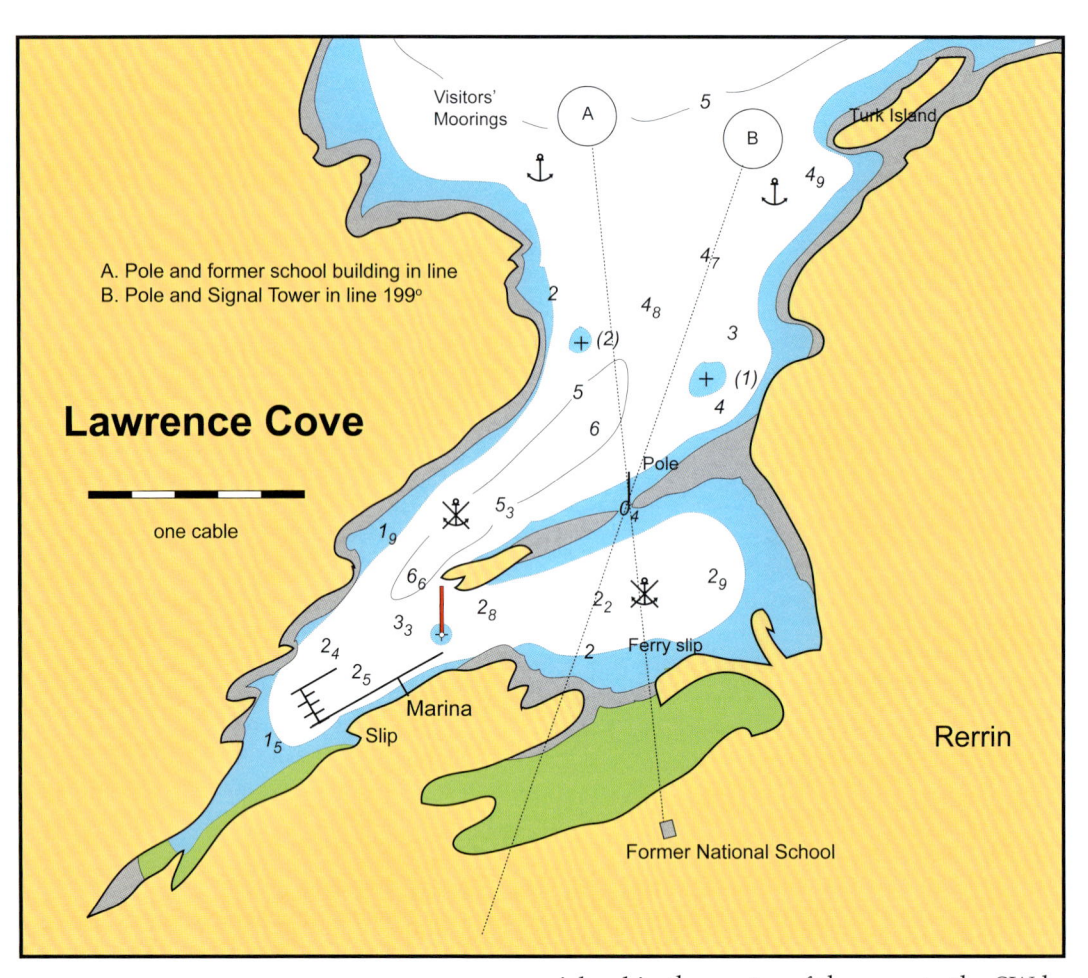

Lawrence Cove

A. Pole and former school building in line
B. Pole and Signal Tower in line 199°

Lawrence Cove

one cable

Tides
Lawrence Cove

Constant
-0035 Cobh
MHWS 3·2m,
MHWN 2·6m,
MLWN 1·2m,
MLWS 0·4m

Entering Lawrence Cove, with the pole marking the gap in the reef (centre) midway between the former school (the two-storey grey building, extreme L) and the ruined tower on the hilltop, R

LAWRENCE COVE

51°38'·4N 9°49'·3W
AC1840, SC5623·7 and Plan

Lawrence Cove (Lawrence's Cove on the chart), on the S side of Berehaven, is a good anchorage except in winds from a N'ly quarter, and has a small marina which is completely secure in all winds. From the W, the Bere Island shore is clean to within a cable; from the E, give the shore a berth of 2 cables to clear Palmer Rock and another rock N of Turk Island. Both these rocks have 1·8m at LAT. Turk Island is shown on the charts as 2m high but is actually about 6m.

SW of Turk Island the bay is narrowed by two rocks, one on the W side with 2m and one on the E side with less than 1m. The low island in the centre of the cove to the SW has the remains of a pier on its W end, and is joined to the E shore by a reef which almost entirely dries. The gap in the reef, with 0·4m at LAT, is marked by a slim pole. The ferry uses this passage near HW but at other times passes between the island and the marina.

Enter the cove in mid-channel between Turk Island and the W shore. If the pole beacon on the reef can be identified, keeping it between the two-storey former school building and the ruined tower on the hilltop to the SW clears the dangers in the approach *(see photographs)*. Note that this is not the Martello tower marked on the charts - from the close approach, the Martello tower is behind the skyline.

130

Lawrence Cove

Lawrence Cove Marina: note the red perch marking the rock off the NE pontoon

Marina

Lawrence Cove Marina occupies the SW corner of the cove. The marina has a least depth of 2·3m alongside. A rock with 1·5m, near the NE end of the long pontoon, is marked by a red pillar; there is 2·5m of water between the pontoon and the rock. Water and shore power on the pontoons. Slipway and 14t travelhoist, hardstanding for 20 boats; showers, toilets and laundry. Diesel. VHF Ch 16 & 37. Phone and fax 027 75044, mobile 087 912 5930, www.lawrencecovemarina.com.

Anchorage

Anchorage in the narrow part of the channel or in the pool SE of the island is not feasible due to the ferry and marina traffic. Anchor in 4 to 6m in the outer part of the cove (where there are also visitors' moorings) or in the bay S of Turk Island, staying well out of the fairway.

Facilities – Bere Island

Shop (also serving teas and snacks), PO and pub at Rerrin. Bere Island Boatyard, 027 75975, is on the Berehaven shore S of the *Bardini Reefer* wreck. Ferries from the NW end of the island (5·5 km by road) to Castletownbere and from Lawrence Cove to Pontoon Pier (4 km by road from Castletownbere). Restaurant at the NW ferry slip.

Lawrence Cove from the SW; the marina has been extended since this picture was taken

131

Eastern Entrance to Berehaven

Dangers
E and S of Bere Island

Carrigavaddra, rocks drying 2·7m, extending 5 cables ESE of Lonehort Point
Wrinkle Rock, dries 0·3m, between Lonehort Point and Carrigavaddra
Rock drying 0·6m, 0·5 cable S of Roancarrigmore
Sunken rocks extending 1·5 cables S of Roancarrigbeg
Wreck between Roancarrigmore and Roancarrigbeg
Doucallia Rock, dries 1·2m, 6 cables ENE of Roancarrigmore
Bulliga Ledge, 3·7m, 2·5 cables SE of Bulliga Point
Feagh Rock, 0·9m high, 4 cables S of the centre of Bere Island, with Greenane Rock (12m high) inshore of it.

Lights and Marks

Danger Zone buoys, three yellow Special Marks Fl Y 5s synchronised, within a mile E and SE of Lonehort Harbour
Carrigavaddra, S Card perch, unlit
Roancarrigmore, disused lighthouse, white tower, black band, unlit

Roancarrigmore, steel tower Fl WR 5s 7m, W11M R9M, W 312°–050°, R 050°–122°, R (unintens) 122°–207°, obscured 207°–246°, R 246°–312°. Reserve light W8M, R6M, obsc 140°–220°. Shows white to seaward S of Bere Island, red elsewhere. Obscured from the NE by the old lighthouse buildings. AIS.

Danger Zone

The yellow buoys S of Lonehort mark a Danger Zone arising from the military firing range at Leahern's Point on Bere Island. The approach to Lonehort (but not the harbour itself) lies within the Danger Zone. The range is used for small-arms training and the defined area reflects the risk of stray projectiles out to sea. A red flag is flown ashore when firing is in progress, and a lookout is kept from shore for vessels straying into the danger zone.

Carrigavaddra perch: Lonehort Point, beyond

Lonehort harbour from the S: the military firing range building on Leahern's Point, bottom R

EASTERN ENTRANCE to BEREHAVEN

51°38'·9N 9°45'·8W
AC1840, SC5623·7, Imray C56

Lonehort Point, the E end of Bere Island, is a long low point with a shelf of rock running out for a distance of 0·5 cable. There are the 2·7m-high remains of an old lighthouse on the point. The islets of Roancarrigmore and Roancarrigbeg are 1·3M to the ENE.

Directions - Eastern entrance to Berehaven

Give Carrigavaddra beacon a berth of a cable, and do not attempt to pass between it and Lonehort Point. Roancarrigbeg, 3 cables N of Roancarrigmore, is an irregular patch of rocks, 2 cables long and 1 cable wide. At HW it forms four flat-topped islets 6m high, with the conspicuous remains of a wreck on it. The channel between Roancarrigmore and Roancarrigbeg is fouled by rocks and a wreck, and is not navigable without local knowledge.

Carrigavaddra beacon is scheduled to be replaced by a lighted south cardinal buoy.

South side of Bere Island

Between Doonbeg Head (84m), the island's S point, and Cloonaghlin Head (2M E of it and with a Martello tower on its summit) lies **Feagh Rock** (0·9m high), S of Greenane Rock (12m high). As it lies 1 cable outside the direct line of the heads it is important to keep well out from and between Doonbeg and Cloonaghlin Heads, especially at night. There is an islet, Carrignanean, close S of Doonbeg Head.

Lonehort

⊕ *LH 51°38'·1N 9°47'·5W*
AC1840, SC5623·7 and Plan

This cove 7·5 cables SW of Lonehort Point offers splendid shelter in reasonable weather, but as there are no marks in the entrance it must be entered with caution. The line on the plan indicates the course to follow; the entrance is N of the conspicuous firing range structure on Leahern's Point. Carrigavaud, the rock in the entrance, dries about 1·2m. Its position when covered is often indicated by weed. The rock on the S side, which never covers, runs out below water at its E and W ends and extends as a half tide reef (drying 1·4m) about 30m N into the channel at its E end. Steer to pass 50m N of this rock to clear its half-tide portion. As the W end of this rock comes abeam and the small creek in the SW corner opens up, close the W shore to clear Carrigavaud before turning NW. Then keep the N shore close aboard. There is a least depth of 1·9m in the entrance.

Anchor in the centre of the pool at the NE end of the cove in about 3m.

Berehaven to Adrigole

East of Roancarrigmore and Roancarrigbeg the position of Doucallia Rock must be noted as it is in the direct approach to Adrigole, and on the course up Bantry Bay to Glengarriff. Bulliga Ledge, with 3·7m, 7 cables NNE of Doucallia and 3 cables offshore, should not trouble a yacht except in a heavy swell. To pass between Doucallia and Bulliga Ledge, bring Leahern's Point, S of Lonehort Harbour, just open S of Roancarrigmore bearing 238°. The centre of the entrance to Adrigole Harbour bearing due N leads E of Doucallia. In addition, Mehal Head just open S of Shot Head 077° leads between Bulliga Ledge and Doucallia, and a waypoint of 51°39'·15N 9°43'·7W gives Doucallia a berth of 2 cables on its SE side. Note that Roancarrig light is obscured from the approaches to Adrigole.

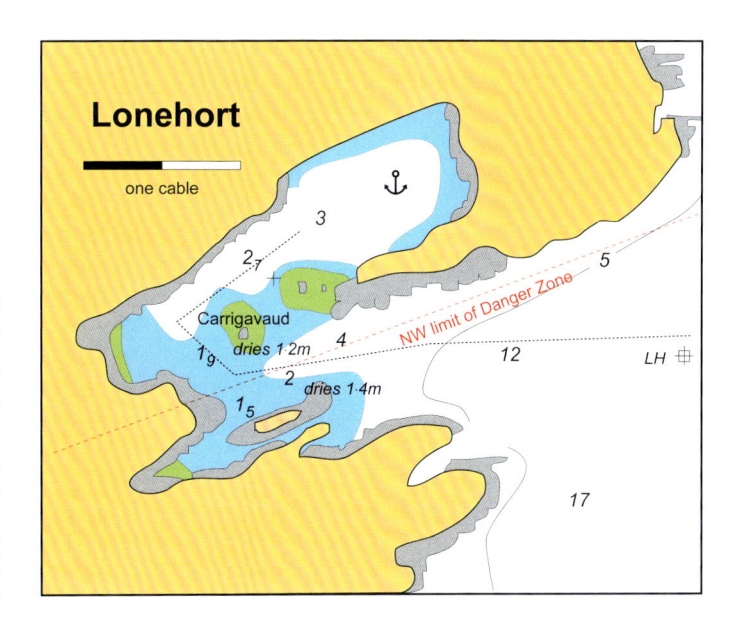

Approaching Lonehort: the entrance R centre

Roancarrigmore: lighthouses new and old

Entering Lonehort: Carrickavaud, R centre

133

Adrigole

Leahern's Point just open of Roancarrigmore leads between Doucallia Rock (breaking, L) and Bulliga Ledge

ADRIGOLE

⊕ *AD* 51°40'·3N 9°43'·1W
AC1840, SC5623·5, Imray C56 and Plan.

This is one of the most beautiful anchorages on the coast. The entrance NE of Bulliga Point is 2 cables wide and the harbour then opens out. Orthon's Island shelters the inner part of the harbour. There are mussel rafts on the W side of the entrance, which should be left to port. The passage between Orthon's Island and the W shore is obstructed by rocks. Enter on a mid-channel course and then steer to pass midway between the island and the E shore, giving the S end of the island a berth of 1·5 cables. There are rocks extending 1 cable off the N, W and S sides of the island. The innermost portion of the harbour near the N shore dries out.

Anchorage

Depending on wind direction, anchor in 4 to 5m, 0·5 cable NW of the pier on the E side, or 1·5 cables N of Orthon's Island in 4m, or (in strong W winds) closer to the W shore NW of the island. Holding good in soft mud. There are visitors' moorings NE of Orthon's

Adrigole

Adrigole

Adrigole

Island. In gales between W and N very heavy squalls come down from the high hills which surround the harbour. Pub at Drumlave, 800m from the pier; shop, pubs, restaurants, PO at Adrigole village at the head of the bay. West Cork Sailing Centre (027 60132 and VHF Ch 72), on the pier, offers dinghy and kayak rental and can supply diesel. Water at the pier. Buses to Bantry and Cork (Harringtons, 027 74003). The pier has a slipway on its S side.

Dangers
Adrigole to Glengarriff

Drying and below-water rocks extending 2 cables NE and 1 cable S from Sheelane Island

Carrigathowder Rock (dries 0·8m), 0·5 cable off the mainland shore NW of Sheelane Island

Rocks drying up to 3m within 2 cables E and NE of Garinish West

Coulagh Rocks (drying 1·4 to 1·7m), S of Coolieragh Harbour

Muccurragh Rock (dries 1·1m), 1 cable offshore, NE of Coolieragh Harbour

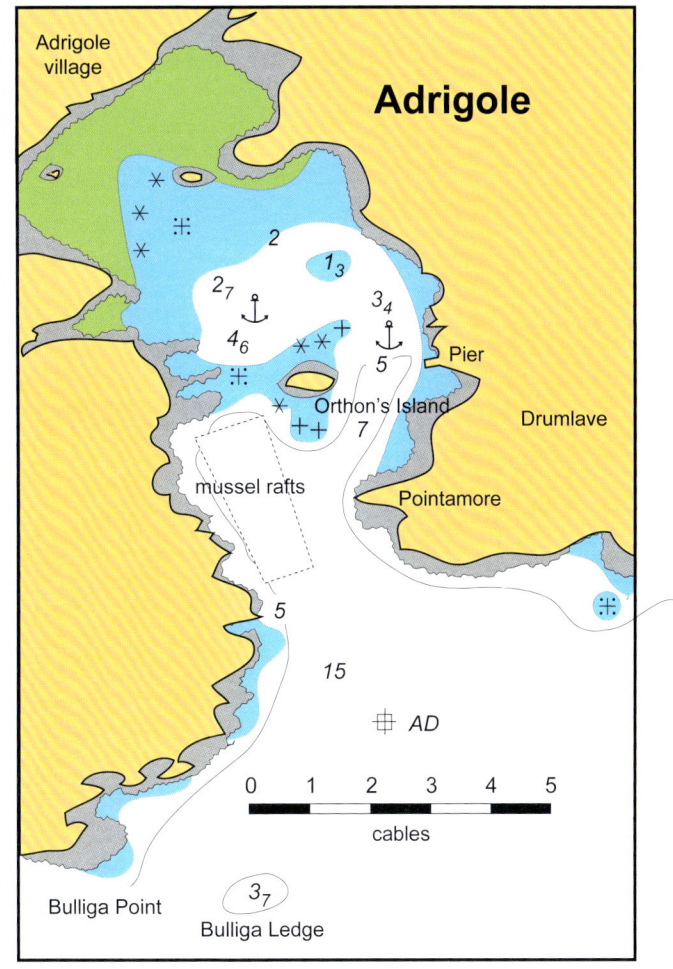

Lights and Marks

Sheelane South buoy, PHM Fl(2)R 6s, 2 cables S by W of Sheelane Island
Coulagh Rocks buoy, PHM Fl R 3s, 6 cables SSE of Muccurragh Point
Indigo North buoy, N Card Q, 3M SW of Whiddy Island
League buoy, SHM Fl(3) G 6s, 1·1M W of Whiddy Point West

Gerane North buoy, SHM Fl G 3s, 6 cables NW of Whiddy Point West
Tanker Mooring Buoy, Mo(U) 15s, AIS, between Four Heads Point and Whiddy Island.
Carrigskye buoy, Isolated Danger BRB Fl(2) 10s, 7 cables SW of Carrigskye Rock.
Glengarriff No 1 buoy, SHM L Fl G 4s
Glengarriff No 2 buoy, PHM L Fl R 4s
(these two synchronised)
The buoyage W and SW of Whiddy Island marks the limits of deep water (more than 25m) for very large tankers.

Adrigole to Glengarriff

Garinish West (L) and Sheelane (R) from the W

Approach to Garinish West anchorage from the SE: note the drying rock, centre

ADRIGOLE to GLENGARRIFF

AC1838, SC5623, Imray C56

The N shore of the upper bay is fringed by low cliffs, and the headlands are clean and steep-to. There are several attractive bays, and Glengarriff Harbour is considered by many to be the most beautiful anchorage in Ireland. Heading E from Adrigole, give the shore a berth of 2 cables to avoid a rock awash at LW, 1·5 cables offshore and nearly 5 cables E of the entrance, and the drying Corrigna Ledge, 3 cables further E. Leahill Jetty, 2·5M E of Shot Head, is a disused quarry jetty. There is a clear passage in mid-channel between Sheelane Island and the shore, but beware rocks on either hand and also the outermost of the Coulagh Rocks and Muccurragh Rock to the E. There are fish farms or mussel rafts at Coolieragh Harbour and on both sides of the entrance to Glengarriff. These are marked by lit yellow buoys, but the lights may not be entirely reliable. The large yellow Tanker Mooring Buoy 6 cables N of the oil jetty on Whiddy Island has a restricted area of radius 3 cables round it.

Trafrask Bay

51°40'·3N 9°40'·8W

This bay faces SW but nevertheless offers pleasant anchorage in settled conditions. Anchor in 3 to 6m in mid-channel, SW of the moorings. There is a single visitors' mooring.

Garinish West

51°41'·8N 9°35'·1W

There is good anchorage in the inlet N of Garinish West. The safest approach passes E of the rocks to the E of the island. Enter the cove steering 255° in mid-channel and anchor in 3 to 4m, mud, off the middle of the island. There is a small drying pier at the head of the cove, labelled Derreenacarrin Quay on the chart but locally known as Zetland Pier. A submarine power cable crosses the cove a cable NE of the pier.

Coolieragh Harbour

51°42'·2N 9°34'·7W

This is a feasible anchorage, with the Coulagh Rocks providing a measure of shelter in moderate SW'ly weather. From the SW, do not turn in until Muccurragh Point bears due N (long 9°34'·4W) to avoid the Coulagh Rocks, and stay E of the mussel rafts. The E side of the bay is foul for a distance of 1·5 cables offshore. Anchor in 5m at the head of the bay.

Glengarriff

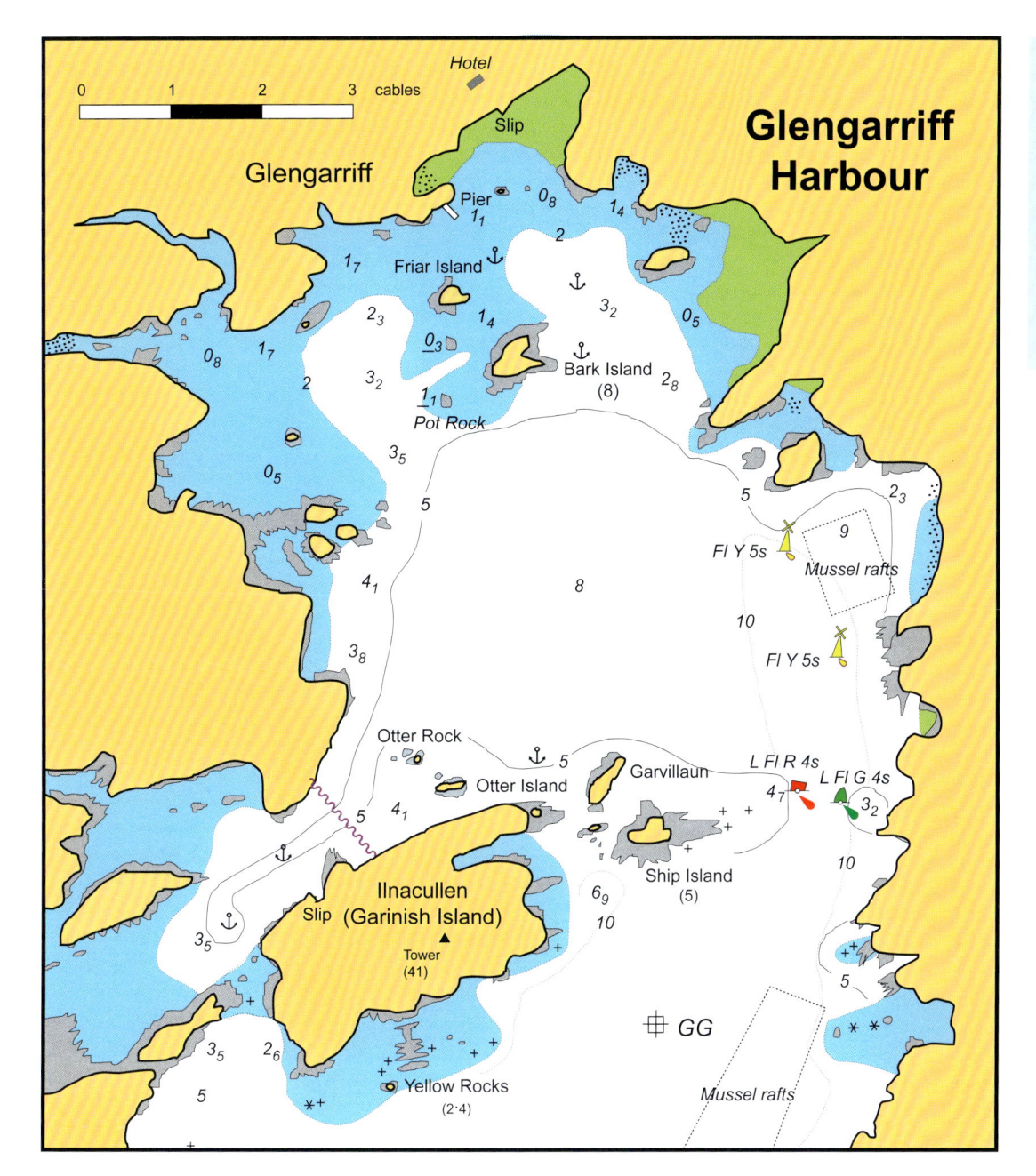

Tides
Glengarriff

Constant
−0044 Cobh
MHWS 3·4m,
MHWN 2·6m,
MLWN 1·1m,
MLWS 0·5m

GLENGARRIFF

⊕GG 51°44'·1N 9°32'·2W

AC1838, SC5623·4, Imray C56 and Plan

Glengarriff Harbour was the birthplace of the Irish Cruising Club, which was founded by 19 yachtsmen who met there on 13th July, 1929, aboard five cruising yachts. The harbour, sheltered by tree-clad islands, is one of the prettiest in Ireland. **From the SW**, after passing Four Heads Rocks, the entrance to the harbour is clear and course may be shaped to leave Gun Point to starboard. Ilnacullen (Garinish) is 41m high with a conspicuous Martello tower on its summit. Ship Island (5m high), which is close to the E side of Ilnacullen, is foul on its E side and should be given a berth of 1 cable. Pass between the port- and starboard-hand buoys, and then alter course for Bark Island (8m high). Do not go between Bark Island and Friar Island (to the NW) as there is a drying rock in mid-channel. Also beware **Pot Rock** (Pot Island on the older charts) which dries 1·1m, 0·5 cable WSW of Bark Island. Pot Rock may be unofficially marked by a buoy.

Anchorage

There is a delightful anchorage in perfect shelter in 3m, NE of Bark Island, or further NW closer to the pier. A tripping line is advised. There are visitors' moorings, also NE of Bark Island. Anchorage is also available anywhere S of Bark Island in 7 to 8m. Near Ilnacullen, anchor about 0·5 cable N of its

Glengarriff

Glengarriff from the SW: Ilnacullen R foreground with Garvillaun and Ship Island beyond; Bark and Friar Islands upper L

NE point, E of Otter Rock, in 4m; or NW or W of the slip on the island, taking cvare to stay well clear of the line of the underwater cable. The slip must not be obstructed. With sufficient rise of tide the slipway in front of the Eccles Hotel is suitable for trailer sailers. A dinghy may be left at the deep-water pier further W but check first if possible with the ferry crews.

Facilities

Water on the pier; shops, PO, pubs, restaurants, hotels, filling station. Buses to Bantry, Killarney and Cork.

Glengarriff from the SSE

Glengarriff to Bantry

Glengarriff anchorage: Friar Island, centre R

BANTRY

⊕BY 51°42'·4N 9°28'W
AC1838, SC5623·4, Imray C56 and Plan
Whiddy Island, 2·75M long, lies NE – SW in the SE corner of Bantry Bay, sheltering Bantry Harbour to the SE.

Directions – Glengarriff to Bantry

After passing Gun Point, steer 140° to clear Carrigskye (1·2m high) by 1 cable and pass 2 cables SW of Morneen Rocks. (Carrigskye BRB buoy, for the benefit of very large tankers, marks a rock with 21m, standing several metres above the prevailing 27 to 30m bottom, is not related to Carrigskye Rock and is of no particular significance to yachts.) After passing Carrigskye Rock steer for the East Battery (22m high) near the NE corner of Whiddy Island; this avoids Castle Breaker and Felaun Rocks. The islands in Bantry Harbour are generally foul all round and should be given a berth of a cable (1·5 cables E and W in the case of Horse Island), but the area around them is in any case almost entirely taken up with mussel rafts. The buoys lead in W of Gurteenroe Point.

Ardnagashel Bay

51°43'·5N 9°27'·5W
There is a pleasant anchorage at the head of this bay NE of Ardnamanagh Point. Most

Dangers
Whiddy Island and Bantry

Morneen Rocks (dry 1·1m), 7 cables SE of Gun Point
Castle Breaker (3·8m), SW of Ardnamanagh Point
Carrignagappul (dries 2m), 1M NE of Ardnamanagh Point
Carrignafeagh (dries 2·1m), 3 cables S of Whiddy Point East
Seliboon Rock (2·3m), 1 cable W of Bantry Town Pier
Black Rock (dries 0·3m), close inshore below Bantry House
The Beaches, bar with least depth 2m, S of Whiddy Island
Cracker Rock, (1·7m), 2 cables N of Relane Point
East, Middle and West Gerane Rocks, drying and above-water reefs extending 5 cables WSW of Whiddy Point West.
There are mussel rafts in Ardnagashel Bay (the inlet NE of Ardnamanagh Point), N and S of Gurteenroe Point, between Whiddy Point East and Horse Island and all round Chapel Island. These are marked by lit yellow buoys, but the lights may not be entirely reliable.

Lights and Marks

Tanker Mooring Buoy, Mo(U) 15s, AIS
Carrigskye buoy, Isolated Danger BRB Fl(2) 10s, 7 cables SW of Carrigskye Rock.
Horse Island buoy, SHM Fl G 6s
Gurteenroe buoy, PHM Fl R 3s
Chapel Island buoy, SHM Fl G 2s
Fundy buoy, SHM Fl(2) G 10s
Outfall buoy, yellow, Fl Y 5s, in the west entrance to Bantry Harbour
Whiddy Island W Clearing Light, white mast Oc 2s 22m 3M, vis 073°–106°
Whiddy Oil Terminal, 2×QY 10m 2M
Whiddy Point West, Y col Fl Y
Gerane West buoy, W Card Q(9) 15s

Carrigskye, L, and Whiddy Island, R: view from the NW

Bantry

Bantry Harbour from the E: Bantry Town Pier centre, Whiddy Island top R

of the bay is occupied by mussel rafts but there is a clear passage along both shores, which also leads clear of the drying rock Carrignagappul. Anchor in 3 to 6m, mud, E or W of the reef at the head of the inlet. Filling station, shop, pub and restaurant at Ballylickey, 1km.

West Entrance to Bantry Harbour

⊕ BW 51°40'·3N 9°30'·8W
AC1838, SC5623·4

The channel S of Whiddy Island is relatively shallow and the bar, with 2m least depth, may break in a heavy swell. The deepest water is between Cracker Rock (1·7m) and the S shore, where there is 4m. From a position 1·5 cables NW of Relane Point, identify the cliff of Reenbeg Point on the far side of Bantry Harbour, and bring it in line 063° with the HW mark of South Beach *(see photograph)*. There is 3·5m least depth on this line, E of Cracker Rock. Give North Beach a berth of at least 0·75 cable.

Anchorages

- 1·5 cables NNW of the Town Pier, soft mud. Stay more than 1 cable from the pier at Reenrour Point on the N side as it is foul. There is also room to the W of the Town Pier between it and Seliboon Rock.
- NW of Bantry House outside moorings in 3m, fair holding. Abbey Slip, close by, is suitable for launching trailer sailers.

Bantry

Bantry Harbour

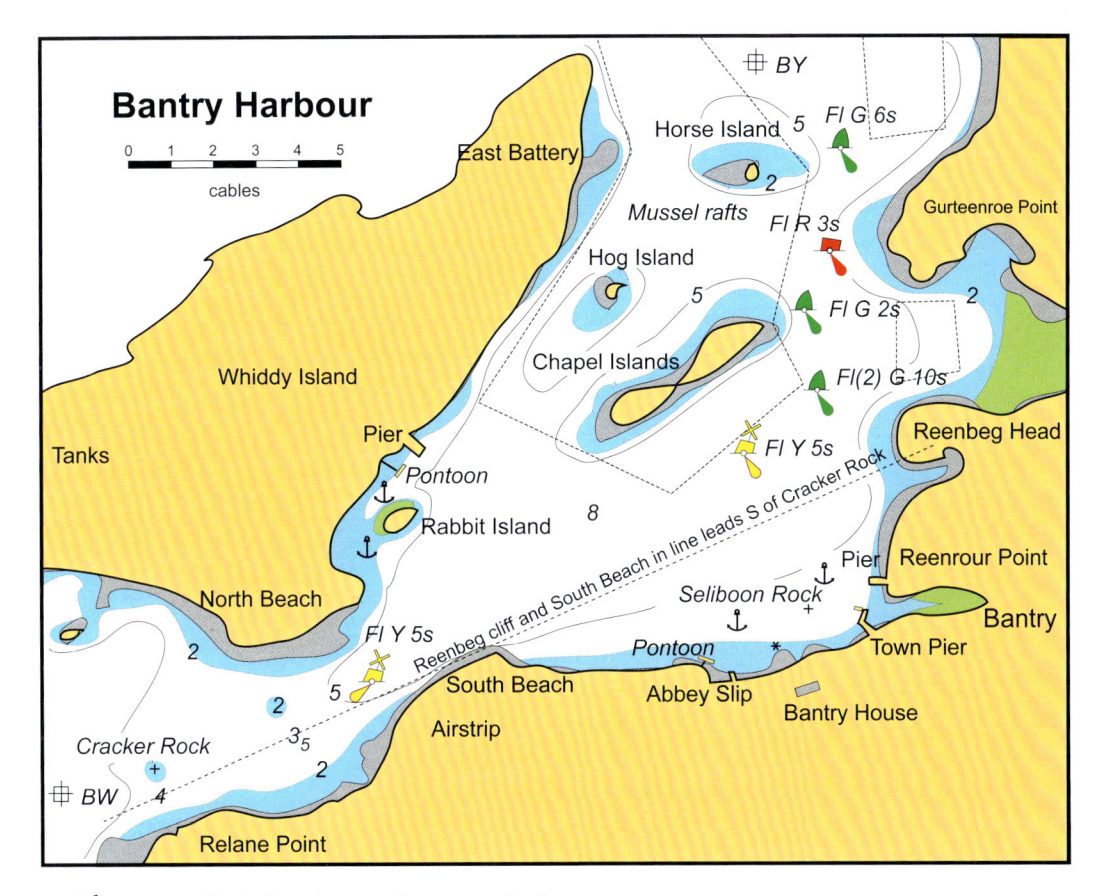

HW mark of South Beach in line with Reenbeg cliff leads S of Cracker Rock

- There are 8 visitors' moorings; contact the HM 027 53277 or VHF Ch 14.
- The pontoon W of Abbey Slip has 1·1m and is suitable for landing or temporary berthing.
- The Town Pier is not recommended as an overnight berth; the outer berth and steps must be kept clear for workboats, and the pontoon at the end is used by the tug and the Whiddy Island ferry. The inner part of the pier dries; however there is 2m at the second and third berth. The dredged area of the basin is narrow so keep close to the pier.

Facilities

Water, diesel from Town Pier, shops, PO, pubs, restaurants, hotels; laundrette at Bantry Photo. Bus services to Cork. Bantry Bay Sailing Club.

Bantry: the pontoon W of Abbey Slip

Bantry Town Pier

141

Coast Westward of Bere Island

The pontoon at Bantry Town Pier

Whiddy pontoon

Whiddy Island

Whiddy is a delightful and welcoming island. The 25m pontoon SW of its pier is used by the ferry but yachts are welcome to use it as an overnight berth; it has 2m at LAT. The end of the pier has 2·1m. Anchorage is available SW or NW of Rabbit Island in 1·5 to 4m, mud. This anchorage offers the best shelter in Bantry Harbour in W to NW winds.

Water on the pier. Pub with pub food, bicycle hire. Ferry to Bantry.

COAST WESTWARD of BERE ISLAND

AC1840

From Fair Head, at the W entrance to Berehaven, past Black Ball Head to Crow Head, there are no dangers.

Pulleen Harbour

51°36'·8N 9°58'·1W
AC1840

Pulleen Harbour, 1·5M W of Pipers Sound, is a narrow cove suitable for exploration only in settled weather. Beware of lobster pots. The outer anchorage is between the 4·6 and 8·2m soundings on AC1840, bottom weedy. There is a very restricted inner anchorage NE of the 4·6m sounding which can be entered by a yacht of modest draft after half flood, staying close to the W shore to avoid drying rocks in mid-channel. This inner pool has about 2m, clean bottom, but there is scarcely room for even a small yacht to swing safely to one anchor. It is sheltered except from due S and normally swell-free except near HW. It would be prudent to reconnoitre the inner anchorage by dinghy.

Black Ball Head

Black Ball Head is a bold, dark headland 81m high with an old watch tower on its summit. Off this head there is sometimes a tidal race with both streams but more particularly with the W-going stream opposed to the wind. There is a small cove on the W side of the head called Black Ball Harbour but the anchorage is unsafe and there is an above-water rock which narrows the entrance.

Crow Head

Crow Head, with Crow Island (62m high) and Leamascoil Rock (18m high) close to it, is bold and cliffbound. Two cables S of Crow Island is **Cat Rock** (dries 3·3m) which almost always shows or breaks. There is a clear passage between Cat Rock and Crow Island *(see photograph)*. **Bull's Forehead** (0·9m) lies

Pulleen Harbour: the inner pool near LW

Pipers Sound to Dursey Sound

Black Ball Head from the W: Bere Island beyond

Cat Rock (breaking, L), the Calf (L centre), Dursey island (R) and Crow Island (extreme R)

1·5 cables to the W of Crow Island, and is particularly dangerous since it frequently does not break. A berth of 3 cables will clear the dangers off Crow Island. From outside Cat Rock, a course towards Dursey Tower (250m) leads well clear of the Bull's Forehead.

The Calf (21m) and the Heifer (10m), almost a mile SW of Dursey Head. The cast-iron lighthouse on the Calf was built in 1866, strengthened in 1870 and swept away by a gale in 1881. Miraculously, the keepers survived. The light was replaced by a new tower on the Bull, three miles to the NW, in 1882. The stump on the Calf remains.

143

4 Dursey to Cahersiveen

Derrynane

The Kenmare River, like its neighbours to north and south, is a beautiful inlet with magnificent scenery and a character all of its own. It gives the enduring impression of being a great and well-kept secret. Although its shores are on well-trodden tourist routes – the Ring of Beara to the south and the Ring of Kerry to the north – and they have some of the finest anchorages in Ireland, the visiting yacht will often have a bay to herself. And as it happens, the two Rings are much better seen from the sea than from the land. Local usage is "Kenmare Bay", which is at least more logical, and consistent with the inlets to north and south – it is rumoured that the official name was insisted upon by a landowner of former times in order to extend his salmon fishing rights to the whole bay.

Derrynane Harbour, NW of Lamb's Head, is a splendid anchorage, and the nearby Derrynane House was the family home of the great 19th-century orator and reformer Daniel O'Connell. The house and gardens are open to the public.

Towering cliffs are the salient feature of the coast from here all the way to Dingle and Brandon Bay. Seven miles offshore are the Skelligs, not only breathtaking in their scenery but a UNESCO World Heritage site, and treasures in their bird life and antiquities. Valentia Island's coastguard radio station can trace its origins back to the earliest days of the transatlantic telegraph, and the island shelters an excellent natural harbour. The picturesque town of Cahersiveen, two miles up-river from Valentia Harbour, has a small marina.

> **"Cruising Ireland"**
> *This coast is described on pages 68 to 80 of*
> **Cruising Ireland**

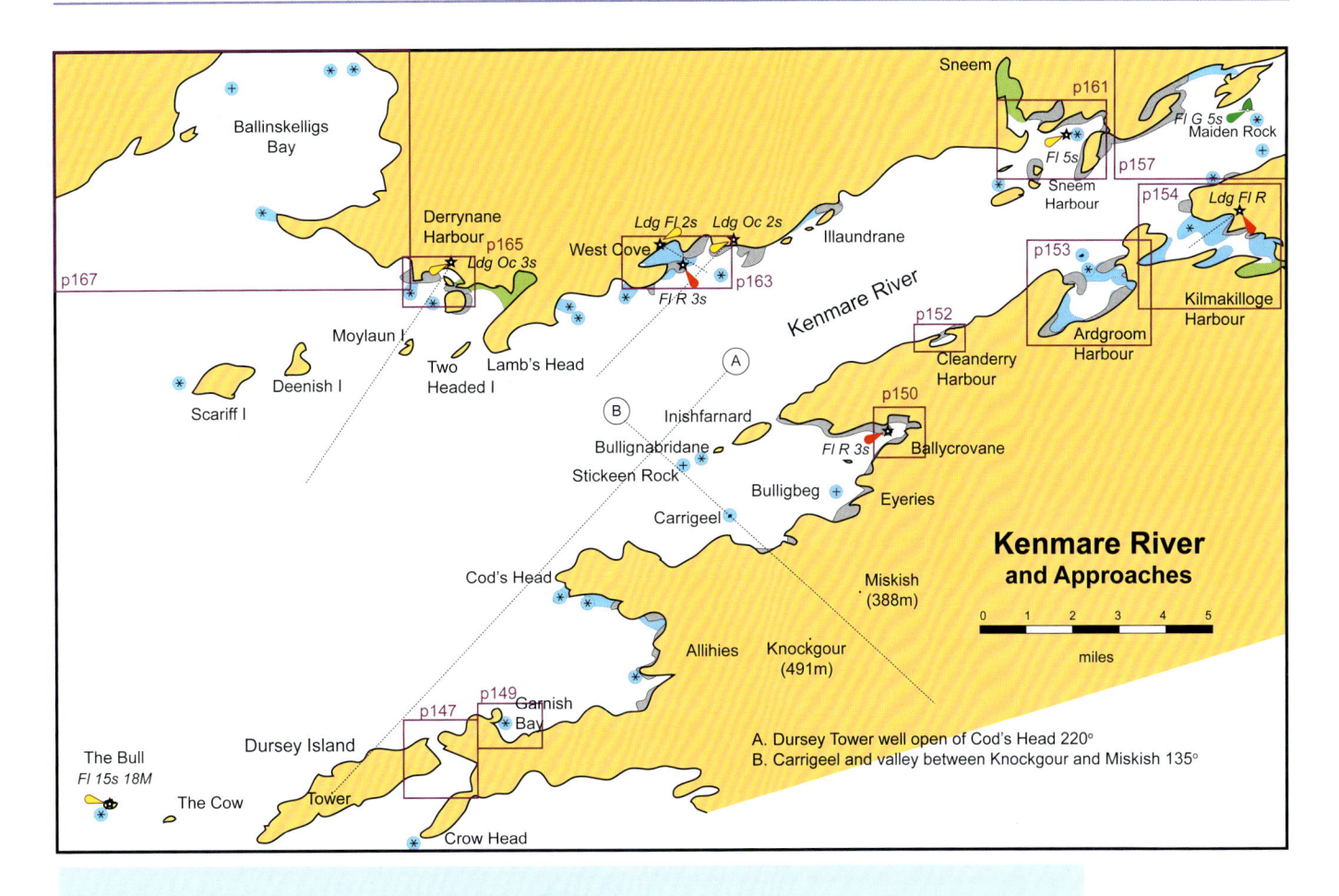

Kenmare River

A. Dursey Tower well open of Cod's Head 220°
B. Carrigeel and valley between Knockgour and Miskish 135°

Tides
Kenmare River and Approaches

Tidal Streams set fairly into and out of the Kenmare River. The ingoing stream makes at +0505 Cobh and the outgoing at –0120 Cobh. The spring rate is 0·5 to 0·8 kn in the outer bay, increasing to 1·5 kn in the inner bay with turbulence off Dinish and Dunkerron Islands on the ebb with strong W winds. Between Scariff and Dursey Islands the streams run N and S, running N on the flood. Between Dursey Head and The Bull the S-going stream makes at –0350 Cobh and the N-going at +0235 Cobh, spring rate about 3 kn. The streams run in the directions of the channels between the rocks, causing a turbulent sea and often a race near Gull Rock and S of the Cow.

Constant (West Cove) –0053 Cobh; MHWS 3·5m, MHWN 2·8m, MLWN 1·2m, MLWS 0·5m. The same data apply, to a good approximation, to Sneem, Ardgroom and Kilmakilloge.

Dangers
Dursey to Ballycrovane

Flag Rock, 0·3m, in Dursey Sound

Lea Rock (dries 3·4m), 1·5 cables SW of Dursey Head

Tholane Breaker (dries 0·3m), 1·5 cables offshore 5 cables S of Cod's Head

Bulligmore, 2·1m, midway between Carrigeel and Eyeries Island at the entrance to Ballycrovane

Bulligbeg, 0·6m, 3 cables NW of Eyeries Point

Stickeen Rock, 1·5m, 7 cables WSW of Inishfarnard

Bulligabridane (dries 1·2m), 4 cables ENE of Stickeen Rock

Lights and Marks

The Bull, white tower Fl 15s 91m 18M, Racon (N), AIS.

Carrigduff, grey concrete beacon, unlit, in Garnish Bay

Illaunnameanla, red square tower Fl R 3s, in Ballycrovane Bay.

Paper Charts

The general chart AC2423 Mizen Head to Valentia, and Imray's C56, cover the area of this chapter. The Imray chart has several useful harbour plans, but AC2495 Kenmare River, with five insets, is essential. AC2125 is the only Admiralty chart which shows any detail of Valentia Harbour.

Dursey Sound

Dursey Island from the E, with the Cow and the Bull beyond, and the Calf top L

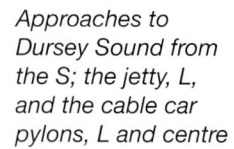

Approaches to Dursey Sound from the S; the jetty, L, and the cable car pylons, L and centre

KENMARE RIVER
AC2495, Imray C56

The inlet extends 28M ENE of the line of Scariff and Dursey Islands, at which point it is 7·5M wide. There are many unmarked hazards and the shores must, in general, be approached with caution, but there is no danger in a mid-channel course as far as Sneem and Kilmakilloge, the most popular anchorages, 16M from the entrance. The S shore up to Kilmakilloge Harbour is described first, followed by the upper bay and then the N shore.

Dursey Sound

⊕DY 51°36′N 10°09′W
Inset on AC2495, and Plan

Dursey Sound, between Dursey Island and the mainland, is 1 cable wide at the narrows, which are further constricted by **Flag Rock** (0·3m) in mid-channel. The tide runs strongly *(see panel)*. A cable car crosses the sound, with a clearance of 21m under the car itself and 25m under the cables. **From the S,** the narrows are difficult to discern until well into the bay, when the channel opens up to the NW. Having cleared the Bull's Forehead

146

Dursey Island

> **Tides**
> *Dursey Sound*
>
> In Dursey Sound the tide runs at 4 kn at springs, turning N at +0135 Cobh and S at -0450 Cobh, setting across Flag Rock and forming eddies and overfalls there. There are eddies on both sides of the S entrance during the S-going stream.

off Crow Head, steer for Illanebeg on the island shore. Look out for lobster pots SW of the entrance to the sound. Keep very close to the island shore going through the narrows, and if marginal in headroom take care not to pass while the cable car is crossing. There is usually a disturbed sea at the N entrance to the Sound, which could become dangerous in strong to gale force winds. The sea rebounds from the cliffs of **Glasfeactula Rock**, 9m high, at the E side of the N entrance. Be prepared for sudden changes in wind direction going through the sound, especially near the N entrance where heavy squalls from the high ground may be met. **From the N**, the approach is clear.

In fine weather it is possible to anchor off the jetty in Dursey Sound.

Dursey Island

Dursey Island is 3·5M long and its highest point, on which stands an old watch tower, is 250m high. On its N side are the highest cliffs in County Cork. Its shores are clear of danger except off Dursey Head, where **Cuckoo Rock** is close inshore but **Lea Rock**, which dries 3·4m, is 1·5 cables SW of the Head. The N side of the Bull open S of the Cow 300° leads S of Lea Rock; Scariff Island, 9M N, open of Mealbeg Point (2 cables NW of Dursey Head), bearing 003°, leads W of it.

Dursey Sound from the mainland

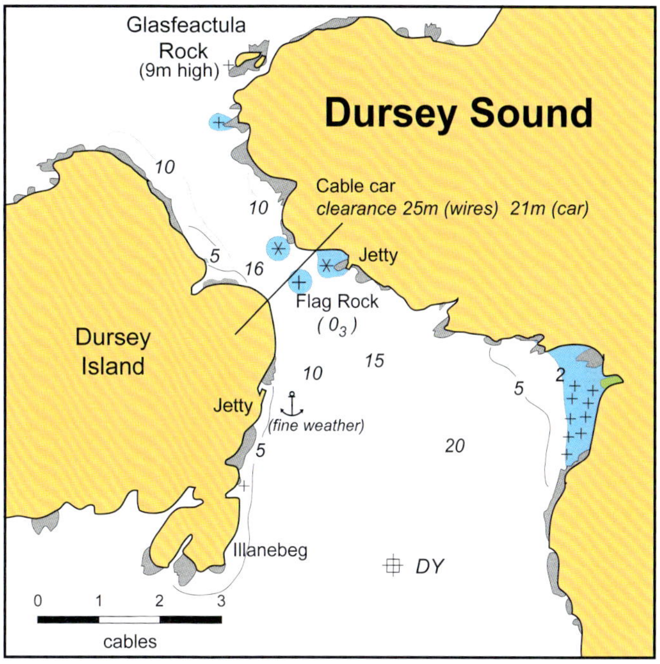

Dursey Sound: the island jetty at LW

Dursey Sound from the N

147

Dursey to Ardgroom

The Bull. The light is now shown from a small structure on the very summit and is visible through 360°

The Cow

The Bull, the Cow, the Calf and the Heifer

The Bull lies 2·5M WNW of Dursey Head and is 89m high. It is perforated SE–NW by an arched cavern through which breaking seas roll in bad weather. There are two detached rocks W of The Bull, one of which, the **Gull**, is 6m high. The Bull has an increasing gannet colony, which has claimed one of the two helicopter pads, forcing the lighthouse authority to depend solely on the other one.

The Cow lies between the Bull and Dursey Head, but slightly closer to the Bull, and is 62m high. It also has arched caverns. The Calf (21m high) and the Heifer (10m high) lie close together 7·5 cables SW of Dursey Head. There is often a considerable rebound of the waves in the channels between Dursey Island and the Cow and Calf.

Dursey Head to Ardgroom

The N side of Dursey Island is steep-to. Ballydonegan Bay, between Dursey Sound and Cod's Head, is entirely exposed and offers only limited shelter in Garnish Bay, *see below*. Beyond Cod's Head is Coulagh Bay, with Ballycrovane Harbour in its NE corner. **Carrigeel** (2·4m high) is 4 cables N of Rahis Point, on the S side of Coulagh Bay. **Bulligmore**, midway between Carrigeel and Eyeries Island at the entrance to Ballycrovane, breaks in a heavy swell. Between Bulligmore and the shore at Eyeries Point to the SE are several shallow patches, including **Bulligbeg** (0·6m). The N side of Coulagh Bay is formed by a series of islands and rocks which extend for 2M W from Kilcatherine Point. **Stickeen Rock**, the W'most of these, has 1·2m and may not break. **Bulligabridane** (dries 1·2m) is 4 cables ENE of Stickeen Rock. Dursey Island tower well open of Cod's Head, 220° leads N of it. Carrigeel, 2·4m high, in line with the bottom of the valley between Miskish and Knockgour Hills and bearing 135° just clears Stickeen to the W. In line with the summit of Knockgour, bearing 146°, it leads between Stickeen and Bulligabridane. In clear weather Miskish and Knockgour are easily recognised

148

Garnish and Ballydonegan Bays

Dursey tower and Cod's Head in line (R). Come a little further N to clear Stickeen Rock. Inishfarnard, L: the Bull just visible at extreme R

but Carrigeel can be hard to pick out against the land. Note that in a heavy sea the breakers extend W and N of Stickeen so give it a berth of at least 2 cables in these conditions.

Garnish Bay

⊕ *GB* 51°37'N 10°07'·3W
AC2495 and Plan

Garnish Bay is an open roadstead in the SW corner of Ballydonegan Bay. It can be used for anchorage only in settled weather and with the wind between SE and W. **Carrigduff** (dries 2m), marked by an unlit concrete beacon, divides the bay in two. There are two anchorages:

- W of the Carrigduff beacon. It is important to find an area clear of weed and the water is usually clear enough to allow this. There is the least swell in this anchorage and it is convenient for landing. The approach N of Carrigduff beacon is reportedly kept clear of pots; stay close to the shore of Long Island to the N when entering.
- 1 cable S of the beacon in 5 to 7m, sand. There is more room in this anchorage and the holding appears to be good.

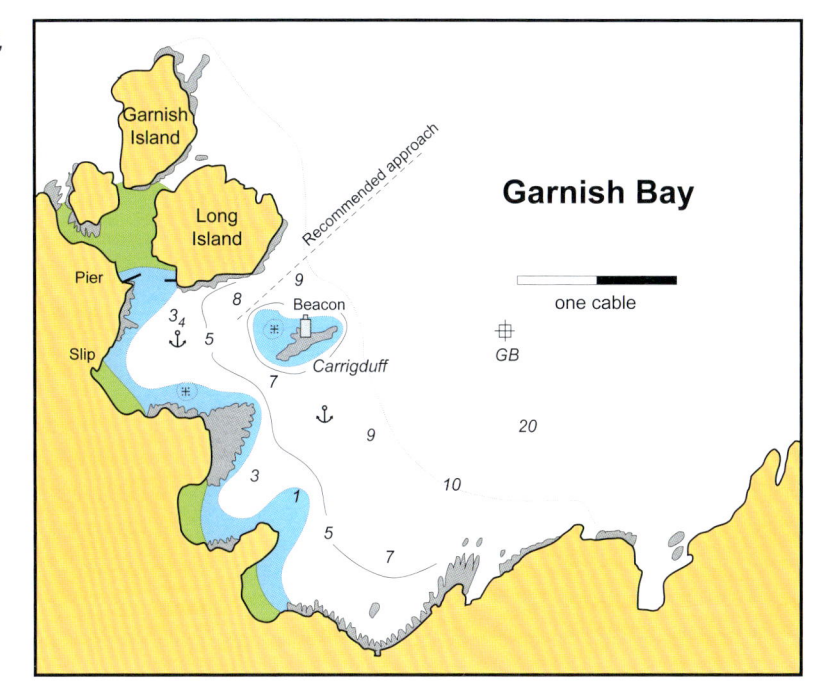

Ballydonegan Bay

51°37'·8N 10°04'·3W

In swell-free conditions this bay S of Cod's Head offers attractive temporary anchorage. Approach from the WSW and anchor off the beach in 3 to 5m. sand. Bird Rock, on the N side of the bay, does not cover as shown on the chart but stands 1·2m above HW.

Shops, pubs, PO at Allihies, 2km.

Garnish Bay from the NE; Garnish and Long Island R, Carrigduff beacon L centre

149

Ballycrovane

Garnish Bay from the E: Carrigduff beacon, R

Ballydonegan Bay from the W

Ballycrovane Pier

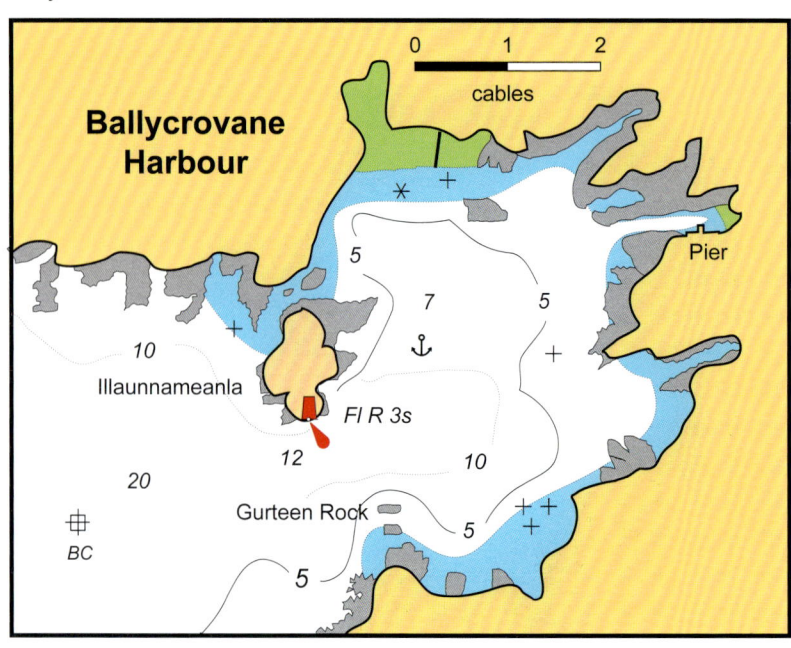

Ballycrovane Harbour

⊕BC 51°42'·6N 9°58'W
Inset on AC2495, and Plan

From the W and Cod's Head, steer 057° with The Bull just showing astern till the summit of Inishfarnard is abeam, then steer to pass midway between Eyeries Island and the mainland N of it. **From the E,** use the passage between Inishfarnard and Kilcatherine Point, which has a least depth of 7·8m in mid-channel. See above for clearing lines for Stickeen Rock. There is a fish farm close S of Inishfarnard.

Eyeries Island is 4m high and has rocks all round it for a distance of 1·5 cables. After passing it, identify Illaunnameanla, with its red pillar beacon, at the NW side of Ballycrovane Harbour. **Gurteen Rock** is 0·75 cable off the S shore and dries 3·4m. The N and E shores of the harbour are foul for over a cable.

Anchorage

One cable NE of Illaunnameanla in 4 to 5m, stiff mud. The bay is exposed to W winds and subject to swell after bad weather from that direction. Constant –0055 Cobh; MHWS 3·5m, MHWN 2·8m, MLWN 1·2m, MLWS 0·5m.

The inlet leading to the pier, in the NE corner of the bay, is much less obstructed than AC2495 would suggest. There is deep water for a width of 50m as far as the pier, and a depth of 2m at the end of the pier. A temporary alongside berth may be available. Shops and pubs at Eyeries, 3 km.

Cleanderry Harbour

51°45'N 9°56'W
AC2495 and Plan

Cleanderry Harbour is 3M NE from Kilcatherine Point. Its entrance is concealed behind the low-lying Illaunbweeheen, which is long and grass-covered. It can be identified by Shamrock Hill to the W and a big patch of scrubby trees on the hillside above it. The

Ballycrovane and Cleanderry

Ballycrovane from the E; Eyeries Island top, Illaunnameanla R centre and the pier in the inlet, bottom

entrance is only 7m wide at LW with low rocks on either side, and has a least depth of 2m. The pool inside has depths up to 13m, but it is heavily obstructed by mussel rafts and their associated plant and hardware. The W end of the harbour is exposed at HW when the rocks cover, and the best shelter is at the E end where there is space to anchor clear of a few moorings, but not much room to swing. Smooth water and a very careful, slow approach are essential. There are two drying reefs just inside the entrance and to port, and the course to the E end lies between them.

Entering Ballycrovane Harbour: Illaunnameanla beacon, L

Cleanderry Harbour from the E

151

Cleanderry and Ardgroom

Cleanderry Harbour (map)

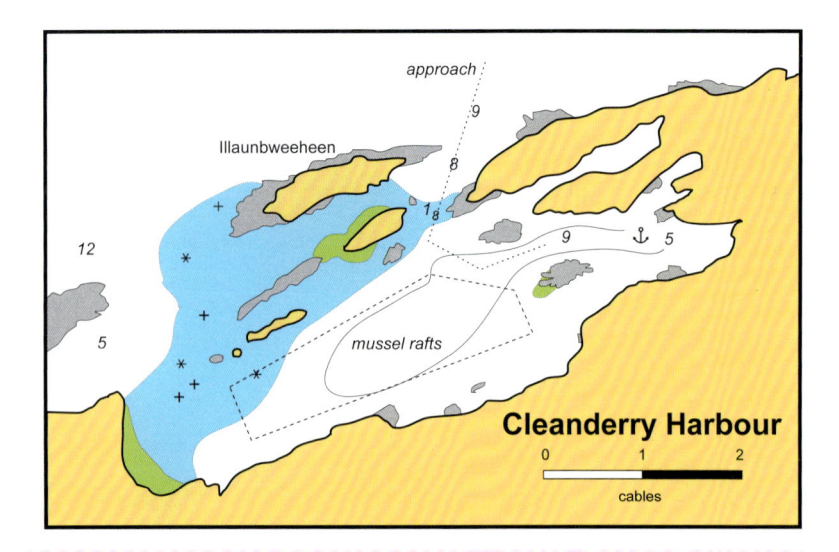

ARDGROOM HARBOUR

⊕ *AG* 51°46'·2N 9°53'·1W

Insets on AC2495 and Imray C56, and Plan

Ardgroom Harbour, on the S side opposite Sneem, offers excellent shelter but the entrance is narrow and intricate. **Kidney Rock** (0·5m high) is a cable offshore, 4 cables SW of Dog's Point. **Carravaniheen** (1m high), with submerged rocks extending NE and SW, lies N of the entrance, and 3 cables NE of Carravaniheen is a rock with 2·4m, which sometimes breaks. Across the mouth of the bay and protecting the harbour is a ridge of rocks and islets; the entrance channel lies in the centre of this ridge and has a rocky bar with least depth 2·4m. Unlit beacons, including two pairs of leading beacons, mark the channel.

Dangers
Ardgroom Harbour

The rocks are too numerous to list individually but the principal dangers are as follows:

Ship Rock (dries less than 0·5m), 4 cables E of Dog's Point and a cable NW of the bar
Halftide Rock (dries) 1·5 cables SW of Ship Rock, with a beacon on it
Skellig Rock, 1m high, 2·5 cables E of Ship Rock, with drying and sunken rocks extending a cable W and marking the NE side of the bar
Sko Rock (dries), 2 cables SW of Skellig Rock, marking the SW side of the bar
Unnamed rocks with 1·5 and 0·9m, 1·5 to 2·5 cables SE of the bar
Black Rock (dries 2·1m), 3·5 cables ESE of the bar
Yellow Rock (awash at HW), 2·5 cables E of Skellig Rock

There are mussel rafts between Dog's Point and Halftide Rock, and in the SW arm of the bay, S of Cus Island.

Lights and Marks

Halftide Rock, black beacon, unlit
Leading beacons, unlit stone pillars, first pair 099°–279° on Black Rock and the mainland to the E, second pair 206°–026° on Yellow Rock and the mainland to the NE.

Directions

Enter between Carravaniheen and Dog's Point, steering 155° for the beacon on Halftide Rock. Mussel rafts surround the beacon and extend a short distance to the NE. Skirt the rafts and identify the white pillar on Black Rock. A bearing of 099° on Black Rock, with the Halftide Rock beacon almost directly astern, leads across the bar and clear N of the 1·5m and 0·9m rocks. The rear beacon of this leading pair is difficult to distinguish; it looks out through a tunnel of trees and is visible only when very close to the line. Once across the bar, identify the second pair of leading marks to the NE. The front mark is the pillar on Yellow Rock and the rear mark is on the shore 1·5 cables beyond it. As soon as these

Ardgroom from the E; Dog's Point, top R, Cus Island, centre, Bird Island, lower L. Note the mussel rafts, L

152

Ardgroom

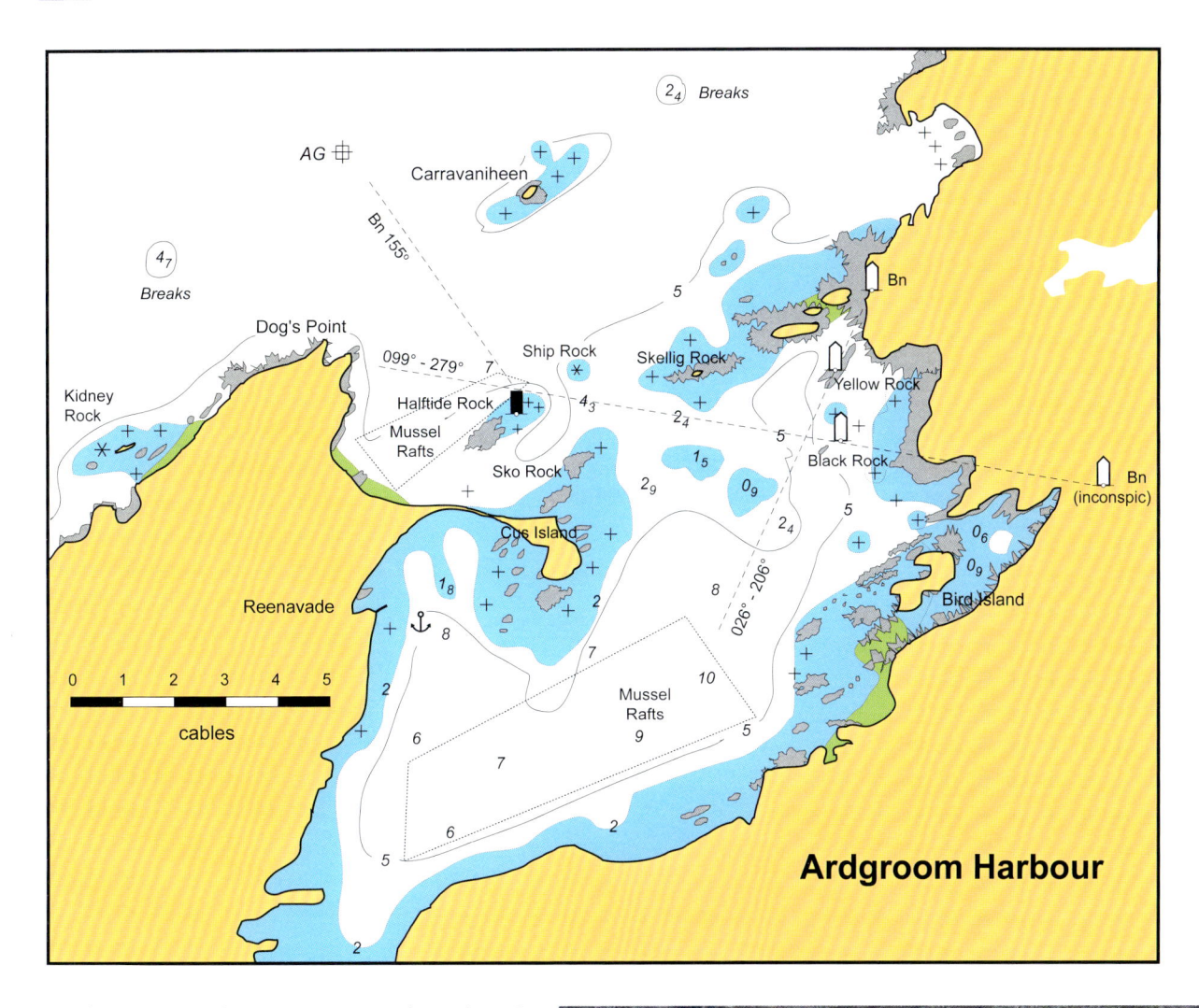

marks come in line, turn to starboard and steer 206° keeping the beacons in line astern. Skirt the mussel rafts on the S side of the bay and steer for the pier at Reenavade when it bears NW.

(right) The first pair of leading beacons at Ardgroom, the front one on Black Rock and the rear one among the trees, leading 099°/279°

(right) The second pair of leading beacons at Ardgroom, the front one on Yellow Rock, leading 206°/026°

(below) Halftide Rock beacon from the NW

Ardgroom and Kilmakilloge

Reenavade pier (L) and Ardgroom anchorage, from the SE

Anchorage – Ardgroom

Anchor 0·5 cable E of the pier at Reenavade in 4m, fair holding. Shop/PO/cafe and Internet access at Ardgroom village, 3 km by road, but the head of the inlet to the SW is accessible by dinghy and is only 500m from the village.

Dangers
Kilmakilloge Harbour

Most of the shore of the Harbour is foul to a distance of a cable off. The principal dangers are:
Book Rocks (dry 0·3m), extending 2·5 cables offshore, 4 cables S of Laughaun Point
Cuskeal (dries 0·3m), a rocky spit extending 3 cables offshore and forming the W side of Bunaw Harbour
Drying and below-water rocks extending 2 cables SW from Battle Point, S of Bunaw
Unnamed rock with 1·8m, 2·5 cables S of Battle Point
Carrigwee (dries 3·4m), 3 cables N of Doorus Point at the E end of the Harbour

KILMAKILLOGE HARBOUR

⊕ KM 51°47′N 9°50′·3W
Insets on AC2495 and Imray C56, and Plan

Kilmakilloge, including also Bunaw and Collorus Harbours, is one of the most attractive inlets on the coast, and offers access in all weathers, and excellent shelter. The entrance, between Collorus Point and Laughaun Point, is 1·5M NE of Ardgroom and 7·5M from Kilcatherine Point. There are fish farms and mussel rafts in the bay, but these do not impede access to the best anchorages and the pier at Bunaw.

Collorus Harbour

From the NW, Collorus Point should be given a berth of 1·5 cables. From the NE, give

Lights and Marks

Book Rocks buoy, PHM Fl(2) R 10s
Cuskeal buoy, PHM Fl R 5s
Bunaw, ldg lts, yellow poles, black bands, front Oc R 3s 9m, rear Iso R 2s 11m

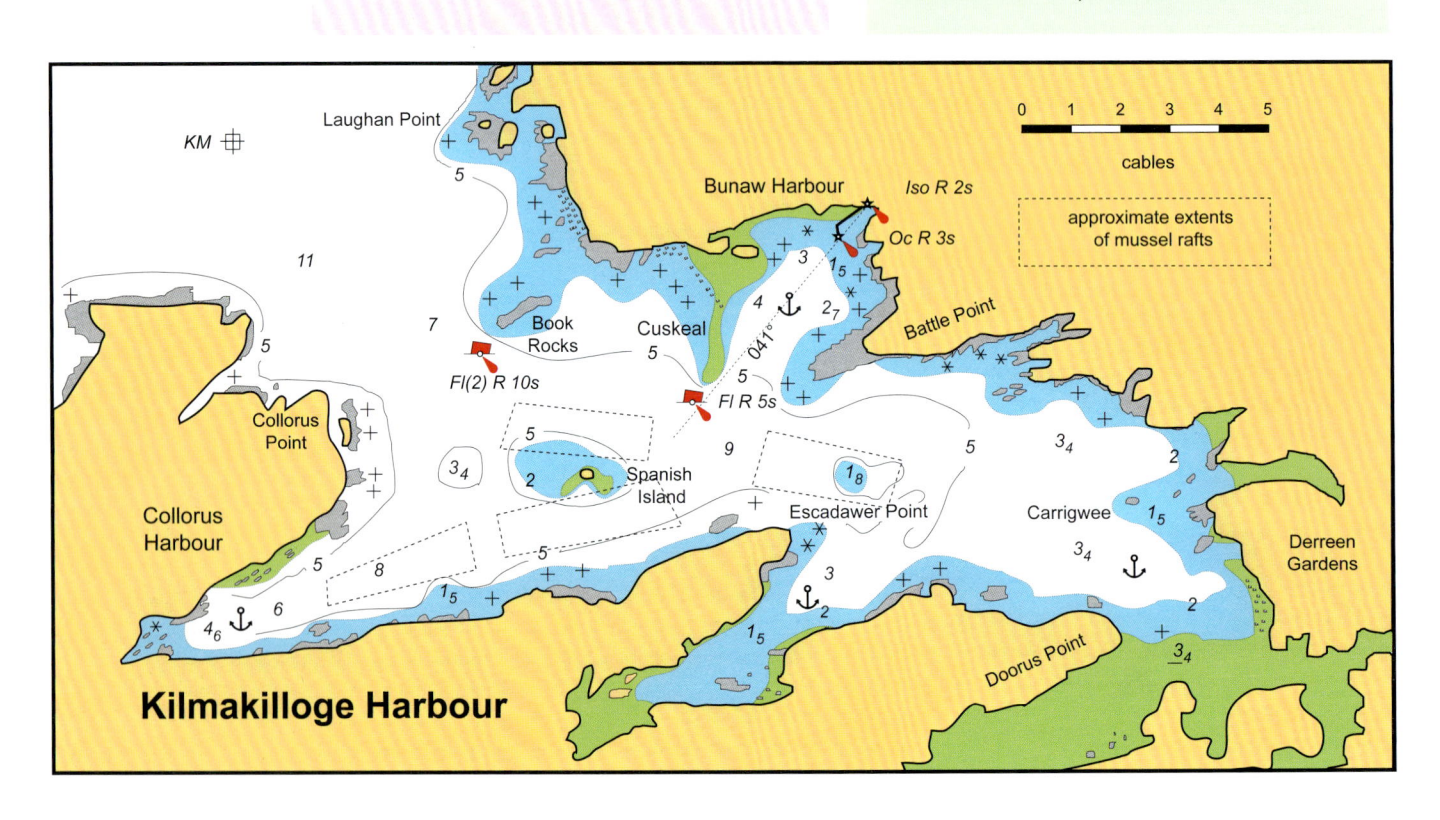

154

Kilmakilloge

(above) Kilmakilloge Harbour. from the SE; Escadawer Point centre with Doorus Point lower L and Collorus Point upper R. Note the mussel rafts

(right) Collorus Harbour

(below right) Bunaw Harbour and pier; note the fish cages, lower L, off Battle Point.

Laughaun Point a berth of 2 cables. Steer to pass midway between Collorus Point and Spanish Island (4·3m high). Identify Book Rocks buoy and leave it to port.

Bunaw

Leave Book Rocks and Cuskeal buoys to port, identify the Bunaw Pier leading marks and steer in on their line.

Kilmakilloge

Follow the directions for Bunaw as above but hold a course of 102° towards Derreen Woods to pass clear N of the mussel rafts, and the 1·8m rock 1·7 cables off Escadawer Point. Nearly 1 cable SE of Escadawer Point there is a small white perch which marks the extremity of a reef off the point.

Anchorage

- In the middle of Collorus Harbour in 5m, abreast a small disused boat slip on the S shore. The holding is rather soft and unreliable, with weed
- In Bunaw Harbour, NW of the leading line between the pier and Cuskeal in 3 to 4m. There is 0·4m alongside the pier, on

155

Kilmakilloge and the Upper Kenmare River

(top) Bunaw pier, with the front leading light, L

(above) Kilmakilloge

Carrignaronebeg from the SW

the village side, and 0·8m N of the steps, with a clean gravel bottom suitable for drying out alongside. The steps should be kept clear.
- 1 cable SW of Carrigwee in 3 to 4m.
- S of Escadawer Point in 1·5 to 3m, avoiding the perch mentioned above.

There is a convenient landing above half tide near a road bridge SE of Derreen. No facilities at Collorus Harbour; pub/restaurant at Bunaw; filling station, pub/restaurant and PO at Lauragh village, E of Derreen. Derreen gardens are open to the public.

Constant (approx) –0053 Cobh; MHWS 3·5m, MHWN 2·8m, MLWN 1·2m, MLWS 0·5m.

UPPER KENMARE RIVER

AC2495

The N shore is clean for 5M above Coongar Harbour, opposite and N of Kilmakilloge, but the S side is foul up to 2 cables offshore, and there are several hazards in mid channel.

Directions

A course of 066° from Maiden Rock buoy leads clear of all dangers to the mouth of Dunkerron Harbour. The narrows N of Brennel Island is 3 cables wide, marked by Carrignaronebeg perch and buoy to the N and Bat Rock buoy to the S.

Coongar Harbour

51°48'·7N 9°49'W

Coongar Harbour, on the N shore, provides sheltered anchorage in winds between W and SE. Its shores are foul all round and there is no convenient landing. Give the shore of Rossmore Island, to the E, a berth of 2 cables on entering, and anchor in 3·5 to 9m towards the head of the bay.

Lehid Harbour

51°48'·2N 9°47'·2W

Lehid Harbour, on the S side opposite Rossmore Island, should be approached from the W, leaving Church Rocks to port. It has an extremely narrow entrance between rocky ledges on either side, and is accessible only by the smallest yachts in settled weather. Preliminary reconnaisance by dinghy is strongly recommended. There is anchorage in the centre of the harbour in 3m.

Ormond's Harbour

51°49'·3N 9°45'·8W

Ormond's Harbour is sheltered by Ormond's Island (10m) on its N side and by Hog Island (3·3m) on its SW side. Ormond's Island has rocks extending 1·5 cables W and 0·5 cable

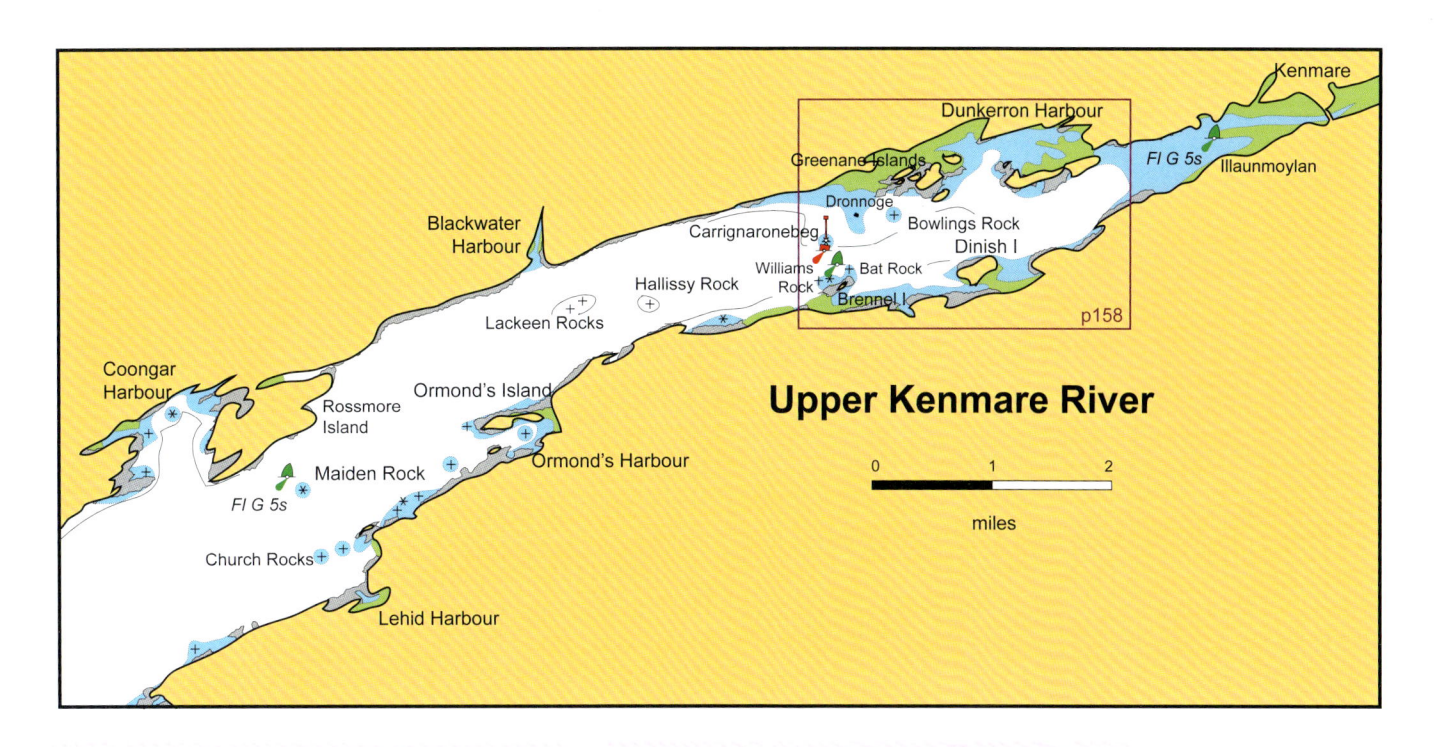

Upper Kenmare River

Dangers
Upper Kenmare River

The following are the principal dangers in the fairway.

Church Rocks, 1·4m, 5 cables NW of Lehid Harbour

Maiden Rock (dries 0·5m), in mid-channel S of the summit of Rossmore Island

Unnamed rock with 1·4m, 4 cables WSW of Ormond's Island

Lackeen Rocks, 2·4m, and **Hallissy Rock**, 3·4m, in mid-channel NE of Ormond's Island

Carrignaronebeg (dries 2·6m) in mid-channel 3M ENE of Ormond's Island, with foul ground extending ENE to the Greenane Islands, and including the above-water heads of **Carrignaronemore** and **Dronnoge**

Bowling's Rock, 0·8m, 3 cables E of Dronnoge

Brennel Island (3m high), 6 cables S of Dronnoge, with drying and submerged rocks extending 2 cables to the NE, NW and SW.

Lights and Marks

Maiden Rock buoy, SHM Fl G 5s, AIS, 3 cables NW of the rock

Carrignaronebeg, PHM perch, unlit

Carrignaronebeg buoy, PHM Fl R 5s

Bat Rock buoy, SHM Fl G 5s, N of Brennel Island

Illaunmoylan buoy, SHM Fl G 5s, in the approaches to Kenmare Quay

Blackwater Harbour

Ormond's Harbour to Dunkerron Harbour

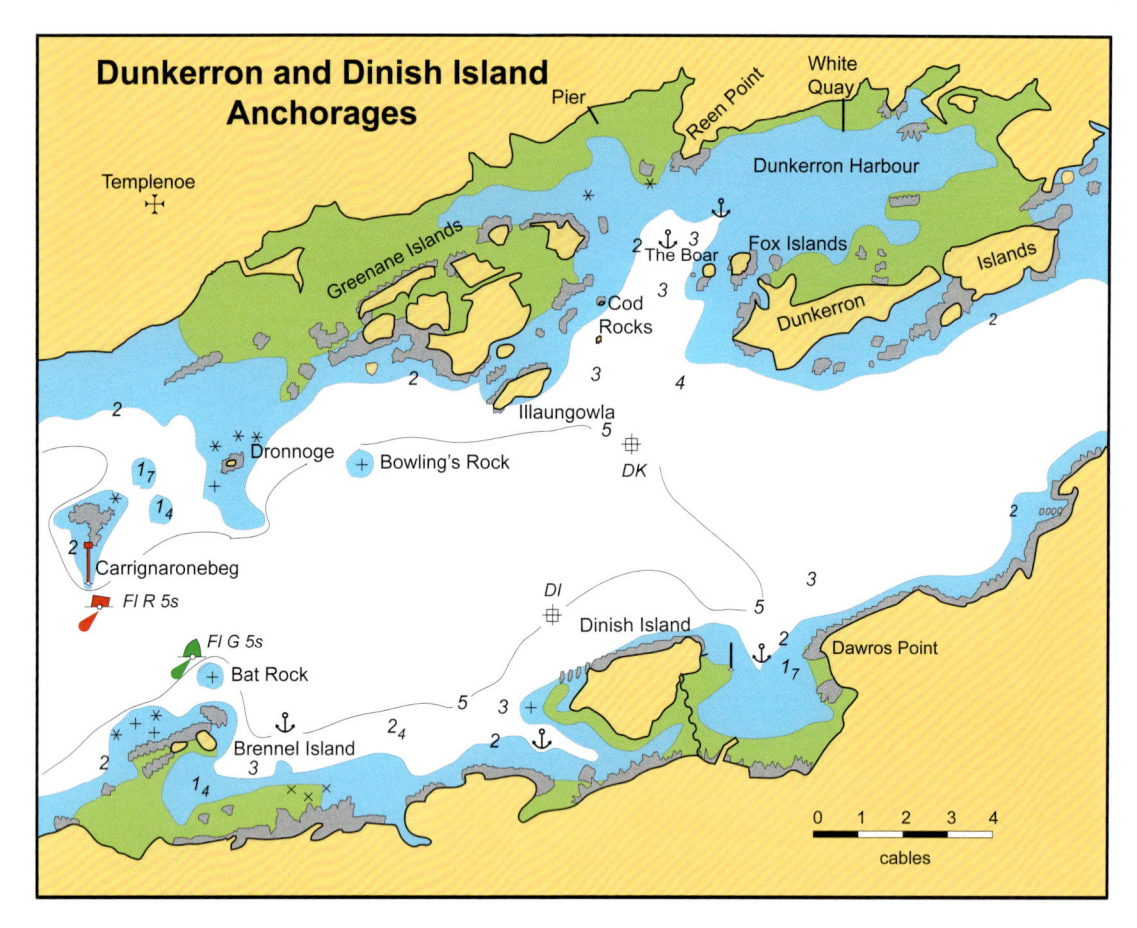

N and S. The bar between it and the E shore dries 2·8m. There is foul ground between Hog Island and the shore. The entrance is 1 cable wide, and has a least depth of 2·3m over a rock in mid-channel. There is a rock awash at LW just NE of the centre of the harbour. Enter in mid-channel and anchor E of Hog Island in 5m, mud. No facilities.

Blackwater Harbour

51°50'·7N 9°44'·6W

Blackwater Harbour is a very pretty river mouth on the N shore 2·6M NE of the Maiden Rock buoy. There is a stone pier on the W side with 1·2m at the end, sand bottom. The channel beyond the pier is shallow with no room to swing and many small-boat moorings. Anchor just outside the point S of the pier in 3·5 to 7m, where there is good shelter in W winds.

Dinish Island

⊕ DI 51°51'N 9°39'·8W

Anchorage is available E or SW of Dinish Island, as appropriate for shelter. Beware of rocks on either side of the approach to the SW anchorage. The E anchorage is in 2m, midway between the quay on the E of the island and Dawros Point to the E. The spit on the E end of the island is marked by a black-and-white banded pole. There is a new pier in this bay which is the base of a watersports centre, but the pier is not available as an alongside berth and the depth is limited. Pub/restaurant on the mainland.

Dunkerron Harbour

⊕ DK 51°51'·4N 9°39'·4W

Dunkerron Harbour, 2M from Kenmare on the N side of the bay, is a very pretty harbour and offers good shelter, particularly for a shallow-draft yacht. The entrance is between Illaungowla on the W and Dunkerron Island on the E. **Cod Rocks** (2·4m and 3m high) on the W side have foul ground on their NW sides. The Fox Islands (4·9m high) on the E side have a reef extending 1 cable W terminating in the **Boar**. Enter close E of the Cod Rocks or leave Dunkerron Island West and the Boar 1·5 cables to starboard. There is a dredged channel leading S into deep water from the pier (known as the White Quay) 4 cables E of Reen Point; the channel follows the projection of the E side of the pier. This channel is narrow and should be attempted only above half tide.

Dunkerron to Kenmare Quay

Dunkerron Harbour: White Quay, R

Anchorages

- Between Cod Rock and the Boar in 2·5 to 3·5m.
- Midway between Reen Point on the N shore and the Fox Islands in 1·8m.
- An alongside berth in 1·8m is available on the W side of a pontoon moored E of the pier and at the end of the dredged channel. The pier is in the grounds of Dromquinna Manor Hotel.
- There are visitors' moorings, provided by the hotel.

Constant –0052 Cobh; MHWS 3·9m, MHWN 3·0m, MLWN 1·4m, MLWS 0·5m.

Facilities

Water on the pontoon, hotel facilities including showers. Pub and PO at Templenoe village, 1·5 km W.

Kenmare Quay

51°52'·3N 9°35'·3W

Kenmare Quay, 1 km from the town, may be reached at HW but it is not recommended for drying out. The bottom is mud. Anchorage is possible SE of the quay although depths are restricted. Dunkerron Harbour, although further from the town, may be a more attractive base from which to visit Kenmare. Shops, PO, pubs, restaurants, hotels, filling station in Kenmare.

Kenmare Quay

Sneem

Sneem Harbour; Oysterbed Pier centre, Illaunsleagh R, Garinish anchorage L and Sneem village top R

KENMARE RIVER, NORTH SHORE - SNEEM to DERRYNANE

AC2495

The SE sides of Rossmore, Rossdohan and Sherky Islands are clean and steep-to, and a berth of 3 cables clears all dangers on the direct course of 250° from S of Sherky Island to Lamb's Head. W of Lamb's Head are Two Headed Island, Moylaun, Deenish and Scariff, with deep channels between each one. The beautiful and secure natural harbour of Derrynane lies 3M N of Two Headed Island.

Sneem

⊕SN 51°47'·8N 9°52'·8W

Insets on AC2495 and Imray C56, and Plan

Sneem Harbour is entered between Sherky Island to the SW and Rossdohan Island to the NE. There are drying and sunken rocks up to 2 cables SW of Rossdohan, but the W side of the entrance is clean. **From the S**, steer due N midway between the islands until the channel NW of Inishkeragh opens up to the SW, and identify the channel ahead to the N between Garinish on the port hand and Illaunslea on the starboard. Leave the two Special Mark beacons to port. Rocks extend 1·5 cables SW of Illaunslea. To avoid them stay 0·5 cable off the NE point of Garinish while steering NW. As the inlet on the N side of Garinish opens up, identify Oysterbed Pier in the NW corner of the anchorage. **From the W**, identify Inishkeelaghmore, 4 cables NW of Sherky, and shape a course one-quarter of the channel's width SE of Inishkeelaghmore to avoid the Cottoner Rock. A mid-channel course from there between the little Potato Island and Inishkeragh leads NE to the anchorages.

Constant (approx) –0053 Cobh; MHWS 3·5m, MHWN 2·8m, MLWN 1·2m, MLWS 0·5m.

Sneem

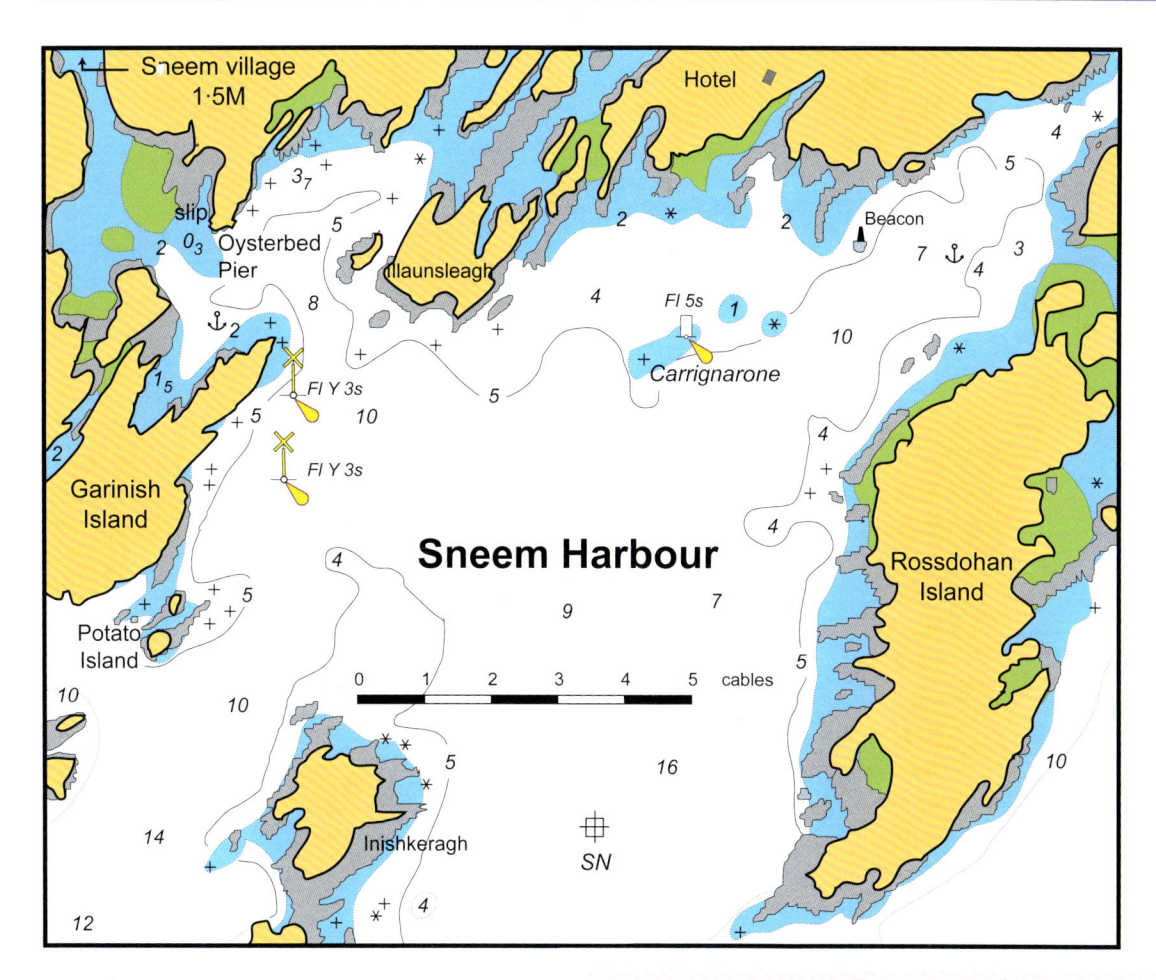

Anchorage

Anchor in the mouth of the N bay on Garinish, 3m, or to the SE of Oysterbed Pier, 5m. Good holding in mud. The N bay on Garinish is well occupied with moorings, and is a thriving seal colony. Visitors' moorings.

Anchorage is also available N of Rossdohan Island in 7m. Give the shore of the island a berth of 2 cables all the way round. Carrignarone (dries 3m) is marked by a lighted beacon, and there is a rock awash at LW, 1·5 cables E of it.

Pier

Oysterbed Pier has 3m at LAT on its front face. Approach at a sharp angle to clear the shore on either side. There is a slip suitable for trailer sailers on the W side of the same promontory.

River channel to Sneem

The river is navigable with care by dinghy four hours either side of HW as far as Sneem Quay, 1·5M from Oysterbed Pier. Submerged rocks in the river are usually indicated by patches of weed. The village of Sneem is 500m from the quay.

Dangers
Sneem to Derrynane

Cottoner Rock (dries 0·6m), off Sherky Island
Carrigheela (dries 2·9m), 5 cables SW of Daniel's Island and 4M ENE of Lamb Head
Beara Rocks (3m high), 3 cables offshore SW of a sharp peak (Knocknasullig) 116m high, at the W side of West Cove
Brigbeg (dries 0·3m), 3 cables E of Illaunaweelaun and 1M E of Lamb's Head
Blackhead Rock (6m high) and **Carrigatemple** (dries 3·4m), close S of Lamb's Island, on the SE side of Lamb's Head
Scariff Hedges, drying rocks extending 2 cables W from Scariff Island
Bulligmore (dries 0·3m) and **Muckiv Rocks** (dry 3·6m), respectively SE and NW of the entrance to Derrynane.

Lights and Marks

Carrignarone beacon, Fl 5s 2m 2M, in Sneem Harbour
West Cove and approaches:
West Cove outer leading beacons, square white pillars Oc 2s. front on Burnt Island
Limpet Rock beacon, red perch on concrete base PHM Fl R 3s
West Cove inner leading beacons, white cols Fl 2s,
Derrynane:
Derrynane, ldg lts 034°, Oc 3s 4M, front 10m rear 16m
Derrynane entrance beacons, SHM green concrete pillar, PHM red concrete pillar, unlit.
Bunavalla Pier, 2FR vert

Sneem to West Cove

(above) Garinish Bay, Sneem Harbour

(below) Oysterbed Pier

Sneem Quay, 1·5M up-river from the anchorage

Illaundrane

Facilities

Water on Oysterbed Pier. Hotel on N shore. Shops, pubs, restaurants, PO at Sneem village.

Illaundrane (Bunnow Harbour)

51°46'·4N 9°59'·5W

Illaundrane anchorage is well sheltered from all winds, but entry requires great care since the rocks are unmarked. The entrance is 3M W of Sherky Island. Enter in mid-channel between Leaghcarrig and Illaunsillagh, and steer due north until the NW side of Illaundrane island is well open. Turn to starboard for the W end of Illaundrane and leave its shore (which is clean) 50m to starboard. Anchor half way along the island in 4m.

West Cove

⊕WC 51°45'·7N 10°00'·9W

See Plan

West Cove is a very well sheltered but shallow harbour in the NW corner of the bight behind Carrigheela, 6M SW of Sneem. The approach is marked by lighted beacons but strewn with rocks, and a stranger should not attempt entry after dark. The entrance is narrow and has a least depth of 0·6m, sand bottom.

Directions

From the E, leave Daniel's Island and Noon Island (2 cables W) a cable to starboard, passing between Noon Island and Coosane Rock (which never covers) to the SW. There is a sunken rock 0·5 cable N of Coosane Rock. Steer to pass a cable SW of Burnt Island, and when the lower leading beacon (a white square pillar) comes into view from behind the island, turn to port bringing the two beacons in line 045° astern. A large white house among the trees above West Cove is conspicuous in this approach. Identify Limpet Rock beacon and the inner leading beacons and turn on to their line *(see photograph)*. Leave Limpet Rock beacon close

162

West Cove

(above) West Cove from the E; Leaghillaun and Grey Island L, Angle Rock breaking lower L, Limpet Rock beacon centre and the rear leading beacon upper R.

West Cove, from the E; Knocknasullig, L, and Burnt Island, R. Note the conspicuous white house among the trees, R

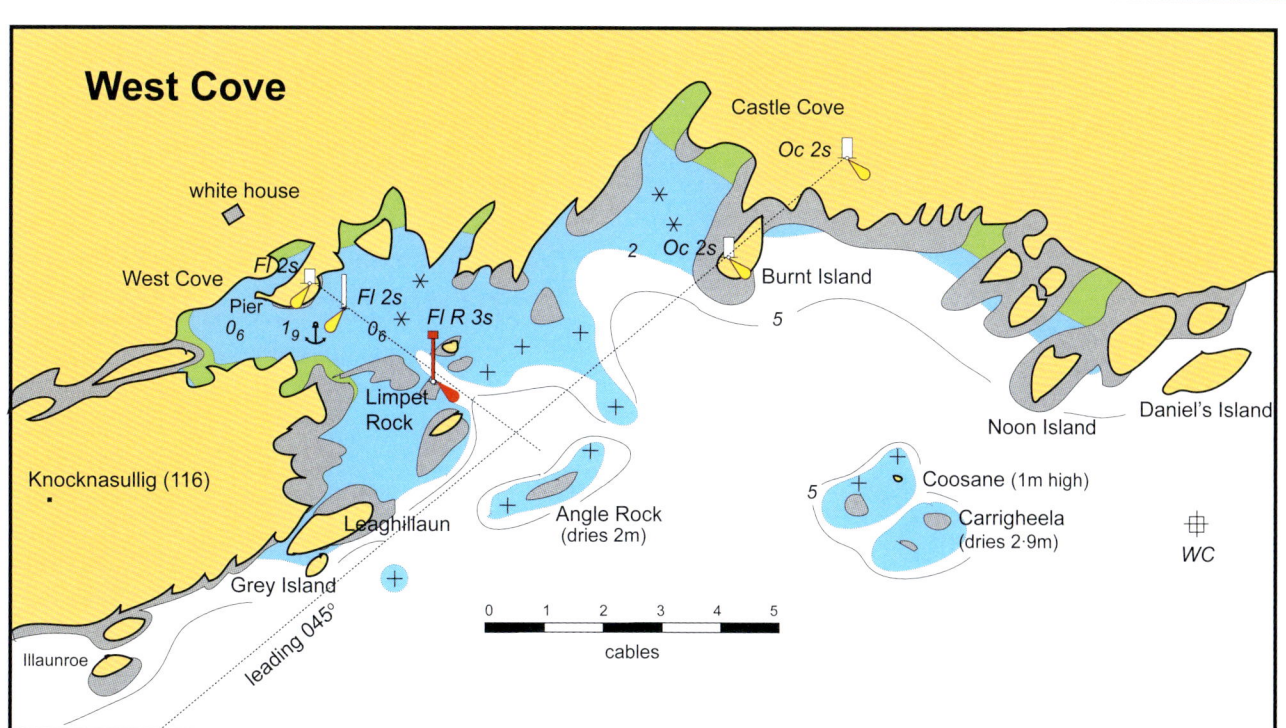

West Cove to Derrynane

West Cove: (above) the outer leading beacons from the SW

(L to R) the inner set of beacons from the landward side; the outer (red) beacon, on Limpet Rock; and the outer leading mark, from seaward (Dept of Agriculture, Food and Marine)

to port. When 20m from the outer leading beacon, turn to port for the anchorage.

From the W, identify the sharp peak of Knocknasullig (116m), 3M ENE of Lamb's Head, and approach the shore just E of its summit between Illaunroe and Leaghillaun. Identify the two grey leading beacons, about 1M to the NE bearing 045°. The front leading beacon is on Burnt Island and the rear beacon on the mainland just NE of it *(see photograph)*. Enter on this line, which is close to Leaghillaun and Grey Island and inshore of the breaker 1·5 cables E of them. Identify the inner beacons, and proceed as above.

Note that Angle Rock ("Carriganglee" on the chart) dries only 2m, and Carrigheela dries 2·9m, not 3·3m for both, as charted.

Anchorage

The only place with more than 1·5m at LAT is abreast the grey cottage E of the quay; the deep area here is narrow. Further up is mostly 0·4 to 0·7m, sand in the middle or mud NW of the quay, and there are small-craft moorings. Shop and filling station at Castlecove, 1·5 km. Constant −0053 Cobh; MHWS 3·5m, MHWN 2·8m, MLWN 1·2m, MLWS 0·5m.

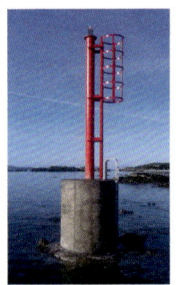

Scariff (L) and Deenish Islands, from the SE. Hog's Head is just closed behind Deenish

Lamb's Head – channels between the islands

There is deep water in mid-channel between all the islands outside Leaghcarrig, W of Lamb's Head. The shortest cut, the channel between Leaghcarrig and Two Headed Island, is 1·5 cables wide and 14m deep, and is navigable in the absence of a heavy swell. The bay on the E side of Deenish Island offers a pleasant temporary anchorage in settled weather.

Derrynane Bay

51°44'·7N 10°09'W

Derrynane Bay (Darrynane on the chart), N of Lamb's Head, is exposed to the prevailing wind and swell, but with settled offshore winds and no swell there is very pleasant anchorage in 9m, E of the abbey ruins on Abbey Island. The N and SE sides of the bay are foul for 2 cables, and the E side, which is sandy, dries out. The sandy beaches are conspicuous from seaward.

DERRYNANE HARBOUR

⊕DN 51°45'·3N 10°09'·8W
AC 2495 and Plan. Additional photo on p144

This spectacular anchorage is sheltered in all winds, but the entrance, although well

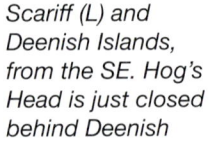

Derrynane

Derrynane Harbour

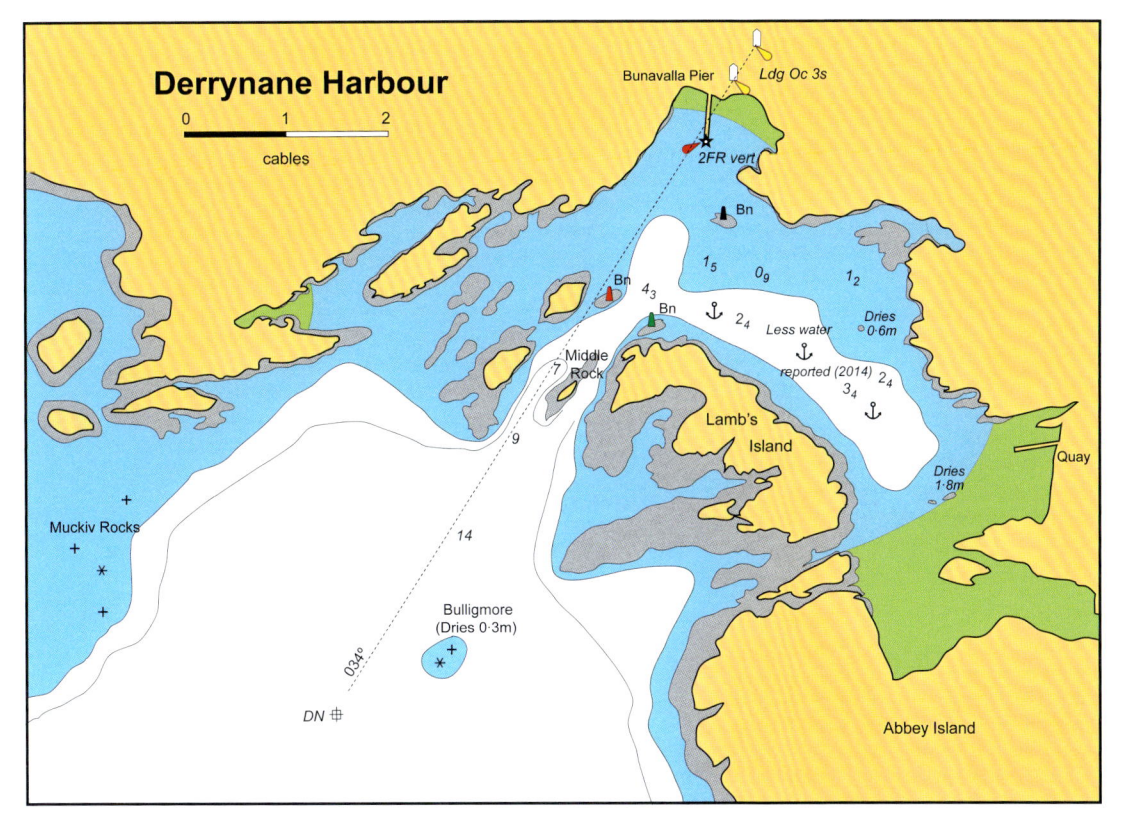

marked, is close between rocks and should not be attempted in a heavy swell from the W or SW. The leading beacons are lit, but a stranger is cautioned against attempting the entrance at night. Depths in the anchorage have been reported as reduced but plenty of usable space remains. **From the S**, from a position close W of Two Headed Island, steer 350° and identify the entrance NW of Abbey Island. Muckiv Rocks to the NW almost always break, and in any swell Bulligmore to the SE also breaks. **From the NW**, stay 5 cables SW of Kid's Island (10m high) and Carrigsheehan (9m high), 2·5M ESE of Hog's Head, and keep Leaghcarrick Island closed with Lamb's Head to the SE.

Identify the leading beacons bearing 034°, and steer in on the leading line, leaving Muckiv Rocks to port and Bulligmore to starboard. Bulligmore is particularly dangerous since it may not be breaking, so do not err to the SE of the leading line. The line leads between Middle Rock (0·5m high) to the SE and drying and above-water rocks to the NW. Approaching the entrance, identify the red beacon on the rocks just inside and almost on the leading line. Leave this beacon close to port and Middle Rock to starboard. The corresponding green starboard-hand beacon is on the rocks close N of Lamb's

(below) Derrynane entrance, from the landward side to the NE; Bulligmore breaking, L centre, and Muckiv Rocks breaking, top R. Bunavalla pier, foreground, and Moylaun Island, top L

165

Derrynane

Derrynane Harbour from the NW, with Middle Rock in the entrance, bottom. Derrynane Bay beyond the sandspit

(below) entering Derrynane: the leading beacons above Bunavalla Pier, L, the port-hand beacon, centre, and Middle Rock, R.

Derrynane to Valentia

Island. Turning to leave this beacon close to starboard opens up the anchorage. A third beacon to the NE marks a drying rock, and a further drying rock lies 2 cables to the SE. These are marked on AC2495.

When leaving Derrynane, Middle Rock appears to be much more obviously in mid-channel, and it is easy to be struck by an attack of last-moment confusion. Leave the rock to port when heading out, and keep the leading beacons in line astern. There is a narrow deep channel E of Middle Rock; it should be attempted with great care in settled weather only, staying close to the rock.

Anchorage

Anchor in the SE half of the harbour, anywhere clear of moorings, in 2 to 3m, sand. There is a drying pier and small slip in the SE corner of the harbour. Bunavalla Pier, in the N corner below the leading beacons, is 75m in length and has 0·5m at its head and 0·1m on each side, and is used by small fishing vessels and the tourist boats to the Skelligs. There is a slip beside this pier.

Constant -0055 Cobh: MHWS 3·5m, MHWN 2·7m, MLWN 1·2m, MLWS 0·4m

Facilities

Pub at Derrynane. Shop, pubs, restaurant at Caherdaniel, 3 km. Derrynane House and gardens are open to the public.

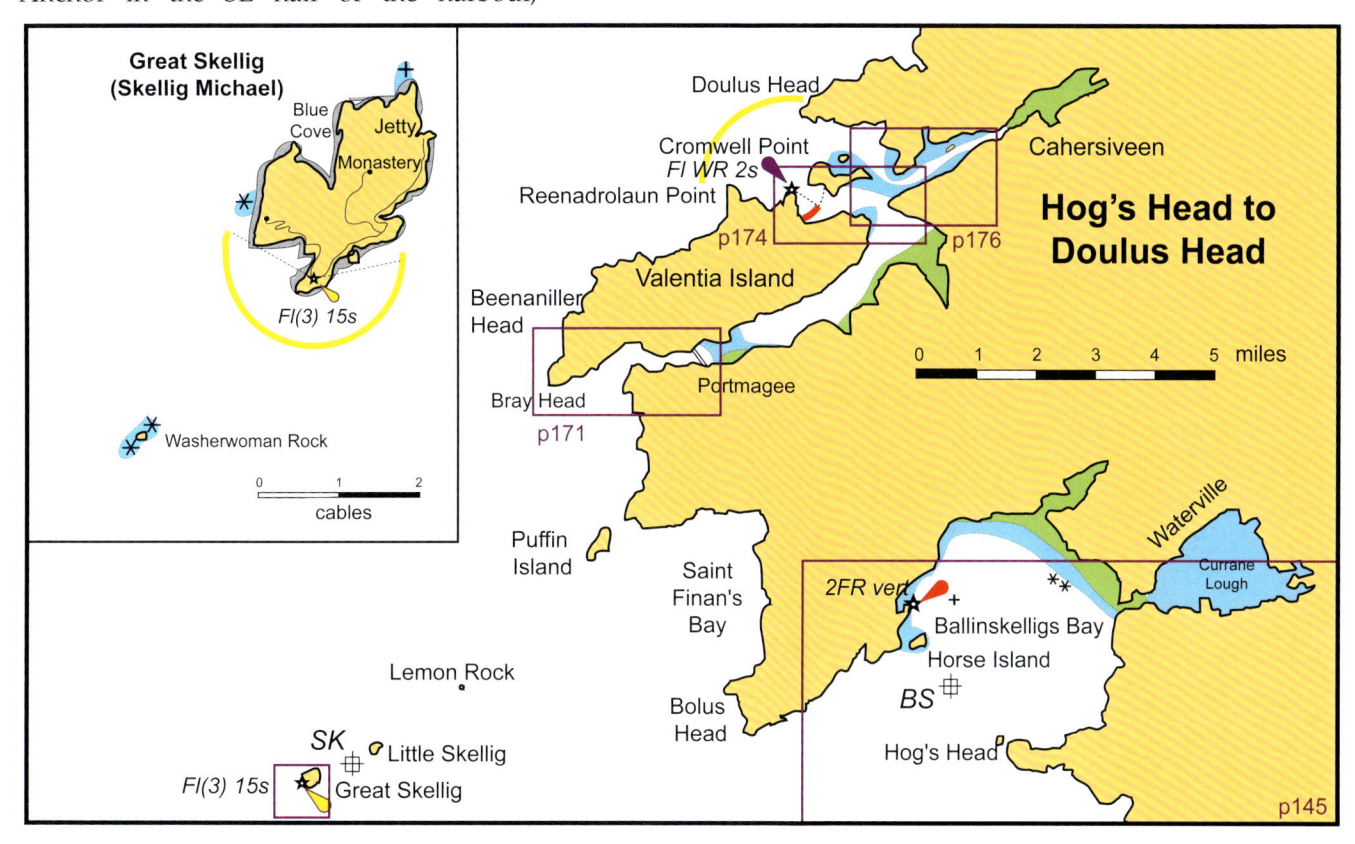

Lights and Marks

Ballinskelligs Pier, 2 FR vert
Skelligs Rock, white tower on the SW side of Great Skellig, Fl(3) 15s 53m 12M. Visible 262°–115°, partially obscured within 6M between 110° and 115°. AIS.
Inishtearaght, Fl(2) 20s 84m 18M, AIS, on the Blasket Islands to the NW *page 27*
Cromwell (Fort) Point, white tower Fl WR 2s 16m, W17M R15M, W 102°–304° R 304°–351°. Shows red over Harbour Rock and the SW corner of Valentia harbour, white elsewhere. AIS.

DERRYNANE to VALENTIA and CAHERSIVEEN

AC 2423, 2495, 2125

Leaving Derrynane with the leading beacons in line astern, do not alter course to the W until the gap closes between Leaghcarrig Island and Lamb's Head, to the SE. This leads clear SW of the Muckiv Rocks. The cliffs from here to Valentia are 150 to 240m in height and very spectacular, and in moderate to good visibility the craggy pyramids of the Skelligs are conspicuous to the W. Bolus Head, 6·5M WNW of Derrynane, is steep-to, and a berth

Ballinskelligs Bay and the Skelligs

Horse Island anchorage, Ballinskelligs Bay, from the SE

of 2 cables clears a drying rock off Ducalla Head further NNW. Canduff, the SW point of Puffin Island, is also clean. In fresh onshore winds and swell there can be a very disturbed sea between Bolus Head and Bray Head on Valentia Island.

The W part of Portmagee Sound, S of Valentia Island, offers sheltered anchorage but the bridge across the Sound no longer opens. Bearhaboy Rocks, SW of Bray Head, always show; **Gallaunaniller Rock,** which dries, lies 1·5 cables N of Beenaniller Head. The NW coast of Valentia is generally clean to within 2 cables of the shore; there is a rock with 2·6m, 1·3 cables NE of Reenadrolaun Point, the NW tip of the island. Identify Cromwell (Fort) Point, and leave it close to starboard. **By night**, the Skelligs light is obscured N of Bolus Head, and Inishtearaght light is obscured E of Beenaniller Head on the NW side of Valentia, while Cromwell Point light is not visible until clear NE of Reenadrolaun Point; this leaves a 3M gap along the NW coast of Valentia Island where no lights are visible at all.

Tides
Derrynane to Valentia

Inshore of the Skelligs the N-going stream makes at +0500 Cobh and the S-going at −0110 Cobh, spring rate 1·5 kn. W of the islands the tides are complex but do not exceed 1 knot.
Constant (Valentia) −0058 Cobh: MHWS 3·8m, MHWN 3·0m, MLWN 1·2m, MLWS 0·4m.

Ballinskelligs Bay

⊕ BS 51°48′N 10°15′W

Ballinskelligs Bay is open to the prevailing wind and swell from the SW, but offers the possibility of a visit in settled conditions with an offshore wind. Hog's Head to the SE has spectacular 160m cliffs; Pig's Rocks (4·6m high), 1·5 cables NW, have a drying reef extending 1 cable W. There are rocks on the NE side of the bay, and **Bay Rock**, with 1·2m, lies 7 cables NE of Horse Island, on the W side.

Anchorage

In settled weather there is temporary anchorage in 4m just N of Horse Island.

THE SKELLIGS

⊕ SK 51°46′·5N 10°31′W

The Great Skellig, or Skellig Michael, 214m high, is a remarkable rocky island 7·5M W by S of Bolus Head. It appears conical from E and W but its two summits with a saddle between are visible from other viewpoints. The Little Skellig, 130m high and 1·4M to the ENE, is similar in profile to its larger neighbour. Lemon Rock, 20m high and 2·3M ENE of the Little Skellig, is an isolated stack, while the Washerwoman Rock, 1·8m high, is 3 cables SW of the Great Skellig, and has two sunken rocks 0·5 cable off its N end. The Little Skellig is a nature reserve, and home to puffins, fulmars, razorbills, guillemots and 20,000 pairs of gannets; landing on it is prohibited, and in any case very difficult. The ancient monastic remains on the Great Skellig

The Skelligs

attract a steady stream of visitors, mostly in small passenger boats from Portmagee, Ballinskelligs and Derrynane. There is no anchorage, but there is a jetty in a rocky gut called Blind Man's Cove on the NE side, which, although naturally subject to swell, gives straightforward dinghy access. There is a resident maintenance team in summer, who also act as guides, and access hours are restricted, normally 0900 to 1400. The island is closed to visitors in winter (the end of October until mid-May). When securing a dinghy at the landing be sure to leave ample room for the ferryboats to berth and manoeuvre.

The island is a UNESCO World Heritage Site. Its five 1400-year-old monastic beehive huts and two oratories, in an astonishing state of preservation, are 150m above sea level and are reached by a flight of 600 steps cut into the rock. The climb demands care and stamina but is not unduly vertiginous. At the very pinnacle of of the island is an extraordinary hermit's cell, to which it is presumed a monk could retire when the pace of life on metropolitan Skellig Michael grew

Skellig Michael from the SW; Washerwoman Rock, lower L, and Bray Head (Valentia Island) in the distance. Note the flotilla of small ferryboats standing off while their passengers explore the island. The landing is just beyond the point to the R

169

The Skelligs

(above) Little Skellig from the E

(below) Skellig Michael from the SW, with the Little Skellig beyond

Puffin Sound and Portmagee Sound

too hectic.

The lighthouse 50m above sea level at the S end of the island was built in 1966, replacing a tower built in the 1830's. This was originally one of a pair, the other being 65m higher on the rock and further to the NW. The upper light was discontinued in 1866.

The recent use of the island in the making of *Star Wars* films may be expected to generate a surge in tourist volume, and possibly more controls as a result.

Puffin Sound

51°50'·4N 10°23'·8W
AC2495, 2125

Puffin Sound, between Puffin Island and the shore, is obstructed by rocks but has a narrow passage, 50m wide, through which the tides run rapidly. The tide is reported to turn N at +0135 Cobh and S at -0450 Cobh; this is 3·5 hours earlier than offshore. It is a very imposing place and the passage is possible only in moderate conditions. Keep a quarter of the width of the sound from the island side. In bad weather it breaks right across, a most formidable sight.

Portmagee Sound

⊕PM 51°52'·5N 10°25'W
AC2125, Imray C56 and Plan

Portmagee Sound, S of Valentia Island, provides excellent shelter with pontoon accommodation, but access to Valentia Harbour is restricted by a low bridge which used to open but is now permanently closed. The shores at the entrance are high cliffs and there is often a steep and confused sea here. The rocks and islets on the S side of the entrance all show above HW. Reencaheragh Point (21m) on the mainland is foul for a distance of 0·25 cable, and there are above-water rocks off Scughaphort Reef on the N side. There is the ruin of a fort on this point.

Enter midway between Reencaheragh and Scughaphort Reef and steer 110°. **Anchor Rock**, which dries, lies 0·25 cable off Quay Brack, 4 cables beyond Skuagh Point. When Quay Brack is abeam, alter course to 065°; this leads up parallel to the island shore about 0·5 cable off and to the N of a shallow rocky patch 1·25 cables ESE of Quay Brack. Identify Loughan Islet (4m high) to starboard, and when it comes abeam alter course for the pier at Portmagee on the S shore. There is foul ground around Loughan Islet.

(top) The landing place, Skellig Michael

(above) Puffin Sound from the SE; Bray Head on Valentia Island, beyond. Wind SW force 4 and swell at Portmagee Sound and Derrynane 1·5m, from the WSW

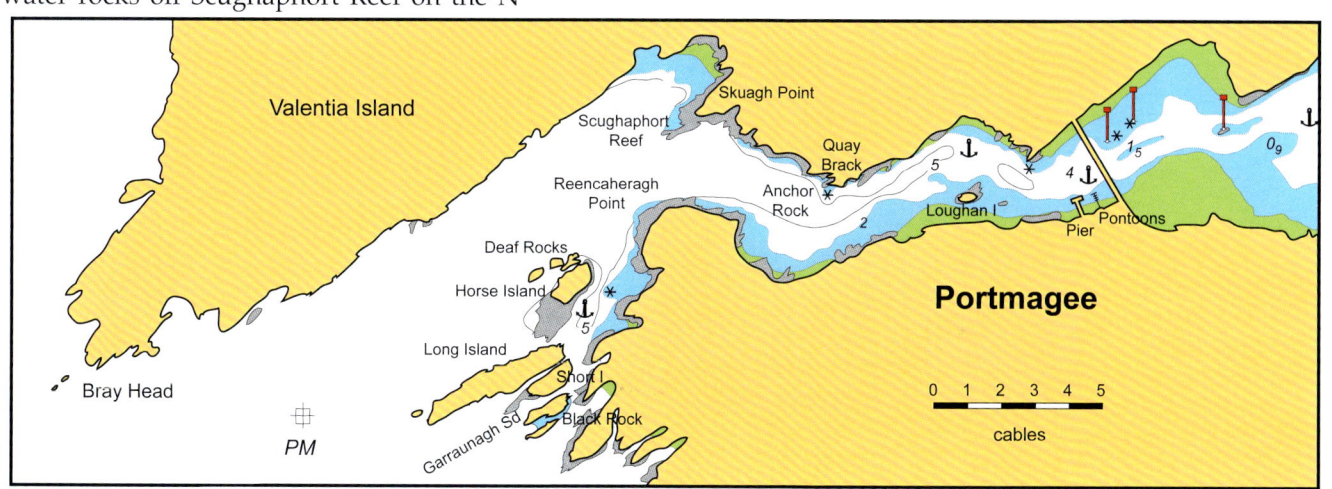

Portmagee Sound

Valentia and Portmagee Sound from the W: Bray Head, foreground

Portmagee Sound: Loughan Islet, centre

Berthing & Anchorage

The finger pontoons on the gangway E of Portmagee pier provide accommodation for the sea angling boats and the Skellig Michael ferries, but the T-head has room for two yachts, or more rafted up. There is anchorage off the pier in 5m, although the tide runs strongly and the holding is reported middling. The pier is used by fishing vessels. The N- and E-facing walls of the pierhead have deep water at all states of the tide, but yachts should not be left unattended. Diesel, water, showers, mechanical repairs, shop, restaurant, pubs.

Beside the bridge on the N side is the Skellig interpretive centre, which also has a pontoon. This is not available to visiting yachts.

The pool SE of Horse Island, in the entrance to Portmagee Sound, is a lovely spot in moderate weather and offers good temporary anchorage when the reefs S of the island are uncovered. Pass about 50m off the E side of Horse Island to avoid the rocks opposite.

Garraunagh Sound, ("Garracinagh Sound" on the chart) SE of Short Island, in the entrance, is a pass no more than 10m wide between cliffs on either side. Shown on the

Portmagee pontoon and pier

Valentia Harbour

old charts as having a least depth of three fathoms, and formerly described as a channel used by local boats, it is now reported as encumbered with boulders. Recent survey information is lacking.

VALENTIA HARBOUR

⊕ VL 51°56'·3N 10°19'·5W
AC2125, Imray C56 and Plan
The main entrance lies between Cromwell (Fort) Point on the W side and Beginish Island on the E.

Directions

Steer a mid-channel course in the white sector of the Port Entry Light, visible by day. Cromwell Point is low and has sunken rocks extending 0·5 cable NNE of it, and there are rocks which show and a sunken rock extending 0·75 cable off the Beginish Island shore. There is often a confused sea at the entrance, which can be dangerous in NW gales. The dangers within the harbour are generally well marked and lit.

Harbour

The harbour at Knightstown is formed by floating breakwaters. This was originally planned as a 200-berth marina but the pontoons were not installed. An alongside berth is available as convenient, inside the breakwaters. The car ferry to Reenard Point uses a slip inside the harbour and should not be obstructed.

Pool SE of Horse Island, Portmagee Sound

Tides
Valentia Harbour
In Valentia Harbour the tides set fairly through both the N and S entrances to the harbour, meeting about 2·5M SW of Reenard Point. The ingoing stream makes at +0450 Cobh and the outgoing at –0135 Cobh. The spring rate is 2 kn off Cromwell Point and 1·5 kn off Knightstown. The same times apply to the Fertha River, where the tides run strongly in the channel and off the marina entrance at Cahersiveen. Constant –0058 Cobh; MHWS 3·8m, MHWN 3·0m, MLWN 1·2m, MLWS 0·4m.

Dangers
Harbour Rock, dries 2·6m, 3 cables SE of Cromwell Point
Ledges and sunken rocks up to 2 cables W of Cruppaun Point on Beginish Island
The Foot, gravel spit drying 1·2 to 0·6m in places, extending 1·5 cables ENE from the N pier at Knightstown.

Lights and Marks
Cromwell (Fort) Point, white tower Fl WR 2s 16m, W17M R10M, W 102°–304° R 304°–351°. Shows red over Harbour Rock and the SW corner of the harbour, white elsewhere. AIS
Harbour Rock, perch E Card Q(3) 10s 4m 5M
Valentia Port Entry Light 141°, white tower, red stripe 25m, Oc WRG 4s W11M R8M G8M, G 136°–140°, W 140°–142°, R 142°–146°. Shows green close NE of Cromwell Point, white in mid-channel and red close SW of Beginish. Visible by day, range 2M
The Foot buoy, E Card VQ(3) 5s, AIS.
Knightstown Harbour N entrance, Iso R 2s and Iso G 2s, synchronised; **S entrance,** Fl(2) R 10s and Fl G 10s, synchronised.

For the dangers and marks in the N entrance from Doulus Bay and in the Fertha River, see the directions for Cahersiveen, below.

Cromwell Point lighthouse, from the N

Entrance to Valentia Harbour: Harbour Rock, R, the Port Entry Light, L

173

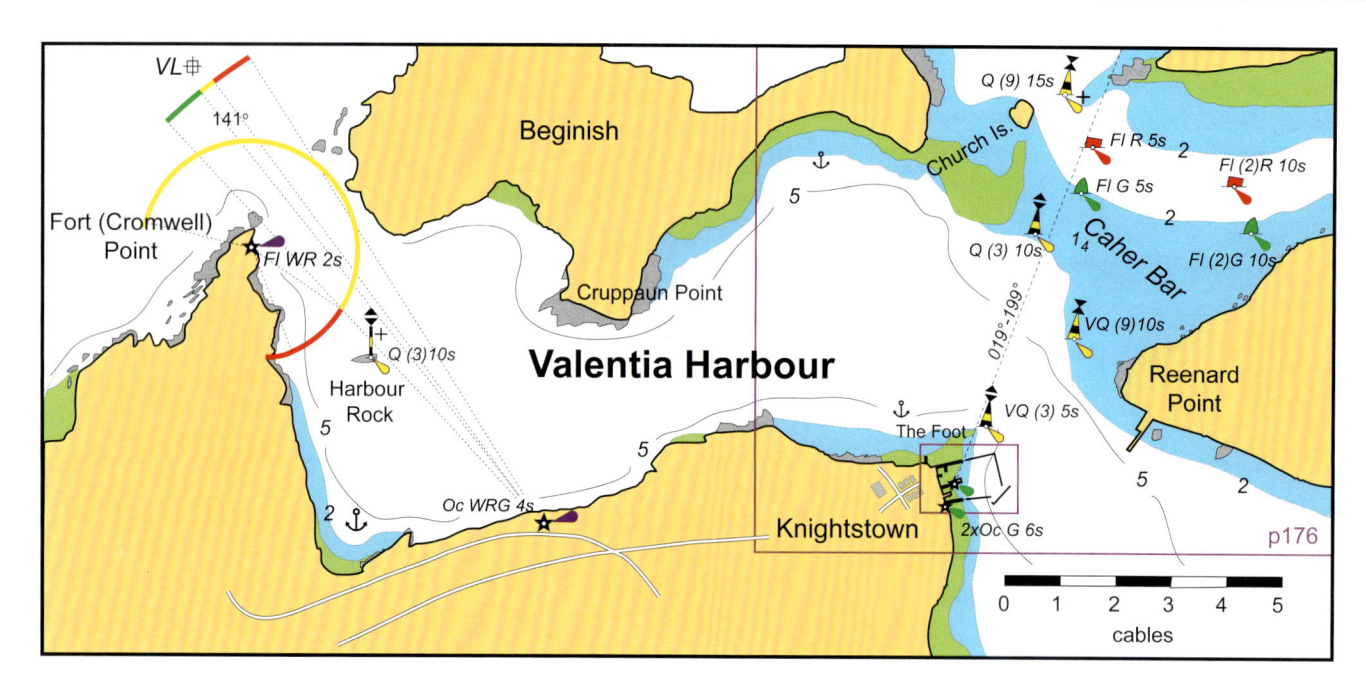

Valentia

Valentia Harbour from the SE: Knightstown, centre, with Beginish beyond. Reenard Point, R. This picture and the one opposite (top) were taken in 2008 before the breakwaters (opposite, bottom) were installed

Anchorage

- Anchorage is available S of the harbour entrance, staying well clear of the ferry's track. There are visitors' moorings
- Just W of the Foot, good holding in 2·5m. Well sheltered in winds from SE to SW. Land on the pebble beach at the back of the harbour pier. Visitors' moorings.
- In strong NW winds better shelter can be obtained in the sandy bay at the SE end of Beginish Island.
- In winds from SE to W, in Glanleam Bay S of Harbour Rock. Anchor in 4m, 1 cable from the head of the bay opposite Glanleam House. The bay is reported subject to downdraughts in gales from S and SW, and the bottom at the NW end is reported weedy.
- The pier at Reenard Point is used by the car ferry, which has a slip on the NW side. A temporary alongside berth may be available on the SE side. The pierhead has 5m at LAT.

Facilities

Shops, pubs, PO, filling station at Knightstown. Water on S pier. Ferry (in summer) to Reenard Point. RNLI all-weather lifeboat station. Slipway travelhoist, chandlery, hull and mechanical repairs at Murphy Marine Services 066 9476365 or 087 280 9861. HM 066 9476124.

E part of Portmagee Channel

The channel is clean to within 0·5 cable of both shores for 3·5M SW of Reenard Point. An underwater cable and pipeline cross 6 cables E of the bridge, and there are fish

Fertha River and Cahersiveen

Knightstown (in 2008, without its breakwaters)

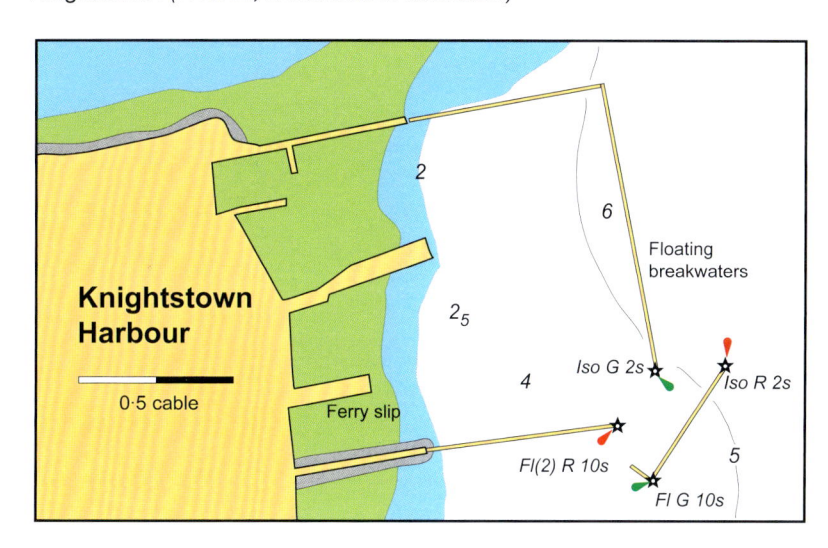

farms in the channel. Anchorage in 3m, with easy access to Portmagee village, is available in mid-channel, well clear W of the pipeline and cable, with Reenarea Point bearing 300°.

FERTHA RIVER and CAHERSIVEEN

AC2125 and Plan

Properly called the Fertha River, the waterway between Valentia and Cahersiveen is labelled "Valentia River" on the charts and is also referred to as the Caher River. Cahersiveen is 2M up the Fertha River from Valentia Harbour and can be approached over Doulus Bar in 2·4m or across the sheltered Caher Bar in 1·4m. The buoyed channel above Caher Bar has least depth 3m. The town has comprehensive facilities and an 80-berth marina.

Directions

From Valentia (Knightstown harbour), with sufficient height of tide to cross Caher Bar (least depth 1·4m at LAT), leave Canganniv Spit W Card buoy to starboard, heading 019°. Identify the Canganniv Spit E Card buoy and the first pair of lateral marks to the N, and leave the starboard-hand buoy to starboard. Then turn on to a heading of 101° and follow the buoyed channel to Cahersiveen. **From Doulus Bay,** the entrance is straightforward except in heavy weather from the W or

Knightstown Harbour from its SE corner

175

Cahersiveen

The Fertha River, looking downstream; Cahersiveen Marina, foreground, Foughil Island centre, Caher Bar and Valentia top L.

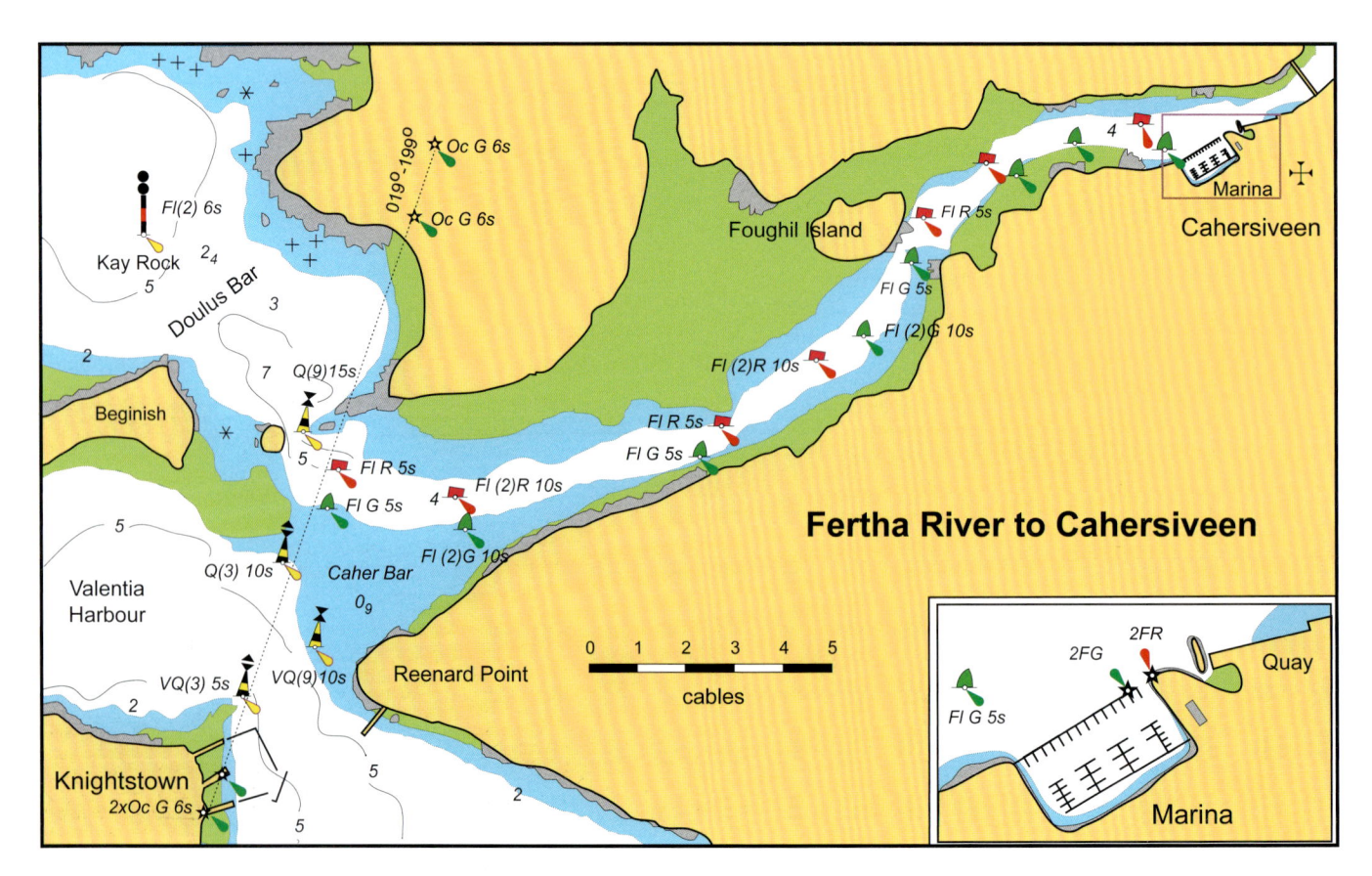

Fertha River to Cahersiveen

Cahersiveen

Dangers
Doulus Bay to Cahersiveen

Kay Rock (0·9m), 3 cables ENE of Lamb Island
Doulus Bar (2·4m), between Beginish and the mainland 2 cables ESE of Kay Rock
Passage Rock (dries 1·5m), 1 cable E of Church Island.

Lights and Marks

Kay Rock beacon, BRB Isolated Danger, Fl(2) 6s 4M
Passage Rock buoy, W Card Q(9) 15s
Canganniv Spit West buoy, W Card VQ(9) 10s
Canganniv Spit East buoy, E Card Q(3) 10s
Beginish Bar ldg lts, BY poles Oc G 6s (N end of line) bns Oc G 6s (S end of line at Knightstown harbour)
The river channel to Cahersiveen is marked by 8 starboard- and 7 port-hand buoys, Fl G and Fl R respectively.
Cahersiveen Marina entrance, 2FG vert and 2FR vert
Note that the former Ballycarbery Spit beacon is no longer lit or maintained.

NW or in a high swell, when there may be breakers on Doulus Bar. Enter in mid-channel between Black Rocks (N of Lamb Island) and the shore to the N, and identify the beacon on Kay Rock. Giving it a berth of 0·5 cable on either side, head for Passage Rock W Card buoy, leave it close to port and follow the buoyed channel round to port and up-river. The tide runs at 2 kn at springs in the river.

Shrimp pots are laid just outside the channel. The small and inconspicuous buoys may drift into the channel on long lines, and a good lookout should be kept for them.

Marina

The marina is on the S side 3 cables downstream of the bridge. Diesel (by tanker or in cans), water, shore power, showers, some chandlery. Marina office 06694 72777, manned Monday-Friday 0900-1700, info@cahersiveenmarina.ie

Anchorage

Anchorage is possible just S of midstream abreast the quay. The projecting breakwater gives some shelter in W winds to the most W'ly berth at the quay, which has 5m. There is a small drying reef on the N shore opposite this breakwater.

Facilities

Shops, PO, pubs, restaurants, filling stations in Cahersiveen, 1 km. Marine engineer J. Kelly 066 9472502. Buses to Tralee & Killarney. Taxis.

(top) Canganniv Spit and its E Card buoy

(above) Kay Rock beacon, from the W in 2012. This beacon was destroyed in 2015 and at the time of writing (January 2016) is about to be reinstated.

Cahersiveen Marina

5 Valentia to Loop Head

The cliffs of Inishtooskert in the Blaskets, with Sybil Point and Ballydavid Head in the distance

North of Valentia Harbour, the eastern part of the wide inlet of Dingle Bay has little to offer in the way of shelter, but the almost landlocked harbour of Dingle on its north shore is an important fishing port and a magnet for yachts. Dingle (1,920) is justifiably famous on two counts: its restaurants are renowned for their seafood, and its harbour entrance has been – since 1984 – home to a stage-struck male bottlenose dolphin by the name of Fungie.

The Dingle peninsula ends at Dunmore Head, at 10°29′W the westernmost point of the mainland of Ireland, but a mile across a tideswept sound to the west lie the fabulous Blasket Islands. Exploring these islands to the full demands seamanship, vigilance and not a little athletic ability, but they reward the effort tenfold. Everything about the Blaskets is stupendous: the wildlife, the dazzling beach, the towering cliffs, the breathtaking views. The last of the islanders left Great Blasket in 1953, taking with them a rich literature, in Irish and English, recording the lifestyle that died on that day. If you are from Scotland, this is Ireland's St Kilda; if you are Faroese, you may find the landscape familiar.

The port of Fenit, in Tralee Bay, has a marina and some specialised cargo traffic. The long estuary of the Shannon, Ireland's greatest river, is the major port on the west coast, with most vessels using the harbour of

"Cruising Ireland"
*This coast is described on pages 81 to 91 of **Cruising Ireland***

Paper Charts
On the smaller scale, AC2254 Valentia to the Shannon covers the area described in this chapter. The Imray chart C55 Dingle Bay to Galway Bay has plans of Dingle, Fenit and several of the Shannon harbours. AC2789 Dingle Bay and Smerwick Harbour is essential, and gives adequate detail for a passage of the Blasket Islands, but for exploration of the islands AC2790 is preferable. Fenit is accessible with AC2254, but AC2739 Brandon and Tralee Bays is better, and essential for exploring the Magharees. The passage anchorages of Kilbaha Bay and Carrigaholt, in the Shannon estuary, are likewise accessible with AC2254, but AC1819 Approaches to the River Shannon is preferable. For the Shannon above Carrigaholt, the large-scale charts AC1547, 1548 and 1549 are essential, with 1540 needed only if going to Limerick.

Valentia to Dingle and the Blaskets

Valentia to Kerry Head

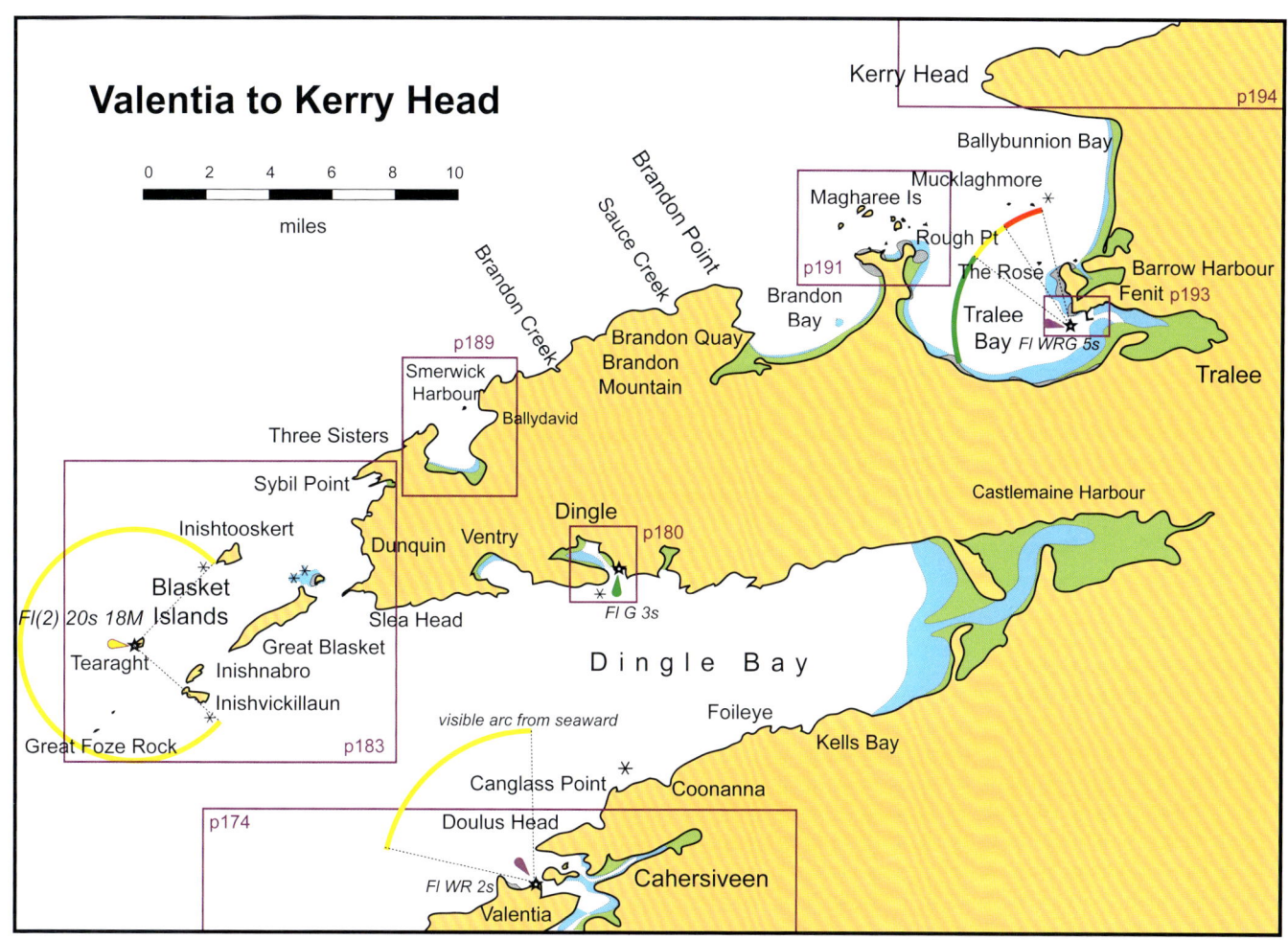

Foynes on the south shore but the largest ones bringing coal to the power station at Money Point. At Limerick the river gives access (subject to draft and headroom restrictions) to the Shannon Navigation, Ireland's most extensive inland waterway network.

VALENTIA to DINGLE and the BLASKETS

AC2125, 2789

From Valentia, the simplest route N is through the main entrance at Cromwell Point, but from Cahersiveen the channel E and N of Beginish offers a shorter passage and obviates the crossing of Caher Bar. See the previous chapter for detailed directions.

The shores of Dingle Bay are generally

Tides - Dingle and Dingle Bay

Across the entrance to Dingle Bay the streams run N and S. There is little stream in the bay. The streams are strong in the entrance to Dingle Harbour, changing at LW and HW by the shore.
Constant (Dingle) –0056 Cobh; MHWS 3·9m, MHWN 3·0m, MLWN 1·5m, MLWS 0·7m.

Dangers - Dingle Bay

Breaker Rock (awash at LW), 3 cables NE of Canglass Point
Crow Rock (dries 3·7m), 5 cables SW of Reenbeg Point, W of Dingle Harbour
Colleen Oge Rock, 1·8m, 2 cables NE of Crow Rock.
Rock with 0·8m, one cable NE of Colleen Oge Rock and one cable offshore

Lights and Marks

Dingle, NE side of entrance, white tower Fl G 3s 20m 6M
Dingle, SW side of entrance, white pole beacon Fl 5s 5m 3M
Black Point buoy, SHM Fl(3) G 5s
Flaherty Point buoy, PHM QR
The channel to Dingle pier and marina is marked by 4 more SH and 2 more PH buoys
Dingle pier channel ldg lts astern 182° Oc 3s
East Pier Heads, 2×2FG vert 5m 2M
Marina Breakwater, 2FR vert
Dingle Pier, Port Entry Light Dir Oc WRG 4s, white 002° over the channel, green to E, red to W.

Dingle

Kells Bay and pier

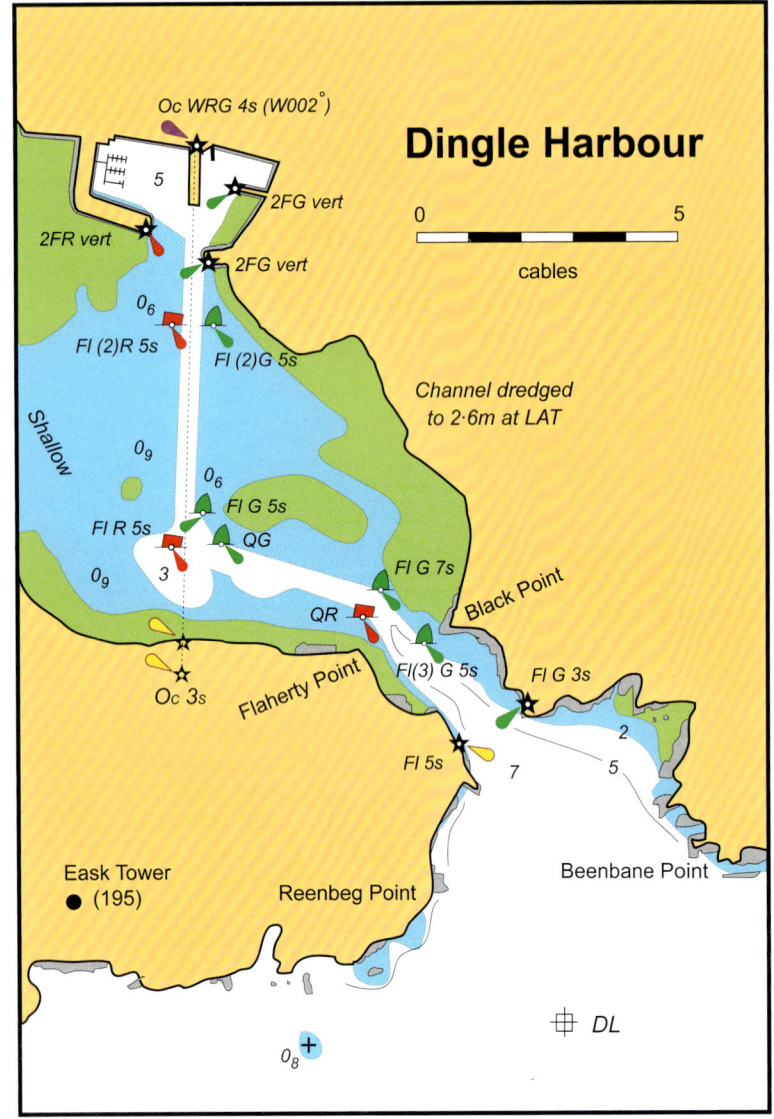

Dingle Harbour (chart)

Entrance to Dingle harbour, from the S

Eask Tower on the hilltop: Crow Rock, breaking, foreground

clean. Reenadrolaun Point on Valentia Island open NW of Doulus Head 223° clears Breaker Rock, 3 cables NE of Canglass Point on the S shore, and Crow Rock seldom covers. On the coast NE of Doulus Head are several attractive temporary anchorages in small inlets, usable in settled conditions. **Coonanna Harbour** has a pier at its head with 0·6m. **Foileye** is a pretty bay and free of dangers. **Kells Bay,** on the S shore 6M E of Canglass Point, offers shelter in winds between SE and W. The pierhead just dries at LAT.

The extensive and mostly drying inlet of Castlemaine Harbour, at the head of Dingle Bay, lies E of Rossbehy and Inch Points. Extensive drying sandbanks extend W from both points for about 2M. The tidal streams run at 3 to 4kn through the entrance at springs. The ingoing stream makes at +0605 Galway and the outgoing at +0005 Galway. The bar is subject to movement of the sandbanks, and no reliable directions can be given for entry.

DINGLE

⊕ DL 52°06'·7N 10°15'·5W
AC2789, 2790, Imray C56 and Plan

The town of Dingle, at the head of its almost landlocked harbour, is an important fishing port as well as a major tourist centre. Dingle Marina, W of the main pier, has 80 berths.

Directions

The entrance to Dingle Harbour lies between Reenbeg Point to the W and Beenbane Point to the E, and is clean, free of dangers, well marked and straightforward by day or night. The entrance is 7·5 cables E of the conspicuous Eask Tower, 195m. The NE light tower open E of Reenbeg Point 024° leads SE of Crow Rock and the rocks to the NE of it. **From the W**, and if Crow Rock is showing, pass within a cable N of it, or stay well S of it. The channel, 40m wide, is dredged to 2·6m at LAT and is marked by five starboard- and three port-hand buoys, all lit. The channel

180

Dingle

Dingle Harbour from the S: the pier and marina, upper L centre

(below) Dingle Harbour and Marina

runs NW from the entrance buoys and then N. Leading beacons on the S shore and a directional light at the pier root lead through the dredged section. The pier itself has heavy fishing vessel traffic and is available to yachts only in emergency. The harbour and marina are managed by the Department of Agriculture, Food and the Marine.

Anchorage

There is depth to anchor outside the dredged channel, S of the second port-hand buoy. Contact HM for advice. Anchoring is not permitted in or near the dredged channel.

Marina

HM phone 066 9151629, e-mail dingleharbour@agriculture.gov.ie. Marina 087 925 4115. VHF Ch 16 and 14 (not continuously manned). A peculiarity of VHF reception in Dingle harbour is that the Shannon CG Radio transmitter is frequently clearer than the Valentia one.

Facilities

Water, shore power, showers at the marina. Diesel by tanker or in cans. Supermarket, shops, pubs, restaurants, PO, laundry, filling station, car rental in town, all within 800m. Radio and electronic repairs, Tom Hand Electronics; mechanical repairs at Griffin's garage. Small chandlery, Dingle Marine & Leisure, 066 915 1344. Dingle Sailing Club is based at the marina.

Dingle Marina (photo W.M.Nixon)

Ventry

Ventry Harbour from the SE: Ventry Pier, upper R

Dangers
Blasket Islands and Sound

Wild Bank, 6·2m, 2·5M SW of Slea Head, and **Barrack Rock**, 8·2m, 3·5M SW of Wild Bank, break in gales.

W and NW of Beginish in the Blaskets is an area of stacks, drying and underwater rocks, with **Ballyclogher Rocks** (dry 3m) at their S end, **Connor Rocks** (above HW) at their NE end and a **rock** drying 0·3m at the NW end. Overfalls occur up to 1·5M N to NW of these shoals. A rock with 7·2m was discovered in 2013 midway between Great Blasket and Inishtooskert, where the seabed had been charted at 50 to 60m.

Scollage Rock (dries 3·7m), 0·5 cable W of Lure, the 44m stack off Dunmore Head

Stromboli Rock, 1·8m, 3 cables W of Lure, with another 1·8m rock 1 cable ENE of it

Rock with 1·5m, 5 cables WNW of the landing place at Dunquin

Fohish Rocks (dry 2·7m), 5 cables SSE of Inishvickillane

Unnamed rock (dries 0·3m), 3 cables W of Inishvickillane

Sound Rocks (dry 0·8m), 1 cable E of the N end of Inishnabro

Unnamed rock (drying 0·3m), 2 cables SW of Inishtooskert

Unnamed rocks (drying 2m and 0·8m), 3 cables WSW of Tearaght

Great Foze Rock (27m high), 2·8M WSW of Inishvickillane, **Little Foze Rock** (7m high), 2·1M W by S of Inishvickillane, and **Tearaght Rocks** (13m high), 5 cables W of Tearaght, are all conspicuous by day but are unmarked, and dangerous at night.

A local magnetic abnormality is reported around the Blaskets.

Lights and Marks

Inishtearaght, Fl(2) 20s 84m 18M, Racon (O), on Tearaght Island. Visible from 318° through N to 221°; obscured from NE through E to SE. AIS. 📷 (pages 27 and 185)

Ventry Harbour

52°06'·5N 10°20'W
AC2789, 2790

This delightful broad bay has an entrance nearly a mile wide facing SE. It gives good shelter in SW to N winds though there can sometimes be a swell. It is also subject to heavy squalls from the high ground to the W in strong winds. Ventry Strand, on its W shore, is a superb sandy beach.

Directions

The entrance is easily recognised 2M W of the prominent Eask Tower. Parkmore Point on the W side of the entrance is at the E end of a long line of diminishing cliffs. Valentia lighthouse (Cromwell Point) open of Doulus Head leads to it. The only danger in the entrance is the 2·9m ridge extending SW from the shore 2·5 cables S of Ballymore Point. This ridge will break heavily in a big swell. It can be avoided by keeping S of the line joining Paddock Point, the E side of the entrance, and the conspicuous church W of the centre of Ventry Strand.

Anchorages

- Off the NE end of the beach in 4·5m, sand. The pier and slip offer a convenient landing and access to the village.
- On the S side of the bay about 1 cable N of the pier at Cuan (Coon on the chart) in 3m, sand.

Facilities

Restaurant, shop, pub and PO in the village. Shop and pub 1·5 km from the S anchorage.

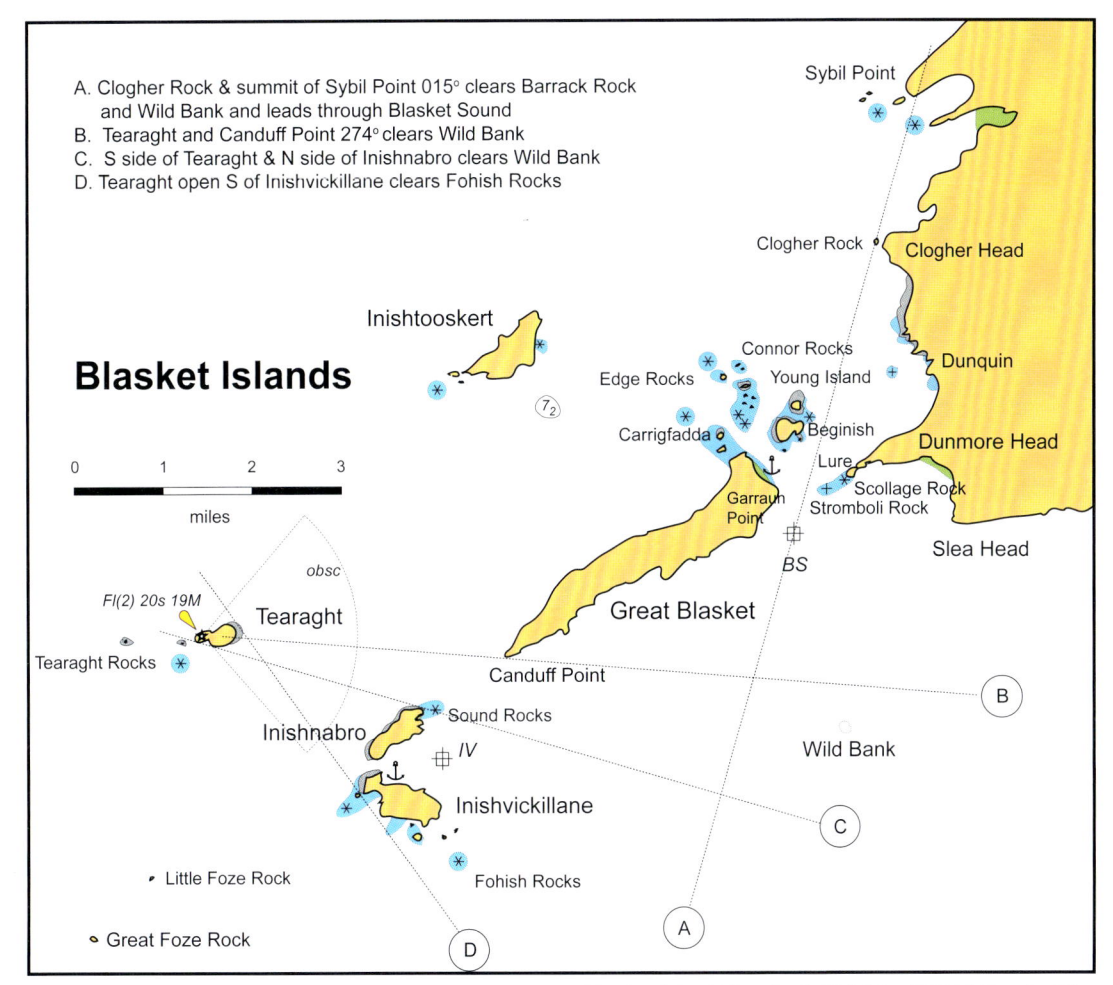

Blasket Islands; Inishvickillane

A. Clogher Rock & summit of Sybil Point 015° clears Barrack Rock and Wild Bank and leads through Blasket Sound
B. Tearaght and Canduff Point 274° clears Wild Bank
C. S side of Tearaght & N side of Inishnabro clears Wild Bank
D. Tearaght open S of Inishvickillane clears Fohish Rocks

BLASKET ISLANDS

AC2790

Approach from the S and E

Clogher Rock, the stack off Clogher Head N of Blasket Sound, in line with the summit of Sybil Point 015° leads 2 cables E of Barrack Rock, 1·5M W of Wild Bank and mid-channel through Blasket Sound. Tearaght over Canduff Point (the SW extremity of Great Blasket) 274° leads 0·5M N of Wild Bank. The S end of Tearaght touching the NE end of Inishnabro 287° leads 1M S of Wild Bank.

Inishvickillane

⊕ *IV* 52°03′N 10°36′W

Inishvickillane, 134m high, in the shape of a long ridge when viewed from the SE, and Inishnabro, 174m high, rising towards its N end, are the southernmost of the islands. The SW and SE sides of Inishvickillane are foul with stacks, rocks and breakers for 4·5 cables. From the SE, Tearaght open S of Inishvickillane clears Fohish Rocks to the S, while keeping the channel between Inishvickillane and Inishnabro open clears all dangers E and S of Inishvickillane.

Anchorage

Anchorage is available in 10 to 12m in the bay on the NE side of Inishvickillane. Give the N shore of the island a berth of 2 cables in the approach from the E, and anchor at least a cable offshore, as the bottom is foul with weed and rocks inside the 10m line. The bay is sheltered from winds between SE and N, and with relatively weak tidal streams

---

Tides
Blasket Islands

In Blasket Sound the N-going stream makes at +0445 Galway and the S-going stream at −0140 Galway. The spring rate is from 2 to 3 kn. The duration of these streams can be much affected by the wind. There are overfalls on Wild Bank and on the uneven bottom among the islands (particularly NW of Great Blasket), and a pronounced S-going eddy off the strand at Great Blasket during the N-going tide. The tidal stream is always to the W at up to 2 kn in the sound between Inishvickillane and Inishnabro.
Constant (Dingle) −0056 Cobh; MHWS 3·9m, MHWN 3·0m, MLWN 1·5m, MLWS 0·7m.

Inishvickillane and Inishnabro

(above) Inishvickillane anchorage: Tearaght, top L, and Inishnabro, top R (photo Mike Balmforth)

(above R) The landing place at An Leirigh, Inishvickillane

(below) The cave (L) leading to the landing place on Inishnabro

it is the best anchorage in the Blaskets, but it has little competition for the title and is (of course) subject to swell. In fine weather landing is easy on the small shingle beach but the steep path which winds up the cliffs is in a dangerous state and should not be attempted. An outcrop of rock at the N end of the bay, known locally as An Leirigh, provides an alternative landing place but even in fine weather a surge or swell can make landing difficult, and in fresh easterlies, impossible.

Traditionally, the island is regarded as home of the fairies and today it is also home to a more visible herd of red deer. There are several important archaeological features including the remains of an early Christian monastic settlement. The island is privately owned and has a single house which is occasionally occupied.

In moderate weather the passage in mid-channel between Inishvickillane and Inishnabro presents no difficulty.

Inishnabro

The only possible landing place on Inishnabro (in very settled weather) is through a cave in the middle of the SE side of the island, N of the 14·3m sounding on AC2790. The cave is about 2m wide and 5m high. It leads into a tiny rocky pool open to the sky, with enough flat rock to land and pull up a dinghy. It is possible to scramble up a gulley above the pool and reach the flat middle neck of the island by a dry stone wall. Even on a very calm day there is a surge and scend in the cave.

The N tip of the island is formed by superb cliffs and arches *(see photograph on page 11)*. There is a strong tide rip on its NE side, and Sound Rock (dries 0·8m) lies just over a cable E of the cliffs.

Blasket Sound from the SE: Great Blasket and Inishtooskert, L, Beginish, centre, Lure and Dunmore Head R

The N landing, Tearaght

Tearaght

Tearaght is pierced by a tunnel running N–S. There are landings and steps both N and S of the tunnel, seldom usable because of the nearly continuous swell. The S side has a hoist and funicular formerly used to supply the lighthouse. The island has large puffin and storm petrel colonies *(see photograph also on p27)*

Tearaght: the S landing, centre

Inishtooskert and Great Blasket

Landing place at Leac na Caoraigh, Inishtooskert (photo Dick Lincoln)

Inishtooskert

Inishtooskert lies 4M N of Inishnabro and is 171m high, with steep cliffs on its NW side and a conspicuous cockscomb pinnacle on its N end *(see photograph on page 178)*. There is no anchorage or convenient landing place. In very calm weather it is possible to jump from a dinghy on to rocks on the SE side, but the swell and surge in normal conditions make this difficult and often dangerous. The ruin of an oratory stands on the top of the island: the climb is steep and is made hazardous by nesting seabirds erupting from their burrows in the slope.

Great Blasket

52°06'·5N 10°30'·4W

Great Blasket is separated from the mainland by Blasket Sound, 1M wide. The NW side of the island is precipitous and rises to 280m at Slievedonagh. At the NE end of the island is the old village, above a sandy bay which offers reasonable shelter and easy landing. In summer, and subject to weather conditions, tourist boats visit daily and a visitor centre and tearoom are opened.

Both sides of Great Blasket are clean as far as the N point of the island, and all dangers show above HW. There is a rock with 3·7m close inshore at Garraun Point, the E point of the island.

Anchorage

Anchor in 5m, sand, off the bay at the NE end. There is a strong tide and a pronounced S-going eddy into the bay on the N-going tide. Land at the slip S of the beach *(see photograph, opposite)*.

Great Blasket from the W

Blasket Sound

Blasket Sound

⊕ BS 52°05'·8N 10°30'·3W
AC 2790, 2789

The passage of Blasket Sound is straightforward in daylight. From the S, transits to avoid Wild Bank are given above. The Sound, with its exposed position, uneven bottom and strong tides, can be rough at times. Beginish (13m) and Young Island (11m, "Young's Island" on the chart) form the W side of the sound and appear as one island from N or S. **Theogh Rocks** extend SE of Beginish, and there is a rock awash at LW 1·75 cables NE of Young's Island. Clogher Rock, the stack off Clogher Head to the N, in line with the summit of Sybil Point, 015°, leads between Garraun Point and Stromboli Rock, and 2 cables E of Theogh Rocks and the rock NE of Young's Island. The two minor channels N of Great Blasket are navigable with care in moderate weather. The wider one, 2 cables wide, runs between Beginish Island and Ballyclogher Rocks, which dry about 3m. There are uncharted rocks within 50m of the above-water rocks W of Beginish. Give these above-

(above) The NE end of Great Blasket, with the old village, the anchorage and (at centre L) the landing place

(left) The landing place on Great Blasket (photo Niall Quinn)

(below) The minor channels through Blasket Sound, from the E: Beginish and Young Island, bottom L, Carrigfadda upper centre and Edge Rocks, R

Blasket Sound, minor channels

View NE from the passage between Beginish and Ballyclogher Rocks: the rocks W of Beginish, from the SW. Beginish, R, with Clogher Head beyond, and Sybil Point, L

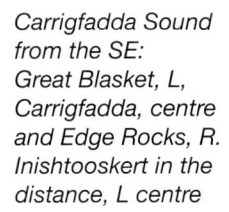

Carrigfadda Sound from the SE: Great Blasket, L, Carrigfadda, centre and Edge Rocks, R. Inishtooskert in the distance, L centre

water rocks a berth of a cable and no more. In Carrigfadda Sound, pass about 50m from Carrigfadda. This passage may be hazardous if Ballyclogher Rocks are not showing. N of Carrigfadda, maintain a NNW'ly heading until well clear of the 0·3m drying rock.

Tides
Blasket Sound to Tralee Bay

Between Sybil Point and Brandon Point the tide runs NE-SW reaching 2 to 3 knots at springs and turning NE about +0450 Galway and SW at −0130 Galway. The E-going flood through Magharee Sound starts at +0505 Galway and the W-going ebb at −0120 Galway, rate 2 to 3 kn. Offshore to the N, the streams are weaker. Leaving Dingle about 2h before LW gives a favourable tide right into Tralee Bay.
Constant (Smerwick) -0047 Cobh; MHWS 3·8m, MHWN 2·9m, MLWN 1·3m, MLWS 0·4m.

Dangers
Clogher Head to Tralee Bay

Between Clogher Head and the Magharees a berth of 3 cables clears all dangers. In Tralee Bay are the following dangers:
Breaker, with 9m, 2M N by E of Rough Point
Breaker, with 4·3m, 1·8M NNE of Rough Point
Rock drying 0·9m, 2 cables N of Mucklaghmore
Breaker, with 3·3m, 4 cables S of Mucklaghmore
Boat Rock, dries 4·3m, 4 cables ENE of Illaunabarnagh
Wheel Rock, dries 3·5m, 1 cable W of Fenit pier head.

Lights and Marks

Ballynagall (Ballydavid) Pier, Fl R 3s 4m 3M
Brandon Pier, 2FG vert 5m 4M
Little Samphire Island, Fl WRG 5s 17m W14M R11M G11M, R 262°–275° and 280°–090°, G 090°–140°, W 140°–152°, R 152°–172°. Shows white over the approach from the NW between the Magharees and Mucklaghmore, green over the Magharees and the peninsula S of them, red over Mucklaghmore and Illaunnabarnagh to the NNW and red also over the S part of Tralee Bay
Great Samphire Island, QR 15m 3M
Fenit pier head, 2FR vert 12m 3M.

Sybil Point from the NE

Smerwick

NORTH COAST of the DINGLE PENINSULA

AC2789, 2739, Imray C55

The mainland coast N and E of Blasket Sound is spectacularly scenic, with towering cliffs, offshore stacks and the remarkable headlands of the Three Sisters, to the W of Smerwick Harbour. Smerwick offers reasonable shelter and is a good point of departure for the Aran Islands or Connemara. Further E, between Ballydavid Head and Brandon Point, is one of the most impressive stretches of coast in the whole of Ireland, rising in 400m cliffs – the highest in Kerry – to Brandon Mountain. In fine weather, with its wonderful scenery and abundant bird life, it makes as fine a point of departure or landfall as anyone could desire; while a dawn landfall on Brandon Mountain will never be forgotten.

East of Brandon Point lies the wide sweep of Brandon Bay, with the Magharee Islands (The Seven Hogs on the chart) off its E point and Tralee Bay beyond. Fenit, at the E end of Tralee Bay, has an excellent marina.

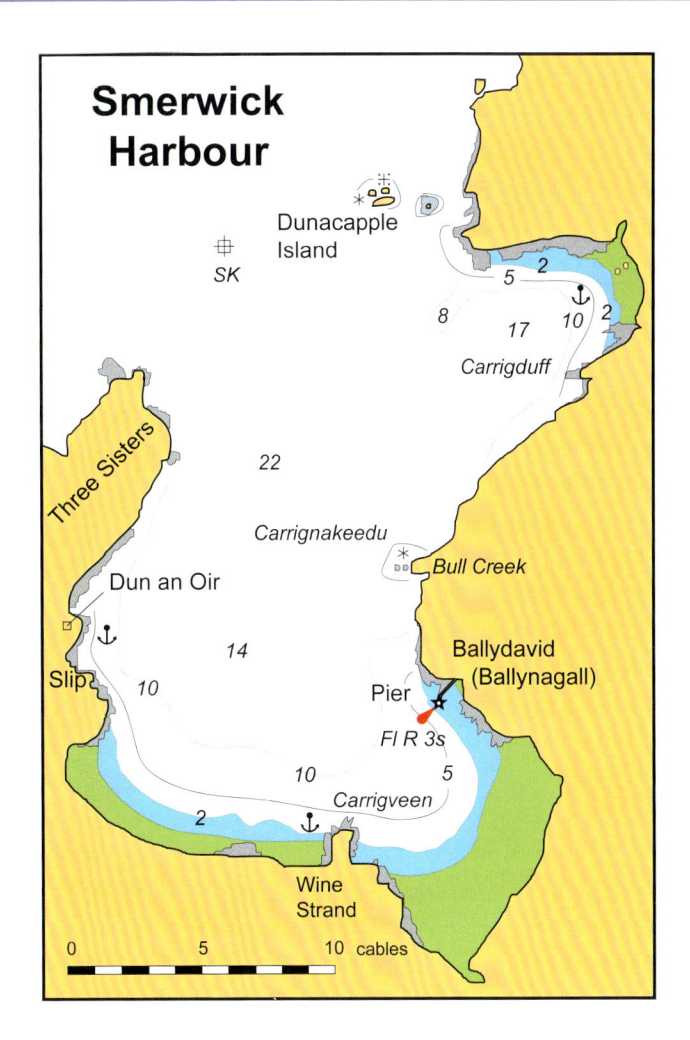

Smerwick Harbour

⊕ SK 52°13′N 10°24′W

AC2789 and Plan

Smerwick Harbour is an open bay between the East Sister and Dunacapple Island, 1M to the NE. The entrance faces NW. There are rocks and breakers between Dunacapple Island and the shore to the E. The harbour is exposed to considerable ground swell and – while not an ideal refuge in bad weather – provides shelter from winds between NE and W. **Carrignakeedu** (awash at LW) is a cable offshore off Bull Creek on the E side of the bay.

Anchorages

- On the W side N of the slip marked "Boat Harbour" on AC2789, about 1·5 cables off the cliffs in 10m, good holding in stiff mud.
- In N winds the bay at the NE corner of the harbour offers shelter, off the mouth of the stream there. The end of Carrigduff reef in the SE corner of this bay is reported to be 0·75 cable further W than charted.
- In SE to SW winds, just W of Carrigveen on the S side of the harbour in 2·5m, sand.

Ballydavid Pier (at Ballynagall on the chart) has 0·5m near the head and may offer a temporary alongside berth, but it is subject to swell.

Facilities

There are roads to the beach at Wine Strand, E of Carrigveen, and 1M further W. Shop, pubs, restaurants, PO at Ballyferriter, 1·5 km SW; filling station 1·5 km from Wine Strand. Shop and pub at Ballydavid (Ballynagall).

Smerwick Harbour from the site of the ruined fort at Dún an Oir: the anchorage on the W side of the bay

Brandon Creek to Magharee Sound

(above) Smerwick Harbour from the S

(right) Ballydavid Pier

(below) Brandon Creek

(bottom) Brandon Quay

Brandon Creek

52°14'·6N 10°18·7'W
AC2789

This tiny inlet between cliffs ("Brandon Cove" on the chart) makes an interesting temporary stop in settled weather with little swell. It was the departure point for St Brendan's legendary voyage in search of the Isles of the Blest, and Tim Severin's Brendan Voyage in 1976.

The pier at the head of the creek dries and is foul, but anchorage (on a boulder bottom) is available.

Sauce Creek, further E, is a spectacular amphitheatre bay and may also offer temporary anchorage in settled weather.

Brandon Bay

52°17'·5N 10°07'W
AC2739

The bay is exposed to the N and a heavy sea can set into it; it is well sheltered from SW to W. At Brandon village, 1·5M S of Brandon Point, there is a drying quay. Anchor in 6m, mud and sand, just NE of the quay; there is a patch of rock just S of the line of the quay. The anchorage is not safe with the wind N of NW or with a heavy swell. Shop, pubs, PO.

Magharee Sound

52°19'N 10°05'W
AC2739 and Plan

The sound provides a simple short cut to Fenit from the W and is easily navigable in moderate weather. It should be avoided in bad weather or heavy swell, which breaks on the banks N of the islands as well as in the sound, especially on the ebb. The W entrance is free of danger if the visible rocks are given a good berth. Steer a middle course between the islands until abreast of **Mucklaghbeg**, 6m high, to avoid **Illaundonnell** and **Illaunlea** on the S side which cover at half tide. The N side of Gurrig Island just open S of Illauntannig astern, 280°, leads through, and course can then be set for Little Samphire Island. If approaching Fenit from the W and passing N of the Magharee Islands, Illaunbarnagh, 9m high and flat in shape, open twice its own length N of Mucklaghmore, 30m high and pudding-shaped, 110°, leads clear N of

The Magharees

Scraggane Bay from the E; Doonagaun, R, Brandon Point, top. Scraggane Point pier, centre R

the banks. Kerry Head and Loop Head in line, 002°, leads clear E of them and W of Mucklaghmore.

Anchorages

In settled weather, temporary anchorage is available E of Illauntannig, on which there are monastic remains including beehive huts and a stone cross. The anchorage is a pool with 2m, off the house on the island; the marks for it are the W point of Scraggane Bay in line with the E point of Illauntannig, and the S side of Illaunturlogh on the middle of Thurran Rock, which dries about 2m and is steep-to. The point of Loop Head on the E point of Reennafardarrig leads W of the rock in 1·2m.

Scraggane Bay, on the mainland side of the sound, provides safe anchorage and good holding in winds between E and SW. Some swell may enter at high water when the rocks inside Doonagaun are covered. There is a pier on the W side. Anchor as close ENE of the pier as draft permits. There is 2m with the pierhead 287° and the E end of Illauntannig 023°. The S and SE sides of the bay are shoal. Pub and restaurant at Fahamore, 1 km.

TRALEE BAY

AC2739

Entry by day in clear weather is straightforward either N of the Magharees or through the Sound. From the W at night, set course to pass 3M N of the Magharee Islands and hold this until the white sector of Little Samphire light is entered. From the N, get into the white sector of Little Samphire light as soon as it is picked up, and head straight

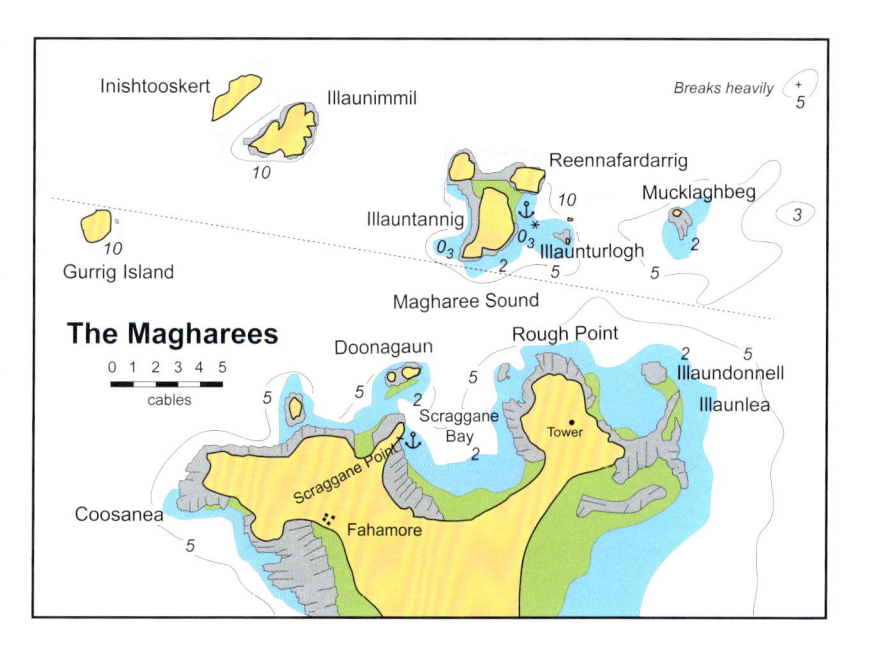

Tralee Bay and Fenit

N side of Gurrig (L) open S of Illauntannig 280° leads through Magharee Sound

(top) Illauntannig anchorage

(above) Scraggane Bay from the N

for the light. As soon as the 10m sounding is reached alter course to 180° and hold this until the red sector is reached bearing 090°, then stand in towards the QR light on Great Samphire Island. Give Little Samphire Island a berth of 2 cables and Great Samphire Island a berth of 1 cable. As Great Samphire Island (the S end of Fenit breakwater) comes abeam, identify the 2 FR vert lights on the pierhead. Be on the lookout for any traffic coming out.

In strong W winds there is good anchorage with very little swell on the W side of Tralee Bay. The best place about 3 cables offshore in 3m is with Little Samphire lighthouse bearing 103°; this is just N of a rocky outcrop 2·5M S of Rough Point.

Fenit Harbour

⊕ FT 52°16'N 9°53'W
AC2739, Imray C55 and Plan

Fenit Harbour is formed by breakwaters running N and E from Great Samphire Island and connected to the N shore by a bridge. Great Samphire Island has a conspicuous statue of St Brendan the Navigator on its summit, its stance and site clearly owing their inspiration to the Metal Men of Sligo and Tramore. The harbour, managed by Tralee & Fenit Harbour Commissioners, has some cargo and fishing vessel traffic and an RNLI all-weather lifeboat. Its N half is occupied by a 140-berth marina.

Marina

VHF Ch. 37 & 80, 066 713 6231. Diesel, water, showers, laundry. Fenit village has shop, pubs, restaurant, PO. Repairs and chandlery, O'Sullivans Marine, Tralee, 066 712 4524. Tralee Bay Sailing Club is based at Fenit.

Constant –0037 Cobh; MHWS 4·6m, MHWN 3·5m, MLWN 1·7m, MLWS 0·6m.

Barrow Harbour

52°18'·5N 9°52'·4W
AC 2739

This beautiful inlet NE of Fenit Island is accessible only with some rise of tide and little or no swell. The entrance, with least depth 2·6m, lies between Illaunnacusha (6m high) and the shore, although the passage between Illaunnacusha and Crow Rock (13m high) is also navigable. Steer for the centre of the gap between the Martello tower and the islet 1 cable off it. Just before bringing the islet abeam turn to starboard to pass close to it, and then follow the slight curve in the channel along the beach on Fenit Island

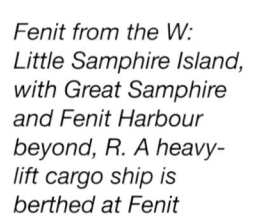

Fenit from the W: Little Samphire Island, with Great Samphire and Fenit Harbour beyond, R. A heavy-lift cargo ship is berthed at Fenit

Fenit; Barrow Harbour

Fenit Harbour and marina from the SE. Crane components built in Killarney await shipment

towards Fenit Castle, a square tower. Anchor opposite the castle in 4m. The channel is 0·5 cable wide and has less than 1m. The inner bay dries out.

(above) Barrow Harbour from the NW: Crow Rock, lower L, Illaunacusha just visible at extreme L

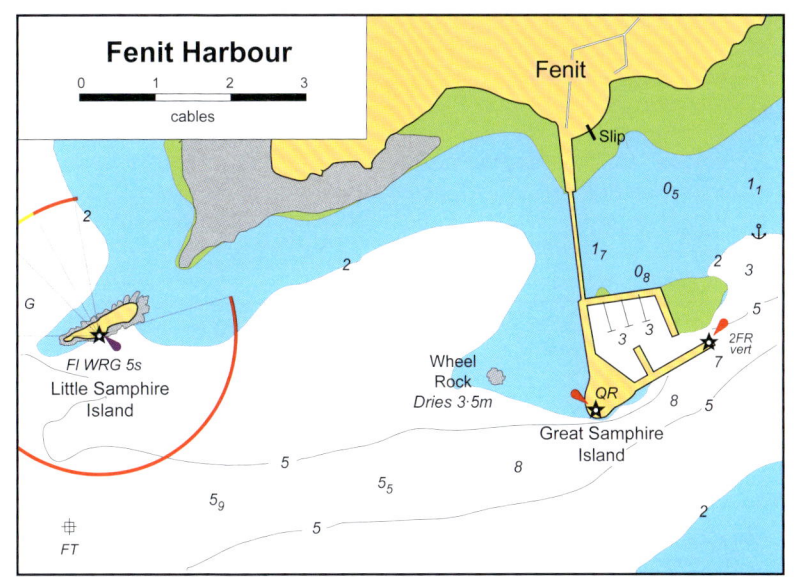

(right) Fenit marina

193

The Shannon Estuary

(top) Entrance to Barrow Harbour: Crow Rock, L

(above) Barrow Harbour anchorage and Fenit Castle

The SHANNON ESTUARY

The Shannon estuary, 50M in length from Loop Head to Limerick, offers a wide variety of anchorages and scenery, and amply rewards the visitor. Its shelter and its gentle shores form a sharp contrast to the exposed and rugged coasts to north and south. There is a marina at Kilrush on the N side 16M from Loop Head. Tides in the estuary are strong, up to 4 kn where it narrows. The outer part of the estuary, below Kilrush, is home to a large pod of bottlenose dolphins.

Directions – main channel

The area between Loop Head, Kerry Head and the Tail of Beal Bar is subject to overfalls and a tide race. To avoid these, stay 0·5 to 1M off the N shore E of Loop Head, or 1M off the S shore between Kerry Head and Beal Point: the N shore is free of off-lying dangers, and the first significant danger on the S shore is Beal Bar. Kilstiffin Bank, which has 7m, breaks in bad weather or a big swell. Kilbaha cliff in line with Kilcloher Head, 260°–080°, leads through the Seven Fathoms Channel N of the bank. Keep 1 cable off Kilcredaun Head to avoid the race on the ebb. Off Kilcredaun Point, 0·5M beyond the head, the ebb runs SW up to 4 to 5 kn, but the tide off Carrigaholt Road is weaker and at Carrigaholt Castle is negligible. In poor visibility Kilcredaun Head can be distinguished by a white stain on the rocks beneath the disused lighthouse and immediately above the HW mark.

Heading seawards with a fresh W wind, or with a swell from the W, it is best to pass

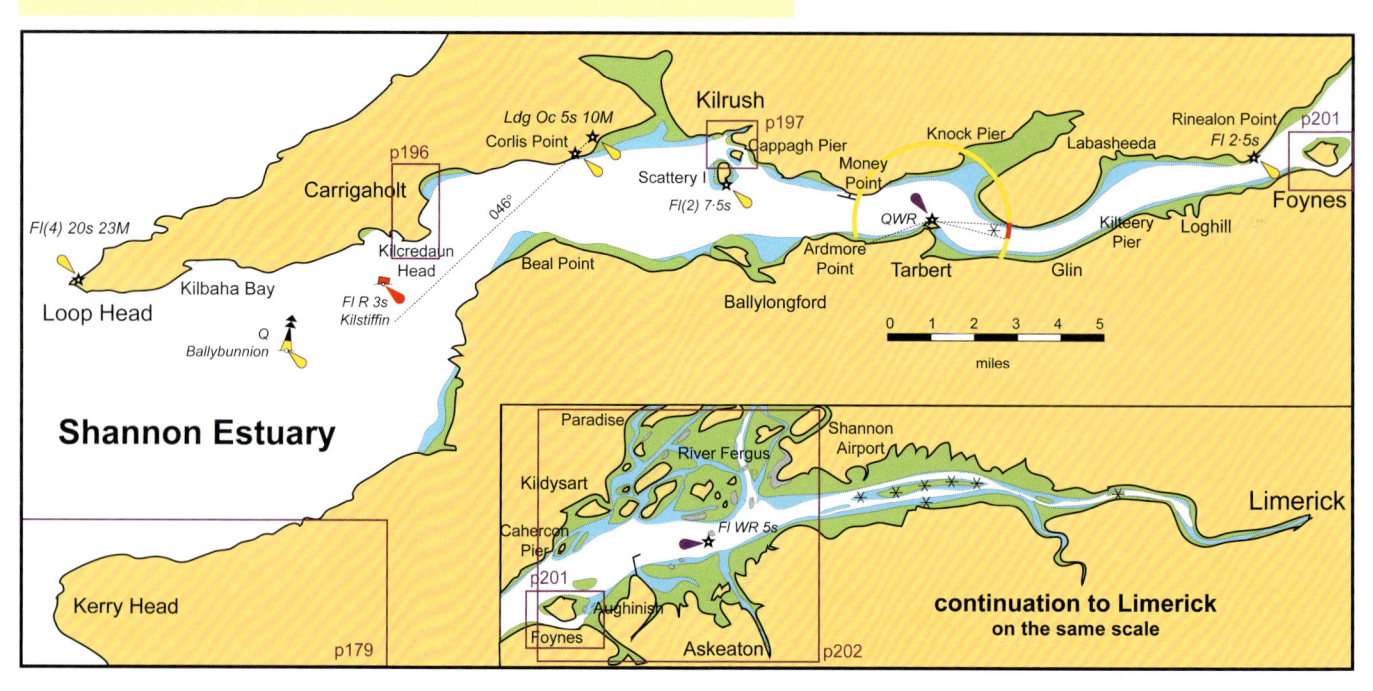

Tides - lower Shannon estuary

Between Kilcredaun Point and Foynes the flood starts between −0515 and −0445 Galway, and the ebb between +0055 and +0120 Galway. The main ebb stream runs SW from Kilcredaun Head, forming a race with heavy overfalls in winds between S and NW. Constant (Kilrush) +0020 Galway; MHWS 5·0m, MHWN 3·7m, MLWN 1·9m, MLWS 0·7m.

Paper Charts

A yacht caught out by bad weather on passage from Kerry to Galway can make Kilbaha or Carrigaholt with AC2254 (Valentia to the Shannon) or 2173 (Loop Head to Slyne Head) but for safe pilotage of the estuary AC1819 (Approaches to the Shannon) is to be preferred. For exploration of the upper reaches of the estuary, the largest-scale charts are essential. There are, unfortunately, no intermediate-scale charts of the Shannon estuary.

194

Kilbaha Bay

Caution

The Shannon estuary is a major port, and very large ships use the channel. The whole estuary should be regarded as a "narrow channel" within the meaning of IRPCS Rule 9, and small craft and yachts should not impede commercial shipping.

Kilcredaun Head at slack water. A yacht leaving with the ebb in these conditions must be prepared to meet very steep short seas in the race. As above, stay within 1M of the N shore to find the calmest water.

Kilbaha Bay

52°34′N 9°51′W
AC1819

This is a useful passage anchorage 3M inside Loop Head, sheltered in winds from W to NE but with indifferent holding, exposed to swell and tidal eddies: a pleasant spot in fine weather, but if unsettled, Carrigaholt is much preferable. There are submerged rocky ledges on both sides of Kilbaha Bay, so keep to the middle approaching the anchorage. Coming in along the line of the local mooring buoys is a good approach. Anchor in 4m in the centre of the bay with the pierhead bearing 250°. SE winds send in a nasty short sea.

The pier is good with a clean sandy bottom. Abreast of the second bollard from the steps it dries 1·4m. In SE winds, when the bay is exposed, the pier offers some shelter.

Water on the pier. Shop, pub, PO, filling station. Constant +0012 Galway; MHWS 4·3m, MHWN 3·3m, MLWN 1·5m, MLWS 0·5m.

(right) Kilcredaun Head from the W, with its now unlit lighthouse tower

(below) Kilbaha Bay and pier

Dangers
Loop Head to Kilrush and Scattery

Beal Bar (dries 0·1m), 8 cables WNW of Beal Point
Baurnahard Spit (dries 2·5m), 1·2M W of Kilrush
Carrigillaun (dries), 2 cables W of Kilrush
Wolf Rock, 1m, 1 cable off the mainland shore opposite Hog Island, 5 cables SE of Kilrush
Carrig Donaun (dries 0·3m), stony patch 1·5 cables E of Scattery Island.

Lights and Marks

Loop Head, Fl(4) 20s 84m 23M (page 210)
Ballybunnion buoy, N Card Q, Racon (M) 6M, AIS
Kilstiffin buoy, PHM Fl R 3s, AIS
Kilcredaun Head, white tower, unlit
Kilcredaun buoy, PHM QR, and **Tail of Beal** buoy, SHM QG, AIS *(these two synchronised)*
Carrigaholt buoy, PHM Fl(2) R 6s, and **Beal Spit** buoy, SHM Fl(2) G 6s *(these two synchronised)*
Beal Bar buoy, SHM Fl G 3s, and **Doonaha** buoy, PHM Fl R 3s *(these two synchronised)*
Corlis Point leading lights 046°, 2×Oc 5s
Letter Point buoy, PHM Fl R 7s
Asdee buoy, PHM Fl R 5s
Scattery Island, white tower, Fl(2) 8s 15m 10M
Kilrush Fairway buoy, L Fl 10s
Kilrush Marina entrance channel, outer leading lights Oc 3s 355°
Kilrush Lock S side, beacon SHM Fl G 6s
Kilrush Marina entrance channel, inner leading lights Oc 6s 070°
Rineanna buoy, PHM QR
North Carraig buoy, N Card Q.

Note that the former lighthouse at Kilcredaun Head is no longer lit.

Carrigaholt and Kilrush

Carrigaholt Bay and New Quay

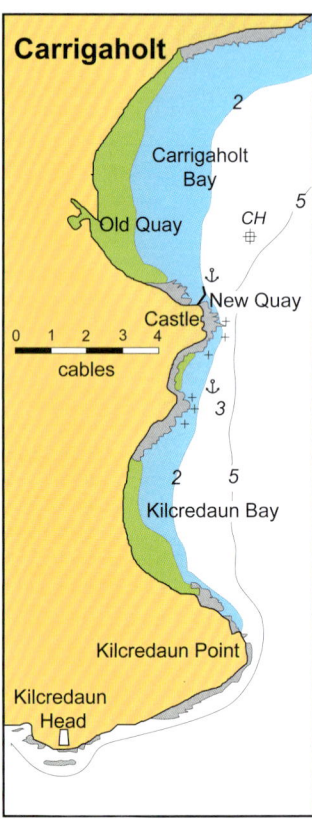

Carrigaholt New Quay

Carrigaholt

⊕ CH 52°36'·2N 9°41'·7W
AC1547, Imray C55 and Plan
This bay, 1·5M N of Kilcredaun Point, gives good protection from all W winds. The most convenient anchorage is 0·5 cable N of the New Quay at the castle, in 3m, excellent holding and no tidal stream to speak of. There are visitors' moorings. Better shelter in W or NW wind may be found off the small bay S of Carrigaholt Castle and N of Kilcredaun Bay, good holding in 3m, sand. Constant +0003 Galway; MHWS 4·9m, MHWN 3·7m, MLWN 1·9m, MLWS 0·7m..

New Quay (Carrigaholt Castle)

The New Quay has 1·7m at the pierhead berth but is unsafe in NW winds. An overnight berth may be available but the fishing boats must be accorded priority. Water on the quay.
The Old Quay, 4 cables NW, dries. Shop and pubs at Carrigaholt.

KILRUSH

⊕ KR 52°37'·6N 9°30'·2W
AC1547, Imray C55 and Plan
Kilrush Channel, between Scattery Island and the shore, is the direct approach from the W to Kilrush Marina and Cappagh Pier (Cappa Pier on the chart). Approaching from the SW on a course of 055° and giving Scattery Island a berth of 2·5 cables, identify the fairway buoy W of Cappagh pier in position 52°37'·6N 9°30'·2W. From there, a line of port- and starboard-hand buoys leads 355° up the channel, which has 2m at its outer end and 1·2m abreast the lock.
In the **approach from the SE** between

196

Kilrush

Hog Island and the mainland, **Wolf Rock**, with 1m, is dangerous near LW and lies 1 cable offshore on the E side of the channel between Hog Island and the shore. Keep well over towards Hog Island; when Scattery Lighthouse is in line with the E part of Hog Island, the rock is abreast.

The water level in the basin is maintained by a barrage and lock. The lock has 3m, can accommodate vessels of 27m overall length and has a pontoon to assist boat handling and provide a temporary berth. It is opened every hour on the half hour from 0830 to 2130 (June to August) and from 0930 to 1730 outside those months. Constant +0020 Galway; MHWS 5·0m, MHWN 3·7m, MLWN 1·9m, MLWS 0·7m.

Marina

Inside the barrage, the inner leading marks lead 070° to the marina, which has 120 berths and 3m least depth. Outside working hours the outer lock gate is left open so that yachts can berth in the lock. Marina VHF Ch. 80, phone 065 9052072, fax 065 9051692, mobile 086 2313870. www.kilrushcreekmarina.ie.

Facilities

Diesel, water, shore power, showers, laundry, chandlery, 45 tonne travelhoist. Supermarkets, shops, pubs, restaurants, filling station, PO, doctors in Kilrush. Hull, mechanical, electrical and electronic repairs

Tides
Kilrush and Approaches

In the channel S of Scattery Island, between the Rineanna and Carrig Shoals, there are heavy overfalls on the ebb with strong W winds; these are worst near the Rineanna buoy. Avoid most of this by keeping between the buoy and Scattery Island. Avoid the windward edge of Rineanna Shoal. Both shoals have least depth 4m. Constant (Kilrush) +0020 Galway; MHWS 5·0m, MHWN 3·7m, MLWN 1·9m, MLWS 0·7m.

Placenames

Note that two distinct places on the Shannon estuary have the name **Rineanna** – the south point of Scattery Island and the headland on the E side of the confluence of the Fergus.

(above right) Kilrush lock from the approach channel

(right) Kilrush Marina

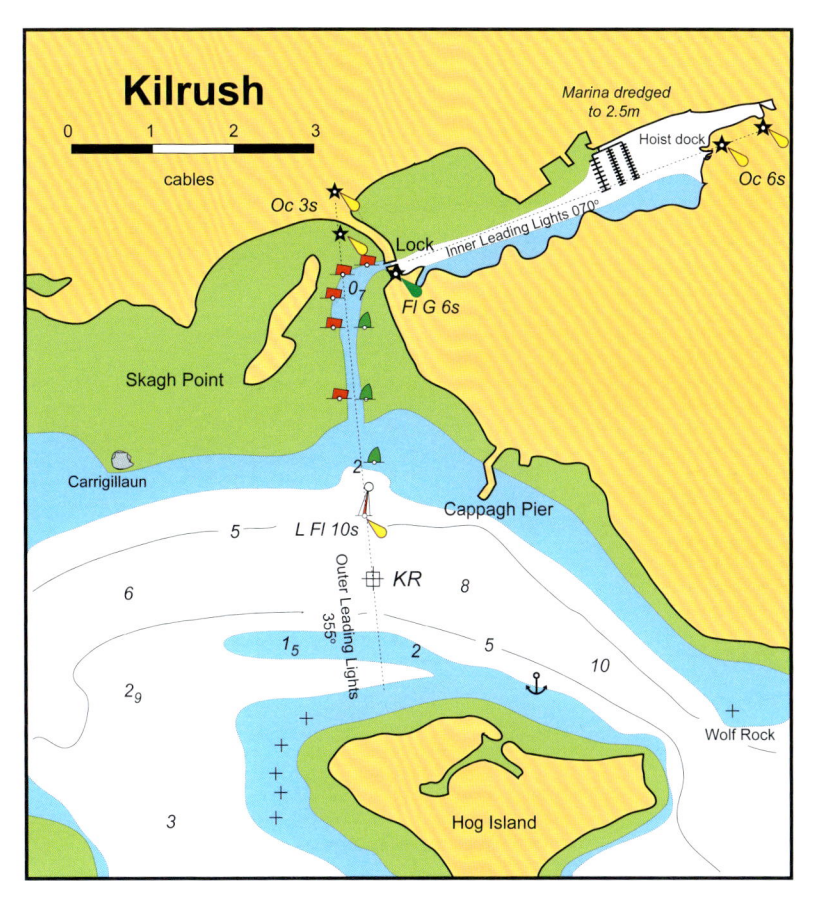

Kilrush fairway buoy and approach: a yacht waits to enter the lock

197

Kilrush and Scattery Island

Kilrush Creek and Marina from the W

by approved contractors; contact the marina office. The Royal Western Yacht Club of Ireland operates from the marina.

Cappagh Pier

Cappagh Pier, 2 cables SE of the entrance to Kilrush, is the pilot station for the Shannon estuary, and the outermost berth at the pier is reserved for the pilot boat; it is clearly marked. The inner berths dry about 0·6m and may be used at suitable rise in reasonable weather. It would not be safe to dry out there.

Water on the pier. Small shop, pub. RNLI inshore lifeboat station (Kilrush).

Scattery Island jetty

Cappagh Pier

Anchorage

- There is temporary or fair-weather anchorage 50m SE of Cappagh pier in 1·5m, fairly good holding.
- A better anchorage is in the bay on the NE of Hog Island with good shelter from SE to SW; the tide here runs SE on both flood and ebb. A green mooring buoy here is used by the pilot boat in SE gales.
- Scattery Roads. There is good shelter from SW to N winds in the bay on the SE side of Scattery Island. Give the S end of the island a berth of 2 cables and anchor in 2 to 3m between 1 and 2 cables NE of the slip near the lighthouse, sand. Note that it shoals quite suddenly from 4 to 1m. Just outside this anchorage there is an eddy on the flood which causes a sea in strong S wind.
- Off the jetty on the E side of Scattery is convenient for visiting the island, but due to the tide is less comfortable than Scattery Roads. Good holding in 2 or 3m, 1·5 to 2 cables from the jetty. S of the line

Kilrush to Foynes; Ballylongford

Tides
Upper Shannon Estuary

Tides run at 3 to 3·5 knots at springs in the channel. The turn of the tide gets later the further up the estuary one goes. At Tarbert the E-going flood begins at −0500 Galway; at Rinealon Point at −0445 Galway; and at Shannon Airport at −0430 Galway. The ebb at the same points begins respectively at +0100, +0120, and +0135 Galway. The range also increases further upstream, from 4·3m at springs at Kilrush to 5·8m at Limerick.
Constant (Foynes) +0100 Galway; MHWS 5·2m, MHWN 4·0m, MLWN 1·6m, MLWS 0·4m.

Dangers
Kilrush to Foynes

Boland's Rock (dries 1·4m), 1·5M E of Tarbert Island
Dillisk Rocks (dry 0·3m), 6 cables E of Labasheeda Point
Long Rock (dries 2·8m), 1M WSW of Garraunbaun Point on the S shore
Carrigeen Rocks (dry 0·3m), 1M ENE of Garraunbaun Point
Elbow Rock (dries 1·4m), in mid-channel between Foynes Island and Durnish Point
Long Rock (dries), 1 cable NE of Elbow Rock.

Lights and Marks

Money Point jetty, 3×2 FR vert
Tarbert tanker jetty, 2×2 FG vert
Tarbert Island, N Point, white tower Iso WR 4s 18m, W14M R10M, W 069°–277°, R 277°–287°, W 287°–339°. Red sector shows over Boland's Rock to the E, white elsewhere 📷 (page 17)
Tarbert Ferry Pier, 2FG vert
Ballyhoolahan Point, Ldg lts 128°, front white tower Iso 3s 13m 3M, rear white beacon, green stripe, Iso 5s 18m 3M
Kilkerin buoy, PHM Fl(2) R 6s
Gorgon buoy, SHM Fl(2) G 6s
Bolands buoy, PHM Fl(2) R 6s
Bolands perch, PHM, red, unlit
Carraig Fada buoy, SHM Fl G 5s
Garraunbaun Point, white beacon, Fl(3) WR 10s 16m W8M R5M, R shore–072°, W 072°–242°, R 242°– shore; red sectors cover Long and Carrigeen Rocks.
Loghill buoy, SHM Fl G 3s
Rinealon Point, black column, white bands, Fl 2·5s 4m 7M.

Entrance to Foynes:
Shannakea Beg, Port Entry Light, on the NW shore of the Shannon opposite Foynes, QWRG 14m 9M. Shows a narrow white sector 288° up the channel to Foynes, with AltWR then R to the N and Alt WG then G to the S
The main entrance, to the SW of Foynes Island, is marked by four pairs of green and red pile beacons, QR, IQR, QG and IQG, including **Hunts (Weir) Point**, red beacon QR 2m 2M and **Colleen Point**, green beacon QG 2m 2M, and by
Barneen Point, red pole beacon L Fl R 5s
Leading lights 108°, grey pole beacons Oc 4s 10M, front 34m, rear 39m
In the channel to the E of Foynes Island are:
Elbow Rock buoy, PHM, unlit
Long Rock buoy, SHM, unlit 📷

of this jetty a shoal extends 2·5 cables from the island shore. About 150m NE of the jetty there is a patch of stones which, like Carrig Donaun further NE, is awash at LWS.

KILRUSH to FOYNES

AC1547, 1548
This 15M stretch of the river has several major landmarks on its banks including the power stations at Money Point and Tarbert, but also delightful and quiet anchorages. A car ferry crosses the river from Tarbert to Killimer. Foynes, behind Foynes Island on the S shore, is the principal commercial port on the Shannon.

Ballylongford Creek and Saleen Quay

52°34'·3N 9°28'·7W (channel entrance buoys)
AC1547
Ballylongford Creek is situated on the S side of the estuary opposite Scattery Island. The entrance, SE of Carrig Island, is marked by a small buoy a cable N of Reenturk Point. The channel to Saleen Quay, 8 cables up-river, has less than 1m and is marked by locally-maintained buoys and perches. It is advisable to enter on a rising tide. Leave the pole on Reenturk Point 30m to port. The quay dries 0·6m, with a good drying berth beyond the first set of steps by the shed. There is also 1m along the S end of the quay but this is usually taken up by local boats. There are oyster beds on the shores beside the channel entrance, and the yellow Special Mark poles on these should be left well to starboard.

Shops, pubs, PO, filling station at Ballylongford village, 1·5 km.

Ballylongford Creek: the pole on Reenturk Point, which should be left 30m to port on entering. Saleen Quay in the distance, centre

Tarbert, Knock Pier and Glin

Tarbert: (above) the inner quay, L, and the ferry pier, R

(above right) Tarbert lighthouse pre-dates the power station by 110 years

(top to bottom) Knock, Glin and Kilteery piers

The Bridge
This rocky ridge about 3M E of Scattery Island, and opposite Ardmore Point on the S shore, extends over halfway across the estuary from the N shore. Although its least depth is 16m there are overfalls with both flood and ebb in strong W winds. It can be avoided by keeping within 0·5M of Ardmore Point.

Tarbert
52°35'N 9°21'·3W
AC1548
At springs the ebb tide runs at 4 kn from the piers out past the lighthouse, causing heavy overfalls in strong NW and W winds. Off the ferry pier the tide always runs NW, as there is an eddy on the flood, and the tide also sweeps through a tunnel in the pier. The S side of the pier must be left clear for the ferry. A berth may be available on the N side of the pier between the steps and the tunnel, or to the E of the steps. There is at least 1·8m at LW and good shelter in all conditions except near slack water in strong NW to NE winds. Constant +0035 Galway; MHWS 5·0m, MHWN 3·8m, MLWN 1·6m, MLWS 0·4m.

Anchorage
S of the elbow of the outer pier with the inner quay in line and with Knock village on the Clare side in line with the end of the outer pier in about 3m, sheltered water in winds between SW and NW, excellent holding. Do not obstruct the ferries. At the time of writing (2015) the power station is not operating.

Facilities
Pub 400m from the pier. Shops, pubs, PO, filling station at Tarbert village, 1·5 km and accessible by dinghy towards HW.

Knock Pier
52°36'·5N 9°21'W, *AC1548*
Clonderalaw Bay, on the N side opposite Tarbert, is a long inlet most of which dries. Knock Pier is 1M within the bay on its NW side and is approached across drying mudflats. When the rock at the base of Tarbert lighthouse covers, which corresponds to HW neaps, there is 1·8m at the pier. Stay close to the pier when going alongside its E side. Pubs and PO.

Caution
The flood sets SSE across Boland's Rock, so avoid passing N of it with the flood, unless with ample wind or power, to avoid being swept onto the rock.

Glin
52°34'·6N 9°17'W
AC1548
Glin Pier is on the S shore 3M upstream of Tarbert lighthouse and 0·25M N of Glin village. The ruined pier extension on iron piles is conspicuous, but the original stone

Kilteery Pier, Labasheeda and Foynes

pier has a clean muddy bottom on its E side and offers shelter in winds between SE and WSW. In summer a pontoon, which dries at LW, is moored to the pier. Be careful not to be set onto the ruined staging by the tide.

Anchorage

Anywhere ENE of the pier in 4m, good holding, well sheltered in S winds, exposed from W to NE. At night Rinealon Point light just open of Garraunbaun Point light is a good anchoring mark. The first half of the ebb runs W but at half tide a strong eddy runs E until LW, when the flood commences and continues running E until HW.

Shops, pubs, restaurants, PO and filling station at Glin village.

Kilteery Pier

52°35′·7N 9°13′·5W
AC1548

Kilteery Pier is on the S side of the estuary opposite Labasheeda. The pier dries about 1·2m but can provide an attractive temporary berth. Loghill village, 1·5 km E, has a shop and pubs.

Labasheeda Roads

52°36′·5N 9°15′W
AC1548

This anchorage on the N shore gives good shelter in W and NW winds with good holding. The best place is NE of Redgap Point as close as possible to the mudbank to avoid the SW-going ebb. Labasheeda village has PO and pub and can be reached by dinghy with sufficient rise of tide. Water tap on the pier.

Anchorage

The bay west of Rinealon Point is well sheltered in N and NE winds and is out of the strength of the ebb tide. It lies off Aillroe Hill which is conspicuous on the shoreline 6·5 cables W of Rinealon Point with the road along its S slope. Anchor abreast the hill about 0·75 cables from the shore in 4m.

FOYNES

⊕FY 52°37′·1N 9°07′·8W
AC1549, Imray C55 and Plan

Foynes Harbour is a commercial port, managed by Shannon Foynes Port Company. The channel between Foynes Island and the S shore is an excellent natural harbour with shelter from all winds, easy access and good facilities; however there is a strong tide through the channel. The port office monitors VHF Ch 16 and 11, 24 hours. HM phone 069 73103.

Labasheeda

Foynes Harbour from the SE; Foynes Island upper R, East Pier, R

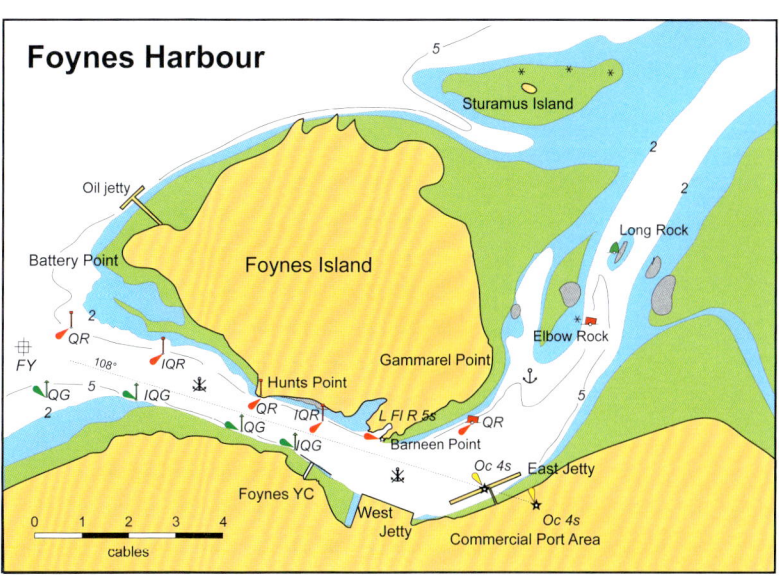

Foynes

(top) Approach to Foynes from the NE: Long Rock buoy, L

(above) Foynes YC pontoon

Directions

Approaching from the W, there is shoal water extending 1 cable off the S shore as far as Poultallin Point at the entrance. From the W end of Foynes Island a shoal runs out for 2 cables with a rock on its S edge. Otherwise the channel is clear, and is well marked.

Approaching from the NE, the channel lies between mudbanks with some rocks and a least depth of 2·1m, and requires more care than the W entrance. Long Rock lies in mid-channel with a green buoy on its W side; leave this buoy to port on entering. Two cables further on a red buoy marks **Elbow Rock.** From the Elbow Rock buoy steer for the East Pier and the anchorage.

Anchorage

Anchor E or SE of Gammarel Point. Foynes YC has a marina pontoon 250m long off the clubhouse at Colleen Point, W of the port area. The clubhouse has the usual facilities during the summer. There are visitors' moorings. Landing is practicable only at the YC pontoon, since the secure commercial port area occupies the entire waterfront at the village.

Constant +0100 Galway; MHWS 5·2m, MHWN 4·0m, MLWN 1·6m, MLWS 0·4m.

Facilities

Filling station, shops, pubs, PO, doctors. Small chandlery at Vincent Kelly supermarket, 069 65183.

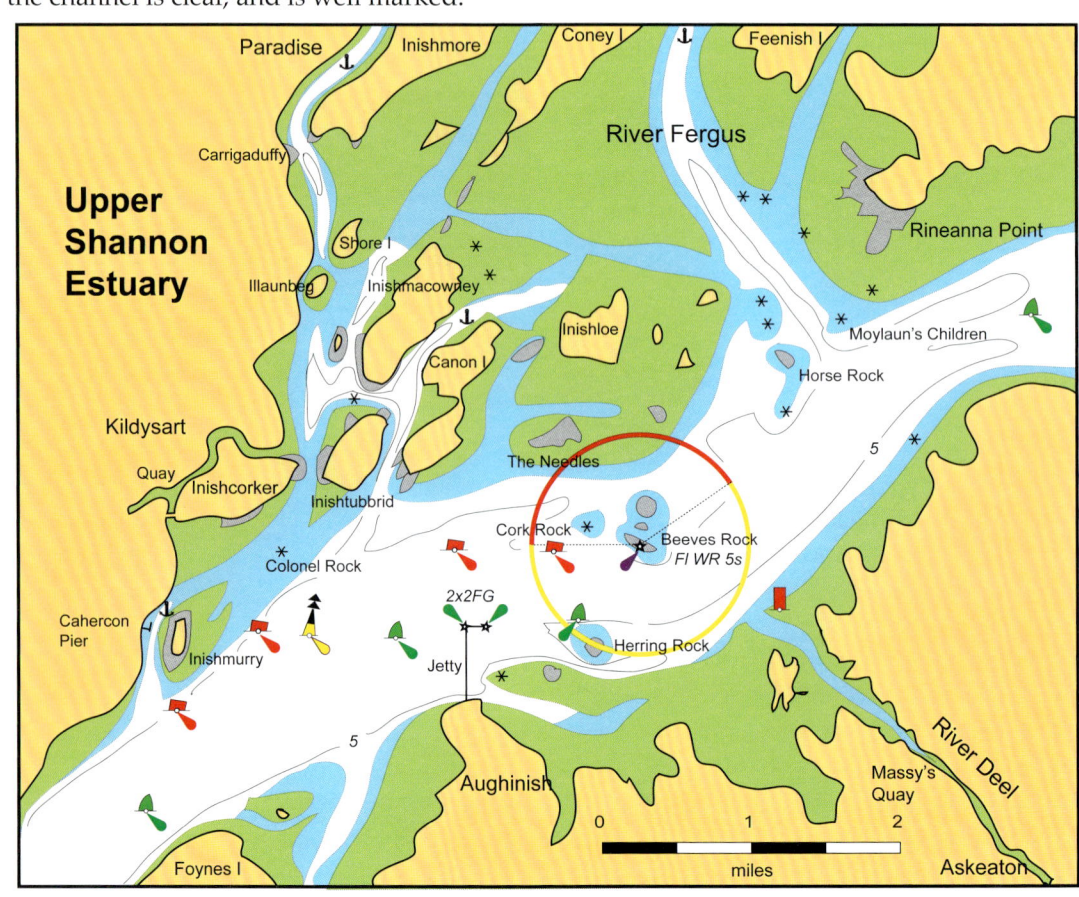

River Deel

Dangers
Foynes to Limerick

The dangers are too numerous to list in exhaustive detail, but the principal ones are as follows:

Colonel Rock (dries 0·3m) 1M NE of Inishmurry

Herring Rock (dries 2·7m), 1M E by N of Aughinish Point

Beeves Rock (dries 1·4m), **Cork Rock** (dries 5·2m) and **Wide Rock** (dries 4m), in mid-channel 1·5M ENE of Aughinish Point

The Needles, extensive drying reef 2M NE of Aughinish Point

Horse Rock (dries 2·8m), 1·4M SW of Rineanna Point

Moylaun's Children (dry 0·3m), at the end of the reef extending 1M SW from Rineanna Point

Roadway Rock (dries 2·4m), in mid-channel of the River Fergus between Coney and Feenish Islands

Carrigkeal (dries 2·1m), **Middle Ground** (dries up to 5·5m at **Bridge Rock**) and **Bird Rock** (dries 2·1m), together extending 3M in mid-channel E of Dernish Island

Logheen Rock (dries 1·3m), 7 cables N of Carrigclogher Point

Carrigdirty Rock (dries 2·7m), 6 cables NE of Carrigclogher Point

FOYNES to LIMERICK

AC1549, 1540

Above Foynes the character of the river changes and there are many drying and submerged rocks, some in mid-channel, and many around the islands in the mouth of the Fergus. Proceeding up-river to Limerick it is advisable to stay in the buoyed channel.

Directions

Aughinish Island, with its conspicuous aluminium works and its jetty projecting 5 cables N from Aughinish Point, lies 2M upstream from Foynes. The confluence of the Shannon and the Fergus is on the N side 3M above Aughinish. The main channel runs N of Aughinish jetty and S of Beeves Rock lighthouse. Under sail in light winds, beware of being swept into the jetty by strong tides. A tail of rock extends 2 cables N from Herring Rock, which is particularly dangerous coming downstream as the strong ebb from Beeves Rock sets directly on to it. Note also the reef extending 4 cables S from Horse Rock. Aughinish N Card buoy marks Aughinish Shoal, which has more than 5m and need not trouble a yacht.

River Deel

52°38'·7N 9°00'·5W
AC1549

The Deel, which joins the Shannon 2M E of

Lights and Marks

The main channel is well marked by lit port- and starboard-hand buoys, and by the following principal fixed marks:

Beeves Rock, stone tower Fl WR 5s 12m W12M R9m, W 064°–091°, R 091°–238°, W 238°–265°, W(unintens) 265°–064°. Shows white over channels to WSW and ENE, red over dangers to the N and unintensified white to S and SE. 📷 *(page 12)*

Dernish Island Pier Head, 2×2FR vert 2m 2M

Conor Rock, white tower, Fl R 4s 6m 6M

North Channel Ldg lts 093°, front white tower on Tradree Rock, Fl R 2s 6m 5M, rear white tower, red bands Iso 6s 14m 5M

Bird Rock, white tower QG 6m 5M

Grass Island, Fl WG 2s 6m 4M, W 146°-339°, G 339°-146°. Shows white over the channel to N, NE and E, green over the shallows to the SW

Logheen Rock, QR 4m 5M

Spilling Rock, Fl G 5s 5m 5M

N Side ldg lts 061°, front on Crawford Rock Fl R 3s 6m 5M, rear Crawford No 2, Iso 6s 10m 5M; ldg lts 302°, front on Flagstaff Rock Fl R 7s 7m 5M, rear Crawford No 2 as above

The Whelps, Fl G 3s 5m 5M

Meelick Leading Lights 106° Iso R 4s 5M (sync), front 6m on Meelick Rock, rear 9m

Aughinish jetty: Beeves Rock lighthouse, L

(right) Deel Bar beacon

(below) Massy's Quay

203

River Fergus; Kildysart

(top) Approaches to Kildysart, from the NE: the Colonel's Point, L, and the first pair of channel marks, centre and R

(above) Kildysart Quay

Auginish Point, has 0·6m at its mouth and a least depth of 0·7m in the channel. A port hand beacon marks the entrance. When the Sheehan, the E point of Beeves Rock, is covered, there is a depth of 2m on the Deel bar NW of the beacon. The channel is marked by small port-hand buoys up to Massy's Quay, which dries. Moorings may be available. Deel Boat Club maintains a private pontoon at Massy's Quay.

Facilities

Askeaton village, 2 km from Massy's Quay, has supermarket, pubs, PO and filling station. Boatyard at Massy's Quay (Ryan & Roberts Marine Services, 061 392198, fax 061 392344, mobile 087 417 9128), hull and mechanical repairs, mobile crane, winter storage, chandlery.

RIVER FERGUS

The mouth of the Fergus is a sandy estuary 5M long by 3M wide, with narrow channels winding among islands and drying banks. Several of these channels are navigable but the limit of safe navigation must be taken as Coney Island, 3M from the main channel of the Shannon, since the river is not charted beyond that. The accessible stretch, however, includes several delightful anchorages. The greatest care is required in pilotage and AC1549 must be closely studied.

Cahercon Pier

52°38'·7N 9°06'·5W
AC1549

This pier ("Cahiracon" on the chart), behind Inishmurry on the Clare side N of Foynes, is unsuitable as an alongside berth due to strong tides, and rocks in the approach and around the pier. Anchorage is possible 1·5 cables NE of the pier abreast the end of the reef running out from Inishmurry, good holding in 2·7 to 5m, with good shelter from WSW to N. No facilities.

Kildysart

52°40'·1N 9°06'W
AC1549

The pretty village of Kildysart (Killadysert on the chart) lies at the head of a narrow creek NW of Inishcorker and is accessible to yachts of moderate draft with suitable rise of tide. The entrance is N of the Colonel's Point, the E end of Inishcorker. The tidal streams among the islands are strong and there are many unmarked hazards demanding the greatest care in pilotage. The narrows between the Colonel's Point and Inishtubbrid have a 5-knot tide and boulder banks on each side, and this approach cannot be recommended to a stranger. The channel W of Inishcorker is closed by a causeway.

The safer approach to the entrance is the passage between Inishtubbrid and Canon Island, then N of Inishtubbrid, keeping to the N side here until past the rock (drying 0·3m) N of Inishtubbrid. Steer W until 1 cable from the mainland shore, then head for the Colonel's Point. There are a couple of large boulders NW of the point which must be given a fair berth when coming round for Kildysart Creek, but more particularly when leaving as the ebb sets down on them. However, do not go too far from this side. The entrance is marked with port- and starboard-hand beacons. The creek dries 1·8m (and

Paradise

*(above and below)
Paradise*

so has 2·2m at MHWN, a metre more at springs) and is well marked by pole beacons. The quay (N of the W point of Inishcorker) is suitable for drying out.

Facilities

Water on the quay. Filling station, shops, PO, pubs, doctor at Kildysart village.

Paradise

52°42'·5N 9°03'·5W
AC1549

Paradise House, now a ruin, was the family home of Lieutenant William Henn RN, whose cutter *Galatea* raced against *Mayflower* for the America's Cup in 1886. The *Galatea*, which drew 13 feet 6 inches and displaced 158 tons, was subsequently sailed up to Paradise. The splendidly sheltered and lovely anchorage is in the channel between Inishmore and the mainland, and the approach requires some care in pilotage. The tricky part is between Illaunbeg and Shore Island, where there is the least depth (0·6m at LAT), and drying rocks project from each side. A bearing of 356° on the end of the quay on Shore Island leads between the rocks. **Carrigaduffy (Paradise Rock),** which dries 1·8m, protrudes a little more into the channel than the chart shows. When approaching Inishmore keep to the island side of mid-channel.

Anchorage

Anchor in 2m in mid-channel, NE of the conspicuous ruin of the old house and S of the slip where the road from Ballynacally meets the shore. Immediately upstream of the (now barely discernible) ruined landing stage below the house there is an underwater pipeline across the channel.

Facilities

Shop, PO, pub at Ballynacally, 1·5 km.

Channel W of Canon Island

52°39'·5N 9°04'W
AC1549

Entering from the Shannon E of Inishtubbrid there is a clear channel between Canon Island and Inishmacowney. E of Inishmacowney are rocks, including **Carriganinneen** (dries

205

River Fergus; River Shannon to Limerick

The River Shannon at Limerick

4·9m). This passage leads to the channel N of Inishloe which runs SE to rejoin the main channel of the River Fergus. It is very narrow between steep, drying banks and has least depth about 1m.

Anchorage

Anchorage is available in 4m, N of Canon Island.

River Fergus, Main Channel

AC1549

Considerable care is needed at the entrance because of the unmarked rocks. The optimum time for entry is within 2 hours of LW so that Horse Rock is uncovered and can be used as a reference point.

Directions

Approach on a course of due N, steering to pass 1 cable E of Horse Rock, and hold this course until Blackthorn Island is abeam to port. Then steer 349° until within 4 cables of Coney Island, and Feenish Island is abeam to starboard. Then steer to pass 1 cable off Curragh Point, the E end of Coney Island, to avoid Roadway Rock.

Anchorage

Anchor E of the island in 2·5 to 5m, sheltered from W to NE. The current here always runs to the S and is not strong.

RIVER SHANNON – RINEANNA POINT to LIMERICK

AC1540

This passage is straightforward with an up-to-date chart showing the latest buoyage. Follow the buoyed channel. The drying harbour E of Dernish Island is part of the precincts of Shannon Airport and is prohibited to yachts.

The limit of navigation for masted yachts is the Shannon Bridge at Limerick. It has a clearance of 3·3m at MHWS.

Limerick – Ted Russell Dock

The wet dock at Limerick, with an area of 2 cables by 0·5 cables, is entered through a lock gate which opens from 1 hour before HW up to HW. The entrance is on the S bank of the river, 4 cables from the Shannon Bridge. The dock might best be described as an industrial environment, but it is possible to berth a yacht there if necessary. The maximum length of stay is three days. All owners must sign an indemnity form which can be obtained from the Dock Gateman upon entry to the dock. Yachts should not be left unattended as there is a frequent requirement to shift around the dock to accommodate the movement of commercial coastal traffic. There is no slipway. A crane is available; contact Limerick Cargo Handling, 061 312733. For vessels which can pass under the Shannon Bridge, alternative berths are available upstream of the bridge at the Custom House Marina, accessed via Sarsfield Lock (see below). Ted Russell Dock is managed by Shannon Foynes Port Company, HM phone 069 73103.

River Shannon above Limerick

Constant +0130 Galway; MHWS 5·9m, MHWN 4·5m, MLWN 1·3m, MLWS 0·1m.

Facilities

Limerick (57,100) has all the facilities of a city, including rail connections to Dublin and Cork and easy access to Shannon Airport.

River Shannon above Limerick

Access from Limerick to the Shannon Navigation and the extensive inland waterway network connected to it is available via a canal system comprising Sarsfield Lock (immediately upstream of the Shannon Bridge), the Abbey River, the tailrace and headrace of Ardnacrusha Power Station, and the locks at Ardnacrusha. The passage is interesting and worthwhile, but also challenging, and is not for the inexperienced. The lock chambers at Ardnacrusha are 32m by 5·9m – Sarsfield Lock is wider. The weir beside Sarsfield Lock maintains a least depth of 1·7m in the canal system; the weir covers towards HW. The headroom limit is imposed by Baal's Bridge on the Abbey River, where there is 3m headroom for a width of 6m when the tide is below the level of the weir; i.e. the bridge arch is 4·7m above the river bed.

Vessels drawing more than 1·5m must obtain permission from Waterways Ireland (090 649 4232) before making the passage,

Limerick; the entrance to Sarsfield Lock, from the seaward end

and all vessels must give 24 hours' notice of intended passage to the lock-keeper at Ardnacrusha (087 997 0131). The passage can be made only when the power station is shut down or running one turbine out of four.

Directions for pilotage of the canal and lock system at Limerick are contained in the booklet "City Cruising" by Edgar Heenan, available free of charge from Waterways Ireland, Carrick-on-Shannon, Co.Leitrim, 071 965 0898.

The weir above Sarsfield Lock; the navigable channel leaves the yellow marks to port. The main channel of the Shannon, with its rapids, and King John's Castle, L. Custom House Marina can just be seen, R

6 Loop Head to Slyne Head

Inishmore, Aran Islands, with its karst landscape: the ancient fort of Dún Aengus on the clifftop. Portmurvy, top L

The long north-west-facing coast of County Clare has few harbours, and no good ones, but is spectacularly scenic from seaward, its most notable feature being the sheer 200m Cliffs of Moher. The limestone geology of this region is remarkable, and results in the extraordinary and valuable *karst* landscape of the Burren, with its unique flora. The Aran Islands have an international reputation as a cultural treasure. Their barren stony landscape and sheer cliffs are awe-inspiring, and their antiquities, including the ancient fortress of Dún Aengus, are unparalleled. The shores of Galway Bay, to the east, are low-lying, with many shallow and stony inlets. Galway is a beautiful and historic city and a vibrant and important commercial and academic centre. West of Galway and Spiddle lies Connemara, a land of water and rock where sea and land interpenetrate to form a maze of islands, reefs, tide-swept channels and sandy bays. This is a Gaeltacht area where spoken Irish may often be heard. In former times it was almost entirely dependent on seaborne transport,

> **"Cruising Ireland"**
> This coast is described on pages 92 to 107 of **Cruising Ireland**

> **Paper Charts**
> On the smaller scale, AC2173 Loop Head to Slyne Head covers the area described in this chapter. Imray's C55 Dingle Bay to Galway Bay and C54 Galway Bay to Donegal Bay may be useful for planning, but for exploring the coast the largest-scale charts, with the exception of AC1904 Galway Harbour, are essential. If making the offshore passage from Kerry or the Shannon to Galway or Connemara, AC3338 is optional if 2173 is carried. For Joyce's Pass, inside Slyne Head, AC2708 is indispensible.

Loop Head to Slyne Head

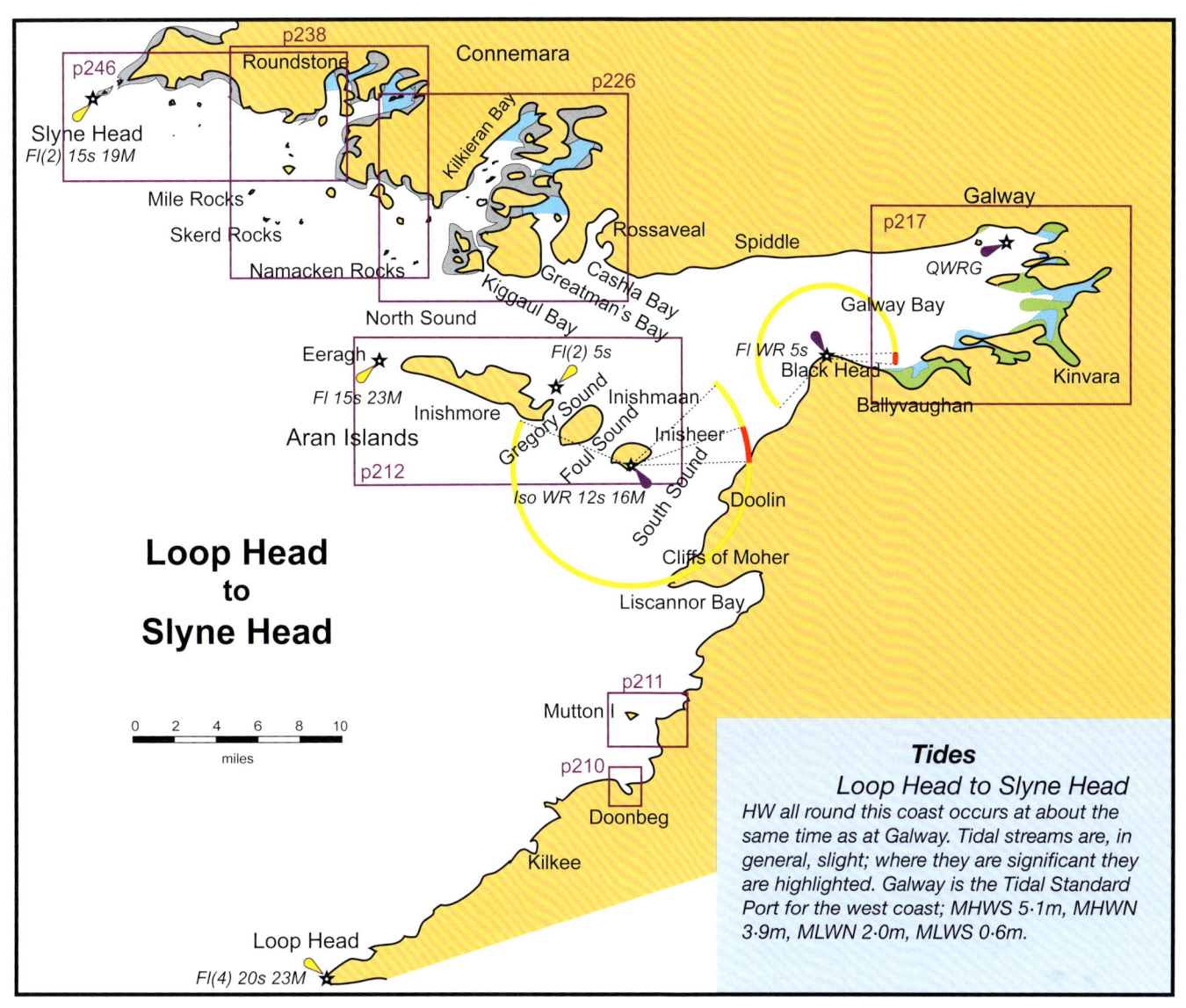

in small vessels under oars and sail, and there are hundreds of ancient stone piers and jetties, many of them utterly inaccessible to anyone without intimate local knowledge. This is the home of the *húicéir* or *bád mór*, the Galway hooker, and every year in the third week of August at Kinvara on Galway Bay is held the Cruinniú na mBád, the traditional boat festival. Hookers and their smaller versions the *leathbád*, *gleoiteog* and *púcán*, the heavy wooden *curach adhmaid* and the light canvas-covered *curach* are encountered all round the coast.

Lights and Marks

Loop Head, white tower Fl(4) 20s 84m 23M
Doolin Pier, 2FG vert
Inisheer, black tower, white band Iso WR 12s 34m, W16M R11M, W 231°–245°, R 245°–269°, W 269°–115°. Shows red to the E over Finnis Rock, white elsewhere.
Black Head, white tower Fl WR 20s 20m W11M R8M, W 045°–268°, R 268°–276°. Shows red to the E over Illaunloo and Finavarra Point, white elsewhere. AIS.

Dangers
Loop Head to Black Head

Grundel Rock (dries 0·3m), 1·2M WSW of Mutton Island
Muirbeg, 0·3m, and **Drumdeirg Rock** (dries 3m), S of Liscannor Bay
Kilstiffin Rocks, 1·5m, 1·5M SSW of Cancregga at the W end of Liscannor Bay.

Caution

In many places on this coast the limited horizontal accuracy of the current charts means that GPS chart plotters must not be implicitly relied upon in close-quarters pilotage. Errors of up to 90 metres have been measured (note that this is **not** due to an offset in horizontal datum, and is not consistent in direction).

Tides
Loop Head to Slyne Head

HW all round this coast occurs at about the same time as at Galway. Tidal streams are, in general, slight; where they are significant they are highlighted. Galway is the Tidal Standard Port for the west coast; MHWS 5·1m, MHWN 3·9m, MLWN 2·0m, MLWS 0·6m.

Harbours on the west coast of Clare

(top) Loop Head from the SW (photo Dick Lincoln)

(above) Moore Bay from the S: Kilkee, bottom, George's Head, top L

The bay close S of Killard Point, shown on the charts as rocky, is in fact a Blue Flag sandy beach

LOOP HEAD to BLACK HEAD

AC3338, 2173

There are half a dozen feasible fair-weather anchorages on the west coast of Clare but no safe havens. The Cliffs of Moher, N of Liscannor Bay, are among Ireland's most famous coastal features although far short of being its highest cliffs – that honour belongs to Croaghaun on Achill Island.

Kilkee

52°41'·5N 9°40'W
AC3338

Moore Bay, with the resort of Kilkee at its head, lies 13M NE of Loop Head and offers possible shelter in offshore winds. Much of the available space in the bay has kelp which may make anchoring difficult. **Black Rocks** (dry 2·1m) are in the centre of the entrance 3 cables N of **Duggerna Rock** (0·6m high, the outer extremity of a drying ledge), and there are drying rocks also 1 cable S of George's Head, on the N side.

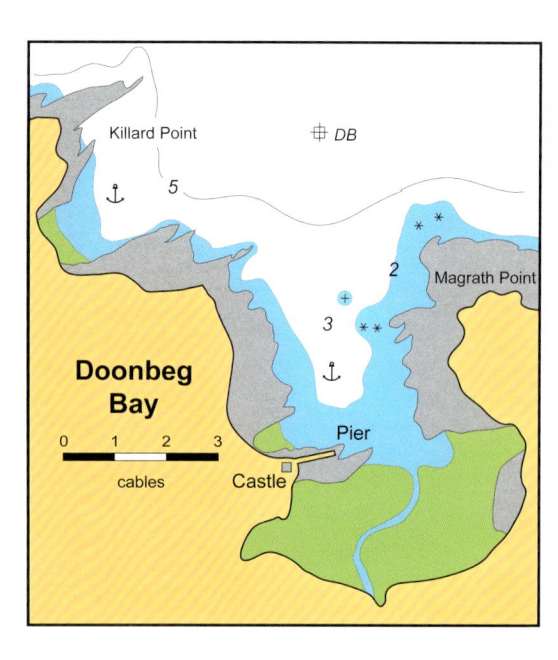

Doonbeg Bay

⊕ DB 52°45'N 9°32'W

This N-facing bay 19M NE of Loop Head provides a feasible temporary anchorage in winds between NE and SW, but is subject to swell. The east side of the bay is foul and the head of the bay is shallower than charted. Approach with the end of the pier bearing 162° and anchor 2 cables N of the pier in 2·5m. There are local boats on moorings here. Pubs and shops at Doonbeg village, 1 km.

In certain swell conditions the bay close S of Killard Point, to the NW, may offer better shelter.

Mutton Island

⊕ MI 52°47'·7N 9°32'W
AC3338 and Plan

Mutton Island, 1M long and 30m high, extends 2M offshore 21M NE of Loop Head. There is no shelter in a heavy onshore swell and this is a lee shore in winds from NW and SW, but nonetheless it offers a feasible anchorage in settled or offshore weather.

Directions

From the SW, identify Mattle Island (10m high) and steer to pass 2 cables W of it. Give the SE side of Mutton Island a berth of 2 cables to clear Mal Rock, which almost always breaks. **From the N**, give the SW corner of Mutton Island a berth of 1·5 to 2 cables to pass between it and Curragh Shoal, 2·1m, then steer E towards Mal Rock until the anchorage opens up. Anchor 1 to 1·5 cables off the ruined cottages at the SE end of the island in 3 to 4m, rock and sand. This anchorage is

Mutton Island and Liscannor; Aran Islands

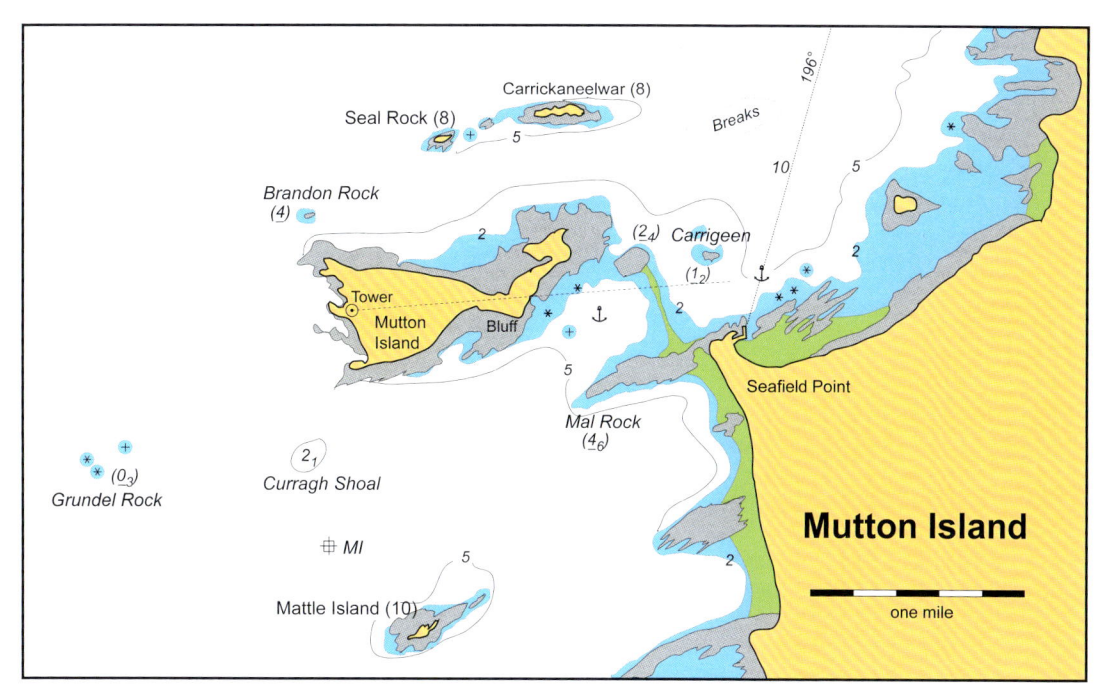

Seafield Pier: the yacht is moored in shallow water

completely exposed to S and SW.

There is also an anchorage E of the rocky spit (which dries 1m in mid-channel) connecting the island with the shore, N of the pier at Seafield Point and E of the drying rocks N of the point. **From the N**, 7 cables E of Carrickaneelwar, steer 196° for the end of the pier. Anchor a little E of this line in 4 to 5m sand, when about 2 cables due N of the pier, with the tower and bluff on Mutton Island in line. There is a swell with winds N of W. A narrow channel with 1·8m between drying rocks runs from seaward to the E side of the pier.

Liscannor

There is a small drying harbour at Liscannor, on the N side of Liscannor Bay. The approach is between two unlit concrete beacons. A rock drying 0·3m lies close NE of the approach line from the SE. The harbour entrance dries 0·6m but the bottom at the pierheads is foul. In settled conditions the outside of the N wall provides a drying berth on a shelving but clean bottom. Anchorage, also in settled conditions, is available S of the harbour. Shops, restaurants, pubs and filling station ashore.

Doolin, in the cove inside Crab Island on the N side of Doonnagore Bay has a pier from which ferries run in summer to the Aran Islands. The pier was reconstructed in 2015 to permit all-tide access but the cove is restricted and rocky, and unsuitable as an anchorage.

THE ARAN ISLANDS

AC3339, Imray C55

The Aran Islands of Inishmore, Inishmaan and Inisheer, with their outliers, make up a group extending 15M NW–SE and sheltering Galway Bay. The three islands have a combined population of 1251. Inishmore has a good harbour and visitors' moorings at Kilronan and a delightful sheltered bay at Portmurvy, and there is a good small harbour at Caladh Mór on Inishmaan. Inisheer has only an open roadstead and pier. Two major lights – Eeragh and Inisheer – mark the NW and SE extremities, respectively, of the island chain. Ferries run to Rossaveal, Galway and

Liscannor Harbour: the yacht is at the drying berth on the outside of the N wall

211

Aran Islands

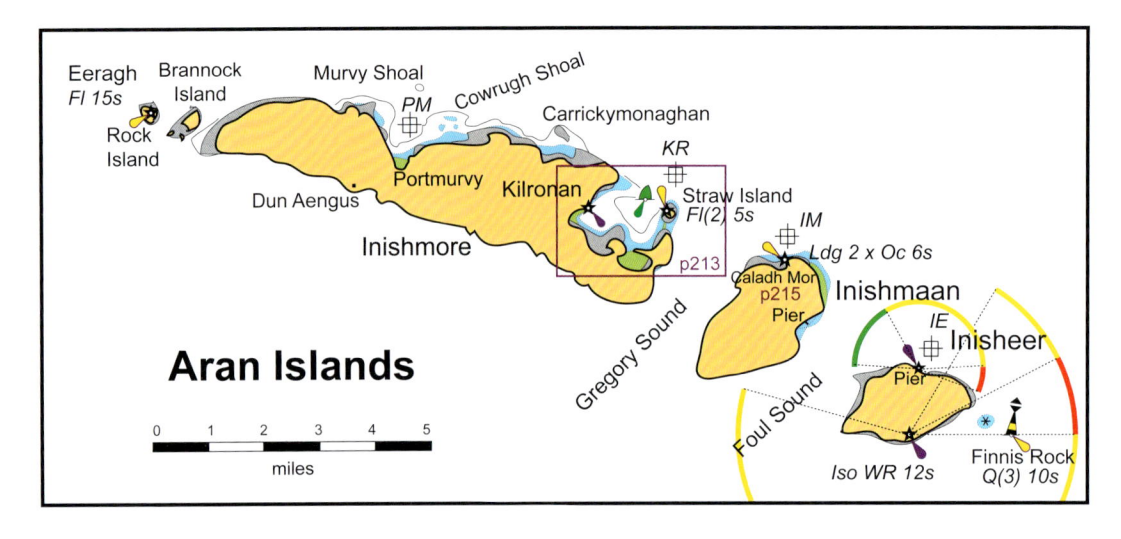

Straw Island from the NW

Lights and Marks

Finnis Rock buoy, E Card Q(3) 10s, AIS
Inisheer, white tower, black band, Iso WR 12s 34m, W16M R11M, W 231°–245°, R 245°–269°, W 269°–115°, AIS. Shows red over Finnis Rock, white elsewhere.
Inisheer Pier, Fl WRG 5s 5m 8M, G 093°–150°, W 150°–266°, R 266°–290°
Inishmaan (Caladh Mór Harbour) leading lights 192·5°, 2 × Oc 6s 8M
Caladh Mór entrance beacons PHM Fl R 5s 6m 4M and SHM Fl G 5s 8m 4M
Killeany buoy, SHM Fl G 3s, AIS
Straw Island, white tower Fl(2) 5s 11m 12M
Killeany ldg lts 192° Oc 5s 3M, front W col 6m, rear W col 8m
Kilronan Breakwater, col Fl G 1·5s 7m 5M
Kilronan N Pier, 2FR vert
Kilronan RNLI pontoon, 2FG vert
Eeragh, white tower, two black bands, Fl 15s 35m 23M.

Tides
Aran Islands

The streams run at 1 kn springs in South Sound and 1·5 kn in Foul Sound and Gregory Sound, the NE-going stream commencing at –0520 Galway and the SW-going stream at +0105 Galway.
Constant (Kilronan) –0005 Galway, MHWS 4·7m, MHWN 3·6m, MLWN 1·8m, MLWS 0·5m.

Dangers

Finnis Rock (dries 0·4m), 4 cables SE of Trawkeera Point, Inisheer
Pipe Rock (dries), 2 cables NW of Inisheer
The Bar of Aran, 3·4m, at the entrance to Killeany Bay, Inishmore
Bar Rock (dries 0·4m), 2 cables SE of Carrickadda Point and 2 cables NW of the Bar of Aran
Unnamed rock (awash at LAT), 2 cables S of Bar Rock
Carrickadda (dries 1·2m) and **Carrickymonaghan** (dries 0·4m), NW of Killeany Bay
Cowrugh Shoal, 0·8m, 5 cables offshore E of Portmurvy
Craghalmon (dries 0·6m), 1M NNW of Portmurvy
Brocklinmore and **Brocklinbeg Banks**, N of Inishmore, may break in gale conditions or a high swell.

Doolin, and an air service links all three islands with Connemara airport at Inverin, 6 km SE of Rossaveal. The islands have an extraordinary *karst* landscape, an island extension of the Burren of County Clare.

Southern Approaches to the Aran Islands

Inishmore presents a wall of rock to the S. Its sheer limestone cliffs rise from 30m at the E end to 80m at the W. The prehistoric fortress of Dún Aengus, and the old lighthouse on the E summit of the island, are conspicuous. A valley running SW–NE at the narrow neck of land between Blind Sound and Portmurvy may make Inishmore appear as two islands when it is first sighted from the S. Inishmaan, also cliffbound, has three large wind turbines near its SW point which provide an excellent landmark. The coast of Inisheer slopes more gradually. The channels between the islands and between Inisheer and the mainland are generally clean and deep; Finnis Rock, E of Inisheer, is marked by a buoy, and a berth of 5 cables clears Pipe Rock, NW of Inisheer. In heavy weather the swell reflected from the

Kilronan

cliffs can raise a confused sea in Gregory Sound, while Foul Sound tends to be calmer.

KILRONAN

⊕ *KR* 53°07'·4N 9°37'·8W
AC3339, Imray C55 and Plan

The village of Kilronan, on Killeany Bay, is the main township and ferry port on the islands. The bay offers all-round shelter in moderate weather, but becomes untenable as an anchorage in strong winds between N and E, while heavy NW weather sends in a considerable swell. The harbour offers perfect shelter; the basin and approach channel were dredged to 3·5m (2010).

Directions

From the E and Gregory Sound, give Straw Island a berth of 3 cables and leave Killeany buoy to starboard, then steer for the end of Kilronan breakwater. From the N or NW, it is usually safe to pass within a cable NW of Killeany buoy, crossing the Bar of Aran in 3 to 4m, but note that the buoy was repositioned a cable NW of its former position in 2012. In a swell, leave the buoy to starboard.

The drying crest of Cush Spit, between Straw Island and Inishmore, is slightly further west than charted. It dries 0·8m (2012). Ferries use this passage near HW.

Anchorage

Anchor S of Kilronan harbour in 3 to 4m, sand. Allow plenty of room for the ferries to manoeuvre. There are visitors' moorings; those nearest the shore are in shallow water.

In SE winds better shelter can be found off Trawmore Strand, 1M SE, in 5m, sand, but this is an isolated spot. Do not anchor near the submarine power cable which comes ashore at the W end of the bay.

Killeany pier, on the S side of the bay, was the traditional emergency shelter in heavy weather, before the present harbour at Kilronan was built. See below for directions.

Harbour

Yachts berth on the SE side of the main pier, usually rafted up. At the time of writing (2015) there are no pontoon berths.

Facilities

Diesel from the fishermen's co-op, water on the pier (tap halfway along). Shops, pubs, restaurants, bicycle hire. Ferries to Rossaveal,

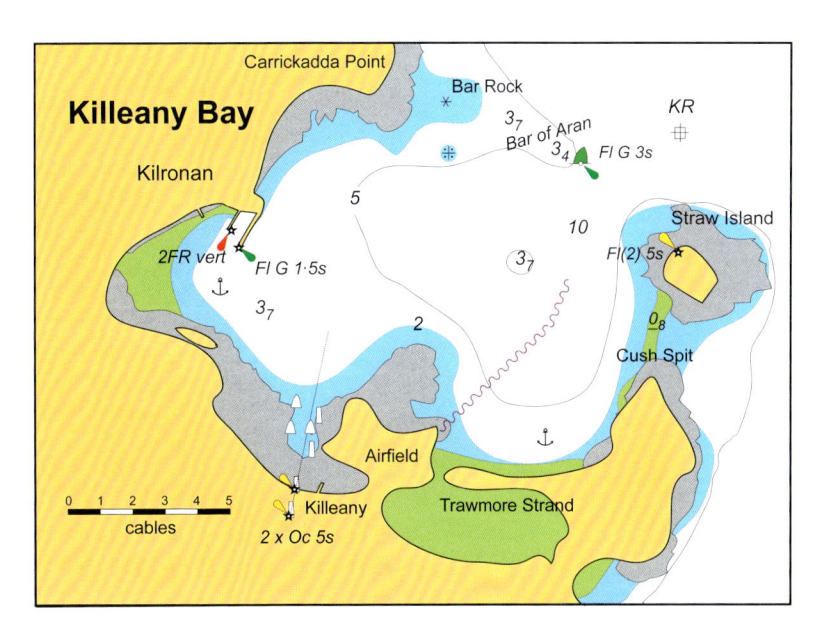

Kilronan Harbour. The ferries now berth on the NW side of the pier, L (photo Galway County Council)

Kilronan Harbour - the approach (above) from the SE

Killeany and Portmurvy

The 2700-year-old Dún Aengus, with (below R) its defensive chevaux-de-frise (photos Dick Lincoln)

Killeany Pier and beacons: the centre beacon on the port hand (entering) has been rebuilt since this photograph was taken

Doolin and Galway, air service to Connemara airport. RNLI all-weather lifeboat station. The ancient fortress of Dún Aengus, with its huge semi-circular walls right on the cliff edge and the *chevaux-de-frise* surrounding them, is not to be missed. Together with the island's other antiquities such as Dún Ducathair (The Black Fort), it places Inishmore on a par with Skellig Michael as one of the world's magical places. The views from the clifftops are superb.

Killeany

AC3339 and Plan

There is a drying harbour formed by a pier projecting NE from the shore on the S side of Killeany Bay. The entrance channel dries 1·9m abreast the first starboard-hand beacon, and the end of the pier dries 1·5m. Two leading beacons 192° lead through the channel which is also marked by two haystack-shaped stone beacons to starboard and one of these plus two concrete pillar beacons to port. Enter on the leading line till the innermost port-hand beacon is abeam, then head for the end of the pier. The lights on the leading beacons should not be depended upon.

Portmurvy

⊕ PM 53°08'·7N 9°44'·4W

AC3339 and Plan of Aran Islands

This bay on the N side of Inishmore offers reasonable shelter in fine weather and moderate offshore winds and is a convenient anchorage for a visit to Dún Aengus. **From Kilronan**, keep 7 cables offshore to avoid Carrickadda, Carrickymonaghan and Cowrugh Shoal. There are patches with less than 2m, inshore of Cowrugh Shoal. **From the W**, keep well clear of Scalraun Point on the W side of the bay to avoid Craghalmon Rock (Cragillaun) which appears surprisingly far offshore.

Brannock Sounds and Inishmaan

To pass between Murvy Shoal (4·9m) and Cowrugh Shoal (0·8m) bring the prominent white Kilmurvy House in line with Dún Aengus bearing 224°. (If either of these shoals is throwing up dangerous seas, the conditions are such that a yacht should not be going into Portmurvy anyway). Anchor in 5 to 7m, sand, off the beach and abreast the small pier on the E side. The bottom alongside the pier is foul, but the pier may offer a temporary alongside berth above half tide to allow a visit to Dún Aengus.

(above) Killeany approaches: the leading beacons, centre

(below) Killeany pier

Channels W of Inishmore

53°08′N 9°51′W
AC3339

Brannock East and West Sounds, between Inishmore, Brannock Island and Rock Island, are navigable with care in moderate weather, although they may break right across in a heavy swell. Stay mid-channel in Brannock West Sound. In Brannock East Sound, hold towards the Brannock Island side to avoid rocks extending 2·5 cables W from Inishmore.

INISHMAAN

⊕ IM 53°06′·4N 9°34′·6W
AC3339 and Plans

The harbour at Caladh Mór on the N side of the island has 3·5m throughout and offers good all-round shelter. Approach on the leading line 192·5°. The ferries must not be impeded, but they do not normally overnight in the harbour. In strong SW winds there may be a steep chop in the harbour for an hour either side of HW, when the reef is covered. Temporary anchorage may be had in fine weather and offshore winds off the pier at Cora Point on the E side of the island. A yacht should not be left unattended at anchor.

Water and shore power at Caladh Mór (for electricity cards contact the HM, 087-6820693). Shop and pub 2 km. Ferries to Rossaveal and Doolin, air service to

Portmurvy Bay and pier (photo Dick Lincoln)

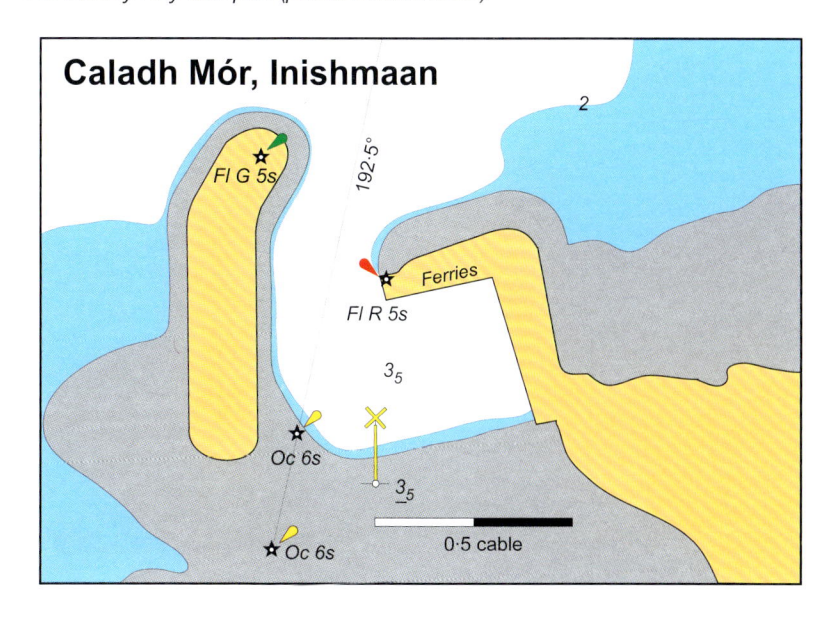

Inisheer; Galway Bay

(right) Approaching Caladh Mór harbour, Inishmaan: the leading beacons, centre R

(lower R) Caladh Mór from the W (photo Galway County Council)

Caladh Mór harbour, Inishmaan (photo Dick Lincoln)

(below) Inisheer roadstead and pier (photo Dick Lincoln)

Connemara airport. There is a very fine ring fort on the summit of the island.

Inisheer

⊕IE 53°04'·5N 9°31'·0W

AC3339 and Plan of Aran Islands

The North Strand provides the best anchorage although exposed and subject to swell. The 120m-long pier has 2·5m at its head and is used by ferries and fishing vessels, but a temporary alongside berth may be available. Shop and pub. Ferries to Rossaveal and Doolin; air service to Connemara airport.

Inisheer has a 15th-century castle and religious buildings dating from the 8th to the 10th centuries.

GALWAY BAY

AC1984, 1904, Imray C55

Galway Bay, 6M wide and 10M long, is sheltered from the ocean swell by the Aran Islands. The S shore of the bay, E of Black Head, is fronted by rocks and shallows within which there are a number of creeks offering excellent shelter, but clearing marks are poor and it is not advisable to close this coast in poor visibility or strong onshore winds. The N shore of the bay is exposed and there are no good harbours in the 20M between Galway and Cashla Bay. The head of Galway Bay has several excellent harbours and anchorages among low-lying islands and headlands, and Galway itself (75,530) is a significant commercial port with a small marina in its wet dock. The principal sailing centre in the bay, and home of Galway Bay SC, is New Harbour (Renville), entered 2M ESE of Mutton Island.

Tides
Galway Bay

The streams in the bay are generally weak. Apart from the upper reaches of the Shannon estuary, Galway Bay has the largest tidal range on the coast. MHWS (Galway) 5·1m, MHWN 3·9m, MLWN 2·0m, MLWS 0·6m.

Galway Bay

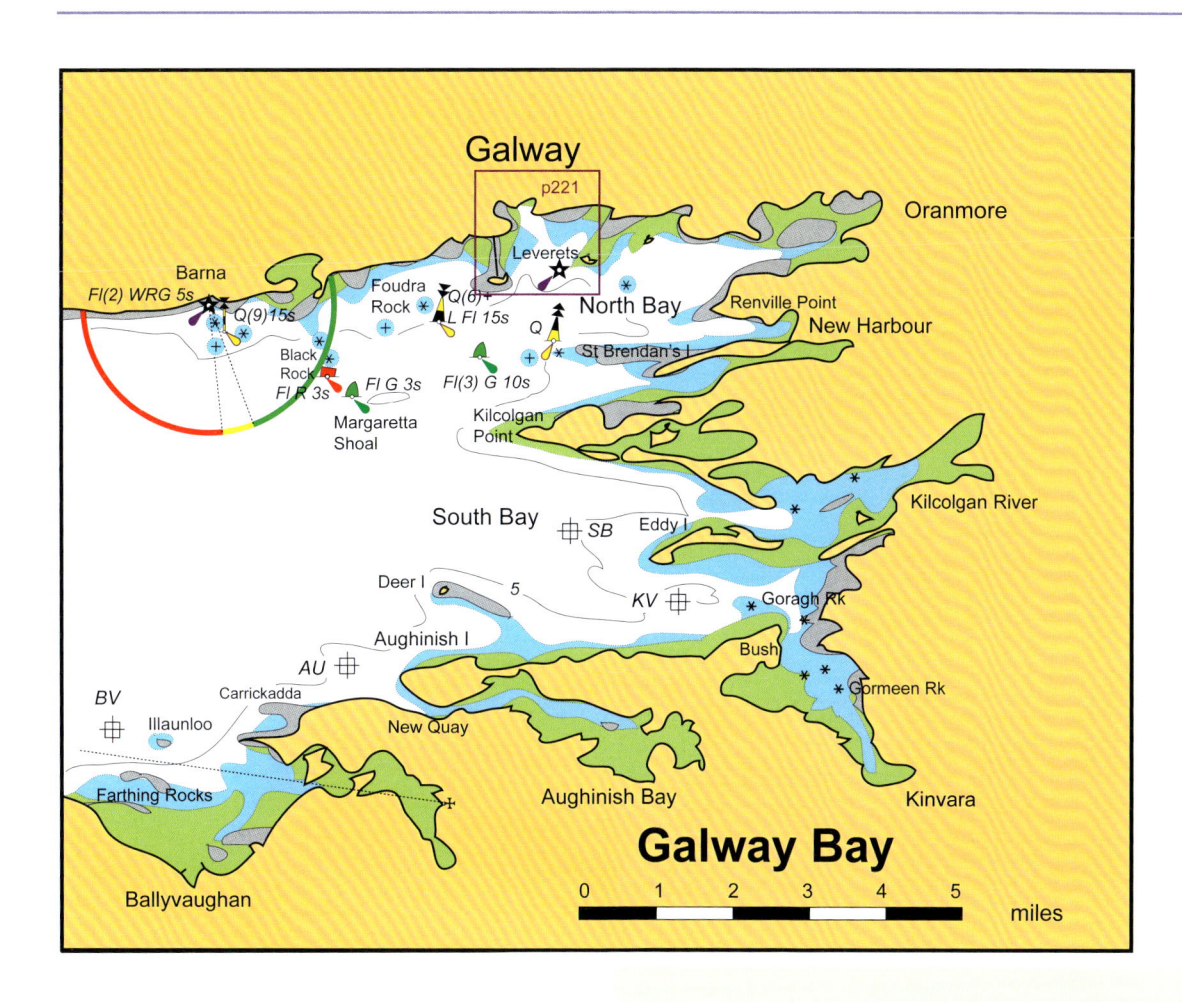

Dangers
Galway Bay

The dangers in the creeks on the S and E sides of the bay are described in the text. The principal dangers in the approaches to Galway and New Harbour are as follows:

Black Rock (dries 1·6m, with a 1·4m patch 3 cables WSW), 2M WSW of Mutton Island
Margaretta Shoal, 2·9m, 2M SW of Mutton Island
Rock with 0·7m, 6 cables NE of Black Rock
Foudra Rock (dries), 1M W of Mutton Island
Trout Rock (dries 1·2m), 5 cables ESE of the Leverets light
St Brendan's Island, a drying reef extending 1M to the W, N of Ardfry Point on the S side of New Harbour, and culminating in **Cockle Rock** (dries 2·3m), 9 cables WNW of Ardfry Point
Ardfry Shoal, 1·9m, 6 cables W by S of Cockle Rock
Tawin Shoals, 2·9m, 8 to 12 cables W of Cockle Rock
Dillisk Rock (dries) and **Renville Spit**, 1·7m, a reef extending 3 cables WSW from Renville Point.

Lights and Marks

Black Head, white tower, Fl WR 5s 20m W11M R8M, W 045°–268°, R 268°–276°. Shows red inshore to the E, white elsewhere. AIS.
Barna Pier Head, Fl(2) WRG 5s 6m W8M R5M G5M, G 250°–344°, W 344°–355°, R 355°–090°. Shows a narrow white sector over the approach from the SSE, green to the E and red to the W.
Black Rock buoy, PHM Fl R 3s
Margaretta Shoal buoy, SHM Fl G 3s, AIS
Tawin Shoals buoy, SHM Fl(3) G 10s
Foudra Rock buoy, S Card Q(6)+L Fl 15s
Mooring Marker 2 buoy, PHM Fl(2) R 6s
Mid-channel buoy, PHM Fl R 4s
Trout Rock buoy, S Card Q(6)+L Fl
Cockle Rock buoy, N Card Q
New Harbour bns, Fl G 5s and Fl R 5s
Leverets, black tower, white bands, Q WRG 9m 10M, G 015°–058° W 058°–065° R 065°–103° G 103°–143·5° W 143·5°–146·5° R 146·5°–015°. Shows white over the approach from the WSW, red over Mutton Island, green over the causeway and Claddagh, white up the channel to Galway Harbour, red to the N, E and S, and green over Tawin and Margaretta Shoals to the SW
Rinmore, white tower, Iso WRG 4s 7m 5M, G 359°–008° W 008°–018° R 018°–027°. Shows white over the approach from the SSW, green to the E, red to the W
Rinmore Spit, green perch Fl G 5s 2m 2M
Nimmo's Pier Head, Fl Y 2s 7m 7M
Galway Approach Channel, Port Entry Light Dir WRG 7m 3M, FG 322·25°–323·75°, AltGW 323·75°–324·75°, FW 324·75°–325·25°, AltWR 325·25°–326·25°, Fl R 326·25°–331·25°, FR 331·25°–332·25°

Galway Bay; Ballyvaughan

Black Head from the NE

Shanmuckinish Castle in line with St Patrick's Church (the blue-grey building, R) leads clear N of Farthing Rocks

Ballyvaughan; the New Pier (above) and Old Pier (below)

(right) Gleninagh Castle in line with the N side of Illaunloo clears Carrickadda

(below) New Quay, Aughinish Bay

Outer approach to Galway Harbour

From the SW, Black Head, steep and bold below the bare rocky Doughbranneen Hill (312m), has a small lighthouse on its shore. The red sector of the light covers **Illaunloo Rock** in Ballyvaughan Bay. Knockavorneen Hill (73m) and the Martello towers at Finavarra and Aughinish are conspicuous. Steering NE, identify the Black Rock and Margaretta Shoals buoys and pass between them, then leave Tawin Shoals buoy to starboard and Foudra Rock buoy to port. The black-and-white banded Leverets beacon is conspicuous, and at night its white sector leads between the buoys. **From the W,** steer 085° from a point 1·3M S of Spiddle to leave the wave energy test area and Black Rock buoys to port, then as above.

SOUTH SIDE of GALWAY BAY

AC1984

Ballyvaughan Bay

⊕ *BV* 53°09′N 9°10′·5W

Ballyvaughan Bay (Ballyvaghan on the charts) lies 3M E of Black Head. In the centre of the bay, **Illaunloo** (0·6m high) is difficult to identify against the land. It is foul for up to 1 cable all round. At the S entrance to the bay the **Farthing Rocks** are an extensive patch, some of which dry 1·7m, and lie up to 4 cables offshore. The inner part of the bay is shallow (with less water than charted) with extensive drying banks, but a yacht of modest draft may cross these safely with sufficient rise of tide. Shanmuckinish Castle ruin in line with St Patrick's church, 096°, leads between Illaunloo and Farthing Rocks *(see photograph)*. At HW it is possible to go up to the old quay by the village and lie alongside its SE side, bottom shingle and small stones. It is also possible to go alongside the "new quay" on its SE side where the shelter is a little better. Both quays dry. There is also a pool with about 3m LWS off the end of the NE ("new") pier near the 3·4m sounding on AC1984. It is about 140m long by 90m wide, its long axis lying NE–SW in continuation of the line of the inner face of the end of the pier. Sound into it and preferably moor with two anchors to reduce swinging. It is very well sheltered at low tide and the NW–SE edges are clean sand. At the E end of the bay Muckinish Strait gives access to a long creek. It is shallow and

Aughinish Bay and Kinvara

not recommended.

Shops, pubs, restaurants at Ballyvaughan.

Carrickadda dries 3·7m and extends 7·5 cables W from the shore NE of Finavarra Point. Gleninagh Castle (which may be hard to identify from a distance) in line with the N side of Illaunloo, 244°, leads just clear of Carrickadda. This line also clears the 2·1m patch NW of Aughinish Point.

Aughinish Bay

⊕ *AU* 53°10′N 9°06′W

The entrance to this bay, S of Aughinish Island, is straightforward with the use of AC1984. Give the S shore a berth of 1 cable and anchor at or above New Quay. There is a strong tide in this anchorage, which may be uncomfortable in NW winds as there are overfalls on the ebb and a yacht will be tide-rode. Under these circumstances go further up the bay, with continuous use of the echosounder, as the channel is unmarked. The ebb continues for some time after LW and the tide turns very suddenly in the channel. The pier at New Quay offers an alongside berth around HW. Pub/restaurant at the pier.

Deer Island (2m high) lies 1M N of Aughinish Point. It is foul all round for 1 cable, and a long, shallow spit, which partially uncovers, runs SE from it to the land. This island may be hard to identify against the shore at HW. Once identified it can be used as a reference point in the entrance to South Bay.

South Bay

⊕ *SB* 53°12′N 9°02′W

South Bay is divided by Eddy Island which can be identified when Deer Island comes abeam. The S part of this bay leads to Kinvara Bay and the N part to the Kilcolgan River.

Kinvara Bay

⊕ *KV* 53°11′·0N 9°00′W

The delightful village of Kinvara is accessible on a high and rising tide. The passage should be made with great care and continuous use of the echosounder, although the Admiralty survey of 1844-50 is still accurate. There are no marks to clear **Goragh Rock**, which dries 1·8m. Steer to pass midway between Fiddoun Island and Doorus Point. When Fiddoun Island is abeam and Doorus Point bears about 205° it is safe to stand into Kinvara Bay, giving Doorus Point a berth of 0·5 cables and less than 2 cables to avoid **Comb Rock** which dries 2·9m. There is good anchorage abreast Parkmore pier (the quay at Bush, 3 cables S of Doorus Point), in 4m. The pier head dries about 1·5m.

To proceed further, first keep Parkmore pierhead 315° astern which leads between **Madden's Island** and **Long Rock**. Identify the small perch on **Gormeen Rock** and leave it to port. After this keep in mid-channel. There are fish cages in the channel. At neaps there is anchorage 2·5 cables from Kinvara, with 2m at LWN, but there is nowhere to land near LW that is free of mud. Alternatively, dry out in the small harbour; the N wall has the most water.

Facilities

Shops, pubs, PO, restaurants at Kinvara.

Kilcolgan River

53°12′·2N 9°00′W

Enter through Mweenish Strait between Mweenish Island and Eddy Island. This passage is fairly straightforward, with regular shorelines of steep, shelving shingle. Favouring the Eddy Island side of the channel, alter to port to pass within 1 cable of Mweenish Point, which is steep-to, thus avoiding **Meelan Rock**, a group of boulders which dries. **Yellow Rocks**, 6 to 8 cables E of Mweenish Point, dry about 3m, and not as charted.

Anchorage

There is good safe shelter NNE of Mweenish Point in Ship Pool. No facilities. Alternatively, if proceeding further and awaiting sufficient rise, anchor in Tyrone Pool, 1M ENE from

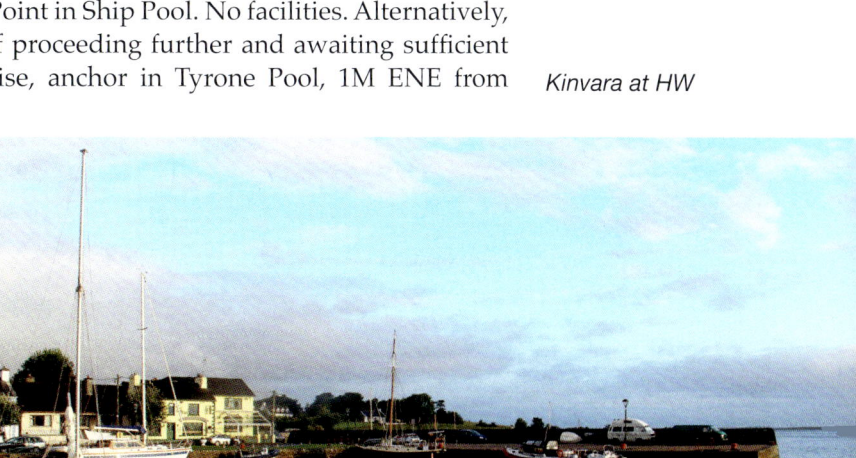

Gormeen Rock perch

Kinvara at HW

The Weir; North Bay and Renville

The Weir, Kilcolgan River (photo David Whitehead)

(below) The conspicuous Marine Institute building on Renville Point

Mweenish Point; **Yellow Slate Rock**, which dries 0·6m, lies on the edge of the shallows on the N side of the pool opposite Bird Island. After half-flood keep 0·5 cable off the S shore and enter the Kilcolgan River S of Corraun Point. Due to scour there is deeper water in the river than charted. Continue in midstream and anchor in 0·5m LWS or 2m LWN 150m short of the quay wall on the N bank of the river at Weir village. The river shallows rapidly abreast the quay.

Facilities

Restaurant/bar at the quay. Shops at Kilcolgan, 1·5 km.

Kilcolgan Point

Kilcolgan Point is deceptive and extends a long way into the bay. It is foul all round and must be given a wide berth. The charted transits are now difficult to discern, but longitude 9°04'·2 clears the point by 5 cables.

NORTH BAY and GALWAY

AC1984, 1904, Imray C55

North Bay is the approach to Galway, and also Oranmore Bay, New Harbour and Mweeloon Bay. Oranmore Bay is open to the W and its head is encumbered with rocks. Mweeloon Bay is also open to the W and dries at its head. There is anchorage 7·5 cables inside the entrance. Keep close to Ardfry Point until the tower on it is passed to avoid the **Creggaun Rocks** (dry 1·5m) in the middle of the entrance. It is not recommended.

New Harbour (Renville)

53°14'·5N 9°00'W
AC1984, 1904

New Harbour, the base of Galway Bay SC, is entered between Cockle Rock buoy and Renville Spit (Rinville on the chart). The inlet offers better shelter than its position would suggest. The dome of Galway Cathedral in line with the W side of Hare Island, 312°, leads clear of Renville Spit, which extends SW from Renville Point. (note that the sand cliff of Renville Point has receded by 50m or so from its charted position in recent years). The white bungalow used as a mark on AC1984

New Harbour (Renville) from the NW: Galway Bay SC, foreground

220

Renville and Galway

Galway Bay SC jetty, from the NE

Approaching Galway Harbour; (L to R) the harbour entrance, the Port Entry Light (showing red, since the view is from slightly west of the leading line), the Aran Islands cargo ship in the "lay-by", and the Leverets tower

no longer exists but the entrance may be identified from seaward by the conspicuous building of the Marine Institute on its N shore. **Black Rock** (dries 4·1m) on the S shore is marked by a starboard-hand perch, Fl G 5s, and there is a corresponding perch Fl R 5s on the point opposite. Once past these marks stay one-third of the channel's width from the N shore to avoid the shallows on the S side.

Anchorage

Anchor SW of the pier in 2m, mud, or outside the moorings where available. There are shellfish beds W of the anchorage and on the N side of the approach channel. It is safe to dry out at the pier where there is 2m at HWN. A wide slip and breakwater extends SE from the pier; the end of the slip is marked with an unlit perch. Galway Bay SC (091 794527) at the pier. A private mooring may be available for a visitor's use; contact the club.

Facilities

Water on the quay. Showers, meals and bar at GBSC clubhouse (most summer evenings and weekends). Shops, pubs and restaurants at Oranmore, 3 km.

Galway Harbour

⊕ GW 53°15'·5N 9°02'·1W
AC1984, 1904, Imray C55 and Plan

Galway Harbour lies behind dock gates which are opened 2 hours before HW and closed at HW, day and night, 7 days a week. The dock on the SW side has a small marina; intending visitors are advised to check berth availability in advance by contacting the Harbour office 091 561874 or 562329 or VHF Ch 12. When the dock gates are open in heavy weather from the S or SE, an irregular swell is reflected around the dock; the marina is relatively protected from this.

A dredged channel 80m wide with a maintained depth of 3·4m runs for 6 cables SE from the outer pierhead, W of Rinmore Point. Steer to pass 0·5 cable W of the Leverets tower, and head 325° for the high intensity directional light, which is easily visible by day. On the ebb or after prolonged rain, there

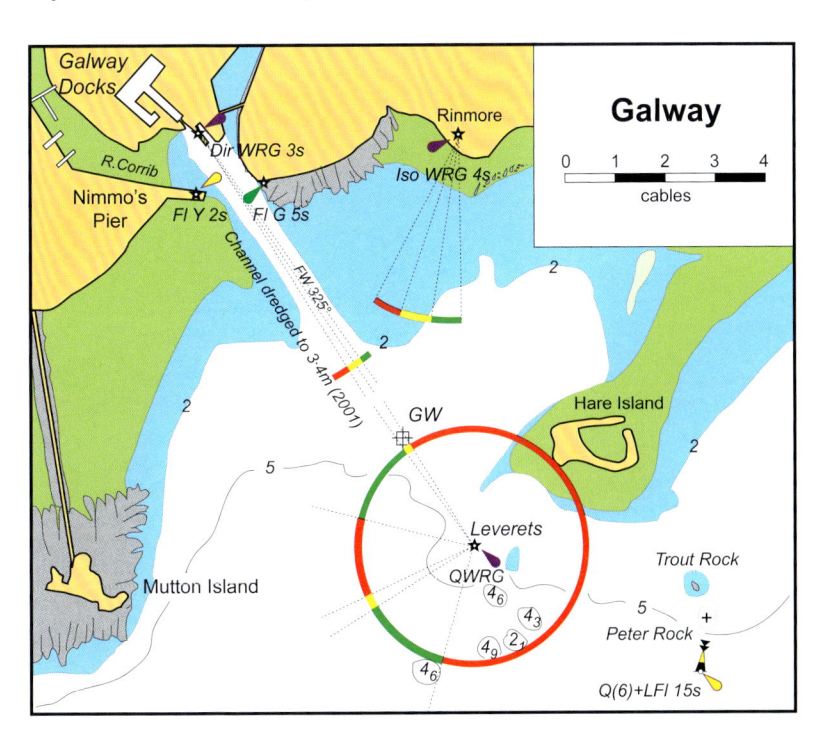

221

Galway

Galway Docks and Marina: the lay-by, upper R, and the boatyard slip, top R. The dock gates are open (photo Galway Harbour Company)

The lay-by (photo Niall Quinn)

is a strong E'ly set out of the River Corrib across the mouth of the harbour. Maintain a listening watch on VHF Ch 12 when entering. On the E side of the pier extending seaward from the dock gates is a narrow dredged cut known locally as the lay-by. This accommodates the Aran Islands cargo vessel, and has a pontoon suitable for a short stay by a yacht. The RNLI inshore lifeboat is davit launched from the head of the lay-by and its passage must not be obstructed.

Marina

The marina has 31 berths. Water and shore power on the pontoons; security gate and CCTV cameras.

Tides

Galway is a Tidal Standard Port. MHWS 5·1m, MHWN 3·9m, MLWN 2·0m, MLWS 0·6m.

Facilities

All the facilities of a port city; supermarkets, shops, pubs, restaurants and PO, train and bus connections. Airport. RNLI inshore lifeboat. HiWay Oil (091 566406) will deliver diesel if the quantity is sufficient; smaller quantities may be obtained at the filling station (between the railway bridge and the coal yard, upper left in the aerial photograph). Boatyard with slipway travelhoist at Rinmore Point. Sailmakers, West Sails, 087 628 9854, yannick@westsails.ie; Hyde Sails Ireland, 087 961 3155, cullensailmakers@gmail.com. Dockside crane, 12t capacity. It is also safe to dry out at Nimmo's Pier, but contact the HM beforehand, 091 561874 or 562329.

GALWAY to CASHLA BAY

AC1984, 3339 and 2096

The N shore of Galway Bay for 20M W of Mutton Island is exposed and apart from the drying harbours at Barna and Spiddle has no safe shelter. Cashla Bay may be entered by day or night in almost any weather, and has the easiest access of any of the Connemara bays. The fishing and ferry port of Rossaveal

222

Galway to Cashla Bay

Dangers
Galway to Cashla Bay

Black Rock (dries 1·6m), 2M WSW of Mutton Island.
Rock with 1·4m, 2 cables WSW of Black Rock
North Channel Rock (dries 0·6m), 3 cables NW of Black Rock
Carrickanoge (dries) 4 cables off Barna village, and rocks with 1·8m and drying 0·1m and 0·5m, SW to NW of Carrickanoge and in the channel to Barna pier
Wave energy test area, with heavy equipment awash, 2M SE of Spiddle
Coddu Rock (above water), 2 cables SW of Cashla Point
Rock with 0·5m, 1·5 cables SSW of Coddu Rock. A rock with 3·3m, 4 cables S of Coddu Rock, may break in bad weather
Cannon Rock (dries 1·7m), 5 cables W of Cashla Point
Carrickmarian (dries 3·7m), 2·5 cables S of Killeen Point
Narien Spit, 1·5m, 2 cables S of Carrickmarian.
Carrickadda (dries 1·5m), 5 cables NNW of Cashla Point, with drying and above-water rocks E and SE of it
Coastguard Rock (dries 1·5m), 2 cables ENE of Carrickadda
Unnamed rock, 0·2m, 2 cables W of Tonacrick Point on the E side of the outer bay
Lion Rock (dries), 1 cable W of Lion Point at the narrows
Ship Rock (dries), 0·5 cable E of Curraglass Point at the narrows
Unnamed rock (dries 0·9m), 3 cables N by W of Curraglass Point, with a series of submerged rocks between it and the shore to the SW.
Haberline Rock (dries), 2 cables NNW of Rossaveal pierhead
  The head of Cashla Bay is heavily obstructed with drying rocks.

Lights and Marks

Tawin Shoals buoy, SHM Fl(3) G 10s
Margaretta Shoal buoy, SHM Fl G 3s
Black Rock buoy, PHM Fl R 3s
Carrickanoge beacon, W Card Q(9) 15s 2m 2M, in the approaches to Barna Pier. There are also two port hand beacons, Fl R, S of the pier
Barna Pier Head, Fl(2) WRG 5s 6m W8M R5M G5M, G 250°–344°, W 344°–355°, R 355°–090°. Shows a narrow white sector over the approach from the SSE, green to the E and red to the W.
Spiddle Pier Head, Y col Fl WRG 3·5s 11m 8M, G 265°–308°, W 308°–024°, R 024°–066°. Shows white over the approach, green over the wave energy test area and inshore to the E, and red inshore to the W
Two N Card and two S Card buoys 2M SE of Spiddle mark a test area for wave energy research.
Cashla Bay Entrance (Killeen Point), W side, white col Fl(3) WR 10s 8m W6M R3M, W 216°–000°, R 000°–069°. Shows red to SW, white over the entrance
Cannon Rock buoy, SHM Fl G 5s, AIS
There is also a perch on Cannon Rock
Cashla Bay (Lion Point), white tower with red high-visibility stripe, dir WRG Iso 5s 6m W8M R6M G6M, G 357·5°–008·5°, W 008·5°–011·5°, R 011·5°–017·5°. White sector leads close W of Cannon Rock buoy, green to E, red to W
Lion Rock buoy, SHM Fl G 3s
Ship Rock buoy, PHM Fl R 3s
A further pair of buoys QR and QG lie to the N of the narrows.
Rossaveal Harbour ldg lts 116° Oc 3s 3M, front white col 12m, rear 14m
Ard Rí beacon, red col Fl(3) R 6s
Rossaveal No.1 beacon, SHM Fl(3) G 6s 4m 3M
Rossaveal No.2 beacon, PHM Fl(2) R 5s 4m 3M
Rossaveal No.4 beacon, PHM Fl R 4s 4m 3M

(Rossaveel on the charts) lies on its E side. Its harbour contains a small marina.

Coast – Mutton Island to Cashla Bay

The area inshore at Salthill, extending for 1·5M W from Mutton Island and 2 cables offshore, is a designated bathing zone between March and October. Powered vessels are prohibited. There is a small drying harbour at Barna, which receives a little protection from Carrickanoge. It has a good sandy bottom and is accessible above half tide. Beware drying and below-water rocks in the approach; give the west cardinal beacon a berth of half a cable and keep the pier head bearing 355° (the W side of the white sector of the pierhead light) until abeam the inner port hand beacon. Shops, PO, pubs and restaurants. Note the wave energy test area SE of Spiddle, 3 cables by 4 and a mile offshore, marked by four small cardinal buoys. Pass either N or S of this area, leaving the buoys on the proper hand. For 4M W of Spiddle a berth of 7 cables clears all dangers, but there are the remains of an abandoned fish farm a mile offshore in approximate position 53°13′N 9°27′W. Either stay within 5 cables of the shore here, or more than 1·5M off to avoid the risk of fouling propellers or rudders.

Spiddle

53°14′N 9°18′W
AC1984, 3339

There is a drying harbour at Spiddle with a clean sandy bottom. The face of the pier is rough and it is subject to scend in winds from E through S to SW. Shops, PO, pubs and restaurants.

Cashla Bay

Spiddle Pier

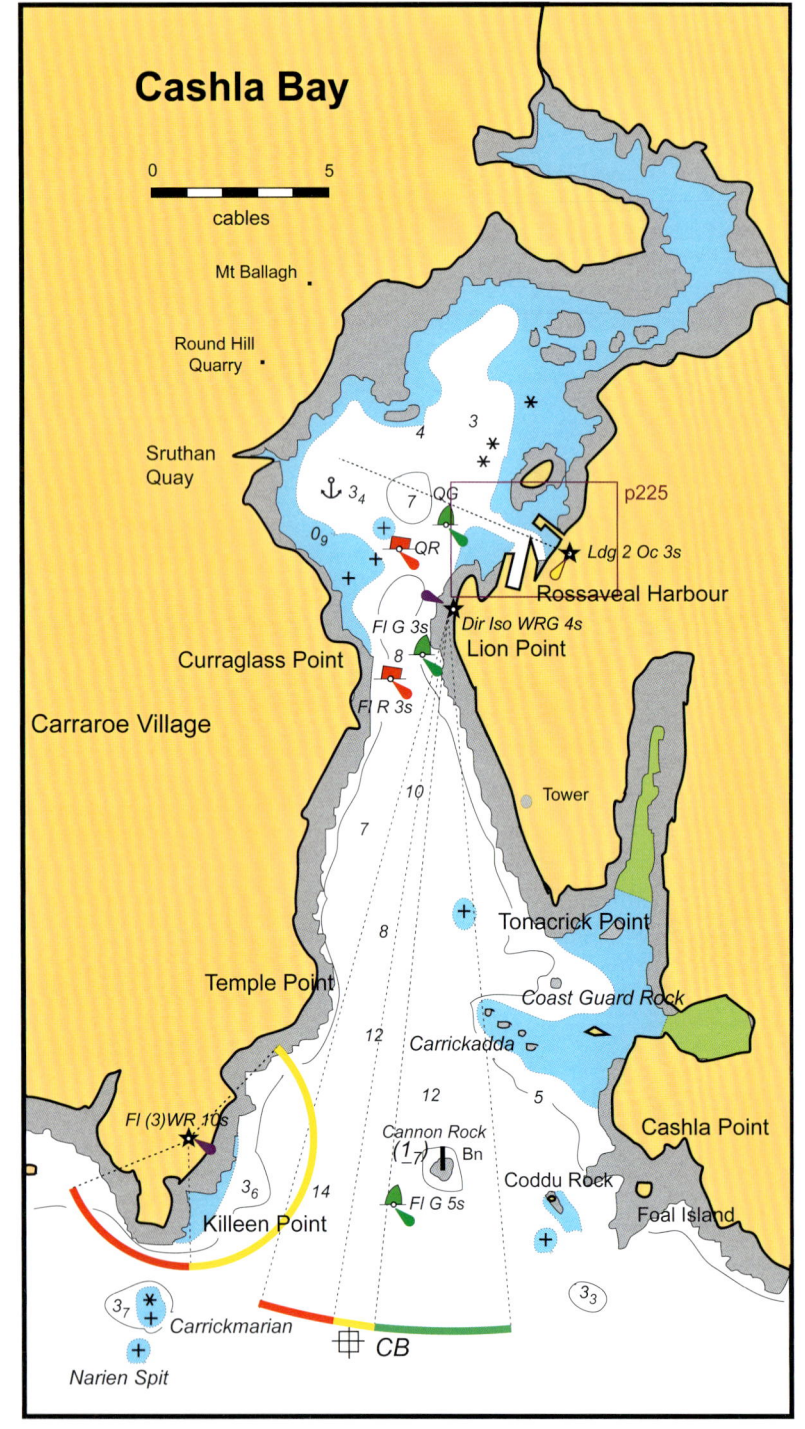

CASHLA BAY

⊕CB 53°13'·8N 9°34'·5W
AC2096, Imray C55 and Plan

From the E, identify Coddu Rock, which never covers, SW of Cashla Point. There is deep water between Coddu and Cannon Rock, or else leave Cannon Rock buoy to starboard. At night, the white sector of Lion Point light leads W of Cannon Rock buoy.
From the W, the summit of Illaunnanownim just open S of Aillewore Point astern 265°, clears Narien Spit, although an easier transit to identify is to keep Cannon Rock perch well open to the R of the buoy. At night, the light on Aillecluggish Point (by Killeen Point) on the W side of the entrance shows red over Carrickmarian and Narien Spit.

Once past Carrickadda head for the middle of the narrows and follow the buoyed channel.

Sruthan Quay

This pier is named on AC2096 and is the quay at Glashnacally shown on AC3339. The end of the quay just dries at LAT.

Anchorage

There is good anchorage midway between the QR port-hand buoy and Sruthan Quay, in 2 to 3m, mud, safe in all weathers though it can be rough in a S or SE gale. There are visitors' moorings.

Facilities

Water on the quay. Filling station and small shop nearby. Shop and hotel at Carraroe, 1·5 km; pub and PO at Costelloe, 2 km.

(above) Cannon Rock perch and buoy from the NE

(left) Coddu Rock from the S

Sruthan Quay and Rossaveal

(left) Sruthan Quay

The head of Cashla bay from the SE: Rossaveal Harbour, foreground, with Ard Ri beacon and Illaunawehichy beyond. Ferry and small-craft pontoons have been installed in the basin (R) since this photograph was taken

(bottom) Rossaveal Marina

Rossaveal

53°16′·2N 9°33′·9W
AC2096

A dredged channel with 3·6m leads into the busy fishing harbour of Rossaveal (Rossaveel on the charts), from where ferries, including high-speed craft, run to the Aran Islands. The ferries use pontoon berths in the SE basin. The NE basin contains a small marina. HM phone 091 572108, VHF Ch 16, 14, 12. The harbour is managed by the Department of Agriculture, Food and the Marine.

Marina

The marina has 24 berths. The finger pontoons are short and closely spaced but the outermost berths can accommodate larger visiting yachts.

Facilities

Water and shore power on the pontoons, diesel by tanker. Mechanical repairs available. Shop, pub, restaurant 800m. Shop will deliver, 091 572292. Buses to Galway.

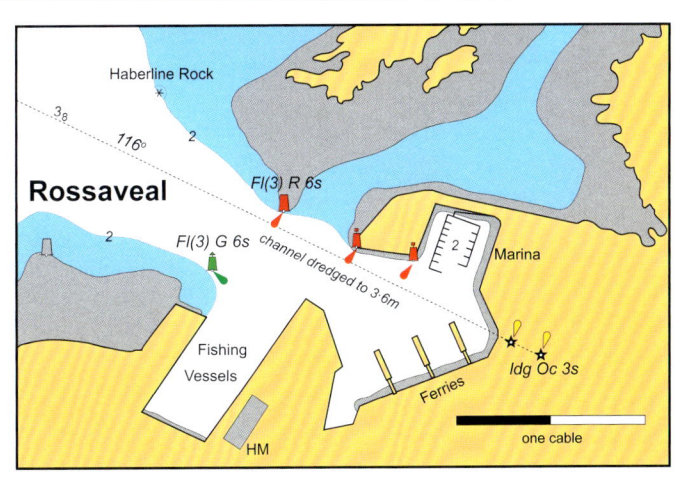

Cashla Bay to Kiggaul Bay

Map: Cashla Bay, Greatman's Bay and Kilkieran Bay

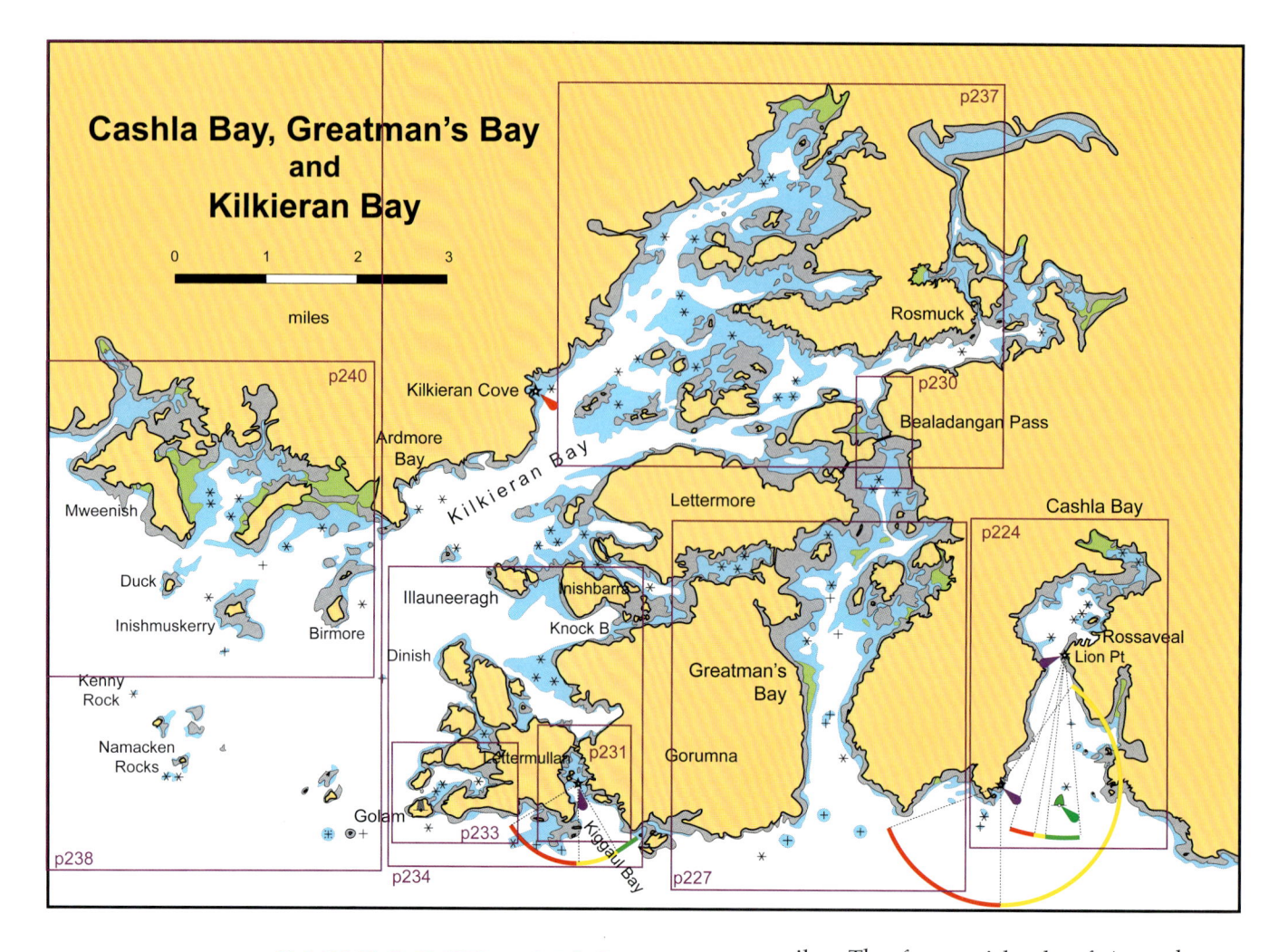

CASHLA BAY to KIGGAUL BAY

AC2096

West of Cashla Bay are so many unmarked rocks and similar small islands that the stranger must continuously relate to the vessel's surroundings, with the largest-scale chart close at hand at all times, and be constantly aware of position. However the Admiralty surveyors in the 1840's did an outstanding job, and the existence and position of the hazards are, for the most part, extremely well documented. It is a fascinating cruising ground for the adventurous sailor. The former islands of Annaghvaan, Lettermore, Gorumna and Lettermullan enclose Greatman's Bay and Kiggaul Bay; these islands are now connected to each other and to the mainland by causeways and bridges, and thus some of the intricate and half-tide channels once used by small craft are now closed off. The old beacons marking Bealadangan Pass, between the mainland and Annaghvaan at the head of Greatman's Bay, are perhaps the most poignant reminders of the former dependence of this coast on seaborne transport by small sailing and rowing craft.

On the coast of Connemara and north into

The old signal tower on Golam Head is the most distinctive landmark on the South Connemara coast. Bringing it open S of Loughcarrick Island (L) clears English Rock, here seen breaking (centre)

226

Greatman's Bay

Dangers
Cashla Bay to Kiggaul Bay

In the recesses of the inlets of Greatman's Bay and Kiggaul Bay the rocks are too numerous to list. The principal offshore dangers are as follows:

Keeraun Shoal, 1·6m, 7 cables SW of Keeraun Point

Trabaan Rock, 0·7m, 4 cables ESE of Trabaan Point

Arkeena Rock, 1·8m, 4 cables S of Trabaan Point

Rin Rocks (dry 1·8m), 2 cables WSW of Rin Point in the entrance to Greatman's Bay

Chapel Rocks, 0·6m, in mid-channel 2 cables NW of Dooleen Point

English Rock (dries 1·2m), 8 cables SW of Trabaan Point

Griffin's Rock (dries 3m), 4 cables S of Lettermullan Island

Griffin's Spit, 0·9m, 2 cables S of Griffin's Rock

Dawsy's Rock (dries 2·4m), 5 cables W of Griffin's Rock. There is a third rock, awash at LAT, midway between them, and a rock with 1·7m 2 cables SE of Dawsy's Rock.

Lights and Marks

Kiggaul Bay, Fl WRG 3s 5m 5M, G 310°–329°, W 329°–349°, R349°–059°. Shows white over the approach, green over the dangers to the SE and red over those to the SW

Golam Tower, unlit 19th-century signal tower, conspicuous on the summit of Golam Island, 2M W of Kiggaul Bay

Caution

Note that prior to 2009 several of the dangers in this section were uncharted, or marked as deeper. The latest information is based on airborne laser bathymetry from 2008, over specific areas. Depths over Keeraun Shoal and Trabaan Rock have been confirmed by echosounder as less than charted prior to 2009.

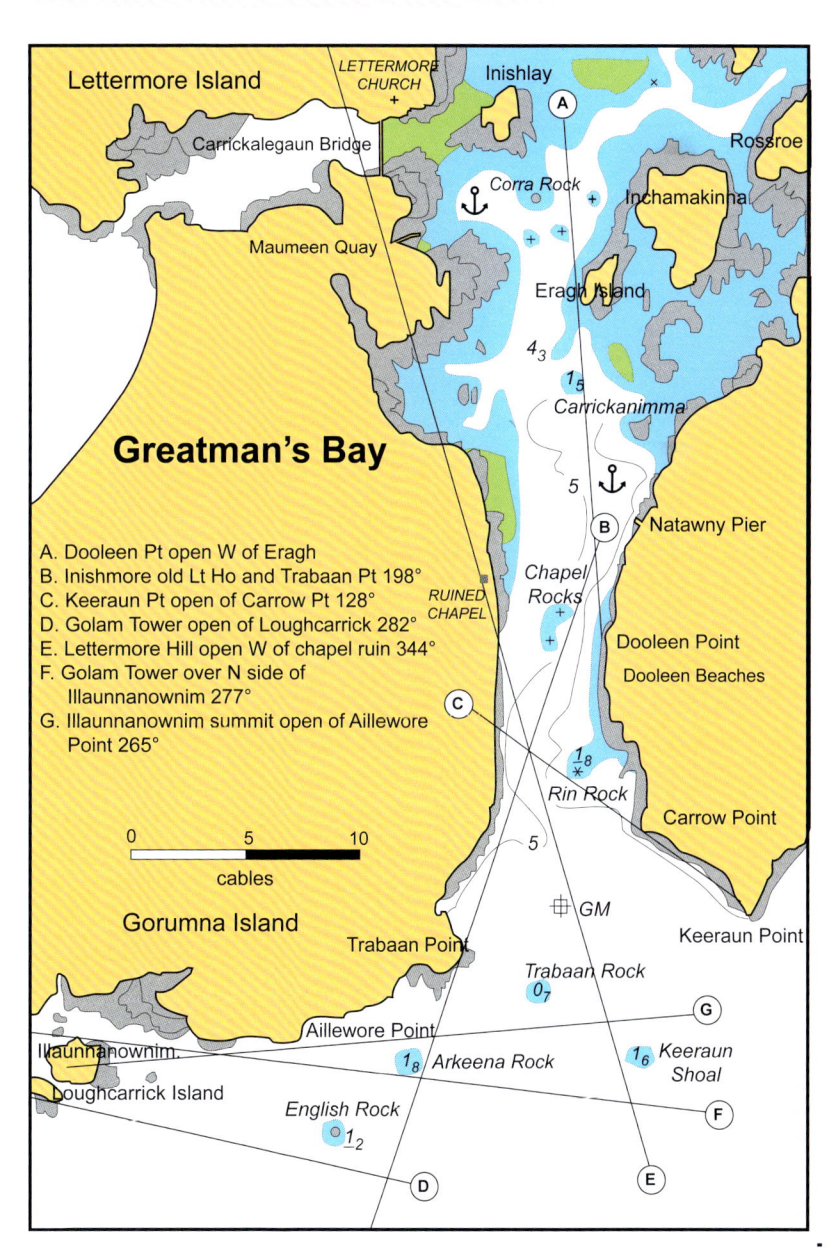

Mayo, sources of supply are relatively few and far between, and there are few piers, and no pontoons, offering an alongside berth. Most piers dry out. A yacht's crew intending to spend a prolonged period in these waters must be prepared to be more than normally self-sufficient and well-stocked, particularly with water and fuel, and seize every opportunity to top up.

GREATMAN'S BAY

⊕ GM 53°14′N 9°38′W
AC2096 and Plan

This bay can be entered in any summer weather but there are more dangers in the entrance than in Cashla Bay, and the shelter is not so good. The entrance is wide and easily identified from seaward.

Directions

From the E, a berth of 2 cables clears all dangers from Keeraun Point to Carrow Point. Keeraun Point just open SW of Carrow Point 128° leads SW of Rin Rock. The building on Inchamakinna (used as a landmark on the charts) is no longer identifiable. **From the W**, beware of English Rock, which frequently does not break. It lies in the red sector of Killeen Point light. Golam Tower open S of Loughcarrick Island 282° leads S

Greatman's Bay

A. Dooleen Pt open W of Eragh
B. Inishmore old Lt Ho and Trabaan Pt 198°
C. Keeraun Pt open of Carrow Pt 128°
D. Golam Tower open of Loughcarrick 282°
E. Lettermore Hill open W of chapel ruin 344°
F. Golam Tower over N side of Illaunnanownim 277°
G. Illaunnanownim summit open of Aillewore Point 265°

Greatman's Bay

Greatman's Bay from N; Lettermore (bottom R) Maumeen Quay (centre R) Inishlay (centre L) Carraveg Bay (top R)

(below) Lettermore Hill open W of Gorumna chapel ruin clears Keeraun Shoal and Trabaan Rock (transit E, plan on p227)

(above) Inishmore old lighthouse in line with Trabaan Point leads clear of Chapel Rocks (transit B, plan on p227)

*(below) Natawny quay; the beacon (L) should be left to **starboard** when approaching the quay.*

of the rock. Golam Tower over the NE point of Illaunnanownim 277° leads N of the rock, and also S of Arkeena Rock. Lettermore Hill open W of Gorumna Chapel ruin 344° leads between Trabaan Rock and Keeraun Shoal.

Once N of Dooleen Point, stay E or W of mid-channel to avoid Chapel Rocks. The old lighthouse on the eastern summit of Inishmore (Aran) in line with Trabaan Point 198° leads E of Chapel Rocks. The modern Lettermore Church with its white tower, just NE of Carrickalegaun bridge, is conspicuous from seaward.

Anchorages

- Temporary anchorage in settled weather is available off Dooleen beaches. The quay at Natawny Point, on the E side of the bay, encloses a tiny drying harbour which services the adjacent fish farm and provides a dinghy landing. N of the quay is a concrete beacon surmounted by a slim perch. It should be left to starboard entering the boat harbour. There is anchorage off the quay but the nearest facilities are at Carraroe, 3 km.

- The best anchorage, which is sheltered in all winds but is approached between unmarked rocks, is off Maumeen Quay, N of Curnaclea Point on Gorumna Island. The reef E of Curnaclea Point ends in a prominent rock which dries about 1·8m. If this rock is showing, leave

Maumeen Quay; Bealadangan

it well to port and steer for the W side of Inishlay. At half-tide and over, when the prominent rock is covered, approach close to Eragh Island as there is then no danger from the sunken rocks S of Eragh Spit and the two 1·5m patches NW of Eragh Island. **Corra Rock** (dries 2m) is bare of weed and has an outlier to the N of it. It is easily avoided approaching the anchorage either by keeping Lettermore Hill bearing 318° or Lettermore church 313°. When the quay is well abeam alter course towards it and anchor 2 to 3 cables off it in 2 to 3m, mud. There are visitors' moorings. Maumeen Quay itself is not suitable for alongside berthing. Shop, hardware store and pub at Lettermore village. Filling station 1·5 km from Maumeen Quay.

- There is a pleasant anchorage N and NW of Rossroe Island. If Corra Rock is showing, leave it close to port and skirt the shore of Inchamakinna staying 2 cables off the HWM. Anchor in mid-channel in Rossroe Bay in 2m, mud.

(above) Corra Rock (foreground) from the SE

(below) The beacon on Nunra Point

(top) Approaching the moorings off Maumeen Quay; the reefs E of Curnaclea Point near LW. Lettermore Church tower, L

(above) Maumeen Quay. Note the drying reef curving E and N from the pierhead

(above left) Maumeen Quay

Bealadangan
53°18'·7N 9°37'·5W
See Plan

The tidal channel of Bealadangan Pass, at the head of the bay, once offered access direct from the head of Greatman's Bay to Camus Bay and Kilkieran Bay, and it still has its stone beacons; the original bridge (connecting Annaghvaan and Lettermore Islands to the mainland) opened, but it has been fixed since the mid-1960's. However there is an attractive temporary anchorage close S of the bridge and the trip, after half flood, is well worthwhile. From the mouth of Rossroe Bay, steer to pass close E of the small pillar beacon off Nunra Point on Lettermore Island then N and NE following the deeper water as charted towards the beacons at the

Approaching Bealadangan from the S

229

Bealadangan and Kiggaul Bay

Bealadangan Pier (L) and bridge, from the S

View from Bealadangan anchorage: the building with six windows, L

Bealadangan, view N from the bridge; the two N'most beacons are left to port going N, which may seem counter-intuitive when the rocks are covered

head of the bay. Leaving the first and second beacons to port, anchor in 2m between the second and third with the next beacon (close S of the quay) in line 289° with a low white building (with six small windows in a row) at the head of the pier. The pier has a rough face and the bottom is foul, so it is unsuitable for drying out, but it may be useful as a berth for about an hour either side of HW. Shop and pub on the mainland (E) side; pub on the Annaghvaan side.

Bealadangan Pass

For vessels of limited air draft, Bealadangan Pass is navigable. It is best to make the passage near HW (+0010 Galway) as the flow reaches 4 to 5 kn under the bridge at half tide, the flood running N. The depth at half tide is 1·8m; the clearance under the bridge should be 2·4m at MHWS, 4m at MHWN and 4·9m at half tide. The first beacon on the N side is tucked close in behind the bridge abutment to the W. The passage between the rocks is very narrow in places. Keep just 5 to 10m from the mainland shore when passing the two N-most beacons. There is 2·5m of water in the pool N of the bridge. For pilotage of Camus Bay and Gurraig Sound leading from Bealadangan to Kilkieran Bay, see page 235.

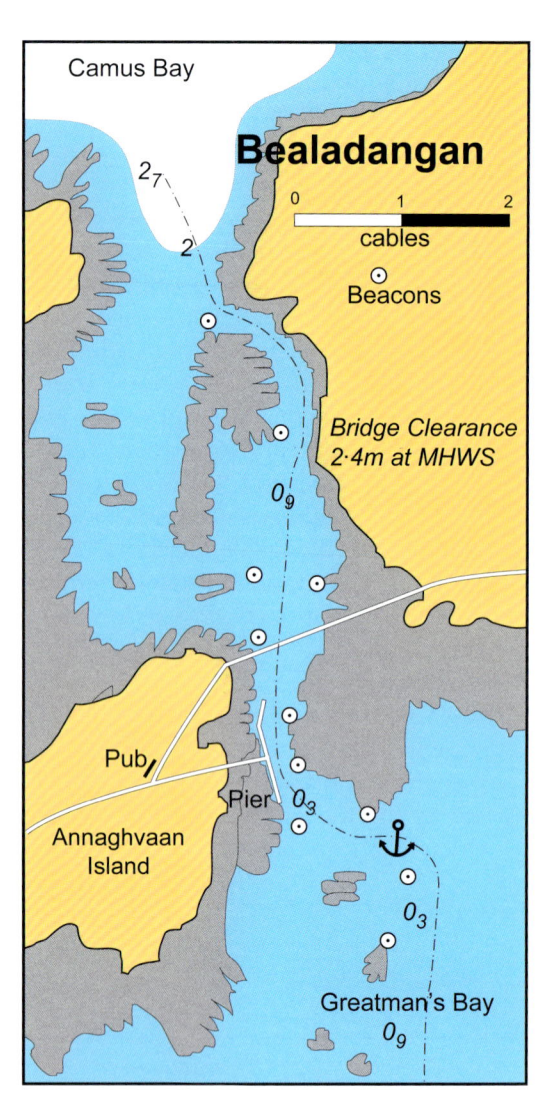

KIGGAUL BAY

⊕ *KG* 53°13'·5N 9°42'·7W
AC2096 and Plan

This bay is situated between Gorumna and Lettermullan Islands, which are joined by a bridge at the head of the bay. It is easily identified from seaward by Illaunnanownim to the E and Golam Head 2M to the W. There is no difficulty in reaching the outer anchorage by day. There are fish cages in the entrance, so at night, stay in the middle of the white sector of the light, bearing 339°. From the E, give Loughcarrick Island a berth of 3 cables. From the W, keep Carricknamackan Rock open S of Eagle Island 290° to clear Dawsy's Rock and Griffin's Spit, and the 1·7m rock between them *(photo on page 232)*.

Anchorage

Anchor close W or NW of the light beacon in 3 to 4m, mud with weed. Good shelter from W and N but untenable in fresh winds between SE and S. Cora Bhuí pier, with 0·5m alongside,

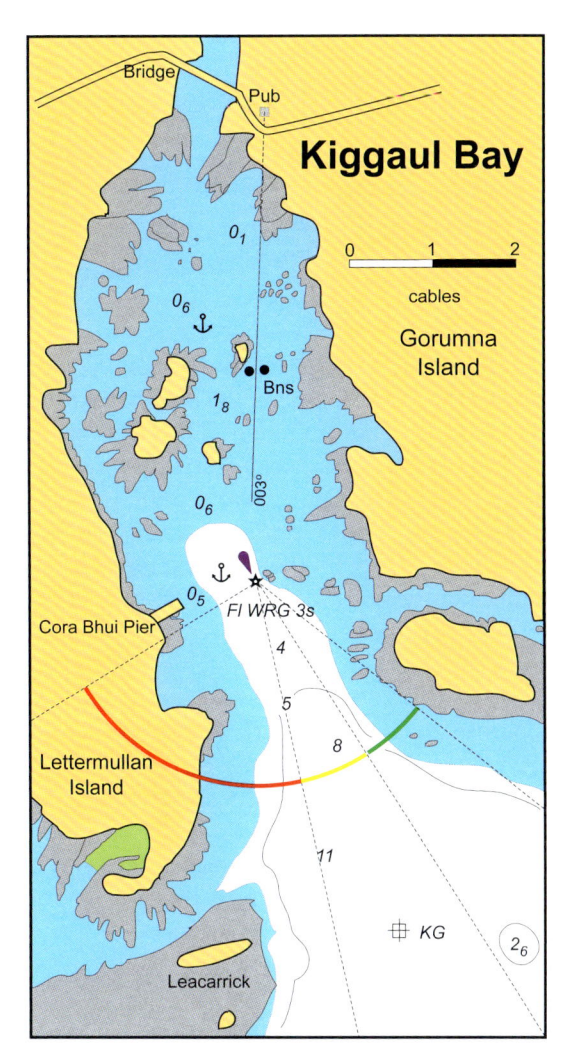

Kiggaul Bay

stands on the shore of Lettermullan Island W of the light beacon, but is remote by road. Water at the pier. Shop and pub at the bridge, accessible by dinghy (see below).

Inner anchorage

The N part of the bay is accessible to small yachts for 2 hours either side of HW, with least depth of 2·4m in the approach but very little room for error. Identify the conspicuous pub building close E of Kiggaul Bridge, and the two stone beacons marking the channel. Leave the light beacon 0·25 cables to starboard and line up the centre of the pub building between the two stone beacons 003°. There are rocks drying 2m, very close W of this leading line. Once past the beacons turn to port round the 12m-high rock N of the west beacon until heading SW towards a grass-topped islet. Anchor in 3m, mud, with the west beacon bearing 132° and the pub 014°, which is very close to the rocks; or in 2m a little NW of this, west beacon bearing 135° and pub 019°. There is a slip 2 cables S of the pub. Shop 200m on the Gorumna (E) side.

(above) Kiggaul Bay from the S; Leacarrick (bottom L), Kiggaul light beacon (centre). Beyond the bridge is Coonawilleen Bay. Inishbarra (top R) and Illauneeragh (top L)

Kiggaul Bay from the SW; the light beacon, R, the pub building and the beacons marking the channel to the inner anchorage, centre

231

Kilkieran Bay and Approaches

Carricknamackan (L centre) open of Eagle Rock (centre) clears Griffin's Spit and Dawsy's Rock. Golam, R, Seal Rock, L

KILKIERAN BAY and APPROACHES

AC2096, see Plan on p226

Kilkieran Bay lies N of Golam Head and extends inland for 14M. It can be entered in any conditions and gives excellent shelter. It is easily identified from seaward by Golam Tower, which is conspicuous all along this stretch of coast. Many of the above-water rocks in the approach, such as **Eagle Rock, Seal Rock** and **Fish Rock,** are easy to identify in clear weather and make good landmarks. **Carricknamackan Little,** square shaped, dries 4·6m and covers only at HWS.

Tides
Kilkieran Bay and approaches

The stream at Golam Head is stronger than elsewhere in North Sound, and may raise overfalls. No accurate information is available on directions and rates at Golam Head. Maximum rates in the bay are 2 kn at the narrows by Kilkieran Point and 1·5 kn near the entrance, off Ardmore Point, and in the narrows of Gurraig Sound and the upper Bay. The ingoing stream commences at –0520 Galway and the outgoing at +0105 Galway.
Constant (Kilkieran pier) +0005 Galway, MHWS 4·8m, MHWN 3·7m, MLWN 1·7m, MLWS 0·6m.

Dangers
Kilkieran Bay

A comprehensive list of the dangers around Kilkieran Bay would be very long indeed. The most significant are the following:
Ullan Rock, (dries), 1 cable S of Golam
Fairservice Rock, 0·9m, 2 cables E of Seal Rock and 6 cables WSW of Golam
Seal Breaker (awash), 2 cables W of Seal Rock
Namackan Rocks, drying and above-water rocks 2·5M WNW of Golam
Kenny Rock (dries 1·8m), 5 cables NW of Namackan Rocks
Inishmuskerry Shoal, 0·9m, 5 cables S of Inishmuskerry
Dinish Shoals, 1·5m, 1·7M NNW of Golam
Outer Hard Rock (dries 1·8m), 5 cables NE of Ardmore Point
Fork Rocks and **Carrickanella Rocks** (drying), 6 cables N of Illaneeragh
Lettercallow Spit, 1·2m, 1M N of Illauneeragh

Directions

From the E, Golam Head is steep-to but beware of Ullan Rock, S of the island. Redflag Island well open of Golam Head 305° leads just S of Ullan Rock. Keep Carricknamackan Rock open S of Eagle Island 290° to clear Dawsy's Rock and Griffin's Spit, and the 1·7m rock between them. Fairservice Rock is frequently not marked by a breaker even when Seal Breaker is showing. Lettercallow Hill and Dinish Point in line 047° lead between the two shallow heads of Dinish Shoals. Illaunmaan in line with Kilkieran Point 033° leads W of the shoals. The S extremity of Illauneeragh in line with Lettermore Hill 066° leads NW of the shoals. There are some ruined cottages and coral sand beaches at the S end of Illauneeragh. **From the W**, Golam Head well open of Redflag Island 126° leads clear S of Inishmuskerry Shoal *(photo on page 239)*.

Lights and Marks

Golam Tower, unlit 19th-century signal tower, conspicuous on the summit of Golam Island, 2M W of Kiggaul Bay
Kilkieran Pier, Fl R 3s
There are three unlit concrete beacons in Gurraig Sound

Caution

Fish farming is carried out all round this coast, although some charted locations are not currently used. Fish cages do not generally obstruct anchorages but in a few places abandoned moorings or floating ropes may present a hazard. Do not anchor in the vicinity of fish cages, for this reason. Shellfish pots are frequently encountered; beware also of long floating ropes on their buoys.

Golam Tower

Golam Harbour

Approaching Golam Harbour from the SW. The drying rock in mid-channel should be left well to port (photo Ed Wheeler)

Golam Harbour

53°14′N 9°46′·5W, *see Plan*

Immediately N of Golam Head is the entrance to Golam Harbour, which is obstructed by **Binock Rock** (dries about 2·7m), with a further drying rock close S of it. The best water is about one third of the width of the channel N of Golam Island. Note that there are rocks with less than 2m LAT in this fairway, and a close watch should be kept for shellfish pots. As soon as the E side of Golam Island opens up turn sharp to port and keep 0·75 cable off the HW shore of Freaghillaunmore until 2 cables from Crappagh when it is safe to turn E, close S of the fish cages. Anchor anywhere inside but beware of floating ropes. If going right up to the head of the harbour (where shelter is best) take care to avoid the rock SW of the 2·4m sounding. It is usually marked by long streamers of weed. Holding reported good to the NW of this rock in 4 to 5m, grey mud. The shelter is good under all conditions. There is a good slip in the bay at the SE end of the harbour, which gives access to the Lettermullan road. Shop at Lettermullan.

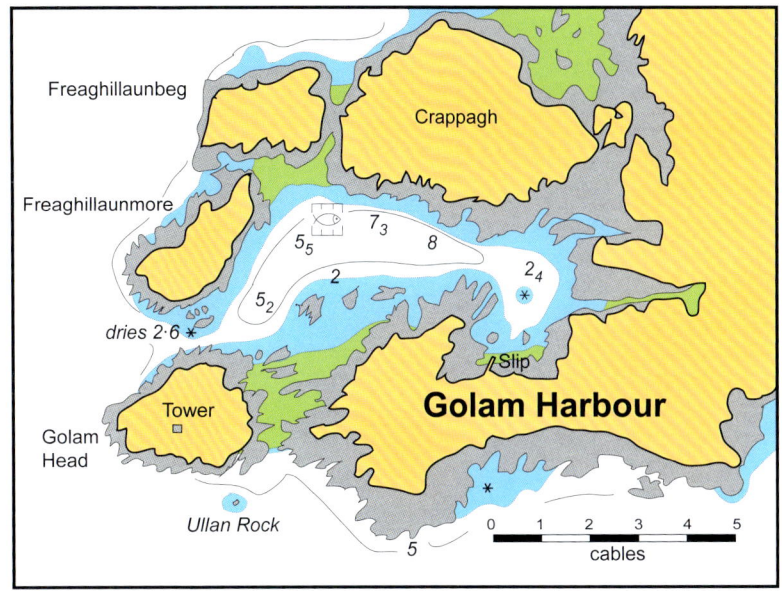

Bollegouh Creek, 53°15′·3N 9°45′·3W, E of Inisherk, affords complete shelter but it is studded with rocks, and for that reason is practicable only as a temporary anchorage for a small yacht in good weather. Approach in mid-channel until the creek narrows, and then stay on the E side, heading for the white house nearest the shore. Proceed at very slow speed and watch the bottom - clean stretches of sand show up clearly. Drying rocks extend from the W side just N of the house, and rocks, with long streamers of weed, from the E side. There is a clean patch opposite the house for an anchorage. The entrance to the S of Inisherk is clearer but is not to be attempted without reconnaissance by dinghy.

Bruiser Rock, marked as "existence doubtful" 0·5 cable W of Dinish Island, almost

Golam Harbour from Golam Tower (photo Ed Wheeler)

Bollegouh Creek; the white house nearest the shore, L

233

Kilkieran Bay anchorages

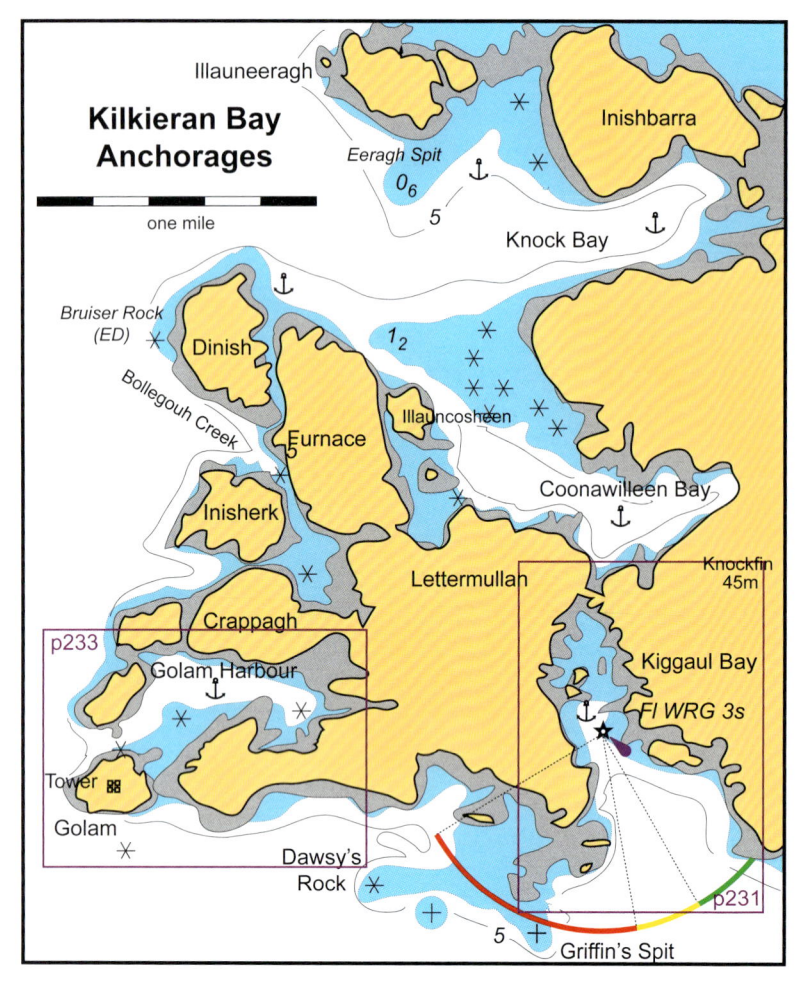

certainly does not exist but it is so close to an exposed shore that this is fairly academic. Lettercallow Hill and Dinish Point in line 047°, as above, clear it. E of Birmore Island there are drying rocks; give the island a berth of at least 4 cables, and stay 4 cables off Ardmore Point (where there are conspicuous sandy beaches) to clear the Inner and Outer Hard Rocks.

Fork Rocks, N of Illauneeragh, are particularly dangerous as the SW rocks cover first. Birmore Island well open to the W of Illaunmaan, 230°, just clears Fork Rocks but leads over the end of Lettercallow Spit.

Anchorages

Latitudes and longitudes are given for ease of location and are not waypoints or recommended anchoring positions.

- **Inside Dinish Point,** 53°16′N 9°44′·7W, in 2 to 3m, sand, off the beach between Dinish and Furnace Islands. Exposed from NW to NE. A lovely anchorage in good weather, with beautiful views up the bay with the Connemara Mountains as a backdrop.
- **Coonawilleen Bay,** 53°14′·9N 9°42′·9W. Leave Illauncosheen close to starboard on entering and anchor at the head of the bay in 4 to 5m, with the quarried hill Knockfin to the SE. There are some fish cages in the bay but these are not a significant obstruction. The Boat Harbour S of Illauncosheen is inaccessible without local knowledge, and the pool to the S of it is fouled with floating ropes and discarded fish farm moorings.
- **Knock Bay,** 53°16′·2N 9°42′·6W, in the bay S of Inishbarra in 6m, halfway between the island and the reef to the SE.
- **E of Illauneeragh,** 53°16′·4N 9°43′·6W. This lovely fine-weather anchorage is off glorious sandy beaches, and the island is uninhabited. Approach S of the 0·6m sounding on Eeragh Spit and keep well clear of the small spit SE of the island. Anchor in 2m, shells, N of this spit with the narrow cleft in the island to the N just closed in. Exposed from SE to SW. There is less than 1·8m at MLWS on the bar S of the anchorage.
- **Ardmore Bay,** 53°18′N 9°45′·8W. Approach with a wide sweep to avoid the Inner and Outer Hard Rocks. Anchor a cable S of the drying pier at the head of the bay to stay clear of fish cage moorings, but N of the conspicuous beach, off which are the Inner Hard Rocks. Shop and pub 500m. A delightful fine-weather anchorage, but in S winds there is a roll.
- **Kilkieran Cove,** 53°19′·2N 9°43′·7W. Approach steering NW to avoid a rock awash at LAT, 1·5 cables ENE of the pierhead. Anchor a cable off the pier with its head bearing 310°, in 2 to 3m, mud, holding suspect. Good shelter from

Birmore Island (R) well open to the W of Illaunmaan clears Fork Rocks. Carricknamackan, further to the SW, is visible through the gap.

234

SE through W to NE, and normally tide-rode. There are visitors' moorings. The pier has 1·8m at its head, but the deep water extends less than 20m from the N side, and the bottom in the shallows opposite is of large boulders. Water on the pier. Pub/restaurant, good shop (one of the few shops on this coast), PO.

Gurraig Sound, Camus Bay and Rosmuck

53°19'·6N 9°38'W
AC2096 and Plan on page 237

Gurraig Sound extends ENE from the main channel of Kilkieran Bay, with Lettermore and Annaghvaan to the S and the Rosmuck peninsula to the N. The deep channel is narrow, with patches of 1·2m on either hand and in mid-channel; care is required in pilotage. The beacons shown on AC2096 on Bird Rock and N of Illaungurraig do not exist; there is instead a single pillar beacon on the reef extending NW from Illaungurraig, which should be left to starboard going E. The similar beacon on Yellow Rock should be left to port. After passing Yellow Rock steer NE towards Garrivinagh on the N side of the bay. Beyond Leighon Island on the S shore the entrance to Bealadangan Pass opens up (see directions on page 229). The channel to the ENE is fairly straightforward though both shores are foul. There is an unmarked rock awash in mid-channel N of Dangan Hill (29m), but a pillar beacon marks the end of the spit extending from the S shore here; leave the beacon close to starboard. Although tidal water extends four miles further inland to the NE and off the charts, the limit of navigation for the stranger is at Rosmuck Quay, SW of Clynagh Island. Beyond this the tides begin to run very strongly, forming rapids in places, and despite a number of beacons, local knowledge is essential.

Anchorage

Anchor a cable SSE of the small quay at Garrivinagh in 2·1m, or 2 cables SE of Rosmuck Quay in 4m, mud. Shop at Turloughbeg, 1 km from Rosmuck Quay.

North Kilkieran Bay

North-east of Kilkieran Cove the Bay, overlooked by the mountains of Connemara, is navigable almost to its head, but the many rocks and shoal patches demand the greatest

(top) The anchorage at Illauneeragh

(above) Ardmore pier

(left) Kilkieran pier

(left) Gurraig Sound; Illaungurraig beacon

(below) Garrivinagh Quay

(bottom) Rosmuck Quay

North Kilkieran Bay; Kilkieran to Roundstone

Marks for the passage to the head of Kilkieran Bay: (above) The west end of Illauneeragh West bearing 037°

(right) Steering 001° for a prominent clump of trees (R) on the N shore at Kylesalia

(right) View ahead on 057°; steer for the house

(top) View ahead on 068°; steer for the house

(above) Illaunrossalough from the SW

of Illauneeraghwest, passing between Oyster Bank and the shoals opposite, to 53°20'·75N 9°41'·25W, 1·5 cables NNW of Iris Rock, then

• 001° for 7 cables towards the north shore, passing through the narrows between Cummer Rock and Cummerkilsalia Rock, much of which show at half flood, to 53°21'·40N 9°41'·20W, 3 cables E of Kylesalia Creek, then

• 057° for 6 cables in relatively deep water to 53°21'·75N 9°40'·33W, 1 cable NNW of Knocknavranka, then

• 068° for 5 cables to 53°21'·90N 9°39'·63W, 1 cable short of Lackatragall, then

• 029° for 5 cables to the centre of the basin SW of Illaunrossalough.

The greatest accuracy is required on the last change of course since Lackatragall and the rocks opposite are covered at half flood.

Anchorages

Anchorage is available almost anywhere on this passage. There is a pub at Kylesalia.

KILKIERAN BAY to ROUNDSTONE

AC2096, 2709

The coast from Kilkieran Bay to Slyne Head is fronted by a maze of rocks, islands and breakers, and navigation marks are few and far between. It provides a challenging and rewarding cruising ground for the adventurous. The picturesque village of Roundstone, N of Bertraghboy Bay, is a popular weekenders' retreat.

Inner Passage

53°15'N 9°48'W
AC2096 and Plans on pp226 and 238

This channel, inside Eagle, Namackan and Tonyeal Rocks, is the shortest route into Roundstone from the E, offers a small degree of extra shelter to a yacht heading for Slyne Head and presents no difficulty in reasonable visibility. As on the coast further E, the above-water rocks and islets offshore provide good reference points in clear weather. **Eagle Rock** (8m high), **Carricknamackan** (6m high), and (further W) **Skerdmore** (18m high), **Doonguddle** (12m high) and **Mile Rock** (4·4m high) are relatively easy to identify.

care in pilotage. A passage to the head of navigation at Illaunrossalough may be made in a least depth of 2·4m at half flood with the aid of the following courses and waypoints, and is best done on a high and rising tide. Among the significant hazards, Iris Rock (dries 0·6m), and Lackatragall and the drying rocks opposite it, are covered at this state of the tide. Knocknavranka rock, shown on AC2096 as 1·8m high and thus apparently a useful landmark, is also below-water. From 53°19'·40N 9°43'·00W, approximately 5 cables E of Kilkieran Pier, steer:

• 037° for 1·7M towards the west HWM

236

Kilkieran Bay to Roundstone

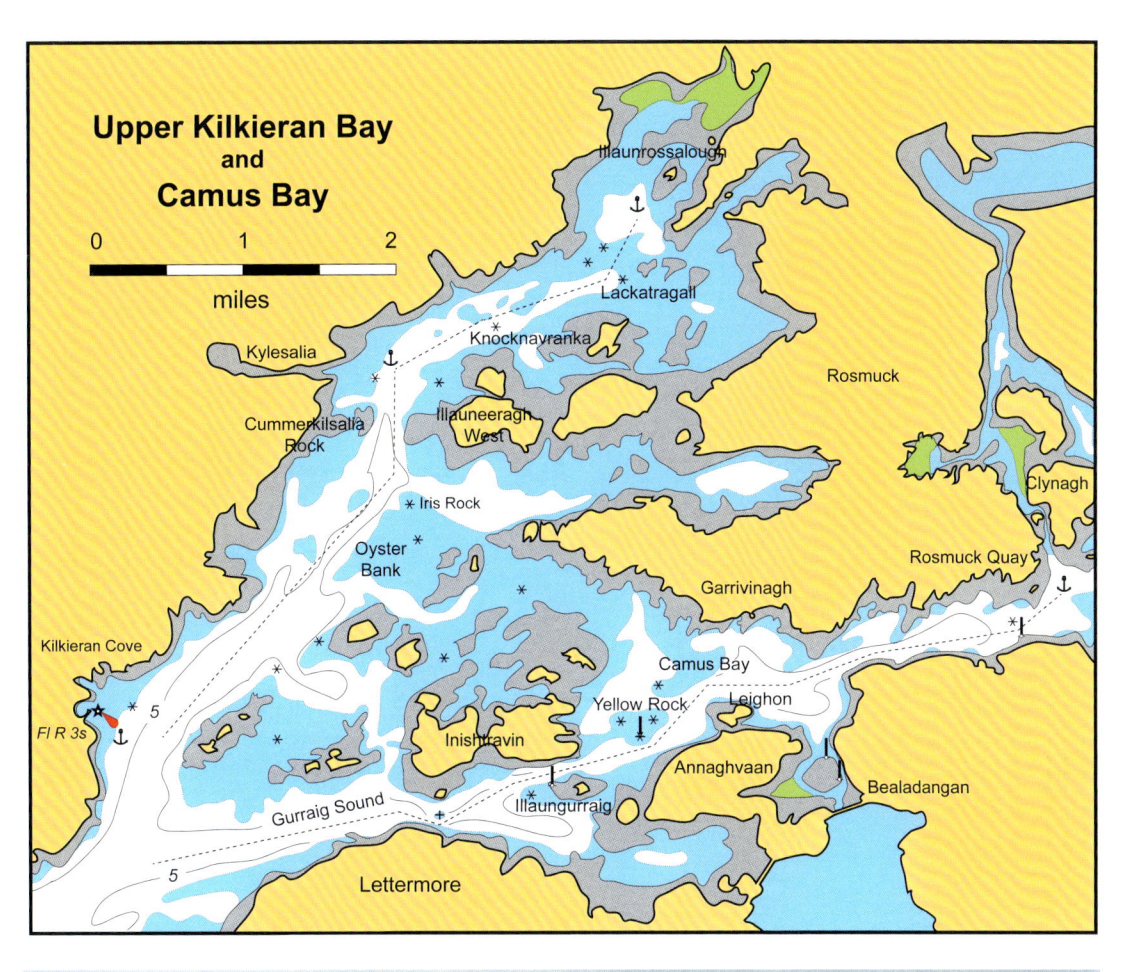

Upper Kilkieran Bay and Camus Bay

Channels W of Kilkieran Bay, from the W. Duck Island R foreground, Mulroa Point (Mweenish) with Finish Island and Ardmore Point beyond, L; Inishmuskerry and Carrigalusk with Birmore and Birbeg beyond, R; Illauneeragh, Inishbarra and Lettermullan Island, top.

237

Inner Passage

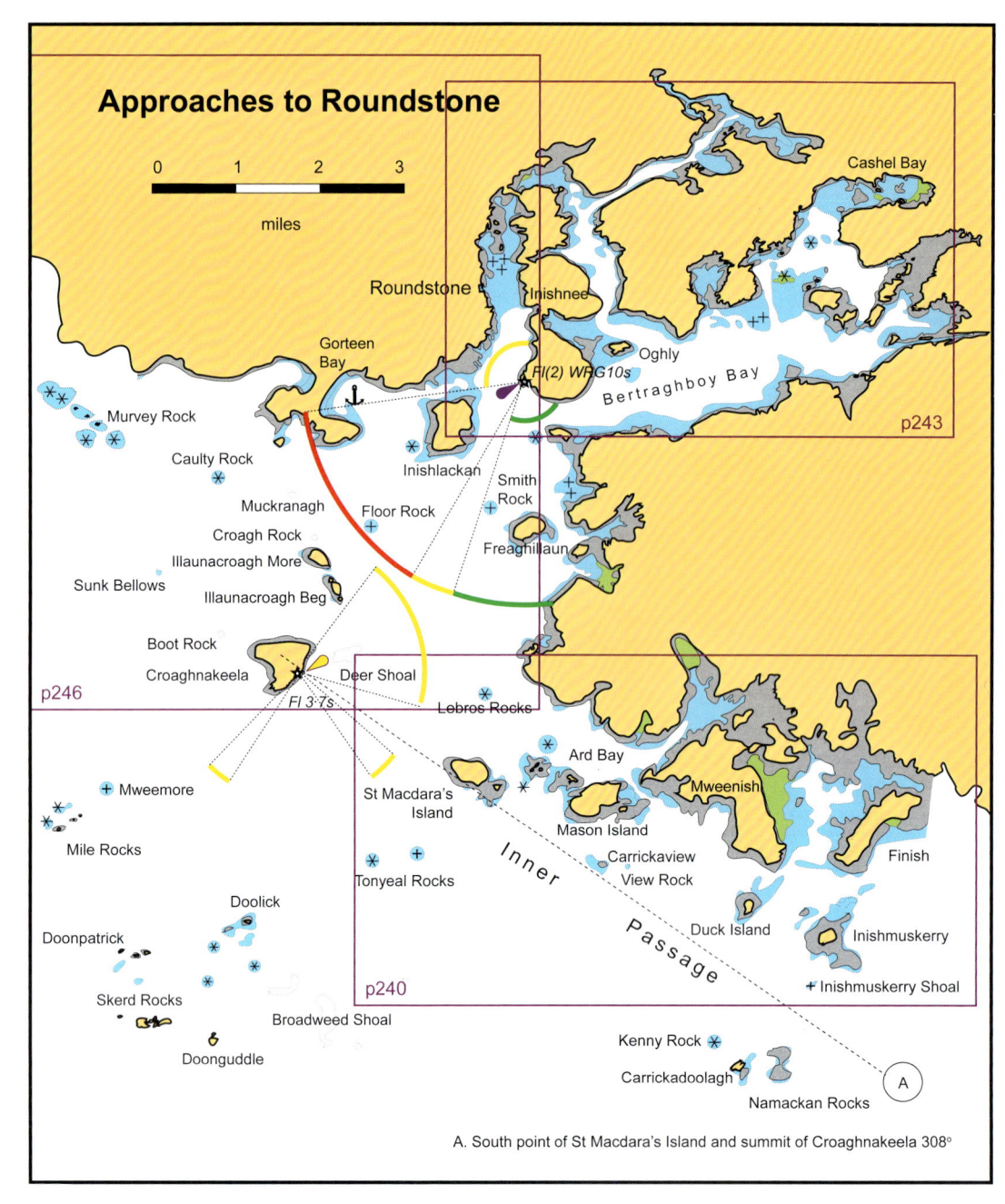

Tides
Kilkieran Bay to Roundstone

The tidal stream in the Inner Passage is insignificant. The general stream runs NW and SE, and turns in and out of the bays and sounds. Off the Skerd Rocks the NW-going stream begins at −0320 Galway and the SE-going stream at +0305 Galway. In the narrows at the entrance to Bertraghboy Bay, the tide runs at 2 kn, and possibly a little more at springs; the ingoing stream starts at −0520 Galway and the outgoing at +0105 Galway.

Constant (Roundstone Bay) +0003 Galway; MHWS 4·4m, MHWN 3·4m, MLWN 1·6m, MLWS 0·6m.

Directions

Golam Head well open N of Redflag Island 126° leads through the Inner Passage. Alternatively bring the summit of Croaghnakeela over the S point of St Macdara's Island, 308°. Feraun North Rock (dries 4·9m) shows except at highest springs when it is almost always marked by a breaker. Kenny Rock and Inishmuskerry Shoal are also usually marked by breakers. The shallowest parts of the Tonyeal Rocks usually break, but these are very dangerous rocks which cover a wide area and are liable to break anywhere in a high swell. Waypoint ⊕TR, 53°17'·6N 9°55'·4W is midway between the rocks and Saint Macdara's Island. At night, Croaghnakeela light, visible 311°–325°,

Finish and Mweenish

Golam Head well open of Redflag Island leads through the Inner Passage

leads through.

There is a clear channel into the Inner Passage between the Namackan Rocks and the Eagle Rock group. Give Seal Rock (2·4m high), W of Golam, a berth of 3 cables on its W side; there is deep water close W of Fish Rock (4m high), 7 cables to the NW. From the W, Golam Tower open S of Eagle Rock 094° clears the breakers to the S of Namackan Rocks. It is also possible to enter W of Namackan Rocks, avoiding Kenny Rock by keeping Carrickadoolagh (2·1m high), close to starboard.

Finish Island

53°17'·6N 9°48'·45W

There is a pleasant anchorage at the above position, E of Finish. From the S, enter in mid-channel between Birmore and Inishmuskerry, steering 341° for waypoint 53°17'·28N 9°48'·77W, then 034°. Anchor in 2·5m, sand. Finish Rock South (dries 1·8m) lies to the E of the track and rocks, with less than 2m, to the SW of it. There is also a clear passage between these rocks and the reefs S of Finish, at a waypoint of 53°17'·93N 9°48'·96W. From this waypoint, steer 252° towards Duck Island (or Mullanegerne, which dries 3·4m, if it is showing) to 53°16'·90N 9°49'·98W, NNW of Carrickalusk, and then SW between Inishmuskerry and Duck Island. Duck is easily identified by the conspicuous remains of a wreck near the summit of the island. Carrickalusk dries more than 4m and covers only at HWS.

It is also possible in fine weather to anchor off the NE side of Inishmuskerry and land on the beach of this delightful little island.

Mweenish Bay

53°16'·2N 9°50'·5W
AC2096, 2709

This bay opens to the N of the Inner Passage and can be entered either N or W of Inishmuskerry. The bay is shallower in places

Dangers
Kilkieran Bay to Roundstone

An exhaustive list would be very long indeed. The most significant hazards on the coastal passage are as follows:

Inishmuskerry Shoal, 0·9m, 5 cables SSW of Inishmuskerry
Namackan Rocks, drying and above-water rocks 2·5M WNW of Golam
Kenny Rock (dries 1·8m), 5 cables NW of Namackan Rocks
Carrickaview (dries 1·8m) and **View Rock** (0·9m), 6 cables S of Mason Island
Fraghan Rock (dries), 4 cables E of Saint Macdara's Island
Tonyeal Rocks (1·5m and drying 0·6m), 1M SW of Saint Macdara's Island
Lebros Rocks (dry 0·6m), 5 cables SW of Mace Head
Rourke's Slate (dries 0·5m), on the S side of Ard Bay
Floor Rock, 1·2m, 6 cables NE of Illauncroaghmore
Smith Rock, 2m, 4 cables NW of Freaghillaun
Oghly Shoal, 1·2m, 3 cables S of Oghly Island in Bertraghboy Bay.

The dangers on the offshore passage to Slyne Head are listed below under **Roundstone to Slyne Head**.

Lights and Marks

Croaghnakeela, white beacon Fl 3·7s 7m 5M, vis 218°–286°, 311°–325°, 034°–045°. Shows narrow sectors between Skerd and Mile Rocks to the SW and between Tonyeal Rocks and St Macdara's Island to the SE, and a broader sector to the E and NE, obscured elsewhere.
Inishnee, white pillar Fl(2) WRG 10s 9m 5M, G 314°–017° W 017°–030° R 030°–080° W 080°–194°. Shows white over the approach from the SSW, green over Smith Rock and E of it, red over the islands and rocks to the SW and white over Roundstone Bay to the W and N
The **church** on Saint Macdara's Island is conspicuous from the S

Caution

It is particularly necessary on this coast to be conscious of the difference between the horizontal chart datum and WGS84, which is the datum used by the GPS system. This offset is documented on up-to-date copies of the charts, and on some recently issued editions it is zero. Where specific waypoints are given in this section, they have been established and validated by a 12m vessel drawing 1·6m. However in the absence of horizontal datum information, the greatest caution is advised.

239

Straddle Pass

Mweenish and adjacent islands

The wreck on Duck Island

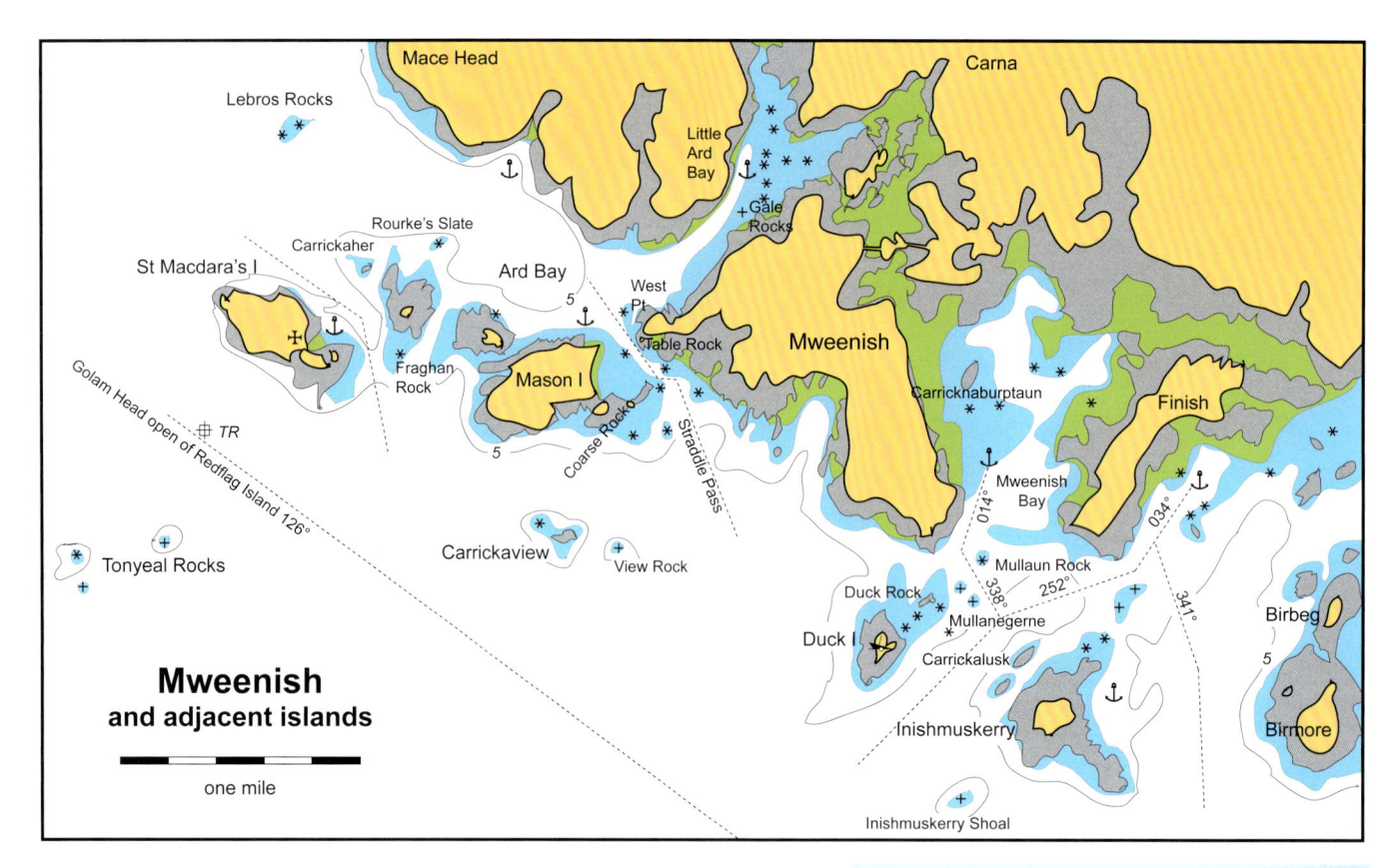

Straddle Pass from the NW; Table Rock, extreme L, and Coarse Rock, R. Golam (L) and Duck Island, with its conspicuous wreck, in the distance, centre.

than charted, and has several uncharted rocks in addition to the charted Mullaun Rock (dries 0·6m). There is a rock with 1·3m, 1·5 cables ENE of Duck Rock, and there are two rocks drying 0·5m, a cable SE of the S'most head of Carricknaburptaun. From 53°16'·90N 9°49'·98W, NNW of Carrickalusk, steer 338° for 3·5 cables to 53°17'·22N 9°50'·20W, then 014° for a further 2 cables and anchor in 2m, sand.

Straddle Pass

53°17'·75N 9°52'·10W
AC2096

The channel between Mweenish and Mason Islands is narrow and constricted by drying rocks at each end. It is navigable in settled weather, with great care, using the following waypoints. From the SE, from a point (53°17'·75N 9°52'·10W) 5 cables SE of West Point on Mweenish, steer 333° for 3 cables to waypoint 53°18'·00N 9°52'·26W; then turn to port and steer 292° for one cable to waypoint 53°18'·05N 9°52'·46W, then turn to starboard and steer 324°, passing 50m from Table Rock (the above-water head of the reef S of West Point) and the drying rock 2 cables NW of it. Least depth on this track is 1·8m at LAT. Proceed under power and cautiously, with constant attention to the depth. From the NW, steer 144° from waypoint 53°18'·46N 9°52'·95W 4 cables NW of West Point, and leave Table Rock 50m to port.

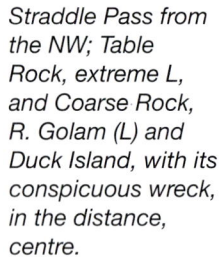

Mason and St Macdara's Islands; Ard Bay and the Skerds

Macdara Sound

53°18'N 9°54'·4W
AC2709

This sound is navigable in any reasonable weather, staying 1·5 to 2 cables off the summit of the 2·7m-high islet SE of Saint Macdara's Island in order to clear Fraghan Rock. Once the church comes abeam, keep the island shore close aboard to port, to avoid Carrickaher (dries 3m). It was customary for vessels passing the church to dip the peak of the mainsail three times in reverence to the saint.

Saint Macdara's is a lovely island with wonderful views of the mountains and the coast. The restored church dates from the 6th century and is one of the oldest in the country. Anchor in the little bay off the beach in the Sound, but not too close in as there are isolated boulders near the beach.

Ard Bay

53°18'·6N 9°53'·4W
AC2709

Ard Bay affords shelter in all except NW winds, and its continuation, Little Ard Bay, is sheltered in all winds. From the mid-channel in the entrance to Little Ard Bay (N of West Point on Mweenish), steer to pass close to the point S of the quay on the W side to avoid Gale Rocks opposite.

Lebros Rocks, drying 0·6m, are a significant hazard in the approach from the W. Golam Tower in line with the SW point of Mason Island 131° leads S of Lebros Rocks; Inishnee light, a small white column, in line with the SW point of Freaghillaun 003° leads E of them. Carrickaher and Rourke's Slate on the S side of the bay can be avoided by keeping over to the mainland shore, which is clean to within 1 cable.

Anchorages

- Off the N shore of Mason Island. Mason is a beautiful and peaceful place, uninhabited since 1952, with lovely beaches on its NE corner. On its NW side there is a tiny drying harbour which is suitable only for small boats. Two houses have recently been restored.
- In N winds there is good anchorage off the quay in the unnamed bay NE of Rourke's Slate.
- In Little Ard Bay, in front of a cottage with a conspicuous model lighthouse as a garden ornament. A yacht will normally be tide-rode here. It is possible above half flood to take a dinghy with a dependable outboard from here 1M to the quay at Carna. Shops, PO and pubs at Carna.

Skerd Rocks

53°15'·2N 10°03'W
AC2709

There is a pool between Skerdmore and Skerdbeg, entered from the S, in which it is possible to land a dinghy at any state of the tide in settled weather with little swell. The islands are a seal colony. Beware a rock drying less than a metre and uncharted until 2011, in 53°16'·327N 9°59'·311W, 1·5 cables SW of Doolickbeg.

(above) The anchorage in Macdara Sound (photo Dick Lincoln)

(left) Beach at the NE point of Mason Island; Ard Bay, L, Straddle Pass to the R

Approaching the anchorage in Little Ard Bay

The pool between Skerdmore and Skerdbeg

241

Roundstone and Bertraghboy Bays

Roundstone from the S; Mace Head, foreground, Freaghillaun centre, Inishtreh, Inishnee and Roundstone Bay beyond. Inishlackan top L and Bertraghboy Bay top R

(below) Mile Rock seen between Illaunacroagh More and Illaunacroagh Beg leads over Floor Rock (seen breaking)

(bottom) Bringing Slyne Head lighthouse towers in line with Caulty Rock (centre) leads N of Floor Rock. Murvey Rock, R. Near low water.

ROUNDSTONE and BERTRAGHBOY BAYS

AC2709 and Plan

These bays offer complete shelter and can be approached and entered in almost any weather. They are easily identified from seaward by Cashel Hill (307m) and Mount Errisbeg (296m), and by Croaghnakeela Island and the Skerd and Mile Rocks offshore.

Directions

From the E, leave Saint Macdara's Island 2 cables to starboard and head for the E end of Inishlackan, or else use Macdara Sound and head for Croaghnakeela before turning N. Longitude 9°55'·5W leads 5 cables W of Lebros and Smith Rocks. The charted transit on Roundstone church is hard to see. **From the S**, identify Skerdmore (18m high) and Mile Rock (4·4m high) and steer to pass 5 cables W of Skerdmore. Once clear N of Doonpatrick (2m high) alter course to pass close E of Croaghnakeela. Deer Shoal can be ignored in normal summer weather. Illaunacroaghmore and Illaunacroaghbeg are steep-to on their E sides, where landing can be made in fine weather. **From the W**, the major hazards apart from Floor Rock are **Wild Bellows, Sunk Bellows, Caulty Rock** and **Murvey Rock** (*see the next section* **Roundstone to Slyne Head** *for detailed directions for avoiding these*).

Mile Rock in view between Illaunacroaghmore and Illaunacroaghbeg 222° leads **over** Floor Rock: Slyne Head lighthouse towers in line with Caulty Rock (which normally shows) clears Floor Rock to the N. Treh Point on Inishtreh is a boulder beach; it should be given a berth of 2 cables to clear the Small Breakers, on its SW side. The SE and SW points of Inishlackan are foul for 2 cables offshore.

Bertraghboy Bay

53°22'·4N 9°54'W
AC2709 and Plan

This bay offers a choice of anchorages and shelter against all winds and sea, with lovely views of the mountains. The W part of the bay is relatively free of dangers, except for Oghly Shoal which can be ignored above half tide. The water tank on Inishlackan is no longer in the charted position, but in transit with the S point of Inishnee, it still leads S of Oghly Shoal. Steer 084° from mid-channel between Inishnee and Inishtreh until the E tip of Oghly Island bears 330°. There is a fish farm S of Salt Point.

Bertraghboy Bay

Bertraghboy Bay from the SW; Inishtreh centre, Inishnee L with Oghly Island beyond, Illaungorm top R. Note the fish cages.

Anchorages

- Off a bold bluff on the S shore halfway between the entrance and Rusheen Point, in 2 to 3m.
- E of Croghnut (28m high) at the E end of the bay, in 3 to 6m. Beware of the drying rock S of Croghnut and leave it to starboard when entering. The holding is reported (2010) poor, with a rocky bottom.
- NE of Salt Point in 3 to 4m, with good shelter in W winds. Note the rock 1 cable offshore at this anchorage.
- NE of Canower in 3 to 5m. This anchorage and the one below are best approached

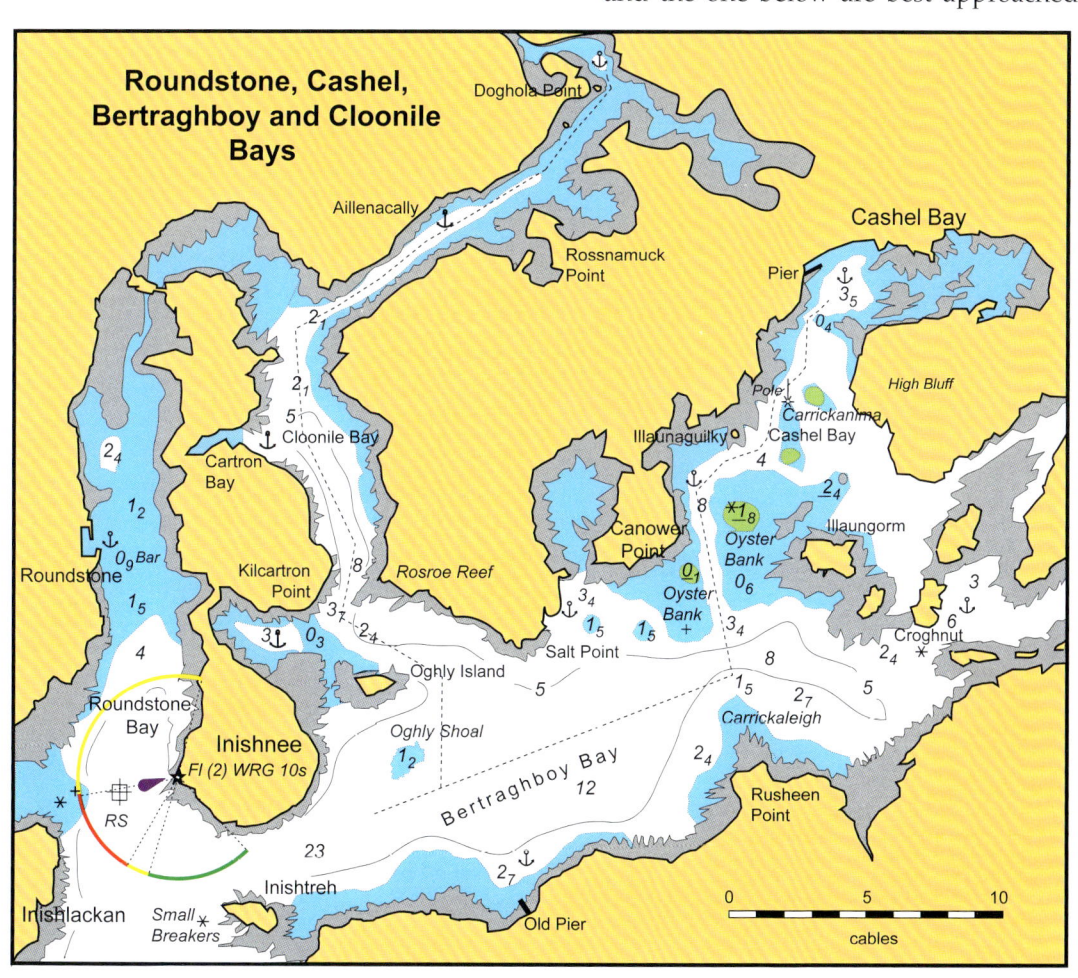

243

Cashel and Cloonile Bays

Inishlackan water tank and the S point of Inishnee lead S of Oghly Shoal

View NW over Bertraghboy Bay: Croghnut, L centre and Mount Errisbeg in the distance

E of Canower, looking N; heading a little to the R of the prominent white house leads up the deep channel

Carrickanima and its pole marker

Cashel Bay and pier (photo Galway CC)

after half flood, and the charted depths in the channels may have reduced. From the entrance, head for Croghnut until Carrickleagh is abeam, then steer for the channel between the E and W Oyster Banks, course 350° with Carrickleagh astern. A conspicuous white cottage makes a good mark to head for. Anchor just beyond the two roofless cottages on Canower.

- Off the quay at the head of Cashel Bay. From the anchorage NE of Canower, head for Illaunaguilky, the above-water head of the reefs to the NE. Steer E then NE and N round these reefs giving the summit of Illaunaguilky a berth of 1·5 cables. Carrickanima, the drying rock to the NE, has a pole marker. Steer to pass NW of Carrickanima (note that there is a small drying outlier 10m W of the rock) then swing to starboard to avoid a sunken rock on the W side. Then steer for the pier ("Quay" on AC2709), staying close to the NW shore to avoid the 0·4m sounding on the E side. Anchor in 3·5m, mud, a cable off the quay. Hotels with restaurants and bar food, 1·5 and 2 km, at the head of the bay.

Cloonile Bay

Several lovely anchorages are available in this arm of Bertraghboy Bay. Follow the deep water as charted, staying close to the NE side of Oghly Island and then keeping Church Point close aboard to avoid Rossroe Reef. Then stay in mid-channel. In the NE arm of the bay many depths are less than charted, and the inner part, above Rossnamuck Point, is safely navigable only above half flood. Keep the NW shore close aboard at the narrows at Rossnamuck Point, then head for the first of two flat-topped above-water rocks on the NW side, 4 cables further. Leave it 10m to port and head for the second one, 2 cables NE off Doghola Point. Leave it 20m to port.

Cloonile Bay and Roundstone

Anchorages

- In the wide bay N of Kilcartron Point, in 3m, mud; the bar at the entrance has 0·3m.
- In the next bay to the N (Creevecartron).
- Off the quay at Aillenacally in 3m, mud. Despite being only a mile from the main Roundstone road, this is a remarkable spot in being a deserted village with no modern houses whatsoever in view.
- In a pool with 3·5m, one cable N of the second above-water rock at Doghola Point, and 2 cables SE of Cloonile Quay.

Note that the Ballynahinch River, which drains the mountains to the N, runs into the head of Cloonile Bay. With the river in spate after heavy rain, the anchorages in the upper part of the bay may be subject to strong currents.

ROUNDSTONE

⊕ RS 53°22'·7N 9°54'·6W
AC2709, Imray C54 and Plan. Additional photo on p13

The W side of Roundstone Bay, N of Inishlackan, is fringed with half-tide rocks, and there is a bar with least depth 0·9m close S of the harbour. Leave Inishnee Point 1 cable to starboard then steer 353° over the bar. The drying rock charted close to mid-channel in 53°23'·6N does not exist, and the bar has the same depth all the way across from E to W.

Anchorage

Anchor off the harbour, to the S of the moorings. There is reported to be foul ground off the N quay, and the W side of the bay shallows N of here, with a drying reef (see the aerial photograph) running out from the shore. There are visitors' moorings on the E side of the bay, but these are a long and exposed dinghy trip from the harbour. Constant +0005 Galway, MHWS 4·4m, MHWN 3·4m, MLWN 1·7m, MLWS 0·5m.

Harbour

The best drying berth is inside the S quay. The end of this quay has 1·2m but is used by sea angling boats. The bottom inside the N quay is also suitable for drying out.

Facilities

Water on the S quay. Shops, PO, pubs, restaurants. Buses to Galway.

Aillenacally anchorage in Cloonile Bay

(above) Head of Cloonile Bay; the second above-water rock at Doghola Point. Cloonile Quay, extreme L

(left) Roundstone Harbour; the yacht is at the best drying berth

(below) Roundstone from the SE

Roundstone to Slyne Head

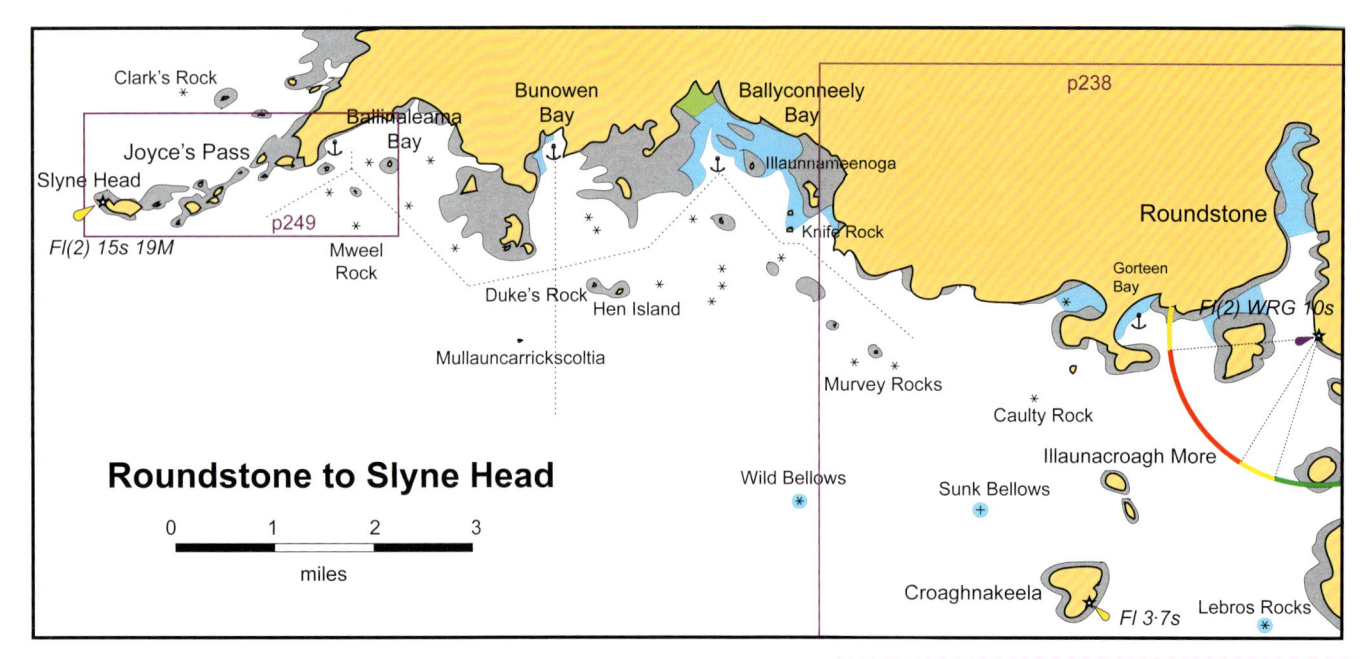

ROUNDSTONE to SLYNE HEAD

AC2709, 2708

The key to pilotage of this section is again to identify the above-water rocks offshore and use them as reference points. There are beautiful and accessible anchorages at Gorteen Bay and Bunowen Bay. Slyne Head is actually on an island – Illaunamid (23m high), at the end of a string of islets and rocks extending 2M WSW from the mainland. Its black lighthouse tower and the disused tower close SE of it are unmistakable. There is one navigable channel through the reefs, known as Joyce's Pass or Joyce's Sound, which is not for the faint-hearted.

Lights and Marks

Slyne Head, black tower Fl(2) 15s 35m 19M, AIS
Disused lighthouse tower on Slyne Head
The following above-water rocks provide useful points of reference:
Skerdmore (18m high), **Doonguddle** (12m high) and **Mile Rock** (4·4m high), S of Croaghnakeela, and **Murvey Rock** (6m high), 8 cables SW of Murvey Point. **Mullauncarrickscoltia** (1·1m high), 1·1M S of Illaunurra, is the key to the coast.

Dangers
Roundstone to Slyne Head

An exhaustive list would be very long indeed. The most significant hazards on the coastal passage are as follows:
Floor Rock, 1·2m, 6 cables NE of Illaunacroagh More
Muckranagh, 6·4m, 6 cables NNW of Illaunacroagh More, may break unexpectedly on the ebb tide.
Caulty Rock (dries 4·3m), 1·2M NW of Illaunacroagh More
Sunk Bellows, 1·8m, 1·5M W of Illaunacroagh More
Above-water, drying and sunken rocks extending in a wide arc of 3M from **Murvey SE Rock** (awash at HW), 1M S of Murvey Point, to **Duke's Rock**, 1M SE of Illaunurra and S of Bunowen Bay
Wild Bellows (dries 3m), 2·1M SW of Murvey Point
Cromwell Shoal, 2·4m, 6 cables WSW of Duke's Rock
Mweel Rock (dries 4m), 7 cables SSW of Carrickfia, in Ballinaleama Bay
Mweel Breaker, 3·7m, 5 cables SW of Mweel Rock.

Inishnee beacon between the right-hand pair of three small humps on the skyline leads through Inishlackan Sound. Not perhaps the most distinct transit in the world, but it works

Ballyconneely and Bunowen Bays

Directions

Heading W from Roundstone, give Inishlackan a berth of 3 cables. The SE points of Inishlackan and Inishnee in line 064° lead S of Muckranagh (6·4m, which is rarely a hazard in summer weather) but dangerously close to Sunk Bellows; once Illaunacroagh More is abeam, alter course to the W to pass S of Caulty Rock, which almost always shows, and identify Murvey Rocks to the NW. Wild Bellows, to the SW, is always marked by a breaker, but Sunk Bellows may break only intermittently. The NE sides of Saint Macdara's Island and Croaghnakeela in line 130° lead N of Sunk Bellows, while the whole of St Macdara's Island open S of Croaghnakeela, 110°, leads S of Sunk Bellows, Wild Bellows and all the dangers to Slyne Head. A confused sea can be met N of Illaunacroaghmore in fresh W winds, especially on the ebb.

Channels between the islands

Inishlackan Sound is navigable with care. Coming from Roundstone, keep well out in the middle of Roundstone Bay to avoid the drying rocks on the W side. Bring the light beacon on Inishnee in line 083° with the gap between the right-hand pair of three small humps on the skyline near the summit of the island. This line leads clear through the sound. Coming E from Gorteen Bay, keep well out from Inishlackan until the marks come in line so as to avoid **Gun Rock** (dries 2·7m) and the breakers around it.

Deer Pass is free of danger but the sound between Illaunacroaghmore and Illaunacroaghbeg is very narrow, and lobster pots are often set in it. It can break right across in bad weather.

Gorteen Bay

53°22'·4N 9°56'·5W

This is a delightful anchorage in crystal clear water with a magnificent sandy beach, and is sheltered from most summer winds. Anchor in 3m off the beach. Somewhat subject to swell.

Ballyconneely Bay

53°22'·6N 10°04'W
AC2708

This large bay offers a pleasant temporary anchorage in settled weather, but it is completely exposed to the S. From the E, leave Murvey Rock 3 cables to port and steer 313° for Knife Rock (2·3m high) 1·5M to the NW. Leaving Knife Rock close to starboard, steer 318° for the white sand beach until the top of Illaunnameenoga is abeam. Anchor in 4 to 5m, sand.

From the W, identify Duke's Rock (1·1m high), W of Hen Island, and leave Duke's Rock 2 cables to starboard (waypoint 53°23'·30N 10°05'·20W) steering 081° for 6 cables to waypoint 53°23'·43N 10°04'·60W, then 042° for 4 cables to waypoint 53°24'·10N 10°04'·25W. The rocks W of Whermine Island dry less than 1·5m, Carrickandrew dries 2·2m, Carricknabud dries 1·8m, Minnanballyconneely dries 2·8m, and the rocks ESE of Carricknabud dry 1·6m.

Bunowen Bay

53°24'N 10°06'·6W
AC2708

This bay offers good shelter in winds from W through N to NE but becomes untenable in a S gale. Giving Hen Island a berth of 4 cables, identify Mullauncarrickscoltia (1·1m high) and when Bunowen House bears due N over a small beach, steer into the bay on this course. This leads clear of Cromwell Shoal, Carrickcummer and Fortune Rock (dries 0·6m) to the W and the above-water rocks to the E. Anchor N of the pier in the SW corner in 3 to 4m, sand. It is possible to lie alongside the N side of the outer pier, which dries, or

(top) Duke's Rock (L) and Hen Island (centre) from the W; Croaghnakeela, R. Tidal height about 1·5m

(centre) Bunowen House ruins over the beach leads into Bunowen Bay. Doon Hill, L

(bottom) Bunowen pier

Ballinaleama Bay and Slyne Head

Anchored at the W end of Ballinaleama Bay; Carrickdown Rock, R centre. Tidal height 1·5m

alongside the outer, NE end, where a yacht might remain afloat in 1·8m at LWN. Weed off this pier may foul intakes or propellers. Water on the pier. No facilities nearer than the shop and pub at Ballyconneely, 5 km.

Ballinaleama Bay

53°23'·8N 10°09'·5W
AC2708

This bay has long sandy beaches and is generally exposed to S and SW, but there is a handy temporary anchorage NW of Carrickdown Rock in the W corner of the bay, providing a convenient place to wait for the tide or assess the conditions in Joyce's Pass. This anchorage is not accessible in a heavy swell from the S or SW. From the E, identify Mweel Rock (dries 4m) and Horse Rock (0·8m high), and steering 320° leave Horse Rock 2 cables to port. Waypoint ⊕CD, 53°24'·33N 10°10'·08W is 2 cables E of Carrickdown. From there, steer 016° for 2·5 cables to waypoint 53°24'·60N 10°09'·94W. Carrickdown Rock dries more than 3m, but the rock 2 cables W of Carrickfia dries less than 1·5m. Anchor in 3m, off the beach in the bay N of Carrickdown. It is a short walk over the sandhills for a view of conditions to the NW, although Joyce's Pass itself cannot be seen. From the W, steer 060° for the waypoint E of Carrickdown. Carrickmweelrough dries 2·5m. From this track, conditions in Joyce's Pass may be observed through the gap between Doonglush and Carrickcluma Beg.

In the E corner of Ballinaleama Bay, NE of Horse Island, there is a drying quay at Aillebrack. The approach is intricate, and no adequate directions can be given to a stranger.

SLYNE HEAD

AC2708

With its strong tides, and long projection from the shore, this is a formidable headland and should be given a wide berth in bad weather.

Directions

From the SE, from a position close S of Mullauncarrickscoltia, steer 282° to give the Head a berth of 1M. **From the N,** from a position 1M SW of the lighthouse and if bound E or SE, identify Croaghnakeela Island, 11M ESE and set course accordingly. A course of 102° passes S of Mullauncarrickscoltia,

---

Tides - Slyne Head

The N-going stream commences at –0320 Galway and the S-going at +0305 Galway. The rate is 3 to 4 kn at springs off the head and in the channels between the islets inside the head. The streams become weak 2 to 3M offshore. The streams are considerably affected by the strength and direction of the wind. There is a race off the head which can become dangerous in heavy weather or a high swell.
Constant (Roundstone) +0005 Galway, MHWS 4·4m, MHWN 3·4m, MLWN 1·7m, MLWS 0·5m.

Slyne Head from the S

248

Slyne Head; Joyce's Pass

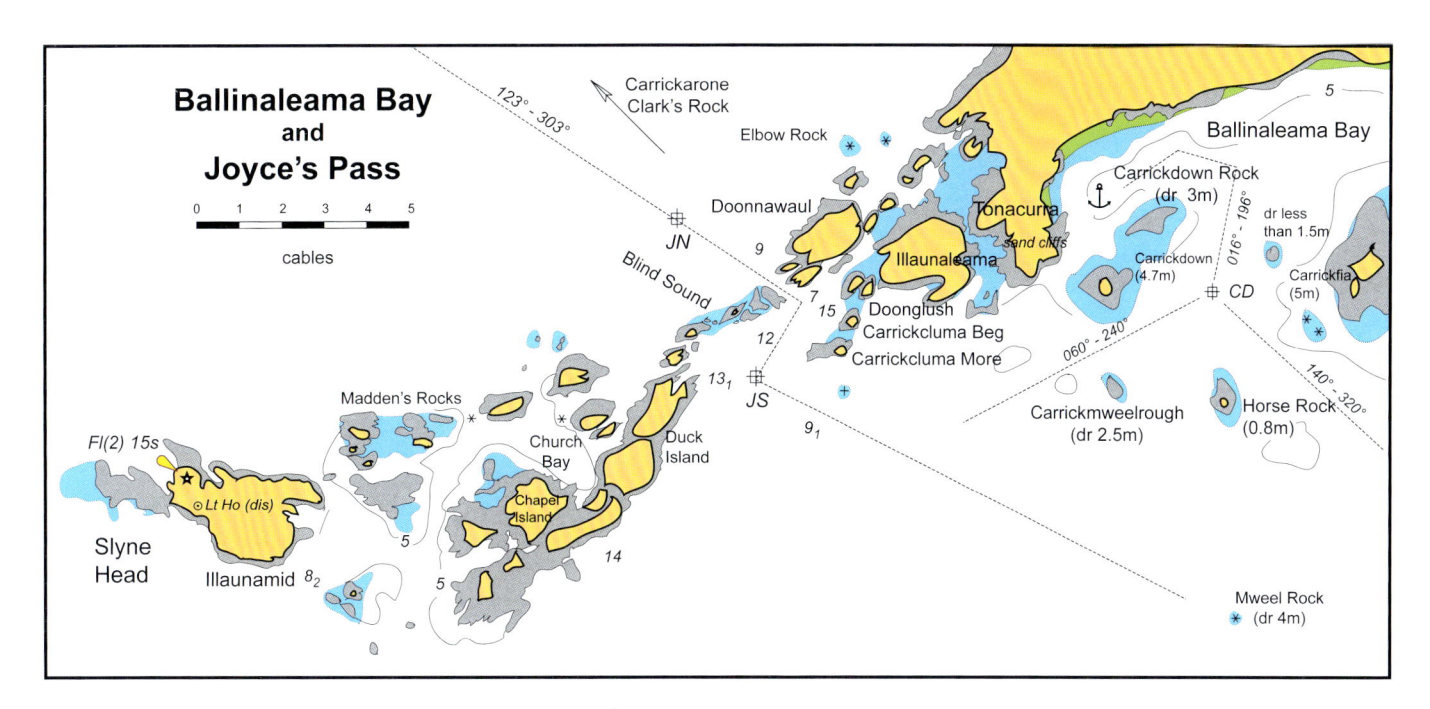

Murvey Rocks and Caulty Rock and so into the approaches to Roundstone. Alternatively, steer 130° to pass S of Skerdmore (18m high). This course also leads N of Eeragh light, W of the Aran Islands.

Joyce's Pass

53°24'·2N 10°11'·7W
AC2708 essential

Joyce's Pass, or Joyce's Sound, SW of Doonnawaul, is the only navigable channel inside Slyne Head. It has a least depth of 5m and is short, but very narrow, and in bad weather and wind against tide it frequently breaks right across. Even on a calm day the sea is confused. The tide runs at 3 to 4 knots, turning N at –0320 Galway and S at +0305 Galway. In assessing the feasibility of the passage, the swell is a more important factor than the wind, and a big swell will make the channel impassable even in light winds. (Swell forecasts are available on websites such as www.passageweather.com). The Pass is also dangerous with a strong wind against the tide; a powerful sea angling boat, making the passage in force 7 NW against the N-going tide, has reported being swept by a wall of breaking water. Lobster pots, many with long floating lines, are often set in the Pass, and for this reason it is best to avoid the period of slack tide, when the trend of these lines will be unpredictable. The SE-NW passage, against the prevailing swell, is easiest since the conditions can be more clearly assessed and the landmarks are clearer. A prior landing at Tonacurra from Ballinaleama Bay allows conditions to the W to be observed, while a preview of the Pass can be had through the gap between Doonglush and Carrickcluma Beg *(see photograph below)*.

Chartplotters are not to be trusted in the Pass since (at the time of writing) the precision of navigation required is beyond the accuracy of the charts, some electronic charts represent the channel badly, and chartplotter tracks frequently (and wrongly) suggest that the vessel has passed over the rocks. Implicit faith in the chartplotter may lead a vessel on to the ledge on the SW side.

(below) Preview of Joyce's Pass from the E; view of the Pass, to the R of the islet at L centre, looking between Doonglush (R) and Carrickcluma Beg (L). The channel in the foreground between these two is not navigable. Conditions in the Pass appear favourable. Tidal height 1·8m (4 hours before HW), tide running SE, wind NW force 4, swell height 1·5m from the W.

Joyce's Pass

Joyce's Pass from the S; Doonnawaul is the large islet, centre R, with the Pass between it and the two small rocks at centre. The wider channel at lower L centre is Blind Sound, which is not navigable. The N tip of Duck Island shows at bottom L; Carrickcluma More at bottom R, with Barrnacarrick beyond Doonnawaul, and the Carrickarone group top L. Note the overfalls in and NW of Blind Sound on what appears to be a N-going tide.

East to west transit of Joyce's Pass: (1) the yacht heading NNE with Carrickcluma More abeam to starboard and Illaunaleama on the starboard bow; the RIB is cutting the corner to port. This and the following photographs show the Pass at LW with tidal height 1·0m, tide running SE, wind SW force 3, swell height 1·5m from the W.

East to west transit of Joyce's Pass: (2) the Pass opening up

Directions from the SE

First identify Mweel Rock, which almost always shows. Mweel Breaker to the SW of Mweel Rock may not be showing if the sea is smooth. Illaunaleama (18m high) and Doonnawaul (15m high) can then be recognised and from them the line of rocks terminating in Carrickcluma More (4·7m high) with a below-water rock 1 cable S of it.

Pass close SW of Mweel Rock (waypoint 53°23'·65N 10°10'·1W), then steer 292° to pass 1·5 cables S of Carrickcluma More. Giving Carrickcluma More a berth of 1 cable on its W side, turn NE and steer towards Doonnawaul, leaving Carrickcluma Beg also to starboard. The waypoint for this turn is ⊕JS 53°24'·15N 10°11'·85W. At this point, observe the sea state through Blind Sound, SW of Joyce's Pass, and make the decision to proceed or not. Note that there is a pronounced tidal set through Blind Sound. As Carrickcluma Beg comes abeam the Pass will open up. Turn hard to

Joyce's Pass; North Sound to Slyne Head, offshore

port and keep in mid-channel steering 303° with plenty of way on. In particular do not err to the SW since a ledge extends from the reef on that side. Once through, Carrickarone West (5m high) will be seen 1M away bearing 338° with Clark's Rock (dries 1m) 2 cables NW of it and bearing 324°. Clark's Rock may not show near HW with a smooth sea. Both of these rocks should be left to starboard.

Directions from the NW

Identification from the NW is not so easy, and this may be a lee shore with a long string of similar-looking islets fronted by breakers and half-tide rocks. Wind, tide and sea state are even more critical when heading SE. If in doubt, stay outside Slyne Head.

Doonnawaul and Illaunaleama are considerably higher than the rocks immediately to the SW near Blind Sound. However, Duck Island and Chapel Island may be confused. Approach on a course which will allow identification of Keerhaunmore Hill, 36m high, and possibly the sand cliffs at Tonacurra, which will then allow Carrickarone to be picked up as the land comes closer. With a firm fix on Carrickarone there should be little difficulty in identifying Joyce's Pass. From a position 5 cables SW of Carrickarone (waypoint 53°24'·8N 10°12'·7W), and in good visibility, Croaghnakeela Island (9M distant) will be seen over Carrickcluma Beg bearing 123°; this line leads to the Pass. Waypoint ⊕*JN* 53°24'·5N 10°12'·10W is close NW of the entrance to the Pass. Carrickcluma More has a flat top which may provide a useful landmark. Once through, turn hard to starboard, leave Carrickcluma More a cable to port and head S into clear water.

Offshore passage - North Sound to Slyne Head

On the direct passage from Cashla Bay, Kilronan or Galway, give the Connemara coast E of Golam Tower a berth of 1M to clear all dangers. Identify Seal Rock (2·4m high), 1M W of Golam, and leave it well to starboard. A course from here to Skerdmore

East to west transit of Joyce's Pass: (3) the narrows

East to west transit of Joyce's Pass: (4) the view back SE; Carrickcluma Beg, centre. Note the flat top of Carrickcluma More, R

Joyce's Pass (centre) from the NW; the flat top of Carrickcluma More is often a good landmark. The wider Blind Sound, R, is not navigable.

(18m high) with Skerdmore and Doonguddle (12m high) in line 286° clears all the dangers except for Wild Shoals (16·2m), which are not hazardous except in gale conditions. There are no dangers on the direct course from Skerdmore to Slyne Head.

Offshore Weather Buoy M1, yellow, Fl(5) Y 20s, is moored 40M W by S of Slyne Head in position 53°07'·6N 11°12'W.

7 Slyne Head to Erris Head

Inishbofin from the SW; Inishturk and Clare Island, top R, Achill Head, top L

The west coasts of Galway and Mayo are deeply indented, with many bays offering excellent shelter, and magnificent scenery. Long stretches are fronted by islands and rocks which give protection from the Atlantic swell to the channels and bays behind them. The populated islands include Inishbofin, Inishturk and Clare. Inishbofin has an excellent natural harbour and is the single most popular port of call for yachts cruising this coast. Clare Island was the stronghold of Gráinne Ni Mhaille – Granuaile – the feisty 16th-century chieftainess who was among the most renowned of all the Irish leaders of her day. Her tower houses on Clare and at Rockfleet still stand with walls intact. The few towns on the coast are all 18th and 19th-century foundations of the landowners, and particularly in the case of Westport, retain the regular layout and much of the classical architecture of planned settlements. Clifden hosts the annual Connemara Pony Show each August, and Clifden and Westport are popular and cosmopolitan tourist destinations. Both towns lie at the head of drying inlets but Clifden in particular has comprehensive and convenient shops and supermarkets accessible to a yacht of moderate draft which can dry out alongside - the best source of supplies in Connemara. The mainland coast is mountainous; Diamond Mountain and Tully Hill dominate the coast by Ballynakill Bay, while the square massif of Mweelrea rises north of Killary Harbour, and is the most imposing feature of the whole coast. The superb cone of Croagh Patrick overlooks the south side of Clew Bay. To the

"Cruising Ireland"

This coast is described on pages 108 to 127 of **Cruising Ireland**

Tides - offshore

The streams offshore are weak, running S from about +0400 Galway to –0330 Galway and N at other times. Near the coast and around salient points, particularly Achill Head and Erris Head, they may attain 1·5 knots.

Paper Charts

The general chart AC2420 Aran Islands to Broad Haven Bay spans the whole area of this chapter. For an offshore passage, this chart, together with 1820 Aran Islands to Roonah Head and 2704 Blacksod Bay and Approaches, is adequate, but for detailed exploration of the coast the largest scale charts are all essential.

Slyne Head to Inishbofin

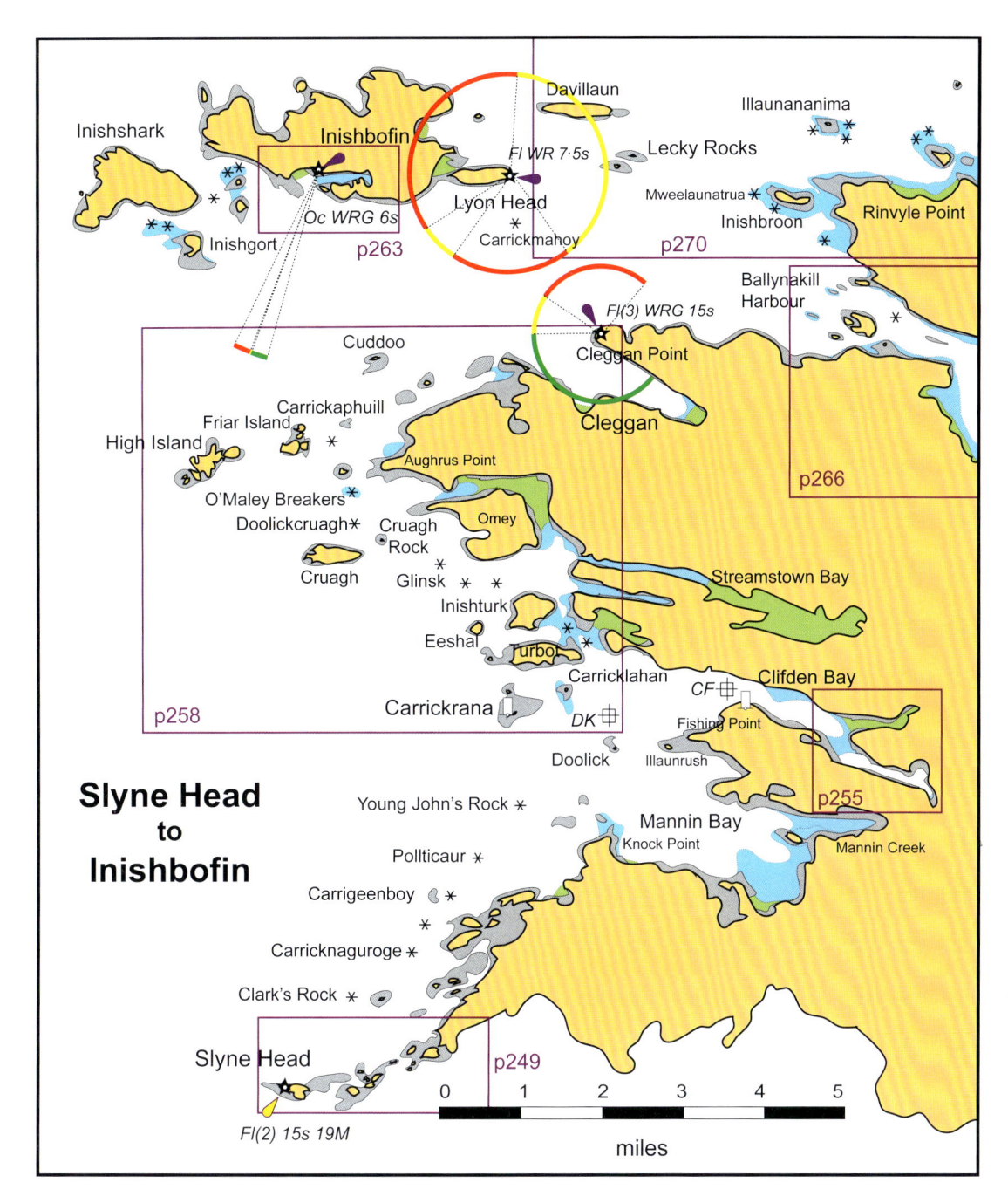

north, Achill Island rises to 664m and slopes west in a ridge to Achill Head. Its terrific cliffs, the highest in the British Isles, form the south side of the entrance to Blacksod Bay. To the west of the bay the low-lying Mullet Peninsula, the remotest part of mainland Ireland, extends with its offshore islands to Erris Head. The coast is exposed to the full rigours of the ocean weather, and Slyne Head, Achill Head and Eagle Island can raise steep and confused seas. In recent years there has been a great improvement in the provision of local navigational aids, particularly in Mayo, but there are still hundreds of unmarked dangers. This is a fabulous and challenging cruising ground.

Caution

*In many places on this coast the limited horizontal accuracy of the current charts, both paper and electronic, means that GPS chart plotters must not be implicitly relied upon in close-quarters pilotage. Errors of up to 90 metres have been measured. Note that this does **not** represent an offset in horizontal datum, which - where it exists - must also be taken into account.*

Mannin and Clifden Bays

Tides
Slyne Head to Clifden Bay
The N-going stream at Slyne Head commences at −0320 Galway and the S-going at +0305 Galway. The spring rate is 3 to 4 kn off the head but less 2 to 3M offshore. The streams are considerably affected by the strength and direction of the wind. There is a race off the head which can become dangerous in heavy weather or a high swell. Precise information on the timing and strength of the streams among the small islands to the NE is lacking, but for all practical purposes the tide may be assumed to turn at the same time as at Slyne Head. Constant (Clifden) +0005 Galway; MHWS 4·4m, MHWN 3·4m, MLWN 1·6m, MLWS 0·6m.
For details of tidal streams around Inishbofin, see below.

Dangers
(above-water rocks are not included)
Barret Shoals, 22m, 3M NNW of Slyne Head and **Shoal** with 12·2m, 1M NE of Barret Shoals.
Drying rocks up to 1·2M offshore, of which the outermost are **Clark's Rock** (dries 1m), 4 cables W of Carrickarone and 1·5M NNE of Slyne Head; **Carricknaguroge** (dries 4m); **Carrigeenboy**, and **Pollticaur** (dries 1·8m). Extending for 1M NW of Knock Point are **Mullaunacrick** (dries 2·7m), **Carrickawollawaun** (dries 3·7m), **Crowneen Rock** (dries 1·5m), and **Young John's Rock** (dries 0·4m).
Drying reefs extend 2 cables N of Doolick and between Carrickrana and Carricklahan.

(top) The peak of Cruagh Island in line with Waverymore

(above) Carrickrana beacon from the N, seen between Waverybeg (L) and Waverymore

SLYNE HEAD to INISHBOFIN
AC1820, 2708, 2707
For 6M NE from Slyne Head the coast is fronted by a maze of rocks and islets, and the only safe advice to the stranger is to stay far enough offshore. North of Clifden, islands and above-water rocks provide enough landmarks to facilitate intricate pilotage in favourable weather.

Lights and Marks
Slyne Head, black tr Fl(2) 15s 35m 19M, AIS

Disused lighthouse tower on Slyne Head
Carrickrana beacon, white tower, unlit
Fishing Point beacon, white tower, unlit

Coast NE of Slyne Head
AC2708
The coast between Slyne Head and Mannin Bay should be given a berth of at least 1·5M. Clark's Rock, Carrigeenboy, Pollticaur and Young John's Rock are the outermost of the dangers. Further offshore, Barret Shoals and the 12m patch NE of them raise overfalls and a confused sea in heavy weather.

The key to the pilotage of Mannin and Clifden Bays is the prominent 11m-high white beacon on Carrickrana (Seal Rocks), 53°29'·2N 10°09'·5W. From a position 2M W of Slyne Head a course of 043° leads to the beacon. The direct course from Slyne Head to Inishbofin passes 3M W of Carrickrana and through High Island Sound.

Mannin Bay
53°27'·5N 10°06'W
AC2708
Mannin Bay is exposed to the prevailing swell and offers only modest shelter, but is a lovely bay with superb sandy beaches. From a position 5 cables S of Carrickrana, head for Doolick until the peak of Cruagh Island (3M NW of Carrickrana beacon) comes in line with Waverymore 315°, and keep this transit in line astern. From Clifden, hold mid-channel between Doolick and Illaunrush, the islet off Errislannan Point to the E. The best anchorage for a short stay is inside Knock Point in 3 to 4m, a beautiful spot. More secure anchorage can be found in Mannin Creek; its bar just dries at LAT on a mid-channel course. Anchor in 4 to 6m in the middle of the creek, clean sand bottom. There are fish cages in the bay W of Hag Rock, to the NW.

Clifden Bay
⊕ CF (p253) 53°29'·5N 10°05'·2W
AC2708, Imray C54
The transit of Fishing Point beacon with the SE side of Clifden Castle leads between Carrickrana and Doolick. Alternatively, from a position 3 cables S of Carrickrana beacon, a waypoint of 53°29'·2N 10°07'·5W (⊕ DK,

254

Clifden and Ardbear Bays

Fishing Point beacon in line with the SE side of Clifden Castle leads between Carrickrana and Doolick

see plan on p253) provides a berth of 2 cables from the reefs N of Doolick. Fishing Point is clean and may be given a berth of 0·5 cable; the best depth on the bar, about 4m, is on the SW side. The channel to Clifden town dries at LW and there are drying and above-water rocks at the entrance, NW of Faul Point. Two of these, Double Rock (dries 2·1m) and Long Rock (dries about 4m) have unlit white beacons. The drying channel to the town quay is navigable near HW (see below).

Ardbear Bay

There is a bar with least depth 0·9m at the entrance to Ardbear Bay. From a position midway between Double Rock beacon and Drinagh Point, steer 142° for 2 cables to clear Carricknabeartragh (dries 1·4m). When Larner's Rock (1·5m high) bears due N, turn to starboard and steer 160°, with Double Rock beacon directly astern, to cross the bar. There are fish cages S of the bar. Where the bay narrows 5 cables SE of Faul Point, keep the mussel rafts on the SW side close aboard to avoid Yellow Slate Rock (dries 1·2m).

Anchorages

- NW of Double Rock beacon in 3 to 5m, good holding in mud and sand. Clifden Sailing Club has its clubhouse here and maintains a landing pontoon, and the RNLI lifeboat station is here. There are visitors' moorings.
- Between Larner's Rock and Drinagh Point in 5m. This anchorage is reported to have poor holding ground with the ebb overfall from Ardbear Bay, particularly in NW winds.
- In the upper part of Ardbear Bay, W or

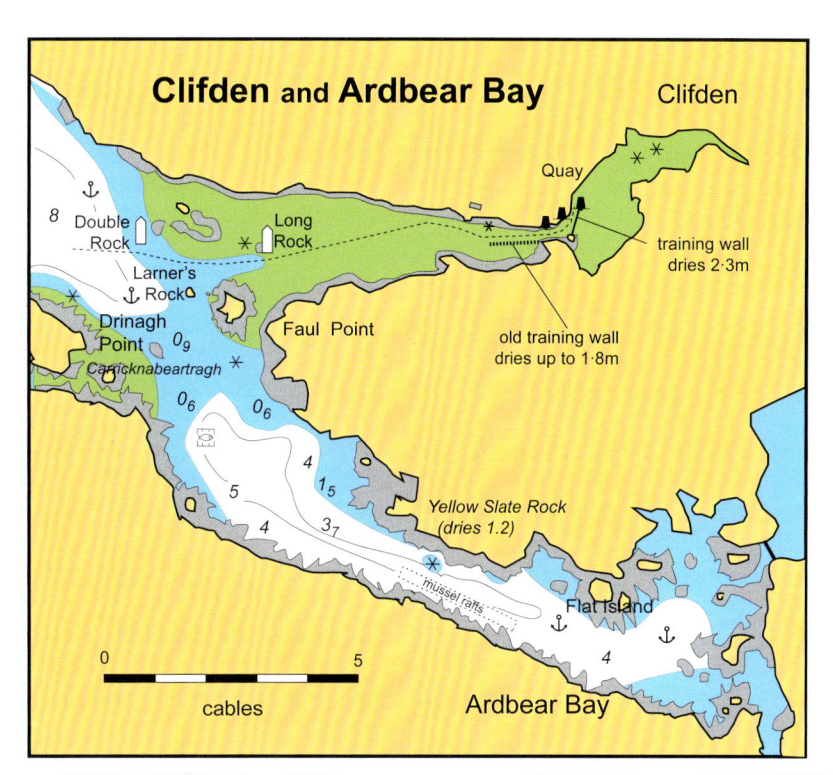

(above) Clifden Bay; Clifden SC, lifeboat station and moorings. Double Rock and Long Rock beacons, extreme R

(below) Double Rock and Long Rock beacons, from the SW

The anchorage at the SE end of Ardbear Bay

255

Clifden

Ardbear Bay (lower R) and Clifden Bay from the SE. Note the mussel rafts

(below) Long Rock beacon; when the rock to the L of the beacon is covered there is at least 1·8m in the channel to Clifden Quay

Channel to Clifden; after passing Long Rock beacon, steer for the white house above the old stone quay on the N bank

Channel to Clifden, upstream of the old stone quay, at LW. The remains of the training wall are visible. These should be left to starboard on entry

SE of Flat Island and about 1·5 cables off the island, in 3m, good holding in mud. A beautiful and tranquil spot, one of the safest anchorages in Ireland.

Clifden Quay

The drying channel to Clifden (pop. 2,610) is accessible for only two hours either side of HW, but the town has the best and most accessible facilities on the coast, and a drying berth on the quay wall is usually available. The channel dries 1·6m; when Long Rock, close N of the beacon, is covered, there is at least 1·8m in the channel. Leave Double Rock beacon close to port and borrow a little to starboard heading for Long Rock to avoid the gravel spit between the two. E of Long Rock, hold mid-channel, heading for a conspicuous white house on the N shore above an old stone quay. The remains of a training wall in mid-channel extend from here to the point W of Black Rock, and from Black Rock N'wards, and there are drying boulders close to the N shore. Once past the old quay, keep 30m off the N shore, then leave Black Rock close to starboard. There are then two stone beacons on the port hand, and one to starboard marking the N end of the training wall, which dries 2·3m here. The bottom alongside the quay wall is suitable for drying out. There is a jetty in the river below the supermarket, accessible by dinghy near HW.

Constant +0005 Galway; MHWS 4·4m, MHWN 3·4m, MLWN 1·6m, MLWS 0·6m.

Coast Northward from Clifden

Clifden from the W; Drinagh Point R foreground, Larner's Rock, Islandagar and Faul Point, R. Clifden SC clubhouse and moorings, L centre

(below) The channel immediately downstream of Clifden quay, at HW; the third beacon (centre) marks the submerged training wall and is to be left to starboard going up-river

Facilities

Diesel (100 litres minimum by tanker, phone 095 21777), water on the quay, supermarkets, shops, pubs, restaurants, filling stations, wifi, PO, laundry, doctors, hospital. RNLI all-weather lifeboat station.

Coast Northward from Clifden

AC1820, 2707

High Island Sound is the normal fair-weather route for a yacht heading N from Slyne Head or Clifden. A course of 011° from a position 2M W of Slyne Head leads to the sound, and also W of Barret Shoals. High Island breaker, with 8·2m, is very close to this line; in a high swell it can be avoided by keeping the E hill of Inishshark in line with the E side of High Island 347°. This also just clears Gur a Mweem breaker, 7·9m, SW of Cruagh Island. From Clifden, the safest course is to leave Carrickrana beacon to starboard and then steer to leave Cruagh Island and Gur a Mweem to starboard and so to High Island Sound. Waypoints ⊕*GM* 53°31'·0N 10°14'·1W, 5 cables SW of Cruagh, and ⊕ *HI* 53°32'·4N 10°14'·3W, 5 cables SW of Friar Island, may be useful *(see plan on p258)*. The N side of Turbot Island open S of Eeshal Island 100° leads S of Mweem Cruagh breaker (3·4m). AC2707 gives clearing marks to pass NE or W of it.

In moderate weather the channel N of Carrickrana is straightforward, leaving Carricklahan (0·8m high) and Waverybeg (1·6m high) one cable to port. In heavy weather or a high swell, Middle Shoals, 2·4m, in mid-channel here, are dangerous, and a yacht should stay S of Carrickrana.

If passing N of Cruagh Island note that Cruagh Rock (1·4 m high) and Carrickaun (2·2m high) will always show, and the drying rocks Sharaghmore, Glinsk and Doolickcruagh must be avoided. Glinsk Rock and Doolickcruagh are usually marked by breakers. Pass 1 cable off Cruagh Island and bring Carrickrana beacon in line with the E end of Cruagh Island astern 141° to pass W

Clifden quay, with drying berths. The channel runs close to the quay and the rest of the basin dries more than 2m. The stone beacons are visible at centre L

257

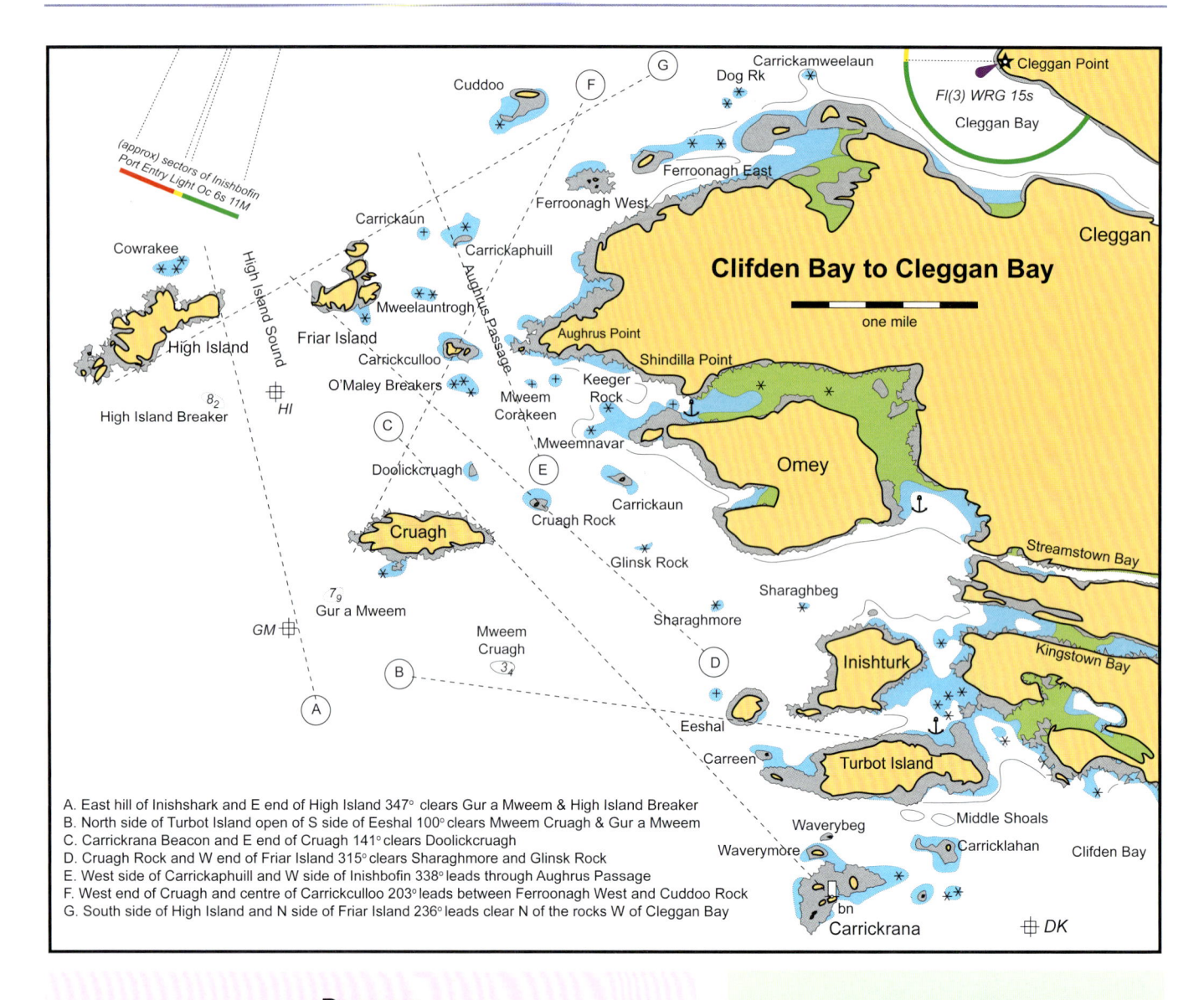

Coast Northward from Clifden

Map: Clifden Bay to Cleggan Bay

A. East hill of Inishshark and E end of High Island 347° clears Gur a Mweem & High Island Breaker
B. North side of Turbot Island open of S side of Eeshal 100° clears Mweem Cruagh & Gur a Mweem
C. Carrickrana Beacon and E end of Cruagh 141° clears Doolickcruagh
D. Cruagh Rock and W end of Friar Island 315° clears Sharaghmore and Glinsk Rock
E. West side of Carrickaphuill and W side of Inishbofin 338° leads through Aughrus Passage
F. West end of Cruagh and centre of Carrickculloo 203° leads between Ferroonagh West and Cuddoo Rock
G. South side of High Island and N side of Friar Island 236° leads clear N of the rocks W of Cleggan Bay

Dangers
Turbot Island to Inishbofin
(above-water rocks are not included)

Mweem Cruagh, 2·2m. 1·2M W of Eeshal Island
Sharaghmore (dries 0·5m) and **Sharaghbeg** (dries) 4 cables SW and S of Omey, respectively
Glinsk Rock (dries 2·4m), 5 cables W of Omey
Doolickcruagh (dries 2m), 3 cables N of Cruagh
O'Maley Breakers (drying), 1 to 2 cables S of Carrickculloo
Mweelauntrogh (dries 1·8m), 4 cables E of Friar Island
Carrickaphuill (dries 4·4m), 6 cables NE of Friar Island
Carrickaun, less than 2m, 4 cables NE of Friar Island
Cowrakee (dries 2·7m), N of High Island
Carrickmahoy (dries 1·9m), 8 cables S of Lyon Head

Anchorage between Turbot and Inishturk; Middle Ship Rock, L centre. View from the SW

Lights and Marks

Bofin Harbour Port Entry Light Dir Oc WRG 6s 22m 11M. Shows a narrow white sector centred on 021° with 5° sectors either side, red to W, green to E

Lyon Head, white col Fl WR 7·5s 13m W7M R4M, W 036°–058°, R 058°–184°, W 184°–325°, R 325°–036°. Shows white over the approach from the SW, red over Cleggan Bay and the dangers to the W of it, white over Ballynakill Harbour, Lecky Rocks and Davillaun, and red inshore to the N and NW.

Cleggan Point, white col on white hut Fl(3) WRG 15s 20m W6M R3M G3M, G shore–091°, W 091°–124°, R 124°–221°. Shows green over the dangers to the W of Cleggan Bay, white to the WNW and a wide red sector to the N.

For the lights in Bofin Harbour see the relevant Directions, below

258

Coast Northward from Clifden; Turbot and Omey Islands

Approaches to Clifden, from the W; Carrickrana foreground, with its white beacon, Waverymore and Waverybeg L foreground, and the rocks Mweelaunawaddra, Carricklahan and Mweelaunmore behind Carrickrana. Doolick with a breaking outlier, upper R. Turbot Island, L, Clifden Bay upper R centre and the Twelve Pins of Connemara on the skyline

of Doolickcruagh, and also W of **O'Maley Breakers,** SW of Aughrus Point. High Island Sound itself is clear but the sea can run high in it with formidable breakers on both shores.

Coast from Turbot Island to Aughrus Point

In settled weather this stretch of coast, with its beautiful sandy beaches, is delightful and provides some good temporary anchorages. It should however be avoided in strong onshore winds or a heavy swell.

Turbot Island (Inishturbot)

53°30'·2N 10°10'·5W
AC2708, 2707
The channel between Turbot Island and Inishturk, entered between Eeshal Island and Carreen, is clean for almost 1M to the E. **Middle Ship Rock**, which usually shows, marks the W side of the reefs at the head of the channel. The rocks SE of the quay on Inishturk extend further than charted, and a submarine power cable crosses the channel 1·5 cables W of Middle Ship Rock. There is anchorage off Turbot Island in 3m with Middle Ship Rock bearing NNE.

Kingstown Bay and Streamstown Bay
53°31'·3N 10°09'·7W
These inlets are not recommended. The channels are narrow, shallow and with fast tidal streams.

Heading W and N from here, stay 1 cable off the S shore of Omey and steer 252° to pass between Sharaghmore and Glinsk Rock. The W point of Friar Island in line with Cruagh Rock 315° clears both rocks to the W.

Omey Island

53°31'·3N 10°09'·7W
AC2707
Omey is joined to the mainland by a beautiful strand which dries up to 2m. There is fine-weather anchorage E of the SE tip of the island in 2 to 3m, sand. The anchorage N of Omey is also a delightful spot in settled weather. In the approach to the N anchorage, O'Maley Breakers and Mweem Corakeen to the N and Keeger Rock and Mweemnavar to the S must be avoided. There is 2m due S of Shindilla Point, and one cable E of the pier dries 0·2m.

259

Aughrus Passage

Coast N of Clifden, from the W; Inishturk centre L, Eeshal, foreground, and Turbot Island, R, with Carreen and Doughty in front. Clifden Bay, top R

Caution

Do not confuse O'Maley Breakers (SW of Aughrus Point) with O'Mallybreaker (off Crump Island, 10M to the NE), or the above-water rock Carrickaun (W of Omey) with the dangerous submerged rock Carrickaun (NE of Friar Island).

(above) The anchorage E of Omey

(below) Omey from the W, with (L to R foreground) the rocks Mweemnavar, Carrickaun and Glinsk. Shindilla Point and Aughrusmore pier, L

Aughrus Passage

53°32'·2N 10°12'·1W *(4 cables S)*
AC2707 essential

Aughrus Passage lies between Aughrus Point and Carrickculloo. With an uneven bottom and an exposed position, the passage can be recommended only in fine weather, moderate winds and little swell. A strong SW wind against a spring ebb could be hazardous. The tide is not restricting but it sets across the rocks at moderate speed and care is required.

The channel is defined on its E side by Mweem Corakeen, with about 1m at LAT, and a 3·7m patch 2·5 cables W of Aughrus Point, and on its W side by Carrickculloo and O'Maley Breakers. O'Maley Breakers almost always show. Drying rocks extend 2 cables W of Aughrus Point, and the channel between the 3·7m patch and Carrickculloo is only 1·25 cables wide. It should not be attempted in moderate or poor visibility since the

260

Aughrus Passage and Friar Island Sound

leading transit (the W side of Inishbofin in line with the W side of Carrickaphuill, 338°) is difficult to discern. Carrickaphuill covers only at high springs and is then marked by a breaker. Once through, bring the W end of Cruagh Island in line with the centre of Carrickculloo astern, 203°, and this line will lead between Ferroonagh West and Cuddoo Rock. A waypoint of 53°33'·9N 10°11'·8W, in mid-channel between Feroonagh West and Cuddoo, may be useful. Tully Mountain open of Cleggan Point 085° leads N of Cuddoo.

Friar Island Sound

53°32'·5N 10°13'·4W *(5 cables S)*
AC2707 essential

Friar Island Sound lies between Carrickculloo and Mweelauntrogh, to the E, and Friar Island to the W. It is also a fine-weather passage, straightforward if course is set to

(above) Aughrus Passage from the S; Aughrus Point, centre, with Carrickculloo L centre. Cruagh Island and Doolickcruagh (breaking), L, Cruagh Rock lower centre, and Carrickaun and Mweemnavar, R. Friar Island, upper L; Carrickaphuill and Cuddoo Rock beyond the Passage. Inishbofin in the distance

(above) The anchorage N of Omey; the pier at Aughrusmore, extreme L

(below) Mweemnavar (foreground) and Carrickaun (R), from the N

(left) Tully Mountain open N of Cleggan Point leads N of Cuddoo Rock

(below) The W end of Inishbofin in line with the W end of Carrickaphuill leads through Aughrus Passage (centre) (transit E, plan on p258)

High Island; Cleggan

Friar Island from the ENE with High Island beyond. Carrickaphuill lower R with Carrickaun (breaking) beyond it. Mweelauntrogh showing, L. The cove on Friar Island, centre L. Cowrakee (breaking) to the R of High Island.

(above) The summit of Carrickculloo in line with the W end of Cruagh leads between Feroonagh West and Cuddoo Rock (transit F, plan on p258)

(right) the E landing on High Island (photo Dick Lincoln)

Transit G, plan on p258; the S side of High Island and the N side of Friar Island in line (L) leads N of the rocks W of Cleggan. Cuddoo, R

Caution
The visibility of many of the transits described and photographed in this section depends critically upon weather and visibility. Islands and rocks may appear to merge into one another, and many of the rocks look similar. While a clear transit is the best position line, full use should be made of GPS and other navigational aids. Chart accuracy here in relation to GPS is reasonably good.

keep close to the island shore. Watch out for the tide which sets across Mweelauntrogh and runs at 2 to 3 knots through the sound. In settled weather, a delightful temporary anchorage is available in 3m in a tiny cove on the E side of Friar Island.

High Island
53°32'·71N 10°15'·07W *(1 cable SE of E landing)*
AC2707 essential

High Island is one of Ireland's most inaccessible islands. There is no anchorage, but two points on the SE side offer the possibility of a dinghy landing in very settled weather. One is approximately as above, the other is a cable NW of 53°32'·51N 10°15'·38W.

Approaches to Cleggan
The S side of High Island in line with the N side of Friar Island 236°, or a waypoint of 53°34'·6N 10°09'·7W, leads clear N of the rocks to the W of Cleggan Bay, the N'most of which are **Dog Rock** (dries 1·2m) and **Carrickamweelaun** (dries). At night, the white sector of Cleggan Point light shows over safe water, and the green sector shows over the rocks and also up the bay.

Cleggan Point is clean, and the approach from the NE is straightforward.

Cleggan
53°34'·4N 10°08'·6W
AC2707, Imray C54

Cleggan Bay is open to the NW but offers reasonable shelter in summer and is easy of access. Anchor off the pier, leaving room for the ferries to manoeuvre. An alongside berth may be available; the outermost one is reserved for the ferries, while the second berth also has deep water and is used by fishing boats. The quay opposite is used by the cargo ferry. The pier is somewhat subject to swell in heavy weather, and the shallow inner harbour can be closed off. Water on the pier, diesel by tanker (Sweeney Oil, 095 21777). Shops, pubs, PO. Small chandlery, Cleggan Marine Supplies, 095 44037. Ferries to Inishbofin and Inishturk.

262

INISHBOFIN

⊕ *IB 53°36'·3N 10°13'·5W*
AC1820, 2707, Imray C54 and Plan. Additional photo on p252

Inishbofin is a very popular and handy port of call for yachts cruising the area or on passage N or S. It is a thriving island with a resident population of 160, lively pubs and good restaurants and a well-deserved reputation as a centre of traditional music. The island lies at the centre of a group of rocks, islets and breakers extending 8M from W to E. The shores and sounds are all foul, and any approach to the group from seaward in poor visibility or a high swell should be made with caution. Bofin Harbour, on the S side of Inishbofin, is one of the best natural harbours on the west coast, although entry and exit can be tricky in heavy weather from the SW or a high swell.

Bofin Harbour (see Plan)

From High Island Sound, a course of 011° leads to the entrance. **From the N**, beware of the drying reef Carrickmahoy (see below), and give the S side of Gun Island a berth of two cables. Two white towers on the N side of the harbour in line 032° lead in close E of a 1·2m patch and then very close to Gun Island with its 12m-high beacon. It is possible to borrow to the E of this line outside Gun Island, and to the W of it when abreast the island. The white sector of the modern Port Entry Light 021°, usually visible by day, is a safer lead. Take care not to be confused by the fact that the two leading lines are different. Continue on either line until the conspicuous ruins of Cromwell's Barracks are abeam, then turn to starboard. Anchor SW of the outer pier in 2 to 4m, clear of the moorings and allowing room for the ferries to manoeuvre. Holding is often rather poor, on hard sand.

The dredged channel 30m wide leads to the refurbished inner quay, N of Glasillan, and there are leading marks on the shore to the E. Avoid obstructing this channel, which may be used by the ferries. There is limited room to anchor in the inner pool, NE of Glasillan, which has 0·2m at LAT, and the S and E faces of the inner quay are available as berths for a yacht if the ferries do not require the berth (they seldom do). The cargo ferry uses the slip on the W side of the inner quay. A fenderboard is recommended if going alongside the main pier. The ferries berth on its E side.

Cleggan pier; the only available deep-water berth is alongside the red fishing boat. The berth at the steps is reserved for the ferries

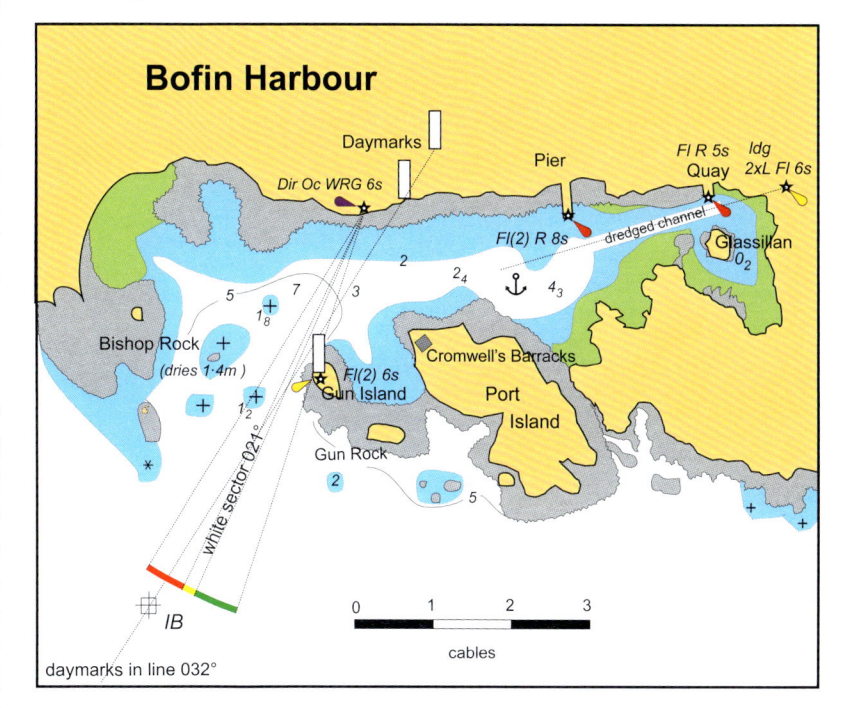

Tides – Inishbofin

In the channel between Inishbofin and the mainland and in Ship Sound the tidal streams run in the direction of the channels. The spring rate in Ship Sound is 2·5 kn and in the main sound 1·5 kn, stronger around Lyon Head at the E end of Inishbofin. The ebb, running SW, sets more strongly across the drying rock Carrickmahoy (in mid-channel S of Lyon Head) than the NE-going flood. The tide turns NE at −0350 Galway and SW at −0120 Galway, running NE for only two and a half hours, or sometimes less. It is frequently rough in this channel due to the long duration of the SW-going ebb against the prevailing wind and swell.
Constant (Inishbofin) +0010 Galway; MHWS 4·1m, MHWN 3·1m, MLWN 1·5m, MLWS 0·5m.

Lights and Marks

Gun Island, white tower, with adjacent bn Fl(2) 6s 8m 4M
Bofin Harbour, leading marks 032°, white towers, unlit
Bofin Harbour Port Entry Light, Dir Oc WRG 6s 22m 11M. Close W of the front leading mark, shows a narrow white sector centred on 021° with 5° sectors either side, red to W, green to E
Inishbofin Main Pier, Fl(2) R 8s
Inishbofin Inner Pier leading beacons, triangles on poles, L Fl 6s
Inishbofin Inner Pier, Fl R 5s

Inishbofin

Bofin Harbour from the SW; Gun Island and its beacon, bottom L, and the leading beacons on the island shore beyond. The dredged channel to the inner quay is clearly visible, upper R. The concrete armouring of the shore below the leading beacons is conspicuous. The ruins of Cromwell's Barracks on the point, L centre

(clockwise from upper L) Bofin Harbour approach; the leading beacons, centre L, Gun Island tower and beacon, centre R. The small light-beacon was destroyed in a storm in 2014 and has been replaced

Bofin Harbour inner leading beacons, R

Bofin Harbour main pier, with the Cleggan ferry

Yachts at Bofin Harbour inner quay

Inishbofin and Inishshark

Facilities - Bofin Harbour
Water on both piers. Shop, pub, hotels/restaurants, cycle hire. Showers at the Community Centre. Ferry to Cleggan. Mechanical and electrical repairs, 095 45807.

Rusheen Bay
53°37'·3N 10°10'·3W

Rusheen Bay, on the E side of Inishbofin, offers sheltered anchorage in offshore winds but is subject to swell in NW'ly weather. There is a fine sandy beach in delightful surroundings. The quay is foul, and dries. Black Rocks, on the NE side of the bay, always show, and New Anchor Shoal (1·5m) on the S side can be avoided by keeping Lyon Head beacon bearing due S until off the centre of the bay. There is a restaurant above the bay.

Inishshark
This island, uninhabited since 1959, has a slip on its SE side (at 53°36'·26N 10°15'·90W) but no good anchorage. There are breakers and rocks to NW, SW and SE. **Kimmeen Rocks** from extend 3 to 6 cables W of the island; the tide runs through the channel at 2·5 kn. **Inishgort**, S of Inishshark, has foul ground all round, and the channel between the two islands is rock-strewn. **Mweemore**, 7·5m, and **Paddy Lenane's Shoal**, 7m, break in heavy weather. The **Stags of Bofin** extend 6 cables from the NW corner of Inishbofin; the **North Stag Rock** (20m high) in line with **Colleen Rock** (12m high) 055°, leads NW of all the dangers W of Inishshark.

Ship Sound, between Inishshark and the islets SW of Inishbofin, is navigable with care, but the 2·5 kn tide and uneven bottom with patches of 3m and 3·4m make the passage possible only in moderate winds and little sea. The isolated, drying **Tide Rock**, 2·5 cables E of Inishshark, normally shows, and defines the E side of the channel. In bad weather Ship Sound breaks right across.

Carrickmahoy, 8 cables S of Lyon Head and drying 1·9m, breaks heavily over an extensive area and is particularly hazardous since it lies in the middle of the main channel SE of Inishbofin. Inishshark well open of Inishbofin 290° leads S of Carrickmahoy, and the W end of Ox Island (W of Davillaun) in line with the cliffs of Dromore Head on Inishturk leads E of it. A waypoint of 53°35'·7N 10°09'·1W, 3 cables SE of Carrickmahoy, may be useful. In a heavy swell there are breakers between Carrickmahoy and Inishlyon.

Rusheen Bay

Ship Sound from the S; Tide Rock, centre

Inishshark (L) well open of Inishbofin 290° leads S of Carrickmahoy

Davillaun
Davillaun (24m high) lies 1·3M E of Inishbofin. There are rocks 2 cables W of it of which the outermost, **Mweeldyon,** dries 1·8m. **Couraghy**, which dries, lies 2 cables E of Davillaun with **Davillaun East Breaker**, 2·1m, a further 2·5 cables to the E. Landing from a dinghy can be made in fine weather in the Port Cove on the S side of the island. **Lecky Rocks,** 5·5 cables SE of Davillaun, consist of two groups with a narrow and shallow channel between them. The N rock is 7m high and the S rock 3·4m. They are foul E and W for about 1·5 cables.

There are deep channels between Black Rock and Davillaun and between Davillaun and Lecky Rocks.

Carrickmahoy breaking; bringing the W end of Ox Island (R) in line with Dromore Head on Inishturk (centre) clears it to the E

265

Ballynakill Harbour

Ballynakill Harbour from the S; Tully Mountain, top, Toneillaun foreground, Barnaderg Bay centre R with Roeillaun beyond, Ross Point upper L with Braadillaun and Inishbroon beyond and Freaghillaun South just visible, top L. Inishturk behind and L of Tully Mountain, and Clare Island on the horizon, top R. Note the fish farm E of Ross Point.

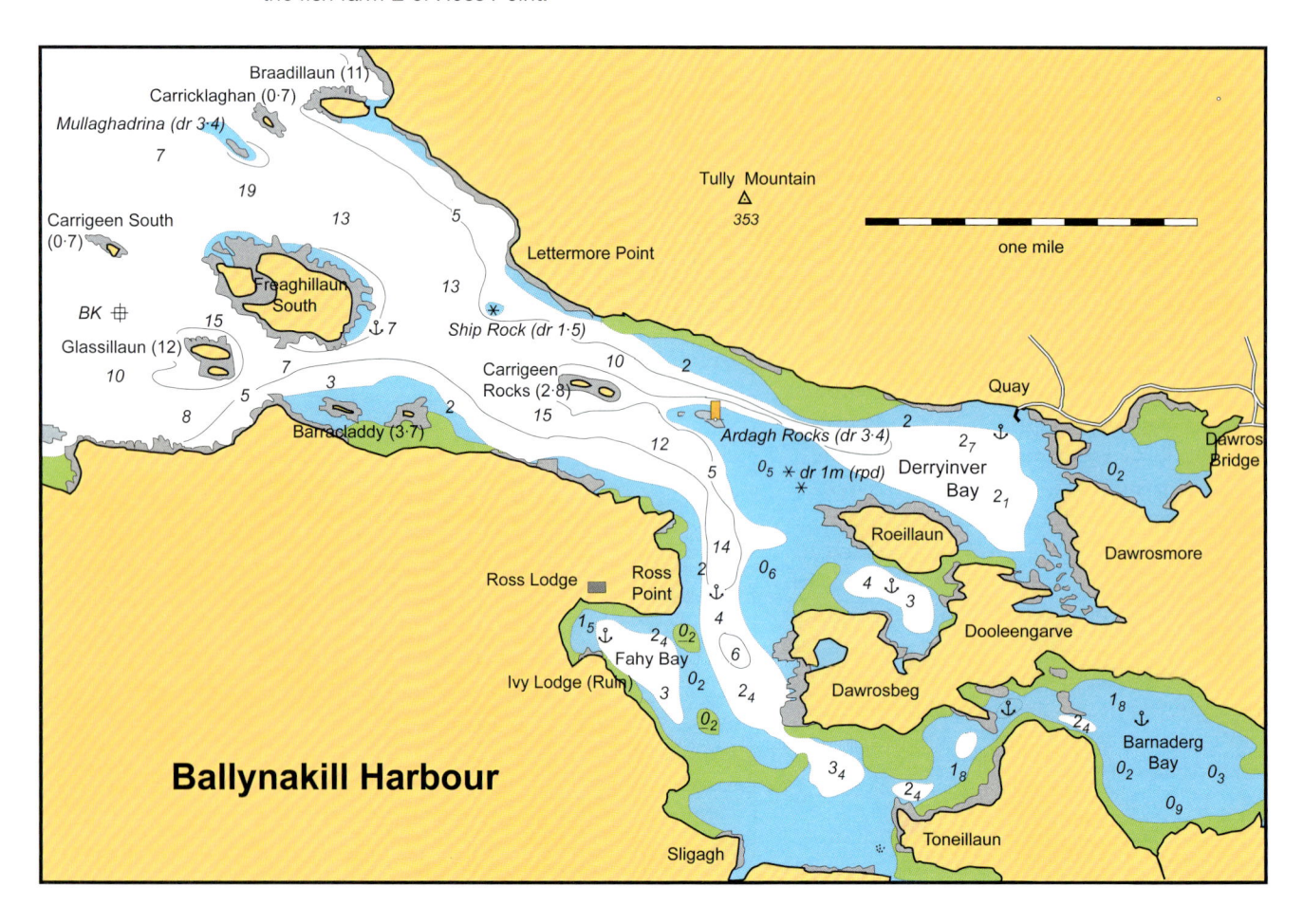

Ballynakill Harbour

Coast – Cleggan to Ballynakill Harbour

Both sides of Cleggan Point and the coast E to Ballynakill consist of cliffs between 15 and 45m high, backed by steep grass slopes with bare rock in places and with occasional guts known as 'ooeys', some with beaches at their heads. A berth of two cables clears all dangers.

BALLYNAKILL HARBOUR

⊕ *BK* 53°34'·6N 10°03'·6W (in approach from W)

AC2706 and Plan

This fine bay is easily entered by day and is a good refuge with excellent shelter, as well as providing scope for day sailing inside in pretty surroundings. The bottom is very irregular, and shoals rise abruptly from deep water.

Directions

There are several above-water rocks in the approach which make useful landmarks, including **Carrigeen South** (0·7m high), **Carricklaghan** (0·7m high), **Glassillaun** (12m high) and the small islet S of it (locally known as the Cow and Calf), a rock at Barracladdy (3·7m high), and (a little confusingly) the **Carrigeen Rocks** (2·2 and 2·8m high). All except Carrigeen South and Carricklaghan have grassy tops.

From the W and Cleggan Point, pass N of Glassillaun and then head for the Carrigeen Rocks, leaving them 0·5 cable to port. When the E Carrigeen Rock comes in line with Braadillaun 357°, keep these marks in transit astern to clear the shallows N of Ross Point. **From the N**, Mullaghadrina usually shows, but the simplest route is in mid-channel between Braadillaun (11m high) and Carricklaghan (0·7m high); then head for the Carrigeen Rocks. The W end of Inishbroon open of Braadillaun 325° leads 1 cable SW of Ship Rock. If heading to Derryinver Bay keep Glassillaun just open S of Freaghillaun 273° to pass between Ship Rock and Carrigeen Rocks.

Anchorages

- **Derryinver Bay** (53°34'·2N 9°59'·2W), at the NE end of Ballynakill Harbour. To pass N of Ardagh Rocks and between the banks in least depth 7·4m, keep the W head of Carrigeen Rocks on Glassillaun

Dangers
Ballynakill Harbour

Mullaghadrina (dries 3·4m), 1·5 cables SW of Carricklaghan

Rock 0·5 cable S of the "Calf"

Drying rock 1 cable NE of the 3·7m rock at Barracladdy

Ship Rock (charted drying 1·5m, but dries no more than 1·1m), 2 cables S of Lettermore Point

Ardagh Rocks (dry 3·4m), with an orange beacon, 3·5 cables E of the E Carrigeen Rock.

Rocks drying 1m are reported to lie between Ardagh Rocks and Roeillaun. There are fish cages E of Freaghillaun South and E of Ross Point, and mussel rafts inshore SE of Braadillaun.

(below) Entrance to Ballynakill Harbour, from the NW; Braadillaun, L, below the cliffs, and Carricklaghan, R

Ballynakill Harbour; Carrigeen Rocks, R

The W end of Inishbroon open of Braadillaun leads SW of Ship Rock

Derryinver Bay; Dawrosmore Hill, sunlit, centre R

Ballynakill Harbour anchorages

(above) Fahy Bay from the SW; Roeillaun and Derryinver Bay beyond

(right) Ardagh Rocks beacon in line with the gable of the stone-faced house leads through the deep channel E of Ross Point

Barnaderg Bay from the SE; Keelkyle Quay, foreground, and Tully Mountain (photo Galway County Council)

276° until Ardagh Rocks are abeam, then steer for Dawrosmore Hill with the N side of Freaghillaun astern 287°. Anchor about 100m SW of Derryinver quay, good holding, but buoy the anchor as there are old mooring chains on the bottom. The quay dries.

- Off **Ross Point** (53°33'·8N 10°00'·4W), always accessible, tide-rode but sheltered from the W. Ardagh Rocks beacon in line with the E gable of a stone-faced house on the N shore (see photograph) leads through the deep water E of Ross Point as far as the entrance to Fahy Bay.
- **Fahy Bay** (locally known as Ross, 53°33'·5N 10°00'·8W), approached over a bar with 0·2m at LWS, is an excellent anchorage, with good holding in 2 to 3m, mud, and pretty, pastoral surroundings. The only bad wind is SE, when it can become surprisingly rough; in these conditions choose a berth on the S side, close to the trees. The bar is quite sheltered and at neaps a yacht drawing 1·5m could enter at LW. It is about the same depth across most of the entrance of the bay, a little deeper towards the S side.
- The **pool S of Roeillaun** (53°33'·7N 9°59'·5W) is accessible at half-tide and offers better shelter than Ross Point or Fahy Bay in strong SE winds.
- **Barnaderg Bay**, in the SE corner (53°33'·3N 9°58'W), offers perfect shelter with enough depth to lie afloat at neap tides, and can be reached on a rising tide with AC2706 and continuous use of the echosounder. Keelkyle Quay dries 0·9m at the head. Anchoring depth may also be found in the pool between the two sets of narrows in the entrance, as shown on the plan. This is a perfectly sheltered spot.

Facilities

PO and shop with petrol pump at Moyard; shop, pub and filling station at Letterfrack, 800m E of Keelkyle Quay.

INISHBOFIN to CLEW BAY

AC1820, 2707, 2706, 2667

This coast includes the magnificent fjord of Killary Harbour and the enchanting islands of Inishturk and Clare, the latter with its 460m cliffs and its historical associations with the warrior-queen Granuaile. Clew Bay has a myriad of low grassy islands and a maze of channels, and the picturesque, historic and busy town of Westport at its head.

Killary Harbour and Approaches

AC2706, and Plan on p270

Killary Harbour and Little Killary Bay may be entered in almost any weather conditions, but note that in heavy weather the whole of Middle Ground, E and S of Caher Island, becomes a mass of breakers and must be avoided.

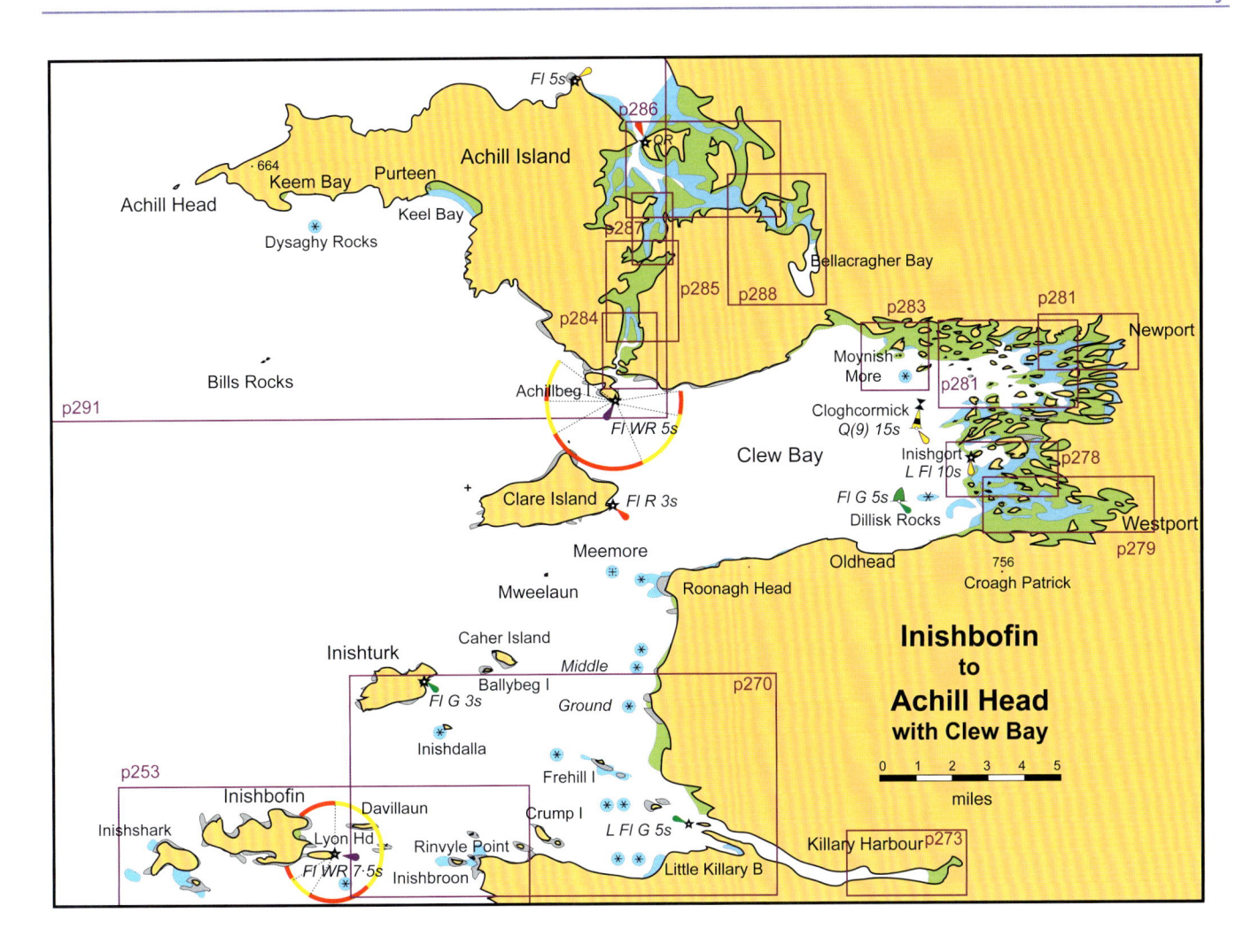

Inishbofin to Clew Bay

Dangers
Inishbofin to Clew Bay

The dangers inshore and in the approaches to the anchorages are described in the individual directions. The major dangers offshore are as follows:

Carrickmahoy (dries 1·9m), 8 cables S of Lyon Head 📷 (page 265)

Mweelaunatrua (dries 1·9m), 3 cables W of Inishbroon

Pollock Shoal, 3·7m, 3·3M N of Rinvyle Point

Blood Slate Rocks (dry 0·5m), 7 cables W of Frehill Island

Middle Ground, 7 to 21m, extensive area S and E of Caher Island which breaks in heavy weather

Meemore (awash), 1·5M W of Roonagh Head

Black Rock (dries 3·2m), 1M W of Roonagh Head 📷 (page 274)

Dillisk Rocks (dry 1·2m), 1·8M SW of Inishgort

Two Fathom Rock (3·4m), 8 cables NNW of the lookout tower on the W end of Clare Island

Lights and Marks

Killary Harbour approaches:
Black Rock buoy, PHM Fl R 6s
Inishbarna, white beacon, L Fl G 5s 45m 4M 📷
Doonee, white beacon, L Fl G 5s 10m 4M 📷

Clew Bay and approaches:
Inishturk Pier, Fl G 3s 3M
Roonagh Quay ldg lts 144° Occ blue 10s 6M sync, front 10m, rear 17m
Clare Island Pier, Fl R 3s 5m 3M
Clare Island Jetty, 2FR vert 2M
Dillisk Rocks buoy, SHM Fl G 5s
Dillisk Rocks perch (derelict), slim iron pole
Inishgort, short white tower L Fl 10s 11m 10M, AIS 📷
Cloghcormick buoy, W Card Q(9) 15s
Achillbeg Island, white tower Fl WR 5s 56m W18M R15M, R 262°–281° W 281°–342°, R 342°–060°, W 060°–092°, R (intens) 092°–099°, W 099°–118°, AIS. Shows red over the shoals in the outer approaches to Newport, white over the deep water NE of Clare Island, red over Clare Island and white to the W, with a narrow intensified red sector over the Bills Rocks. 📷 (page 283)

The lights and marks in Killary Harbour and in the approaches to Westport and Newport are described in the relevant Directions, below.

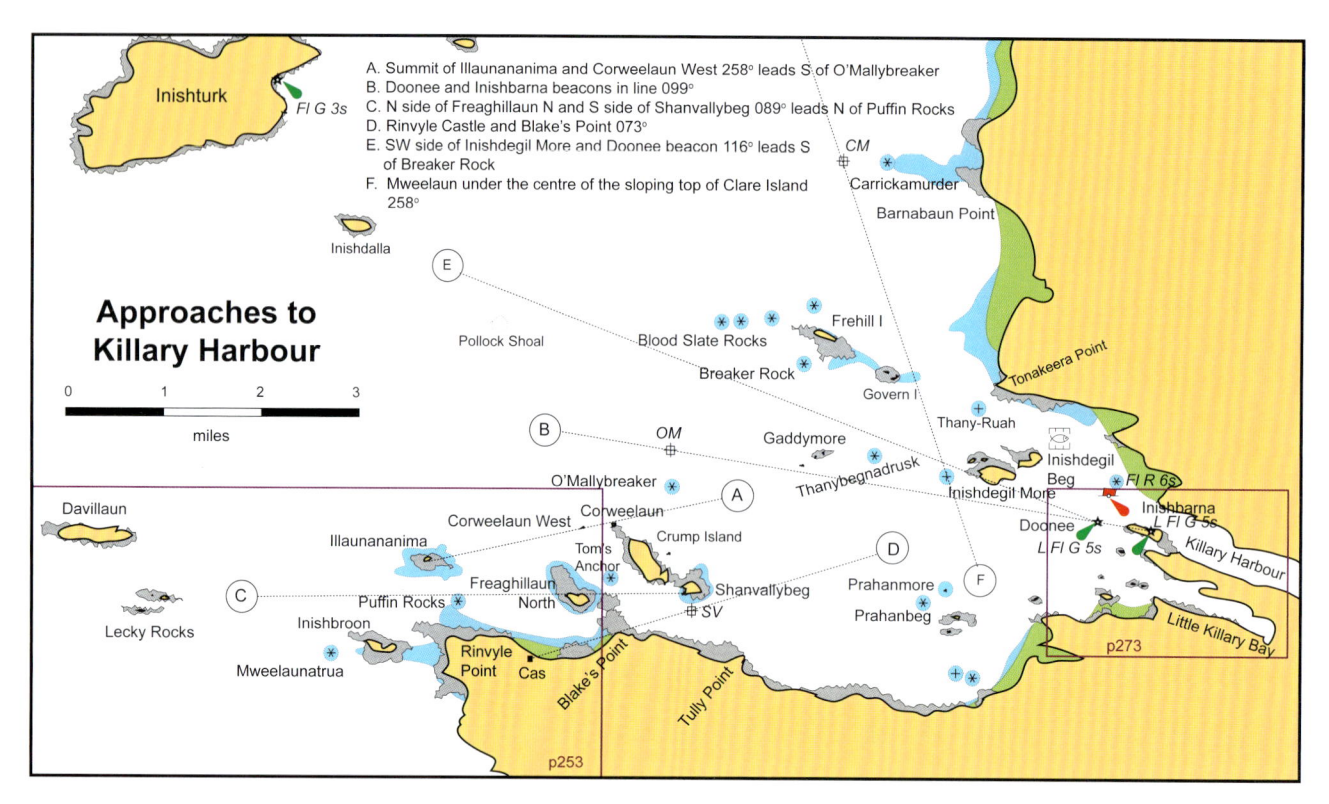

Approaches to Killary Harbour

A. Summit of Illaunananima and Corweelaun West 258° leads S of O'Mallybreaker
B. Doonee and Inishbarna beacons in line 099°
C. N side of Freaghillaun N and S side of Shanvallybeg 089° leads N of Puffin Rocks
D. Rinvyle Castle and Blake's Point 073°
E. SW side of Inishdegil More and Doonee beacon 116° leads S of Breaker Rock
F. Mweelaun under the centre of the sloping top of Clare Island 258°

Tides – S Approaches to Clew Bay

Between Inishturk and the mainland the tides are rotatory and run at less than 0·5 kn at springs. The tides run fairly into and out of Clew Bay, reaching 1·5 kn at springs. Offshore tidal streams are slight. Constant (Killary Harbour) +0018 Galway; MHWS 4·1m, MHWN 3·1m, MLWN 1·5m, MLWS 0·5m.

(L to R) Corweelaun, O'Mallybreaker, Corweelaun West and Crump Island; view from the W

(below) Gaddymore (L) and Gaddybeg, from the W

(right) Inishbarna and Doonee beacons in line lead in to Killary Harbour (transit B, plan above)

Approaching from High Island Sound, Cleggan or Ballynakill, the outermost danger is **Mweelaunatrua**, W of Inishbroon. From Cleggan Point, steer to pass 5 cables NW of Inishbroon, and Illaunananima, 1M to the NE. **From Inishbofin**, and passing either side of Lecky Rocks, leave Illaunananima 5 cables to starboard. Identify Corweelaun West (1·9m high) and Corweelaun (0·7m high), NW of Crump Island, and leave them 2 cables to starboard. The summit of Illaunananima in line with Corweelaun West 258° astern leads S of **O'Mallybreaker** (dries 0·5m) but across a bar with least depth 6m. In heavy weather, steer to pass 5 cables N of Corweelaun West and hold this course, passing well N of O'Mallybreaker, until Gaddymore (6m high) is identified. Waypoint ⊕OM 53°38'·4N 9°59'·5W is 3 cables N of O'Mallybreaker and 1M W of Gaddymore. Steer 099° from here

270

Inshore Passage round Rinvyle Point

on the transit of the beacons on Doonee and Inishbarna to clear all dangers to the entrance to Killary Harbour.

The charted transit of Shanvallybeg and Tully Point, leading SW of O'Mallybreaker, is usually impossible to distinguish.

Inshore passage round Rinvyle Point

In moderate weather it is possible to make the passage S of Illaunananima and between Freaghillaun N and Crump Island. Leaving Mweelaunatrua 2 cables to starboard, alter course for Illaunananima when Rinvyle Point shows N of Inishbroon. The charted transit (the N side of Freaghillaun in line with the S side of Shanvallybeg, 089°) is very difficult to pick out; as an alternative, steer along the latitude line 53°37'·05N, which leads close N of **Puffin Rocks** (dry 0·5m) and across the bar between these rocks and Illaunananima in a least depth of 3·7m. As soon as the depth increases to 6m or more and Rinvyle Castle (a square tower near the shore) is open of the clay cliff of Kanrawer, (at long 10°02'·6W), steer for Corweelaun West (1·9m high), to avoid the rocks extending NW from Freaghillaun North. Cleggan Point over the E point of Inishbroon 233° leads clear of these rocks. When 3 cables from Corweelaun West, close the shore of Crump Island and steer SE *(see photograph)* to pass NE of **Tom's Anchor** (dries 1·6m, marked as "Thos. Anchor" on the chart). Give Shanvallybeg a berth of 2 cables to port. When Blake's Point comes in line with Rinvyle Castle 253° (also difficult to discern, use the waypoint ⊕ *SV* 53°36'·9N 9°59'·3W) steer 073° with the castle astern; this leads clear of all dangers to the entrance to Killary Harbour.

Approaching Killary from the NW and Inishturk, set a course between Gaddymore and Frehill Island, with Inishdalla directly astern and Doonee beacon in line with the SW side of Inishdegil More 116°. This leads N of Pollock Shoal, S of Blood Slate Rocks and **Breaker Rock** (dries, 4 cables SW of Frehill Island), and N of **Thanybegnadrusk** (dries 0·6m, 5 cables E of Gaddymore). When 5 cables from Inishdegil More (in long 9°56'·0W) alter course S to clear the 1·8m sounding W of Inishdegil More.

The 6m-high white beacons on Doonee and Inishbarna in the entrance to Killary Harbour can often be picked out clearly from a distance. They lead between and close to

Inshore passage round Rinvyle Point; Puffin Rocks (breaking) from the W, Kanrawer cliff beyond

Tom's Anchor, breaking, R; view from the NW

Blake's Point in line with Rinvyle Castle (transit D, plan opposite)

Inshore passage round Rinvyle Point; Rinvyle Castle open E of Kanrawer

(above) Bring Doonee beacon (R centre) in line with the SW side of Inishdegil More (centre) to pass S of Blood Slate Rocks and Breaker Rock and N of Thanybegnadrusk (transit E, plan opposite)

(below) Mweelaun under the middle of the sloping top of Clare Island leads W of Carrickamurder and E of Frehill Island (transit F, plan opposite, and text overleaf)

Approaches to Killary Harbour; Little Killary Bay

Killary Harbour and Little Killary Bay from the W: Black Rocks bottom L, Inishbarna centre, Doonee lower R centre, with Carricklea and Carricklass beyond; Little Killary Bay to R

The head of Little Killary Bay

John Keneally's Rock (11m) and Conolly's Rock (10m). In a heavy sea or swell, keep well S of the leading line at this point.

Once Gaddymore is identified, Gaddy Beg (0·4m high) will be seen and course may be set to pass 2 cables W of it to avoid a rock which dries 0·9m, 1 cable to the W of Gaddy Beg.

From the N, bring Mweelaun, 19m high, under the centre of the sloping top of Clare Island 341° astern; waypoint ⊕*CM*, 53°41'·3N 9°57'·3W, on this line, also leads W of **Carrickamurder** (dries 1·1m, 7 cables W of Barnabaun Point). The transit line passes E of Frehill Island, but over the 1·8m patches E of Govern Island and W of Inishdegil More; keep more to the E and W, respectively, passing these two points, but beware of Thany-ruah, with 2m, 3 cables SW of Tonakeera Point. Govern Island and Frehill Island in line 305° lead S of Thany-ruah. Roonagh Head (8M N) just open E of Govern Island 011° leads E of Thanybegnadrusk. There is a fish farm close N of Carricknaglamph, NE of Inishdegil Beg.

In heavy weather, approach W of Caher Island and close E of Inishdalla to avoid Middle Ground.

Little Killary Bay (Salrock)

⊕*LK* 53°37'·2N 9°53'·8W
AC2706 and Plan

The head of this inlet is a fine anchorage which can be entered in any weather and provides excellent shelter; no swell reaches the anchorage, although it appears on the chart to be open to the NW. The shores of the inlet slope steeply, the S side tree-clad and the N bare and rocky.

Directions

From the W, the sandy bays just W of the entrance are conspicuous. Prahanbeg (dries 0·9m, 1M W of Culfin Point) is the only hidden danger in the approach. All the rocks in the immediate approach show at HW and may be passed on either hand. Note, however, that Carricklea is foul all round, and rocks extend 1 cable E and W of Bird Rock. *(Note also that there is another rock called Carricklea, less than a mile to the E in Killary Harbour.)* Illaunmore should be left 1 cable to starboard. **From the N** and Killary Harbour, pass between Inishbarna and Doonee and follow the shore round, staying E of mid-channel between Carricklea and the mainland point to the E. Note Carrickalecky (dries 2·1m), on the S side. Care must be taken at the 0·5 cable wide

Killary Harbour

passage between Ship Rock, (the extension of Salrock Point) and Carrickanoggaril, opposite (Carrickanoggaril is not named on AC2706). Anchor in 2 to 4m, soft mud, on the SE side of the pool E of Salrock Point. The holding has been reported suspect, and in strong winds a second anchor should be used. No facilities ashore.

KILLARY HARBOUR

⊕ KH 53°37'·9N 9°53'·2W
AC2706

This spectacular inlet, 7M long, with mountains falling steeply to the water's edge on either hand, has some of the most remarkable scenery on the coast, and a visit to its head is well worthwhile. In unsettled weather, however, any W wind funnels up the inlet and makes the anchorage at Leenaun uncomfortable. The entrance, between Doonee and Black Rocks (1m high, marked by a port hand buoy), is straightforward. The shores are clean to within 0·5 cable. Mussel rafts occupy the southern side of the harbour for much of its length and are marked on their N sides by ten yellow special mark buoys. All these marks show Fl Y 5s and should be left to starboard when entering. Beware of an unmarked mussel raft on the N side, extending for almost a mile, approximately opposite the third yellow buoy.

Anchorages

- About halfway up on the S side off Dernasliggaun Lodge, in 2 to 4m, where there is a gap in the mussel rafts. The house (now known as Killary Lodge) is an Adventure Centre. There is a small pier to lie alongside at HW. Water on the pier. Visitors' moorings may be available.
- On the N side off Bundorragha, S of the beacon in 5 to 7m. A rock was marked on the old charts 70m W of the beacon, but its existence is doubtful. Landing at the drying quay which is approached along the W shore.

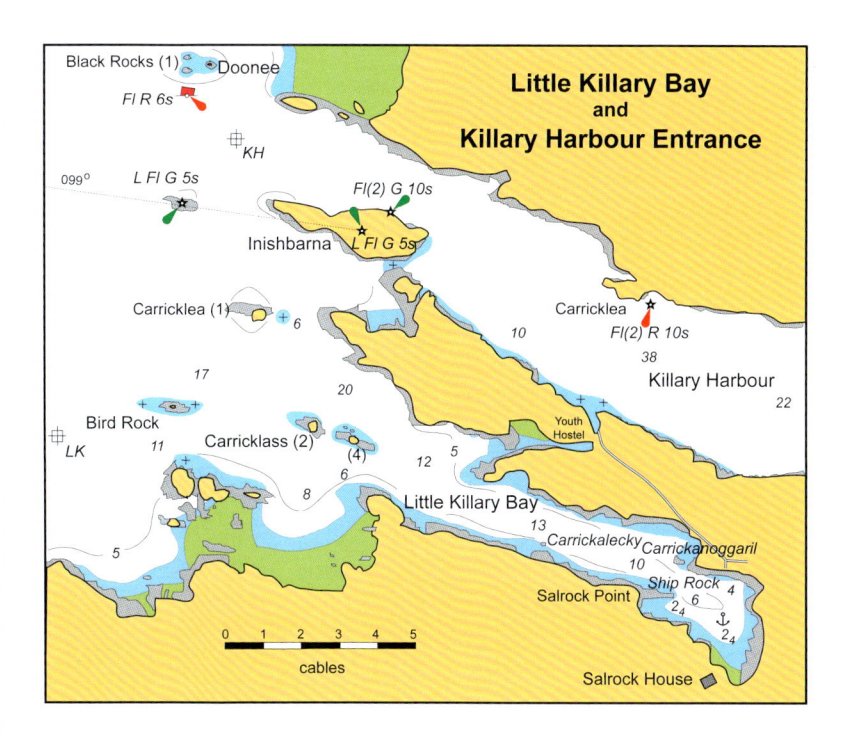

Lights and Marks
Killary Harbour

Black Rocks buoy, PHM Fl R 6s
Inishbarna, white beacon, L Fl G 5s 45m 4M
Doonee, white bn, L Fl G 5s 10m 4M
Inishbarna North beacon, SHM Fl(2) G 10s 6m 3M
Carricklea beacon, PHM Fl(2) R 10s 5M 3M
Illanballa beacon, PHM Fl R 5s
Tully white beacon, Fl(2) 10s
Bundorragha Quay, Fl 5s
Leenaun Quay, Fl G 6s

Bundorragha (Killary Harbour) from the S; Tully beacon, L centre

(bottom left) Leenaun Quay from the SW (photo Galway CC)

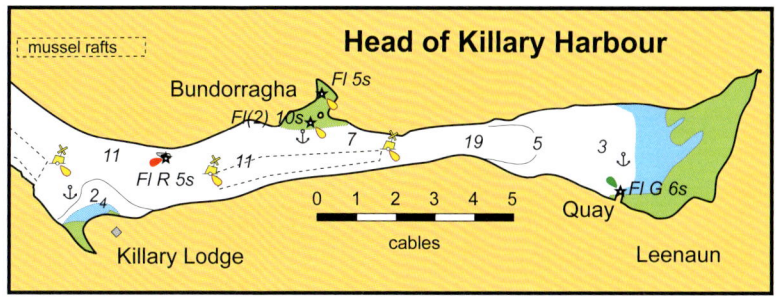

273

Inishbofin and Killary to Clew Bay; Inishturk

- At the head of the Harbour in 2 to 3m about 3 cables NW of Leenaun Quay, which dries. Hotel, shop, PO, filling station at Leenaun.

Constant +0018 Galway; MHWS 4·1m, MHWN 3·1m, MLWN 1·5m, MLWS 0·5m.

Direct Passage - Inishbofin to Clew Bay

In good weather, pass 2 cables S of Lyon Head and leave Carrickmahoy and Lecky Rocks to starboard, then pass 5 cables E of Davillaun and steer 038° to clear Pollock Shoal and Roonagh Head (with **Black Rock** to the W of it), and pass E of Meemore. If there is any uncertainty in position, steer closer to Caher Island and within 1M of Mweelaun (19m high, W of Roonagh Head). Refer to the directions below for rounding Roonagh Head. In heavy weather, avoid Middle Ground altogether; steer close E of Inishdalla, and W of Caher Island and Mweelaun.

Coast – Killary Harbour to Clew Bay

AC2706, 2667

The coast between Killary and the entrance to Clew Bay consists of 6M of sandy beaches broken at intervals by rock outcrops. Several groups of rocks, reefs and shoals extend up to 1·5M out from the beaches and beyond these groups the depths are irregular up to 4M offshore. The beaches are exposed to the W and are subject to nearly continuous surf. In bad weather, the whole coast E of a line joining Mweelaun to Caher Island becomes a mass of irregular breakers and should be avoided, while in the channel between Clare Island and Roonagh Head, patches down to 8m and a SW-going tide of 1·5 kn can give rise to a high and confused sea. In such conditions it may be prudent to sail north-about Clare.

In all normal summer weather, however, the passage SE of Clare Island is the usual approach to Clew Bay from the S and SW. Mweelaun provides a conspicuous mark.

The passage between **Meemore Shoal** and Roonagh Head is a useful short cut in good weather and is easy to identify when leaving Clew Bay, less so when approaching from the SW. Meemore dries at low springs and usually breaks.

The passage lies between **Black Rock** (dries 3·2m), 6·5 cables off the shore between Roonagh Head and Emlagh Point, and Meemore, 7 cables WNW. The key to the passage is the identification of Black Rock, as there are no convenient leading marks in either direction. Covered at HW, it is almost invariably marked by a breaker. Give it a berth of 2 or 3 cables, no more, so as to stay well clear SE of Meemore.

The summit of Croagh Patrick (761m) N of the summit of Carrowmore Hill (170m), 2M E of Roonagh Head, leads N of Meemore.

Roonagh Quay, near Roonagh Head, is the mainland terminal for the Clare and Inishturk ferries but is very exposed, has very restricted room and is not accessible to a yacht.

Inishturk

⊕ 53°42'·2N 10°05'W (2 cables SE of the pier)
AC2706, 2667

Inishturk, 188m high and 2·25M long, with a population of 53, is considered by many to be Ireland's most captivating island. Its coast is, in general, steep-to except at the SE corner where **Floor Shoals** with 6·7m least water extend for 8 cables. There is anchorage, well sheltered from winds between SW and NNW, in Garranty Harbour on its E side, off the pier in 3 to 6m, sand, good holding but somewhat exposed to swell. There are visitors' moorings. Shop and PO. Bar/restaurant at the Community Club. Ferries to Cleggan and Roonagh Quay.

Black Rock from the NW

Garranty Harbour, Inishturk

274

Caher and Clare Islands

Caher Island

53°43′N 10°01′W
AC2667

Caher Island, 57m high and uninhabited, lies 1·5M E of Inishturk. It has steep, high cliffs at its NW end. There are boat landings at Portatemple on the E and Portnacloy on the W, usable in settled conditions only.

Clare Island

⊕ 53°48′·1N 9°56′·6W (3 cables E of the pier)
AC2667

This magnificent island, with a population of 168, has a quieter ambience than the similarly-populated Inishbofin, and many archaeological sites including Granuaile's Castle and a well-preserved medieval abbey with remarkable wall paintings. The island has towering cliffs on its NW side, beneath which there are a few isolated rocks close in. Between Calliaghcrom and Lecknacurra, the N point of the island, there is a 7m rock which breaks in gales. There are fish farms E and NE of the island.

Anchorage

The bay N of the pier is sheltered from winds from S through W to N; a visitor's mooring

Garranty Harbour, Inishturk, from the SE; the visitors' moorings, centre

Ballybeg and Caher Islands (foreground) with Clare Island in the distance and Mweelaun between (centre R)

Clare Island

Clare Island harbour from the SE

(above) Clare Island; Granuaile's Castle overlooks the pier and moorings

(below) Mweelaun (L), Caher Island (centre L) and Inishturk, seen from Clare Island

is normally available. Ferry traffic at the pier is fairly heavy but a temporary berth may be available, and anchorage is possible outside the moorings in 5 to 6m, sand. A submarine power cable runs out from the N corner of the bay. In heavy weather the bay and pier are subject to swell.

There is a temporary anchorage on the NE side of the island in up to 6m, sand, off the beach which has a small pier and slip at its W end. The bottom further W is rock.

Constant +0015 Galway; MHWS 4·1m, MHWN 3·1m, MLWN 1·5m, MLWS 0·5m.

Facilities

Pub at the harbour, shop and PO at Portnakilly, 2 km. Ferries to Roonagh Quay.

Clew Bay; Approaches to Westport

Approaches to Westport, from the WNW. Inishgort lighthouse, bottom L, with Inishlyre beyond; Dorinish, R

CLEW BAY

AC2667

Clew Bay extends 12M E from Roonah Head and Achillbeg. The head of the bay is studded with small islands and there are several good anchorages behind them. The islands are drowned drumlins, composed of boulder clay which has been eroded by the sea to leave steep clay cliffs, particularly on their W sides, and boulder beaches all round. There are shallow channels through the islands to Westport Quay and Newport. The inner part of the bay offers fascinating day-sailing in sheltered water. The S side of the bay is dominated by the cone of Croagh Patrick (756m - *see photograph on p25*).

The coast from Roonagh Head to Oldhead is foul for 6 cables offshore. Oldhead, 146m, is conspicuous and surrounded by trees. There is a pier E of the head which dries, with clean sand bottom along its inner side; to clear the rocks close E and S of the pier approach it near HW on a bearing of 190° and round the pierhead fairly close. The approach is marked by unlit red and green buoys. There is a temporary anchorage NE of the pier, holding poor and subject to swell.

Approaches to Westport

⊕ *WP 53°49'·6N 9°41'W*

AC2667, 2057, Imray C54 and Plan

From the SW, from a position 1M N of Roonagh Head, leave Dillisk Rocks buoy to starboard. From the NW, leave Cloghcormick buoy to port. In rough weather, approach Inishgort lighthouse on a bearing between 080° and 100°. Leave Dorinish buoy close to starboard. The entrance can be rough with wind against tide.

Tides
Clew Bay

The tide sets fairly into and out of Clew Bay, the W-going ebb starting about an hour after HW Galway and the E-going flood about an hour after LW Galway. Rates around Clare Island reach 1·5 knots, and in the entrance to Westport 2 knots, less in open water. Tidal streams among the islands have not been studied but are not strong. Constant (Westport) +0050 Galway; MHWS 4·5m. MHWN 3·4m, MLWN 1·6m, MLWS 0·5m.

Lights and Marks
Westport

Dillisk Rocks buoy, SHM Fl G 5s
Inishgort, white tr L Fl 10s 11m 10M, AIS
Dorinish buoy, SHM Fl G 3s
No 1 buoy, SHM Fl(2) G 10s, 3 cables ESE of Dorinish buoy
No 2 buoy, PHM, Fl(2) R 10s
No 4 buoy, PHM Fl R 4s
No 3 buoy, SHM Fl G 5s
No 6 buoy, PHM Fl R 4s
No 5 buoy, SHM Fl(2) G 5s
Finnaun (No 8) buoy, PHM Fl R 6s
Corrillan (No 7) beacon, SHM Fl G 5s
Carricknamore (No 9) beacon, SHM Fl G 3s
No 10 beacon, PHM Fl R 3s
No 12 beacon, PHM Fl R 6s
No 14 buoy, PHM Fl R 3s
No 11 buoy, SHM Fl G 5s
Carricknacally (No 16) beacon, PHM Fl R 6s
No 18 buoy, PHM Fl(2) R 5s
Illanroe (No 13) buoy, SHM Fl(2) G 5s
Monkelly's (No 20) buoy, PHM Fl R 2s
and six more port- and four more starboard-hand beacons to Westport Quay.

Anchorages in the Approaches to Westport

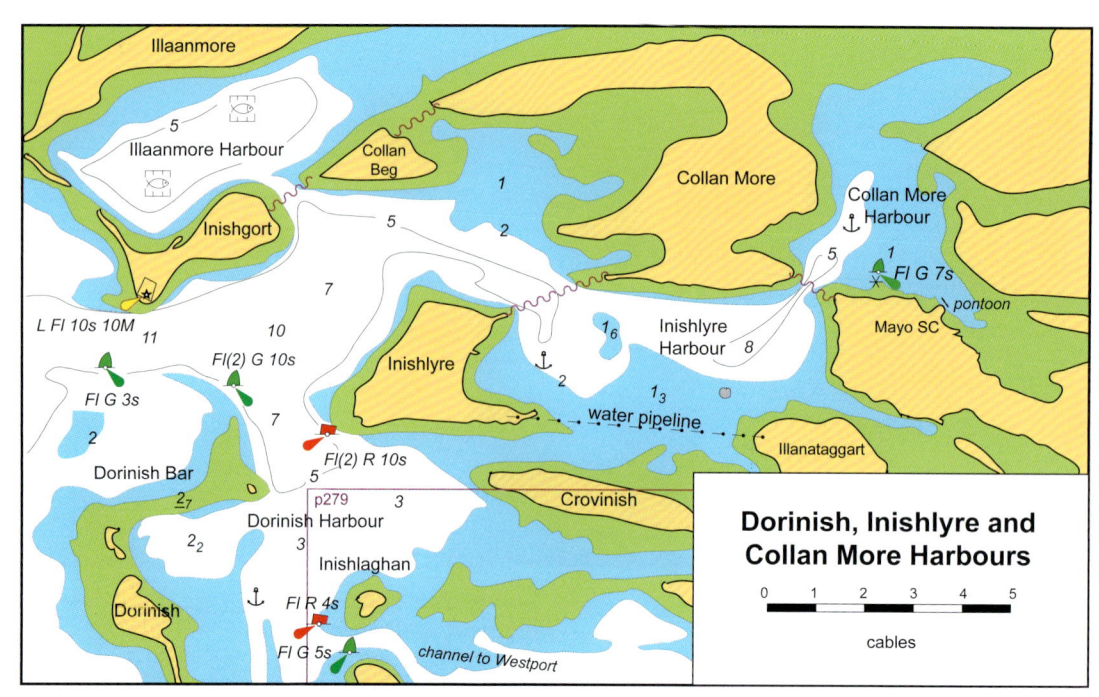

Inishgort lighthouse, from the SW

Mayo SC's pontoon at Rosmoney

Collan More Harbour and Mayo SC

Anchorages among the islands
(see Plan)

- **Dorinish Harbour,** SW of Inishlyre. Anchor 2 to 3 cables off Dorinish More and W to NW of the Inishlaghan (No.4) buoy in 2 to 3m, good holding. Dorinish Bar covers at HWS but still breaks the sea.

- **Inishlyre Harbour.** This natural harbour gives good shelter from W and SW winds. Enter midway between the NE point of Inishlyre and the SW point of Collan More, then turn S and anchor in 2m, 1·5 cables N of the SE point of Inishlyre.

- **Collan More Harbour,** E of Collan More Island, gives the best all-round shelter and offers the easiest access to the mainland. Approach from between Inishlyre and Collan More as above, with the S end of Inishgort in line with the N point of Inishlyre. When the SW point of Collan More comes abeam, bring the N point of Inishlyre in line with the wall N of the lighthouse. This leads well N of the drying rock NW of Illanataggart. The sailing club sometimes has a racing mark just to the north of this rock; keep to the north of the mark. The entrance, between Collan More and Rosmoney Point is 1 cable wide between the HW marks but the shore on either side is foul and the navigable entrance is only 45m wide. Enter in mid-channel in 1·7m;

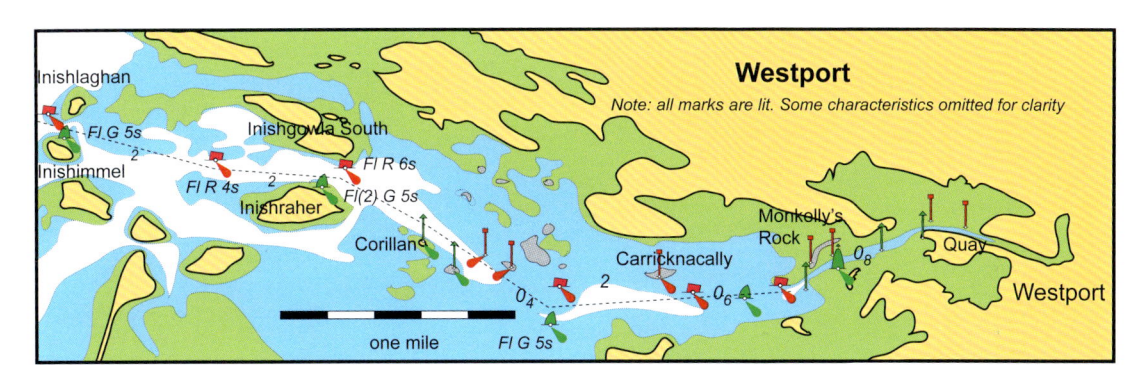

Westport

Westport
Note: all marks are lit. Some characteristics omitted for clarity

the deepest part is NNE of the narrows. There is a drying rock about 120m off the Rosmoney shore, marked by a starboard-hand buoy. The quay, which dries, is on the S side of the harbour near Mayo Sailing Club. The Club has a pontoon at the quay for landing and short-stay berthing. The pontoon is lit at night, 2FG vert. **Anchor** in 2 to 3m.

WESTPORT

AC2057 essential
The channel to Westport has a least depth of 0·1m near the quay, and the quay itself mostly dries but with a clean mud bottom.

Directions

From Dorinish Harbour, the channel passes between Inishlaghan and Inishimmel and then N of Inishraher. Follow the buoys and beacons. Finnaun and Corillan islets are distinctive, top-hat shaped. There is a least depth of 2m in the channel to the quay at half tide, and the pool between Monkelly's buoy (No.20) and Inishmweela beacon opposite has 2·2m at LAT. The best available berth at the quay is just past the last port-hand perch No 32, which is on a rock, and has a tide gauge; there is width to turn, upstream of this. The quay here dries 0·8m, but has no ladders. Sea angling boats use the quay further NW, where it is deeper. Constant +0050 Galway; MHWS 4·5m, MHWN 3·4m, MLWN 1·6m, MLWS 0·5m.

The distinctive Corillan, in the approaches to Westport, from the NW

Westport Quay near HW

Westport from the W

279

Newport

Newport from the E; Burrishoole, extreme R

Facilities

Supermarket, shops, pubs, restaurants, bottle and can bank at the quay. Westport (5,510), 1·5 km from the quay, has all the facilities of a popular tourist town. Supermarkets, shops, PO, pubs, restaurants, doctors. Train and bus connections to Dublin. Chandlery 098 28800, divers 098 41236.

NEWPORT

⊕ *NP* 53°51'·6N 9°40'·9W
AC2667 and Plan

Newport, in the NE corner of Clew Bay, lies behind a labyrinth of low islands and narrow channels which – in moderate weather – offer some fascinating pilotage to the adventurous sailor. The approach channel is marked and lit, but the creek leading to Newport dries at least a metre at LAT. W of the islands, and N and W of the Cloghcormick buoy, is an area of shallow water and irregular bottom which makes the approach from seaward hazardous in heavy onshore weather or a high swell. The main approach passes N of Inishoo and S of a line of rocks and shoals extending 2·5M W from Illanmaw, and comprising the drying rocks **Carrickachorra, Carricklahan, Carrickachaash South, Carrickachaash North** and **Larbaun**, and below-water rocks with 1·4m, 1·7m and 2m. Carrickachaash and Larbaun rocks do not show even at LWS.

All the islands are fringed by boulder shoals, so aim always to keep in the centre of the channels. It is important also to keep a careful tally of the islands, most of which are very similar in appearance.

Directions

From the W, approach with the N sides of Inishoo and Inishgowla in line. **From the S**, leave Cloghcormick buoy close to starboard and steer 051° to pass 3 cables NW of Inishoo. Then follow the marked channel. Note that beyond Muckinish there are patches with least depth 0·3m.

Newport itself is accessible above half tide. There is a landing pontoon opposite and down-river from the quay.

Lights and Marks
Newport

Inishoo beacon, SHM Fl(2) G 6s
Illanmaw buoy, PHM Fl(2) R 5s
Taash buoy, SHM QG
Illanascraw beacon, SHM Fl G 4s
Rosmore Point buoy, PHM Fl R 5s
Rabbit Island buoy, SHM Fl G 5s
Rosmore South buoy, PHM Fl(2) R 10s
The channel to Newport is marked by a further two port- and three starboard-hand marks, all lit.
South of the main approach channel:
Carrigeennafrankagh beacon, Isolated Danger Fl(2) 10s
Carrickwee beacon, E Card Q(3) 10s
Inishcuill East beacon, E Card VQ(3) 5s

Newport

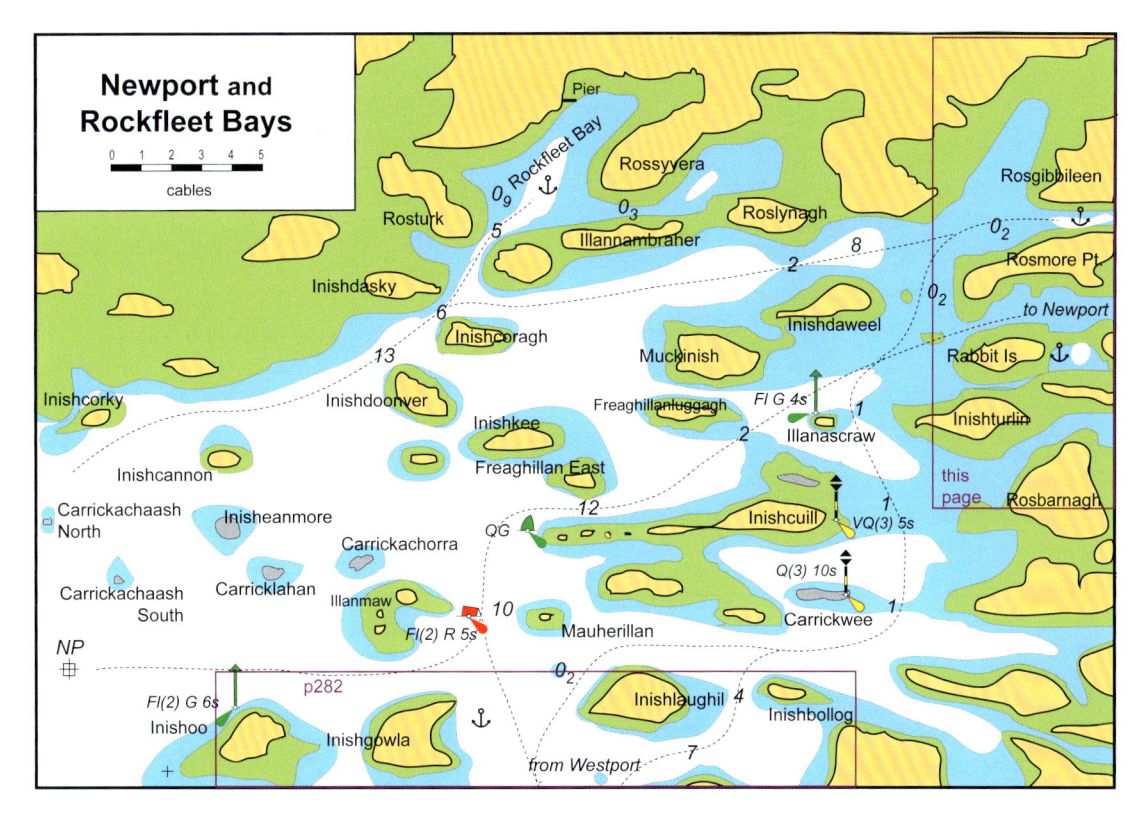

Illanascraw

Anchorages

The following anchorages have sufficient water to lie afloat at LW but can be reached only above half tide.

- S of the E tip of Rabbit Island, in 3m or more. A careful mid-channel course must be kept between Rabbit Island and the island and peninsula to the S of it. Dinghy access to Newport across the spit E of Rabbit Island.
- N of Rosmore Point in the narrows S of Rosgibbileen, with over 3m in midchannel, mud on sand; more exposed in W and SW winds and further from Newport by dinghy than the S anchorage.
- A perfectly sheltered anchorage at Burrishoole has a least depth of only 1.6m at LWS in the pool. From the anchorage between Rosmore and Rosgibbileen, steer between Rosgibbileen and the islets to the E. Anchor either in the pool below

Burrishoole

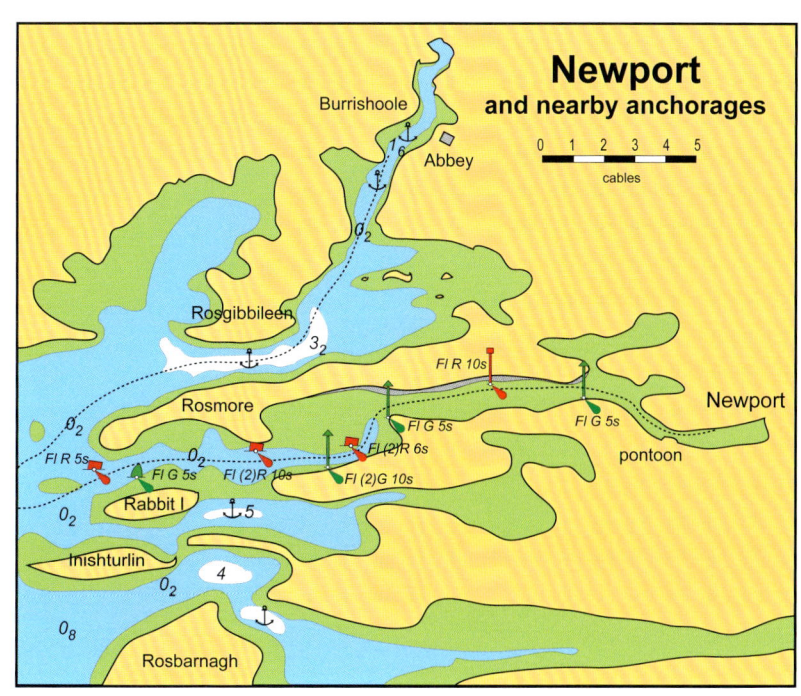

Newport at HW, looking up-river from the landing pontoon

281

Westport to Newport; Rockfleet Bay

Inshore passage North from Westport

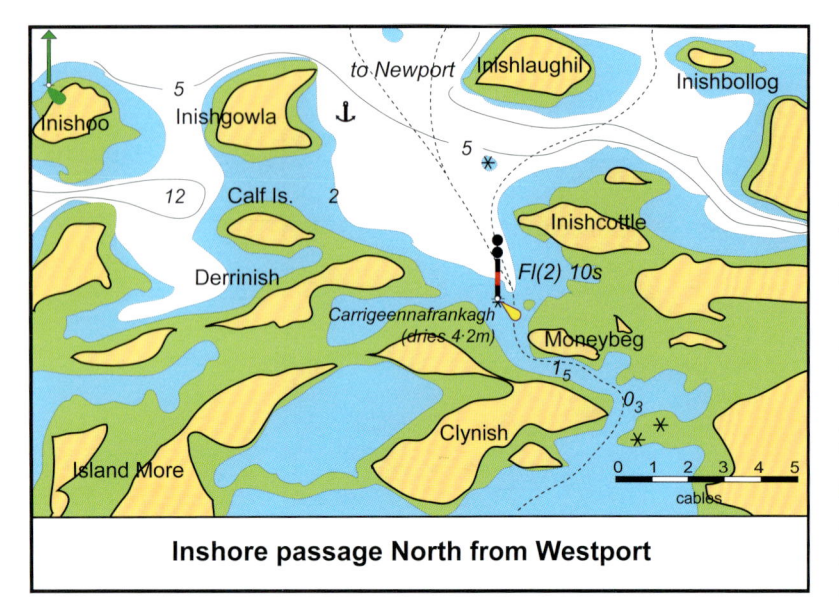

The narrows between Collan More and Clynish

Mauherillan

Carrickwee (R) and Inishcuill (centre R) E Card beacons

Rockfleet Bay; the castle, R

- the abbey ruins or just S of the narrows.
- E of Rosbarnagh Island, where there is a pool with 5m. Note the rocks 2 cables S of Illanascraw.

Facilities

Water on the pontoon; shops, pubs, filling station at Newport.

Inshore Passage North from Westport

AC2057 and Plan

There is an inshore passage among the islands from Inishgort to Inishgowla, offering a short cut from Westport above half tide, with care, and continuous use of the echosounder. The channel leads NW between Inishgort and Collan Beg, then between Collan More and Clynish, where the least depth (it just dries at LAT) is found. Pass between the rocks SE of the E point of Clynish by leaving the point 0·5 cable to port. Then follow the channel S of Moneybeg Island and give the Isolated Danger beacon on Carrigeennafrankagh a berth of 25m on either side. This leads to the anchorage E of Inishgowla, and the channel to Newport and the other anchorages among the islands.

Alternative channels include the passage N or S of Inishlaughil and E of Carrickwee and Inishcuill. Note the 0·2m patch S of Mauherillan.

Rockfleet Bay

53°53'·4N 9°38·5'W
AC2667 and Plan on p 281

Rockfleet Bay is a good anchorage sheltered in all winds, accessible from Newport between the islands but accessible from seaward only in moderate weather. **From the W**, follow the directions below for Moynish More but pass 1 cable S of Roeillaun, then head between Inishcorky and Inishcannon and between Inishdasky and Inishcoragh. When Inishcoragh is abeam head 030° between the next islands 2 cables NE, then steer towards Rockfleet Castle, a well-preserved former O'Malley stronghold. Anchor in 2m, very soft mud, W of Rossyvera Point. There are fish cages in the W arm of the bay.

Going in by the main channel to Newport, or going up to it from Westport entrance, after passing Illanmaw, head NW to join the above entrance; or leave Freaghillanluggagh (close S of Muckinish) to starboard and Inishcoragh to port.

Moynish More; Achill Sound

Moynish More

⊕ *MM 53°52'·7N 9°43'·2W*
AC2667 and Plan

Moynish More is the W'most island on the N shore of Clew Bay. There is anchorage close E of it in settled weather and offshore winds. The dangers in the approach are **Larbaun**, a drying rock 9 cables S of the island, and a 2·9m patch 3·5 cables NW of this rock. **From the S**, steer 001° from Cloghcormick buoy towards Rosturk Castle to leave Larbaun 2 cables to port. **From the W**, a bearing of 078° on the summit of Roeillaun (28m high) leads between Larbaun and the 2·9m patch. When the E side of Moynish More opens up, turn N and leave Moynish Beg a cable to port.

Anchor opposite the first pile of stones on the island, a cable offshore in 3m, sand.

ACHILL SOUND

53°51'·8N 9°56'W
AC2667 and 2704, Imray C54 and Plans

Achill Island is connected to the mainland by an opening bridge, replaced in 2008. There are no headroom restrictions. The channel to the bridge dries more than a metre in places and is strongly tidal, but the marks, at least on the S side, have been upgraded (see plan). Officially, the bridge can be opened during working hours (0900-1630 Mon-Thurs, 0900-1530 Fri) given two working days' notice. However up to the time of writing the installation has been plagued by teething troubles, and this, combined with the tidal restrictions and difficult pilotage of the Sound, makes the through passage a challenging prospect.

Moynish More

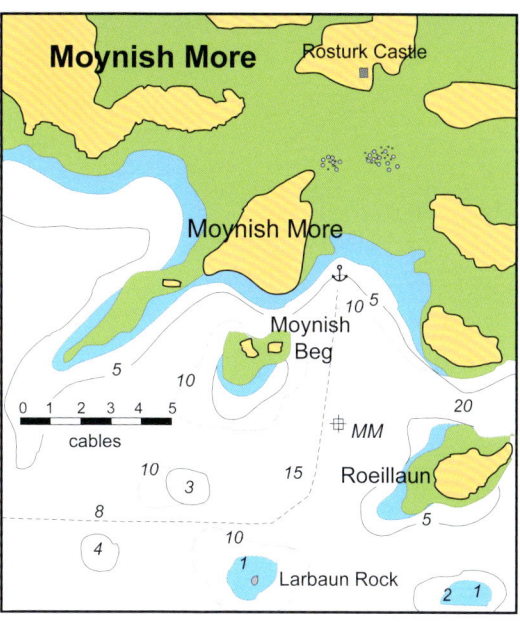

Achill Sound from the S; Achillbeg foreground, with its lighthouse; the narrows between Darby's Point and Gubnacliffamore beyond

Achill Sound

South end of Achill Sound

Tides
Achill Sound and Approaches

N of Clare Island the W-going ebb stream out of Clew Bay reaches 1·5 kn. The stream in the S entrance to Achill Sound runs at 3 kn at springs, increasing to 4 or 5 kn in the narrows off Darby's Point. Slack water lasts for about half an hour; the tide turns N at −0550 Galway and S at +0100 Galway. The N-going flood sets strongly across the shallows NW of Gubnacliffamore, on which it breaks; the S-going ebb sets strongly across Carrigin-a-tShrutha. The Sound fills through both N and S entrances, and the streams meet 5 cables S of the bridge. At the bridge, the S-going flood starts about −0450 Galway and the N-going ebb about +0200 Galway. At the Bull's Mouth, the N entrance to the Sound, the tide turns S at −0550 Galway and N at +0100 Galway, and runs at 5 knots at springs.

Constant (Kildavnet) +0030 Galway; MHWS 3·6m, MHWN 2·9m, MLWN 1·3m, MLWS 0·6m.

Lights and Marks

S of the bridge (from seaward):
Achillbeg Island, white tower Fl WR 5s 56m W18M R15M, R 262°–281° W 281°–342°, R 342°–060° W 060°–092° R (intens) 092°–099° W 099°–118°. Shows red over the shoals in the outer approaches to Newport, white over the deep water NE of Clare Island, red over Clare Island and white to the W, with a narrow intensified red sector over the Bills Rocks.
Achillbeg East, red beacon Fl R 2s 5m
Carrigin-a-tShrutha, red beacon Q(2) R 5s, 2 cables S of Darby's Point
Whitestone Pier ldg lts 330° Oc 4s, front 5m rear 6m
Gubnacliffamore, green bn Fl G 3s
Darby's Point, red beacon Fl R 5s
Gubnaranny buoy, SHM Fl(2) G 6s
Lifeboat Station beacon, PHM Fl R 10s
Kildavnet beacon, PHM Fl(2) R 6s
Glassillaun buoy, SHM Fl G 5s
Dareens beacon, PHM Fl R 3s
Ship Rock beacon, PHM QR
Gubrinnanoyster Buoy, SHM Fl(2) G 5s
Shraheen's Point beacon, PHM Fl R 2s
Dorrary Point beacon Fl(2) R 6s

N of the bridge (S to N):
Achill Sound, red beacon QR
Saulia Pier, green col Fl G 3s 12m
Carrigeenfushta, green concrete beacon, Fl G 3s
Inishbiggle, red concrete beacon QR
Ridge Point beacon, Fl 5s 21m 5M

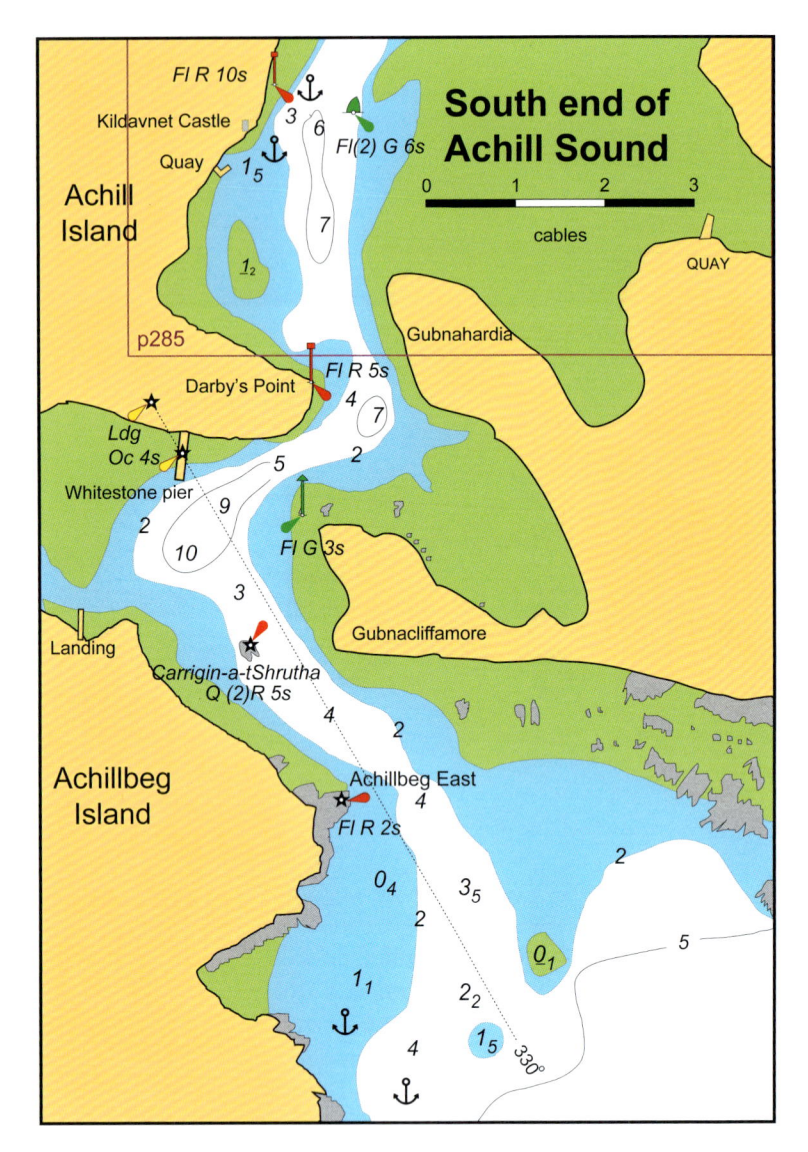

The S end of the Sound also offers the only sheltered anchorage on this part of the coast, and is well marked and lit; the anchorage at Kildavnet is scenic and attractive. Care is however required in dealing with the strong tides in the channel. There is a good supermarket and hardware store at the bridge.

The entrance is E of Achillbeg Island, easily identified by its diminutive lighthouse. The bar, with 1·5m patches, breaks in SW gales, and there is a spit drying 0·1m close NE of it. With offshore winds or in calm weather it is possible to anchor temporarily in the bay SW of the bar to await slack water for entering.

Directions – Achill Sound, south of the bridge

Enter on the leading line with Whitestone Pier, W of Darby's Point, bearing 330° from a waypoint of 53°51'·74N 9°56'·20W; this leads S of the 0·1m drying spit, then close to the

Achill Sound

rocky NE point of Achillbeg, clear between Gubnacliffamore and Achillbeg East port-hand beacon and E of Carrigin-a-tShrutha beacon. (The leading beacons at Whitestone Pier are not easy to see by day from S of the Achillbeg E beacon.) Follow the N shore round from the pier, pass Darby's Point in mid-channel at both narrows to its S and NE, and head for the tower of Kildavnet Castle, close to the W shore 3 cables N of Darby's Point. Continuous monitoring of the echosounder is recommended.

Anchorage

Anchor in 2 to 3m, close inshore on the W side of the channel, off the castle; anchorage further NE in the full run of the tide can be untenable in strong wind-over-tide conditions. There are visitors' moorings, and a landing pontoon alongside Kildavnet quay with enough depth to accommodate a yacht above half tide. Water tap on the quay.

The channel from Kildavnet to the bridge dries more than a metre in places and is marked by six port-hand perches and three starboard-hand buoys. A passage up to the bridge should be made on the last of the flood tide, leaving Kildavnet at HW Galway

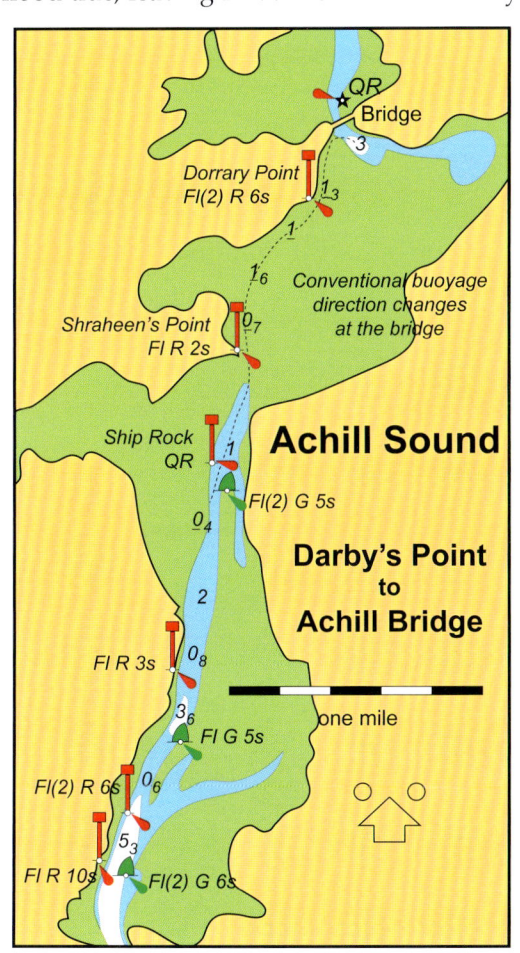

Anchorage on the E side of Achillbeg

(above) On the leading line of the inconspicuous beacons at Whitestone pier, E of Darby's Point; Achillbeg East (centre L) and Carrigin-a-tShrutha (L) beacons

(right) The leading beacons at Whitestone Pier

(below) Approaching the narrows at the S end of Achill Sound; Gubnacliffamore beacon, L centre, Darby's Point beacon, R centre

Darby's Point and beacon from the S; Kildavnet Castle, extreme L

Kildavnet; the lifeboat is alongside the pontoon at the quay, L

Achill Sound

–0030. The Admiralty charts are based on old surveys and no longer accurately represent the sandbanks in the Sound. The greatest caution is advised, with continuous monitoring of the depths. The channel and soundings shown on the plan are based on observations from a yacht in 2011. Leave all marks close on the proper hand but borrow to the E of the direct line between Ship Rock and Shraheen's Point beacons, and to the W of it between Shraheen's Point and Dorrary Point beacons. Between Dorrary Point beacon and the bridge stay 50m from the HWM on the W shore, then turn to starboard when very close to the bridge, to find a pool with 3m of water at LAT, and two visitors' moorings. Supermarket and hardware shop (098 45211) at the bridge, with some chandlery; also shops and pubs. There is no convenient landing on the S side of the bridge, or indeed anywhere at LW, and taking a dinghy to the slip on the N side when the tide is running means negotiating the 4 kn current under the bridge.

Achill Bridge

To request opening phone Mayo County Council, 097 81004 between 0900 and 1300 or 1400 and 1700, Monday to Friday or email belmullet@mayococo.ie, giving at least two working days' notice. The bridge can be opened, weather permitting, at high water, only between 0900-1530 Mon-Thurs, 0900-1430 Fri, except public holidays. (This limits opening opportunities to eight or nine days per month.) It is actually best to transit on the last hour of the flood, after +0100 Galway, and specifically request opening for this time. Transit the bridge on the E (mainland) side of the central pier, whether going N or S; the W side is rocky and dries. From the S, the easiest approach is from the pool with the moorings. Once through, turn immediately to starboard to avoid foul ground close NW of the bridge, and steer for the port-hand beacon.

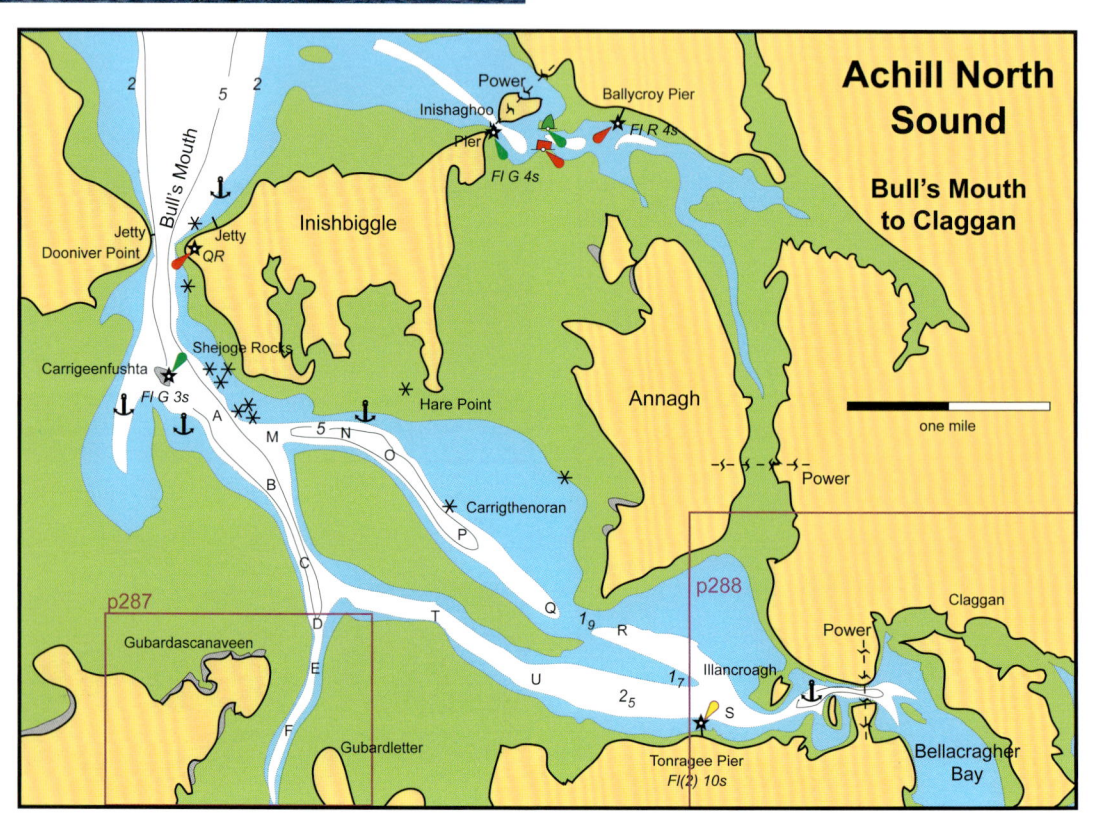

Achill Bridge from the N

The Bull's Mouth, from the S; Carrigeenfushta beacon, L

Achill Sound; Inishbiggle

Achill Sound, north of the bridge

There are also two visitors' moorings N of the bridge, in a pool with 2·9m at LAT. Close N of the bridge is a red port-hand beacon, which should be left to starboard when heading N, since the conventional buoyage direction changes at the bridge. The N part of the Sound is mostly deeper but essentially unmarked; there are beacons on Saulia Pier and Carrigeenfushta Rock, but the only way for a stranger to navigate the sandbanks of the north Sound is by means of GPS waypoints. The ones on the plans were established by a yacht in 2014; they do not necessarily follow the deepest part of the channels, but they provide at least 3m of water up to the bridge at MHWS. Stay 0·5 to 1 cable from Carrigeenfushta to avoid the drying Shejoge Rocks opposite, to the E. Steer 010° for the mid-channel of the Bull's Mouth to avoid the rocks SW of Inishbiggle Point. To avoid the shallow spit extending N, maintain a N'ly heading until Slievemore Point (4M W) is open of Ridge Point (in lat 54°02'N) before turning NW.

Entry from the N should also be made close to slack water, steering 190° until 3 cables past the Bull's Mouth. Anchorage is available 1 to 2 cables S of Carrigeenfushta beacon keeping it in line with Dooniver Point; the deeper water in the channel to the E has a rocky bottom. The anchorage is tidebound and is exposed to a fetch of 1 to 2M at HW, so may be uncomfortable in fresh winds between SE and S.

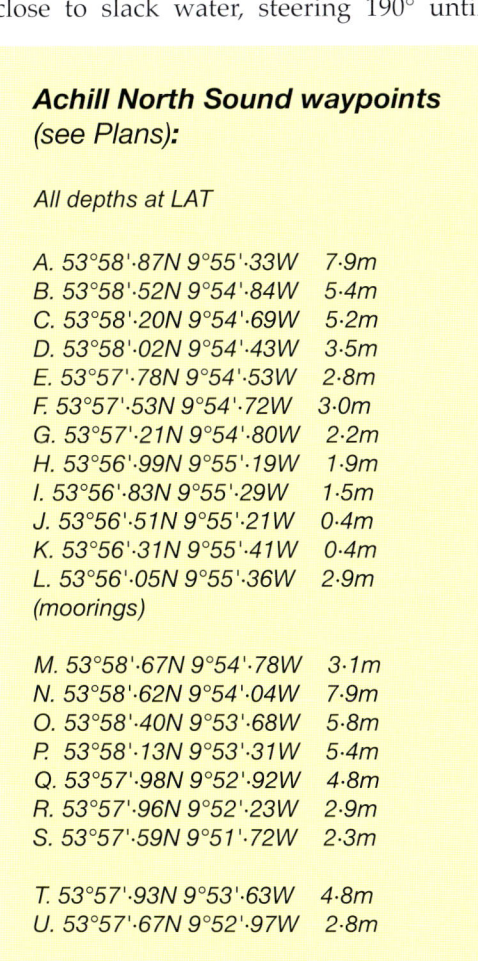

The small drying pier at Bunacurry, on the inlet 1M SW of Carrigeenfushta, is marked by a port-hand beacon Fl R 5s, but access requires local knowledge.

N part of Achill Sound from the SW, at high water. The bridge is the old one, now replaced. The Bull's Mouth and Inishbiggle, top L. Most of the area in the picture dries at LW.

Achill North Sound waypoints (see Plans):

All depths at LAT

A.	53°58'·87N 9°55'·33W	7·9m
B.	53°58'·52N 9°54'·84W	5·4m
C.	53°58'·20N 9°54'·69W	5·2m
D.	53°58'·02N 9°54'·43W	3·5m
E.	53°57'·78N 9°54'·53W	2·8m
F.	53°57'·53N 9°54'·72W	3·0m
G.	53°57'·21N 9°54'·80W	2·2m
H.	53°56'·99N 9°55'·19W	1·9m
I.	53°56'·83N 9°55'·29W	1·5m
J.	53°56'·51N 9°55'·21W	0·4m
K.	53°56'·31N 9°55'·41W	0·4m
L.	53°56'·05N 9°55'·36W	2·9m (moorings)
M.	53°58'·67N 9°54'·78W	3·1m
N.	53°58'·62N 9°54'·04W	7·9m
O.	53°58'·40N 9°53'·68W	5·8m
P.	53°58'·13N 9°53'·31W	5·4m
Q.	53°57'·98N 9°52'·92W	4·8m
R.	53°57'·96N 9°52'·23W	2·9m
S.	53°57'·59N 9°51'·72W	2·3m
T.	53°57'·93N 9°53'·63W	4·8m
U.	53°57'·67N 9°52'·97W	2·8m

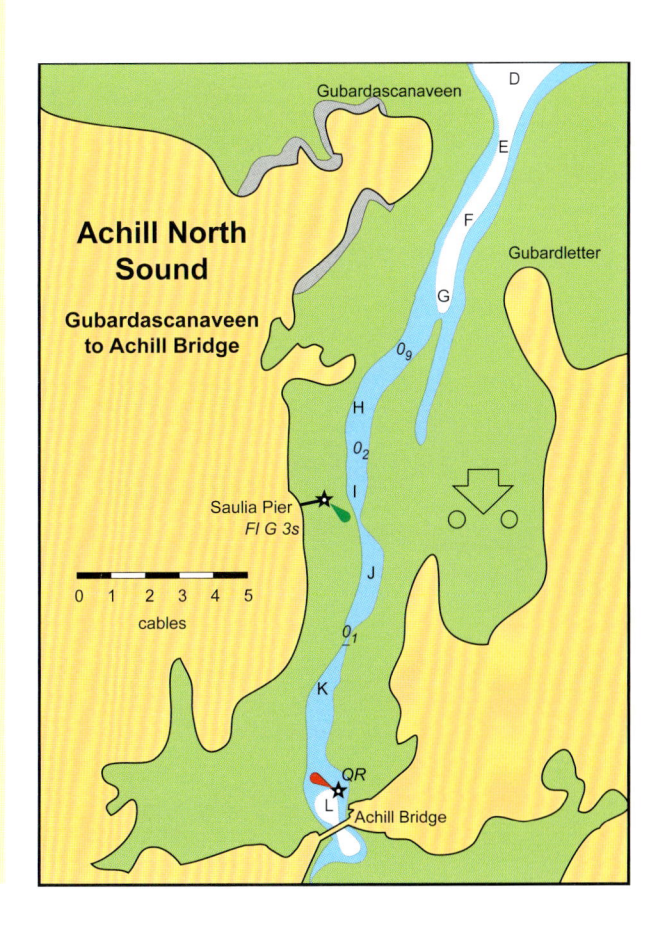

Inishbiggle; Bellacragher Bay

The jetty and anchorage at the W end of Inishbiggle, from the N

The anchorage at Illancroagh. Slievemore (Achill), R

Inishbiggle

Across the Bull's Mouth from Achill, Inishbiggle (pop. 25) is separated from the mainland by two narrow and tideswept channels on either side of the islet of Inishaghoo. Low power cables obstruct these, and also the channel between Annagh (to the SE) and the mainland.

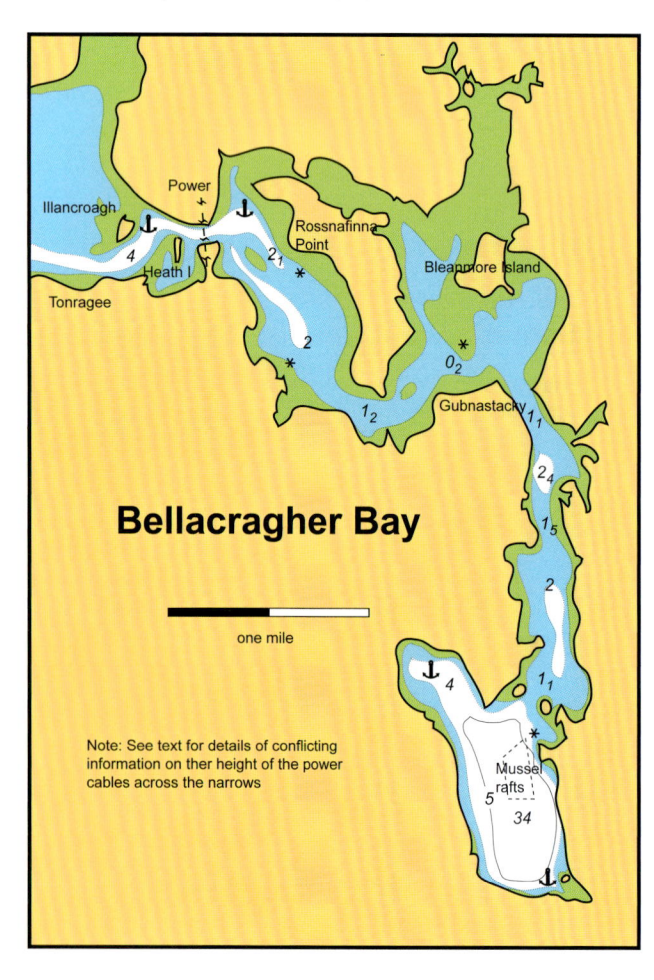

Bellacragher Bay

Note: See text for details of conflicting information on ther height of the power cables across the narrows

Inishbiggle has no anchorage which is both secure and with convenient access to the island. In settled weather temporary anchorage may be available close NE of the jetty on the N side of the Bull's Mouth, but beware of the drying rock 1·5 cables N of the light beacon. A yacht should not be left unattended here. Shallow-draft yachts, or those which can take the ground, can anchor in the shallows to the S of the island, taking care to avoid the uncharted rock drying 1·6m, 1·5 cables W of Hare Point. Deeper-drafted vessels may be able to use this spot around HW. Holding good in sand and mud; the beach is firm sand.

The island's pier is at Gubnadoogha at the NE end but is inaccessible to masted vessels. No facilities ashore.

Bellacragher Bay

Locally called Ballycroy Bay, this beautiful inlet is obstructed at its entrance by overhead 20kV power lines with a safe clearance charted at 10m. Although the cables were raised in 2004, measurements by the power network provider in September 2014 appeared to indicate that their height was unchanged. However a passage had been made safely in August 2014 by a 12m yacht with an air draft of 17·5m, on a tidal height of 2·4m, staying N of mid-channel, which seems to confirm a local report of 20m physical clearance (17m safe clearance). In view of this conflicting information, the greatest caution is advised.

Bellacragher Bay consists of a deep pool 1·5M by 0·5M, enclosed by steep hillsides and connected to Achill North Sound by a narrow and shallow channel 5M in length.

Directions

Entry is best made on a rising tide, with caution and continuous monitoring of the depth. Approach either N or S of the drying sandbank between Gubardletter and Annagh; the more S'ly of these channels has a least depth of 2·4m, N of Tonragee Pier. In the N channel, beware of Carrigthenoran, charted as drying 3·4m, but actually less than that. The channel then leads S of Illancroagh and N of Heath Island. The tide runs at 2 to 3 knots here. Once clear of the power cables, the drying bank W of Rossnafinna Point may be left on either hand. There are uncharted drying rocks 2 cables S of Rossnafinna Point, one cable off the SW shore and 2 cables SSW of Bleanmore Island.

Bellacragher and Tullaghan Bays

Tides
Bellacragher Bay
The narrows attenuate and delay the tide: HW at the entrance is at +0215 Galway (Bull's Mouth +0115) and in the upper Bay at +0300 Galway (Bull's Mouth +0200). Tidal streams run at 2 to 3 knots in the entrance and are significant in the narrow channels. The range in the upper Bay is clearly less than outside but no data are available.

The anchorage at Rossnafinna

The shallowest point is NW of Gubnastacky, where the channel almost dries. Stay 0·5 cables off the S shore on this stretch and hold mid-channel from the narrows at Gubnastacky to the Bay itself. There are mussel rafts and fish cages in the bay – skirt these to the W and keep a lookout for large floating ropes.

Anchorages

- In the pool between Illancroagh and Heath Island, as convenient out of the tide, in 3 to 6m.
- In the bay NW of Rossafinna Point. Bellacragher Bay Boat Club has its base here, and may be able to make a mooring available to a visitor. Phone 087 657 9348 for advice.
- In the N arm of the upper Bay, in 4m, mud.
- In the SE corner of the upper Bay, in 2 to 5m, mud and stones.

Facilities

The village of Mallaranny is a pleasant 1 km walk across the isthmus from the S end of the Bay. Supermarket, pubs/restaurants, hotel, PO and filling station at Mallaranny. The Greenway walking and cycle trail along the line of the old railway from Westport to Achill skirts the W side of the Bay and offers commanding views.

Tullaghan Bay

Tullaghan Bay, the extensive estuary of the Owenmore River, opens into the approaches to Achill North Sound, opposite Ridge Point. The Bay has wide drying sandbanks but is easy of access in moderate weather, and although subject to strong tidal streams, offers a pleasant anchorage in the channel E of Tullaghanbaun.

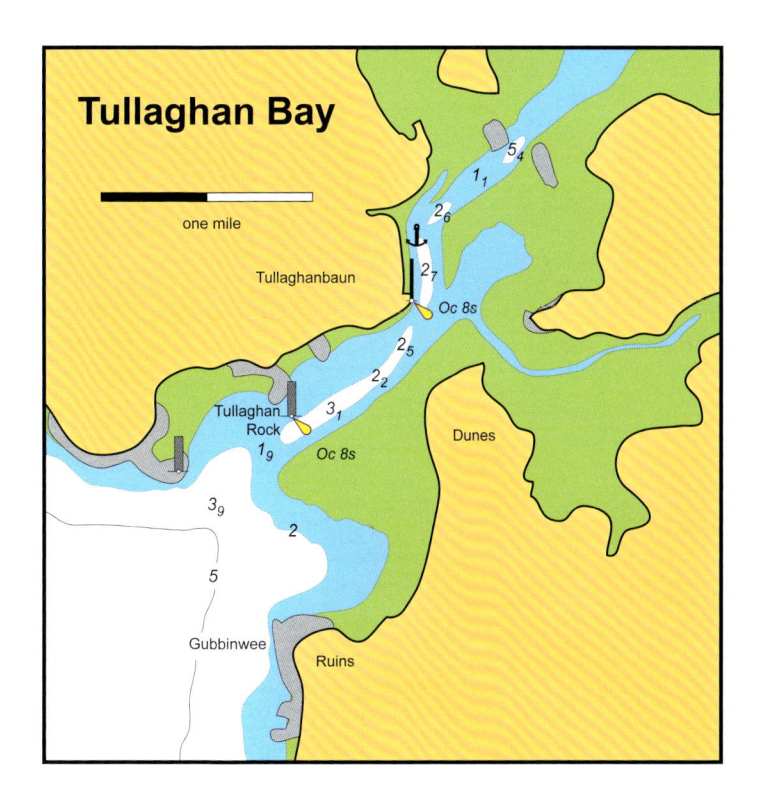

The SE end of Bellacragher Bay. The yacht has a centreboard - most boats would have to anchor further out

289

Clew Bay to Blacksod Bay

Tullaghan Bay from the SE. Gubbinwee, R

Tullaghan beacon from the S

Tullaghan Rock beacon from the S. The back mark at Tullaghanbaun, on the point at L

The anchorage at Tullaghanbaun

The Bills, from the S

Purteen harbour

Directions

The bay may be identified by the conspicuous sand dunes and ruins on Gubbinwee, to the S of the entrance. Approach steering NE and identify the concrete beacon marking the entrance. Leave it 0·5 cable to port, and the beacon on Tullaghan Rock 30m to port. The bar is halfway between the two, with a least depth of 1·9m at LAT. NE of Tullaghan Rock the deepest water is close to the bank on the SE side, but then keep the point at Tullaghanbaun, and the W shore to the N of it, close aboard. The tide runs at 2·5 to 3 knots in the channel. There is navigable water for a further 5 cables to the NE.

Anchor 2 cables N of the point at Tullaghanbaun in 2m, sand. No facilities ashore.

CLEW BAY to BLACKSOD BAY

Offshore passage

This rugged and remote coast is subject to the full rigours of the weather. Between Achillbeg and Clare Island there can be a confused sea on the SW-going tide, and there is a rough and confused sea close W of Achill Head in all but the lightest of winds. Black Rock, 6M NW of Achill Head, once had the dubious distinction of marooning its lighthousekeepers more often than any other station in Ireland. Blacksod Bay offers fine anchorages in one of the remotest parts of the mainland of Ireland. On the west and north coasts of Mayo between Clew Bay and Killala there are no towns or villages directly accessible by sea, and few facilities or sources of supply.

Bills Rocks

The Bills, 5·5M S by W of Keem Bay, are steep-to and 38m high; they are only 1M E of the line from Inishbofin to Achill Head, and though conspicuous by day are unlit and dangerous at night. They lie in a narrow intensified red sector of Achillbeg light.

Clew Bay to Blacksod Bay

Tides
Clew Bay to Blacksod Bay
N of Clare Island the W-going ebb stream out of Clew Bay reaches 1·5 kn. The streams offshore are weak, running S from about +0400 Galway to −0330 Galway and N at other times. Near the coast and around Achill Head they may attain 1·5 knots. The tide sets fairly N and S at the entrance to Blacksod Bay, turning at HW by the shore. The rate is 1 kn at springs.
Constant (Blacksod) +0030 Galway; MHWS 3·9m, MHWN 2·9m, MLWN 1·5m, MLWS 0·5m.

Dangers
Drying ledges 0·5M off shore, 2M NW of Achillbeg
Dysaghy Rocks (dry 3m), 5 cables S of Keem Bay
Drying and underwater rocks extending 2 cables S from Achill Head
Rock with 2·9m, in mid-channel between Achill Head and Carrickakin

Lights and Marks
Achillbeg Island, white tower Fl WR 5s 56m 18M, R 262°–281° W 281°–342°, R 342°–060° W 060°–092° R (intens) 092°–099° W 099°–118°, AIS. Shows white over the deep water NE of Clare Island, red over Clare Island and white to the W, with a narrow intensified red sector over the Bills Rocks.
Purteen leading lights Oc 8s
Purteen harbour, red pillar QR
Black Rock, white tower Fl WR 12s 86m W20M R16M, W 276°–212° R 212°–276°. Shows red to E and NE over Duvillaun and the Inishkeas, white elsewhere. AIS.
Tullaghan beacon, concrete pillar, unlit
Tullaghan leading beacons 047° Oc 8s, front concrete pillar on Tullaghan Rock, rear perch at Tullaghanbaun
Blacksod Point buoy, E Card Q(3) 10s
Blacksod Quay ldg lts 180°, orange triangles on posts Oc 5s 3M, front 5m rear 9m
Blacksod Quay, Fl R 3s 6m 3M
Blacksod Point, white tower Fl(2) WR 7·5s 13m W12M R9M, R 189°–210° W 210°–018°. Shows red over Carrigeenmore and close E of it, white elsewhere
Carrigeenmore perch, E Card VQ(3) 5s 3M
Saleen Pier leading lights 319°, Oc 4s 5M
Saleen Pier, 2FG vert

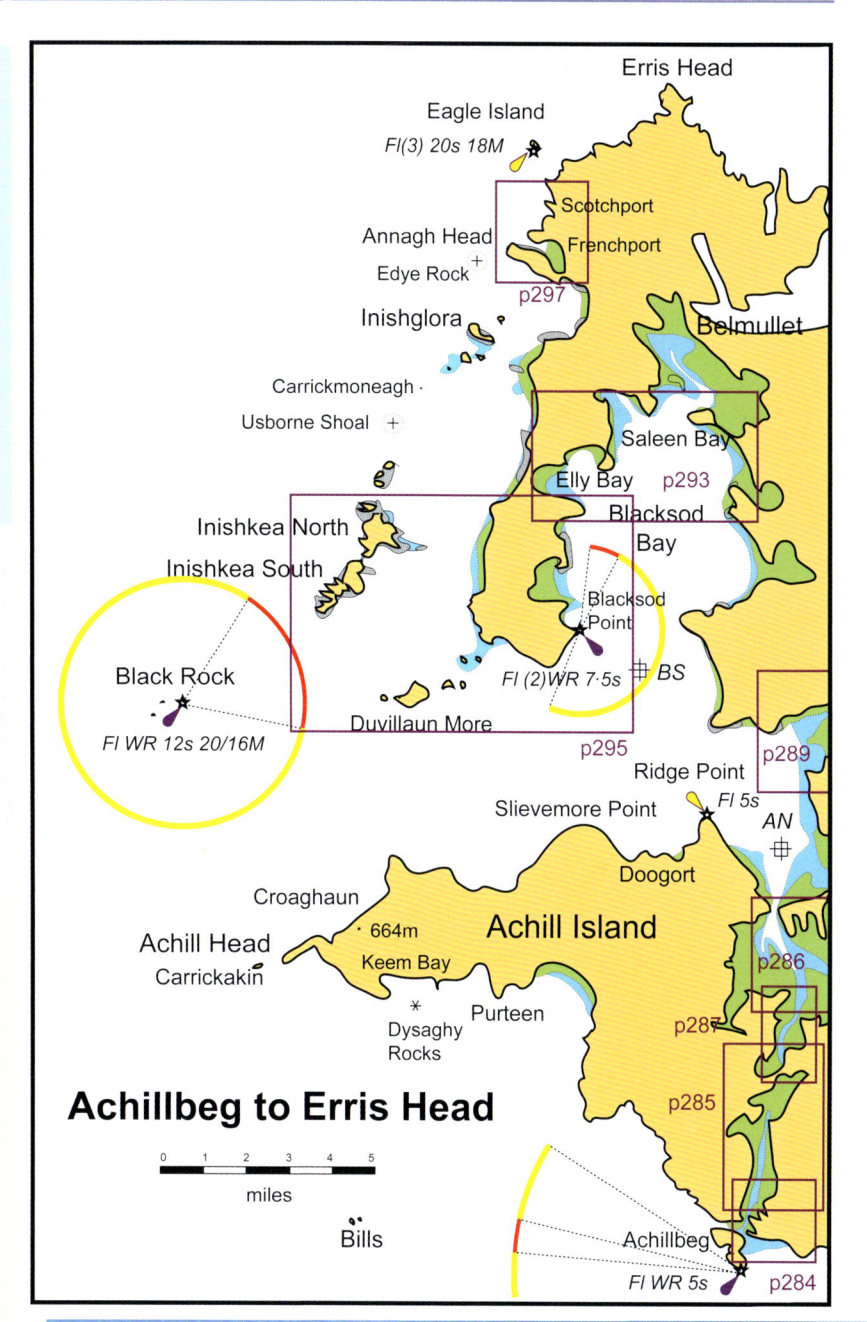

NW coast of Achill Island: the 664m cliffs of Croaghaun are the highest in Ireland, and the British Isles

291

Keem Bay and Achill Head

Keem Bay

Achill Head from the SW

Doogort Bay

Black Rock from the SE

Gubalennaun Beg (Purteen)

53°57'·6N 10°05'·5W

There is a small harbour at Purteen, N of Inishgalloon. The outer part, subject to swell, has about 1·3m at LWS along the W quay. Keel village, 2 km, has shops, restaurants, pubs and filling station.

Keem Bay

53°57'·8N 10°10'·8W

Keem Bay, 2·5M E of Achill Head, is an impressive amphitheatre surrounded by steep slopes rising to 300m cliffs on the seaward side. It offers a convenient passage anchorage in offshore winds but is subject to swell and heavy gusts off the slopes. The beach shelves suddenly; anchor in not less than 5m, sand.

Achill Head

AC2704

In heavy weather give the Head a berth of at least 2M, but in moderate conditions it is sufficient to pass 2 cables W of Carrickakin, and the magnificent spectacle of the Achill cliffs may compensate for any discomfort on the passage. The sea state is almost always confused and lumpy. In calm weather, it is possible to make the passage of the channel between Carrickakin and Achill Head, giving the S side of the Head a berth of 2 cables and staying E or W of mid-channel to avoid the 2·9m rock in the middle. This rock breaks heavily in bad weather. The Priest Rocks, above-water stacks close W of the Head, are steep-to on their W side.

There is anchorage on the N coast of Achill in offshore winds in 5m, sand, in Doogort Bay (Pollawaddy), 1M SE of Slievemore Point.

Achill Head from the N; Carrickakin R, the Bills top centre and Clare Island top L

Blacksod Bay

Black Rock

Black Rock (82m high) is 6M NNW of Achill Head. There are rocks above and below water up to 1·25M W and SW of Black Rock, other rocks close S of it and a clean 12m-high rock 0·5 cable E of it. At night or in heavy weather, it is safest to pass E of Black Rock.

Achill Sound, North Entrance

⊕ AN 54°00'·6N 9°55'·3W
AC2704, Imray C54 and Plan

For directions, see *Achill Sound, North of the Bridge*, above. Note that there are low overhead power cables across the tidal sounds separating Inishbiggle and Annagh and the shore to the E.

Blacksod Bay

⊕ BS 54°05'·2N 10°01'·3W
AC2704 and Plans

Blacksod Bay is accessible by day or night in any weather. A 14m shoal 1M S of Duvillaun Beg breaks heavily in gales but is easily avoided. From the S and Achill Head, steer to pass 5 cables W of Saddle Head, and leave Blacksod E Card buoy to port. **From the N,** give Turduvillaun and Duvillaun More a berth of 3 cables to port. In settled conditions with little swell, Duvillaun Sound, between Duvillaun Beg and Gaghta Island, offers a passage in 7m with the beacons on Inishkea South in line 317°.

Anchorages

- In the bay NW of Blacksod Pier, close NW of Blacksod Point, about halfway between the pier and Doonbeg Point, outside the moorings in 3m, sand. The pier consists of an L-shaped extension of about 50m from the original stone quay, and has a narrow dredged area alongside with enough water to lie afloat. Shop, filling station and PO, 2 km.
- Elly Bay, 3·5M N of Blacksod Point, is the most sheltered anchorage. Give the shore NW of Ardelly Point a berth of 2 cables, head W towards the moored boats and anchor outside them. Water and showers at the Adventure Centre 097 81488. Pub. Filling station and shop at Drum House, 2 km.

Blacksod Bay from the SW; Elly Bay, foreground, with Elly Harbour and Barranagh Island beyond.

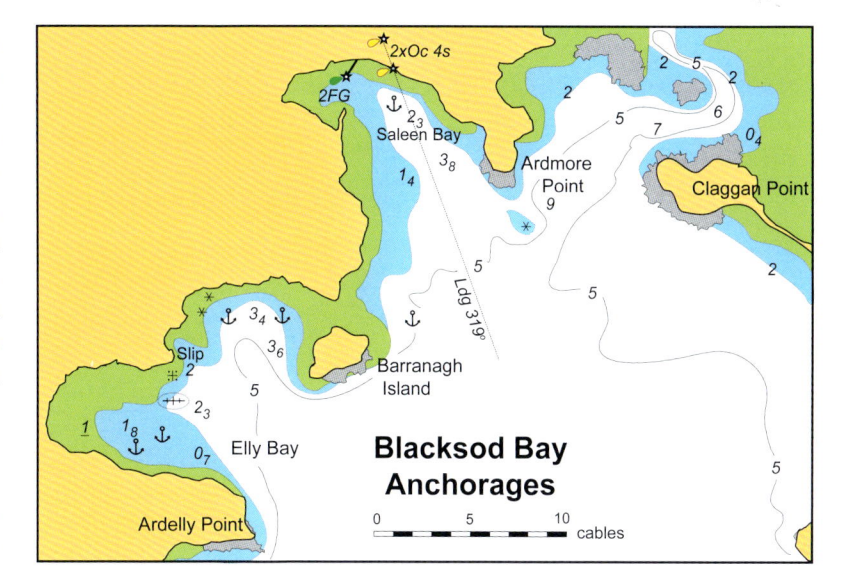

Tides
Blacksod Bay to Erris Head

The streams run S from about +0400 Galway to –0330 Galway and N at other times. Around Erris Head and Eagle Island they can reach 1·5 knots, with overfalls N of Eagle island and NW of Erris Head. There is a N-going eddy inside Eagle Island during the S-going tide. Constant (Blacksod) +0030 Galway; MHWS 3·9m, MHWN 2·9m, MLWN 1·5m, MLWS 0·5m.

Blacksod Bay to Erris Head

The beacons on Inishkea South lead through Duvillaun Sound

The Inishkeas and Rusheen; view from the summit of Inishkea South

Inishkea North

- Elly Harbour, W of Barranagh Island, is usually more liable to swell than Elly Bay but is calmer in N to E winds. Anchor in the middle of the bay.
- Saleen Bay, N of Barranagh Island, offers anchorage sheltered from SW to E, in 3m, sand, in the middle of the bay.

Dangers
Pluddany Rocks (dry 1·8m), 5 cables E of Inishkea North
Usborne Shoal, 2·1m, 2M N of Inishkea North
Carrickmoneagh (1m high), 2M SW of Inishglora
Edye Rock, 2·6m, 1M WSW of Annagh Head

Lights and Marks
Duvillaun Sound leading beacons 308°, white towers on Inishkea South, unlit 📷
Eagle Island, white tr Fl(3) 20s 67m 18M, AIS 📷

BLACKSOD BAY to ERRIS HEAD

AC2704, 2703

There is a clear channel inside the islands, partly sheltered from the swell and easily navigable in daylight.

Directions

Pluddany Rocks extend 6 cables E from Inishkea North; there is no passage between their drying heads and the island. To pass E of the rocks, keep Turduvillaun below the Ears of Achill 198°. The Ears are two prominent summits 7 cables E of Achill Head (*see photograph*). Heading N, it is useful to keep this transit astern until the small islands to the N are identified; then Shiraghy (the pyramidal 41m rock immediately E of Turduvillaun) in line with the Ears of Achill leads to the passage between Inishglora and the mainland, which is otherwise difficult to discern from the S. Duffur Rock (17m high), with its steep cliffs, is more distinctive from a distance than the Carricknaronty Rocks (2m and 3m high) SE of it. Inishkeeragh and the

Turduvillaun on the Ears of Achill leads E of Pluddany Rocks

The Inishkeas

Mullet Peninsula and the Inishkeas

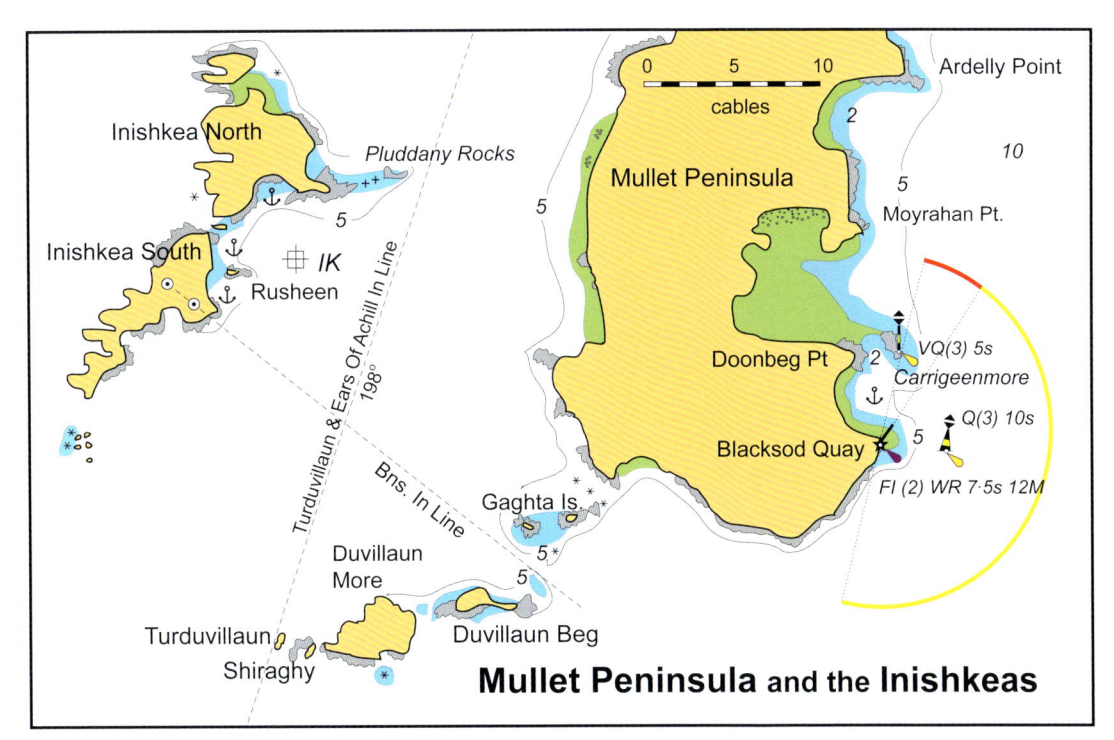

other islands are low and shelve gradually to the shore. Inishglora has ruined buildings on its E end. Heading N, before Inishkeeragh comes abeam, bring Leacarrick just open of Inishglora and then steer to pass close E of Leacarrick as the Mullet side is foul 5 cables offshore. In bad W weather the sea breaks right over Leacarrick and the passage E of it may be covered with foam.

If passing between the Inishkeas and Inishglora, note the **Usborne Shoal** and also **Carrickmoneagh** (1m high), SW of the Inishglora group.

North and South Inishkea

⊕*IK* 54°07'·3N 10°11'·1W
AC2704

These islands have a fascinating history and are well worth a visit. A Norwegian whaling station was set up on Rusheen in 1908, and the rusted remains of equipment may still be seen. The islands were evacuated in 1939. A few houses on Inishkea South are maintained in habitable condition.

Anchorages *(see Plan)*

- The bay N of Rusheen Island is the best anchorage. It is sheltered from S through W to N but is subject to swell, which can roll in through the narrow sound between the Inishkeas.
- Anchorage is also available in the bay SW of Rusheen Island.
- In NE winds better shelter may be found off North Inishkea SW of the 22m sandhill, between the outer ends of two reefs which extend 1·5 cables SW from the shore. The little bay thus formed has more reefs at its head.

Duffur from the S

Shiraghy on the Ears of Achill leads to the passage between Inishglora and Corraun Point

Inishglora

54°12'·1N 10°06'·9W

Inishglora has a hallowed place in Irish legend as the resting place of the mythical Children of Lir. There are ancient monastic remains on the island. Temporary anchorage, in settled weather, is available off the SE end of the island. A tripping line is recommended since the bottom is of rock and boulders.

Inishglora to Erris Head

Eagle Island (L) from the S: Cross Rock, centre

Inishkeeragh (lower L) from the S, with Inishglora and Leacarrick beyond. On the mainland side, Corraun Point, R, Annagh Head (upper L centre) and Eagle Island beyond

Inishglora to Erris Head
AC2703

From Leacarrick steer for Annagh Head. On the south-going tide there is a useful north-going eddy inside Eagle Island. In fine weather pass between Cross Rock and the mainland shore, but there can be a bad sea in this channel, and if at all rough it is better to go outside Eagle Island. Do not pass close to Carrickhesk, and give Erris Head a berth of 5 cables.

(above) Frenchport entrance, from the shore to the SW; Eagle Island in the distance, L. Wind S, force 6. The anchorage was calm.

(right) Scotchport

NW coast of the Mullet Peninsula, from the W; Eagle Island and Cross Rock L, Carrickhesk extreme L, Scotchport centre, Frenchport and Annagh Head R

Frenchport and Scotchport

Frenchport (Portnafrankagh)

⊕ *PF* 54°15'·0N 10°06'·4W
AC2703, Imray C54 and Plan

This inlet, immediately N of Annagh Head, is a popular haven for yachts sailing round Ireland as it involves no detour from the direct route. It provides safe shelter, but is subject to swell and should not be attempted in heavy onshore weather. A rock with 7·4m lies in mid-channel off the entrance, and may break; stay N of this, in the deepest water, in any significant swell. There is a rock drying 3·7m, 1 cable off the inlet on the S side of the entrance; Parson's Rock, awash at LAT, is 0·5 cable off the N point of the entrance. Enter in mid-channel and anchor off the S shore beyond the narrows in 4m, sand. The head of the inlet dries. There are no facilities ashore.

Scotchport (Portnanalbanagh)

54°15'·5N 10°05'·3W

Scotchport, just S of its eponymous rock on the chart, is a clean narrow inlet with rocky sides and a steep boulder beach at its head. It was used in former times as the base for rowing boats supplying the lighthouse on Eagle Island, and the boathouse and winch are still extant, with a memorial stone honouring the boatmen. The boathouse provides a convenient landmark for identifying the cove, which should be entered steering E then SE. Scotchport provides an interesting temporary anchorage in settled offshore weather.

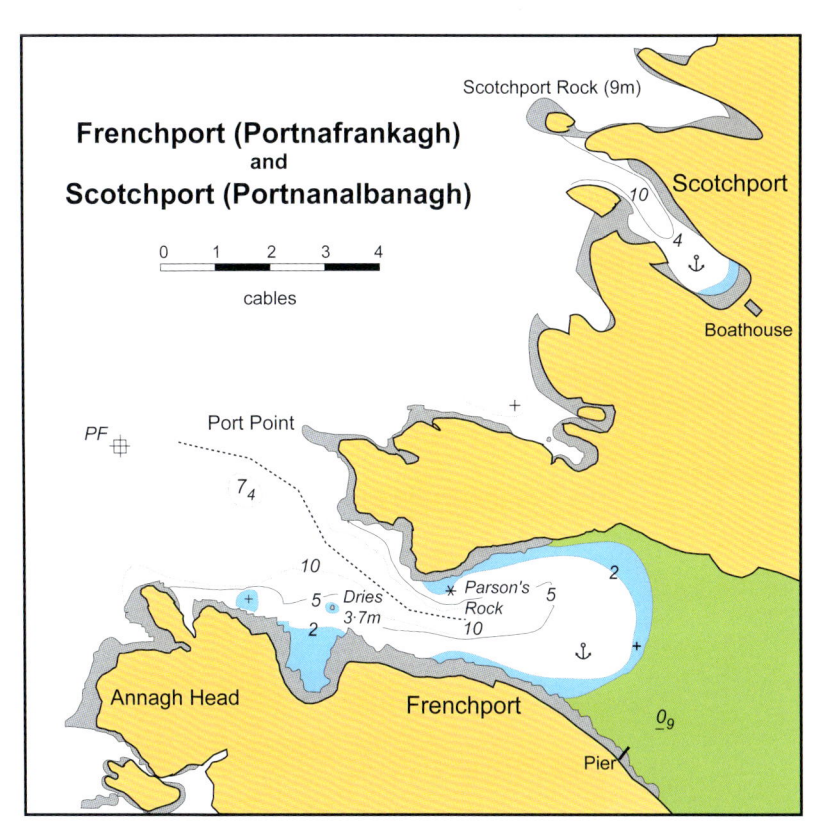

(above) Erris Head from the SW

(below) Frenchport from the SW; Annagh Head, foreground. Scotchport is the next inlet but one to the L

297

8 Broad Haven to Rathlin O'Birne

Anchored under the 597-metre cliffs of Slieve League, W of Killybegs in Donegal

"Cruising Ireland"
This coast is described on pages 128 to 145 of **Cruising Ireland**

The north coast of Mayo has some of the most spectacular cliffs in Ireland, backed by a Gaeltacht area with sweeping moorlands and remote communities. Between Broad Haven and Killala, 24 miles to the east, there are no good harbours, but this coast has some of the oldest known human settlements in Ireland – at the Céide Fields, near Belderrig, a complete Neolithic village has been discovered beneath the peat. Killala, though it can be tricky of access, offers perfect shelter.

The eastern side of the bight has three large sandy inlets leading to Ballysadare, Sligo and Donegal Town, and a stretch of rocky coast with the enchanting offshore island of Inishmurray and the harbour of Mullaghmore. This is Yeats Country, the homeland of Ireland's greatest poet, who is buried in Drumcliff churchyard "under bare Ben Bulben's head". The commercial port of Sligo has a handy yacht pontoon adjacent to its town centre, and the historic town of Donegal is accessible near HW. The fishing port of Killybegs has good technical services and one of the best natural harbours in the country. To the west are the cliffs of Slieve League, the second highest in Ireland, with Teelin nearby providing a convenient landfall or point of departure for a crossing of Donegal Bay. Many yachts choose to make the direct passage from Frenchport or Broad Haven to Teelin, or to Church Pool further north, but the cliff coasts and bays, harbours and Inishmurray to the east are a beautiful and rewarding cruising ground.

Broad Haven to Rathlin O'Birne

Erris Head to Sligo

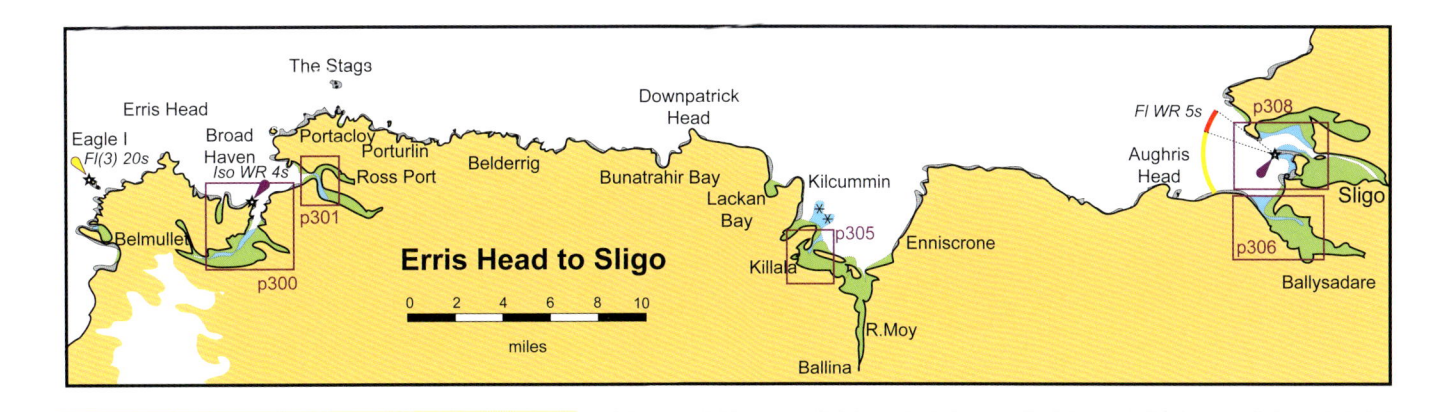

Paper Charts

AC2725 Blacksod Bay to Tory Island is the largest scale chart which shows the passage from Erris Head to west Donegal, and should be carried if passage-making around the coast. The medium-scale charts AC2703, 2767 and 2702 cover the whole coast described in this chapter, and are also essential, except that 2702 need not be carried if simply crossing from Mayo to west Donegal. The large-scale AC2792 is marginally useful for detail of Teelin and Killybegs; AC2715 is essential for Killala and AC2852 for Sligo. The Imray chart C53 Donegal Bay to Rathlin Island may be worth carrying but is no substitute for the Admiralty charts.

Caution

In many places on this coast the limited horizontal accuracy of the current charts means that GPS chart plotters must not be implicitly relied upon in close-quarters pilotage. Errors of up to 90 metres have been observed (note that this is distinct from any offset in horizontal datum). In addition many of the sandy inlets are subject to change, and the surveys may be up to 160 years old. Good visual pilotage must be maintained, with continuous attention paid to the depth.

Tides

On this coast HW occurs between +0035 and +0110 Galway. Spring tides rise between 3·7 and 4·1m and neaps between 2·7 and 3·0m above LAT. Offshore between Erris Head and Rathlin O'Birne the tidal set is negligible, and around the coast it is generally not significant. The tide however runs faster in the narrow harbour entrances, particularly that of Sligo; see below for details.

Broad Haven from the NW; Gubacashel (foreground), Gubaknockan and Ballyglass Pier (centre R), Inver Point (centre L) with Inver hamlet bay beyond. The long inlet (upper L), leading to Barnatra, dries.

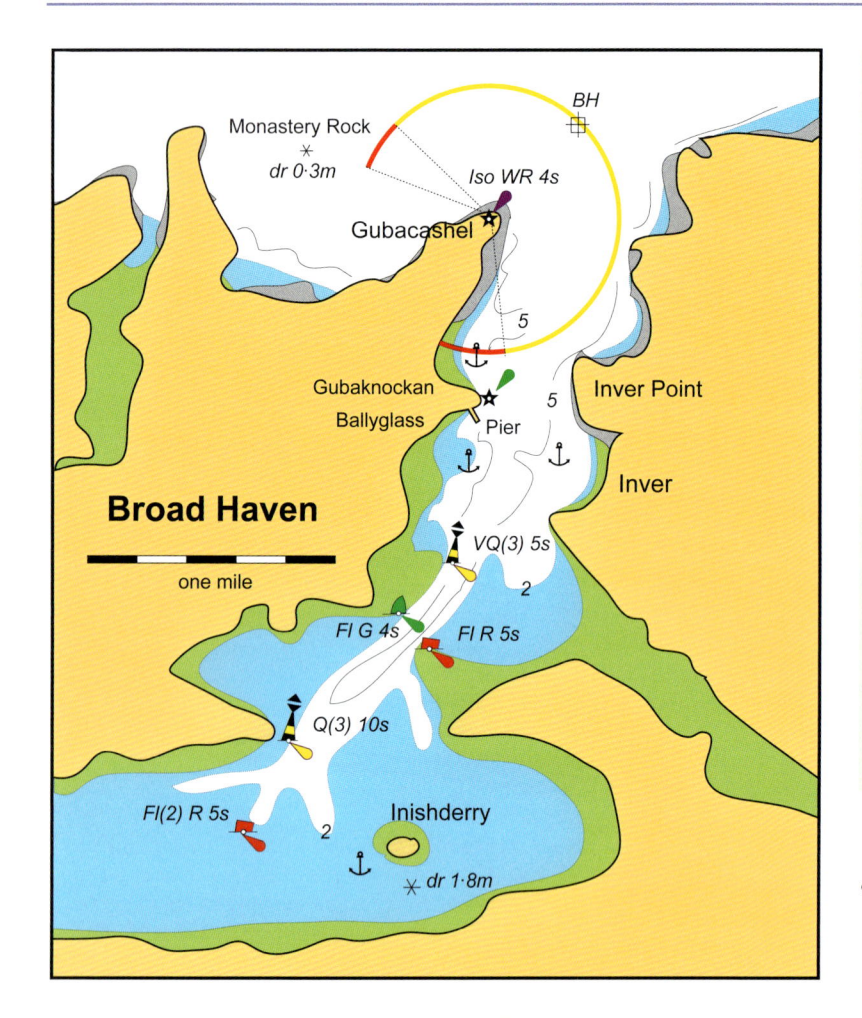

Broad Haven

Lights and Marks
Broad Haven

Gubacashel Point, 15m white tower Iso WR 4s 27m W12M R9M, R 110°–133°, W 133°–355°, R 355°–021°. Shows red inshore to the NW, and to the S over Gubaknockan Point and close E of it, and white elsewhere.
Ballyglass beacon, green pillar Fl G 3s.

Channel to Belmullet
Barret Point Cardinal buoy, E Card VQ(3) 5s
Barret Point Lateral buoy, SHM Fl G 4s
Fox Point buoy, PHM Fl R 5s
Shanaghy Point buoy, E Card Q(3) 10s
The channel to Belmullet is then marked by a further 5 port- and 8 starboard-hand buoys.

Broad Haven Bay
Rinroe Pier, Fl(2) 10s
Ross Port leading lights 082°, orange triangles on poles, Iso 4s

Gubaknockan Point and Ballyglass pier from the SE; Ballyglass starboard-hand beacon, extreme R, the lifeboat station, L. The Severn-class lifeboat lies on a mooring

BROAD HAVEN

⊕ BH   54°16'·6N 9°52'·7W
AC2703, Imray C54 and Plan

Broad Haven is a safe harbour in most summer winds, but a bad NW or N gale can cause the entrance to break right across. The approach across Broad Haven Bay is clear of all dangers except for **Slugga Rock** (1m high), on the E side, with a rock (drying 0·3m) 1 cable NW of it, and **Monastery Rock** on the S side, also drying 0·3m. The first 1·5M of the inlet is clean, but further S the channel leading to Belmullet lies between extensive shallows and is marked by buoys.

Anchorages

- In 3·5m about 2 cables N of Gubaknockan Point with Gubacashel Point in line with the W side of Kid Island. This is the most convenient anchorage, out of the main stream, with good shelter in winds from SW to NW, and accessible at night.
- South of Ballyglass pier in 3m with its outer end bearing 035°. This anchorage is somewhat exposed to the S, but sheltered from the N. The pier has 2m alongside but has sheet piling, so a fenderboard is required unless rafting up, and priority must be accorded to fishing vessels. Water on the pier and diesel by tanker. RNLI all-weather lifeboat. PO.
- In strong E wind the best shelter is in 3·7m, close to shore about 1 cable S of Inver Point, opposite Ballyglass. For convenient landing, anchor further S in 3m about 2 cables offshore in Inver Hamlet Bay. Small shop at Inver; filling station, PO and shop at Barnatra, 5 km S by road and at least partly accessible by dinghy at HW.

All the above are somewhat subject to swell. Anchorage in strong winds from the S is reported to be available near the S shore of Broad Haven, close SW of Inishderry; careful sounding is required to reach this spot from Shanaghy Point buoy. The rock 1·5 cables SSE

Tides - Broad Haven

The tide runs at up to 1·5 kn past the anchorages. Constant +0045 Galway; MHWS 3·7m, MHWN 2·8m, MLWN 1·4m, MLWS 0·5m.

Belmullet and Ross Port

Ross Port from the W; Sandy Point L, Rossport House top R

(below) Ross Port leading beacons (with orange topmarks), centre

of Inishderry dries 1·8m, not 0·3m as on older charts.

Belmullet

The channel to Belmullet, in the SW corner of Broad Haven, is buoyed and lit, but dries at LW and is not recommended for visiting yachts. There is no convenient berth in Belmullet. The buoyage is provided principally for the safety of small fishing craft, which take shelter in Belmullet when moorings at Ballyglass become untenable in winter gales from the S. Belmullet (2,010) has supermarkets, shops, PO, pubs, restaurants, doctors, and is best reached by taxi (097 81176) from Ballyglass.

Broad Haven Bay

In moderate weather or with wind N of W there is a convenient anchorage on the NE side of the bay, E of Rinroe Point. Give the point a berth of 1·5 cables and anchor E of it in 3 to 4m, off the pier. This is a handy place to wait for the tide on the bar to Ross Port. Shop, PO at Carrowteige, 1·5 km.

Ross Port

54°17'·4N 9°50'·4W
AC2703 and Plan

This narrow creek inside the sandbanks offers good shelter but the tide in the anchorage runs at 4 to 5 knots at springs. The outer entrance across a bar with 1m at LAT is navigable only in settled conditions and in daylight (although the leading beacons are accurate). Note that the area on the W side of the narrows, marked on the chart as "Sand Dunes", has suffered erosion and now consists of a high drying sandbank and several grass-topped heads above HW *(see aerial photograph)*. The pipeline from the offshore Corrib gas field comes ashore here.

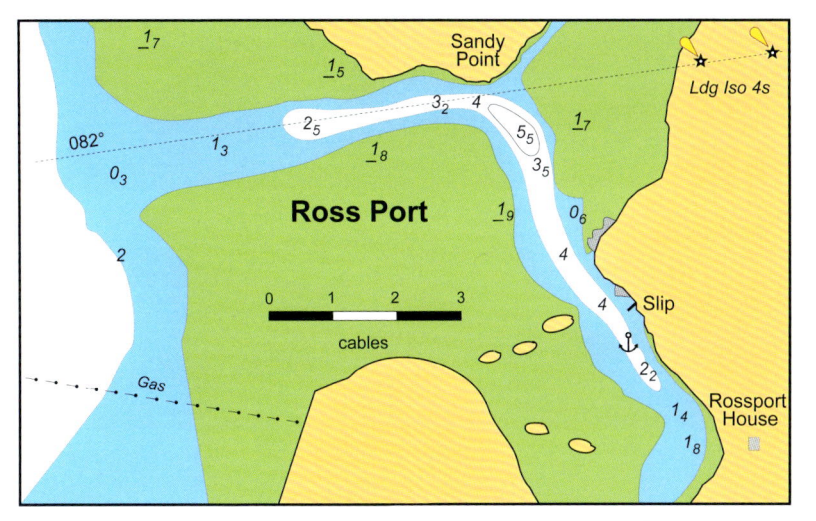

Ross Port

Directions

Identify the leading marks from offshore and follow their line across the bar. When Sandy Point is abeam turn to starboard and head 147° towards the middle of the narrows

301

Broad Haven Bay to Killala Bay; Portacloy

(above) Benwee Head and Kid Island

(below) The Stags of Broad Haven, L; Parson Rock, Knife Rock and Benwee Head, R

The Buddagh (R) at the entrance to Portacloy

Portacloy

Porturlin; Harbour Rock buoy, centre R

View from the NE; entrances to Porturlin (centre) and Portacloy (R)

Lights - *Porturlin*
Carrickduff beacon, PHM Fl R 5s 3M
Glassillaun beacon, SHM Fl(2) G 5s 3M
Harbour Rock buoy, SHM Fl(2) G 10s

between the E shore of the inlet and the grassy sand islets off the W shore. Beyond the narrows and past the slip, keep close to the E shore.

Anchorage

Anchor 1 to 1·5 cables to the S of the slip. There is depth further S but the channel becomes narrow, with sand and gravel banks extending from the W shore, and it may be necessary to moor to two anchors. Do not go further S than the ruined Rossport House.

Facilities

Shop, pub and PO at Ross Port on the E side; pub at Pollatomish further in on the W side and accessible by dinghy, with careful timing to suit the tidal stream. Dooncarton stone circle and megalithic tomb, 1·5 km along the road towards Barnatra on the W side of the inlet, are worth a visit.

BROAD HAVEN BAY to KILLALA BAY

The 24M stretch from Broad Haven Bay to Killala Bay is high, rugged and spectacular, with cliffs up to 300m and offlying stacks, and in most conditions should be given a good berth; there is no good anchorage, no shelter from the usual swell, and often fierce gusts off the cliffs. The coast is sparsely inhabited. There are five bays offering possible passage anchorages; Portacloy and Belderrig are the best of these, though somewhat subject to swell. The Stags of Broad Haven are a spectacular group of four rocky islets 70 to 92m in height, with deep water all round. There is a clear passage 1M wide between the Stags and the mainland coast. SE of Conaghra Point, the Ceide Fields visitor centre, a conspicuous pyramidal building on the hillside, is a useful landmark.

Portacloy

54°20'·7N 9°46'·3W
AC2703

The inlet, close E of the conspicuous Buddagh stack, is about 1·5 cables wide and has clean rock shores and a beach at its head; plenty of room to anchor, a sand bottom and good holding. It is sheltered from winds from E through S to W although fresh to strong S winds funnel down the inlet. The pier has 0·4m near its outer end.

Porturlin to Killala

Porturlin
54°19'·7N 9°42'·2W
AC2703 and 2767

Porturlin is 2·5M E of Portacloy and is well marked and lit, with better shelter. However the inlet is mostly taken up by fishing-boat moorings and the holding is reported poor.

Belderrig Harbour
54°19'·5N 9°33'·2W
AC2767 and Plan

Belderrig ("Belderg" on the chart) is at the E end of the high cliffs stretching E from Broad Haven Bay. Carrickneill, E of the entrance to Belderrig, covers at HW except for two small heads. The disused boathouse shows up well from due N but is obscured from NE and NW. A newer and similar building stands E of it, at the SE corner of the rocky gut; this gut is too narrow for anchoring, but has a breakwater and a slip for dinghy landing. Anchor in less than 10m off the inner half of the W shore of the bay, good holding on sand. PO, pub and shop at Belderrig village, 1·5 km.

Bunatrahir Bay
54°18'·7N 9°22'·7W

East of Belderrig the coast is lower, with 30m cliffs backed by gentle grass slopes, and the overhanging cliff of Downpatrick Head (35m) is conspicuous. Bunatrahir Bay has gentler surroundings than Belderrig but the bottom is rock and provides poor holding. Hotel on W side of the bay; shops, pubs and PO at Ballycastle, 2 km.

Lackan Bay
54°17'·6N 9°14'W

Lackan Bay is exposed and subject to swell. Rathlackan Pier, on its W side, is not normally suitable for alongside berthing. No facilities ashore. In most winds, Kilcummin offers better shelter.

KILLALA BAY
54°15'·5N 9°08'·4W
AC2715 and Plan

The historic village of Killala, with its small fishing harbour, lies behind a bar with 0·3m, in the SW corner of Killala Bay, 5M wide between Kilcummin Head and Lenadoon Point and exposed to the N. The 13th-century Round Tower at Killala is a prominent landmark.

(top) Belderrig; the newer boathouse, L centre

(above) Bunatrahir Bay

(left) Downpatrick Head

Kilcummin

Caution
As of 2011 GPS chart plotters cannot be implicitly relied upon in the close approaches to Killala due to the limited horizontal accuracy of the charts. It is essential to maintain good visual pilotage with continuous use of the echo sounder.

Kilcummin Roads
54°16'·3N 9°12'·2W

This passage anchorage on the W side of Killala Bay 1M S of Kilcummin Head gives a surprising amount of shelter in winds from SW through W to N. Anchor S of the pier, which has 0·6m at LAT alongside. There are visitors' moorings. Pub above the pier.

303

Killala

Killala from the SW; Bartragh Island centre and River Moy entrance top R. The training walls are visible, L centre. The Round Tower, lower R centre

Dangers - Killala Bay

Unnamed rocks with 1·6 and 1·8m, 1 cable offshore E and SE of Kilcummin Head.
St Patrick's Rocks, a drying reef extending 1M N and 9 cables E of Ross Point, has two principal heads in **Bone Rock** (dries 3m) and **Carrickpatrick** (dries 1·5m). The E side of the bay is foul up to 5 cables offshore for 2M S of Lenadoon Point.

Lights and Marks

Bone Rock perch, N Card Q
Carrickpatrick buoy, E Card Q(3) 10s
Killala buoy, SHM Fl G 6s
Killala leading beacons, white pillars with red triangles, three pairs as follows:
Rinnaun Point Idg Its 230°, Oc 10s 5M, front 7m, rear 12m
Inch Island, rear Dir WRG 2s 6m 3M, G 205°–213° W 213°–217° R 217°–225°. Shows white over the approach channel, green to W, red to E; front leading beacon, unlit
Kilroe Idg Its 196°, Oc 4s 2M, front 5m, rear 10m
Killala Pier Idg Its 236°, white diamonds on poles, Iso 2s 2M, front 5m, rear 7m.

Entrance to Killala; Rinnaun Point leading beacons, R

Killala

⊕KL   54°14'·2N 9°10'·7W
AC2715 and Plan

The bar should not be attempted with a fresh NE wind, and is best negotiated on a high and rising tide. **From the N or NE**, head for Carrickpatrick buoy, then steer 210° past Killala buoy and identify the white-painted leading beacons on Rinnaun Point. Steer across the bar on the leading line of these beacons 230° until the Inch Island beacons come in line bearing 215°. Hold this course for 2 cables, then turn on to the line of the Kilroe beacons on the S shore, 196°. This line leads close W of the steep beach on Bartragh Island; when immediately S of the W tip of the island, identify the leading beacons on the pier and steer on their line, 236°. The channel to the pier is bordered by old training walls which cover at HW but are clearly marked by poles.

From the W, give Bone Rock beacon a berth of 5 cables. It is normally possible to pass up to 3 cables W of Carrickpatrick buoy, but Carrickpatrick Rock is dangerous if it is not showing up by breaking.

Anchorage

Anchor in 5 to 7m, sand, in Bartragh Pool, 1 cable SW of the W tip of Bartragh Island. Tidal streams here are strong and the sandbanks steep-to, so adequate swinging room must

Killala; River Moy; Enniscrone; Pollacheeny

be assured. Anchorage further down the channel inside the bar is possible, but be sure to show an anchor light. The bay to the N of the bar offers a feasible passage anchorage but is very subject to swell.

Harbour

A depth of 1·5m at LWS is available only at the N end of the pier; if there are fishing boats alongside, raft up to the outermost trot with permission, but in any case be prepared to move at short notice. There is a wide slipway on the NW side of the pier. The S and E parts of the harbour are shallow. Constant +0045 Galway; MHWS 3·8m, MHWN 2·7m, MLWN 1·5m, MLWS 0·4m.

Facilities

Water on the pier. Diesel by tanker. Shops, pubs, PO, restaurants, wi-fi and laundry in Killala village, 1 km.

River Moy

Before 1940 Ballina (10,360) was a minor commercial port. The Moy has a shallow and very hazardous bar at its mouth, but good unlit marks in the channel as far as Ballina Quay (5M from the entrance), and is used routinely by local small craft. The river marks were replaced in 2011 following damage by floating ice in the fast-flowing river in December 2010. Unfortunately the bar is very mobile and no consistently reliable directions can be provided for a stranger, although the Galway hooker *MacDuach* (see page 23) visited Ballina Quay in 2015. For pilotage assistance phone 096 22183.

Enniscrone (*Inishcrone* on the charts)

54°13'·2N 9°06'·2W

The village is a seaside resort and is conspicuous in the SE corner of Killala Bay. The breakwater runs out 280° and its S side is a quay 130m long, but a yacht can go alongside only at or above half tide when the depth near the outer end just beyond the steps is 2m. Two concrete pillars in line mark the S end of the channel to the slip. The quay is subject to swell.

East side of Killala Bay

This coast is bordered by extensive flat drying reefs. For 3M N of Enniscrone it should be given a berth of 3 cables and between Pollacheeny and Lenadoon Point

Entrance to Killala; (above) Inch Island leading beacons, L

(left) Kilroe leading beacons, centre R

Approach to Killala pier; the SE training wall, L. The Round Tower, extreme L

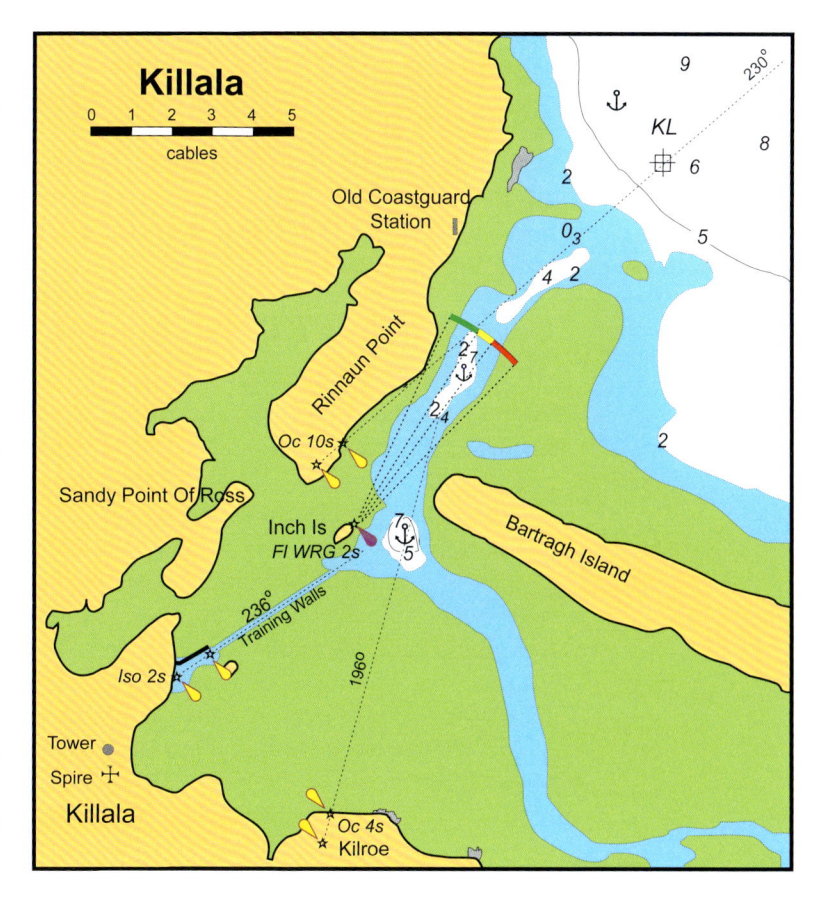

305

Killala to Sligo; Aughris Hole and Ballysadare

Aughris Hole from the NE

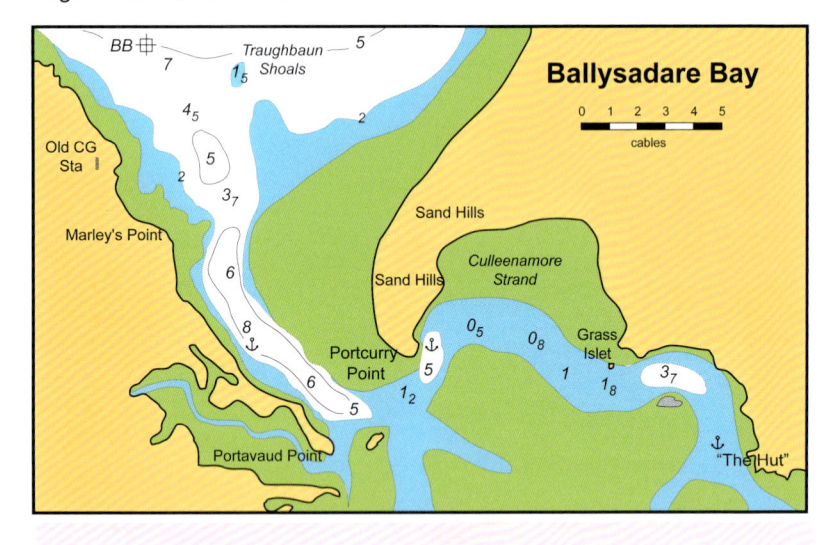

Caution

GPS chart plotters should not be implicitly relied upon in Ballysadare Bay due to the age of the survey data and the likelihood of changes in the channel and sandbanks. It is essential to maintain good traditional pilotage with continuous use of the echo sounder.

a berth of 8 cables. **Pollacheeny Harbour**, named on AC2715, is just a gap between the drying rocks and offers little shelter. For entry (in winds between NE and SE, and no swell) identify the slip from 3 cables out and approach between 085° and 090° to avoid rocks on either side.

Coast between Killala Bay and Sligo Bay

From Lenadoon Point to Aughris Head, 11M further E, the coast is fringed by rocky ledges and should be given a berth of at least 5 cables. Pollnadivva Harbour in Dromore Bay is not recommended even in calm weather; it dries with a rocky bottom alongside. The pier shows a light Fl G 5s 3M. There are no facilities ashore. Aughris Head ends in an overhanging cliff; rocks awash at HW extend 1·5 cables seaward from it. **Cooanmore Bay**, inside **Temple Rock** 1M E of the conspicuous tower at the mouth of the Easky River, offers temporary anchorage from winds from SW through S to SE. Shops and pubs at Easky village, 1·5 km.

SLIGO BAY

AC2767, 2852

The entrance is 4M wide between Aughris Head to the SW and **Seal Rocks** (1m high) to the NE. Midway between these points is **The Ledge** (8m) which breaks with a high swell, when it is simplest to pass S of it. Within the points of the bay are off-shore anchorages in Aughris Hole and Brown Bay. The principal sailing centre is Rosses Point in the entrance to Sligo.

Aughris Hole

54°16'·9N 8°44'·5W

Aughris Hole, on the E side of Aughris Head, provides shelter in winds from SE to SW. At LW a ridge of rock protects the anchorage from the E. Below-water rocks extend halfway from this ridge towards the W shore. Having given Aughris Head a suitable berth the shore is clean to the quay, off which there is anchorage in 2·7m, sand and stones. In W wind, a swell rolls in, particularly with the flood tide. The quay gives no protection from this and a yacht should not attempt to go alongside. Pub 400m, shop 1·5 km.

Ballysadare Bay

⊕BB 54°16'·3N 8°38'·7W
AC2767 and Plan

This large enclosed bay is mostly occupied by drying sandbanks but may be entered in most conditions, has a navigable channel and offers a delightful anchorage in the lee of the sand dunes at Portcurry. Note however that AC2767 is based on a survey carried out in 1852.

Directions

The entrance 3M S of Raghly Point and 4M E of Aughris Head can be approached in any moderate weather but should not be attempted by a stranger in a swell from the NW. The passage over the bar in 3·7m is narrow, so reliable power and good visibility are necessary. Entry near LW is simplest, as

306

Ballysadare and Sligo

the banks and rocks then show, but there is a least depth of 1·2m S of Portcurry Point. The directions below for entry and the channel as far as the Portcurry anchorage, long established, were re-verified by a yacht in 2011.

From the N and Sligo, avoid **Traughbaun Shoals** by staying N and W of a line of bearing 210° on the old Coastguard station (now a private house) S of Derkmore Point. When about 2 cables from the shore steer 153° for the E extremity of Portavaud Point, which is inconspicuous, low and flat with bent-grass; on this bearing it is below Carricknasheeogue, an isolated rock like a tooth on the skyline of the hills 5M away, which is conspicuous unless hidden by cloud. This course of 153° clears stony spits extending more than a cable from Marley's Point. When just past Marley's Point, and before it bears W, alter course to 180° until within a cable of the HW mark of the W shore, and then continue in at that distance off. When Portcurry Point comes in line with the N slope of Knocknarea bearing 062°, steer 096° towards the tree-clad SE slope of Knocknarea. When Black Rock lighthouse (at the entrance to Sligo) closes behind the W side of the sandhills N of Portcurry Point steer 073° towards the middle of Knocknarea. The Golf Club building N of Culleenamore Strand is conspicuous, and beyond it Benbulben Mountain with a 45° slope beneath its vertical brow. When the Golf Club building comes under the centre of this slope, turn on to this transit line (038°) which leads between Portcurry Point and the sandbank E of it.

Anchorage

The best anchorage, sheltered from W and NW winds, is E of Portcurry Point, close to the shore. There is about 3m at LAT opposite the high sandhill behind the NE corner of the point. The beach is very steep-to. There is also a possible anchorage near the moorings SE of Marley's Point, although the tidal stream here is strong.

The Hut, SW of Knocknarea, is an old two-storey house on a point just above the only public slip in the bay; a lane runs up from it to the main road. The anchorage NW of the Hut is sheltered from E winds. To reach this spot, start from Portcurry Point 2 hours after LWS, or at LWN, when the channel should be deep enough but the banks still visible. Steer

(right) Ballysadare; the old CG station S of Derkmore Point

(below) Ballysadare entrance from the NW; Carricknasheeogue (R) on the skyline

(bottom) Knocknarea from the W

(below) Ballysadare; the anchorage E of Portcurry, with the Golf Club building below Benbulben to the N. Portcurry Point beach, L

114° towards the Hut until the grass islet is abeam, then steer 090° until the point E of it is abeam; then head NE to avoid the rocky N end of the bank. When past it, steer SE, and anchor NW of the Hut. Ballysadare village is 5M further SE at the head of the drying bay, and is inaccessible by sea.

SLIGO

⊕ SO 54°18'·7N 8°38'·8W
AC2852, Imray C54 and Plan

The port of Sligo is used by small cargo vessels and is reached by a channel S of Raghly Point and Rosses Point and N of Oyster Island. Sligo (19,450) is the principal town of the region. Sligo YC is located at Rosses Point.

Directions

From the N, keep 2 cables W of Seal Rocks and leave Wheat Rock buoy to port. **From the W** in fine conditions it is simplest to head towards Black Rock lighthouse until Wheat

Sligo

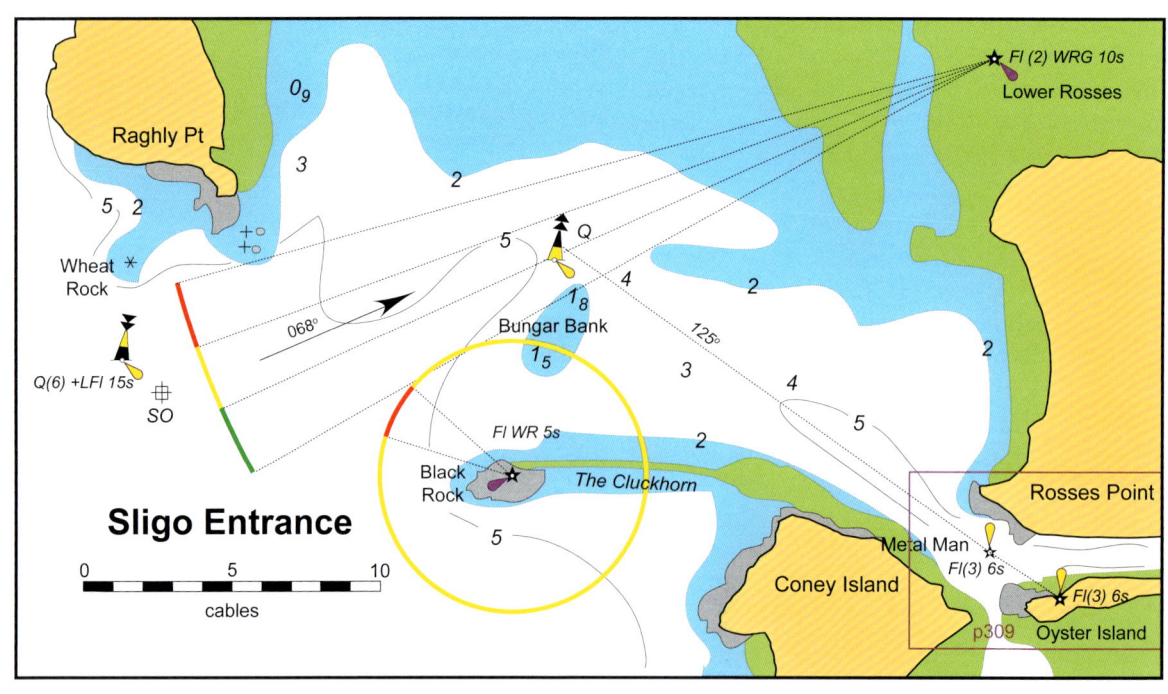

Dangers - Sligo

The Ledge, 8·5m, 2m NE of Aughris Head (breaks in gales)
Wheat Rock, dries, 4 cables SW of Raghly Point
Raghly Ledge, dries 0·3m, 3 cables SE of Raghly Point
Black Rock, dries, 1·2M SE of Raghly Point, with **The Cluckhorn**, drying boulder ridge running E to Coney Island
Bungar Bank, 1·5m, 5 cables NNE of Black Rock
Blennick Rocks, drying, 2 cables E of Oyster Island

Lights and Marks

Wheat Rock buoy, S Card Q(6)+L Fl 15s, AIS
Lower Rosses, white hut on piles, Fl(2) WRG 10s, 8m 10M, G 061°–066°, W 066°–070°, R 070°–075°. Shows white over the approach from the WSW, green to the S, red to the N
Black Rock white tower, black band, Fl WR 5s, W 130°–107° R 107°–130°. Shows red over Wheat Rock, white elsewhere
Bungar Bank buoy, N Card Q, marks the N side of the bank.
Leading lights 125°, Fl(3) 6s, front on **Metal Man Rocks**, rear on **Oyster Island**, lead from Bungar Bank buoy and between Deadman's Point and Coney Island. Metal Man Rocks are marked by a pillar surmounted by a 4m statue of a sailor in 19th-century uniform, with an outstretched arm pointing up the channel to the port of Sligo, and are to be left to starboard
No 2 (YC West) buoy, PHM Fl R 1·5s
No 4 (YC East) perch, PHM Fl R 3s 2M
Lifeboat beacon, PHM QR 2M
No 1 (Oyster NE) beacon, SHM Fl(3) G 4s
No 6 (January) beacon, PHM Fl(2) R 6s
No 8 (Blennick Rock West) beacon, PHM Fl R 2s
No 10 (Blennick Rock East) beacon, PHM Fl(4) R 10s
No 3 (The Pool) buoy, SHM QG
No 5 (Old Seal Bank) beacon, SHM Fl G 1·5s
No 7 (Start Wall) beacon, SHM Fl G 3s, marks the outer end of the training wall. From there to Sligo town the channel is marked by a further 16 beacons and two port-hand buoys
Coney Island Pier, Fl 5s 2m 2M

Rock buoy is visible, and then head for the buoy. If there is appreciable swell, avoid **The Ledge** by keeping 1M off Aughris Head and continuing E for 2M before heading for Wheat Rock buoy; to pass N of The Ledge the N end of Coney Island should be just N of Black Rock lighthouse bearing 098°. From 2 cables S of Wheat Rock buoy, head for Lower Rosses beacon or (if the distant and inconspicuous beacon is not identified) steer 068°. Leave Bungar Bank buoy to starboard and bring the Metal Man and Oyster Island beacons in line to the SE. Follow this line, and when 0·5 cable from the Metal Man, turn to pass close NE of him.

Coney Island, which shelters the harbour from the W, is connected to the S shore by a causeway running 1·3M SE across the drying sandbank. The causeway covers at HWS. There is a pier on Coney Island opposite the Metal Man.

Rosses Point

AC2852 and Plan

This is a less-than-ideal anchorage as the holding is poor in sand, the tide is strong and there is a short, steep chop in a fresh wind.

Tides

In the narrows between Rosses Point and Oyster Island the tide runs at 5 to 6 kn springs, turning at HW and LW by the shore. Constant +0050 Galway; MHWS 4·1m, MHWN 3·0m, MLWN 1·6m, MLWS 0·5m.

Sligo

Rosses Point from the W; the Metal Man, lower centre, with Oyster Island beyond. Coney Island Pier, bottom R; Deadman's Point and Sligo YC clubhouse, bottom L. Sligo town, top R

Anchor in line with the local moored yachts, or just outside them, taking care not to obstruct the shipping channel. A temporary berth may be available at the head of the pier, where the tide is not so strong. In settled weather a temporary anchorage on sand is possible off the Yacht Club at Deadman's Point. RNLI inshore lifeboat. Shops at Rosses Point village, showers and bar at the YC, 071 9177168.

Sligo Harbour

AC2852 essential

The channel to Sligo runs for 4M E and SE from Oyster Island, and for all but the first mile is bounded by training walls. It is well marked by lit perches and buoys. From the perch on the E end of Oyster Island steer 120°, leaving the beacons marking Blennick Rocks to port and the Pool buoy and Old Seal Bank and Start Wall beacons to starboard. For the next 2M the training wall should be left close to starboard. The training wall on the port hand begins where the channel turns SE for the last 1M stretch to the town; here the deepest water is close to the port-hand marks. Stay close to the deepwater quay on the SW side but then leave the last starboard-hand marks, which are in mid-channel, on the proper hand when approaching the pontoon.

Approaches to Sligo; the Metal Man and Oyster Island light in line

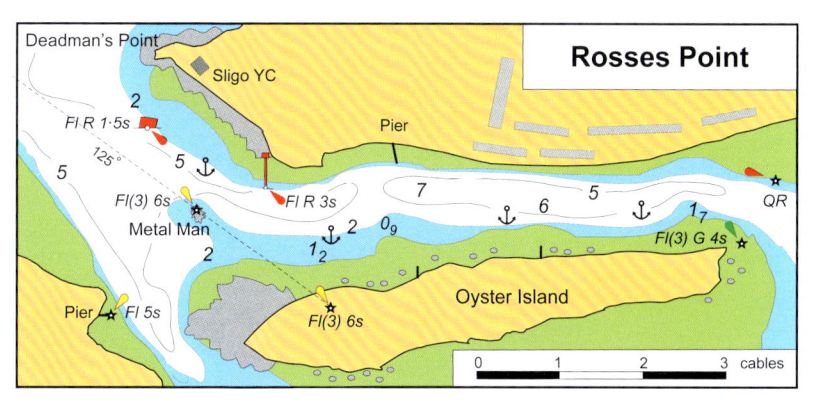

Approaches to Sligo; the Yacht Club at Rosses Point

309

Sligo to Mullaghmore

Pontoon facility

There is a 60m-long pontoon with 2m depth alongside on the SW side of the river at Sligo, with water, shore power and security gate. Contact HM 071 911 1237, mobile 086 089 0767. Sligo has all the facilities of a large port town including medical services, train connections to Dublin and an airport (at Strandhill, N of Ballysadare Bay). Sailmaker, Sunset Sails 071 916 2792. Small chandlery at Inland Inflatables, Cleveragh Business Centre 071 914 4766. Diesel by cans or tanker from Sligo Fuel Sales (500m from the pontoon) 071 916 9552.

SLIGO BAY to MULLAGHMORE

AC2702

From Sligo Bay to Mullaghmore Head the coast should be given a good berth in any height of sea from the W; a course halfway between the shore and Inishmurray is a safe one. **Black Bull Rock**, drying 1·2m, is 7 cables offshore 3M NE of Ardboline Island, and there are rocks 1M offshore at Milk Harbour.

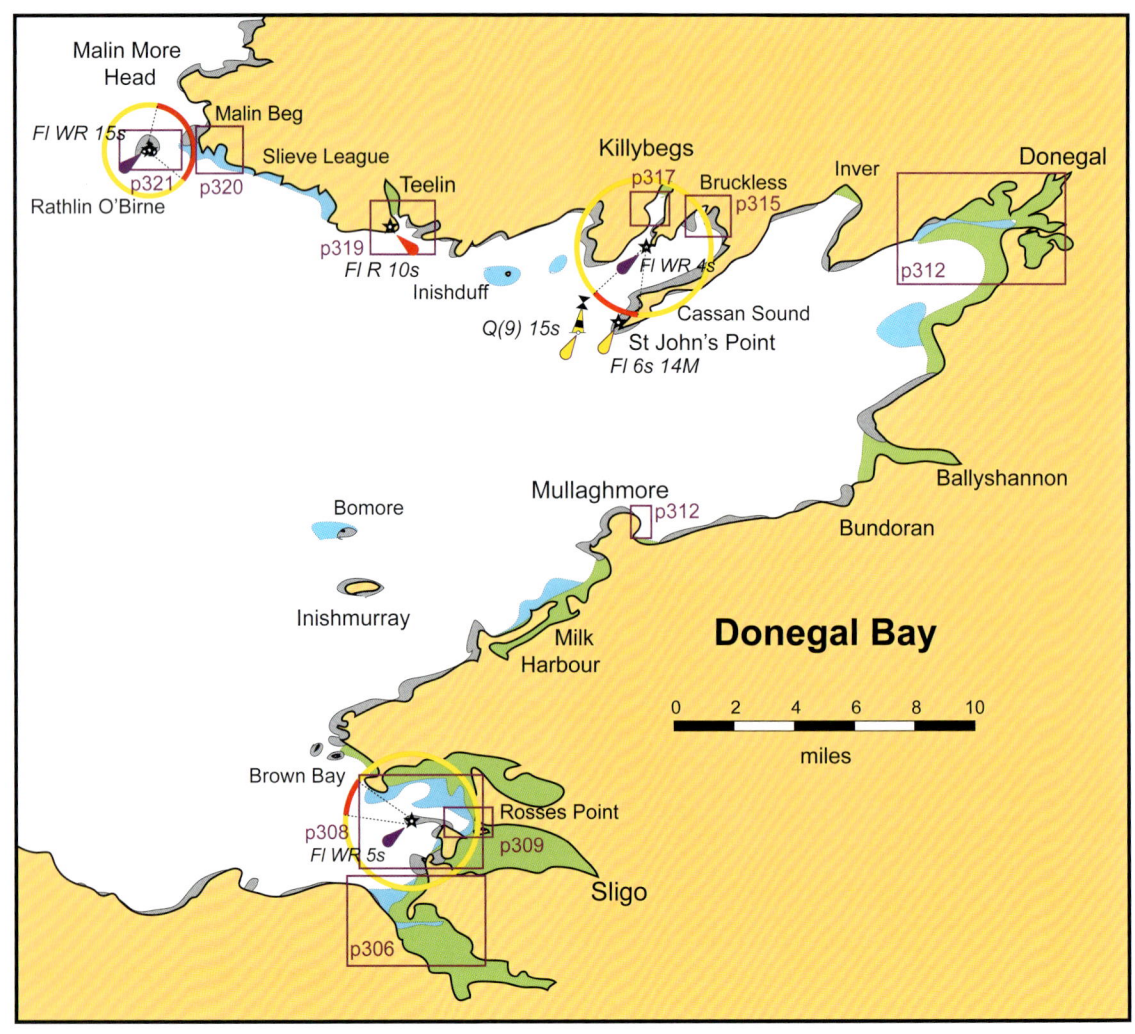

Sligo harbour (top); the training wall

(middle) approaching the town; the old training wall (in line with the eight-storey building, centre) should be left to starboard

(bottom) the pontoon in the town centre

Inishmurray and Mullaghmore

Brown Bay

54°20'N 8°40'W

Brown Bay, between Seal Rocks and Raghly Point, provides reasonably good anchorage and shelter from swell in winds from NW to E, at least 2 cables off the beach in 5m, sand. No facilities ashore.

There is a small drying harbour on the E side of Raghly Point, 6 cables NE of the Wheat Rock buoy. Approaching from the buoy, give the point a berth of 3 cables to avoid Bird Rocks and Raghly Ledge.

Inishmurray

54°25'·5N 8°39'·7W

Inishmurray has been uninhabited since 1950, and is well worth a visit – weather permitting – to see its remarkable and unusually well-preserved 6th century monastic buildings. Clashymore Harbour on the S side is a rocky gut, in the mouth of which, in settled weather with little swell, a yacht may be anchored in 7m, weed over rock. Use a tripping line on the anchor. On the E side of the gut there are natural quays, with mooring rings.

With any sea, or at LW, the shoal patches close E and NE of the island must be avoided. **Bomore Rock** (7m high) and its outliers, 1·5M N of the island, should be given a wide berth.

Mullaghmore

54°28'N 8°26'W

AC2702, Imray C53 and Plan

Mullaghmore is a bustling holiday village, rivalling Rosses Point as the principal sailing centre in Donegal Bay. The bay, on the SE side of the headland, offers secure anchorage in winds from SE through W to N, and the inner harbour is completely sheltered for a yacht that can dry out. Approaching from the W, the headland should be given a berth of 2 cables to avoid rocks to the N. The breakwater end shows Fl G 3s 3M. There are many moorings in the bay, so care is required if approaching after dark.

Harbour

Immediately inside the breakwater is a pontoon 20m in length with 0·6m alongside. The inner harbour mostly dries except for a small pool with 0·5m between and immediately inside the pierheads. There is also a drying shoal in the harbour entrance, one-third of its width from the S pier; so when entering, keep close to the N pier. Local bilge-keel and centreboard yachts are berthed in the harbour, and yachts up to 10m can conveniently dry out alongside the N pier. The pontoon is intended for embarking and disembarking. The Yacht Club has visitors' moorings in the bay – call 087 257 4497 for availability. The best anchorage is off the harbour mouth in 2m but there is plenty of room N or SE of this in 2 to 3m. If bad weather threatens, a yacht should not remain anchored at Mullaghmore but should take refuge in Donegal, Killybegs or Sligo. Constant +0040 Galway; MHWS 3·7m, MHWN 2·9m, MLWN 1·3m, MLWS 0·5m.

Facilities

Water on pontoon, diesel from the boatyard but no petrol. Shops, hotels, restaurants, pubs, Mullaghmore YC Clubhouse, sailing school. Boatyard – hull, mechanical and electrical repairs.

(top) Clashymore Harbour, Inishmurray

(above) Mullaghmore pontoon

(left) Mullaghmore harbour. Most of its area dries

311

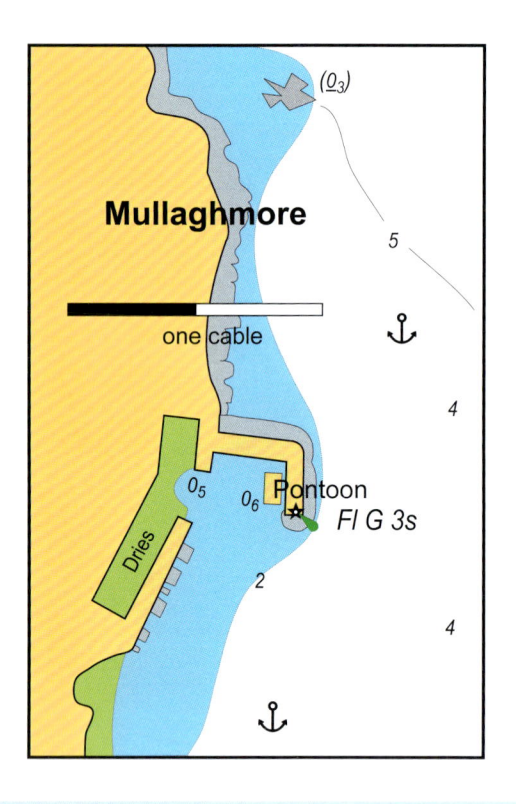

Bundoran, Ballyshannon and Donegal

Bundoran
There is a boat pier at the SW end of the town with about 0·6m LAT where the RNLI inshore lifeboat is stationed. The approach with rocky shoals extending a cable to seaward is shallow, tortuous and not recommended.

Ballyshannon
This was a commercial port long ago but has not been used since 1940. Leading beacons established in 2010, red with yellow stripe, show Iso 6s 7M on the approach 092·5°, and the channel inside the bar has new beacons, but these are principally for the benefit of the inshore lifeboat and the entrance is not advised for a stranger. The bar, with 1m at LAT, is very exposed and hazardous, the depths are limited and there is no easy access to facilities. An overhead power cable with 12m headroom crosses the channel close downstream of the town. The pier at Creevy, 7 cables N of Kildoney Point, offers alternative access to Ballyshannon. There is a hotel at Creevy.

Donegal Harbour
54°36'·7N 8°14'·6W
AC2702 (AC2715 essential above Green Island): see Plan

Donegal Harbour has recently been well buoyed and marked, sheltered anchorages beyond Green Island are in pretty surroundings, and Donegal Town (2,610) has good supermarkets, shops, restaurants and pubs. The entrance lies at the head of the bay framed by Doorin Point to the NW and Rossnowlagh Point to the SE. It is exposed to W and SW and is subject to swell which can sometimes break in apparently safe

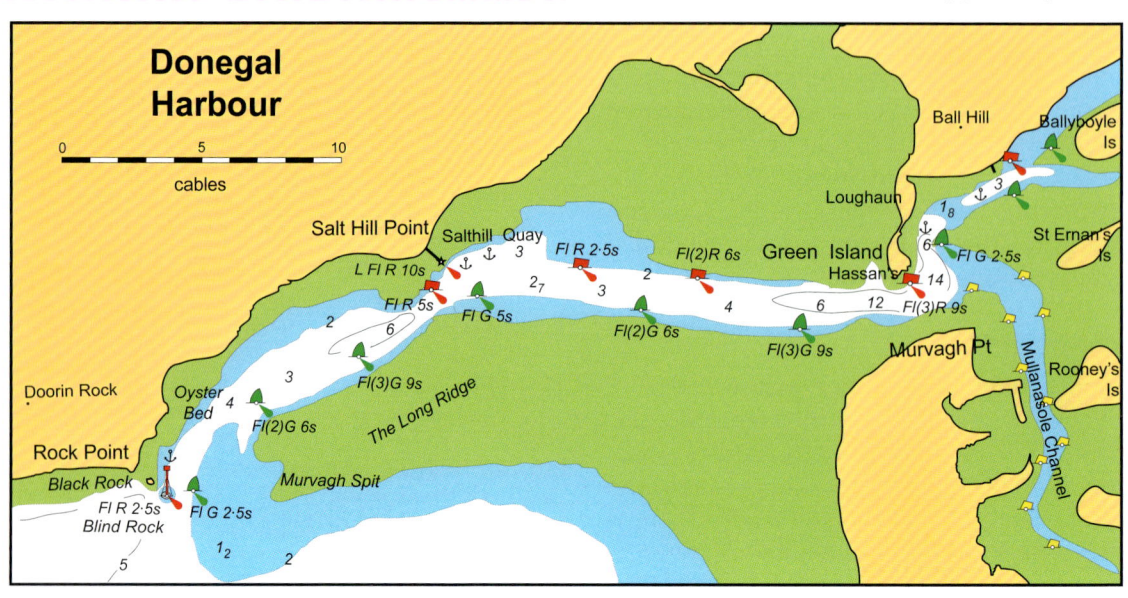

Tides – Donegal Harbour
S of Green Island the tide runs up to 5 kn at springs and the ebb sets towards Green Island from the Mullanasole channel to the S. In that channel the tide runs very strongly W of Rooney's Island. Constant +0045 Galway; MHWS 3·9m, MHWN 3·0m, MLWN 1·5m, MLWS 0·6m.

Caution
GPS chart plotters should not be implicitly relied upon in the narrow parts of the channel to Donegal Town due to the likelihood of changes in the channel and sandbanks. It is essential to maintain good traditional pilotage with continuous use of the echo sounder.

Donegal

Donegal Harbour; Green Island (centre), Murvagh Point and Mullinasole Channel (centre R), Ballyboyle Island and Donegal Town (top L)

conditions. The least depth in the outer part of the channel is 1·5m, between Blind Rock and Salt Hill Quay.

Directions – Salt Hill

Stay within 2M of the coast SE of Doorin Point to avoid **Carrickfad Rocks**. Identify the Blind Rock beacon, and approach it steering NE (note that a survey in 2008 showed the shallows SW of Murvagh Spit extending further than before). Steer to pass between the beacon and the starboard hand buoy. Follow the line of the buoys, keeping each one close aboard.

Anchorages

- It is possible to anchor in the lee of Black Rock. A tripping line is recommended. Exposed from E to S.
- SE or E of the end of Salt Hill quay outside moorings in 2 to 5 m on sand, good holding, but exposed above half tide from E to SW. The quay dries about 0·5m at the outer steps on the E side.

Directions – inner anchorages

From a position off Salt Hill quay, steer straight for the gap between Green Island and Murvagh Point, with Salt Hill Point dead astern, and leave the buoys on the proper hand. The banks off Murvagh Point are steep-to, and if visible can be approached very closely. Once E of Green Island turn to port, steering 353° to leave St Ernan's buoy close to starboard. The deep channel just E of Green Island is only 40m wide. Anchor

Dangers - Donegal and approaches

Carrickfad Rocks, (drying), 1M SW, W and NW of Rossnowlagh Point

The Long Ridge, sandbar drying up to 2m, extending 2M from the E shore, ending in **Murvagh Spit** and forming the S and SE side of the entrance channel

Blind Rock (dries 2·6m), 1·5 cables SE of Rock Point.

Lights and Marks

Blind Rock beacon, PHM Fl R 2·5s, on the rock
Blind Rock buoy, SHM Fl G 2·5s, 0·6 cable ENE
Oyster Bed buoy, SHM Fl(2) G 6s
Long Ridge buoy, SHM Fl(3) G 9s
Salt Hill Port buoy, PHM Fl R 5s
Salt Hill Pier beacon, L Fl R 10s
Salt Hill Starboard buoy, SHM Fl G 5s
Privateer Wreck buoy, PHM Fl R 2·5s
Channel Port buoy, PHM Fl(2) R 6s
Channel Starboard buoy, SHM Fl(2) G 6s
Green Island Starboard buoy, SHM Fl(3) G 9s
Green Island Port buoy, PHM Fl(3) R 9s
St Ernan's buoy, SHM Fl G 2·5s

The channel to Donegal Town quay is marked by a further six starboard- and four port-hand buoys and four beacons, and the Mullanasole channel to the S by ten yellow Special Mark buoys.

Inver Bay: **Rock of the Port** beacon, IDB Fl(2) 10s

Donegal Harbour entrance; Blind Rock beacon, centre

313

Donegal; Inver Bay

Donegal Harbour; the anchorages at Salt Hill Quay (above) and E of Green Island (below)

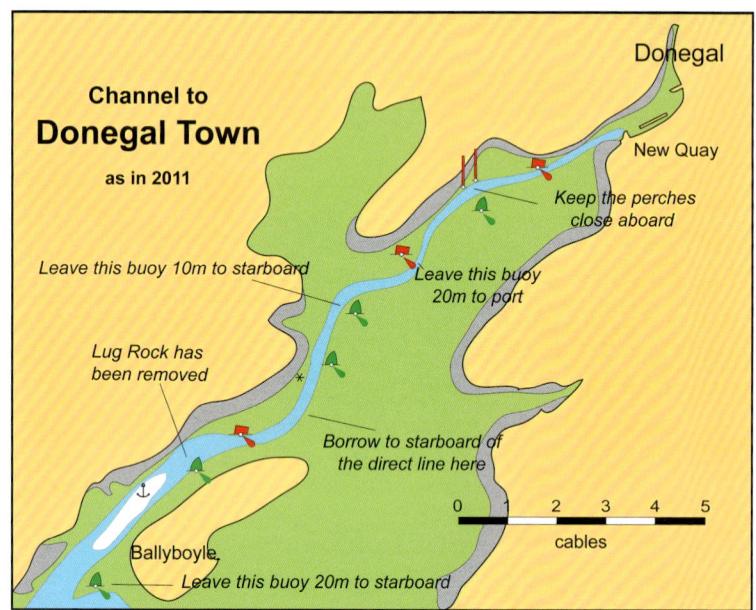

(above and below) Donegal Town

either E of the spit between Green Island and Loughaun in 3·5m, (there are visitors' moorings) or 3 cables further NE in 2·5m. This represents the limit of all-tide access for a deep-keeled yacht.

Donegal Town

The channel to the town is well marked and has a least depth of a metre at LAT, but it is narrow and winding and care is required in pilotage. Lug Rock, a large boulder marked on the charts at 54°38'·40N 8°08'·38W, has been removed, and the bottom is mud and sand. The plan shows the trend of the channel as it was in 2011, and the passage involves borrowing a little to one side or the other between some of the buoys, as shown. Pass very close to the two red perches. A drying berth is available at the steps on the New Quay on the SE side; the pontoon is reserved for the waterbus, whose crew can provide advice.

Facilities

Shops, filling stations, hotels, restaurants, pubs, PO, doctors.

South Channel to Mullanasole
This is pretty at HW but the tide runs very strongly W of Rooney's Island so the channel is unsuitable for anchoring.

COAST between DONEGAL and KILLYBEGS

Doorin Point and the coast for 1M each side of it should be given a good berth as reefs project up to 4 cables seaward from the bottom of the cliffs. Note that there are not nearly as many fish cages in Inver Bay and McSwyne's Bay as are marked on the charts.

Inver Bay

54°37'·2N 8°19'W

Inver Bay is exposed to the SW but provides sheltered anchorage in offshore winds. There are three drying rocks within 3 cables of the NW shore; **Menamny Rock** dries only at very low springs, and the **Whillins**, SW of Inver Port, dries 2m. **Rock of the Port** off the pier is marked by an Isolated Danger beacon. Inver Roads, at the head of Inver Bay, provides safe anchorage in 3 to 5m, well sheltered in offshore winds, but without convenient landing nearby. The fish cages in the bay make an approach by night impracticable.

314

Cassan Sound, Bruckless and Killybegs

Cassan Sound

54°35'N 8°25'W
AC2702, 2792 Killybegs inset

This open anchorage is 1·5M NE of St John's Point. Beware **Black Rock** (dries 2·3m) on the SW side. The bay SW of Black Rock has a rocky bottom, and a golden sand beach. Cassan Sound has a small stony beach beneath an old cottage, and should be approached bearing NW or W to avoid Black Rock. Anchor in 3·5m close inshore between the end of the little breakwater and the shore N of it. The anchorage is unsafe in any swell, but sheltered in winds between W and N, and has a handy slip for landing.

Bruckless

54°37'·2N 8°23'·8W
AC2702 and Plan

This pretty but shallow creek, with trees down to the water's edge, lies at the head of McSwyne's Bay and is well sheltered except from due SW. Green Island, 10m high, is prominent, especially at LW when the extensive reefs on which it stands are uncovered. **Black Rock** (locally known as the Round Rock) stands out well and never covers. Coming in, **Flat Rock** is not easy to see; it covers completely only at very high springs but the small reefs projecting about 20m from its W side cover at half tide. **Middle Boc** is a small isolated rock which dries 1m and lies between Green Island and Black Rock.

Directions

Leave Black Rock 15m to starboard and steer 038° for the head of the pier, with Pound Point (the NW side of the St John's Point peninsula) dead astern. This line passes less than 45m SE of Middle Boc. Anchor in mid-channel just short of the pier, bottom soft mud. The pier dries out to the head at LWS. There is also a passage E of Black Rock, which may be taken with care.

Facilities

Shop, PO and filling station at Bruckless village, 1 km NW. Restaurant 800m S of the pier.

KILLYBEGS

54°36'·8N 8°26'·9W
AC2702, 2792, Imray C53 and Plan

In terms of landed tonnage, Killybegs

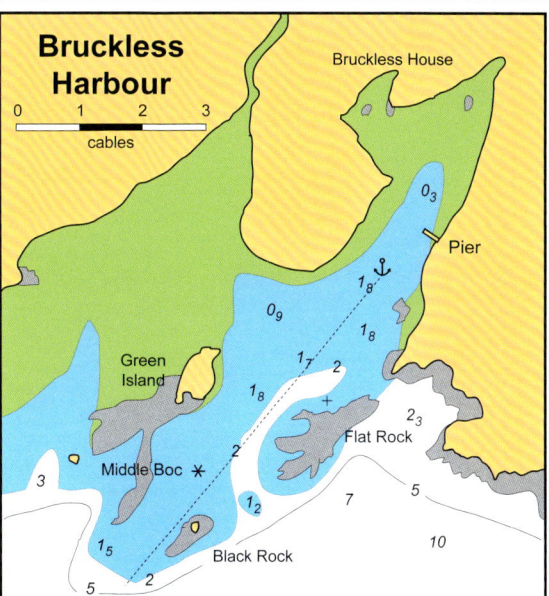

St John's Point

Black Rock, at the entrance to Bruckless Harbour

Bruckless Harbour

is the largest fishing port in the British Isles, and it also has a significant seaborne trade in processed fish and miscellaneous cargo. However, the main fishery is midwater pelagic and is essentially confined to the months of September to April; there is relatively little activity in summer. The port is one of the best natural harbours in Ireland, accessible by day or night in any weather, and offers all services including hull, engine, electrical and electronic repairs, but not sailmakers. (Sail repairs are available in Sligo.) Yachts up to the very largest are welcome and can be accommodated in Killybegs although there are at present no

Killybegs

Killybegs from the SW; East and Town Piers centre, North and South Quays bottom R. Note the projecting shingle bank at the NW end of the North Quay (photo Dept of Agriculture, Food and the Marine)

Dangers - Killybegs and approaches

Manister Rock, 1·8m, 4 cables W of Inishduff
Black Rock, dries 3·4m, 8 cables W of Drumanoo Head
Sharp Rock, 1·8m, 2 cables SSW of Black Rock
Horse Head Rock, dries 2·7m, 1 cable SW of Drumanoo Head
Bullockmore, 2·1m, 1M W of St John's Point
Reefs extending 3 cables NW from St John's Point, ending in
Connellagh Rock, dries 1·5m
Harbour Shoal, 1·5m, in Killybegs Harbour

Lights and Marks

St John's Point, white tower Fl 6s 30m 14M, AIS
Rotten Island, white tower FlWR 4s 20m W15M, R11M, W 255°–008°, R 008°–039°, W 039°–208°. Shows red to the SSW over Bullockmore and St John's Point, white elsewhere
Bullockmore buoy, W Card Q(9) 15s, AIS
Rashenny Point buoy, SHM Fl G 2s
Walker's buoy, SHM Fl G 6s
Lackerabunn beacon, PHM Fl R 3s 5m 2M
Killybegs port entry light, white lattice tower Dir Oc WRG 6s, G 328°–334° AltWG 334°–336° FW 336°–340° AltWR 340°–342° R 342°–348°
South Quay, 2×2FR vert
North Quay, 2×2FR vert
Black Rock Pier, 2FR vert
Smooth Point buoy, PHM Fl R 7s
Black Rock beacon, Isolated Danger mark, Fl(2) 10s
Town Pier, 2FR vert
Killybegs Outer buoy, S Card VQ(6) + L Fl 10s
Killybegs Inner buoy, N Card VQ

specific facilities for them. The Harbour is managed by the Department of Agriculture, Food and the Marine.

Directions

From the S, leave Bullockmore buoy (1·5M W of St John's Point) 1·5 cables to starboard and steer for Rotten Island. Alternatively, the NE peak of Crownarad (490m) well W of Drumanoo Head bearing 349° leads clear W of St John's Point shoals and E of Bullockmore. Stay on this heading till St John's Point bears SE, then head for Rotten Island.

Approaching from Teelin or close inshore at Muckros Head, a bearing of 309° on Slieve League summit or Dundawoona Point leads clear SW of **Manister Rock**, which is always covered. Alternatively, steer into Fintragh Bay well N of Manister Rock, and when **Black Rock** is seen (it only covers at HWS) steer to leave it close to starboard and then pass 2 cables from Drumanoo Head to clear **Horse Head Rock**.

Leave South and North Quays and Smooth Point buoy to port and Harbour Shoal (Killybegs Outer) S Card buoy to starboard. Beware the drying spit extending NE from the inner end of North Quay. Constant +0045 Galway; MHWS 4·1m, MHWN 3·0m, MLWN 1·6m, MLWS 0·5m.

Killybegs, Walker's Bay and Port Roshin

Anchorage

The best anchorage, clear of traffic and moorings, is E of the East Pier and S of the fish factory, as shown on the plan, in 2 to 5m. Anchorage may also be available in the small bay between the Town Pier and Black Rock Pier, although this area has many moorings, and traffic at both piers may be heavy. The holding ground in Killybegs is excellent, but the chain and anchor must be thoroughly rinsed on weighing, since the bottom mud tends to have a fairly pungent odour.

An alongside berth may be available on one of the piers; contact HM by VHF (Ch 14,16) or by phone 074 973 1032 for advice and instructions. The piers are open-piled and a fenderboard is advisable; however an alongside berth will normally mean rafting up to another vessel. The slipway W of the Town Pier is used by sea-angling boats but is a convenient place to land by dinghy.

There are also two visitors' moorings.

Facilities

Diesel by tanker on piers, or cans from filling station, 1 km. Petrol from filling station. Bottled gas. Water on slipway W of Town Pier. All amenities, shops, hotels, pubs and restaurants, banks, hospital. Ship chandler; Mooney Boats (074 973 1152) mechanical, electrical and electronic supplies and repairs, 75t travelhoist (the largest in Ireland). Atlantic Marine, electrical and electronic supplies 074 9731440. Buses to Donegal Town and Sligo.

Walker's Bay

Walker's Bay, on the E of the entrance, is a pleasant overnight anchorage. It is well sheltered in SW or W winds and Killybegs offers an easy alternative if the wind veers NW. The area with suitable depths is narrow and it shoals quickly inside. Anchor in 5 to 8m, NW of the slip, but keep clear of local moorings.

Port Roshin

On the W side opposite Rotten Island, Port Roshin has minimum depth 2m. The entrance is only 20m wide at LAT and is not difficult; however, care should be taken to avoid rocks to the S which cover shortly after MLWS. This is a quiet and beautiful, if somewhat small, anchorage.

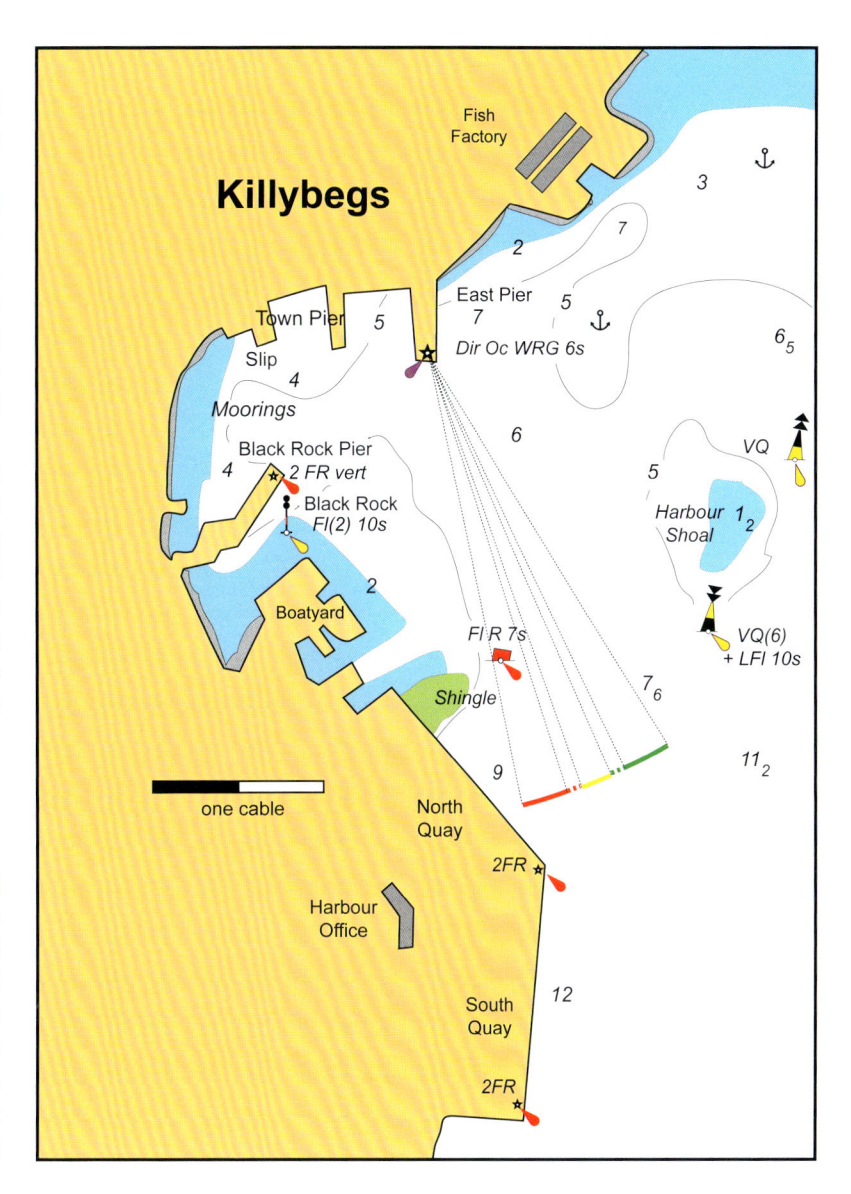

Entrance to Killybegs; Rotten Island, R

Port Roshin

317

Teelin

Teelin Harbour from SW. The inner bay (upper L) largely dries

Approaching Teelin from the S; Teelin Point beacon, centre R

Teelin; the main (west) pier

Teelin

⊕ *TL* 54°37'·2N 8°37'·5W
AC2702, 2792, Imray C53 and Plan

Teelin is a good natural harbour and a handy point of departure for the crossing to NW Mayo, with a deep-water pier offering an alongside berth with perfect shelter in all summer weather. The bay is exposed to S and SW swell. In NW winds very severe squalls can come down off the mountain. Sea angling and sightseeing boats use the pier.

Directions

The entrance is hard to discern until fairly close. From the E, it does not open up until Dundawoona Point is abeam; from the W, Tawny Bay, the inlet E of Teelin, is conspicuous from a position close inshore E of Carrigan Head. The entrance, which faces SE, is 2 cables wide and steep-to on both sides.

Anchorage

Off the moorings on the W side, depth 3 or 4m, not too far N of the pier as there is more

Teelin to Rathlin O'Birne; White Strand Bay

Lights and Marks

Teelin Point, the W side of the entrance, shows Fl R 10s from a red structure which is inconspicuous by day. The **pier light** shows Fl(2) R 5s.

Rathlin O'Birne, white tower Fl WR 15s 35m W12M R10M, R 195°–307°, W 307°–195°. Shows white to seaward and red inshore between Carrigan Head and Malin More Head. Racon (O) 13M, AIS.

Offshore weather buoy M4, yellow, Fl(5) Y 20s, is moored 45M WNW of Glen Head in position 55°N 10°W.

swell further N. There are visitors' moorings, somewhat exposed, but the pier has 3m at LAT and offers excellent shelter alongside. The E side of the bay is foul with discarded moorings and is not recommended.

Facilities

Water on the pier. Diesel by tanker or at Carrick village, 5 km. Pub at Teelin village, 1·5 km.

TEELIN to RATHLIN O'BIRNE SOUND

The coast between Teelin and White Strand Bay, 6m to the WNW, presents a fine spectacle, with the cliffs of Slieve League sweeping 597m almost sheer to the sea, the second highest cliffs in Ireland. The coast is clean to within 3 cables of the shore, but uncharted rocks are reported to exist. A reef of five rocky heads locally known as "the Boys" extends ESE from the point at 54°38'·50N 8°42'·43W. Close E of this point are two pebble beaches accessible only from seaward, and in very settled weather it is possible to anchor under the cliffs, off the more W'ly beach. Approach the cliffs about a cable to the E of the point, skirt the coast westwards, and anchor in 10m. The beaches, of large pebbles, are very steep and in any swell and surf are dangerous for swimmers.

In all but the calmest weather, the only sensible advice to a stranger is to admire the view from a safe distance.

White Strand Bay

⊕ *MB* 54°39'·3N 8°47'W
See Plan
White Strand Bay offers temporary anchorage in N winds in about 5m, sand, in pretty surroundings. From the E, stay 5 cables offshore, identify **Candle Rocks** and continue until the W point of the bay is open W of Candle Rocks before turning N, to avoid **Thor-Lea Bullig,** which uncovers only at very low springs. Anchor in the middle of the bay E of the **Stack,** which covers at HW.

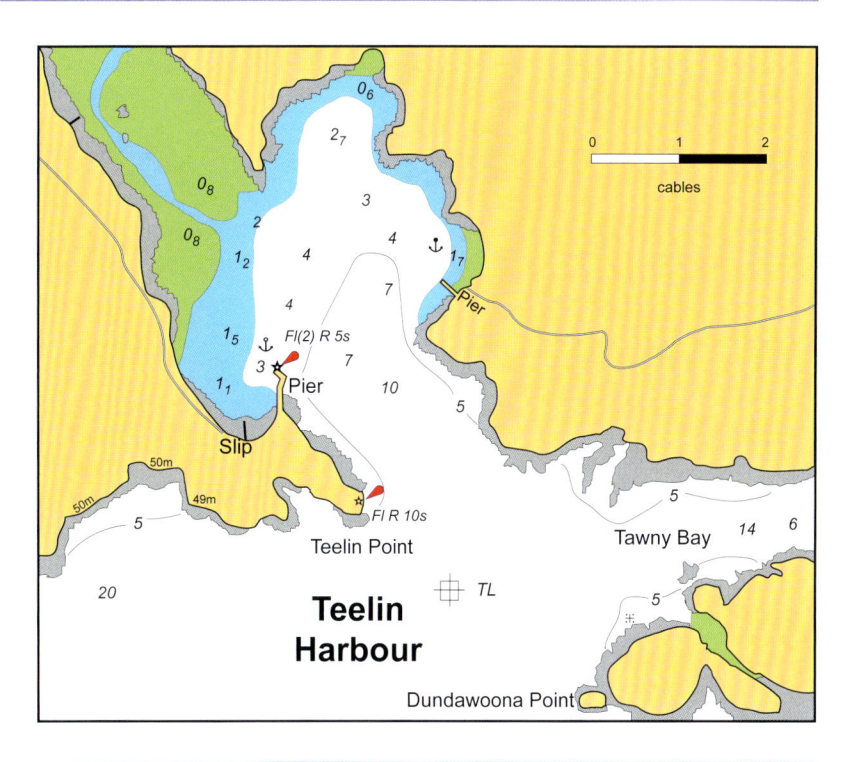

Malin Beg Bay

⊕ *MB* 54°39'·3N 8°47'W
See Plan
Malin Beg Bay has a slip and a small quay

The cliffs of Slieve League

319

White Strand and Malin Beg Bays

White Strand and Malin Beg Bays from the SW; Candle Rocks (breaking) bottom R, Malin Beg village, top L

Malin Beg Bay

with about 0·4m alongside. A yacht should enter only in very settled weather as the head of the bay is less than 0·5 cable wide with three remarkable rock stacks. Temporary anchorage is available just beyond the first stack; with sufficient rise of tide an alongside berth is possible at the quay. Malin Beg village, 400m, has shops and PO.

Rathlin O'Birne

⊕ RB 54°39'·4N 8°48'·7W
See Plan

Rathlin O'Birne is 1M offshore, and the clear passage 5 cables wide through the sound is

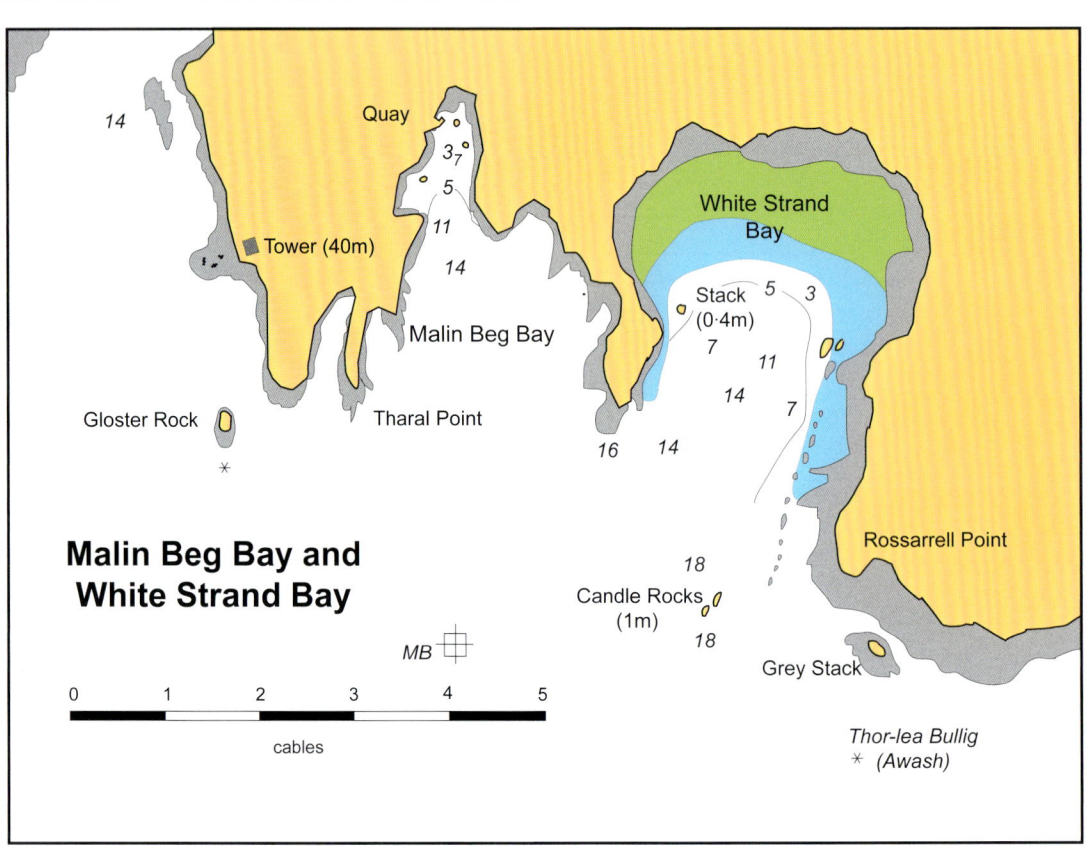

Malin Beg Bay and White Strand Bay

320

Rathlin O'Birne

nearer the island as rocks extend 4 cables from Malin Beg Head. The island is worth a visit on a calm day. Its lighthouse has been a test bed for alternative power supplies. Automated in 1974 and equipped with a nuclear power source, it was converted to wind energy in 1987, and finally in 1993 became the first of Ireland's (now many) solar-powered lighthouses. The best landing is at the steps on the E side. Beware of **White Claddagh Bullig** (dries 1·2m) which extends further S than would appear. It is best to anchor NE of the SE corner where the holding is better than off the landing steps. There is no anchorage or landing off the S shore, where a crane is positioned to service the lighthouse.

Tides - Rathlin O'Birne Sound

The tide runs N at 1·5 kn at springs for 9·25 hours, starting at −0200 Galway. The S going tide is very weak. The streams may be strongly affected by N or S winds. Constant (Killybegs) +0045 Galway; MHWS 4·1m, MHWN 3·0m, MLWN 1·6m, MLWS 0·5m.

The landing steps on the E side of Rathlin O'Birne

321

9 Rathlin O'Birne to Bloody Foreland

South Sound of Aran from the SW; Inishkeeragh, foreground, with Chapel Bay on Arranmore Island, L; The Clutch and Aileen Reef centre R; Eighter and the channel to Burtonport, upper R; Owey at top

"Cruising Ireland"
This coast is described on pages 146 to 155 of **Cruising Ireland**

The west coast of Donegal is breathtakingly scenic. With its necklace of offshore islands, it has, as one marine writer recently put it, "an edge-of-the-world feel". Its cliffs and bays have been moulded by exposure to the full force of Atlantic weather – "strongest in the north west" is one of the most frequent phrases heard on the Irish sea area forecasts.

Towering cliffs extend northeast from Glen Head, and are broken by a pair of sandy inlets, Loughros More and Beg, which have dangerous sandbars. To the north is a broken, rock-strewn coast with many excellent natural harbours. This is the Rosses, a granite coast reminiscent of north Brittany or parts of Scandinavia, with golden beaches and pink rocks with deep water alongside. Arranmore has Ireland's second-largest island community, and shelters an archipelago of smaller islands to the east. A herring fishery was founded here in 1784, and docks, houses and boatyards were built on Edernish, Inishcoo and the large island to the south, Inis Mhic an Doirn, which was renamed Rutland in honour of the Duke of Rutland, who was Lord Lieutenant of Ireland at the time. The enterprise was short-lived, but fascinating relics are still to be found, including many of the old buildings, some recently renovated. On the mainland, Burtonport nestles among the boulders; its deep-water pier shelters a fine little harbour.

To the north is a string of islands of which only one, Cruit, is bridged to the shore and has year-round residents, but Owey, Gola and Inishmeane are all occupied in summer. The people of Gola left their homes and school for the mainland in 1967, but they never lost touch with the island, and some have led a programme which has restored many of the old houses, brought a power cable from the

Rathlin O'Birne Sound to Crohy Head

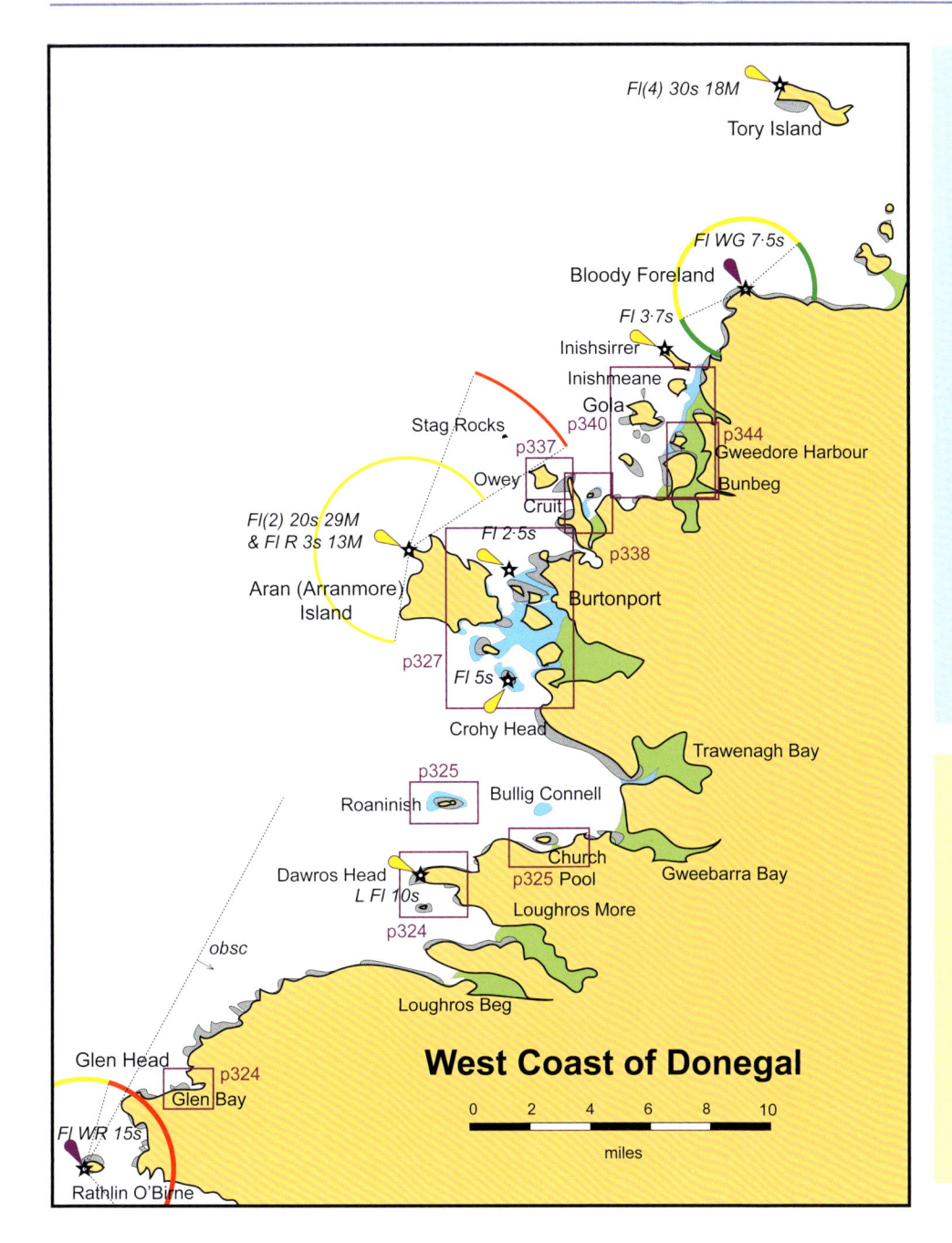

Tides – West Coast of Donegal

On the coast between Glen Head and Bloody Foreland HW occurs between +0040 and +0100 Galway. Spring tides rise about 3·8m and neaps about 2·9m above LAT. The tide outside the islands turns S at +0300 Galway and N at –0300 Galway with a rate of 0·8 to 1 kn. Inshore it turns 1 to 2 hours earlier, and so is in effect running S during the ebb by the shore and N during the flood. Near the salient points the rate reaches 1·5 to 2 kn at springs.
Constant (Burtonport) +0050 Galway; MHWS 3·9m, MHWN 2·9m, MLWN 1·5m, MLWS 0·5m.

Paper Charts

AC2725 Blacksod Bay to Tory Island covers west Donegal, but the medium-scale charts 1879 and 1883 are essential. The large-scale AC2792 is also essential if spending time exploring the Sound of Aran and Burtonport. The Imray chart C53 Donegal Bay to Rathlin Island may be worth carrying but is no substitute for the Admiralty charts.

mainland, and built a tearoom and campsite. The granite coast continues to Ireland's north west corner, which is not as savage as it sounds but took its name from the glorious pink hue which the sunset lends to the rocks. This is a Gaeltacht area; the spoken Irish of west Donegal, and particularly of the islands, is closely akin to the Scots Gaelic of Islay, and the two are quite mutually intelligible.

RATHLIN O'BIRNE SOUND to CROHY HEAD

AC1879

NE from Glen Head there are spectacular cliffs and stacks. The coast is most impressive, but foul up to 5 cables offshore. The only

Dangers - Rathlin O'Birne Sound to Crohy Head

The coast from Glen Head to Loughros Beg Bay has many rocks within 5 cables of the cliffs. The principal offshore dangers between Loughros Beg and Crohy Head are
Meadal Rock, dries 3·9m, in Loughros Beg Bay
Bullig Connell, 0·3m, 8 cables N of Inishkeel
Free Ground Breaker, 1·5m, **Wee Bullig**, 1·5m, and **Middle Bullig**, 2·4m, within 1·4M NE of Roaninish

Lights and Marks

Dawros Head, square white tower L Fl 10s 39m 4M
Dawros Bay, ldg lts 2xOc 6s (synchronised)
Dawros Bay beacon, PHM Fl R 5s 3m 3M

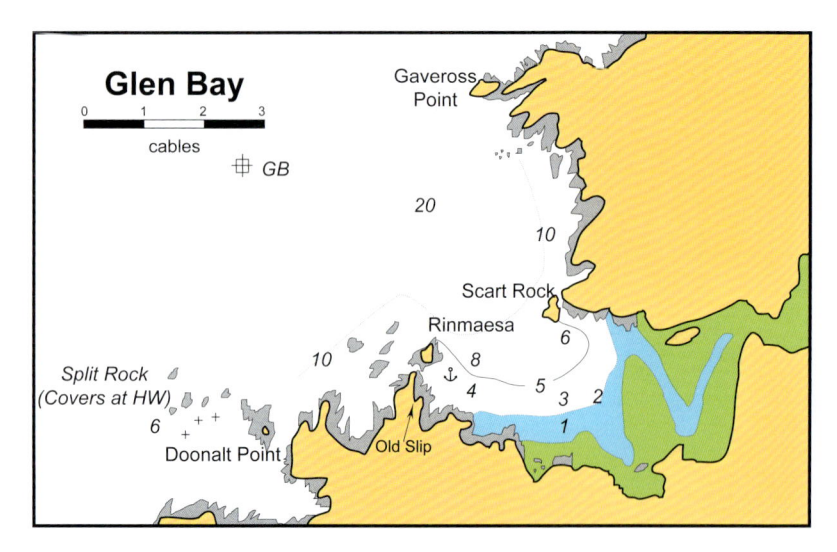

Glen Bay, Dawros Bay and Boylagh Bay

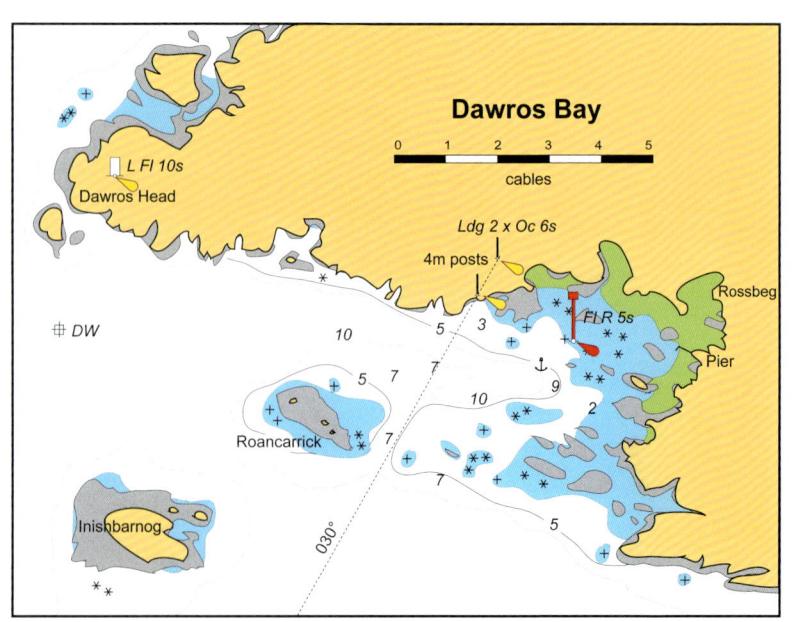

feasible overnight anchorage on this stretch of coast is Church Pool, while in heavy weather the nearest safe anchorage is Aran Road, entered from the N after going west-about Arranmore Island, 28M from Rathlin O'Birne. Loughros More and Beag, and Gweebarra and Trawenagh Bays, to the E, have dangerous bars and are not navigable.

Glen Bay

⊕ GB 54°43'·0N 8°45'·8W
AC1879 and Plan

Glen Bay provides temporary anchorage in winds from NE through SE to S. Anchor close to Rinmaesa Point in 7m, sand. The bay is unsafe in winds between SW and N or a swell from the W. Shops, pubs and restaurants at Glencolumbkille, 2 km.

Dawros Bay (Rosbeg)

⊕ DW 54°49'·2N 8°33'·9W
AC1879 and Plan

Dawros Bay provides temporary anchorage in calm sea conditions with N or E winds. The bay is best entered from the W; the approach from the S is on the line of the leading beacons, 030°. These are difficult to pick out by day. The pier dries at LW and is inaccessible without local knowledge. Anchor in 4m, close SW of the port-hand perch. Hotel and PO; small shop at Rosbeg village, 800m SE.

Boylagh Bay

54°51'·5N 8°30'·2W
AC1879, 2792

There is a string of shoals and rocks stretching into the bay from **Bullig More**, 11m, 4M NW of Dunmore Head. These should all be avoided though some of them are dangerous only in a big sea or swell. **Roaninish**, 4·6m high, is clean on its S side but has reefs extending up to 7 cables N and W. Landing on Roaninish is possible at the gut N of the

The anchorage E of Rinmeasa Point in Glen Bay

The inconspicuous leading beacons in Dawros Bay

> **Caution**
>
> As of 2011, GPS chartplotters cannot be implicitly relied upon in the close approaches to Dawros Bay due to the limited horizontal accuracy of the charts. It is particularly essential to maintain good traditional pilotage with continuous use of the echo sounder.

Dawros Bay, Church Pool and Portnoo

Dawros Bay from the SE; Rosbeg Point centre L, Dawros Head and Roancarrick top L

W end of the island; the bottom all along the N side is foul, and there is no anchorage. The innermost danger in Boylagh Bay is **Bullig Connell**, 0·3m, 8 cables N of Inishkeel. The flood tide sets strongly into Boylagh Bay.

Approach

From the S, give Dawros Head a berth of 3 cables and stay within 5 cables of Dunmore Head and Inishkeel, to avoid the rocks close NW of Dawros Head and Dawros Island, and the shoals in Boylagh Bay to the north. The approach **from the N** has no good leading lines. From Crohy Head, steer 160° towards the rocky shore at Carrickfadda, E of Church Pool, with Illancrone beacon astern, so as to pass well E of Bullig Connell; the chart shows clearance marks to pass E or W of this rock.

Anchorages

- Church Pool, E of Inishkeel, offers excellent shelter in winds from SE through SW to WNW, and good holding in about 3m, sand. There are visitors' moorings. This is the first good anchorage N of Glen Head.
- Portnoo, SW of Inishkeel, is more exposed to swell than Church Pool. However it provides better shelter in NE wind and in really calm conditions it is a pleasant place to stay overnight. Anchor 0·75 cable E of the end of the pier in more than 2m, or further out in less than 5m.

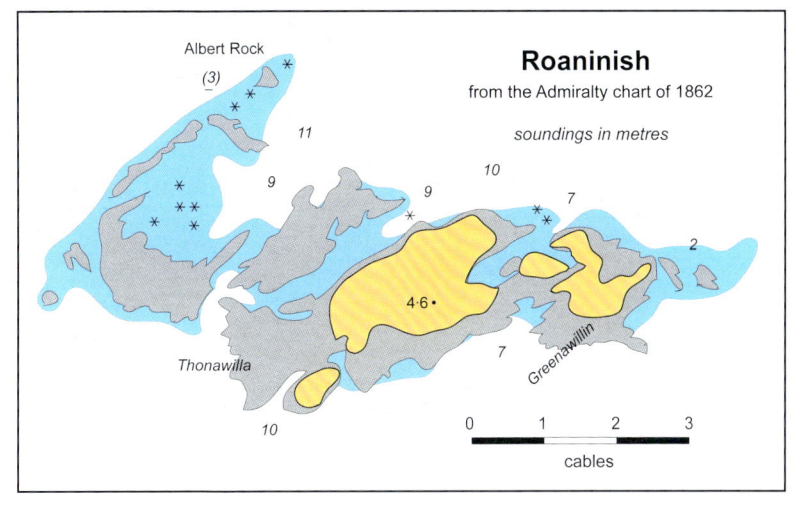

Hotel, shops, PO at Narin, beside the bay.

The Gweebarra River, in the SE corner of Boylagh Bay, is not navigable, has a dangerous and very shallow bar and should be avoided. The entrance to Trawenagh Bay, to the NE, is not safely navigable. The bay largely dries.

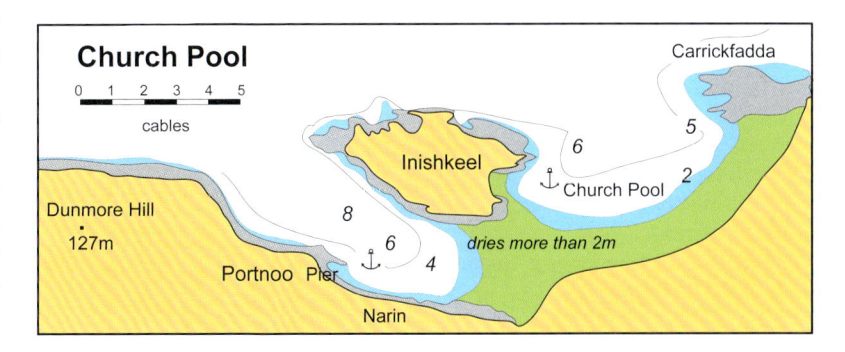

325

CROHY HEAD to BLOODY FORELAND

AC1883, 2792, Imray C53

The coast from Illancrone, 2M S of Arranmore, to Bloody Foreland is sheltered by a string of islands. The largest and most populous of these is Arranmore (Aran on the charts, and often also spelt Aranmore). The islands sheltering Burtonport have summer residents, and others, including Owey, Gola and Inishmeane, are seasonally occupied. The coast has a number of excellent anchorages and harbours amid beautiful scenery, with some splendid sandy beaches, and is a most attractive cruising ground. The islands give a useful amount of shelter for coastwise passages, and the pilotage, while interesting and challenging, is not unduly difficult. Despite the age of some of the survey data the depths shown on the charts are still remarkably accurate.

Lights and Marks
Arranmore and Aran Sound

Aranmore (Rinrawros Point), 23m white tower Fl(2) 20s 71m 29M, AIS. Auxiliary light Fl R 3s 61m 13M, vis 203°–234°. The red light shows NW of Owey and over the Stag Rocks.

S Approaches to Aran Road (all 📷 pp329-332):
Wyon Point, white tower Fl(2) WRG 10s 8m W6M R3M; vis G shore–021°, W021°–042°, R042°–121°, W121°–150°, R150°–shore. Shows white over the approach from SW, green inshore to the S and SE, red over Illancrone and Middle Sound, white to the NW and over Inishkeeragh, and red over Turk Rocks, Aileen Reef and the South Sound of Aran to the N
Illancrone, white tower Fl 5s 7m 6M.
Turk Rocks, green tower Fl G 5s 6m 2M.
The Clutch buoy, PHM QR, 5 cables NW of Turk Rocks
Aileen Reef, red tower QR 6m 1M.
Carrickbealatroha Upper, white tower Fl 5s 3m 2M.
Lackmorris, stayed perch Isolated Danger mark, unlit.
Carrickbealatroha Lower, stayed perch W Card, unlit.
Black Rocks, red tower Fl R 3s 3m 1M.

N Approaches to Aran Road (both 📷 p332):
Ballagh Rocks, 10m conical beacon, white with black band, Fl 2·5s 13m 5M
Aran leading lights Oc 8s 3M 186° from bns, black with white band, S of Charley's Point. Front 8m, rear 17m

Channels S of Arranmore (all 📷 p329-330):
Chapel Sound (Cloghcor) leading lights Iso 8s 2M 048·5° from black and white banded bns NE of Chapel Bay
Rossillion Bay (Aphort) leading lights Oc 4s 308·4° from black and white banded bns N of Rannagh Pt.
Leac na bhFear, white tower Q(2) 5s 4m 2M, 2 cables W of Aileen Reef beacon.
Aphort, unlit beacon 1·5 cables NW of Leac na bhFear beacon.

Offlying dangers – passage W of the islands

Leenon More, 2M W of Inishkeeragh, has 8m at LAT but breaks with a heavy swell. The **Stag Rocks**, 1·25M NW of Owey, consist of three rocks 9m high and one, SW of these, which dries 1·2m. **Bullogconnell Shoals,** locally called **the Blowers**, are 1M NW of Gola and are the most dangerous. A small portion of the N shoal dries 1·4m and the middle and S shoals have depths of 2m and 3m. They break heavily and should be given a wide berth. Keeping Bloody Foreland closed behind Inishsirrer, 045°, leads between them and Gola, and also NW of **Rinogy Rock** N of Gola. To pass outside the shoals keep Cluidaniller, the summit of Arranmore Island, open W of Owey. At night the secondary light on Aranmore lighthouse (Fl R 3s, vis 203°–234°) shows over all these dangers, and they may be avoided by staying W of the arc of visibility of this light.

In gales from SW through W to NW the whole coast is subject to very heavy swell and the sea state can be high, confused and dangerous, especially close W of the islands and salient points. If making the passage around the coast in such conditions it is prudent to stand several miles out to sea.

Dangers - Approaches to Aran Sound

The rocks E and S of Arranmore are too numerous to list but are referred to in the text. The principal dangers in the approaches are

Southern approach, S of Wyon Point:
Bullig-na-naght, 3m, 1·5M W of Crohy Head
Leenon-rua, dries 0·9m, 5 cables NW of Crohy Head
Carrickgilreavy, dries 2·7m, 5 cables S of Illancrone

Northern approach, N of Calf and Eighter islands:
Rinnagy, dries 2·4m, 1M N of Eighter
Bullignamirra, dries 3·7m, 7 cables N of Eighter
Blind Rocks, 0·9m, 2 cables ENE of Calf Island

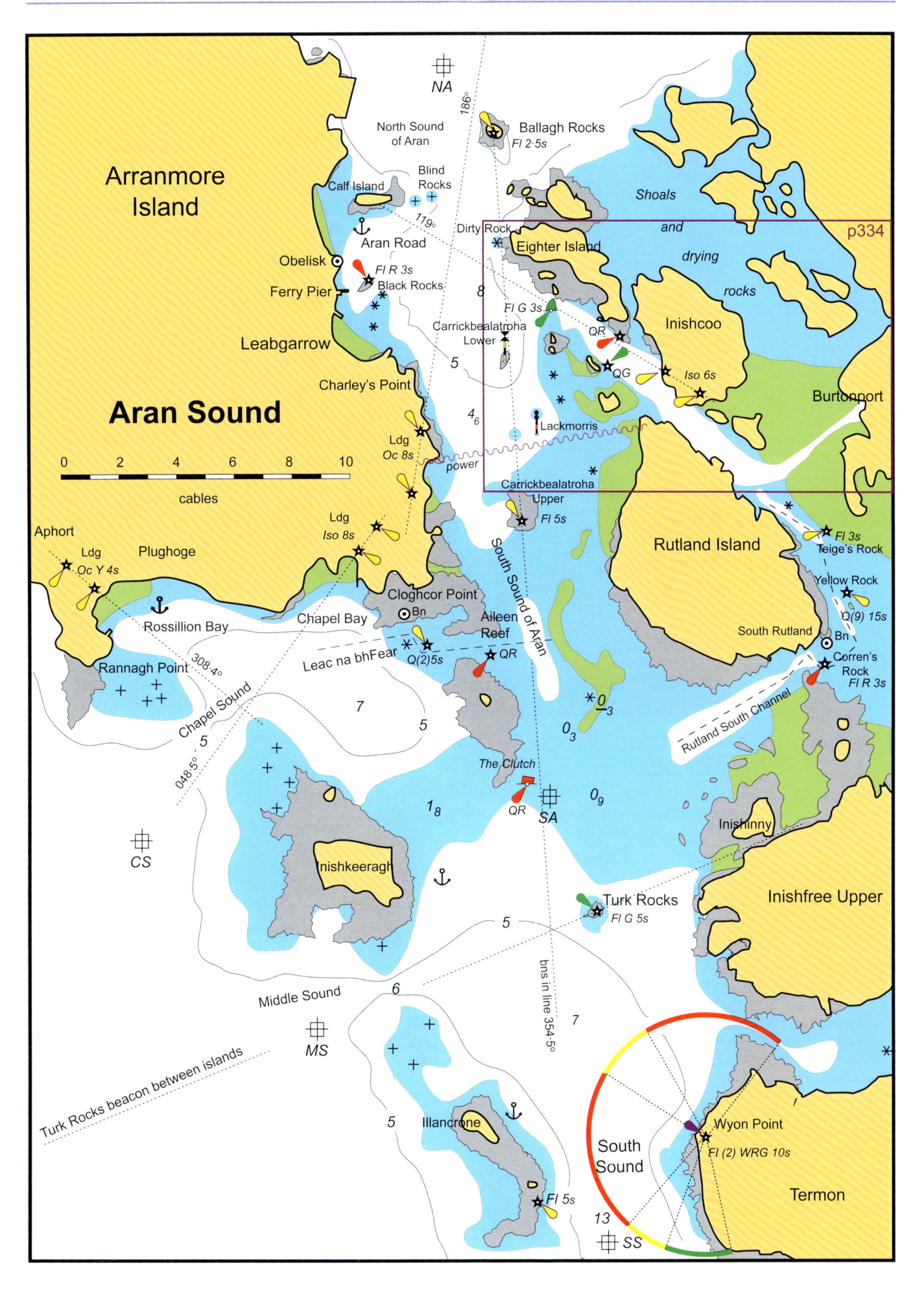

Aran Sound

Approaches to the South Sound of Aran

Approaches to Aran Sound from the S; South Sound, foreground; Illancrone and its offlying reefs centre L, Middle Sound, Inishkeeragh, Chapel Sound and Arranmore top L, Crohy Head bottom R, Wyon Point centre R, Inishfree Upper and Rutland top R, Owey in the distance.

ARRANMORE ISLAND and SOUND

The west side of Arranmore has some very fine cliff scenery. In the Sound and between the islands within it there is a wide choice of anchorages. The North Sound of Aran has good depth and provides the safest access to Aran Road and Burtonport. The South Sound of Aran has a least depth of only 0·3m and many rocks; it should be attempted only in daylight with an adequate rise of tide, but in moderate weather it is straightforward. There are many beacons and leading marks inside Arranmore, most of them with lights, but visiting yachts unfamiliar with the area should not attempt to use the minor channels after dark.

Approaches to the South Sound of Aran

54°55'·4N 8°29'W
AC1883, 2792, Imray C53 and Plan
Between Crohy Head (on the mainland) and Rannagh Point (the S point of Arranmore Island) are three channels: Chapel Sound, Middle Sound and South Sound.

South Sound

⊕SS 54°56·1'N 8°28'W
From the SW, identify Crohy Head and the beacon on Wyon Point. Approach with Roaninish astern and Wyon Point beacon

Place Names

*Nomenclature can be a little confusing on this coast. Distinguish between **South Sound**, which is the channel between Illancrone and Wyon Point, and the **South Sound of Aran**, the shallower and rock-strewn channel between Cloghcor Point and Rutland Island. The general term **Aran Sound** is here used to describe the entire passage between Arranmore Island and the mainland. Distinguish also between **Bullig Connell** in Boylagh Bay and **Bullogconnell Shoals** NW of Gola, and between **Rinogy Rock**, N of Gola, and **Rinnagy Rock**, N of Aran Sound (note also that on AC2792, Rinnagy Rock is spelt Rinnogy). The major island is here referred to as **Arranmore**, which is the locally favoured name and spelling, used by the lifeboat station. However the Commissioners of Irish Lights use the spelling **Aranmore** for the lighthouse.*

Middle and Chapel Sounds

bearing 032°; this leads clear E of **Bullig-na-naght** and **Carrickgilreavy** and W of **Leenon-rua**. Carrickgilreavy is often marked by breakers, and **Meadalmore**, the S extremity of Illancrone, covers only at very high spring tides. When Illancrone beacon is abeam, turn N, leaving the beacon 3 cables to port. Identify Turk Rocks beacon, one mile N, and steer to pass 2 cables W of it. The transit of Carrickbealatroha Upper and Ballagh Rocks beacons, 354°, leads clear W of Turk Rocks.

Note that these directions lead over Middle Shoals, with a least depth of 5·5m, and which break in heavy weather or a high swell. However in such conditions a yacht should not in any case attempt the approach to Aran Sound from the S, but should proceed outside Arranmore Island.

Middle Sound

⊕MS 54°56·9′N 8°30′W

Middle Sound is scarcely more than a cable wide between underwater rocks extending from the islands on each side. It is navigable only in settled conditions, and from seaward only with judicious use of GPS. For a vessel bound S out of Aran Sound it may provide an attractive option: the leading line is Turk Rocks beacon astern in line between Inishfree Upper and Inishinny (and in line with the peak of Errigal). The beacon 069° in line with the S end of Inishinny gives a least depth of 5m but leads close S of a 0·6m rock; the beacon 066° in line with the W point of Inishinny gives a least depth of 3m but a slightly greater margin for error on each side. It is essential to establish the identity and continued visibility of the leading marks before commencing the passage: from a distance the low islands merge into each other.

Chapel Sound

⊕CS 54°57′·7N 8°31′·2W

Chapel Sound is 1·5 cables wide between dangerous rocks and has a shoal with 2·4m at its SW end. The leading beacons NE of Chapel Bay lead through it, but for the stranger, it is to be approached from seaward only in clear visibility and with judicious use of GPS. When the Aphort beacons line up 308° it is safe to turn into Rossillion Bay.

Outward bound, the leading marks must be clearly identified to begin with, and must remain visible.

Wyon Point beacon from the W; Mount Errigal, R

Illancrone from the E

Turk Rocks beacon from the SW; the wind turbine at Burtonport, L

Carrickbealatroha Upper beacon (R) in line with Ballagh Rocks beacon (centre R) leads W of Turk Rocks and through the South Sound of Aran. Carrickbealatroha Lower beacon, L

(left) Turk Rocks beacon between Inishfree Upper and Inishinny and in line with Errigal leads through Middle Sound.

(below) Chapel Sound leading beacons 048° (centre)

South Sound of Aran

Aphort leading beacons in line lead 308° clear NE of Black Rocks, SW of Rannagh Point

Charley's Point beacons, from the E: the N one (above) and the S one (below)

Aileen beacon, from the E

*Passage west to east, Chapel Bay to the South Sound of Aran; Leac na bhFear beacon, R, Aileen beacon, centre L. Transiting W to E, the fishing boat has left Leac na bhFear to **port**, is borrowing to the N to find the deepest water, and will leave Aileen beacon close to **starboard**.*

Aphort beacon (R), from the S

Anchorages south of Arranmore

- 1·5 cables NE of Illancrone in 3m, sand.
- Between 1·5 and 2·5 cables E of Inishkeeragh in 2·5 to 3·5m, sand.
- Rossillion Bay (Aphort, 54°58'·3N 8°30'·8W) is sheltered from winds between W and NE and may be reached by crossing the shoal between Inishkeeragh and the Clutch in a least depth of 1·8m keeping Turk Rocks beacon bearing 128°. Anchor in 2m, sand, clear of the moorings in the bay. The pier immediately N of Rannagh Point has 1m alongside and room for a 10m yacht to tie up for a short visit. Pub at Plughoge, 400m.
- Chapel Bay (54°58'·3N 8°29'·7W) is well sheltered from winds between NW and NE. Anchor one third of a cable S of the 2m-high rock in 4·3m, or SW of this position in 2·7m. Small pier.

All these anchorages are somewhat exposed to swell.

South Sound of Aran

⊕ SA 54°57'·7N 8°28'·4W
AC2792

The South Sound of Aran, N of Turk Rocks, is navigable by a yacht only above half tide and in reasonably settled weather. Leaving Turk Rocks beacon not less than 1 cable to starboard, bring Carrickbealatroha Upper beacon in line with Ballagh Rocks beacon 354° to leave Clutch buoy to port, and Aileen beacon 1·5 cables to port. Keep on this line until Cloghcor Point, the SE corner of Arranmore Island, comes abeam, then steer 325° for the more N'ly of the two leading beacons on the Arranmore shore S of Charley's Point. When the S leading beacon comes abeam, turn to starboard and head N, giving Charley's Point a berth of two cables to avoid the rocks off it. Note that Carrickbealatroha Upper rocks extend 1·5 cables N and NW of their beacon.

Caution

Note that (unusually) the navigable channel lies between Aileen Reef (to the N) and the Aileen Reef port-hand beacon. There is foul ground S and E of the beacon.

Passages in Aran Sound

Arranmore lifeboat heading W from Aileen Reef towards Chapel Sound. The lifeboat has left Aileen Reef beacon (bottom R) close to port and is heading for Leac na bhFear beacon (centre). Aphort beacon is just visible above and to the right of Leac na bhFear. Rossillion Bay (Aphort) top L

South Sound of Aran to Chapel Bay

54°58'·2N 8°28'·6W *see photos above and opposite*

The sound SW of Aileen Reef and W of Aileen Reef beacon is a useful short cut. Heading W, approach Aileen Reef beacon steering 260° and leave it close to port. Borrow a little to the N between there and Leac na bhFear beacon, then leave Leac na bhFear beacon close to starboard, and head towards Aphort beacon. When 50m from Aphort beacon, turn on to a course of 250°, with the Burtonport wind turbine directly astern, until Chapel Bay opens up. The photograph above shows the lifeboat using this channel.

Caution

As of 2011 GPS chart plotters cannot be implicitly relied upon in narrow channels around Aran Sound and Burtonport due to the limited horizontal accuracy of the charts. Where precision of half a cable or better is required it is particularly essential to maintain good visual pilotage with continuous use of the echo sounder.

NORTH SOUND of ARAN

⊕*NA* 55°00'·2N 8°29'·1W
AC1883, 2792 and Plan

This is the normal approach to Aran Road and Burtonport. It is safe in almost any weather, the exception being NW gales; a prolonged NW winter gale can cause the entrance to break right across.

Directions - North Sound to Aran Road anchorage

The entrance is marked by the 9m high **Ballagh Rocks** beacon, a dominating feature of the Sound, which should be approached from due N so as to leave **Rinnagy** and **Bullignamirra** well to port. There are two alternative leading lines. **Lackmorris** perch a little to the left of **Carrickbealatroha Lower** beacon 161° leads W of **Leenane na Mallagh**, a 5·5m patch which breaks in heavy weather. The leading beacons on the Arranmore shore S of Charley's Point in line 186° lead over Leenane na Mallagh. Both lines lead close E of **Blind Rocks** (0·9m), E of Calf Island.

Approaching from the N: once past Ballagh

331

North Sound of Aran and Aran Road

Ballagh Rocks

The leading beacons S of Charley's Point 186° lead between Ballagh Rocks and Blind Rock

Arranmore Obelisk (lower R) from the E; Moylecorragh (L) and Cluidaniller (R) on the skyline.

Arranmore ferry pier (R), from the NW; Black Rock beacon, L. Leave the beacon to port and head straight for the end of the pier.

(below) Carrickbealatroha Lower (L) and Lackmorris beacons, from the W

Rocks, borrow a little to the left of the leading lines to give a good berth to Blind Rocks, and as Calf Island comes abeam identify the Obelisk on the Arranmore shore. Do not turn to starboard until the peak of Moylecorragh (162m) comes in line with the Obelisk, 241°; this leads S of Blind Rocks and N of **Calf Island Shoal**, which has a least depth of 3·4m. There is however no harm in continuing S until the Obelisk bears W before turning in to the anchorage, but beware **Dirty Rock** to the SE.

Anchorage

The best area is NE of the Obelisk and S of Calf Island. There are a good many moorings there, but room to anchor outside them. This is a safe anchorage, usually comfortable in settled or W weather, but sometimes subject to swell. There are visitors' moorings. There is also plenty of room to anchor E of the Obelisk but this area is more exposed. Stackamore quay is just W of the Obelisk with a slip and FY light. There is 0·7m alongside at the steps and a little less along the inner half. The ferry pier and slip are 1·5 cables S of this quay. The ferry pier has deep water alongside and is a handy place for a short visit to pick up stores; do not leave a yacht at the steps, but the large car ferries use the slipway. A fenderboard is required. Approaching the ferry pier, leave Black Rock beacon close to port and steer for the pierhead. Note that drying rocks extend 60m SE from the beacon.

The bay close to the old drying pier further S at Leabgarrow is encumbered with rocks and unsuitable for anchoring.

Facilities

Water at ferry pier. Diesel (in cans), contact Arranmore Co-op (diesel is available by hose at Burtonport). Small shop, restaurants, pubs, PO. Doctor. Car ferry to Burtonport. RNLI all-weather lifeboat station.

Arranmore ferry pier; the car ferry uses the slip, L

North Sound of Aran from the SW; Leabgarrow foreground, with the ferry pier lower R and Black Rock beacon beyond it; Calf Island centre, Ballagh Rocks upper R centre, Owey top L and Bloody Foreland Hill in the distance. The entrance to Burtonport S of Eighter Island, middle R

BURTONPORT

AC2792, Imray C53 and Plan
54°59'·5N 8°29'W

Burtonport (Ailt an Chorráin) is the principal mainland harbour on this coast and the ferry port for Arranmore. The harbour is also used by sea angling, diving and shellfish boats, offers excellent shelter in all weathers and welcomes yachts; it is the only place on the NW coast where water and diesel are both available by hose at the pier. The ferries (in particular) must not be obstructed. They monitor VHF Ch 16 and 11.

Main approach – Rutland North Channel

Rutland North Channel has a least depth of 2·5m at LAT and is well lit and beaconed, but may be challenging for a stranger at night since - particularly with a flood tide - the lights appear in rapid succession and the shores are extremely close in places. The passage should be made under power only, due to the presence of ferry and other traffic in this narrow channel. **Dirty Rock** (dries 2m), 0·5 cable W of the W end of Eighter Island, is particularly dangerous since it is close to the channel, covers at HW and in calm weather does not break. From S of

Lights and Marks
Burtonport

Rutland North Channel
Torban buoy, SHM Fl G 3s
Carrickatine red beacon, No 2, QR 6m 1M.
No.3 beacon SHM QG
Inishcoo leading lights Iso 6s 1M 119·3° from bns on Inishcoo Island. Front 6m white with black band, rear 11m black with yellow band
Inishcoo red beacon, No 4, QR 3m 1M
Rutland leading lights Oc 6s 1M 137·6° from bns on Rutland Island. Front 8m white with black band, rear 14m, black with yellow band
Nancy's Rock, green beacon, No 1, QG 3m 1M.
Edernish Rock, red beacon, No 6, QR 3m 1M
Burtonport leading lights FG 1M 068·1° from bns above harbour. Front 17m, grey with white band, rear 23m, grey with yellow band. Same line, bns on Rutland Oc 4s, yellow with black bands.
Burtonport Pier Channel, red conical stone bn, PHM Fl R 3s 3M

South Channel or Duck Sound (photo p336):
South Channel red PHM perch, unlit, 2 cables E of Lackmorris.

Rutland South Channel (photos p336):
Corren's Rock, red tower Fl R 3s 4m 2M.
South Rutland, unlit conical bn 0·5 cable N of Corren's Rock.
Yellow Rock, grey tower, W Card Q(9) 15s, on the E side of the channel E of Rutland Island.
Teige's Rock, grey tower Fl 3s 4m 2M.

Burtonport

Map: Rutland North Channel to Burtonport

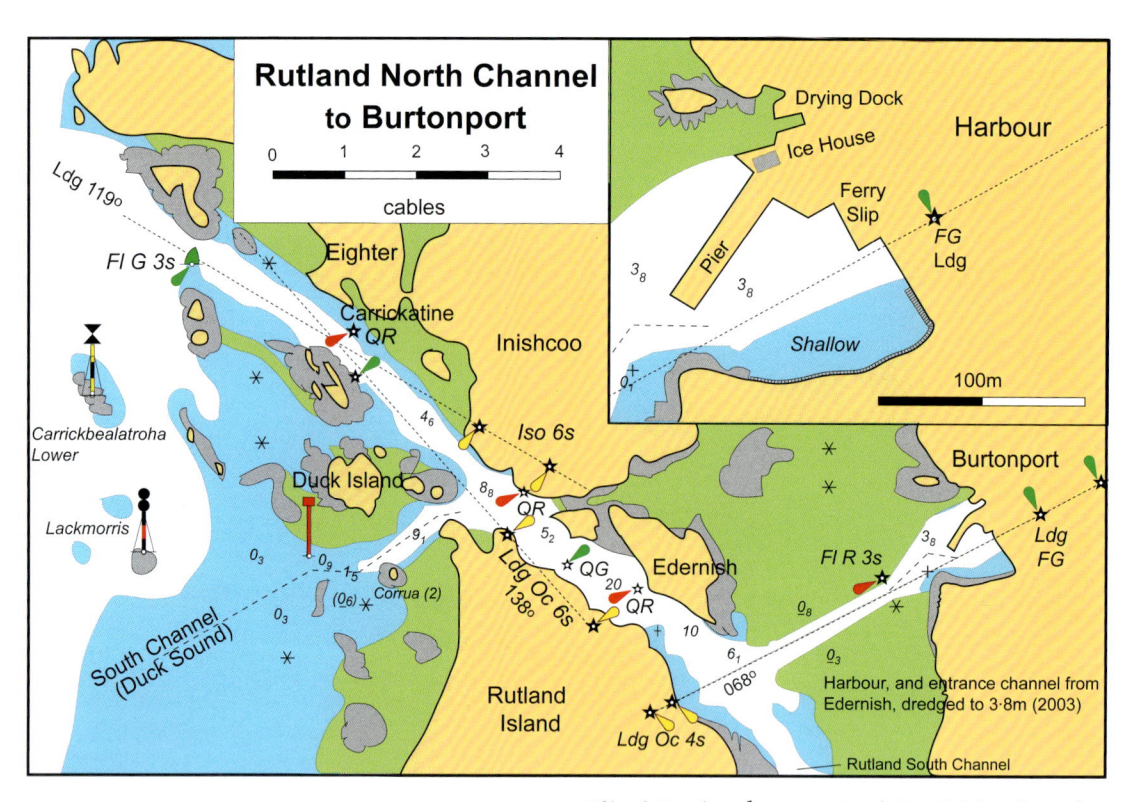

Bring Carrickbealatroha Lower beacon (foreground) slightly to the right of Lackmorris beacon to avoid Leenane na Mallagh, Blind Rocks and Dirty Rock

Rutland North channel, the main approach to Burtonport. The Inishcoo leading beacons, centre, Carrickatine beacon, L, and No.3 starboard-hand beacon, R. The deeper water lies slightly to the NE (left) of the leading line at this point.

Rutland North channel; the Rutland leading marks. From left of the line, the house obscures all but the top of the back mark

Blind Rocks, the transit of **Carrickbealatroha Lower** and **Lackmorris** perches leads clear W of Dirty Rock. On this transit, pick up the **Inishcoo** leading beacons, 119°, which lead in and very close S of **Carrickatine** beacon (QR). It is prudent to borrow to the SW of the leading line in the outer approach, but leave **Torban** starboard-hand buoy on the proper hand. Immediately beyond Carrickatine, the leading line of the **Rutland** beacons, 137°, must be followed closely, in particular erring nothing to starboard (note that from the NE side of the line the characteristic lower (yellow) part of the rear beacon of the Rutland pair is obscured by a new house). Then steer for **Nancy's Rock** beacon (QG), leave it close to starboard and **Edernish Rock** beacon (QR) close to port. Keep to the Edernish side of the channel until the **Burtonport** leading beacons line up. Turn on to the leading line steering 068° and proceed up the dredged channel leaving the pier channel beacon to port. Leave the leading line at this point and steer for the conspicuous ice house on the NW side of the harbour until the entrance is well abeam, then turn in. The SE side of the channel has rocky shallows.

There is a feasible and pleasant temporary anchorage in 1·5m, on the SW side of Eighter on the extension of the Rutland leading line, NE of the main channel.

Burtonport

Burtonport Harbour from the NW in 1997. The area of reefs and islets to the right of the picture has since been reclaimed and fronted with rock armouring facing the harbour, and a wind turbine stands to the right of the large sheds, top R

Burtonport Harbour

The SE part of the harbour is shallow and encumbered by small craft moorings; the NW part, with both sides of the pier, and the approach channel, is dredged to 3·8m. Yachts may have to raft up to fishing boats against the pier. In settled weather it is possible to lie against the outer (NW) side of the pier. A fenderboard is recommended if lying directly against either side of the pier. The E wall of the harbour, SE of the ferry berth, is available as a temporary berth at high tide. To the N of the root of the pier is a small drying dock with up to 4m at MHWS and a clean, gently shelving concrete bottom. This is available for emergency repairs.

Harbour dues may be levied. Contact HM (phone 086 831 0121) for advice on berthing and facilities. Constant +0050 Galway; MHWS 3·9m, MHWN 2·9m, MLWN 1·5m, MLWS 0·5m.

Facilities

Pubs, restaurants, PO, mechanical and electrical repairs. Bottled gas. Water and diesel (by hose) on the pier. Petrol and shop at filling station, 1 km. Buses to Letterkenny, Fintown and Dublin. Airport at Carrickfin, 13 km. Car ferries to Arranmore.

Rutland North channel; Inishcoo (No.4) and Edernish Rock (No.6) port-hand beacons, L; Teige's Rock and Yellow Rock beacons in Rutland South channel, R

South Channel (Duck Sound)

54°58'·9N 8°28'·3W

This channel, between Duck Island and the N tip of Rutland Island, should not be confused with Rutland South Channel. Pilotage of Duck Sound is tricky and it is simpler and safer to use the N channel for access to Burtonport. The narrow and shallow part of Duck Sound

Burtonport; the pier channel port-hand beacon. Steer from here for the old ice house (L centre) to avoid the shallows off the point, R

335

Duck Sound and Rutland South Channel

Duck Sound; leave the South Channel port hand perch 40m to port and steer for Corrua (L, below)

Entering Rutland North channel from Duck Sound; Inishcoo rear leading beacon, L centre, Toninishgaun Point, R

Rutland South Channel, passage N to S; leave Teige's Rock 20m to port

Rutland South Channel, passage N to S; leave Yellow Rock 60m to port

(below L) South Rutland beacon   (R) Corren's Rock beacon from the E

is just SE of the South Channel red perch, where there is 0·9m. Approaching through the South Sound of Aran, and with sufficient rise of tide, turn to starboard when Cloghcor Point is abeam, leave Carrickbealatroha Upper beacon 0·5 cable to port and then head for a point midway between Lackmorris and South Channel perches. Pass 40m S of the South Channel perch and head E towards Corrua (the 2m-high rock W of Rutland). When the Inishcoo rear leading beacon is in line with Toninishgun Point (the N point of Rutland) steer towards it, pass close to the point and join the main channel. If turning N wait until Nancy's Rock beacon is visible; this avoids a rock extending ESE from Duck Island. Going out, use the same line until the NW corner of Duck Island bears N, then turn to pass 40 m S of the red perch.

Rutland South Channel

54°57'·8N 8°27'·6W

The south entrance to Burtonport is hazardous on account of the many unmarked rocks and the strong tidal stream, which runs on to the reefs N of Inishfree at up to 6 knots. Strangers are strongly advised to use the North Channel in preference. The passage should be attempted only around HW as there are patches, including the narrows, with as little as 0·3m at LAT, and the channel at the narrows is only 30m wide.

Inbound for Burtonport, from a position 5 cables NE of Turk Rocks beacon, identify Corren's Rock red beacon and steer for it on a bearing of 060°. When 2 cables from it (long. 8° 26'·88), turn to port and steer 032° for the SE point of Rutland Island. When Corren's Rock beacon is abeam to starboard, turn hard to starboard towards it. Leave it close to **port**, then steer NE for a further cable, also leaving South Rutland conical beacon to port. Then steer to leave Yellow Rock beacon 60m to starboard and Teige's Rock beacon 20m to starboard, then stay close to the Rutland Island shore to avoid Walker's Rock (dries 0·9m). The photographs show a passage in the opposite direction.

The bathymetry of the channel on AC2792 and electronic charts derived from it (most recent survey 1966) is still valid, but (in addition to any difference in horizontal datum) there is an inaccuracy in charted positions around Rutland Island and Burtonport which makes full reliance on GPS and chartplotters hazardous.

Owey and Cruit Bay

OWEY ISLAND and SOUND
AC1883

Owey Island is free of offlying dangers except on the SW side where a number of rocks terminate in Tornagaravan, 9m high, and on the SE where a spit extends part of the way across the sound. Red granite cliffs with many caves on the W and N sides make impressive scenery. There is no secure anchorage but in settled sea conditions there can be good shelter in W wind on the SE side of the island off the village in 5m. There is a small pier on the SE shore, not recommended, and a small quay at the boat landing in the deep, narrow gut just N of the E point. The island has occasional summer residents but no facilities.

Owey Sound

⊕OS 55°02′·7N 8°27′W

Owey Sound presents no difficulty except in high swell or strong SW or N winds, but should not be used at night. It is however possible to go through in strong W winds when it would be particularly unpleasant W of the island. Heading straight from Aran Sound identify **Tornamullane Rock**; if it does not show up well, the gut on the SE coast of Owey is conspicuous and makes a good mark. Do not err to the E of a bearing of 190° on **Ballagh Rocks,** in order to avoid **Bullignamirra** (dries 3·7m) and **Rinnagy Rock** (dries 2·4m) and the area S and SE of them, which is incompletely surveyed. Approaching Owey Sound, leave **Tornamullane Rock** 1 cable to starboard and

Lights and Marks
Owey Sound and Cruit Bay
Owey Sound leading bns, 2 x Oc 10s
Horse Rock leading bns 2 x L Fl 8s
Rinnalea Point bn, Fl 7·5s 19m 9M, visible between 132° and 167°. Inconspicuous by day as it does not break the skyline.
Gortnasate Quay Fl R 5s.
Nicholas Rock, concrete beacon, unlit

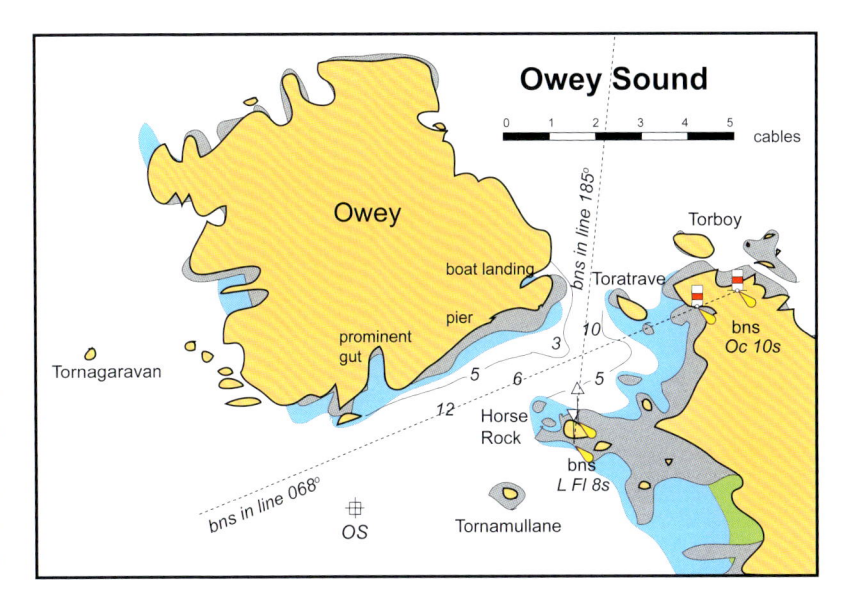

then steer N until the red and white banded leading beacons near the N point of Cruit Island come in line 068°. Steer on this transit until the sound is well open to the N, and identify the leading marks on Horse Rock to the S. When these come in line 185°, turn to port and keep them in transit astern until clear to the N. A spit with 3m extends 2 cables SE from Owey; the leading marks lead clear of it. The Horse Rock pair are hard to discern in the approach from the N; in this case a mid-channel course between Toratrave and Owey is safe until the much more obvious beacons on the mainland are identified.

CRUIT BAY

⊕CB 55°02′·8N 8°24′W

AC1883 and Plan

Cruit (pronounced "Critch") Bay is a beautiful spot, normally the best anchorage

(above left) The boat landing at the E end of Owey

(above) Owey Sound; the leading beacons on Horse Rock 185°

Owey Sound; the leading beacons on Cruit Island 068°

337

Cruit Bay

Cruit Bay; Nicholas Rock beacon, from the NW

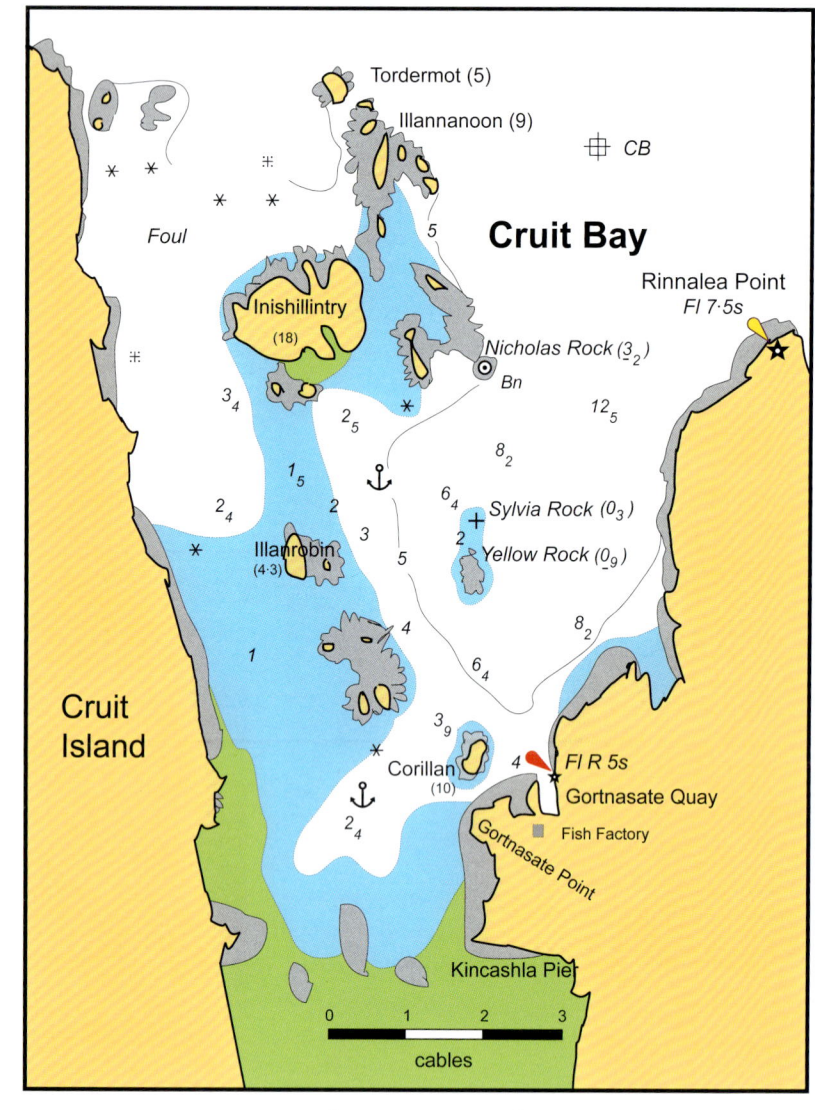

on the coast, easy of access and secure in all summer winds, although swell in N winds makes it uncomfortable at times. The channel to the W of Inishillintry has more rocks than are shown on AC1883 and is not navigable by yachts. A stranger should not attempt to enter Cruit Bay at night.

Directions

From Owey Sound or the W there are no offlying dangers apart from the **Stag Rocks,** well offshore. The sound W of Tordermot and Inishillintry should not be mistaken for Cruit Bay. Leave Tornamuldoo, Tordermot (5m high) and Illannanoon (9m high) a cable to starboard. Leave **Nicholas Rock** beacon to starboard and steer towards **Corillan**, 10m high and rocky. To pass well E of the unmarked **Sylvia** and **Yellow Rocks** keep the E side of Corillan in line with Gortnasate Point. Sylvia Rock has 0·3m and Yellow Rock dries 0·9m. Passing W of Corillan, stay within 0·5 cable of the island to avoid a drying rock less than a cable to the WNW. Approaching from the N, give the shore S of Rinnalea Point a berth of a cable. The ebb tide runs out strongly.

Anchorages *(all on sand)*

- One to two cables SW of Corillan.
- With careful pilotage it is possible to reach an anchorage S of Inishillintry. Enter close SE of Nicholas beacon and keep the beacon bearing between 045° and 055°. This leads between two rocks and beyond them there is an area about 3m deep and good room to anchor. The best sheltered part is reported to be NW away from the rocks with Nicholas beacon bearing 065° and Gortnasate Quay bearing between 150° and 156°. There is also an entrance to this anchorage from Corillan keeping Gortnasate Quay bearing 151° and heading towards the right hand of two rocks just S of Inishillintry's S point, passing through a 0·5 cable gap between Yellow Rock and the rocky area SW of it.

Gortnasate Quay

55°02'·2N 8°24'·3W

On the E side of a narrow inlet E of Corillan is a 100m-long quay, with a road connecting it to Kincashla village 1 km to the SE. The quay has deep water alongside and there is a fish factory at the head of the inlet. Water is available at the fish factory; shops and PO at Kincashla. The disused Kincashla pier ("Kincasla" on the chart), just SE of Gortnasate Point, dries.

Carnboy Channel

⊕CC 55°03'N 8°21'·6W

AC1883, and Plan of Gola Sound

Carnboy Channel is the passage between the mainland and the rocks to the S and SE of Inishfree. From the S, **Rabbit Rock**, which always shows, should be left close to port. The main challenge lies in negotiating the 1-cable-wide gap between (on the E) the rocks extending 2 cables out from Carnboy

Cruit Bay and Carnboy Channel to Gola

Cruit Bay from SW; Corillan and Gortnasate Point centre R, Inishillintry upper L; Inishfree, Gola and Inishmeane top centre, Bloody Foreland Hill top R

Point and (on the W) **Bullignagappul** (dries 0·3m) and **Bullignamort** (0·3m). A stranger should not attempt this passage in poor visibility due to the difficulty of identifying the leading line, and it is not navigable by night. The summit of Inishmeane, 3M to the N, just open of Gubnadough, the E extremity of Gola, 012°, leads through the gap. The former leading beacons on Mullaghdoo Point, 184°, no longer exist. Once N of Carnboy Point, identify Middle Rock buoy at the S end of Gola Roads and steer to leave it close on either hand.

GOLA ISLAND and SOUND

55°04'·7N 8°21'W
AC1883 and Plan

There are many dangers N and S of Gola and several channels inside the island. None of the approaches is simple for a stranger and in bad weather and especially in poor visibility a yacht coming from the S would be safer to make for Cruit Bay or Aran Road.

Cruit Bay; the E side of Corillan in line with Gortnasate Point clears Sylvia and Yellow Rocks

(above) Cruit Bay; the anchorage SW of Corillan

(right) Carnboy Channel; the summit of Inishmeane just open of Gubnadough (the E end of Gola) leads E of Bullignagappul and Bullignamort. The yacht is about to cross the transit line

Gola Sound

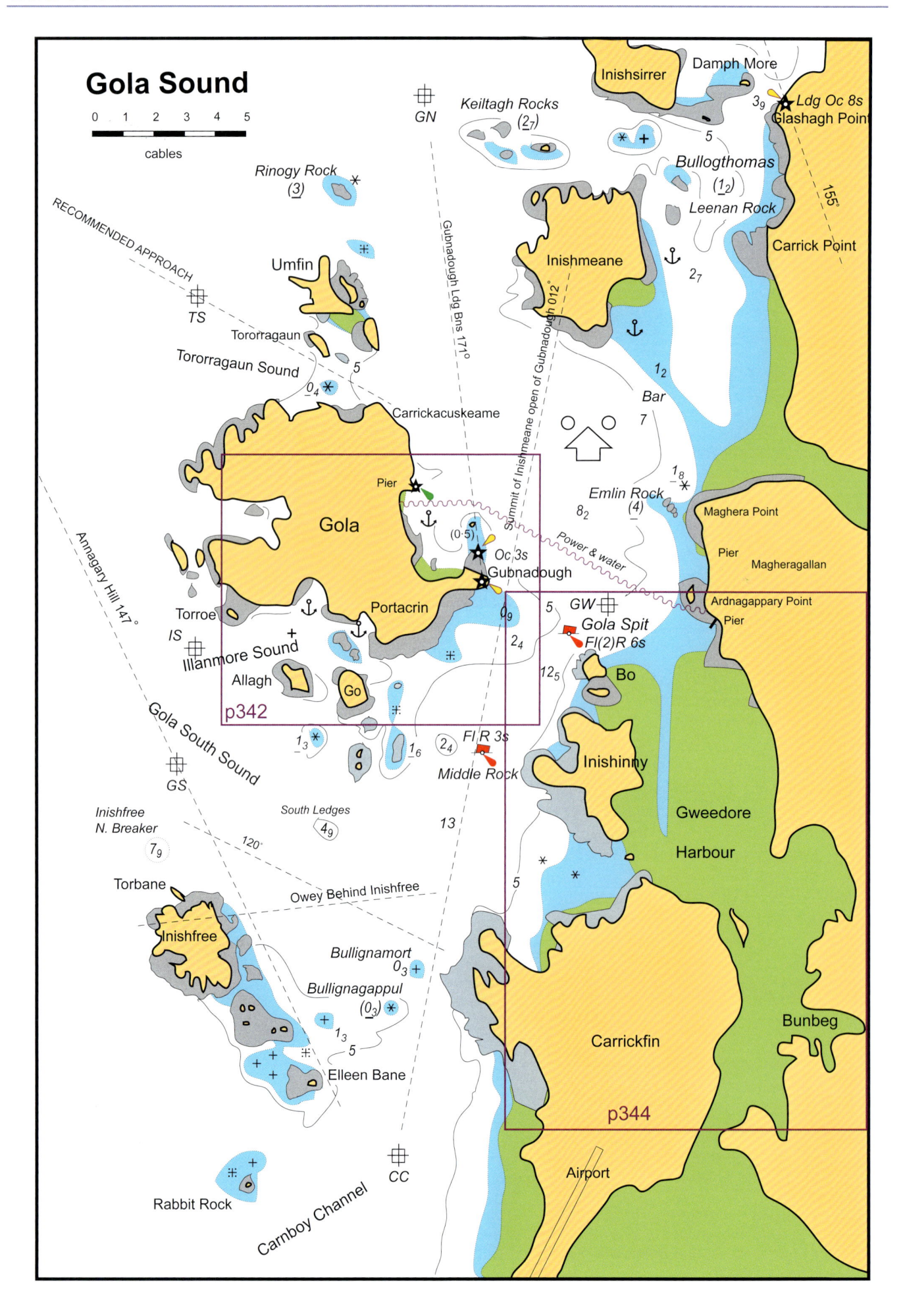

Gola

Dangers
Cruit Bay to Bloody Foreland
There are many rocks and shoals around the islands. The principal dangers from the point of view of pilotage are:

Carnboy Channel:
Bullignagappul, dries 0·3m, 3 cables W of Carnboy Point
Bullignamort, 0·3m, 1 cable NE of Bullignagappul

S and N of Gola:
Leonancoyle, dries, 1 cable E of Go Island
Passage Rock, 1·2m, in Illanmore Sound
Drying rocks in the S half of Tororragaun Sound
Rinogy, dries 3m, 3 cables N of Umfin
Keiltagh Rocks, dry 2·7m, 5 cables NW of Inishmeane

Offshore:
Bullogconnel Shoals, 3 groups with 2·4m, 2·4m and drying 1·4m, 1·2m NW of Gola

Lights and Marks
Middle Rock buoy, PHM Fl R 3s
Gola Spit buoy, PHM Fl(2) R 6s
Gola North Sound leading bns on Gubnadough Oc 3s 2M, front white pillar with black band 9m, rear black pillar with white band 13m
Gola Pier, Fl G 3s
Glashagh Point leading beacons Oc 8s 3M, front white pillar with black band 12m, rear black pillar with white band 17m
Inishsirrer, NW point, white pillar Fl 3·7s 20m 4M
Bloody Foreland, 4m white pillar Fl WG 7·5s 14m W6M G4M, W 062°-232°, G232°-062°. Shows green over the islands and rocks to the SW and NE, white elsewhere
Tory Island, black tower, white band, Fl(4) 30s 40m 18M, Racon (M) 12-23M

In Gweedore Harbour:
Bo Island, green beacon SHM Fl G 3s 3m
Inishinny (no.1), green beacon SHM QG
Inishinny (no.3), green beacon SHM unlit
Carrickbullog (no.2), red beacon PHM QR
Inishcoole (no.4), red beacon PHM QR
Bluff buoy, SHM Fl G 3s
Yellow Rocks (no.6) red beacon PHM QR
Bunbeg buoy, PHM Fl R 3s
Magheralosk (no.5) green beacon SHM QG

Coming from the N in good visibility it is safe to go in through Gola N Sound. Gola lost its permanent population in 1967 but has recently been the focus of much excellent restoration work led by former residents and their families. Houses have been refurbished for seasonal occupation, there is a campsite and tearoom, and a passenger ferry runs from Magheragallan and Bunbeg.

Gola South Sound
⊕ GS 55°04'·4N 8°23'·1W

Rocks and breakers extend almost a mile south of Gola. In settled weather it is safe to pass 5 cables N of Inishfree and 4 cables from Allagh and Go. In heavy weather or a large swell it is advisable to stay well outside Inishfree North Breaker, 2 cables NNW of Inishfree. Approach with Annagary Hill bearing 147°, open left of Inishfree, until 2 cables N of Inishfree, then steer 120° until Owey Island is just shut in behind the height of Inishfree. Then steer 085° until Gubnadough is below the top of Inishmeane, and turn to port leaving Middle Rock and Gola Spit buoys close on either hand.

Illanmore Sound
⊕ IS 55°04'·9N 8°22'·9W

Illanmore Sound is the most direct passage from seaward but has several hazardous rocks. From the W, to avoid **Passage Rock**, in the middle of the channel N of Allagh Island, first identify **Torroe** off Gola at the entrance to the Sound. Leaving Torroe 0·5 cable to port, turn to port towards the large bay on Gola. When off the middle of the bay turn to starboard and head towards the NW point of Go Island. Give Go Island a berth of 50 to 80m to starboard, then keep the N point of Allagh Island just open of Go Island so as to pass N of **Leonancoyle Rock**. Continue on this line until Gubnadough (the E point of Gola) is open W of the top of Inishmeane before turning to port.

Tororragaun Sound
⊕ TS 55°06'·2N 8°22'·8W

Tororragaun Sound is the gap between the N side of Gola and **Tororragaun Rock**, 19m high. It is easy to identify and in fine weather is the shortest and simplest route from Owey to Gola Pier. It may be hazardous in a significant swell as there is a ridge of rocks right across it, with less than 1m and two drying rocks in the S half, but with 4·6m least charted depth on the N half. Enter just 50m off the SW side of Tororragaun, which is steep-to, and then steer for the NE point of Gola, labelled Carrickacuskeame on the chart.

Tororragaun Sound from the E; the mid-channel drying rock, breaking, L centre. Tororragaun, R, Gola L

341

Gola

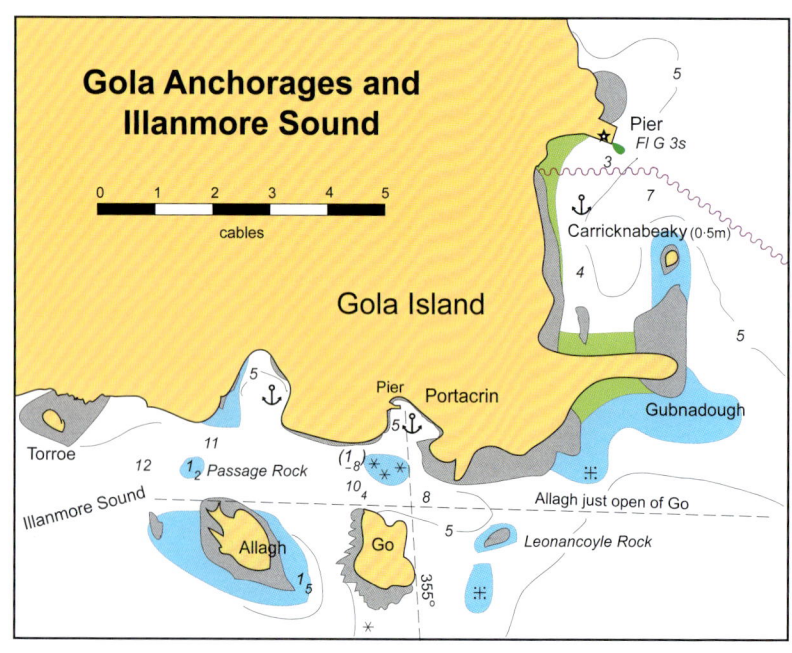

View NE over Illanmore Sound and Gola North Sound. Go Island foreground, Gola centre, with Portacrin L and Gubnadough R; Inishmeane and Inishsirrer top centre and Bloody Foreland and Tory Island in the distance

Gola North Sound – Approach from the N

⊕GN 55°06′·9N 8°21′·5W

The entrance lies between **Keiltagh Rocks** (dries 2·7m) to port and **Rinogy Rock** (dries 3·0m) to starboard. The line of the leading beacons on Gubnadough, 171°, leads midway between these dangers. If the beacons cannot be distinguished, steer towards the N point of Umfin Island until Inishsirrer light beacon bears 050° and Gubnadough 171° (Illancarragh just open of Gubnadough), then steer direct for Gubnadough.

Gola Anchorages; Gweedore Harbour

Gola Anchorages
AC1883 and Plan

- In the bay on the E side of the island, in 3m, sand. Stay at least a cable S of the pier to avoid the underwater power cable and water pipe, which come ashore here. The bay may be subject to swell. The pier has sufficient depth alongside towards HW to offer a temporary berth in swell-free conditions. Beware of the rock ridge in the south arm of the bay, which just covers.
- In winds from NW through N to E, the bay on Gola N of Allagh Island is a very suitable anchorage and easy to enter using the directions for Illanmore Sound. Anchor in 5m staying more than 0·5 cable from the W side and giving the NE side a fair berth as well.
- The anchorage off the pier at Portacrin, N of Go Island on the S side of Gola, is smaller and more difficult to enter but offers good shelter and is convenient for going ashore. Approach from the NE point of Go Island and head 355° towards the pier, which is behind a rocky spit and not obvious from seaward. The channel is very narrow so it is simplest to enter near LW when the rocks show clearly. Anchor in 4·5m in line with the pier and opposite the other possible entrance from the W.

GWEEDORE HARBOUR and BUNBEG

⊕GW 55°05′N 8°20′·2W
AC1883, Imray C53 and Plan

The entrance to Gweedore Harbour crosses a shallow bar, and the channel, which dries 0·8m at one point, requires care and has strong tidal streams, but it is well marked and leads to a secure and attractive anchorage. The harbour at Bunbeg, offering perfect shelter, is used by a number of small fishing boats, and the Tory Island ferry has her overnight berth here. Yachts are welcome, but despite the lights, a stranger should not attempt entry by night.

Directions

The entrance lies between Bo Island and Ardnagappary Point, and has a depth of 1m at LAT. The best depth is close to the rocks extending E of Bo; these can usually be seen below water. As soon as the E end of Bo is

Gola; the leading beacons on Gubnadough

Gola; the anchorage in the bay N of Allagh Island

Portacrin, Gola; the small pier is behind the boulder spit, centre

Caution
GPS chart plotters should not be implicitly relied upon in Gweedore Harbour and its approaches due to the age of the survey data and the changes in the channel and sandbanks. It is essential to maintain good traditional pilotage with continuous use of the echo sounder.

Gola; the anchorage S of the pier on the E side. Carricknabeaky, L centre

Gweedore Harbour; No.1 (L centre) and No.3 beacons

343

Gweedore Harbour

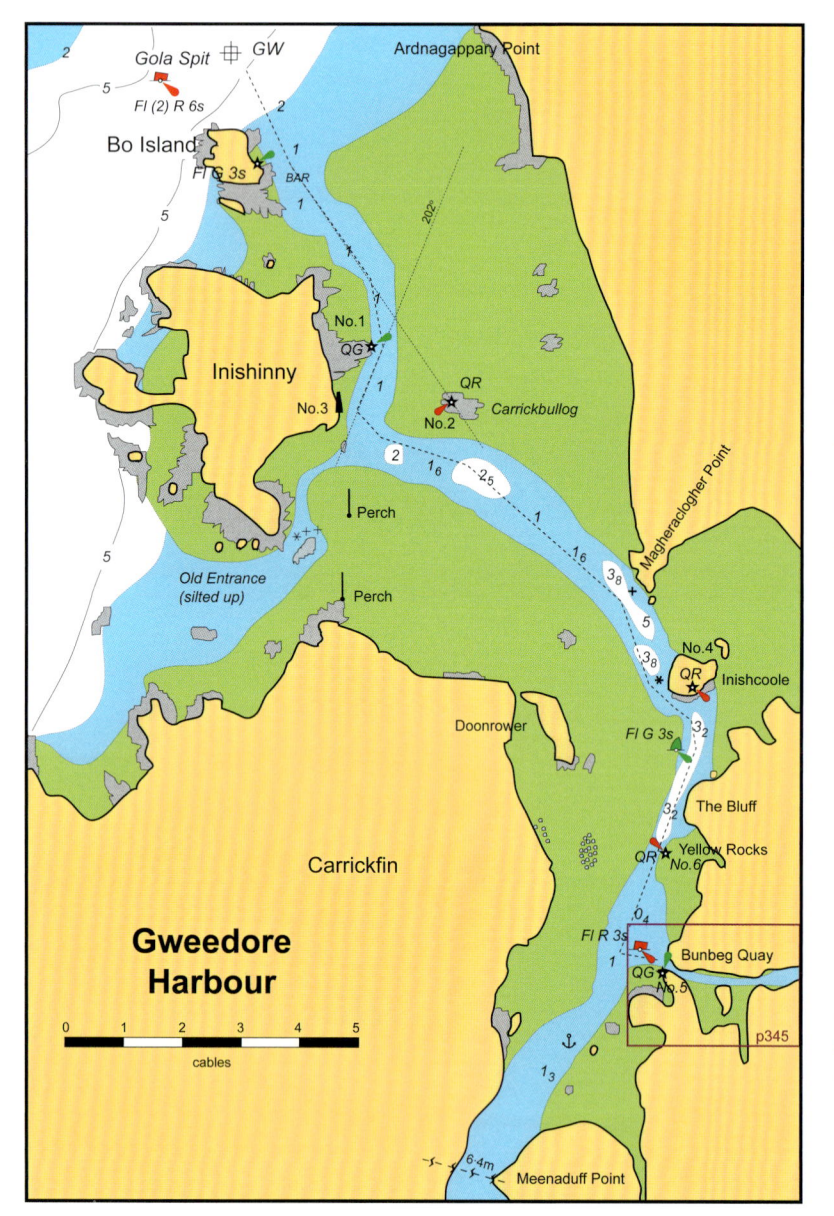

abeam, steer towards Carrickbullog, and when E of the NE point of Inishinny turn S to pass just 12m E of No.1 beacon. From here steer 202° and when abeam of No.3 beacon (on the E point of Inishinny), turn SE for about 60m, then turn to pass 120 to 150m S of No.2 beacon on Carrickbullog. When the E of Carrickbullog is abeam turn on to 140°. Give Magheraclogher Point a berth of 100m to clear the submerged rock about 50m off it, then stay 70m W of Inishcoole to clear the rock there, which just dries; the tidal current may indicate its position. Leave the Bluff starboard-hand buoy 20m to starboard then head past the Bluff, which is steep-to, and W of No.6 beacon. This beacon is on a rock, and all the area to the E of it dries. The channel between here and No.5 beacon, at the entrance to Bunbeg, now has at least 0·4m and does not dry as shown on AC1883. From No.6 beacon head for the mid-channel between Meenaduff Point and the shore opposite.

Anchorages

Anchor 2 cables SW of No.5 beacon, 1·5m, sand. Tidal streams here are still significant, so a second anchor may be advisable. Anchoring in the channel N of Bunbeg entrance is not recommended because of the fishing and ferry traffic. Constant +0055 Galway; MHWS 3·8m, MHWN 2·9m, MLWN 1·5m, MLWS 0·6m.

Gweedore Harbour from the NE; Inishinny, centre R, with Inishfree, Cruit and Arranmore top R

Bunbeg

Bunbeg from the S at LW; Yellow Rock and the No.6 beacon, L centre. Inishmeane, Inishsirrer and Bloody Foreland Hill in the distance

Caution

A power cable with a clearance of 6·4m crosses the channel at Meenaduff Point, 5 cables S of Bunbeg entrance.

Bunbeg

55°03'·5N 8°19'W
See Plan

Bunbeg Harbour occupies the inlet between steep rocky shores at the mouth of the Clady River, E of the No 5 beacon in Gweedore Harbour. Leave Bunbeg buoy to port and No 5 beacon 10m to starboard on entering. The quay, on the N side of the inlet, is 300m in length and has a depth of 2m alongside.

Gweedore Harbour; Carrickbullog from the SW

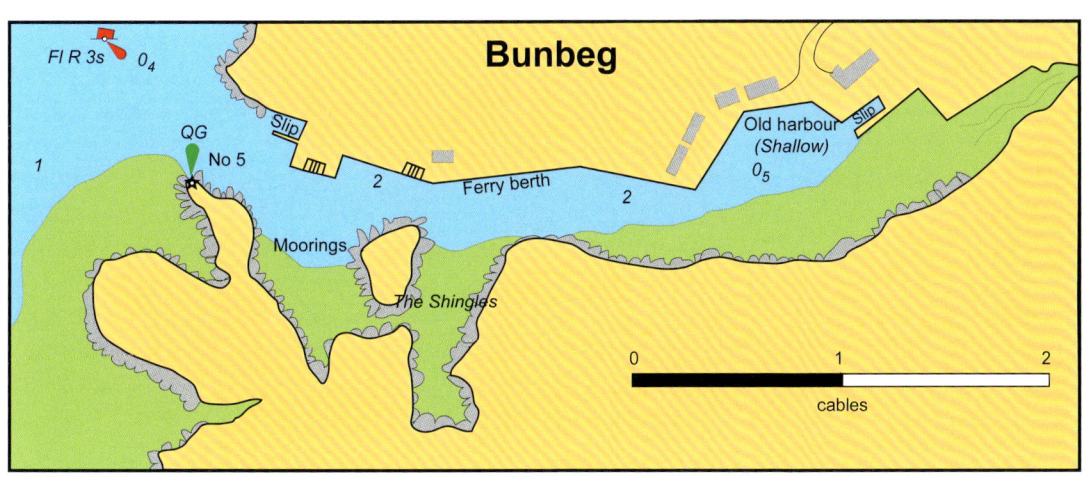

Gweedore Harbour; Yellow Rocks beacon and the Bluff, from the SW

345

Inishmeane and Inishsirrer; Bunaninver and Bloody Foreland

Bunbeg harbour

The leading beacons on Glashagh Point

Bunaninver Port from the NW

There is limited but adequate turning room between the quay and the shore on the S side. The ferry's berth is near the centre of the quay, where the crane is positioned, and should be left unobstructed. The tiny bays on either side of the islet opposite the quay are shallow; the W one has some small-boat moorings in it and the E one, known as the Shingles, dries out. The old harbour further up the creek also dries.

Facilities

Water on the quay. Diesel by tanker. Shops, pubs and PO at Bunbeg village, 1 km. This is the nearest harbour to the airport at Carrickfin, on the W side of Gweedore Harbour.

Inishmeane

55°05'·7N 8°20'W
AC1883

Passage between Inishmeane and the mainland is straightforward in swell-free conditions with sufficient rise of tide. Heading N give Maghera Point a berth of 3 cables to clear Emlin Rock, then hold mid-channel to find the deepest water. There is a small pier on the E side of Inishmeane, and anchorage is available either ESE of the island, south of the bar, or just N of its E point, N of the bar, taking care to stay well clear of Leenan Rock.

Inishsirrer

Locally known as Inishutter, the island has a slipway at its SE end. A white concrete tower on the NW end of the island shows Fl 3·7s.

Inishsirrer Strait

55°06'·6N 8°19'·4W
AC1883

A safe and simple passage except in strong onshore wind or high swell when it should not be attempted. **Damph More** always shows, but all the other rocks SW of it cover. From the S, enter the strait with E side of Damph More bearing 000° to pass between the spit E of **Damph Beg** and the reefs SW of Glashagh Point. Then steer 030° to leave Damph More 0·5 cable to port. Two black and white banded concrete beacons on the shore N of Glashagh Point, in line 137·25° lead NE of the small rocks N of Damph More and SW of **Bunaninver Shoal**, in bad weather keep a bit nearer to Inishsirrer in the outer approach. Northbound in settled conditions it is however possible to head N for Bloody Foreland as soon as the leading beacons come in line; this takes a yacht inside Bunaninver Shoal.

Anchorage in 3m, sand, is available E of the old kelp store building. Approach from the NE keeping the island shore close aboard to avoid the reefs SW of Damph More. The above-water boulder spit to the SW is shorter than charted and its extension towards Damph More covers at half tide.

Bunaninver Port

55°07'·4N 8°18'·7W
AC1883

Bunaninver Port is a pleasant temporary anchorage in good weather. The entrance breaks right across in any rough sea. Approach from well offshore to the NW steering 134° so as to avoid the outer rocks on either side. Anchor outside the narrower part. There is a slip on the N side.

Inishsirrer beacon (centre) from the SW; Bloody Foreland Hill beyond

Bloody Foreland

Bloody Foreland Hill, 315 m high, slopes down gradually to the low point of the headland from which reefs extend for 1 cable. Swell is apt to run high off the point, so it should be given a berth of at least 5 cables.

Inshore Passage South from Bloody Foreland

AC1883 and 2792, and see also Plans of Gola Sound and Aran Sound

If there is sufficient height of tide to pass inside Inishmeane, steer from Bloody Foreland towards the NW end of Inishsirrer until the leading marks on Glashagh Point come into line, then head in on this line 155° until **Damph More** is well abeam. Turn SSW, giving Carrick Point a berth of 2 cables, and hold mid-channel between Inishmeane and the mainland. Give Maghera Point a berth of 3 cables to clear **Emlin Rock**, then leave the two red buoys in Gola Roads close to starboard. With Gubnadough under the summit of Inishmeane, 012°, pass inside **Bullignamort** and identify **Elleen Bane** and **Rabbit Rock** to the SW. Leave each of these a cable to starboard, and once round Rabbit Rock head for the N end of Owey.

If there is sufficient height of tide to negotiate the South Sound of Aran, proceed via Owey Sound; when this Sound opens up, leave Torboy close to port and hold mid-channel between Owey and Toratrave until the leading beacons S of Torboy come in line, 068°. Turn to starboard on this line steering 248°. When **Tornamullane** is abeam, steer 213° for the summit of Arranmore until **Ballagh Rock** with its conspicuous light beacon, at the entrance to the North Sound of Aran, is identified. When Ballagh Rock bears 190°, steer to pass close W of it, erring nothing to port in order to avoid **Rinnagy** and **Bullignamirra** and the incompletely surveyed area S and SE of them. Approaching Ballagh Rock bring the leading marks on Arranmore in line 186° and steer on this line. This passes very close to **Blind Rocks**, 2 cables SW of Ballagh Rock, so in a swell it may be advisable to borrow a little to the left of the line, but beware of **Dirty Rock** to the W of Eighter Island. Keep **Carrickbealatroha Lower** beacon slightly to the right of **Lackmorris** beacon 161°, then leave Carrickbealatroha Lower to port and turn to starboard to pass 1·5 cables W of Lackmorris and **Carrickbealatroha Upper** beacons. Once past Carrickbealatroha Upper beacon, turn to port to bring it in line with Ballagh Rock astern, and steer 174° on this transit to pass W of **Turk Rocks** and out through South Sound.

For detailed descriptions and photographs of the marks in Aran Sound and elsewhere, refer to the main text.

10 Crossing to and from England and Wales

Gateholm Bay, Pembrokeshire: Skokholm (L) and Skomer, on the horizon (photo Wikimedia Commons)

The crossing to or from the neighbouring island involves essential preparation and passage planning, but is comfortably within the capability of a well-found yacht. Those crossing to and from France may or may not choose to stop over in Cornwall or the Isles of Scilly, but these will be waypoints on virtually any course between France and Ireland.

WALES

In Ireland, Kilmore Quay is a strategically-positioned port of arrival or departure, and normally the harbour of choice, but Rosslare is a handy alternative in difficult conditions of weather or tide. Both places are accessible by day or night although (temporarily, at the time of writing in 2015) Kilmore Quay may be inaccessible to deeper drafted vessels around low water. Distances to Rosslare are: from Pwllheli 83 miles, from Aberystwyth 85 miles, from Fishguard 54 miles and from Milford 63 miles. Kilmore Quay is 94 miles from Pwllheli or Aberystwyth, 60 miles from Fishguard or 75 miles from Milford. A few extra miles may be logged by having to negotiate the TSS off the Tuskar Rock, but this scheme is not usually busy. For a vessel crossing from Ireland, the Pembrokeshire coast presents a bold and rocky aspect, but sheltered anchorages and harbours are closely spaced. The best of these are within the long inlet of Milford Haven, which is of course also a major commercial port. The marina at Milford Dock is accessible above half tide, and Neyland marina has all-tide access.

Traffic through and across St George's Channel is fairly constant, but not nearly as heavy as in the English Channel. Large RoRo ferries sail from Fishguard and Pembroke to Rosslare and from Rosslare to Cherbourg and Roscoff. The major Welsh lights are on

To and from Wales

Crossings to and from England and Wales

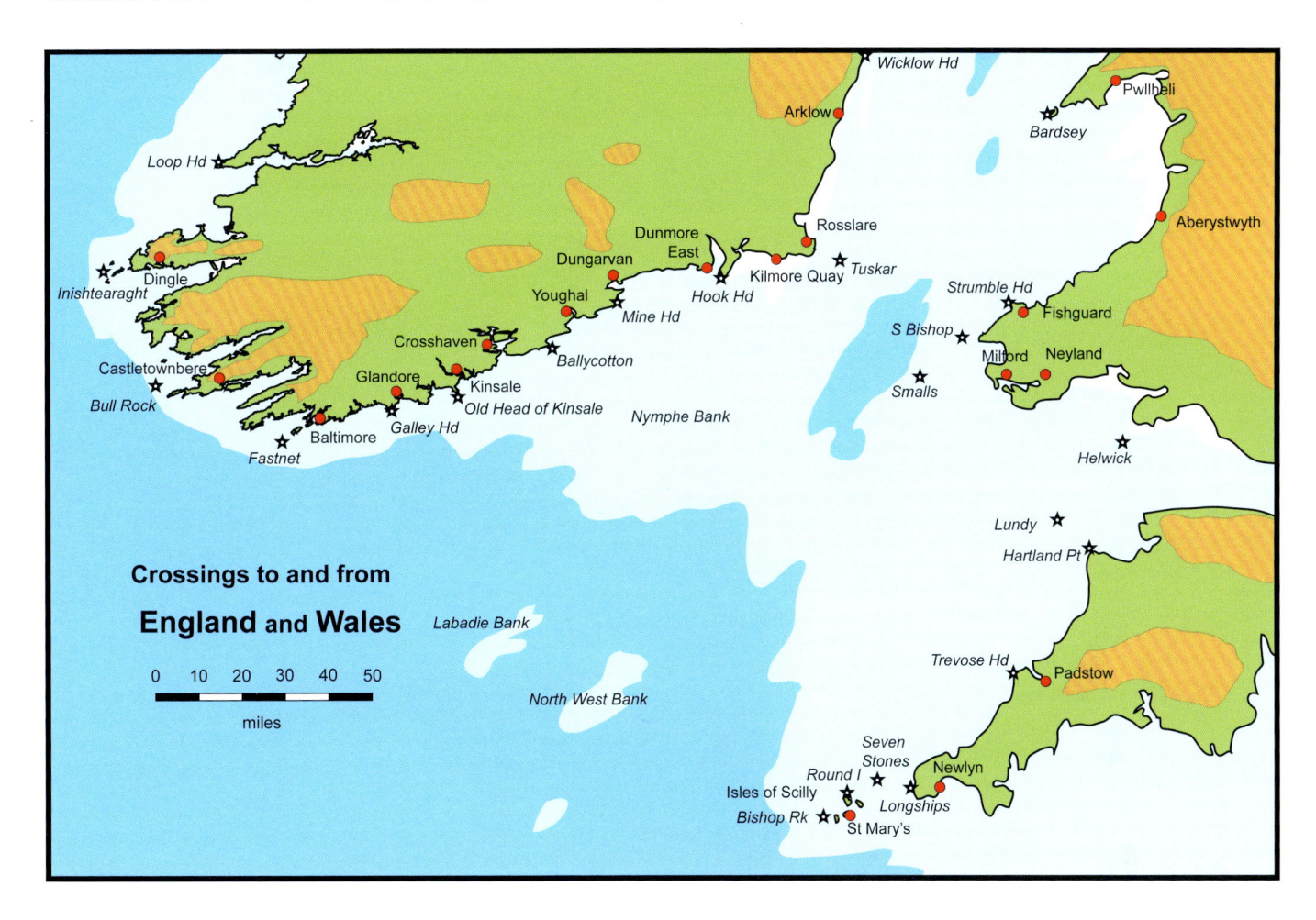

Bardsey, Strumble Head, the South Bishop and the Smalls, and on the Irish side, Tuskar Rock and Hook Head. A buoy with 9-mile range marks the Coningbeg Rock, south of Kilmore Quay.

Both coasts are fringed by offshore islands and reefs, and characterised by strong tidal streams. This can make for demanding pilotage at either end of the voyage.

A vessel crossing from south Wales and intending to make landfall further west on the Irish coast - say in Cork - may find it to her advantage first to close the Irish coast further east. In typical conditions the inshore waters are subject to less in the way of swell - see page 15 for the rationale.

The tide in St George's Channel is a primary consideration in planning a crossing to or from any Welsh port. Particularly fast tides, up to 7 knots at springs, occur off the Welsh headlands, and in the narrow sounds among the islands. From Milford Haven, the simplest course takes a yacht south of Skokholm and north of Grassholm and the Smalls TSS. Assuming a fair wind and six knots through the water, departure from St Ann's Head two to four hours before local HW may require the Wild Goose Race (off Skomer and Skokholm) to be given a fair berth but provides the ideal arrival at Kilmore Quay on a high and rising tide. Eastbound for Milford Haven, leaving Kilmore Quay at local HW means a fair tide round the Welsh islands and arrival near HW. On a direct course between Pwllheli and Carnsore Point, the tide races off Bardsey are easily avoided.

Pwllheli Marina (photo Hafan Pwllheli)

349

To and from Cornwall

Tresco, Isles of Scilly (photo Tom Corser)

CORNWALL

The trend of the south coast of Ireland from ENE to WSW means that the yacht crossing the Celtic Sea has a choice of departures or landfalls in Ireland, with little difference in the distance. Land's End (the Longships light) to Kilmore Quay is 132 miles, to Dunmore East 134, to Helvick or Youghal 138, to Crosshaven or Kinsale 144, to Castlehaven 156 and to Baltimore 162. To or from Newlyn, add 14 miles. From the Isles of Scilly the distances to west Cork are shorter; to Kinsale 136 miles, Castlehaven 146 and Baltimore 150.

An overnight passage is thus almost inevitable. Routing via Padstow and Milford Haven shortens the longest leg to 75 miles but adds considerably to the overall distance.

Well offshore, north of Land's End, the tides are insignificant, but between Land's End and the Isles of Scilly the tides are rotatory and run at up to 3 knots in places at springs. Streams around the Isles of Scilly are also considerable. The prevailing ocean swell is felt almost all the way across, normally diminishing only near the Irish coast.

Newlyn, as one of England's largest fishing ports, has good services, and a sheltered deep water harbour accessible day or night at any state of the tide and in virtually all weathers. In the Isles of Scilly, New Grimsby Sound and Old Grimsby Sound, respectively west and east of Tresco, and Tean Sound, west of St Martin's, offer secure anchorage, but are accessible only in daylight. The roadstead at St Mary's can be accessed by day or night from north and south, and St Mary's has good sources of supplies including fuel.

On the north coast of Cornwall the bays at St Ives and Newquay are possible anchorages but are open to the NW and very subject to swell. The only good harbour on the coast is Padstow, which is accessible two hours either side of HW, with a shallow bar at the entrance and a flap gate on its dock.

The coast around Land's End and the Isles of Scilly is very well marked and lit, the major lights being on Trevose Head, Pendeen Head, and Tater-du (on the mainland), the Seven Stones, the Longships and Wolf

To and from Cornwall

Rock (between Land's End and the Scillies) and Round Island and the Bishop Rock, respectively N and W of the Scillies.

There are Traffic Separation Schemes E and W of the Scillies, and while the traffic density in the Celtic Sea is relatively light, fishing activity takes place all the way across. If passing close to the two Kinsale Field gas rigs, 28M S of Ballycotton, bear in mind that sailing between them is prohibited.

The usual landfall ports for a yacht crossing to Ireland are Crosshaven and Kinsale, and these are handy places for crew transfers and to restock. But if wind and weather permit, there is a case to be made for aiming further west. The prevailing west to south-west winds may make hard work of a passage west along the Irish coast, but starting from Baltimore, it is always possible to shape a cruise, either north and west or eastwards, depending on the weather.

Newlyn Harbour
(photo Marktee 1)

Appendix 1 – PAPER CHARTS AND ADMIRALTY PUBLICATIONS

Standard Admiralty (UK Hydrographic Office) Charts

No	Title	Scale 1:	Pub date
1123	Western Approaches to St George's Channel and Bristol Channel	500,000	12-2006
1787	Carnsore Point to Wicklow Head	100,000	11-1991
1772	Rosslare Europort and Wexford Harbour, with Approaches; plan of Rosslare	30,000	07-2005
2049	Old Head of Kinsale to Tuskar Rock	150,000	10-2010
2740	Kilmore Quay including the Saltee Islands	25,000	12-2012
2046	Waterford Harbour, New Ross and Dunmore East; plans of New Ross and Dunmore East	25,000	12-2009
2017	Dungarvan Harbour	15,000	11-1998
2071	Youghal Harbour	12,500	10-1991
1765	Old Head of Kinsale to Power Head	50,000	02-2010
1777	Port of Cork, Lower Harbour and Approaches	12,500	03-2005
1773	Port of Cork, Upper Harbour	12,500	03-2005
2424	Kenmare River to Cork Harbour	150,000	10-2010
2053	Kinsale Harbour and Oyster Haven	12,500	06-2013
2081	Courtmacsherry Bay	25,000	11-1977
2092	Toe Head to Old Head of Kinsale; plan of Glandore Harbour	50,000	09-1993
3725	Baltimore Harbour	6,250	11-1991
2129	Long Island Bay to Castle Haven	30,000	02-2002
2184	Mizen Head to Gascanane Sound	30,000	08-2012
2423	Mizen Head to Dingle Bay	150,000	12-1981
2552	Dunmanus Bay; plans of Dunbeacon Harbour, Kitchen Cove and Dunmanus Harbour	30,000	07-2011
1840	Bantry Bay – Black Ball Head to Shot Head; plan of Castletownbere	30,000	02-2013
1838	Bantry Bay – Shot Head to Bantry; plan of Whiddy oil terminal	30,000	02-2013
2495	Kenmare River; plans of Dursey Sound, Sneem, Ballycrovane, Ardgroom and Kilmakilloge	60,000	11-1981
2125	Valentia Island; plans of Valentia Harbour and Cahersiveen	30,000	09-2012
2789	Dingle Bay and Smerwick; plan of Smerwick	60,000	11-2002
2790	Ventry and Dingle harbours, Blasket Islands; (Blaskets at 1:37,500)	15,000	01-2014
2739	Brandon and Tralee Bays; plan of Fenit Harbour	37,500	10-2012
2254	Valentia to the Shannon	150,000	11-1981
1819	Approaches to the River Shannon	50,000	05-2006
1547	River Shannon – Kilcredaun Point to Ardmore Point; plan of Kilrush	20,000	01-2012
1548	River Shannon – Ardmore Point to Rinealon Point	20,000	12-1986
1549	River Shannon – Rinealon Point to Shannon Airport; plan of Foynes	20,000	11-2013
1540	River Shannon – Shannon Airport to Limerick	12,500	06-1981
1125	Western Approaches to Ireland	500,000	01-1985
3338	Kilkee to Inisheer	50,000	09-2012
2173	Loop Head to Slyne Head	150,000	07-1984
3339	Approaches to Galway Bay and the Aran Islands	50,000	10-2011
1820	Aran Islands to Roonagh Head	75,000	03-1984
1984	Galway Bay	30,000	09-2011
1904	Galway Harbour; plan of New Harbour	10,000	07-2011
2096	Cashla Bay to Kilkieran Bay; plan of Rossaveal	30,000	08-2011
2709	Roundstone and Approaches	30,000	11-1983
2420	Aran Islands to Broad Haven Bay	150,000	07-1984
2708	Ballyconneely Bay to Clifden Bay, with Slyne Head	25,000	11-1983
2707	Kingstown to Cleggan Bays and Inishbofin to Inishturk	25,000	11-1983
2706	Ballynakill and Killary Harbours and Approaches	25,000	08-2012
2667	Clew Bay and Approaches; plan of Newport	50,000	02-1983
2057	Westport Bay	15,000	08-2005
2725	Blacksod Bay to Tory Island	200,000	10-1999
2704	Blacksod Bay and Approaches	50,000	11-1981
2703	Broad Haven and Approaches; plan of Portnafrankagh	50,000	02-1980
2767	Porturlin to Sligo Bay and Rathlin O'Birne Island	75,000	02-2013
2715	Killala and Donegal	25,000	05-2010
2852	Approaches to Sligo; plan of Sligo Harbour	20,000	08-2006
2702	Donegal Bay	60,000	08-2011
2792	Plans on the North West Coast; Teelin, Church Pool, Killybegs, Aran Sound and Burtonport	various	08-2012
2723	Western Approaches to the North Channel	200,000	07-2015
1879	Rathlin O'Birne Island to Aran Island	75,000	10-1979
1883	Crohy Head to Bloody Foreland	30,000	08-2012

Maritime Safety Information

Admiralty Small Craft Folios

No	Title	Pub date
SC5621	*Ireland, East Coast, Carlingford Lough to Waterford*	2010
SC5622	*Ireland, South Coast, Kinsale to Waterford*	03-2012
SC5623	*Ireland, South West Coast, Bantry Bay to Kinsale*	11-2011

Agents for Admiralty Charts and Publications

Viking Marine, The Pavilion, Dun Laoghaire, 01 280 6654, www.vikingmarine.ie
Todd Chart Agency Ltd, Navigation House, 85 High Street, Bangor BT20 5BD, Northern Ireland, 028 9146 6640, todd@intelligentnavigation.com, www.toddchart.com *(Principal Admiralty Chart Agents for Ireland)*
Union Chandlery Ltd, Penrose Quay, Cork, 021 427 1643, www.unionchandlery.ie
Galway Maritime, Lower Merchants Road, Galway, 091 566568, www.galwaymaritime.com

Imray Charts

No	Title	Scale 1:	Pub date
C57	*Tuskar Rock to Old Head of Kinsale; plans of Kilmore Quay, Dunmore East, Waterford, Dungarvan, Youghal, Cork Lower Harbour, Crosshaven and Kinsale*	167,000	07-2011
C56	*Cork Harbour to Dingle Bay; plans of Kinsale, Courtmacsherry, Glandore, Castle Haven, Baltimore, Schull, Crookhaven, Castletownbere, Glengarriff, Bantry, Ardgroom, Kilmakilloge, Sneem, Portmagee, Valentia and Dingle*	170,000	04-2012
C55	*Dingle Bay to Galway Bay; plans of Dingle, Fenit, the Shannon, Kilrush, Foynes, Limerick, Galway Bay, Galway Harbour, Kilronan and Cashla Bay*	200,000	07-2010
C54	*Galway Bay to Donegal Bay; plans of Roundstone, Clifden Bay, Inishbofin, Cleggan Bay, Westport, Achill Sound, Portnafrankagh, Broad Haven and Sligo*	200,000	08-2007
C53	*Donegal Bay to Rathlin Island; plans of Killybegs, Teelin, Sound of Aran, Burtonport, Gweedore Harbour and Approaches*	200,000	03-2010

Appendix 2 – MARITIME SAFETY INFORMATION

WEATHER FORECASTS

The principal sources of weather forecast information are the Coast Guard Radio stations, national and local public broadcast radio stations, smartphone services and the Internet.

Coast Guard Radio Stations

Garda Costa na hÉireann, the Irish Coast Guard, has its National Maritime Operations Centre and Marine Rescue Co-ordination Centre in Dublin, and Marine Rescue Sub-Centres at Malin Head (Co. Donegal) and Valentia Island (Co. Kerry). These three stations maintain a continuous listening watch on VHF, including VHF DSC. MRSCs Malin Head and Valentia also listen on MF and are Navtex broadcast stations. There are sixteen remotely controlled transmission sites which are individually named. Weather forecasts and navigational warnings are broadcast every three hours on working channels, following a DSC alarm call and an announcement on Ch 16 and 2182 kHz (MRCC Dublin uses VHF only). Broadcast times are 0103, 0403, 0703, 1003, 1303, 1603, 1903 and 2203.

MRCC Dublin (phone 01 662 0922, operations room 01 662 0923, VHF channel 83, MMSI 002500300) also remotely controls stations at Carlingford (channel 04), Wicklow Head (02), Rosslare (23) and Mine Head (83).
MRSC Valentia (phone 066 94 76109, VHF channel 24, MMSI 002500200) remotely controls stations at Cork (channel 26), Mizen Head (04), Bantry (23), Shannon (28) and Galway (04).
MRSC Malin Head (phone 074 93 70103, VHF channel 23, MMSI 002500100) remotely controls stations at Clifden (channel 26), Belmullet (83), Donegal Bay (02) and Glen Head (24).

Forecasts from Met Éireann, the Irish weather service, are provided for the coastal waters of Ireland up to 30M offshore and the Irish Sea, updated four times daily, valid for 24 hours and including an outlook for the following 24 hours. The forecast information is given clockwise around the coast, with the whole area divided into between one and four forecast areas, depending on the weather, using major coastal features as boundaries. The features used are shown on the chart overleaf. Weather reports are given for six shore stations and six weather buoys; the positions of these and of the radio stations are also marked on the chart.

MSI broadcasts from Belfast MRCC are routinely received in Donegal Bay (via the Navar transmitter) and often elsewhere as well.

Maritime Safety Information

[Map of Ireland showing Irish Coast Guard Radio Stations, coastal features, British shipping forecast areas and MRCC Belfast transmitters. Labels include: MALIN, MALIN HEAD (MRSC) Ch 23, BLOODY FORELAND, FAIR HEAD, West Torr Ch 86, Limavady Ch 84, LOUGH FOYLE, M4, ROCKALL, ROSSAN POINT, Glen Head Ch 24, BELFAST LOUGH, Black Mountain Ch 23, Orlock Head Ch 84, Navar Ch 86, ERRIS HEAD, Donegal Bay Ch 02, Belmullet Ch 83, Slievemartin Ch 86, M6, Carlingford Ch 04, CARLINGFORD LOUGH, 200 M, Clifden Ch 26, HOWTH HEAD, M2, Dublin (MRCC) Ch 83, M1, SLYNE HEAD, Galway Ch 04, IRISH SEA, WICKLOW HEAD Ch 02, LOOP HEAD, Shannon Ch 28, Rosslare Ch 23, SHANNON, DUNGARVAN, CARNSORE POINT, VALENTIA (MRSC) Ch 24, Cork Ch 26, HOOK HEAD, Bantry Ch 23, Mine Head Ch 83, ROCHE'S POINT, M5, M3, MIZEN HEAD Ch 04, FASTNET, LUNDY.]

Irish Coast Guard Radio Stations in *Italics*, coastal features used in Irish sea area forecasts in UPPER CASE, British shipping forecast areas and MRCC Belfast transmitters in RED

A larger version of this chart, for easy reference when receiving weather forecasts, appears on the inside back page, p368

Navtex

Portpatrick and Malin Head are Navarea 1 Navtex stations, and transmit both Irish and British forecasts and navigational warnings.

Telephone

Met Éireann provides the sea area forecast on the premium-rate number 1550 123855. A mobile weather service for smartphones is available on m.met.ie, with the full range of weather services, as on their website. For older mobile phones a more limited range of service is available on mobile.met.ie.

Internet

Sea area forecasts and isobaric weather charts are available on many websites. The principal ones are those of Met Éireann (www.met.ie/forecasts/sea-area.asp) and the British Met Office (www.metoffice.gov.uk/weather/marine). The European Centre for Medium-range Weather Forecasting (www.ecmwf.int) is also reliable, as is www.theyr.com. Pressure charts for up to six days ahead are on www.weathercharts.org/ukmomslp.htm, and www.passageweather.com is particularly useful for swell forecasts. Detailed URLs are of course subject to change.

Broadcast media

RTÉ1 broadcasts the sea area forecast for the coastal waters of Ireland and the Irish Sea three times daily on 88–90 MHz FM and 252 kHz AM. Broadcast times are 0602, 1254 and 2355. The RTÉ broadcast includes the reports from the shore stations but not the weather buoys.

Some of the local radio stations, notably Radio Kerry (88-90 and 95 MHz FM), also broadcast the sea area forecast.

BBC Radio 4 (198 KHz AM in Irish waters) broadcasts the British shipping forecast for all the sea areas around the British Isles four times daily, at 0520, 1201, 1754 and 0048. Sea area Fastnet covers Carnsore Point to Valentia, Shannon covers Valentia to Slyne Head, and Malin covers Slyne Head northwards. Sea area Rockall is immediately offshore to the northwest of Slyne Head.

NAVIGATIONAL WARNINGS

Navigational warnings for the coastal waters of Ireland and for the the Irish Sea are regularly broadcast by the Irish and UK Coastguard Radio stations on their working channels.

Gunnery exercises by ships of the Irish Naval Service are notified by VHF warnings from the ship herself.

In the Republic, MRCC Dublin is responsible for pollution and salvage operations, and pollution reports should be passed via a Coast Guard Radio Station.

The Irish Coast Guard advises all vessels on passage that in the interests of safety they should pass a Traffic Route (TR) message via their nearest Coast Guard Radio Station. There is no charge for this service. Overdue reporting remains the responsibility of the vessel's shore contact, and the Irish Coast Guard will not initiate overdue procedures unless contacted.

Abbreviations

MANDATORY SAFETY EQUIPMENT

In the Republic of Ireland it is mandatory for every vessel, regardless of size, to carry a lifejacket or personal flotation device for every person on board. On board leisure craft, young persons under 16 must wear these when on deck, when the vessel is under way. On a vessel under 7m in length, lifejackets or personal flotation devices must be worn by everyone on board.

Appendix 3 – SYMBOLS and ABBREVIATIONS

AC	Admiralty Chart		MHWN	mean high water neaps
AIS	Automatic Identification System(s)		MHWS	mean high water springs
Alt	alternating		MLWN	mean low water neaps
			MLWS	mean low water springs
Bn	beacon		Mo	Morse
Card	cardinal		N	north
CG	Coast Guard			
Ch	channel		obsc	obscured
col	column		Oc	occulting
			Or	orange
Dir	directional			
			PEL	Port Entry Light
E	east		PHM	port-hand mark
			PO	Post Office
F	(wind) Beaufort force; (light) fixed			
Fl	flashing		Q	quick-flashing
G	green		R	red; (in captions) right
			RoRo	roll-on, roll-off
h	hour(s)		RWVS	red and white vertical stripes
HM	Harbour Master			
hor	horizontal		S	south
HW	high water		s	second(s)
HWM	high-water mark		SC	sailing club
HWN	high water neaps		SHM	starboard-hand mark
HWS	high water springs		sync	synchronised
IQ	interrupted quick-flashing		t	tonne
Iso	isophase		TSS	Traffic Separation Scheme
			twr	tower
kHz	kilohertz			
kn	knots		unintens	unintensified
L	(in captions) left		vert	vertical
LAT	lowest astronomical tide		vis	visible
Ldg	leading		VHF	very high frequency
LÉ	Long Éireannach (Irish Ship)		VQ	very quick-flashing
L Fl	long flash			
lt	light		W	west; white
LW	low water			
LWM	low-water mark		Y	yellow
LWN	low water neaps		YC	yacht club
LWS	low water springs			
			⊞	waypoint appears on plan(s)
m	metre(s)		📷	(in lists of Dangers, Lights and Marks): object appears in photograph(s)
M	mile(s)			
MF	medium frequency			

A key to chart symbols appears on the back cover flap.

Appendix 4 – TIDAL STREAMS

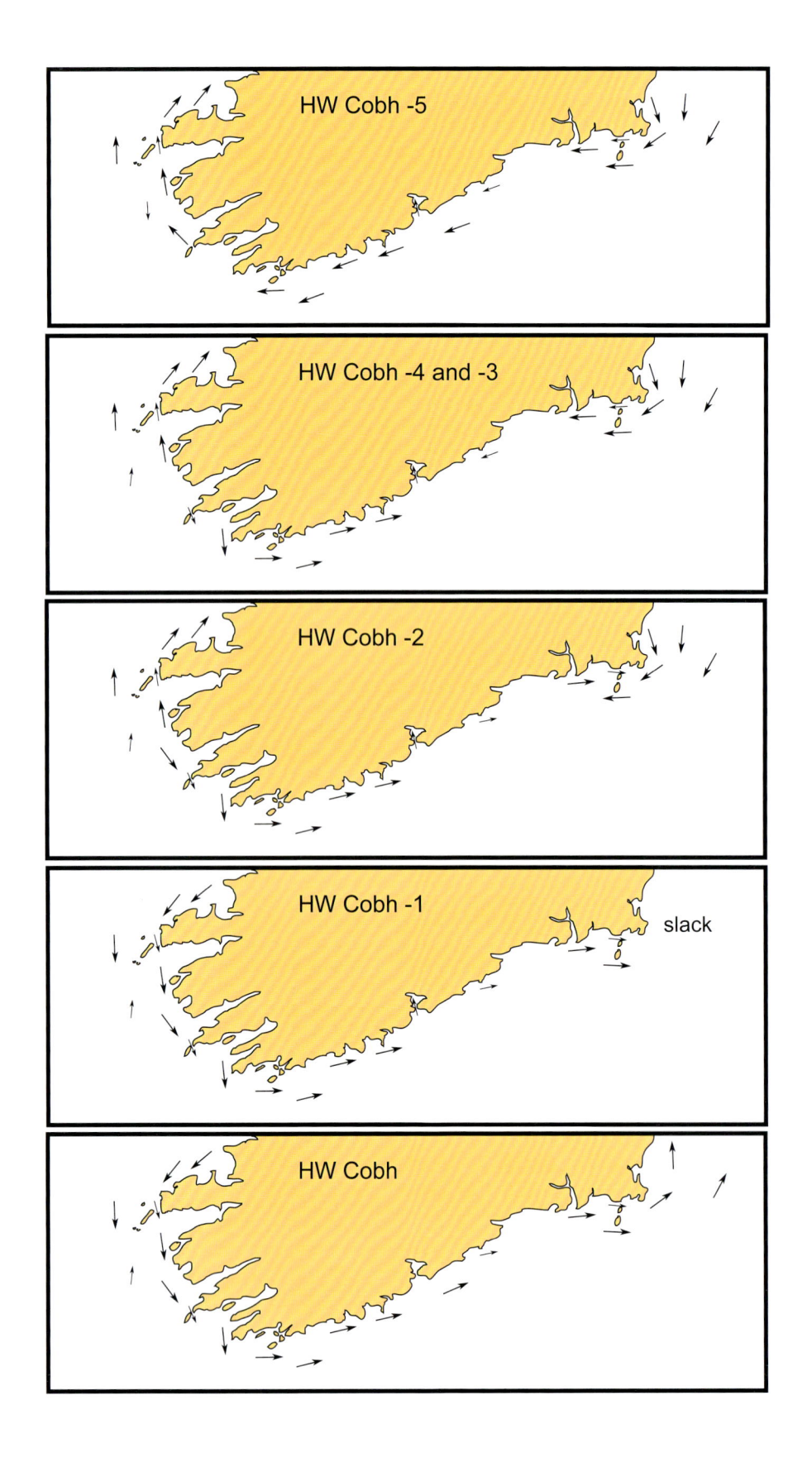

Tidal Streams

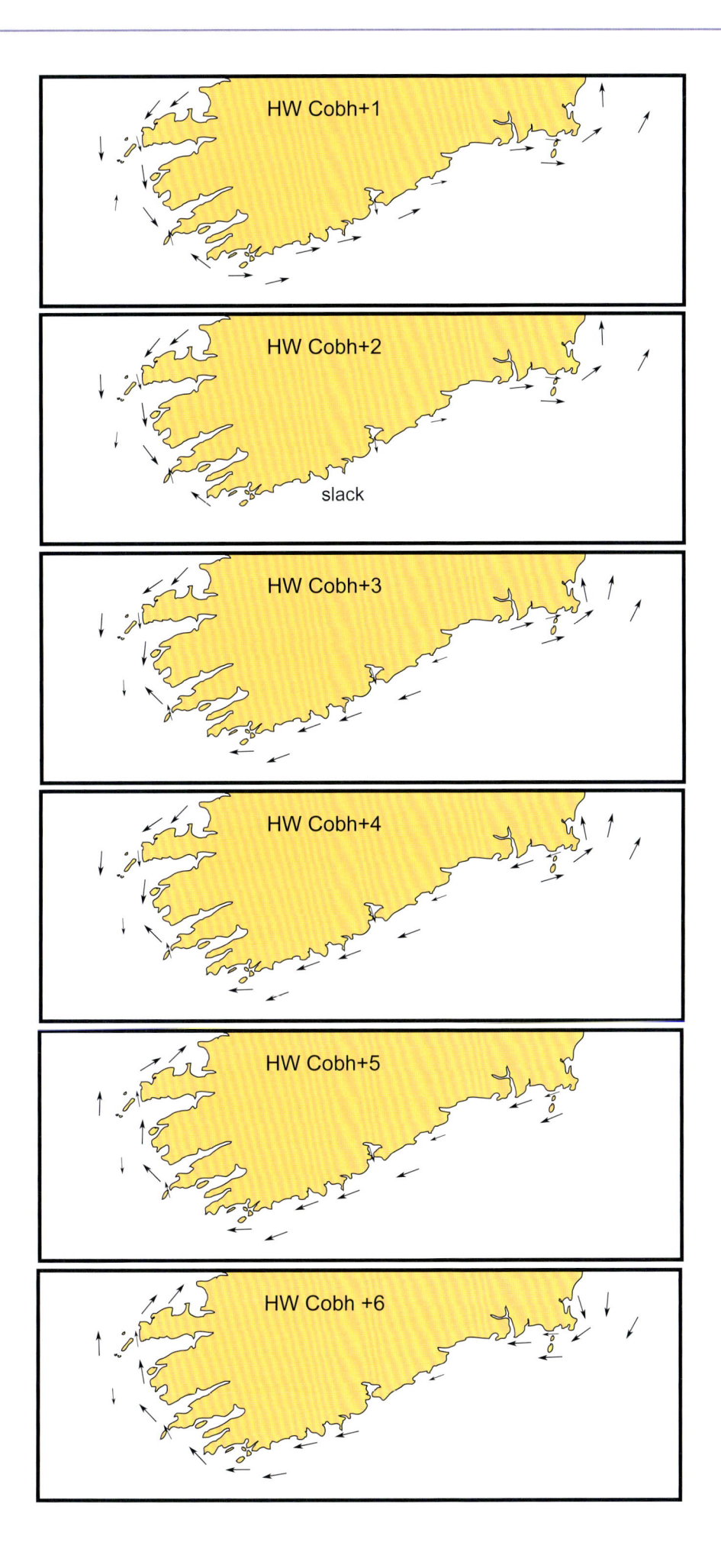

- HW Cobh+1
- HW Cobh+2 — slack
- HW Cobh+3
- HW Cobh+4
- HW Cobh+5
- HW Cobh +6

Tidal Streams

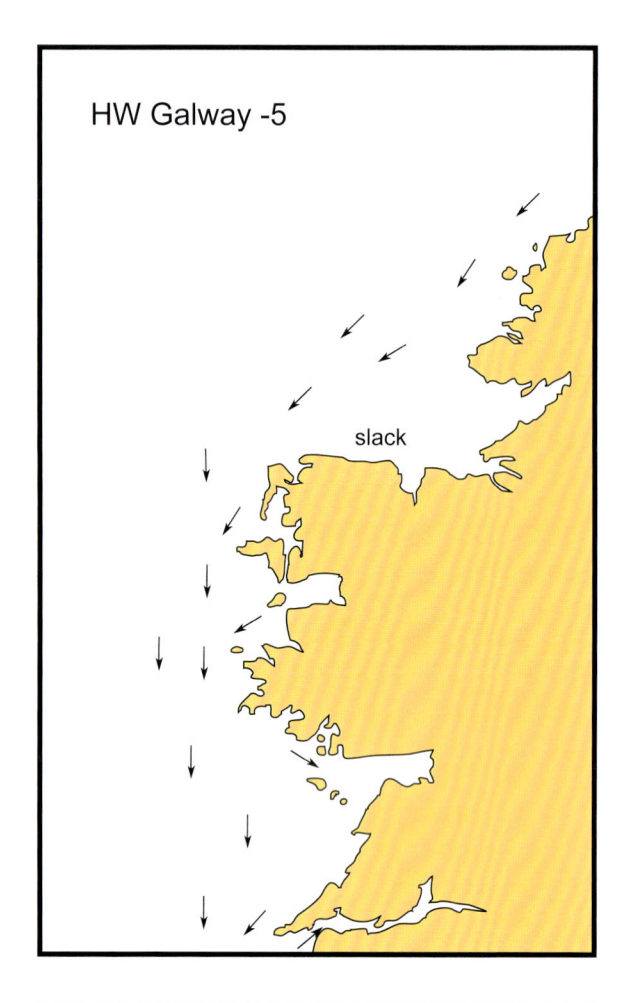

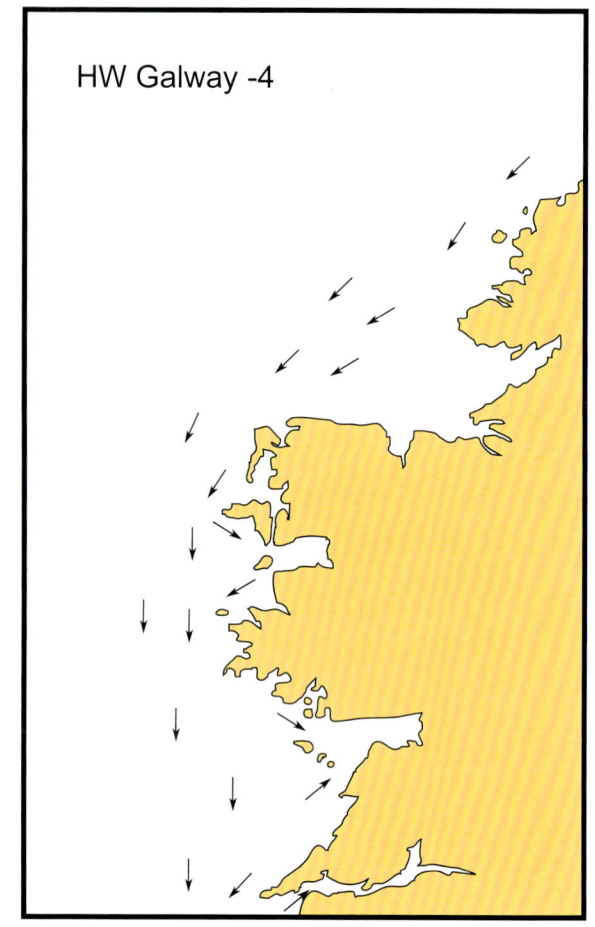

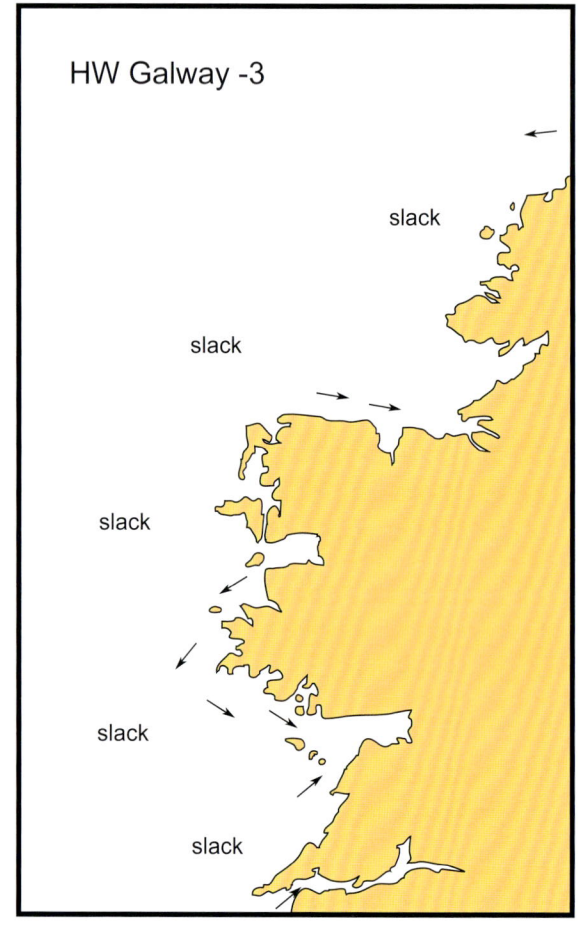

HW Galway -5

HW Galway -4

HW Galway -3

HW Galway -2

Tidal Streams

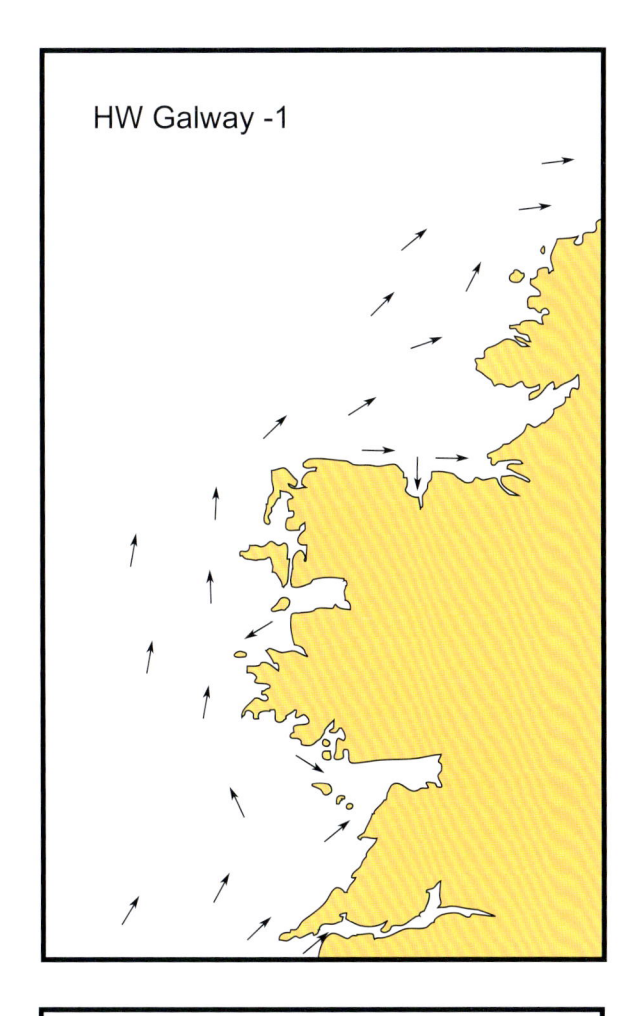

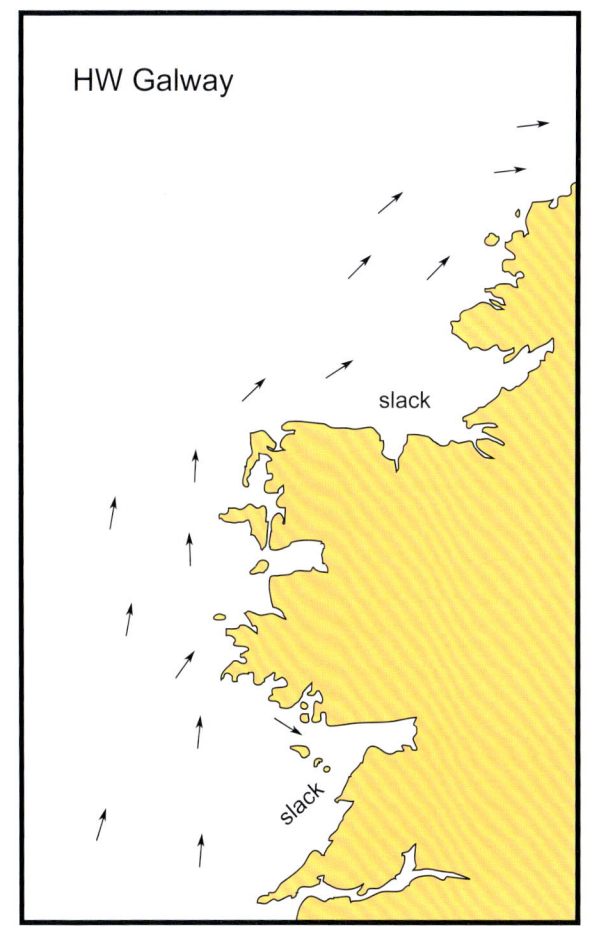

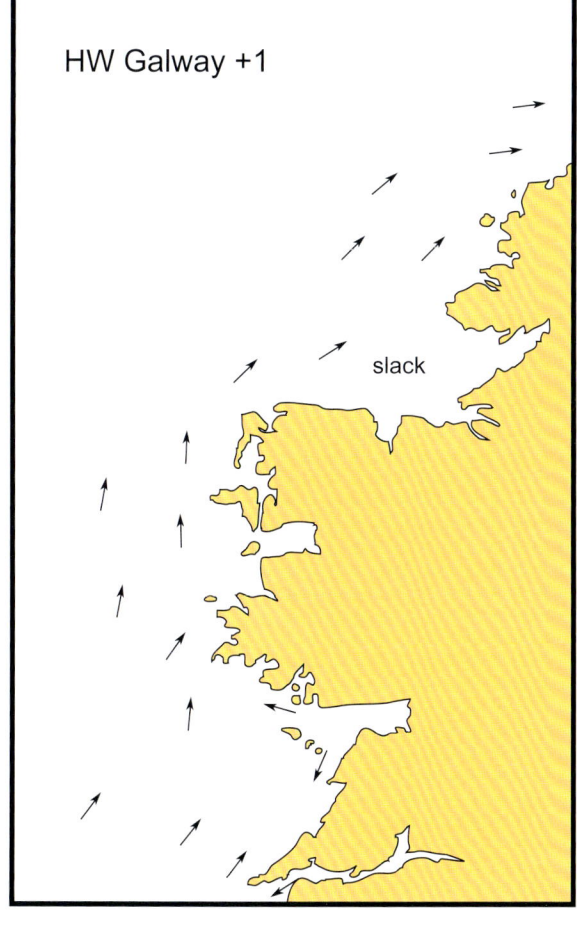

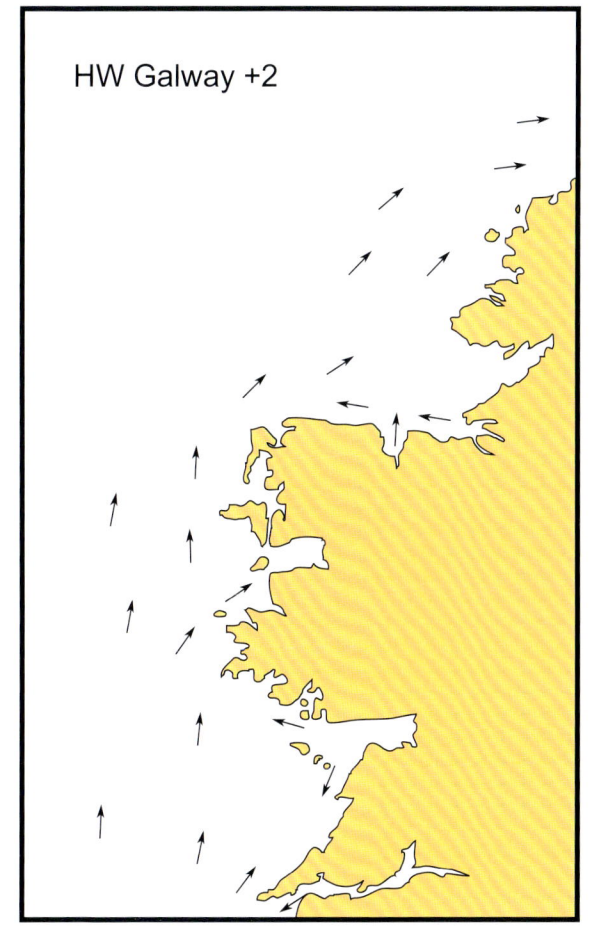

HW Galway -1

HW Galway

HW Galway +1

HW Galway +2

Tidal Streams

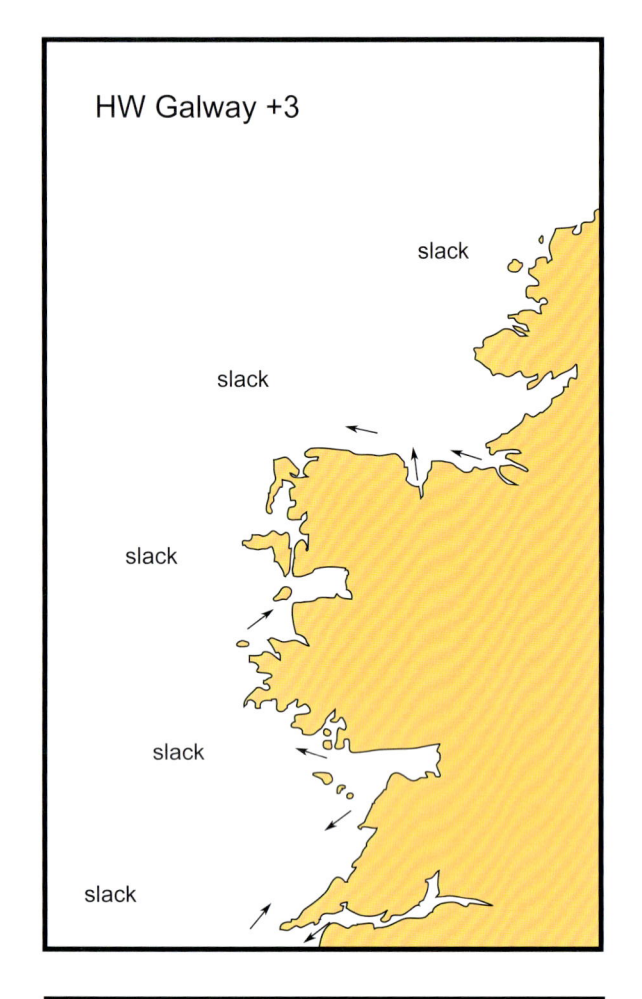

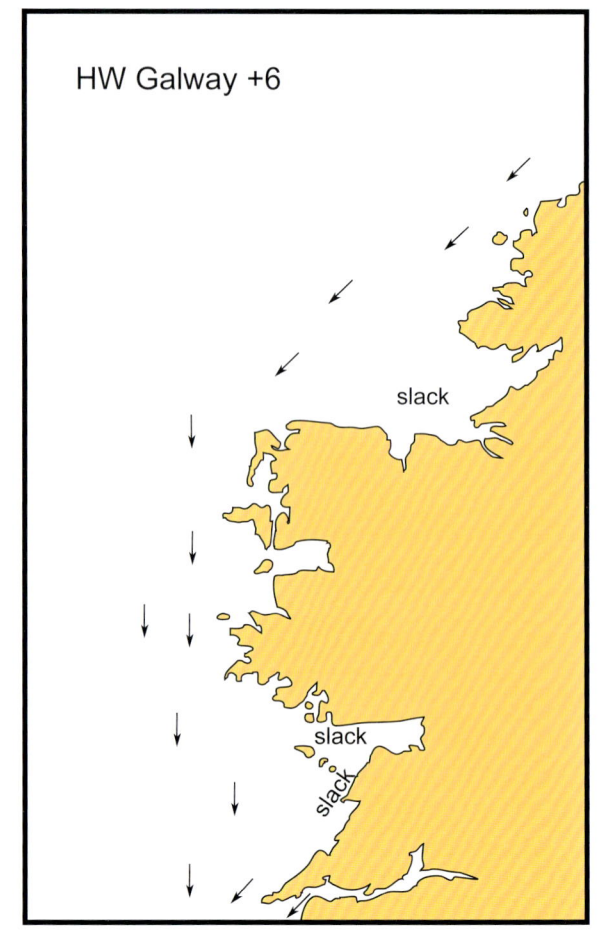

360

Appendix 5 – TABLE of DISTANCES (nautical miles)

The two parts of this table are divided at **Dunmore Head** (Blasket Sound). Where applicable, distances on either side of Dunmore Head should be added. Thus Kinsale to Galway = 197 miles (Kinsale to Dunmore Head, from upper table, 91 + Dunmore Head to Galway, from lower table, 106)

361

Appendix 6 – IRISH LANGUAGE GLOSSARY

The following table lists some of the placename elements found in the area of this book, with their Irish Gaelic word origins and English translations. Also included are some of the Irish words commonly met with on signs, particularly in Gaeltacht areas.

English rendering	Gaelic	English translation	Examples of derived placename/ expression
	abhaile	homewards	Slán abhaile! - Safe home!
	aerfort	airport	
agh, agha	achadh	field	Aghada - long field
ail-, alt-	ailt	ravine	Ailroe - red ravine
aille-	aill	cliff	Aillenacally - cliff of the hag
	aimsir	weather, season	
aird-, ard-	ard (noun)	height, top, highest point	Ardmore - the high headland
	aire	notice, attention	Pobal ar Aire - Neighbourhood Watch Area
-ane, ana, anna	éan	bird	Illauneana - bird island
-anima, -animma	anam	soul, spirit	Illaunanima - island of the soul
anna, annagh	eanach	marsh	Annagh Point
ard-	ard (adjective)	high, (of a person) chief	
ass-, assa-	eas	waterfall	Assaroe; Easky
bad, vad, vaud	bád, bhád	boat	Carrickavaud - boat rock Reenavade - boat point
bal-, bally-	baile	town, townland	Ballynakill - Churchtown
bal- , bel- , val-	béal	mouth, entrance	Bealadangan - fortress entrance
-ban, -bane, -van, -vane, bawn	bán	white, fair	Trawbawn - white beach
ban, ben	bean (pl mná)	woman	Mná - Ladies
	barnog	barnacle	Inishbarnog - barnacle island
beg	beag	small	Inishbeg - little island
bo	bó	cow	Inishbofin - white cow island
boher	bothair	road (literally, cow path)	
brack, breck	breac	speckled, dappled	Illaunbreck - speckled island
brock	broc	badger	Illaunbrock - badger island
	bruscar	litter	
bullig-	bolg	bulge, blister; hence underwater rock, breaker	Bulligmore - the big breaker
bun-	bun	base, bottom, (of a river) mouth	Bunbeg - the little river mouth
bwee, boy (suffix)	buí	yellow	Illaunbweeheen - little yellow island
caher	cathair	fort	Cahersiveen - the fort of little Sive
cairn, carn	carn	heap, mound, cairn	Carnboy - yellow cairn
camus	camas	bay, cove	Camus Bay
can-, ken-, kin-	ceann	head	Canduff - black head
capull, gappul	capall	horse	Bullignagappul - horse rock
carrick, carraig	carraig	rock	Carraig Fada - long rock
	ceol	song, music	ceol agus craic - songs and laughter
claddagh	cladach	rocky shore	Claddagh
clogh, cloy	cloch	stone	Clifden
cloon	cluain	meadow	Cloonile Bay
colleen	cailín	girl	Colleen Og Rock - young girl's rock
	comhairle	council	Comhairle Chontae Chorcaí - Cork County Council
cool, cul, cole	cúl	back, corner	Coolieragh - sheep corner
coon	cuan	haven, harbour	Coongar Harbour
coor, cuar, cour	cur	foam	Couraghy - foamy place
crack	craic	fun, jokes, laughter	ceol agus craic - songs and laughter
dangan	daingean	stronghold	Dingle - the fortress

Irish Language Glossary

	deas	south	
	deoch	drink	
derg, derrig	dearg	red	Belderrig - the red river mouth
derry, darry	doire	oakwood	Derrynane - oakwood of the birds
dillisk	duileasc	dulse, edible seaweed	Dillisk Rock
doo, duff, duv	dubh	black	Carrickduff - black rock
drum-, drom-	druim	ridge	Dromadda - the long ridge
dun, doon	dún	fort	Dunboy - yellow fort
dysart	díseart	hermitage	Kildysart - hermitage church
-een	-ín	little (diminutive suffix)	Carrigeenboy - little yellow rock
fad, fadda, adda	fada	long	Carrigfadda - long rock
	fáilte	welcome	Bord Fáilte - the Irish Tourist Board
fer, var	fear (pl fir)	man	Fir - Gents
fin	fionn	white, fair	Carrickfin - white rock
freagh, free	fraoch	heather	Freaghillaun - heathery island
frankagh	francach	Frenchman	Portnafrankagh - Frenchport
gall	gall	stranger	Donegal - fort of the stranger
gar-	gearr	short	Garinish - short island
garve, garriff	garbh	rough, rugged	Glengarriff - the rough glen
glas, glass	glas	green	Glassillaun - green island
glinsk	glinn uisce	clear water	Glinsk Rock
gola, gowla	gabhlóg	fork	Inishgowla - forked island
gore, gower	gobhar	goat	Carrignagower
gorm	gorm	blue	
	go mall	slowly	on the roads in Gaeltacht areas
gub	gob	point, promontory	Gubacashel - castle point
gwee	gaoth	wind	Carrigwee - windy rock
	iar	west	Iarthair Chorcaí - West Cork
illan, illaun, illane	oileán	island	Freaghillanmore - big heathery island
inish, innis, ennis	inis	island	Inishmore - big island
inver	inbhir	river mouth	Derryinver - rivermouth of the oakwood
	mullan	hillock	
keel, kill, kyle	caol	strait, narrows	
keeragh, cooragh	caorach	sheep	Carrigieragh - sheep rock
kil-	cill	church, monk's cell	Killeany - St Enda's Church
kil-, -kilty	coillte	woods	Clonakilty - fort of the woods
knock-, crock-, croagh	cnoc	hill	Croagh Patrick - St Patrick's Hill
lack-, lackan	leaca	stony slope	Inishlackan
lahan	leathan	broad	Carricklahan
league, legaun		pillar, pile of stones	Carrickalegaun
leck, lick	leac	slab, flat rock	Doolick - black slab
lee, lea	liath	grey	Ringlea - grey point
lenan, leenan		weed-covered rock	Leenan-rua - red weedy rock
letter	leitir	hillside	Lettermore - big hillside
lis-	lios	ring fort	Liscannor - Fort of Ceannúr
long	long	ship	LÉ=Long Éireannach - Irish Ship, a Naval Service vessel
maan	meán	middle	Inishmaan - midddle island
mac, mic, vic-, vick-	mac, mhic-	son of	Macdara's Island - island of the son of Dara
magher, maghera	machair	grassy plain	Magheragallan
mara	mara	of the sea	Kinvara - head of the sea
meal	meall	lump	Mealbeg - little lump
more, vore	mór, mhór	big	Inishmore - big island
muck	muc	pig	Rosmuck - pig promontory
mullagh	mullach	summit	Mullaghmore - big summit
mullaun	mullan	hillock	Mullauncarrickscoltia - split hillock rock
murren, murrisk		low seashore	
mweel, mwale	maol	bare	

363

Irish Language Glossary: Customs and Immigration Requirements

mweel	maoil	breaker	Mweelanatrua - breaker in the tide
oge	óg	young	
oir, -eer	oir	east	Inisheer - eastern island
ooey, owey	uaimh	cave	Owey - island of caves
owen-, own- avon-,	abhainn	river	Owenboy - yellow river
pool, poll	poll	pool	Pollatomish - Thomas's pool
reen, ring, rin	rinn	point, promontory	Rineanna - bird point
	rogha	choice	rogha bia - choice of food, menu
ron	rón	seal	Carrignaronemore - big seal rock
roo, row, roe	rua	red	Rossroe - red promontory
ross	ros	promontory	Rosbeg - small promontory
scolt	scoilt	split; cleft	Mullauncarrickscoltia - split hillock rock
shan-, shen-	sean	old	Shanmuckinish - old pig island
shoonta	siunta	cleft, crevice	Carrigashoonta - cleft rock
skellig	sceilg	steep rock, crag	Skellig Michael - St Michael's crag
	slán, sláinte	health	slán abhaile - safe home. Sláinte! - Cheers!
slieve	sliabh	mountain	Slieve League - pillar mountain
stack, stag	stac	pinnacle rock	The Stags of Broad Haven
ti-	teach, tí	house	Timoleague - St Molaga's house
tober-, tubber-	tober	well	Inishtubbrid - island of the well
tooskert	tuaisceart	north	Inishtooskert - north island
tor, tur	tor	clump, tower	Turduvillaun - black tower island
tra	trá	beach, shore	Tralong - ship beach
-trua	sruth	stream, tide	Mweelanatrua - breaker in the tide
turk	torc	boar	Inishturk - boar island
wheelaun	faoilean	seagull	Carrickaweelaun - seagull rock

Appendix 7 – CUSTOMS and IMMIGRATION REQUIREMENTS

We are obliged for the following to the Revenue Service of Ireland

Yachts arriving in the Republic of Ireland from other countries of the European Union are normally required to report to Customs only if they have on board persons who do not have right of residence in the EU. This requirement is, however, waived in the case of voyages between the United Kingdom (including Northern Ireland and the Isle of Man) and the Republic of Ireland, since there are normally no immigration formalities between the two jurisdictions. Yachts arriving from outside the European Union must report to Customs on arrival. Yachts with goods to declare, or carrying restricted items such as firearms, must also report. The report should be made by telephone to the nearest customs office to the port of arrival: there are offices at Rosslare 05391 61310, Waterford 051 862145 or 087 642 6753, Cork 021 602 7700, Bantry 027 53210, Tralee 066 716 1000, Limerick 061 488000, Galway 091 536000, Sligo 071 914 8600 and Letterkenny 07491 69400. In the event of difficulty the report may be made at the nearest Garda station or by telephoning 1800 295 295. Harbourmasters can also provide advice. Yachts required to report should fly flag Q until clearance is obtained. Yachts being permanently imported from outside the State are also required to notify Customs within 3 days of arrival.

Under international law, the Customs authorities of a state have the right to examine any yacht within the territorial waters of the state, and in exceptional circumstances (such as suspicion of illegal goods on board) in international waters as well.

Yachts owned by EU residents should carry proof of VAT-paid status at all times. For further information see www.revenue.ie.

INDEX

Abbey River, 207
Abbreviations, 355
Achillbeg, 283
Achill Bridge, 286
Achill Head, 290
Achill Island, 283
Achill Sound, North, 286
    South, 284
Adrigole, 134
Aghada, 66
Ahakista, 122
Aillenacally, 245
Airports, 26
Alderman Sound, 115
Allihies, 149
Anchoring, general
    advice, 19
Aphort, 330
Aran Island (Donegal), 328
Aran Islands (Galway), 211
Aranmore (Arranmore), 328
Aran Road, 332
Ard Bay, 241
Ardbear Bay, 255
Ardgroom, 152
Ardmore Bay (Galway), 234
Ardmore (Waterford), 53
Ardnacrusha, 207
Ardnagashel Bay, 139
Ardnakinna Point, 126
Argideen, River, 81
Arranmore, 316
Arthurstown, 42
Askeaton, 203
Audley Cove, 108
Aughinish Bay, 219
Aughris Hole, 306
Aughrus Passage, 260

Ballina, 305
Ballinaleama Bay, 248
Ballinskelligs Bay, 168
Ballyconneely Bay, 247
Ballycotton, 56
Ballycrovane, 142
Ballydavid, 189
Ballydehob, 102
Ballydonegan Bay, 141
Ballyglass, 300
Ballyhack, 42
Ballylongford, 199
Ballynacally, 205
Ballynagall, 189
Ballynakill Harbour, 267
Ballysadare Bay, 306
Ballyshannon, 312
Ballytrent Bay, 34
Ballyvaughan Bay, 218
Baltimore, 94
Bandon, River, 77

Bannow Bay, 38
Bantry Bay, 126
Bantry Harbour, 139
Barloge, 92
Barna, 222
Barnaderg Bay, 268
Barrel Sound, 113
Barrow Harbour, 193
Barrow, River, 46
Bealadangan, 229
Beal Lough, 129
Beeves Rock, 203
Belderrig (Belderg), 303
Belfast Lough, 354
Belgooly, 73
Bellacragher Bay, 288
Belly Rock, 89
Belmullet, 301
Bere Island, 131
Berehaven, 126, 129
Bertraghboy Bay, 242
Bills Rocks, 290
Black Ball Head, 142
Black Head, 218
Black Rock (Cork), 89
Black Rock (Mayo), 292
Black Rock (Sligo), 308
Blacksod Bay, 293
Blackwater Harbour
    (Kerry), 158
Blackwater, River (Cork), 54
Blasket Islands, 183
Blasket Sound, 187
Blind Harbour (Cork), 83
Blind Harbour
    (Waterford), 48
Blindstrand Bay, 81
Bloody Foreland, 347
Boatstrand Harbour, 47
Bofin Harbour, 263
Bollegouh Creek, 233
Bolus Head, 168
Boylagh Bay, 324
Brandon Bay, 190
Brandon Creek, 190
Brannock Sound, 215
Brennel Island, 156
Broad Haven, 300
Broad Haven Bay, 301
Broadstrand Bay, 81
Brow Head, 120
Brown Bay, 311
Bruckless, 315
Bull, The, 148
Bull's Mouth, 287
Bunatrahir Bay, 303
Bunaw, 155
Bunbeg, 345
Bundoran, 312
Bundorragha, 273

Bunaninver, 346
Bunowen Bay, 247
Burrishoole, 281
Burtonport, 333

Caher Island, 275
Caher River, 175
Cahercon Pier, 204
Cahersiveen, 175
Caladh Mór
    (Inishmaan), 215
Calf Islands, 107
Calf, The, 143, 148
Camus Bay, 235
Canon Island, 205
Canower, 243
Cape Clear Island, 96
Capel Island, 56
Cappagh Pier, 198
Carbery Island, 121
Carlingford Lough, 354
Carne, 34
Carnboy Channel, 338
Carnsore Point, 33
Carrigaholt, 196
Carrigaline, 63
Carrigfadda Sound, 187
Carrigillihy Cove, 89
Carthy's Island, 107
Cashel Bay, 244
Cashla Bay, 224
Cassan Sound, 315
Castle Haven, 90
Castle Island, 108
Castlemaine Harbour, 180
Castlepark Marina, 76
Castletownbere, 127
Castletownshend, 90
Catalogue Islands, 103
Celtic Sea, crossing, 350
Chandlery, availability, 25
Chapel Bay, 330
Chapel Sound, 329
Charts, general info, 17
Charts, list, 352
Cheek Point, 44
Church Pool, 325
Circumnavigation, 21
Clare Island, 275
Cleanderry Harbour, 150
Clear Island, 96
Cleggan, 262
Clew Bay, 277
Clifden, 254, 256
Cliffs of Moher, 200
Clonakilty, 83
Clonderalaw Bay, 192
Cloonile Bay, 244
Coast Guard service, 353
Cobh, 66

Collan More Harbour, 278
Collorus Harbour, 154
Commercial shipping, 22
Communications, 26
Coney Island (Clare), 204
Coney Island (Cork), 112
Coney Island (Sligo), 308
Coningbeg Rock, 32
Cooanmore Bay, 306
Coolieragh Harbour, 136
Coonanna Harbour, 180
Coonawilleen Bay, 234
Coongar Harbour, 156
Cork City, 68
Cork Harbour, 57
Cork Harbour Marina, 66
Courtmacsherry, 79
Cow, The, 148
Creevecartron, 245
Croagh Bay, 112
Croaghnakeela, 238
Croghnut, 243
Crookhaven, 115
Crosshaven, 58
Crow Head, 142
Cruit Bay, 337
Cuan, 182
Cunnamore Pier, 105
Customs and
    Immigration, 26, 364

Davillaun, 265
Dawros Bay, 324
Deel, River, 203
Deenish Island, 164
Dernasliggaun, 273
Derryinver Bay, 267
Derrynane, 164
Dingle Bay, 179
Dingle Harbour, 180
Dinish Island (Cork), 127
Dinish Island (Kerry), 158
Dinish Point, 234
Dirk Bay, 84
Distances Table, 361
Diving, 23
Donegal Harbour, 312
Doogort Bay, 292
Doolin, 211
Doonbeg Bay, 210
Dooneen Pier, 122
Dorinish Harbour, 278
Doulus Bay, 175
Drake's Pool, 62
Duck Island, 246
Duck Sound, 335
Duffur, 294
Dunbeacon Cove, 124
Dunbeacon Harbour, 125
Dunboy Bay, 126

365

Index

Duncannon, 40
Dungarvan, 48
Dunkerron Harbour, 158
Dunmanus Bay, 120
Dunmanus Harbour, 121
Dunmore East, 38
Dunnycove Bay, 84
Dunworley Bay, 83
Durrus, 125
Dursey Island, 147
Dursey Sound, 146

Eagle Island, 296
East Ferry, 65
East Grove Quay, 65
Eeragh Island, 212
Eeshal Island, 259
Eighter Island, 333
Electronic charts, 18
Elly Bay, 293
Enniscrone, 305
Erris Head, 296

Fahy Bay, 268
Fair Head (Antrim), 354
Fastnet Rock, 101
Fenit, 192
Fergus, River, 204
Ferries, 22
Fertha, River, 175
Fethard-on-Sea, 38
Finish Island, 239
Fishing Industry, 22
Flea Sound, 92
Foileye, 180
Foul Sound, 212
Foynes, 201
Frenchport, 297
Friar Island, 261
Frolic Point, 99
Fuels, availability, 25

Galley Head, 84
Galway Bay, 216
Galway Harbour, 221
Garinish Island, 137
Garinish West, 136
Garnish Bay, 149
Garranty Harbour, 274
Garraunagh Sound, 172
Garrivinagh, 235
Gascanane Sound, 97
Glandore, 85
Glen Bay, 324
Glengarriff, 131
Glin, 200
Glossary, Irish, 362
Goat Island Sound, 112
Gola Island, 339
Golam Harbour, 233
Goleen, 114
Goose Island Channel, 105
Gorteen Bay, 247
Gortnasate, 338
Great Blasket, 186

Greatman's Bay, 227
Great Saltee, 36
Great Skellig, 168
Gregory Sound, 212
Gubalennaun Beg, 290
Gurraig Sound, 235
Gweebarra Bay, 324
Gweedore Harbour, 343

Heir Island, 102
Haulbowline Island, 64
Helvick, 50
High Island (Cork), 89
High Island (Galway), 262
Hook Head, 38
Horse Island, 108
Horseshoe harbour, 96
Howth Head, 354
Hyne, Lough, 93

Ilen, River, 102
Illancroagh, 289
Illancrone, 329
Illanmore Sound, 341
Illaunagrogh, 106
Illaundrane, 162
Illauneeragh, 234
Illaunrossalough, 235
Illauntannig, 190
Illnacullen, 137
Inishbiggle, 287
Inishbofin, 263
Inishcorker, 204
Inisheer, 216
Inisherk, 233
Inishfarnard, 150
Inishglora, 295
Inishgort, 277
Inishkea, N and S, 295
Inishkeel, 325
Inishkeeragh (Donegal), 330
Inishkeeragh (Mayo), 296
Inishlackan Sound, 247
Inishlyre, 278
Inishmaan, 215
Inishmeane, 346
Inishmore, 212
Inishmurray, 311
Inishmuskerry, 239
Inishnabro, 184
Inishnee, 242
Inishshark, 265
Inishsirrer, 346
Inishtearaght, 185
Inishtooskert, 186
Inishtubbrid, 204
Inishturk (Galway), 259
Inishturk (Mayo), 274
Inishvickillane, 183
Inistioge, 46
Inner Passage, 236
Inver Bay, 314
Irish language glossary, 362

Jarley's Cove, 77
Joyce's Pass, 249

Kedge Island, 93
Keem Bay, 292
Kells Bay, 180
Kenmare Quay, 159
Kenmare River, 146
Kerry Head, 194
Kiggaul Bay, 230
Kilbaha, 195
Kilcolgan River, 219
Kilcrohane, 122
Kilcummin, 303
Kildavnet, 285
Kildysart, 204
Kilkee, 210
Kilkieran Bay, 232
　Head of, 235
Kilkieran Cove, 234
Killala, 304
Killary Harbour, 273
Killary, Little, 272
Killeany, 214
Killybegs, 315
Kilmacsimon, 77
Kilmakilloge, 154
Kilmore Quay, 35
Kilronan, 213
Kilrush, 196
Kilteery Pier, 199
King's Channel, 44
Kingstown Bay, 259
Kinsale, 74
Kinsale Field gas rigs, 53
Kinvara, 219
Kitchen Cove, 122
Knightstown, 173
Knock Bay, 234
Knock Pier, 200
Kylesalia, 236

Labasheeda, 201
Lackan Bay, 303
Lamb's Head, 164
Lawrence Cove, 130
Leahill Jetty, 136
Lee, River, 66
Leenaun, 274
Lehid Harbour, 156
Lifeboats, 21
Lights and buoys, general information, 17
Limerick, 206
Liscannor, 211
Little Island (Waterford), 44
Little Killary Bay, 272
Little Saltee, 36
Little Samphire Island, 192
Little Skellig, 168
Lonehort, 133
Long Island, 112
Long Island Bay, 106
Loop Head, 210
Lough Hyne, 93

Loughros Beg, 324
Loughros More, 324

Macdara Sound, 241
Magharee Islands, 190
Malin Beg, 320
Malin Head, 354
Mannin Bay, 254
Man of War Sound, 112
Marinas,
　general information, 20
Maritime Safety Information, 353
Mason Island, 241
Massy's Quay, 203
Maumeen Quay, 228
Metal Man, 48, 309
Middle Cove (Kinsale), 77
Middle Sound, 329
Mill Cove (Berehaven), 128
Mill Cove (Glandore Bay), 84
Mine Head, 52
Mizen Head, 120
Monkstown, 66
Moore Bay, 210
Moy, River, 305
Moynish More, 283
Mullaghmore, 311
Mullet Peninsula, 293
Mutton Island (Clare), 210
Mweenish Bay, 239

Natawny Quay, 228
Navigational aids (general description), 17
Navtex Stations, 354
New Harbour, 220
Newport, 280
New Quay, 219
New Ross, 46
North Bay, 220
North Harbour (Cape Clear), 100
North Passage (Baltimore), 102
North Sound of Aran, 331

Oldcourt, 104
Old Head of Kinsale, 78
Oldhead (Mayo), 277
Omey Island, 259
Oranmore Bay, 220
Ormond's Harbour, 156
Owenboy River, 62
Owey Island, 337
Oysterbed Pier, 161
Oyster Haven, 72

Paradise, 205
Passage East, 42
Passage West, 68
Passagemaking, general advice, 21
Pilotage, general advice, 19

366

Index

Pipers Sound, 126
Placenames, 24, 362
Pollacheeny Harbour, 305
Pollnadivva, 306
Portacloy, 302
Portacrin, 343
Portmagee, 171
Portmurvy, 214
Portnafrankagh, 297
Portnanalbanagh, 297
Portnoo, 325
Port Roshin, 317
Porturlin, 303
Poulgorm Bay, 108
Power Head, 56
Pubs and Restaurants, 25
Puffin Sound, 171
Pulleen Harbour, 142
Purteen, 290

Rabbit Island (Glandore Bay), 89
Rabbit Island (Bantry Bay), 142
Rabbit Island (Mayo), 281
Radio Communications, 21
Radio channels, 353 & front cover flap
Raghly Point, 299
Ram Head, 52
Rathlin O'Birne, 321
Reen Pier (Castle Haven), 85
Reenavade Pier, 153
Renville, 220
Restaurants and pubs, 25
Rinealon Point, 201
Ring (Co.Cork), 83
Ringabella Bay, 72
Ringaskiddy, 64
Rinvyle Point, 271
Roancarrigmore, 133
Roaninish, 324
Roaringwater Bay, 108
Roche's Point, 58
Rockfleet Bay, 282
Roeillaun, 268
Roonagh Head, 274
Rosbarnagh Island, 281
Rosbeg, 324
Rosmoney, 278
Rosmore Point, 281
Rosmuck, 235
Rossafinna, 289
Rossan Point, 354
Rossaveal, 225
Rossbrin, 109
Rosses Point, 308
Rossillion Bay, 330
Rosslare, 29
Ross Point, 268
Ross Port, 301
Rossroe Bay, 229
Roundstone, 245
Royal Cork YC Marina, 62

Royal National Lifeboat Institution, 21
Rushbrooke, 67
Rusheen Bay, 265
Rusheen Island, 295
Rutland North Channel, 333
Rutland South Channel, 336

Sailmakers, 25
St George's Channel, crossing, 348
St Macdara's Island, 241
St Margaret's Bay, 34
St Mullins, 46
St Patrick's Bridge, 33
Saleen Bay, 293
Saleen Quay, 199
Salrock, 272
Saltee Islands, 36
Saltee Sound, 34
Salt Hill, 313
Salt Point, 242
Salve Marina, 62
Sandy Cove, 77
Scarriff Island, 164
Scattery Roads, 198
Schull, 110
Scotchport, 297
Scraggane Bay, 191
Seafield Quay, 211
Search and Rescue, 21
Seven Heads, 82
Seven Hogs, 190
Shannon Estuary, 194
Shannon Navigation, 207
Sheep's Head, 125
Sherkin Island, 96
Ship Sound, 265
Shipping, commercial, 22
Skeam Islands, 105
Skellig Michael, 168
Skerd Rocks, 241
Skibbereen, 104
Sligo Bay, 306
Sligo Harbour, 309
Slyne Head, 248
Smerwick, 189
Sneem, 160
South Bay, 219
South Harbour (Cape Clear), 101
South Sound (Arranmore), 328
South Sound of Aran, 330
Sovereigns, 72
Spiddle, 223
Spike Island, 64
Squince Harbour, 89
Sruthan Quay, 224
Stags (Cork), 92
Stags (Donegal), 326
Stags of Broad Haven, 302
Straddle Pass, 240
Streamstown Bay, 259
Suir, River, 45

Summer Cove (Kinsale), 76
Supplies, general information, 25
Sybil Point, 188
Symbols, 355 & back cover flap

Tarbert, 200
Tearaght, 185
Teelin, 318
Three Castle Head, 120
Three Sisters (Kerry), 189
Three Sisters Marina, 46
Tidal Streams, 356
Tides, general description, 16
Timoleague, 81
Toe Head, 92
Toe Head Bay, 92
Toormore Bay, 107
Tororragaun Sound, 341
Tory Island, 341
Traditional boats, 23
Trafrask, 136
Tragumna Bay, 92
Tralee Bay, 191
Tralong Bay, 84
Tramore Bay, 47
Tranabo Cove, 92
Travel, 26
Trawenagh Bay, 324
Trident Marina, 76
Tullaghan Bay, 289
Turbot Island, 259
Tuskar Rock, 30

Union Hall, 87

Valentia Harbour, 173
Valentia Island, 173
Ventry Harbour, 182
Villierstown, 56

Walker's Bay, 317
Waste disposal, 26
Waterford Harbour, 40
Waterford City, 45
Weather, general description, 14
Weather forecasts, 353
Weaver's Point, 58
Weir, The, 220
West Cove, 162
Westport, 279
Whiddy Island, 142
White Strand Bay, 319
Whiting Bay, 56
Wicklow Head, 354
Wildlife, 23

Youghal, 53

Zetland Pier, 137

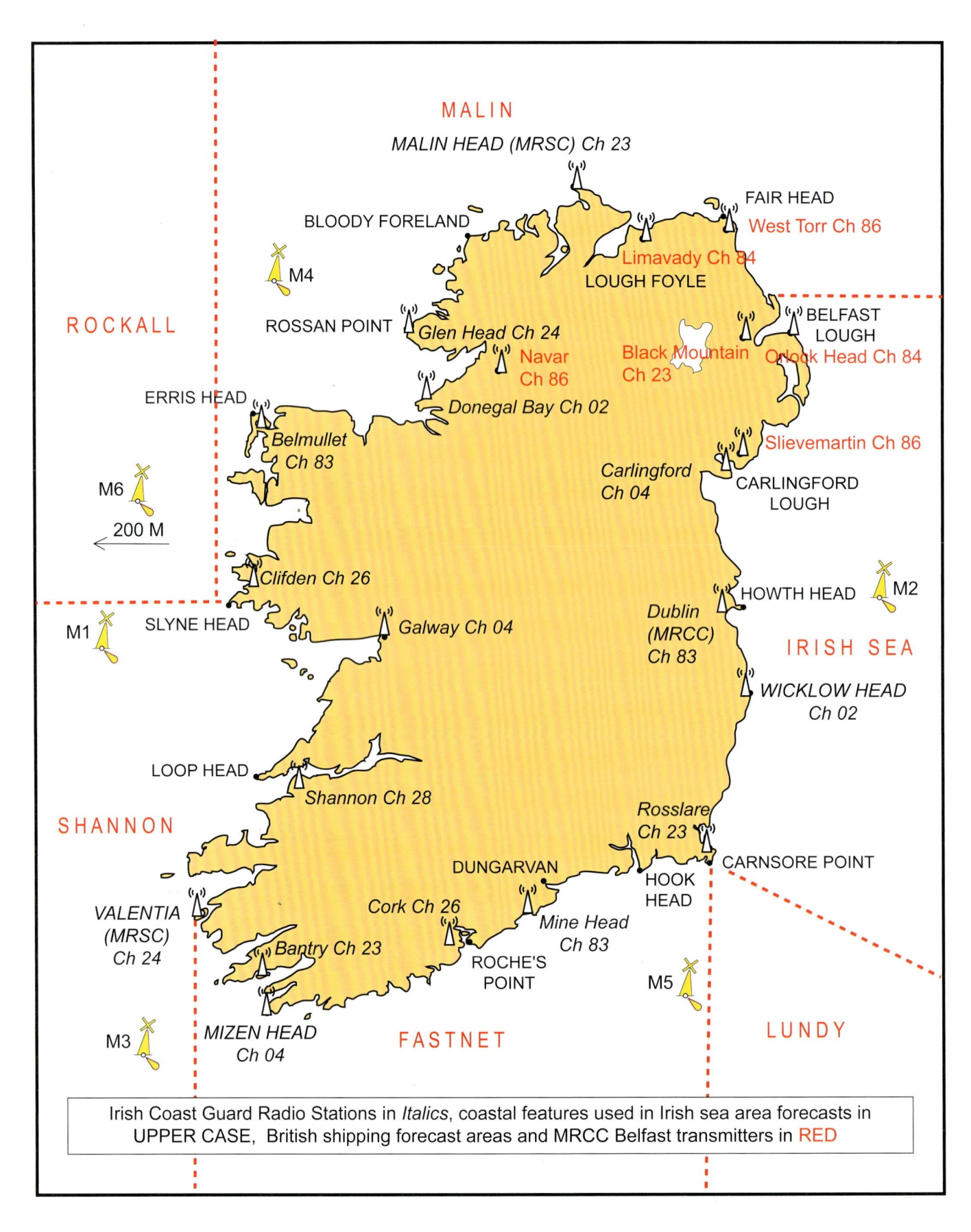

Quick-reference Weather Forecast chart

MALIN
MALIN HEAD (MRSC) Ch 23
FAIR HEAD
West Torr Ch 86
BLOODY FORELAND
Limavady Ch 84
LOUGH FOYLE
M4
ROCKALL
ROSSAN POINT
BELFAST LOUGH
Glen Head Ch 24
Navar Ch 86
Black Mountain Ch 23
Orlock Head Ch 84
ERRIS HEAD
Donegal Bay Ch 02
Slievemartin Ch 86
Belmullet Ch 83
Carlingford Ch 04
CARLINGFORD LOUGH
M6
200 M
Clifden Ch 26
HOWTH HEAD
M2
M1
SLYNE HEAD
Galway Ch 04
Dublin (MRCC) Ch 83
IRISH SEA
WICKLOW HEAD Ch 02
LOOP HEAD
Shannon Ch 28
Rosslare Ch 23
SHANNON
DUNGARVAN
CARNSORE POINT
VALENTIA (MRSC) Ch 24
Cork Ch 26
Mine Head Ch 83
HOOK HEAD
Bantry Ch 23
ROCHE'S POINT
M5
M3
MIZEN HEAD Ch 04
FASTNET
LUNDY

Irish Coast Guard Radio Stations in *Italics*, coastal features used in Irish sea area forecasts in UPPER CASE, British shipping forecast areas and MRCC Belfast transmitters in RED